Other Kaplan Books for College-Bound Students

Test Prep and Admissions

SAT® Subject Test: U.S. History

2006–2007 Edition

Mark Willner, Joann Peters, Eugene V. Resnick, and Jeff Schneider
and the Staff of Kaplan Test Prep and Admissions

Simon & Schuster

NEW YORK · LONDON · SYDNEY · TORONTO

Kaplan Publishing
Published by SIMON & SCHUSTER
Rockefeller Center
1230 Avenue of the Americas
New York, New York 10020

Contributing Editor: Jon Zeitlin
Editorial Director: Jennifer Farthing
Project Editor: Sheryl Gordon
Production Manager: Michael Shevlin
Content Manager: Patrick Kennedy
Interior Page Layout: Jan Gladish
Cover Design: Mark Weaver

Manufactured in the United States of America.
Published simultaneously in Canada.

March 2006
10 9 8 7 6 5 4 3 2 1

ISBN-13: 978-0-7432-8003-7
ISBN-10:   0-7432-8003-2

For information regarding special discounts for bulk purchases, please contact Simon & Schuster Special Sales at 1-800-456-6798 or business@simonandschuster.com.

Mark Willner is assistant principal and chairman of the social studies department at Midwood High School in Brooklyn, NY. He has also taught at Morris High School in the Bronx, Wadleigh (Harlem) Evening High School in Manhattan, and Temple Emanu-El Religious School, also in Manhattan. He was selected as "Outstanding Social Studies Supervisor in the United States" for the year 2000. Similar honors were bestowed upon him by New York State (1991) and by New York City (1984, 1988). In addition, New York State chose him as its "Distinguished Social Studies Educator" in 1997 and, in 1995, he was awarded the Louis E. Yavner Teaching Award for Outstanding Contributions to Teaching about the Holocaust and Other Violations of Human Rights by the New York State Education Department. Mr. Willner has a bachelor's degree from Queens College and a master's degree from Yeshiva University. As a recipient of Fulbright and other grants, he has studied and traveled extensively in Asia and Europe. He is a past President of the New York City Social Studies Supervisors Association (SSSA), and has sat on the executive boards of the New York State SSSA and the New York City Association of Social Studies/United Federation of Teachers. He has been a frequent presenter at social studies conferences on the national, state, and local levels.

Joann Peters teaches AP U.S. History, U.S. Government, and Economics at Midwood High School in Brooklyn, NY. At Midwood, she was instrumental in developing an interdisciplinary course in American History and piloting an interactive program in economics using computer technology in the classroom. Involved in education for over thirty years, Ms. Peters has also taught American history at John Kennedy High School in the Bronx and Brandeis High School in Manhattan. While living in England, she organized several youth programs for the American School in London. Ms. Peters has bachelor's and master's degrees in secondary education as well as a professional diploma in administration and supervision from Fordham University, where she has also served as an adjunct professor and guest lecturer.

Eugene V. Resnick has been teaching for nine years at Midwood High School in Brooklyn, NY. He received a B.A. in history from the University of Vermont and a master's degree in urban history from Empire State College in New York. He was selected to participate in two seminars sponsored by the National Endowment for the Humanities, and has worked on curriculum development projects in European and Untied States history.

Jeff Schneider graduated from Columbia College in 1967, passed his oral examination in the Ph.D. program in American History in 1988 at the Graduate Center of the City University of New York, and received his master's in American history from Hunter College in 1995. He did research for the Public Broadcasting System series by David Grubin on Lyndon Johnson and presented a paper at the Society for the History of the Early Republic. He has attended seminars sponsored by the Gilder Lehrman Institute of American History. Since 1987 he has taught American History at Hunter College and Adelphi University and is currently teaching AP U.S. History, Intel Social Science Research, and Great Speeches and Debates in American History at Midwood High School in Brooklyn, New York.

AVAILABLE ONLINE

FOR ANY TEST CHANGES OR LATE-BREAKING DEVELOPMENTS

kaptest.com/publishing

The material in this book is up-to-date at the time of publication. However, the College Board and Educational Testing Service (ETS) may have instituted changes in the test after this book was published. Be sure to carefully read the materials you receive when you register for the test. If there are any important late-breaking developments—or any changes or corrections to the Kaplan test preparation materials in this book—we will post that information online at **kaptest.com/publishing**.

FEEDBACK AND COMMENTS

kaplansurveys.com/books

We'd love to hear your comments and suggestions about this book. We invite you to fill out our online survey form at **kaplansurveys.com/books**. Your feedback is extremely helpful as we continue to develop high-quality resources to meet your needs.

Section One

THE BASICS

CHAPTER 1

About the SAT Subject Test: U.S. History

- Frequently Asked Questions on the SAT Subject Test
- Understanding the SAT Subject Test: U.S. History

You're serious about going to the college of your choice. You wouldn't have opened this book otherwise. You've made a wise choice, because this book can help you to achieve your goal. It'll show you how to score your best on the SAT Subject Test: U.S. History. The first step to a better score is to understand the test.

FREQUENTLY ASKED QUESTIONS ON THE SAT SUBJECT TEST

The following information about the SAT Subject Test is important to keep in mind as you get ready to prep for the SAT Subject Test: U.S. History. Remember, though, that sometimes the test makers change the test policies after a book has gone to press. The information here is accurate at the time of publication but it's a good idea to check the test information on the College Board website at collegeboard.com.

> Originally, SAT stood for *Scholastic Aptitude Test*. Then, when the test changed in the mid-1990s, the official name was changed to *Scholastic Assessment Test*. Finally, in 1997, the test makers announced that SAT no longer stands for anything, officially.

What Is the SAT Subject Test?

The SAT Subject Test is actually a set of more than 20 different Subject Tests. These tests are designed to measure what you have learned in such subjects as literature, physics, biology, and Spanish. Each test lasts one hour and consists entirely of multiple-choice questions. On any one test date, you can take up to three Subject Tests.

How Does the SAT Subject Test Differ from the SAT?

The SAT is largely a test of verbal and math skills. True, you need to know some vocabulary and some formulas for the SAT; but it's designed to measure how well you read and think rather than how much you remember. The SAT Subject Test tests are very different. They're designed to measure what you know about specific disciplines. Sure, critical reading and thinking skills play a part on these tests, but their main purpose is to determine exactly what you know about writing, math, history, physics, and so on.

> Colleges use your SAT Subject Test scores in both admissions and placement decisions.

How Do Colleges Use the SAT Subject Test?

Many people will tell you that these standardized tests are flawed—that they measure neither your reading and thinking skills nor your level of knowledge. But these people don't work for colleges. Those schools that require SATs feel that they are an important indicator of your ability to succeed in college. Specifically, they use your scores in one or both of two ways: to help them make admissions and/or placement decisions.

Like the SAT, the SAT Subject Tests provide schools with a standard measure of academic performance, which they use to compare you with applicants from different high schools and different educational backgrounds. This information helps them to decide whether you're ready to handle their curriculum.

> Many colleges require you to take certain SAT Subject tests. Check with all of the schools you're interested in applying to before deciding which tests to take.

SAT Subject Test scores may also be used to decide what course of study is appropriate for you once you've been admitted. A low score on the Literature Test, for example, might mean that you have to take a remedial English course. Conversely, a high score on an SAT Subject Test: Mathematics might mean that you'll be exempted from an introductory math course.

Which SAT Subject Test Tests Should I Take?

The simple answer is: those that you'll do well on. High scores, after all, can only help your chances for admission. Unfortunately, many colleges demand that you take particular tests and some schools will give you a degree of choice in the matter, especially if they want you to take a total of three tests. Before you register to take any tests, therefore, check with the colleges you're interested in to find out exactly which tests they require. Don't rely on high school guidance counselors or admissions handbooks for this information. They might not give you accurate or current information.

> You can take up to three SAT Subject tests in one day.

When Are the SAT Subject Test Tests Administered?

Most of the SAT Subject Tests, including U.S. History, are administered six times a year: in October, November, December, January, May, and June. A few of the tests are offered less frequently. Due to admissions deadlines, many colleges insist that you take the SAT Subject Test no later than December or January of your senior year in high school. You may even have to take it sooner if you're interested in applying for "early admission" to a school. Those schools that use scores for placement decisions only may allow you to take the SAT Subject Test as late as May or June of your senior year. You should check with colleges to find out which test dates are most appropriate for you.

How Do I Register for the SAT Subject Test?

The College Board® administers the SAT Subject Tests, so you must sign up for the tests with them. The easiest way to register is to obtain copies of the *SAT Registration Bulletin* and *Taking the SAT Subject Tests*. These publications contain all of the necessary information, including current test dates and fees. They can be obtained at any high school guidance office or directly from the College Board. You can also find information online at collegeboard.com.

In fact, with a credit card, you can register online rather than through the mail. You can also reregister by telephone if you have previously registered for an SAT or SAT Subject Test. If you choose these options, you should still read the College Board publications carefully before you make any decisions.

> Want to register for the SAT Subject Test or get more info? Ask your school counselor's office for the *SAT Registration Bulletin*, which contains a Registration Form, test dates, fees, and instructions.
>
> **By mail:** Mail in the Registration Form to the College Board.
>
> **Online:** With a credit card, you can register online at collegeboard.com.
>
> **By phone:** You can register by phone *only if* you have registered for an SAT test in the past.
>
> College Board SAT Program
> (609) 771-7600
> collegeboard.com

How Are the SAT Subject Tests Scored?

Like the SAT, the SAT Subject Tests are scored on a 200–800 scale.

What's a "Good" Score?

That's tricky. The obvious answer is: the score that the colleges of your choice demand. Keep in mind, though, that SAT Subject Test scores are just one piece of information that colleges will use to evaluate you. The decision to accept or reject you will be based on many criteria, including your high school transcript, your SAT scores, your recommendations, your personal statement, your interview (where applicable), your extracurricular activities, and the like. So, failure to achieve the necessary score doesn't automatically mean that your chances of getting in have been damaged.

> The mean SAT Subject Test: U.S. History Test score for 2003 college-bound seniors was 589.

What If I Get Sick During the Test or Really Blow It?

If, after taking the test, you have serious doubts about your performance on the test and believe for any reason the score will not reflect your abilities, you may cancel your score. Cancelling your score means that the score will not become part of your test record or be reported to colleges. You must submit the necessary paperwork by the Wednesday after the test. Once your scores are cancelled you may not reinstate them. If you took more than one SAT test on the same date, you must cancel all scores for that date. More information is available at collegeboard.com.

The College Board used to offer a service known as Score Choice™ that allowed you to look at your scores and then decide whether or not you wanted the score on a particular SAT test to be included on your permanent score record that colleges get. That option is no longer available. Unless you cancel your score, it will automatically become part of your permanent record to be reported to schools.

What Should I Bring to the SAT Subject Test?

Gather your test materials the day before the test. You'll need:

- Your admission ticket
- A proper form of I.D.
- Some sharpened No. 2 pencils
- A good eraser

It's a good idea to get your test materials together the day before the tests. You'll need an admission ticket; a form of identification (check the *Registration Bulletin* to find out what is permissible); a few sharpened No. 2 pencils; and a good eraser. (Note that calculators are not allowed on any of the SAT Subject Tests except for Math Level 1 and Math Level 2.) If you'll be registering as a standby, collect the appropriate forms beforehand. Also, make sure that you know how to get to the test center.

UNDERSTANDING THE SAT SUBJECT TEST: U.S. HISTORY

Now that you know the basics about the SAT Subject Tests, it's time to focus on the U.S. History test. What's on it? How is it scored? After reading this chapter, you'll know what to expect on Test Day.

Content

The SAT Subject Test: U.S. History expects you to have a mastery of the concepts and principles covered in a one-year, college-prep U.S. history class. This one-hour exam consists of 90 to 95 multiple-choice questions covering topics from our nation's earliest days through the present. It covers items of social, economic, political, intellectual, and cultural history, and foreign policy. An approximate percentage of questions covering these items that appear on the test is listed on the next page.

Topics	Approximate Percentage of Test
Political History	32–36%
Economic History	18–20%
Social History	18–22%
Intellectual and Cultural History	10–12%
Foreign Policy	13–17%

Preparation

The best preparation is to complete a one-year survey course in American history at the college-preparatory or AP level. A great majority of the test questions are derived from commonly taught subject matter in such a course in secondary schools. No one text or mode of instruction is better than another. The test questions are written to measure knowledge, skills, and abilities. According to the College Board, the questions may:

- Challenge you to recall standard information concerning facts, dates, people, terms, concepts, and generalizations.
- Ask you to analyze and interpret visual material, including charts, cartoons, graphs, paintings, photographs, and maps.
- Require you to relate to given data.
- Direct you to evaluate data for a specific purpose. This would be done as you make your judgment on evidence such as proof and consistency, or on external criteria, i.e., via comparison with other theories, works, and standards.

Scoring Information

This exam is scored in a range from 200–800 (in multiples of ten), just like a section of the SAT. Your raw score is calculated by subtracting 1/4 of the number of questions you got wrong from the number of questions you got right. If you answered 70 questions correctly and 25 questions incorrectly, your raw score would be:

Number correct:	70
1/4 × Number incorrect:	− 6.25
Raw score:	63.75 (rounded to 64)

This raw score is then compared to all the other test takers' scores to come up with a scaled score. This scaling takes into account any slight variations between test administrations. On a recent administration, it was possible to miss 10 questions and still receive a scaled score of 800. A raw score of 65 on a 1995 SAT Subject Test: U.S. History translated into a 730. So, you can miss a few questions and still receive a competitive score.

CHAPTER 2

Strategies to Test Your Best

- Know the Directions
- Know the Format
- Skip the Difficult Questions; Come Back to Them Later
- Be a Good Guesser
- Be a Good Gridder
- Think About the Questions Before You Look at the Answers
- Pace Yourself
- Two-Minute Warning
- Stress Management
- The Days Before the Test
- The Next Step

Now that you know a little about the SAT Subject Tests, it's time to let you in on a few basic test taking skills and strategies that can improve your performance on them. You should practice these skills and strategies as you prepare for the SAT Subject Tests.

The SAT Subject Tests are different from the tests that you're used to taking. On your high school tests, you probably go through the questions in order. You probably spend more time on hard questions than on easy ones, since hard questions are generally worth more points. And you often show your work, since your teachers tell you that how you approach questions is as important as getting the right answers.

None of this applies to the SAT Subject Tests. You can benefit from moving around within the tests, hard questions are worth the same as easy ones, and it doesn't matter how you answer the questions—only what your answers are.

KNOW THE DIRECTIONS

The SAT Subject Tests are highly predictable. Because the format and directions of the SAT Subject Tests remain unchanged from test to test, you can learn the setup of each test in advance. On Test Day, the various question types on each test shouldn't be new to you.

Learn SAT Subject Test directions as you prepare for the tests. That way, you'll have more time to spend answering the questions on Test Day.

One of the easiest things you can do to help your performance on the SAT Subject Tests is to understand the directions before taking the test. Since the instructions are always the same, there's no reason to waste a lot of time on Test Day reading them. Learn them beforehand as you work through this book and the College Board publications.

KNOW THE FORMAT

The questions on the SAT Subject Test: U.S. History generally get harder as you work through the test. This pattern can work to your benefit.

When working on more basic questions near the beginning of the test, you can generally trust your first impulse: The obvious answer is likely to be correct. As you get to the end of a test section, you need to be a bit more suspicious. Now the answers probably won't come as quickly and easily; if they do, look again because the obvious answers may be wrong. Watch out for answers that just "look right." They may be *distracters*: wrong answer choices deliberately meant to entice you.

Do the questions in the order that's best for you. Skip hard questions until you've gone through every question once. Don't pass up the opportunity to score easy points by wasting time on hard questions. Come back to them later.

SKIP THE DIFFICULT QUESTIONS; COME BACK TO THEM LATER

There's no mandatory order to the questions on the SAT Subject Test. You're allowed to skip around on the SAT Subject Tests. High scorers know this fact. They move through the tests efficiently. They don't dwell on any one question, even a hard one, until they've tried every question at least once.

When you run into questions that look tough, circle them in your test booklet and skip them for the time being. Go back and try again after you've answered the easier ones if you've got time. After a second look, troublesome questions can turn out to be remarkably simple.

If you've started to answer a question but get confused, quit and go on to the next question. Persistence might pay off in high school classes, but it usually hurts your SAT Subject Test scores. Don't spend so much time answering one hard question that you use up three or four questions' worth of time. That'll cost you points, especially if you don't even get the hard question right.

Don't guess, unless you can eliminate at least one answer choice. Don't leave a question blank unless you have absolutely no idea how to answer it.

BE A GOOD GUESSER

You might have heard it said that the SAT Subject Test has a "guessing penalty." That's a misnomer. It's really a *wrong-answer penalty*. If you guess wrong, you get a small penalty. If you guess right, you get full credit.

The fact is, if you can eliminate one or more answer choices as definitely wrong, you'll turn the odds in your favor and actually come out ahead by guessing. The fractional points that you lose are meant to offset the points you might get "accidentally" by guessing the correct answer. With practice, however, you'll see that it's often easy to eliminate *several* answer choices on some of the questions. Eliminate the answer choices you can, then guess.

BE A GOOD GRIDDER

The answer grid has no heart. It sounds simple, but it's extremely important: Don't make mistakes filling out your answer grid. When time is short, it's easy to get confused going back and forth between your test booklet and your grid. If you know the answers, but misgrid, you won't get the points. Here's how to avoid mistakes.

Always circle the questions you skip. Put a big circle in your test booklet around any question numbers that you skip. When you go back, these questions will be easy to relocate. Also, if you accidentally skip a box on the grid, you'll be able to check your grid against your booklet to see where you went wrong.

Always circle the answers you choose. Circling your answers in the test booklet makes it easier to check your grid against your booklet.

> A common mistake is filling in all of the questions with the right answers—in the wrong spots. Whenever you skip a question, circle it in your test booklet and make doubly sure that you skip it on the answer grid as well.

Grid five or more answers at once. Don't transfer your answers to the grid after every question. Transfer them after every five questions. That way, you won't keep breaking your concentration to mark the grid. You'll save time and gain accuracy.

THINK ABOUT THE QUESTIONS BEFORE YOU LOOK AT THE ANSWERS

The test makers love to put distracters among the answer choices. Distracters are answers that look like they're correct, but aren't. If you jump right into the answer choices without thinking first about what you're looking for, you're much more likely to fall for one of these traps.

> Try to think of the answer to a question before you shop among the answer choices. If you've got some idea of what you're looking for, you'll be less likely to be fooled by "trap" choices.

Predict your answer before you go to the answer choices so you don't get persuaded by the wrong answers. This helps protect you from persuasive or tricky incorrect choices. Many wrong answer choices are logical twists on the correct choice.

PACE YOURSELF

The SAT Subject Tests give you a lot of questions in a short period of time. To get through the tests, you can't spend too much time on any single question. Keep moving through the tests at a good speed. If you run into a hard question, circle it in your test booklet, skip it, and come back to it later if you have time.

You don't have to spend the same amount of time on every question. Ideally, you should be able to work through the easier questions at a brisk, steady clip, and use a little more time on the harder questions. One caution: Don't rush through basic questions just to save time for the harder ones. The basic questions are points in your pocket, and you're better off not getting to some harder questions if it means losing easy points because of careless mistakes. Remember, you don't earn any extra credit for answering hard questions.

TWO-MINUTE WARNING

Some questions can be done more quickly than others because they require less work or because choices can be eliminated more easily. If you start to run out of time, look for these shorter, quicker questions.

STRESS MANAGEMENT

You can beat anxiety the same way you can beat the SAT Subject Test in U.S. History—by knowing what to expect beforehand and developing strategies to deal with it.

Sources of Stress

In the space provided, write down your sources of test-related stress. The idea is to pin down any sources of anxiety so you can deal with them one by one. We have provided common examples—feel free to use them and any others you think of.

I always freeze up on tests.

- I'm nervous about timing.
- I need a good/great score to get into my first choice college.
- My older brother/sister/best friend/girlfriend/boyfriend did really well. I must match their scores or do better.
- My parents, who are paying for school, will be quite disappointed if I don't do well.
- I'm afraid of losing my focus and concentration.
- I'm afraid I'm not spending enough time preparing.
- I study like crazy but nothing seems to stick in my mind.
- I always run out of time and get panicky.
- The simple act of thinking, for me, is like wading through refrigerated honey.

My Sources of Stress

_____

_____

_____

_____

_____

Read through the list. Cross out things or add things. Now rewrite the list in order of most disturbing to least disturbing.

My Sources of Stress, In Order

_____

_____

_____

_____

_____

Chances are, the top of the list is a fairly accurate description of exactly how you react to test anxiety, both physically and mentally. The later items usually describe your fears (disappointing mom and dad, looking bad, etc.). Taking care of the major items from the top of the list should go a long way towards relieving overall test anxiety. That's what we'll do next.

Strengths and Weaknesses

Take 60 seconds to list the areas of U.S. History that you are good at. They can be general such as "Colonialism" or specific like "Foreign Policy in the 1930s." Put down as many as you can think of, and if possible, time yourself. Write for the entire time; don't stop writing until you've reached the one-minute stopping point. Go!

Strong Test Subjects

_____

_____

_____

_____

_____

_____

Now take one minute to list areas of the test you struggle with or simply do not understand. Again, keep it to one minute, and continue writing until you reach the cutoff. Go!

Troublesome Test Subjects

_____

_____

_____

_____

_____

_____

Taking stock of your assets and liabilities lets you know the areas you don't have to worry about, and the ones that will demand extra attention and effort. It helps a lot to find out where you need to spend extra effort. We mostly fear what we don't know and are probably afraid to face. You can't help feeling more confident when you know you're actively strengthening your chances of earning a higher overall score.

Now, go back to the "good" list, and expand on it for two minutes. Take the general items on that first list and make them more specific; take the specific items and expand them into more general conclusions. Naturally, if anything new comes to mind, jot it down. Focus all of your attention and effort on your strengths. Don't underestimate yourself or your abilities. Give yourself full credit. At the same time, don't list strengths you don't really have; you'll only be fooling yourself.

Expanding from general to specific might go as follows. If you listed "politics" as a broad topic you feel strong in, you would then narrow your focus to include areas of this subject about which you are particularly knowledgeable. Your areas of strength might include specific presidencies, legislative acts or Supreme Court decisions, etc. Whatever you know well goes on your "good" list. OK. Check your starting time. Go!

Strong Test Subjects: An Expanded List

_____

_____

_____

_____

_____

After you've stopped, check your time. Did you find yourself going beyond the two minutes allotted? Did you write down more things than you thought you knew? Is it possible you know more than you've given yourself credit for? Could that mean you've found a number of areas in which you feel strong?

You just took an active step towards helping yourself. Enjoy your increased feelings of confidence, and use them when you take the U.S. History SAT Subject Test.

How to Deal

Visualize

This next little group of activities is a follow-up to the strong and troublesome test item lists you completed above. Sit in a comfortable chair in a quiet setting. If you wear glasses, take them off. Close your eyes and breathe in a deep, satisfying breath of air. Really fill your lungs until your rib cage is fully expanded and you can't take in any more. Then, exhale the air completely. Imagine you're blowing out a candle with your last little puff of air. Do this two or three more times, filling your lungs to their maximum and emptying them totally. Keep your eyes closed, comfortably but not tightly. Let your body sink deeper into the chair as you become even more comfortable.

With your eyes shut you can notice something very interesting. You're no longer dealing with the worrisome stuff going on in the world outside of you. Now you can concentrate on what happens inside you. The more you recognize your own physical reactions to stress and anxiety, the more you can do about them. You may not realize it, but you've begun to regain a sense of being in control.

Let images begin to form on TV screens on the back of your eyelids. Allow the images to come easily and naturally; don't force them. Visualize a relaxing situation. It might be in a special place you've visited before or one you've read about. It can be a fictional location that you create in your imagination, but a real-life memory of a place or situation you know is usually better. Make it as detailed as possible and notice as much as you can.

Stay focused on the images as you sink farther into your chair. Breathe easily and naturally. You might have the sensations of any stress or tension draining from your muscles and flowing downward, out your feet and away from you.

Take a moment to check how you're feeling. Notice how comfortable you've become. Imagine how much easier it would be if you could take the test feeling this relaxed and in this state of ease. You've coupled the images of your special place with sensations of comfort and relaxation. You've also found a way to become relaxed simply by visualizing your own safe, special place.

Close your eyes and start remembering a real-life situation in which you did well on a test. If you can't come up with one, remember a situation in which you did something that you were really proud of—a genuine accomplishment. Make the memory as detailed as possible. Think about the sights, the sounds, the smells, even the tastes associated with this remembered experience. Remember how confident you felt as you accomplished your goal. Now start thinking about the SAT Subject Test: U.S. History. Keep your thoughts and feelings in line with that prior, successful experience. Don't make comparisons between them. Just imagine taking the upcoming test with the same feelings of confidence and relaxed control.

This exercise is a great way to bring the test down to earth. You should practice this exercise often, especially when you feel burned out on test preparation. The more you practice it, the more effective the exercise will be for you.

THE DAYS BEFORE THE TEST

As the test gets closer, you may find your anxiety is on the rise. To calm any pretest jitters you may have, let's go over a few strategies for the days before and after the exam.

Three Days Before the Test

It's almost over. Eat an energy bar, drink some soda—do whatever it takes to keep going. Here are Kaplan's strategies for the three days leading up to the test.

Take a full-length practice test under timed conditions. Use the techniques and strategies you've learned in this book. Approach the test strategically, actively, and confidently.

WARNING: DO NOT take a full-length practice test if you have fewer than 48 hours left before the test. Doing so will probably exhaust you and hurt your score on the actual test. You wouldn't run a marathon the day before the real thing.

Two Days Before the Test

Go over the results of your practice test. Don't worry too much about your score, or about whether you got a specific question right or wrong. The practice test doesn't count. But do examine your performance on specific questions with an eye to how you might get through each one faster and better on the test to come.

The Night Before the Test

DO NOT STUDY. Get together an "Exam Kit" containing the following items:

- A watch
- A few No. 2 pencils (pencils with slightly dull points fill the ovals better)
- Erasers
- Photo ID card
- Your admission ticket from ETS

Know exactly where you're going, exactly how you're getting there, and exactly how long it takes to get there. It's probably a good idea to visit your test center sometime before the day of the test, so that you know what to expect—what the rooms are like, how the desks are set up, and so on.

Relax the night before the test. Read a good book, take a long hot shower, watch some bad television. Get a good night's sleep. Go to bed early and leave yourself extra time in the morning.

The Morning of the Test

First, wake up. After that:

- Eat breakfast. Make it something substantial, but not anything too heavy or greasy.
- Don't drink a lot of coffee if you're not used to it, Bathroom breaks cut into your time, and too much caffeine is a bad idea.
- Dress in layers so that you can adjust to the temperature of the test room.
- Read something. Warm up your brain with a newspaper or a magazine. You shouldn't let the exam be the first thing you read that day.
- Be sure to get there early. Allow yourself extra time for traffic, mass transit delays, and/or detours.

During the Test

Don't be shaken. If you find your confidence slipping, remind yourself how well you've prepared. You know the structure of the test; you know the instructions; you've had practice with—and have learned strategies for—every question type.

If something goes really wrong, don't panic. If the test booklet is defective—two pages are stuck together or the ink has run—raise your hand and tell the proctor you need a new book. If you accidentally misgrid your answer page or put the answers in the wrong section, raise your hand and tell the proctor. He or she might be able to arrange for you to regrid your test after it's over, when it won't cost you any time.

After the Test

You might walk out of the exam thinking that you blew it. This is a normal reaction. Lots of people—even the highest scorers—feel that way. You tend to remember the questions that stumped you, not the ones that you knew. We're positive that you will have performed well and scored your best on the exam because you followed the Kaplan strategies outlined in this section. Be confident in your preparation, and celebrate the fact that the U.S. History SAT Subject Test is soon to be a distant memory.

Work quickly on easier questions to leave more time for harder questions. But not so quickly that you make careless errors.

THE NEXT STEP

When you take the SAT Subject Tests, you have one clear objective in mind: to score as many points as you can. It's that simple. The rest of this book is dedicated to helping you review the content that will be covered on the SAT Subject Test: U.S. History.

Next you're ready to tackle our diagnostic practice test. This test will probe your mastery of the various U.S. history topics on the SAT Subject Test: U.S. History. Use it to identify areas in which you need to refresh your knowledge. If you have limited time to review, focus on the chapters in this book that deal with the content areas in which your performance was weakest.

Section Two

DIAGNOSTIC TEST

HOW TO TAKE THE DIAGNOSTIC TEST

Before taking this diagnostic test, find a quiet room where you can work uninterrupted for one hour. Make sure you have several No. 2 pencils with erasers.

Use the answer grid provided to record your answers. Guidelines for scoring your test appear on the reverse side of the answer grid. Time yourself. Spend no more than one hour on the 90 questions. Once you start the diagnostic test, don't stop until you've reached the one-hour time limit. You'll find an answer key and complete answer explanations following the test. Be sure to read the explanations for all questions, even those you answered correctly. Finally, you'll learn how the diagnostic test can help you in your review of U.S. history.

Good luck!

HOW TO CALCULATE
YOUR SCORE

Step 1: Figure out your raw score. Refer to your answer sheet to determine the number right and the number wrong on the test you're scoring. You can use the chart below to figure out your raw score. Multiply the number wrong by 0.25 and subtract the result from the number right. Round the result to the nearest whole number. This is your raw score.

SAT Subject Test: U.S. History Diagnostic Test

Number right	Number wrong	Raw score
□	$- \left(0.25 \times \square \right) =$	□

Step 2: Find your test score. Find your raw score in the left column of the table below. The score in the right column is an approximation of what your score would be on the SAT Subject Test: U.S. History.

A note on your test scores: Don't take these scores too literally. Practice test conditions cannot precisely mirror real test conditions. Your actual SAT Subject Test: U.S. History score will almost certainly vary from your practice test scores. However, your scores on the practice tests will give you a rough idea of your range on the actual exam.

Conversion Table

Raw	Scaled	Raw	Scaled	Raw	Scaled	Raw	Scaled	Raw	Scaled	Raw	Scaled
90	800	72	770	54	680	36	580	18	470	0	350
89	800	71	760	43	670	35	570	17	460	−1	350
88	800	70	760	52	670	34	570	16	460	−2	340
87	800	69	750	51	660	33	560	15	450	−3	340
86	800	68	750	50	660	32	550	14	450	−4	330
85	800	67	740	49	650	31	550	13	440	−5	330
84	800	66	740	48	650	30	540	12	430	−6	320
83	800	65	730	47	640	29	540	11	430	−7	320
82	800	64	730	46	640	28	530	10	420	−8	310
81	800	63	720	45	630	27	520	9	410	−9	310
80	790	62	720	44	630	26	520	8	410	−10	300
79	790	61	710	43	620	25	510	7	400	−11	300
78	790	60	710	42	610	24	510	6	390	−12	290
77	790	59	700	41	610	23	500	5	390	−13	280
76	780	58	700	40	600	22	490	4	380	−14	280
75	780	57	690	39	600	21	490	3	370	−15	270
74	780	56	690	38	590	20	480	2	370	−16	270
73	770	55	680	37	580	19	480	1	360	−17	260

Answer Grid
Diagnostic Test

1. Ⓐ Ⓑ Ⓒ Ⓓ Ⓔ	31. Ⓐ Ⓑ Ⓒ Ⓓ Ⓔ	61. Ⓐ Ⓑ Ⓒ Ⓓ Ⓔ
2. Ⓐ Ⓑ Ⓒ Ⓓ Ⓔ	32. Ⓐ Ⓑ Ⓒ Ⓓ Ⓔ	62. Ⓐ Ⓑ Ⓒ Ⓓ Ⓔ
3. Ⓐ Ⓑ Ⓒ Ⓓ Ⓔ	33. Ⓐ Ⓑ Ⓒ Ⓓ Ⓔ	63. Ⓐ Ⓑ Ⓒ Ⓓ Ⓔ
4. Ⓐ Ⓑ Ⓒ Ⓓ Ⓔ	34. Ⓐ Ⓑ Ⓒ Ⓓ Ⓔ	64. Ⓐ Ⓑ Ⓒ Ⓓ Ⓔ
5. Ⓐ Ⓑ Ⓒ Ⓓ Ⓔ	35. Ⓐ Ⓑ Ⓒ Ⓓ Ⓔ	65. Ⓐ Ⓑ Ⓒ Ⓓ Ⓔ
6. Ⓐ Ⓑ Ⓒ Ⓓ Ⓔ	36. Ⓐ Ⓑ Ⓒ Ⓓ Ⓔ	66. Ⓐ Ⓑ Ⓒ Ⓓ Ⓔ
7. Ⓐ Ⓑ Ⓒ Ⓓ Ⓔ	37. Ⓐ Ⓑ Ⓒ Ⓓ Ⓔ	67. Ⓐ Ⓑ Ⓒ Ⓓ Ⓔ
8. Ⓐ Ⓑ Ⓒ Ⓓ Ⓔ	38. Ⓐ Ⓑ Ⓒ Ⓓ Ⓔ	68. Ⓐ Ⓑ Ⓒ Ⓓ Ⓔ
9. Ⓐ Ⓑ Ⓒ Ⓓ Ⓔ	39. Ⓐ Ⓑ Ⓒ Ⓓ Ⓔ	69. Ⓐ Ⓑ Ⓒ Ⓓ Ⓔ
10. Ⓐ Ⓑ Ⓒ Ⓓ Ⓔ	40. Ⓐ Ⓑ Ⓒ Ⓓ Ⓔ	70. Ⓐ Ⓑ Ⓒ Ⓓ Ⓔ
11. Ⓐ Ⓑ Ⓒ Ⓓ Ⓔ	41. Ⓐ Ⓑ Ⓒ Ⓓ Ⓔ	71. Ⓐ Ⓑ Ⓒ Ⓓ Ⓔ
12. Ⓐ Ⓑ Ⓒ Ⓓ Ⓔ	42. Ⓐ Ⓑ Ⓒ Ⓓ Ⓔ	72. Ⓐ Ⓑ Ⓒ Ⓓ Ⓔ
13. Ⓐ Ⓑ Ⓒ Ⓓ Ⓔ	43. Ⓐ Ⓑ Ⓒ Ⓓ Ⓔ	73. Ⓐ Ⓑ Ⓒ Ⓓ Ⓔ
14. Ⓐ Ⓑ Ⓒ Ⓓ Ⓔ	44. Ⓐ Ⓑ Ⓒ Ⓓ Ⓔ	74. Ⓐ Ⓑ Ⓒ Ⓓ Ⓔ
15. Ⓐ Ⓑ Ⓒ Ⓓ Ⓔ	45. Ⓐ Ⓑ Ⓒ Ⓓ Ⓔ	75. Ⓐ Ⓑ Ⓒ Ⓓ Ⓔ
16. Ⓐ Ⓑ Ⓒ Ⓓ Ⓔ	46. Ⓐ Ⓑ Ⓒ Ⓓ Ⓔ	76. Ⓐ Ⓑ Ⓒ Ⓓ Ⓔ
17. Ⓐ Ⓑ Ⓒ Ⓓ Ⓔ	47. Ⓐ Ⓑ Ⓒ Ⓓ Ⓔ	77. Ⓐ Ⓑ Ⓒ Ⓓ Ⓔ
18. Ⓐ Ⓑ Ⓒ Ⓓ Ⓔ	48. Ⓐ Ⓑ Ⓒ Ⓓ Ⓔ	78. Ⓐ Ⓑ Ⓒ Ⓓ Ⓔ
19. Ⓐ Ⓑ Ⓒ Ⓓ Ⓔ	49. Ⓐ Ⓑ Ⓒ Ⓓ Ⓔ	79. Ⓐ Ⓑ Ⓒ Ⓓ Ⓔ
20. Ⓐ Ⓑ Ⓒ Ⓓ Ⓔ	50. Ⓐ Ⓑ Ⓒ Ⓓ Ⓔ	80. Ⓐ Ⓑ Ⓒ Ⓓ Ⓔ
21. Ⓐ Ⓑ Ⓒ Ⓓ Ⓔ	51. Ⓐ Ⓑ Ⓒ Ⓓ Ⓔ	81. Ⓐ Ⓑ Ⓒ Ⓓ Ⓔ
22. Ⓐ Ⓑ Ⓒ Ⓓ Ⓔ	52. Ⓐ Ⓑ Ⓒ Ⓓ Ⓔ	82. Ⓐ Ⓑ Ⓒ Ⓓ Ⓔ
23. Ⓐ Ⓑ Ⓒ Ⓓ Ⓔ	53. Ⓐ Ⓑ Ⓒ Ⓓ Ⓔ	83. Ⓐ Ⓑ Ⓒ Ⓓ Ⓔ
24. Ⓐ Ⓑ Ⓒ Ⓓ Ⓔ	54. Ⓐ Ⓑ Ⓒ Ⓓ Ⓔ	84. Ⓐ Ⓑ Ⓒ Ⓓ Ⓔ
25. Ⓐ Ⓑ Ⓒ Ⓓ Ⓔ	55. Ⓐ Ⓑ Ⓒ Ⓓ Ⓔ	85. Ⓐ Ⓑ Ⓒ Ⓓ Ⓔ
26. Ⓐ Ⓑ Ⓒ Ⓓ Ⓔ	56. Ⓐ Ⓑ Ⓒ Ⓓ Ⓔ	86. Ⓐ Ⓑ Ⓒ Ⓓ Ⓔ
27. Ⓐ Ⓑ Ⓒ Ⓓ Ⓔ	57. Ⓐ Ⓑ Ⓒ Ⓓ Ⓔ	87. Ⓐ Ⓑ Ⓒ Ⓓ Ⓔ
28. Ⓐ Ⓑ Ⓒ Ⓓ Ⓔ	58. Ⓐ Ⓑ Ⓒ Ⓓ Ⓔ	88. Ⓐ Ⓑ Ⓒ Ⓓ Ⓔ
29. Ⓐ Ⓑ Ⓒ Ⓓ Ⓔ	59. Ⓐ Ⓑ Ⓒ Ⓓ Ⓔ	89. Ⓐ Ⓑ Ⓒ Ⓓ Ⓔ
30. Ⓐ Ⓑ Ⓒ Ⓓ Ⓔ	60. Ⓐ Ⓑ Ⓒ Ⓓ Ⓔ	90. Ⓐ Ⓑ Ⓒ Ⓓ Ⓔ

Diagnostic Test

1. The discovery of the New World resulted from the desire of many Europeans to

    (A) establish a place where they could practice their religion freely
    (B) find an all-water route to the East
    (C) end the practice of primogeniture
    (D) spread Christianity around the world
    (E) uplift and civilize other peoples of the world

2. Which event was the most important cause of the Nullification Crisis?

    (A) The passage of the Force Act under Andrew Jackson
    (B) The debates between Robert Y. Hayne and Daniel Webster
    (C) The Treaty of Ghent after the War of 1812
    (D) The passage of the Compromise Tariff of 1833
    (E) The passage of the Tariff of Abominations

3. Why did Stephen Douglas support the idea of Popular Sovereignty in dealing with the question of slavery in Kansas in 1854?

    (A) It allowed "free-staters" to exclude slavery from Kansas and Nebraska.
    (B) It was outlined in the Constitution as a method for creating new states.
    (C) It allowed pro-slavery settlers to expand slavery.
    (D) It seemed a fair way to resolve a difficult controversy.
    (E) It let the Congress decide on slavery in the territories.

4. Which of the following developments is NOT associated with the Gilded Age?

    (A) Relations between workers and owners became increasingly contentious.
    (B) African Americans' migration to industrial cities led to "white flight."
    (C) New inventions made communication between cities easier.
    (D) Many industries came to be dominated by a small number of large companies.
    (E) Corruption in politics became more public and widespread.

GO ON TO THE NEXT PAGE

5. The publication of *The Jungle* contributed to rapid passage of the

   (A) Interstate Commerce Act
   (B) Wade-Davis Bill
   (C) Pure Food and Drug Act
   (D) 15th Amendment
   (E) Clayton Antitrust Act

6. A philosophical basis of Franklin D. Roosevelt's New Deal was the

   (A) philosophy of Herbert Hoover
   (B) practice of *laissez-faire* by the government
   (C) combination of relief, recovery, and reform
   (D) idea that wars end depression
   (E) importance of gaining the approval of Congress before he established his programs

7. In response to the Japanese invasion of Manchuria in 1931, the United States

   (A) issued a document refusing to recognize Japanese actions as legitimate
   (B) called a special session of the League of Nations
   (C) sent General MacArthur to command U.S. forces in the Pacific
   (D) engaged in a policy of watchful waiting
   (E) sent the *Panay*, a naval vessel, to the coast of Japan

8. During the years of Lyndon Johnson's presidency, all of the following were enacted EXCEPT for

   (A) Medicare
   (B) Medicaid
   (C) the Elementary and Secondary Education Act
   (D) the Constitutional Amendment eliminating the poll tax
   (E) the Alliance for Progress

9. For which of the following ideas in the 1970s was Gloria Steinem most noted?

   (A) Freudian psychology was anti-woman.
   (B) Women should convince men to help with the housework.
   (C) Blacks and whites should have equality in the work place.
   (D) Women should have equal rights with men.
   (E) The use of pesticides was harming the environment.

10. An example of the change in U.S. policy toward Vietnam since the end of the Vietnam War was best demonstrated by

    (A) increased aid given to North Vietnam by George H. Bush
    (B) trade restrictions placed on Vietnam by George W. Bush
    (C) recognition of the Vietnamese Government by Richard Nixon
    (D) criticism of Vietnam for its human rights violations by Jimmy Carter
    (E) visits and trade talks conducted by Bill Clinton with Vietnamese leaders

GO ON TO THE NEXT PAGE

KAPLAN

11. The New England colonists seemed to thrive in the early years of colonization as compared to the Southern colonists. The longer life spans and the overall growth of the population in New England have been attributed to the

    (A) participation of New Englanders in transatlantic trade

    (B) lack of slavery and indentured servitude in New England

    (C) strong religious beliefs and the family units with which they traveled to the New World

    (D) larger number of single men in the New England colonies

    (E) temperate climate of New England

12. The Northwest Ordinance of 1787 was significant because it

    (A) ended British control of the Ohio Valley

    (B) prohibited the extension of slavery into the Northwest Territory

    (C) prevented slavery north of the 36° 30' north latitude line

    (D) secured peaceful relations between the colonists and the Native Americans

    (E) settled a dispute over the location of the boundary between Canada and the United States

13. In the 1829 *Appeal to the Colored Citizens of the World*, David Walker called for

    (A) gradual abolition of slavery

    (B) a return to Africa for all African Americans

    (C) abolition of slavery and an end to the proposals for colonization of free blacks in Africa

    (D) slaves to wait until the time was right to ask the U.S. government for emancipation

    (E) a separate state for freed people to live in

14. Which of the following is an important reason the South lost the Civil War?

    (A) The South did not have enough guns to prevent the Union from overpowering it

    (B) Slaves ran away so there were fewer and fewer hands to do the work on the home front

    (C) Union generals were better, so they continually out-maneuvered the southern forces

    (D) The South was unable to ship out any cotton because the Union blockade was so effective

    (E) The issues of slavery and states rights were not important to the majority of Southerners

GO ON TO THE NEXT PAGE

15. Which of the following best expresses the point of view of the above cartoon?

(A) The working class and the poor had good reason to oppose immigration to the United States because new immigrants would compete with them for jobs.

(B) The government should enact restrictions on the number of immigrants allowed in the United States because immigrants were lazy and immoral.

(C) Nativists who opposed allowing immigrants into the country were hypocrites because they themselves had humble, foreign origins.

(D) Immigration contributed to the cultural diversity of the United States.

(E) The United States should avoid getting involved in foreign conflicts because it would then feel obliged to accept refugees from these conflicts.

GO ON TO THE NEXT PAGE

16. One reason Woodrow Wilson was able to win the presidency in 1912 was that

    (A) Americans rallied around him during World War I.
    (B) a majority of African Americans voted for the Democratic Party.
    (C) Wilson's humble origins endeared him to working class Americans.
    (D) There was a major split in the Republican Party.
    (E) His opponent died two weeks before the election.

17. Which of the following best describes the differences that existed between the American Federation (AFL) and the Congress of Industrial Organizations (CIO) in the 1930s?

    (A) The AFL had a huge membership, while the CIO never developed a mass following.
    (B) The AFL had its strength east of the Mississippi River, while the CIO was strongest west of the Mississippi.
    (C) The AFL was more cautious in its approach to conflicts with management, while the CIO was willing to use more militant tactics such as the sit-down strike.
    (D) The AFL was actually a coalition of "company unions," organized by management to placate worker resentment, while the CIO was composed of actual worker organizations.
    (E) The AFL was dominated by Communist Party members, while the CIO, fearing government reprisals, excluded Communists from leadership positions.

18. In the "Letter from Birmingham Jail," Martin Luther King Jr. discussed the "strangely irrational notion that there is something in the flow of time that inevitably cures all ills…. We must come to see that human progress never rolls on the wheels of inevitability."

    Which of the following represents the main idea of the above excerpt?

    (A) Nonviolence is the key to success for the civil rights movement.
    (B) The white moderates are obstacles to our victory.
    (C) We must act now.
    (D) Injustice must be eradicated everywhere.
    (E) Breaking unjust laws is justified.

19. The women's movement that emerged in the 1970s was called the second wave of feminism because it

    (A) took its name from the title of a book by Simone de Beauvoir
    (B) built on the women's movement of the 19th century
    (C) built on the women's movement of the 1930s
    (D) took inspiration from the women's movement in Europe
    (E) took its name from the title of a book by Kate Millett

20. Ronald Reagan was called the "Teflon President" because he

    (A) was the Great Communicator
    (B) told the truth without embellishment
    (C) always had everything under control
    (D) was never held responsible for the failures of his administration
    (E) did not need special handling

GO ON TO THE NEXT PAGE

21. Rhode Island and the Massachusetts Bay Colony differed in that Rhode Island

    (A) was a theocracy
    (B) was a royal colony
    (C) lacked religious freedom
    (D) practiced a policy of separation of church and state
    (E) was located in New England

22. The First and Second Great Awakenings were similar in that both

    (A) made use of revivals to attempt to convert the sinful
    (B) enforced the Puritan use of incense
    (C) encouraged long periods of silence during services so that the congregation felt the spirit of God
    (D) were purely American phenomena
    (E) employed deistic approaches to religious belief

23. The implied powers clause of the United States Constitution was used to justify the

    (A) suppression of the Whiskey Rebellion in 1794
    (B) addition of the Bill of Rights to the Constitution in 1791
    (C) signing of Jay's Treaty with England in 1794
    (D) passage of the Judiciary Act of 1789
    (E) establishment of the Bank of the United States in 1791

24. The 13th, 14th, and 15th Amendments are similar in that all three

    (A) extended voting to different groups in the United States
    (B) were ratified during the Civil War
    (C) expanded the rights of African Americans
    (D) were ratified despite opposition from the Republican Party
    (E) protected the rights of property holders

GO ON TO THE NEXT PAGE

Corn Production and Prices 1865–1900

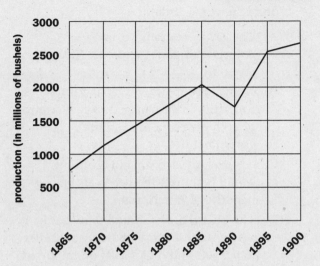

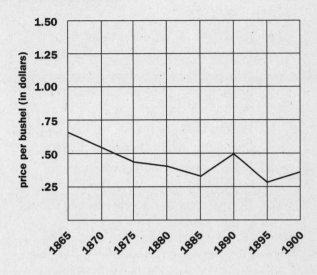

25. Which of the following statements is consistent with the data in the graphs above and with trends in American history from 1865 to 1900?

(A) Mechanization greatly benefited farmers, as output of corn nearly tripled between 1865 and 1900.

(B) American tastes shifted from corn to wheat in the second half of the 19th century, which resulted in reduced demand and reduced prices for corn.

(C) Corn yields per acre stayed stagnant between 1865 and 1900, but the number of acres under cultivation vastly increased.

(D) The inflationary policies of the government between 1865 and 1900 did not benefit farmers.

(E) Mechanization led to a glut of corn on the market and to reduced prices per bushel.

GO ON TO THE NEXT PAGE

26. Wilson's idea of a "peace without victory" failed to become a reality in the Treaty of Versailles because

    (A) the Triple Alliance was totally responsible for the events leading to World War I

    (B) England and France wanted Germany to pay for starting the war

    (C) Wilson failed to pursue his ideas actively during the negotiations for the treaty

    (D) the League of Nations was not established

    (E) Germany refused to take part in the negotiations

27. The use of the atomic bomb by the United States in 1945 was significant in that it

    (A) hastened the end of World War II

    (B) caused the defeat of Harry Truman in the election of 1948

    (C) led to the formation of the United Nations

    (D) ushered in the computer age

    (E) was the direct cause of the Cold War

28. Which of the following is a central argument of the 1958 book, *The Affluent Society*, by John Kenneth Galbraith?

    (A) The key to economic growth is government noninterference in the economy

    (B) A small group of wealthy and influential Americans had managed to gain control of both the economy and the government

    (C) A Soviet-style command economy would best meet the needs of the majority of Americans

    (D) The United States should reinvigorate its agricultural sector with heavy subsidies to farmers and high tariffs on imported agricultural products

    (E) American society was ignoring social goods in the pursuit of private material gain

29. All of the following Cold War ideas involved Europe EXCEPT

    (A) the Truman Doctrine

    (B) the domino theory

    (C) Mutually Assured Destruction (MAD)

    (D) containment

    (E) détente

GO ON TO THE NEXT PAGE

30. All of the following people play important roles in the book *All the President's Men* by Bob Woodward and Carl Bernstein EXCEPT

    (A) Richard Nixon
    (B) John Dean
    (C) Sam Ervin
    (D) Lyndon Johnson
    (E) G. Gordon Liddy

31. As a result of the French and Indian War, the American colonists developed a

    (A) hostile attitude toward the Indians
    (B) greater sense of self-confidence
    (C) greater respect for the British
    (D) desire to create a strong army
    (E) desire to ally with Spain

32. The beginnings of a uniquely American culture in the 1700s was seen in the

    (A) success of the American generals who fought in the French and Indian War
    (B) John Locke's views regarding human rights
    (C) development of the belief in transcendentalism
    (D) works of artists and poets like John Trumbull and Phillis Wheatley
    (E) writing of the *Star-Spangled Banner* by Francis Scott Key

33. The constitutionality of the Bank of the United States was upheld in the Supreme Court decision in the case of

    (A) *McCulloch v. Maryland*
    (B) *Marbury v. Madison*
    (C) *Plessy v. Ferguson*
    (D) *Dred Scott v. Sanford*
    (E) *Brown v. Board of Education of Topeka*

GO ON TO THE NEXT PAGE

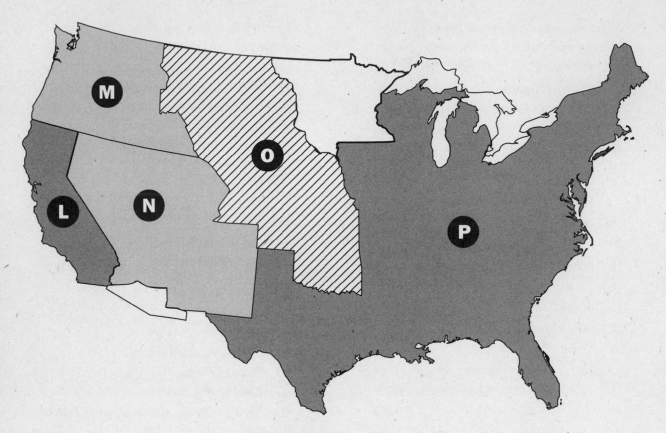

34. To which sections would the Wilmot Proviso
    have applied in the map above?

    (A) L and M
    (B) M and N
    (C) L and N
    (D) O and N
    (E) P and O

GO ON TO THE NEXT PAGE

35. An unintended consequence of the implementation of the 1862 Homestead Act was that

    (A) very few people volunteered to participate in the program
    (B) much of the land that was intended for homesteading ended up in the hands of large agricultural firms
    (C) the land that was involved in the program was incapable of producing crops
    (D) the homesteaders often had clashes with Native Americans
    (E) corrupt politicians sold the best land to speculators

36. Joseph Pulitzer and William Randolph Hearst were similar in that both were

    (A) muckraking journalists who wrote articles that exposed government corruption
    (B) moralizing commentators who chastised the public for its vices
    (C) anti-imperialist editorial writers who pushed the United States in an isolationist direction
    (D) publishers who owned newspapers, which sensationalized accounts of events
    (E) writers of non-English newspapers that appealed to recently arrived immigrants

37. There were protests against the "Palmer Raids" of the late 1910s and early 1920s on the grounds that they

    (A) blurred the separation of church and state
    (B) discriminated against women
    (C) violated protections against unwarranted search and seizure
    (D) discriminated against African Americans
    (E) failed to protect the rights of Native Americans

38. Which of the following was the reason the Supreme Court decided that prayers could not be required in public schools?

    (A) Church membership had declined
    (B) Atheism had spread throughout American society
    (C) Prayer in public schools violated the 1st Amendment
    (D) Prayer in public schools would lead to a renewal of religious tests for public office
    (E) Americans no longer considered prayer to be important in their lives

39. The main purpose of the Free Speech Movement of 1964 was to

    (A) make unions more democratic and give workers more power
    (B) support the American Civil Liberties Union
    (C) remove the censorship from rock and roll lyrics
    (D) change radio programming
    (E) allow college students to support civil rights and political causes

GO ON TO THE NEXT PAGE

40. The high gasoline prices that occurred during the administration of Jimmy Carter caused

    (A) deflation because the value of the dollar was falling
    (B) inflation because prices were rising and the value of the dollar was falling
    (C) depression because the bottom fell out of the stock market
    (D) stagnation because employment was so high
    (E) a rise in the value of the dollar because the prices were so high

41. The fact that Spain, rather than its rival, Portugal, was the dominant power in the Americas in the fifteen the fifteenth and sixteenth centuries was largely the result of the

    (A) fact that Spanish ships were faster than Portuguese ships
    (B) large numbers of Spanish settlers who arrived in the New World
    (C) Treaty of Tordesillas, signed in 1494
    (D) success of Christopher Columbus in the New World
    (E) large treasury that had been accumulated by King Ferdinand and Queen Isabella

42. The creation of the Electoral College and the indirect election of Senators demonstrates that the framers of the Constitution were concerned with the

    (A) effects of a strong central government
    (B) problems created by weak state governments
    (C) possibility of corruption in the election process
    (D) excesses of democracy
    (E) need to protect the rights of the majority

43. The Northwest Ordinance and the Missouri Compromise of 1820 were similar in that both documents

    (A) set guidelines on the number of new states to be established
    (B) admitted new states into the Union
    (C) established public schools in new territories
    (D) provided for the fair treatment of the Native American population
    (E) restricted slavery in areas yet to be admitted as states

44. "The owner fed us regular on good food just like you would a good horse if you had one."
    —*An escaped slave (explaining why he ran away)*
    This quotation reflects the ex-slave's belief that

    (A) the slave owner was a good master
    (B) he should be treated as more than a piece of property
    (C) if slaves are treated well they will be happy
    (D) his owner took proper care of his slaves
    (E) he was always satisfied as a slave

45. Which of the following quotes comes from Abraham Lincoln's First Inaugural Address of March 1861?

    (A) "A house divided against itself cannot stand."
    (B) "Government of the people, by the people, and for the people shall not perish from the earth."
    (C) "Liberty and union, now and forever, one and inseparable."
    (D) "You can have no conflict without being yourselves the aggressors."
    (E) "With malice toward none and charity for all."

GO ON TO THE NEXT PAGE

46. Most of the prominent labor battles of the late 19th century, such as the Railroad Strike of 1877 and the Pullman Strike of 1894, occurred in the aftermath of

    (A) government recognition of workers' right to organize unions
    (B) deadly accidents
    (C) production speedups
    (D) wage cuts
    (E) the formation of the Congress of Industrial Organizations

47. After Spain's defeat in the Spanish-American War in 1898, the Philippines

    (A) became an independent republic with a democratic constitution
    (B) ceased to exist as a political entity, becoming a string of independent islands
    (C) fought against the United States to gain independence, but became a U.S. colony
    (D) stayed within the strategic orbit of Spain
    (E) became the first satellite nation of the Soviet Union

48. Booker T. Washington and W. E. B. DuBois differed in their approaches to addressing discrimination against African Americans. Which statement below best represents Washington's position?

    (A) "Since racial integration is not possible in the United States, African Americans should go back to Africa."
    (B) "The best way for African Americans to improve their position in society is to gain vocational training in order to obtain jobs in agriculture, crafts, and manufacturing."
    (C) "African Americans should engage in nonviolent civil disobedience to put pressure on the federal government to end discriminatory practices."
    (D) "African Americans should pursue equality 'by any means necessary,' including violence in self-defense."
    (E) "African Americans could best achieve their goals by running candidates for public office to vote out those who discriminate against them in state and federal government."

49. President Franklin D. Roosevelt's New Deal programs, which were designed to end the Great Depression,

    (A) were overwhelmingly effective in ending unemployment
    (B) had a limited effect on ending the Depression
    (C) led the United States into World War II
    (D) were strongly supported by the Supreme Court
    (E) led to the establishment of the Federal Reserve System

50. The Supreme Court's decision in the case of *Roe v. Wade* was based on

    (A) freedom of the press
    (B) the right of *habeas corpus*
    (C) executive privilege
    (D) the right to privacy
    (E) eminent domain

51. The adoption of the Barbados Slave Codes by South Carolina in 1696 resulted in

    (A) an increased number of indentured servants
    (B) the development of the abolition movement in the North
    (C) the development of chattel slavery in the colonies, which centered on race
    (D) Bacon's Rebellion
    (E) the development of a paternalistic view of slavery in South Carolina

52. Which of the following was one of the main legal objections that the colonists made to Parliament in regard to the Stamp Act?

    (A) It taxed too many items used by the colonists in their daily lives
    (B) It constituted an attempt to coerce the colonists to obey the crown
    (C) It was a direct tax on the colonists
    (D) It restricted colonial trade
    (E) It placed extremely high taxes on colonial goods

53. President Washington's actions in the Whiskey Rebellion in 1794 demonstrated the power of the central government to

    (A) suspend habeas corpus in times of extreme danger
    (B) enforce the laws of the land
    (C) prohibit the sale and consumption of liquor
    (D) control the production of whiskey
    (E) subsidize the production of grain used to make whiskey

GO ON TO THE NEXT PAGE

54. "Pompey, how do I look?"

    "Mighty massa, mighty."

    "What do you mean mighty, Pompey?"

    "Why massa you look noble."

    "What do you mean by 'noble'?"

    "Why you look just like one lion."

    "Now Pompey, where have you ever seen a lion?"

    "I saw one down in yonder field the other day."

    "Pompey, you foolish fellow, that was a jackass."

    "Was it massa? Well, you look just like him."

    Who would be most likely to have related this dialogue to whom?

    (A) a slaveholder to his son
    (B) a white overseer to his son
    (C) a slave mother to her son
    (D) a Confederate schoolboy to his friends
    (E) a white overseer to another white overseer

55. President Andrew Johnson's Reconstruction plan called for the former Confederate states to

    (A) pass the Civil Rights Act
    (B) support the Freedman's Bureau
    (C) endorse the 13th Amendment, which abolished slavery
    (D) arrest all the men who served in the Confederate government
    (E) guarantee that the freedmen would attain the right to vote

56. During the Gilded Age, the U.S. economy

    (A) faltered because industries failed to convert from wartime production to peacetime production after the Civil War
    (B) grew at a rapid pace, but the gap between the wealthy and poor widened
    (C) was characterized by a growing agricultural sector and a back-to-the-land movement
    (D) suffered because of the nation's over-dependence on the slave trade
    (E) was cut off from the world economic system due to high tariffs and isolationist policies

57. "Blue laws," supported by the Republican Party in many states during the Gilded Age,

    (A) regulated the number of hours children could work
    (B) mandated that producers honestly portray the contents of their products
    (C) provided price supports for struggling farmers
    (D) reformed civil service procedures
    (E) made illegal certain activities that were seen by some as immoral

GO ON TO THE NEXT PAGE

58. Which of the following is NOT a reason for the growth of the Communist Party in the United States in the 1930s?

    (A) The Communist Party tapped into many people's doubts about the efficacy of the capitalist system during the Great Depression.

    (B) The Communist Party, as part of its Popular Front strategy, avoided talk of impending revolution, and advocated forming alliances with anti-fascist liberals.

    (C) The Communist Party's work on behalf of African Americans, as is evident in the Scottsboro case, won it many adherents.

    (D) The Communist Party's espionage work on behalf of the Soviet Union created an aura of dedication and audacity.

    (E) The large number of Eastern European immigrants who had supported communism back home gravitated toward the Communists Party in the United States.

59. The most important impetus behind the emergence of the modern Civil Rights Movement was

    (A) the founding of the NAACP
    (B) lynchings
    (C) the March on Washington
    (D) the experience of African Americans in World War II
    (E) the Freedom Rides

60. In his farewell address, President Dwight D. Eisenhower

    (A) urged future administrations to avoid entanglements with European powers
    (B) predicted that environmental issues would become more important in the nation's future
    (C) castigated Joseph McCarthy for his excessive zeal
    (D) advocated that the government wage a war on illicit drugs
    (E) warned the nation of the power of the military-industrial complex

GO ON TO THE NEXT PAGE

61. The French and Indian War, which ended in 1763, greatly affected the American colonists because it

    (A) removed the French threat against the colonists

    (B) resulted in the expansion of the colonies east of the Appalachian Mountains

    (C) marked the beginning of the British policy of salutary neglect in the colonies

    (D) removed the Indian threat from the frontier settlements

    (E) marked the end of mercantilism

62. Tensions between England and the United States grew between 1790 and 1812 for all of the following reasons EXCEPT the

    (A) impressment of U.S. seamen into British service

    (B) British incitement to violence of the Indian population on the frontier

    (C) British military occupation in the Ohio Valley

    (D) XYZ Affair

    (E) Americans' continued holding of Loyalists' lands

63. The most important result of the development of interchangeable parts in the early 19th century was that it allowed

    (A) printers to make newspapers more easily

    (B) farmers to harvest crops more easily

    (C) manufacturers to make their assembly lines more efficient

    (D) children to have safer toys

    (E) coopers to cut staves in their barrels more precisely

64. The Compromise of 1850 included all of the following EXCEPT

    (A) a strengthened Fugitive Slave Law

    (B) permission to continue slavery but not slave auctions in Washington, DC

    (C) resolution of the Texas–New Mexico border dispute

    (D) postponing a decision on the question of slavery in the California territory

    (E) postponing a decision on the question of slavery in the Utah territory

65. An important result of the impeachment crisis of 1868 was that

    (A) President Andrew Johnson was removed from office

    (B) power shifted in the government from President Andrew Johnson to Congress

    (C) President Andrew Johnson was able to defeat the Radicals' plan for Reconstruction

    (D) impeachment proceedings motivated by political differences became common in subsequent years

    (E) impeachment rules were rewritten to preclude another politically motivated impeachment

66. In order to remedy problems American farmers faced in the last quarter of the 19th century, the Populist Party advocated a policy of

    (A) increasing the amount of currency in circulation

    (B) raising interest rates on bank loans

    (C) raising tariffs to keep foreign agricultural products out of the United States

    (D) helping farmers resettle in urban areas

    (E) curbing inflation

GO ON TO THE NEXT PAGE

67. The reasons for the United States' entry into World War I included the goal of

   (A) destroying Germany and its people
   (B) organizing a "Great Parade" for freedom
   (C) protecting U.S. interest in the Far East
   (D) protecting freedom of the seas
   (E) retaliating for the attack on the United States by Japan

68. After World War II, NATO was formed primarily to

   (A) assist emerging nations in Asia
   (B) stop the spread of Communism in Europe
   (C) promote democratic reforms in Latin America
   (D) provide economic aid to war torn nations in Europe
   (E) halt the growth of fascism in southern Africa

69. The 1954, Vietnam peace negotiations in Geneva provided for all of the following EXCEPT

   (A) elections in 1956
   (B) the elimination of a French presence in Vietnam
   (C) a U.S. role in the future of Vietnam
   (D) the temporary division of Vietnam into North and South
   (E) political power for the Communist Party in Vietnam

70. In the "smoking gun" tape, Richard Nixon discussed the possibility of asking the Central Intelligence Agency to stop the Federal Bureau of Investigation from investigating Watergate matters. In the language of the Articles of Impeachment against Nixon, this charge became

   (A) breaking and entering
   (B) taping people without their knowledge
   (C) firing the Special Prosecutor
   (D) obstruction of justice
   (E) lying to the American people

71. According to John Adams, "The Revolution was effected before the war commenced." By this he meant

   (A) taxation without representation was the real issue that led to the Revolutionary War in 1776
   (B) the colonists in America had developed a unique character, independent of Great Britain, before the actual revolution had taken place
   (C) the American colonists had reached a point in their development in which a separation from England was necessary
   (D) the American Revolution was the result of the American policy of salutary neglect
   (E) the Battle of Lexington and Concord had taken place before the signing of the Declaration of Independence

GO ON TO THE NEXT PAGE

72. The "Era of Good Feeling" can best be characterized as years of

    (A) active participation by the United States in world affairs
    (B) economic growth within the United States
    (C) lower tariffs on imported goods
    (D) harmony over the issue of slavery
    (E) political control of the government by the Federalist Party

73. The accusation of a "corrupt bargain" in the election of 1824 was significant because

    (A) it marked the beginning of the spoils system in the administration of Andrew Jackson
    (B) it was a cross-party agreement between Andrew Jackson and John Quincy Adams
    (C) it led to the overwhelming election of Andrew Jackson in 1828
    (D) John Quincy Adams had a majority of the popular vote, but not a majority of the electoral vote
    (E) it led to the political demise of Henry Clay

74. "I stood alone on that wild prairie. Looking westward I saw my husband driving slowly over the plain[.] [T]urning my face once more to the east, my dear sister's footsteps were fast widening the distance between us. For the time I knew not which way to go, nor whom to follow. But in a few moments I rallied my forces… and soon overtook the slowly moving men who were bearing my husband and child over the prairie."

    Which of the following statements is NOT true of the above excerpt from the diary of a woman beginning her journey to the West?

    (A) It reflects the pioneer spirit.
    (B) It describes a conflict between a husband and wife about going west.
    (C) It shows how irrationally indecisive some people were.
    (D) It describes the fear of going into the unknown.
    (E) It shows that the wife ultimately chose her husband and child over her sister.

GO ON TO THE NEXT PAGE

75. The effect of Jim Crow laws, passed by Southern states after the Reconstruction period, was

    (A) stricter voting requirements for African Americans

    (B) the loss of citizenship for many African Americans

    (C) separate economies—one run by and for whites and one run by and for African Americans

    (D) a shift in African American loyalties from the Republican Party to the Democratic Party

    (E) racial segregation in public facilities

76. Why did the Ghost Dance movement thrive among Native Americans in the 1880s?

    (A) Many Native Americans believed that it would protect them in conflicts with whites.

    (B) It became a popular tourist attraction.

    (C) Many Native Americans believed it would end a severe drought.

    (D) It was a way for a younger generation of Native Americans to resist the authority of their elders.

    (E) Native American culture was finally given respect and recognition in mainstream American culture.

77. Senator Henry Teller agreed to vote for a declaration of war against Spain in 1898 only on the condition that

    (A) Cuba would be granted its independence if the United States defeated Spain

    (B) the United States would give up all claims to overseas possessions

    (C) all of Spain's possessions would become U.S. possessions if the United States won the war

    (D) President McKinley would initiate a Progressive domestic agenda

    (E) racially integrated units would be used in the war

78. Henry Ford's financial success can be attributed to all of the following EXCEPT

    (A) using an assembly line to produce an automobile every 93 minutes

    (B) reducing the price of a model-T from $850 to $300

    (C) attracting workers to his work force by paying them five dollars per day

    (D) retaining skilled European craftsmen and mechanics at his factories to ensure quality

    (E) creating efficient work processes, based on the ideas of Frederick Winslow Taylor

GO ON TO THE NEXT PAGE

79. All of the following increased participation in the political process in the 20th century EXCEPT the

    (A) 19th Amendment, giving women the right to vote
    (B) 17th Amendment, providing for the direct election of U.S. senators
    (C) 14th Amendment, granting civil rights to freedmen and women
    (D) Voting Rights Act of 1965
    (E) passage of state referendum acts

80. Which of the following organizations advocated carrying guns for self-defense?

    (A) Students for a Democratic Society
    (B) Congress of Racial Equality
    (C) National Association for the Advancement of Colored People
    (D) Black Panther Party
    (E) Vietnam Day Committee

81. Samuel Adams and Patrick Henry objected to the proposed Constitution in 1787 because they felt that the Constitution would

    (A) undermine the principles for which the Revolutionary War was fought
    (B) create too much democracy
    (C) support slavery
    (D) support states' rights
    (E) create a weak executive

82. I. "The Kansas-Nebraska Act authorizes the further extension of slavery and we have, do now, and will continue to protest most emphatically against… slavery." (1854)

    II. "The territories were the common property of the several states. As a joint agent of the states, Congress has no power to deny the citizens of any state the right to take their property into a territory… Therefore slavery is legal in the territories. If Wilmot carries, woe, woe I say to the union." (1850)

    III. "We beg the slave owners to pause before they proceed further to disturb the peace we had hoped the Compromise of 1850 would have made perpetual." (1854)

    Which of the above statement(s) would John C. Calhoun have supported?

    (A) I
    (B) II
    (C) III
    (D) I and III
    (E) II and III

83. Which of the following provisions would NOT be found in the various Black Codes passed after the Civil War?

    (A) A ban on African Americans carrying weapons.
    (B) A prohibition on interracial marriages.
    (C) A requirement that African Americans serve in the state National Guard units for two years.
    (D) A requirement that African Americans attain a permit if they wished to travel.
    (E) A ban on African Americans serving on juries.

GO ON TO THE NEXT PAGE

84. The federal government helped with the building of the transcontinental railroad by

    (A) providing the railroad companies with free iron and steel
    (B) organizing a publicly owned railroad company
    (C) raising the tariff to fund the project
    (D) providing the railroad companies with land grants
    (E) setting up the Interstate Commerce Commission to oversee the project

85. The Treaty of Paris, which concluded the Spanish-American War in 1898, contained all of the following provisions EXCEPT that

    (A) Spain cede Puerto Rico to the United States
    (B) Spain cede the Hawaiian Islands to the United States
    (C) the United States agree to pay $20 million to Spain for the Philippines
    (D) Guam become a U.S. territory
    (E) Cuba would be granted its independence

86. Which of the following was a reason the Democratic Party failed to win the presidency in the 1920s?

    (A) Its opposition to Jim Crow laws alienated Southern voters.
    (B) Internal splits existed between urban moderates and rural conservatives.
    (C) It had opposed U.S. involvement in World War I.
    (D) Voters saw the party as responsible for the Great Depression.
    (E) Voters perceived that the party was overly friendly to big business.

87. Herbert Hoover's idea of "rugged individualism" suggested that

    (A) people were able to survive hard times through their inner strength and resources
    (B) the government should give direct aid to the people in hard times
    (C) all of the basic needs of the people are the sole responsibility of the government
    (D) difficult times called for exceptional individuals to exercise power
    (E) the government and the people are partners who must share equal responsibility for the well being of the populace

88. The U.S. government allocated massive sums of money to math and science the 1950s in response to which of the following?

    (A) The Soviet Union landing men on the moon.
    (B) Fidel Castro coming to power in Cuba.
    (C) The Soviet Union developing the world's first hydrogen bomb.
    (D) The Soviet satellite *Sputnik* successfully orbiting the earth.
    (E) The United States failing to produce a Nobel Prize winner in science.

GO ON TO THE NEXT PAGE

89. Which chief justice of the Supreme Court was said to be the leader of a very activist court?

    (A) William Rehnquist
    (B) Earl Warren
    (C) Felix Frankfurter
    (D) Roger Taney
    (E) Warren Burger

90. The New Right of the 1990s could best be described as

    (A) a group of conservative Democrats who sought to move their party away from its liberal agenda
    (B) a liberal reaction to the conservative direction of the Democratic Party
    (C) popular support for President Clinton's welfare reform policies
    (D) an ultraconservative group within the Republican Party that gained control of Congress in 1994
    (E) a group of Richard Nixon Republicans who opposed the impeachment of President Clinton

STOP!

**If you finish before time is up,
you may check your work.**

Answer Key
Diagnostic Test

1. B	31. B	61. A
2. E	32. D	62. D
3. D	33. A	63. C
4. B	34. C	64. D
5. C	35. B	65. B
6. C	36. D	66. A
7. A	37. C	67. D
8. E	38. C	68. B
9. D	39. E	69. C
10. E	40. B	70. D
11. C	41. C	71. B
12. B	42. D	72. B
13. C	43. E	73. C
14. B	44. B	74. C
15. C	45. D	75. E
16. D	46. D	76. A
17. C	47. C	77. A
18. C	48. B	78. D
19. B	49. B	79. C
20. D	50. D	80. D
21. D	51. C	81. A
22. A	52. C	82. B
23. E	53. B	83. C
24. C	54. C	84. D
25. E	55. C	85. B
26. B	56. B	86. B
27. A	57. E	87. A
28. E	58. D	88. D
29. B	59. D	89. B
30. D	60. E	90. D

ANSWERS AND EXPLANATIONS

1. B

As a result of the Crusades in the 11th century, the Europeans had been exposed to the goods available in the East. This paved the way for the Renaissance and the Age of Exploration as the European nations sought to find an all–water route to the East. The discovery of the New World was the direct result of these explorations. Many English Puritans came to the New World to be able to worship freely (A), but that occurred over a century after the discovery of the New World. Primogeniture (C) was the medieval practice by which only the firstborn son could inherit the family wealth. As a result, many men came to the New World in search of their own land and fortune. However, the practice of primogeniture could not be ended by the discovery of the New World. Spreading Christianity (D) was a thought in the minds of the early explorers, but was not the main reason for the beginning of the exploration that led to the discovery of the New World. The desire to "civilize" other peoples (E) developed after the discovery of the New World.

2. E

The Nullification Crisis (1832–1833) occurred when the South Carolina legislature insisted on its right to declare federal tariff laws "null and void." The first and most famous protest by South Carolina was against the Tariff of Abominations (1828). The crisis was one of the most important events of the Jacksonian period. The Force Act (A) was one of Jackson's reactions to the nullification attempt. The debates between Hayne and Webster (B) were about the Nullification Crisis, not its cause. The Compromise Tariff of 1833 (D) was the resolution of the crisis. The Treaty of Ghent, which ended the War of 1812 (C), had nothing to do with nullification.

3. D

Popular Sovereignty was a provision placed in the Kansas-Nebraska Act by Stephen Douglas. Douglas was not concerned with the morality of slavery. Popular Sovereignty seemed democratic and fair because it allowed the citizens of the Kansas Territory to decide by voting whether or not to have slavery in their future state. However, it also repealed the Missouri Compromise line, which had excluded slavery in that very territory. It did not let Congress decide on slavery (E). It was not a part of the U.S. Constitution for admitting new states (B). The end result of the Kansas-Nebraska Act could have been either (A) or (C), but these were not Douglas's concerns.

4. B

All the other choices are important features of the "Gilded Age" (1875–1900). There was not a large migration of African Americans to Northern cities until the Great Migration of the World War I era; nor was there a substantial "white flight" of middle class whites out of urban areas until the 1940s and 1950s. The Gilded Age was characterized by highly contentious and sometimes violent classes between workers and owners (A), such as the Pullman Strike. A host of new inventions (C) such as the telephone made communication easier. Consolidation and monopolization in business (D) were hallmarks of the era. The era also was known for corruption (E), from the Credit Mobilier scandal to the notorious activities of "Boss" Tweed.

5. C

The vivid descriptions of meatpacking in Upton Sinclair's 1906 novel turned many readers' stomachs. The public wanted some sort of regulation of the industry. Many businesses within the industry itself did not object to the act, as they were eager for the industry to shed its bad image. The novel falls within the category of muckraking, even though it is a fictionalized account. The Interstate Commerce Act of 1887 (A) was a response to abuses by the railroads. The Wade-Davis Bill (B) was a Reconstruction proposal that Lincoln refused to sign. The 15th Amendment (D) was also a Reconstruction era action. The Clayton Antitrust Act of 1914 (E), dealt with trusts and monopoly practices—issues not central to *The Jungle*.

6. C

Relief, recovery, and reform were the cornerstones of the New Deal. Roosevelt sought to help people in need survive, stimulate the economy, and change the practices that led to the Depression in the first place. Hoover did not believe in direct government involvement in the lives of the people (A), while Roosevelt was ready to use the power of the government to solve the economic problems of the 1930s. *Laissez-faire* (B), a term coined by the British economist Adam Smith, meant that there would be little or no government interference in business. This was the direct opposite of FDR's New Deal. Some believe that the war finally ended the Depression (D), but that was not the basis of the New Deal. Roosevelt made it clear in his Inaugural Address of 1933 that he would take action whether Congress supported him or not (E).

7. A

Secretary of War Henry Stimson issued a response to the Japanese aggression in Manchuria which stated that the United States did not "intend to recognize any situation, or agreement" which Japan might enter as a result of this aggression. It was a doctrine of non-recognition which was intended to establish a moral argument against aggression. The United States was not a member of the League of Nations (B). General MacArthur (C) was the commander of the Allied troops in the Pacific during World War II, but not in 1931. The policy of watchful waiting (D) was associated with Woodrow Wilson and the problems in Mexico, which existed in the 1910s. The *Panay* (E) was fired upon by the Japanese in 1937, resulting in an apology from the Japanese. It was not related to the Manchuria problem.

8. E

The Alliance for Progress was an idea of John F. Kennedy's. All the other choices describe measures adopted during Lyndon B. Johnson's presidency.

9. D

Gloria Steinem, founder of *Ms.* magazine, fought for the Equal Rights Amendment. Kate Millet and others discussed Freud's anti-women ideas (A). Convincing men to participate in housework (B), though an important idea, was not central to the women's rights movement. Black and white equality in the workplace (C), a Civil Rights idea that Steinem supported, was not her principal cause. Concern about pesticides (E) is associated with environmentalists like Rachel Carson.

10. E

Bill Clinton, the President criticized for not serving in Vietnam, normalized relations with that nation more than 25 years after the war had ended. He visited Vietnam during his second term as president. George H. Bush did not increase aid to North Vietnam (A). In fact, North Vietnam no longer existed as a separate entity after the Vietnam War ended. There have been no trade restrictions (B) placed on Vietnam by George W. Bush. Richard Nixon was responsible for ending the war in Vietnam (C) through a program of "Vietnamization" giving more responsibility for the war to the South Vietnamese. However, when the American troops were withdrawn, South Vietnam fell to the North. Under Nixon, there was no recognition of that government as being the legitimate government of Vietnam. Jimmy Carter was critical of the actions of the Vietnamese government (D), a policy that represented no fundamental change in the continuing American dissatisfaction with the Vietnamese government after the Vietnam War.

11. C

The New England colonists lived longer and thrived in the harsh climate of New England. This has been attributed to their strong religious beliefs and the communities that supported these beliefs. Many New Englanders came to the New World with their families, which contributed to population growth through reproduction. Early

Southern colonists were predominantly male; natural reproduction was limited. New Englanders did participate in trade with Europe (A), but so did Virginians. This would not cause New Englanders to succeed more than Southerners. There *were* slaves and indentured servants in New England (B). There were fewer slaves in New England, but this has no bearing on overall population growth or longevity. Both (D) and (E) are false. There was a far higher proportion of single men among the Southern colonists as they came without their families (D), and the climate of New England (E) was harsh and cold, while the climate in the South was more moderate.

12. B

The Northwest Ordinance of 1787 established a guideline for the settlement of the Ohio Valley. One of its provisions was the prohibition of slavery in this territory. It also provided that no less than three or more than five states were to be formed in this territory. British control of the Northwest Territory (A) ended with the Revolutionary War. The Missouri Compromise established the 36° 30' (C) as the demarcation point between slave and free states. The ordinance encouraged peaceful relations with Native Americans (D), which were never achieved. The Clayton-Bulwer Treaty (1850) settled the border between Canada and the United States (E) in the Great Lakes region.

13. C

David Walker was a free black who wrote in the New York *Freedom's Journal* that sending African Americans to Africa was wrong because blacks were Americans and that they should be free immediately or they would rebel. He was opposed to gradual abolition as to slow a process (A), and colonization (B) because the Declaration of Independence said, "all men are created equal." He was an American, he reasoned, who should be equal to other Americans, not separate from them (E). He was for immediate abolition; he was not willing to wait until the government was ready (D).

14. B

Slaves were no longer doing the work, and the Southern economy suffered for it. Running away was an act of war. The one supply the South *did* have was guns (A). The consensus among historians is that the Confederate generals were better (C). Some cotton was getting through (D) because the blockade was not effective. The dedication of white Southerners to their cause (E) was legendary.

15. C

The people holding up their hands to stop immigration are comfortable or even affluent. In the shadows are their former, poorer, selves. The well-to-do individuals are demonstrating their hypocrisy by forgetting that they too had been poor immigrants. All the other choices were ideas held by some individuals during the Gilded Age. Choices (A), (B), and (E) are anti-immigrant sentiments. Choice (D) represents a pro-immigration point of view, but it does not represent the specific viewpoint of the cartoonist.

16. D

Theodore Roosevelt formed the Progressive Party, also called the Bull Moose Party, in 1912 when he lost the Republican nomination to the incumbent President Howard Taft. Taft's manipulation of the convention, as well as his conservative policies, had convinced Roosevelt and his allies to form a third party. Roosevelt did quite well at the polls, getting more votes and more electoral votes than Taft, but the split in the Republican Party allowed Democrat Woodrow Wilson to win the race with just 42 percent of the popular vote. World War I did not start until 1914 (A). African Americans (B) did not abandon the party of Lincoln until 1936, when they overwhelmingly supported the Democratic president, Franklin D. Roosevelt. Wilson was not of humble origins (C); he was the son of a minister and went to Princeton and Johns Hopkins. Neither of his opponents died before the election (E).

17. C

The two umbrella groups for labor unions had radically different approaches to union organizing. The AFL was the older, more conservative union, focusing mainly on skilled workers. The CIO was more brash and militant. It organized assembly line workers and skilled workers into the same unions. Both had large memberships in the 1930s (A). There was no significant East coast/West coast division (B) between the two unions. A "company union" (D) is an organization established by management to supposedly deal with worker grievances; both the AFL and CIO were made up of legitimate unions, organized by workers. The AFL was not dominated by Communist Party members (E).The Communist Party played a greater role in the CIO in the 1930s than it did in the AFL.

18. C

The quote refers to the relationship between time and action. King said the request that the movement wait "almost always means never." Time is neutral according to King. If people don't act, nothing good will happen. Martin Luther King wrote the "Letter from Birmingham Jail" in 1963 during the drive to desegregate the first capital of the Confederacy. The quote is not a discussion of nonviolence although King was an advocate of social change through nonviolent means (A). King did plea for action from white moderates (B) who were more concerned about calm than justice. He believed that all humanity was connected (D), and that it is morally right (E) to break the segregation laws since they were unjust. However, the ideas in (B), (D), and (E) do not refer to the central idea of the quote.

19. B

The Seneca Falls Declaration (1848), the great speeches of Elizabeth Cady Stanton (1848–1902) and the works of Susan B. Anthony, Lucretia Mott, and Harriet Tubman (all 19th-century thinkers and activists), were part of the first wave on which the feminism of the 1970's was based. Simone de Beauvoir (A) was the author of the ground breaking *Second Sex* (1950). There was only a small women's movement in the 1930s (C); and the women's movement in America was the precursor of the European movement (D). Kate Millet's famous book (E) is *Sexual Politics* (1970).

20. D

Teflon is a nonstick substance used on frying plans. Some of Reagan's detractors called him the Teflon President because he was never held accountable for any of the failures of his administration. In other words, he was the Teflon President because nothing stuck to him. Reagan was known as the great communicator (A) because he connected with his audiences, but that was not a characteristic of Teflon. Reagan consistently embellished his stories (B), blurring the line between fact and fiction. He had an endearing grandfatherly demeanor and his popularity remained very high during most of his administration, but he was not always in control (C). He depended heavily on the advice of others (E).

21. D

Roger Williams, the founder of Rhode Island, had been banished from the Massachusetts Bay Colony because he disagreed with the government-supported church established there. He believed in the separation of church and state. It was Massachusetts that was a theocracy (A), not Rhode Island. Massachusetts was a royal colony (B), while Rhode Island was a self-governing colony. All groups, including Quakers, enjoyed religious freedom (C) in Rhode Island. Both colonies were located in New England (E).

22. A

The First and Second Great Awakenings were characterized by large-scale revival meetings. The Puritans opposed the Catholic and Anglican use of incense (B). It was the Quakers who had long periods of silence (C), not the evangelicals of the Second Great Awakening, nor the fiery preachers of the First Great Awakening. Both Great Awakenings were *international* phenomena (D), not purely

American. Both Awakenings were emotional expressions of faith. Deism (E) was a highly rational approach to religion developed during the 18th century.

23. E

The implied powers are embodied in the elastic clause in the Constitution in Article I Section 8. It provides that Congress can make laws that are "necessary and proper" to carry out its delegated powers. This clause was used by Hamilton to justify the establishment of the Bank of the United States and then by Thomas Jefferson when he purchased the Louisiana Territory. The Whiskey Rebellion (A) was suppressed when Washington used his powers as commander in chief, to quell an uprising of Pennsylvania farmers. The Bill of Rights (B), the first ten amendments, was adopted according the ratification procedures specified in the Constitution. Jay's Treaty (C) was ratified by the Senate as outlined in the Constitution. The Constitution empowers Congress to establish a system of courts (D). The elastic clause, therefore, was not required to justify the passage of the Judiciary Act of 1789.

24. C

The 13th Amendment abolished slavery; the 14th Amendment extended citizenship right to African Americans and guaranteed all people "equal protection under the law" as well as due process; and the 15th Amendment gave African American men the right to vote. The 15th Amendment is the only one of the three that specifically addressed the issue of voting rights (A). The amendments are all from the Reconstruction era, not the Civil War (B). The Republican Party (D) supported all three amendments. The amendments did not protect the rights of property holders (E). The 13th actually deprived slave owners of their "property."

25. E

Mechanization was a double-edged sword for farmers. It increased output, but with so much corn and wheat on the market, prices fell. Farmers then had difficulty paying back the loans that they had taken out to buy the new equipment. The graph shows a decrease in prices, which did not benefit farmers (A).

26. B

The Triple Entente, led by France and Great Britain, demanded that Germany pay reparations for the tremendous loss of life and property that had been experienced by the European nations during World War I. Wilson's conciliatory approach under the Fourteen Points (with the exception of the League of Nations) was largely rejected at Versailles. The Triple Entente (A) held Germany totally responsible for World War I, although these nations shared much of the blame for that war. Wilson pursued his policies with great vigor and optimism (C) at the negotiations, but he was unable to convince Lloyd George and Georges Clemenceau to construct a framework for a democratic peace. The League of Nations was established (D) by the Treaty of Versailles, but the U.S. Senate rejected the Treaty and the League of Nations. Germany was not part of the negotiations at Versailles (E).

27. A

Soon after the bombings of Hiroshima and Nagasaki, Japan signed the peace treaty that ended World War II. Truman won the election of 1948 (B). The United Nations was established after World War II, but not as a result of the bombings (C). The computer age began in the 1960s with space exploration (D). The problems over establishing peace, which developed between the democracies of the United States and Europe and the totalitarian government under the Soviet Union, were the fundamental causes of the Cold War (E).

28. E

Galbraith worried in *The Affluent Society* that America was too focused on individual material gain and not enough on social betterment. Statement (A) is a conservative, laissez-faire position; Galbraith, who was considered a liberal, did not support this view. Statement (B) would better describe another 1950s book, *The Power Elite*, by C. Wright Mills. The Communist Party might be advocate a Soviet-style command economy (C), but this was not Galbraith's position. The position of the 19th century Populists is described in statement (D).

29. B

The domino theory of Eisenhower and Kennedy stated that Communism would spread like falling dominoes—a theory that originated as a description for the spread of Communism in Southeast Asia. Containment (D), George F. Kennan's 1947 idea, was the policy of attempting to stop Soviet expansion. The Truman Doctrine (A) was a 1948 Cold War philosophy that America should support free (non-Communist) peoples; it was developed in response to the situation in Greece. Mutually Assured Destruction (MAD) (C) refers to the situation beginning in the 1950s in which the nuclear peace was maintained because both the United States and the USSR were scared by the realization that the use of nuclear weapons would result in a massive nuclear retaliation. Détente (E) was Nixon's overture to the USSR to reduce arms and develop more cordial relations (1972–1974).

30. D

Lyndon Johnson was president before Nixon; he is most remembered for the War on Poverty and the escalation of the Vietnam War. The book *All the President's Men* describes the Watergate scandal during the administration of Richard Nixon (A). John Dean (B) was Nixon's chief counsel. Sam Ervin (C) headed the Senate Watergate Committee. G. Gordon Liddy (E) engineered the break-in at the Watergate Hotel. (The title of the Woodward-Bernstein book alludes to the nursery rhyme: "All the king's horses and all the king's men could not put Humpty Dumpty—i.e., the Nixon administration—back together again.")

31. B

The Americans developed a greater self-confidence after fighting the French and Indian War. They realized that the British were not invincible. Fighting together, the Americans of the 13 colonies also realized that they had much in common and shared many ideas. The hostility against the Indians (A) did not begin with the French and Indian War, although the acquisition of new territory led to Pontiac's Rebellion. The Americans *lost* respect (C) for the British as a result of the war. The Americans were still happy to depend on Britain for protection and, therefore, were not interested in building a strong army (D). However, the colonists need for protection diminished because the French threat had been removed. There was no desire on the part of the Americans to ally with the Spanish (E), although the Americans did want the use of the Mississippi. After the French and Indian War, Spain dominated Mississippi River shipping by virtue of its control of New Orleans (and the land West of the Mississippi).

32. D

John Trumbull was a painter who lived during the late 1700s and painted portraits of Hamilton, Jay, and Washington. Phillis Wheatley, an African slave, was a poetess of the same period. Their works were evidence of the beginnings of a distinctly American culture. John Locke's views (B) influenced American leaders including Thomas Jefferson, who incorporated much of Locke's thought in the Declaration of Independence. Locke, however, was an Englishman, not an American. Transcendentalism (C) was a movement that took place in the 1830s and refers to a belief that people had an inner light that could help them find the truth. *The Star-Spangled Banner* (E) was written by Francis Scott Key during the War of 1812.

33. A

The decision of *McCulloch v. Maryland* (1819), which dealt with the Bank of the United States and upheld its constitutionality, established that the states could not nullify actions taken by the federal government. Stating that the "power to tax is the power to destroy," Marshall upheld the right of the national government to establish the Bank of the United States. *Marbury v. Madison* (1803) established the right of the Supreme Court to exercise judicial review (B). This case resulted from the Midnight Appointments under the administration of John Adams. *Plessy v. Ferguson* (1896) established the doctrine of separate but equal when it came to racial matters (C). The *Dred Scott* Case (1857) established the idea that slaves were property, inflaming the abolitionist's cause (D). *Brown v. the Board of Education of Topeka* reversed the Plessy decision stating that separate but equal was "inherently unequal" (E).

34. C

L and N are correct because they describe the Mexican Cession. The Wilmot Proviso (1846) stated that "there shall be no slavery or involuntary servitude in any territory from Mexico." The so-called Mexican Cession was won in the Mexican War; it included California and the whole Southwest and Mountain West excluding the Oregon Territory. The United States paid Mexico $15 as part of the Treaty of Guadalupe Hidalgo (1848). The other choices include territory from the Louisiana Purchase (O), the Oregon Territory (M), or the Eastern states (P); none of these were part of the Mexican Cession.

35. B

The small entrepreneur was gradually replaced by larger and larger entities—a story that is true of mining and many other American businesses as well. The program was fairly popular, making (A) incorrect. As a whole, the land of the Great Plains, where most homesteads were established, was (and is) incredibly fertile (B). While clashes no doubt occurred (D), the homesteaders usually settled on land that no longer had large Native American populations. There was no large public scandal in regard to the Homestead Act (E), and the land was not *sold* by the government; it was given away after the recipient paid a filing fee.

36. D

Despite the fact that excellent newspapers receive Pulitzer Prizes today, Pulitzer himself and his competitor, William Randolph Hearst, were associated with sensationalistic "yellow journalism." Such journalism is seen as a contributing factor to the United States declaring war on Spain in the Spanish-American War, making (C) incorrect. Progressive era journalists, such as Lincoln Steffens and Ida Tarbell, were considered muckrakers (A). An important public moralizer (B) in the 19th century was Anthony Comstock, founder of the New York Society for the Suppression of Vice. Important anti-imperialists of the late 19th and early 20th century were Carl Schurz and Mark Twain (C). The immigrant, foreign-language press has been vibrant in America from the mid-19th century until the present day— but it was not Pulitzer and Hearst's field (E).

37. C

The Justice Department conducted a series of raids on the homes of suspected radicals and socialists and of the offices of radical organizations. These raids were carried out without search warrants, in violation of the 4th Amendment. The raids were coordinated by the Attorney General, A. Mitchell Palmer. The Palmer Raids involved *both* men and women (B) and did not target churches (A), Native Americans (E), or African Americans (D). The most obvious discrimination against African Americans during this period was caused by Jim Crow laws, which resulted in the separation of the races.

38. C

The 1st Amendment prohibits Congress from establishing an official religion (the so-called "establishment clause"). In *Engel v. Vitale*, the Supreme Court ruled that "it is no part of the business of government to compose official prayers…." The establishment clause is the basis for a separation of church and state. The other choices, whether valid or not, would not come before a court of law for resolution.

39. E

The Free Speech Movement of 1964 at the University of California at Berkeley began as a defense of students who had set up tables for off-campus political organizations on university grounds. The administration attempted to prevent the students from disseminating literature. They were not workers (A) or free speech advocates in the larger society (B). Rock and roll lyrics (C) were not censored until the 1980s. Radio programming (D) did not become an issue until the late 1960s.

40. B

A definition of inflation is rising prices. First, prices go up; then *that* causes the value of the dollar to go down, because it takes more money to buy the same goods. Deflation means a fall in prices and an increase in the value of the dollar (A). There wasn't a depression in the late 1970s (C). Stagnation (of the economy) does not occur when employment is high (D). The value of the dollar *decreases* when prices are high—the opposite of what (E) suggests.

41. C

The Treaty of Tordesillas, signed by Spain and Portugal in 1495, divided the non-European world between Spain and Portugal. Thus Spain was then free to explore the Western Hemisphere without Portuguese interference—except the coast of Brazil, which fell into the Portuguese half of the world. The Portuguese had developed the caravel, a faster sailing ship than those possessed by the Spanish (A). Spanish settlers (B) did not come in large numbers to the New World. Although Christopher Columbus "discovered" the New World, his actions, by themselves, were not very successful in establishing Spain in the New World (D) and only encouraged competitors from other nations to join the search for an all-water route to

the Far East. The wealth accumulated by the Spanish crown (E) was the result, not the cause, of Spanish domination of most of the New World.

42. D

A fear of mobocracy, or excesses in democracy, led the framers of the Constitution to create an indirect process of electing the President through the establishment of the Electoral College. In addition, while the House of Representatives was directly elected by the people, the Senate was to be elected by the state legislatures, placing the Senate out of the direct hands of the people. The 17th Amendment to the Constitution, adopted in 1913, provided for the direct election of U.S. senators by the people. Choices (A), (B), and (C) were not concerns that led to the establishment of the Electoral College or the indirect election of senators. The framers were interested in protecting the rights of the minority, in this case, the aristocrats, from the excesses of democracy and were less interested in protecting the rights of the majority (E).

43. E

Both the Northwest Ordinance of 1787 and the Missouri Compromise of 1820 restricted slavery in areas yet to be admitted as states. The Northwest Ordinance forbade slavery in the Northwest Territory, while the Missouri Compromise forbade slavery north of he 36° 30' line of north latitude across the Louisiana Purchase. The Northwest Ordinance provided that no less than three or more than five states was to be created in that territory, but the Missouri Compromise contained no such guidelines (A). The Missouri Compromise provided for the admission of Maine as a free state and Missouri as a slave state, but no new states were admitted to the Union by the Northwest Ordinance (B). Land for public schools was set aside by the Land Ordinance of 1785 and mentioned in the Northwest Ordinance, but the Missouri Compromise does not discuss this issue (C). The Northwest Ordinance provided for fair treatment of the Native American population, while the Missouri Compromise does not address this issue (D).

44. B

The escaped slave ran away because he considered himself a person, not a piece of property. His former owner treated him like a good horse, not like a human. He was obviously not happy (C) or satisfied (E) as a slave, or he wouldn't have risked his life to run away. The fact he ran away makes it quite clear that he did not consider his master "good" (A) and that he did not believe the owner took proper care of his slaves (D).

45. D

Lincoln's First Inaugural Address took place before the fighting of the Civil War started. Lincoln was trying his best to avoid war. He tried to convince the South that they could have peace, if they didn't attack. Statement (A) is from the Lincoln-Douglas debates and (B) is from Lincoln's Gettysburg Address. The quote in (C) is from Daniel Webster's Second Reply to Hayne and (E) is from Lincoln's Second Inaugural Address.

46. D

A pattern emerged in the Gilded Age of employers cutting wages and the workers rebelling. This occurred with the Railroad Strike of 1877 and Pullman Strike of 1894. Deadly accidents (B) certainly occurred in the 19th century as did speedups (C), but neither sparked major labor battle. The government's recognition of workers' rights to organize unions (A) did not come until the Wagner Act which was passed in 1935. The CIO (E) wasn't formed until 1936.

47. C

The United States would not relinquish control of the Philippines after the Spanish-American War. In response, Filipinos waged an unsuccessful war for independence. President McKinley argued that he was helping a people not yet ready for self-government, but having a toehold in Asia and its markets probably also entered into the calculations. The Philippines continued to exist as a political entity (B), albeit as a U.S. colony, and did not become independent (A) until 1946. Spain had little influence in the area after relinquishing control of the Philippines as a result of the Spanish American War (D). Eastern European countries, not the Philippines, became satellites of the Soviet Union following World War II (E).

48. B

Washington insisted that African Americans accommodate themselves to existing society by learning farming and manual skills. He was challenged by the more radical DuBois who advocated resistance to racist practices. It was Marcus Garvey who attracted a following in the late 1910s and 1920s with his affirmation of racial pride and the "back to Africa" movement (A). Martin Luther King Jr. is closely identified with the nonviolent civil disobedience movement of the 1950s and 1960s that sought to end racial segregation (C). Choice (D) incorporates a famous phrase by Malcolm X. Choice (E) might represent the viewpoint of many contemporary African American politicians.

49. B

Economic figures show that problems of unemployment and production only ended upon the entry of the United States into WWII. The New Deal had some positive effect early on, but seemed less effective later. The economic figures show a decrease in unemployment from 24 percent to 14 percent by 1937, but do not show an end to significant unemployment (A) until the outbreak of WWII. The problems in Europe and the attack by the Japanese on Pearl Harbor (C), not New Deal programs, led the United States into WWII. The Supreme Court was not supportive (D) of all the New Deal legislation and declared the Agricultural Adjustment Act and the National Recovery Act unconstitutional. This led to FDR's attempt to pack the Court. The Federal Reserve System (E) was established in 1913 under the Administration of Woodrow Wilson.

50. D

In *Roe v. Wade* (1972) the Supreme Court, under Nixon's appointee Warren Burger, decided that abortion was protected by the Constitution on the basis of a woman's right to privacy derived from the due process clause of the 14th Amendment. The other rights were not used in the *Roe* case. Freedom of the press (A) was used in the Pentagon Papers case; *habeas corpus* (B) is used in death penalty cases to obtain a new trial. Executive privilege (C) was used by President Richard Nixon to attempt to prevent handing the Watergate tapes to the special prosecutor, and the right of eminent domain (E) allows a government to take over land when it sees fit.

51. C

The Barbados Slave Codes were passed by the British to control the slaves in the West Indies. They were harsh and gave the masters total control over slaves who were described as racially inferior. When South Carolina adopted the Barbados Slave Codes in 1696, it provided a legal basis for chattel slavery (the use of slaves as property) based upon race. Mixing of the races (A) was not encouraged in colonial America. Gradual abolition (B) was not a part of a slave code which legalized slavery. Bacon's Rebellion in 1676 (D) occurred in Virginia and led to an increase in the number of African American slaves, not Indians. The paternalistic attitude (E) of the South toward the slaves was most widely used to justify the continuation of slavery after the 1830s.

52. C

The fact that the Stamp Act imposed *direct* taxes on the colonists was a key source of widespread indignation—second only to the fury provoked by "taxation without representation." In 1767 Parliament passed the Townshend Acts (which were indirect taxes), in an attempt to get around the direct tax argument. Stamps were required for many items used by the colonists but that wasn't their *legal* objection (A). In 1765 the idea of coercion by the king was not the main objection.

Explicit coercion did not come until 1766 in the Declaratory Act (B). The Stamp Act did not restrict colonial trade (D) and the fees were not unreasonably high (E).

53. B

When President Washington used military force to quash the Whiskey Rebellion, he demonstrated the ability of the central government to enforce law and collect taxes. Suspension of habeas corpus, which would allow the government to imprison a person without informing him or her of the charges, was not an issue in the Whiskey Rebellion (A). Washington's actions did not interfere with the sale or consumption of whiskey (C). There was no attempt by the government to control the production of whiskey (D). The government had placed a tax on whiskey and did offer to subsidize grain producers, but the key question in Washington's actions concerned the ability of the government to collect taxes and enforce the law (E).

54. C

Slave mothers tried to boost the confidence of their children and keep them entertained at the same time. If you can figure out how to fool your master or have fun at his expense, it gives you some psychological space of your own. This little dialogue shows how clever slaves could be. Many blacks were familiar with these kinds of things, but it took the Civil Rights Movement to bring material like this into mainstream history teaching. Here, the slave tricks his master by using the knowledge that the master thinks he (the slave) is stupid. A slave holder (A), or white overseer (B) and (E) would be unlikely to recount a story making fun of them and their race. The same holds true for a confederate schoolboy (Confederate schoolboys were white, since slaves could not attend school).

55. C

The 13th Amendment abolished slavery, which was as far as Johnson wanted to go. By the end of the Civil War everyone realized that slavery was a thing of the past; consequently, the amendment abolishing it (C) was not seen as a radical step. All the other actions—the Civil Rights Act (A), the Freedman's Bureau (B), the arrest of Confederates (D), and voting rights for African Americans (E) are more radical steps that Johnson opposed.

56. B

During the era, the slums of New York's Lower East Side existed just a few miles from the lavish mansions of Fifth Avenue. This gap between rich and poor characterized the era. The Gilded Age saw a great deal of economic growth, as the United States produced massive amounts of manufactured goods for both domestic and foreign consumption. The country carried out the transition from wartime production to civilian production quite successfully, making (A) incorrect. There was no "back-to-the-land movement" during the Gilded Age (C); in fact, many rural people moved to the city to work in industry. By the Gilded Age, slavery and the slave trade had been abolished (D). High tariffs and isolationist policies were characteristics of the 1920s (E).

57. E

These activities included gambling and drinking on Sundays. The Democratic Party, with its support among working-class and immigrant city dwellers, tended to oppose "blue laws." Child labor (A) was challenged by the 1916 Keating-Owen Act, which was declared unconstitutional in 1918. Child labor was outlawed by the 1938 Fair Labor Standards Act. Mandating that producers honestly portray the contents of their products (B) was a result of the 1906 Pure Food and Drug Act. The Agricultural Adjustment Act (1933) provided price supports for farmers (C) and the Pendleton Act (1881) reformed civil service procedures (D).

58. D

The Communist Party did engage in spying on the United States for the Soviet Union, but this could not be considered a cause for its growth. This espionage was not known to the public, nor even to most members of the Communist Party. If the public did know of this activity, it would certainly disillusion most would-be sympathizers. The Alger Hiss case of the later 1940s and the Ethel and Julius Rosenberg of the early 1950s drove many people from the party, although loyalists claimed that the defendants were innocent. Choices (A), (B), (C), and (E) are all accurate descriptions of the appeal that the Communist Party held for different people.

59. D

Blacks were shocked when they came back after beating the Nazis and still faced discrimination (D), giving great impetus to the call for Civil Rights. It was the war experience of African Americans (D) that made accepting lynchings as a part of life in the South more difficult after World War II. The March on Washington (1963) (C) and the Freedom Rides (1961) (E) were too late to have started the movement. The founding of the NAACP (1911) (A) occurred long before the movement. Lynchings (B) were a constant threat and a reality from the earliest days of the colonies.

60. E

Eisenhower warned that the power of the "military-industrial complex" was growing virtually unchecked. Arms manufacturers and the military establishment posed a danger, he said, to freedom and democracy. Entangling alliances (A) is a phrase from Washington's farewell address. Environmental questions (B) did not become national political concerns until 1970. Eisenhower turned against Senator McCarthy in 1954 (C). Illicit drugs (D) did not become a major political issue until the 1960s and 70s.

61. A

The Treaty of Paris ending the French and Indian War removed the French presence from North America. This allowed the colonists to depend less heavily on the British for their defense. The colonists desired to settle in areas west, not east, of the Appalachian Mountains (B). However, the British government restricted such settlement by the Proclamation of 1763, which forbade colonists to settle west of the Appalachians. The colonists resented the Proclamation and ignored the King's directive. The end of the French and Indian War marked an end to the salutary neglect (C) and a beginning of greater involvement by the British in the American colonies, which contributed to the colonists' increased resentment against the British. The threat from the Native Americans still existed on the frontier (D). Britain continued its mercantilist policies toward the colonists. However, the American colonists' increasing resentment of the British attempts to enforce this policy contributed to the War for Independence (E).

62. D

The XYZ Affair, which took place in 1797 during the administration of John Adams, resulted in American agitation for war against France, but did not raise tensions with Britain. The British engaged in impressment of U.S. seamen (A) until the War of 1812. The British continually incited the Indians to violence against the Americans after the Revolutionary War (B). Despite the Treaty of Paris in 1783, the British had not removed their forces from the Ohio Valley (C). In the Treaty of Paris of 1783, the Americans had agreed only to *encourage* the states to return land seized from the Loyalists during the Revolutionary War (E).

63. C

Interchangeable parts were machine-made parts for guns or other manufactured devices that could be put together without further work. This enabled workers to assemble mass-produced goods more easily. Printers (A) had had moveable type since the 16th century. Farmers (B) did not directly use interchangeable parts, since they were not manufacturing products. Safe toys (D) are not necessarily the result of mass production. The demand for coopers' skills in making barrels (E) declined as mass production of metal barrels replaced wooden ones.

64. D

California was admitted as a free state in the compromise. All other choices were part of the compromise. The other important parts were (A) the Fugitive Slave Law and (E) leaving the status of Utah to be resolved in the future. The 1850 Compromise put off the major questions, but it did prevent war for 10 years.

65. B

Johnson was virtually silenced after the impeachment process; he was further weakened by the midterm election of 1866, in which the Republicans received an overwhelming mandate. The Senate failed to remove him from office by one vote (A), but he successfully ran for the Senate five years later. The Radicals in Congress implemented their plan without much interference from Johnson after 1866 (C). There was only one other Presidential impeachment after Johnson's— President Bill Clinton's in 1998 (D). There was no major rewriting of the impeachment rules after 1866 (E).

66. A

A solution that the farmers' organizations, the Grangers, the Greenback Party, and the Populist Party proposed was putting more money into circulation so that inflation would occur and it would be easier for farmers to repay their debts. Inflation would not be curbed (E); rather, it would push up the prices they received for their crops. The most widely circulated suggestion was to back up currency with silver at a ratio of 16 parts of silver to one of gold. Farmers' organizations would not support an increase in interest rates (B), as they had to take out loans to purchase equipment and seeds. Farmers have generally supported tariffs on agricultural imports (C), but this was not the main plank of the Populist Party. Urban resettlement (D) was of no interest to the Populists.

67. D

The announcement that Germany would resume unrestricted submarine warfare led the United States into World War I. The use of submarines impaired shipping and travel and thus violated the principle of freedom of the seas. The United States did not wish to destroy Germany or its people (A). Although World War I has been called the "Great Parade" (B), the involvement of the United States in this war was not motivated by a desire to participate in it. The protection of United States' interests in the Far East (C) was more relevant to World War II. The focus of World War I for the United States was in Europe. The Japanese attacked Pearl Harbor, Hawaii, in 1941 (E).

68. B

NATO was a defensive alliance designed to halt Soviet expansion in Europe after World War II. The United States and 11 Western European nations joined NATO, which stood for North Atlantic Treaty Organization. Immediately after WWII, there was no attempt to aid emerging nations in Asia (A) or to help Latin America (C). It was the Marshall Plan, not NATO, that brought economic aid to Europe (D). The United States was not concerned with fascism in Africa (E).

69. C

There was no mention of an official U.S. role in Vietnam in the Geneva Accords, although they initiated a new stage of U.S. imperialism in the area. The 1954 agreement removed the French as a political force in Vietnam (B), divided Vietnam (D) and scheduled elections in 1956 (A). The United States, which did not sign the Geneva Accords, helped prevent the 1956 elections from being held because the Communist leader, Ho Chi Minh, who was given control of North Vietnam, was sure to win (E).

70. D

The "smoking gun" tape showed obstruction of justice because Nixon was trying to stop an investigation into wrongdoing. The Articles of Impeachment passed by the House Judiciary Committee were Obstruction of Justice (interfering with the investigation), Abuse of Power ("dirty tricks"), and the Defiance of Subpoenas (refusal to hand over the tapes). Breaking and entering (A) was a "dirty trick" and an abuse of power but this was not part of the "smoking gun" tape. Taping people without their knowledge (B) and firing the Special Prosecutor (C) were not the "high crimes or misdemeanors" required by the Constitution to impeach a president. Lying to the American people (E) is not a crime.

71. B

By 1776, the colonists had developed a perception of themselves and the world that was quite different from their British brethren. This famous quote of John Adams was written many years after the Revolutionary War and expresses his view that the development of a distinctly American identity was the real American Revolution and underlying reason for the war for independence from Britain. Although answer choices (A) and (C) state reasons for the colonists' rebellion, these do not express the basic idea of the John Adams quote. Salutary neglect (D) was a British—not an American—policy towards its North American colonies in the 1600s and 1700s. By this policy, the British passed laws supporting the system of mercantilism but did not enforce them strictly. John Adams understood that the years of geographical separation from England and the British policy of salutary neglect had allowed the colonies to develop independently of Britain and contributed to the development of an American identity, but the John Adams quote is not specifically about salutary neglect. Statement (E) is a correct statement about the war, but does not reflect the idea expressed by John Adams in this quotation.

72. B

The Era of Good Feeling commonly refers to the years of the Monroe Administration, 1816–1824. It was marked by the economic growth and improvements in the infrastructure. Despite the appearances of "good feelings," there was no harmony on the issue of slavery (D) and controversy arose over the admission of Missouri as a slave state. Americans focused on issues within the country as opposed to the outside world, and the United States was not very involved in world affairs (A). Tariffs were not lowered during this period (C); in fact, the American System, proposed by Henry Clay, supported the idea of a raising tariff rates to encourage the development of American industry. After the Hartford Convention in 1814, the Federalists (E) steadily lost power.

73. C

In the election of 1824, no candidate had a majority of the electoral votes, but Andrew Jackson had more popular votes than anyone else, even though it was not a majority. In the House of Representatives Henry Clay threw his support to John Quincy Adams, making Adams president. When Adams subsequently appointed Clay to the position of Secretary of State, Jackson accused Adams of making a "corrupt bargain" to gain the votes of Clay's supporters in the House. Jackson used this accusation against Adams and this contributed to his landslide victory in 1828. The spoils system (A) of Jackson's administration did not begin until 1828 when Jackson was elected. The "corrupt bargain" was not an agreement between Adams and Jackson (B). No candidate received the majority (D) of the popular or electoral vote in 1824. Henry Clay (E) continued to be a leading statesman despite the accusation.

74. C

This diary entry doesn't provide the usual concept we think about in regard to the exciting Oregon Trail. ("Westward Ho!" is the slogan that usually springs to mind.) After the 1960s, historians began looking at the experiences of ordinary people by reading their diaries, letters, and looking at church records. This passage shows the fear (D) which men and women experienced going west. The woman who is quoted was torn between her sister and all she knew in the East, and her husband who wanted to go west. She clearly hesitated about whether to follow, indicating that it might have been his ambition but not hers (B). This is a description of the pioneer spirit because she gathered her forces and joined her husband and child (A) and (E). Her indecision was NOT irrational; there was a real conflict for her (C).

75. E

Jim Crow laws created separate public facilities for African Americans. These included separate schools, water fountains, and waiting rooms at bus and train station. The facilities were not equal, but such laws stood until the 1950s and 1960s. Stricter voting requirements (A) came about as a result of literacy tests or poll taxes. African Americans were not considered citizens (B) as a result of the *Dred Scott v. Sanford* decision (1857). The economic activities of whites and African Americans were tightly linked (C), with African Americans performing domestic and manual labor for whites. The shift of African American voters from the Republican Party to the Democratic Party (D) did not occur until 1936.

76. A

The ritualistic dance honoring Native American ancestors, known as the Ghost Dance, became a rallying point for Native Americans in their battles against U.S. forces. As such, the United States banned the practice. Native communities did not draw large numbers of tourists in the 19th century (B). The Ghost Dance was not a rain dance (C). There is not much evidence of youthful resistance to the leadership of elders among Native Americans before the 20th century (D). Native American culture has not received recognition or respect in mainstream American society today, and certainly not in the 19th century (E).

77. A

Teller's concerns led to the Teller Amendment, which guaranteed Cuban independence if the United States defeated Spain in the Spanish-American War. Many

Americans did not want to duplicate the imperial policies of the European powers, but they could support helping Cuba gain its independence from Spain. Anti-imperialists argued that the United States should give up overseas possessions (B), but not Teller. As a result of its victory in the Spanish-American War, the United States took control of Puerto Rico and the Philippines, but not Cuba (C). The conditions involved Cuba, not domestic policy (D). African Americans did fight in Cuba, but racially integrated units (E) were not used in the U.S. military until the very end of World War II.

78. D

Ford's policies virtually eliminated the need for skilled craftsmen and mechanics at his factory. The most important achievement is bringing the assembly line to automobile manufacturing (A). Ford created well-built, inexpensive cars that were within the reach of most incomes (B). The "five dollar day" (C) was, in part, an attempt to encourage people to work for Ford despite the repetitive, boring nature of the assembly line. Ford was a follower of Taylor's time-motion studies (E) designed to create an efficient manufacturing system. All of these techniques had the result of "de-skilling" the workplace.

79. C

The 14th Amendment was passed in 1868 and had little effect in increasing political participation in the 20th century. The 19th Amendment (A), ratified in 1920, increased political participation by allowing women to vote. The 17th Amendment (B), ratified in 1913, increased political participation by allowing the voters to directly elect U.S. senators. The Voting Rights Act (D), passed in 1965, was specifically aimed at ending obstructions previously raised against African American voters in the South. Referendum acts (A), which allowed citizens to vote on ballot questions, were 20th century measures passed in the Progressive Era.

80. D

The Black Panther Party was an explicitly revolutionary socialist organization that advocated carrying guns for self-defense. The Congress of Racial Equality (B) and the National Association for the Advancement for Colored People (C) were explicitly nonviolent, while Students for a Democratic Society (A) and the Vietnam Day Committee (E) had no policy on guns. The most famous image of the Black Panthers is a photograph of a group of Panthers standing with rifles on the steps of the California legislature.

81. A

Patrick Henry and other Anti-Federalists viewed the Constitution as a dangerous document that did not fully support the idea of popular rule. They believed that the framers of the Constitution, the Federalists, had compromised the principles for which the Revolutionary War had been fought. They feared the Constitution would restrict democracy (B), not expand it. This debate was not about slavery; in fact, Patrick Henry supported slavery (C). Henry attacked the Constitution because it took power away from the states (D), and he feared that the president might become a king (E).

82. B

John C. Calhoun, after writing the *South Carolina Exposition and Protest* against the "Tariff of Abominations" in 1827, became one of the most prominent leaders of the South. He was strongly pro-slavery and would have supported speaker II. Speaker I opposes slavery in the West, which Calhoun supported. Speaker III is in favor of the Compromise of 1850, which Calhoun opposed. Calhoun had died by the end of 1850.

83. C

While serving in the National Guard for two years might seem like an onerous burden, white Southerners did not want to arm the African American population of the South to protect whites. All the other provisions were part of the Black Codes. The overall effect of the Black Codes was to put African Americans in a secondary position in Southern society and to maintain the economic status quo. In fact, they tried to keep the African Americans as close to slavery as possible.

84. D

The railroads received large swaths of land out West. The rationale was that this was a way to entice the railroads to do something that would benefit the entire public. This procedure amounted to a big giveaway of public lands to wealthy corporations. Choices (A), (B), and (C) did not occur. Of these, choice (B) is the least logical—free enterprise was the rule in the 19th century. The Interstate Commerce Commission (E) was established to regulate abusive railroad practices, not to help railroad companies build.

85. B

The United States obtained the Hawaiian Islands in 1898, but this had nothing to do with the Spanish American War and the Treaty of Paris. All the other choices were important provisions of the treaty. Puerto Rico (A) and Guam (D) are still U.S. possessions. The Philippines (C) fought for its independence from the United States following the Spanish-American War, but lost. It was granted independence in 1946, although the United States exerted influence there afterward. Cuba was granted its independence after the Spanish-American War (E) as a result of the Teller Amendment to the U.S. declaration of war.

86. B

An important issue that split the rural and urban factions of the Democratic Party in the 1920s was Prohibition. The rift within the Democratic Party reflected tensions within society during the 1920s. The Democratic Party of the 1920s was not opposed to Jim Crow Laws (A). It had supported U.S. participation in World War I (C)—after all, Wilson was a Democrat. The Depression did not begin until the very end of the 1920s (D). Both parties were friendly to big business in the 1920s (E).

87. A

Hoover believed that people could survive the worst of times by helping themselves and helping their communities. He did not believe that it was the role of government to give direct aid to people in hard times (B). Hoover did not believe that the government was solely responsible for the basic needs of the people (C); he believed that these were the responsibility of individuals. The idea that exceptional men must rise to power during difficult times (D) is more akin to fascism than it is to Hoover's ideas. The idea of a government partnership with the people, particularly in regard to the economy (E), was not an idea embraced by Hoover and is not representative of the idea of "rugged individualism."

88. D

The orbiting of *Sputnik* shook America's confidence in itself. Americans feared the Soviet Union was surpassing the U.S. in technology, leading to attempts to improve U.S. math and science education. The Soviets did not land men on the moon (A); the United States did in 1969. The Cuban Revolution influenced U.S. policy in the 1960s (B)—but the shift in educational focus was a 1950s phenomenon. It was the United States that developed the first hydrogen bomb (C) in 1952. America has produced more than its share of Nobel Prize winners in science (E).

89. B

Earl Warren headed the Supreme Court from 1953 to 1969. Decisions during his tenure reflected a broad interpretation of the Constitution. Decisions that helped the Warren Court earn its reputation for "activism" include: *Brown v. Board of Education of Topeka* (1954), ruling school segregation unconstitutional; *Gideon v. Wainwright* (1963), mandating counsel for indigent defendants; and *Miranda v. Arizona* (1966), requiring that the police read arrested people their rights. Rehnquist (A) and Burger (E) were conservatives who claimed to be "strict constructionists." Frankfurter (C) and Taney (D) issued very few decisions that could be used to describe them as "activists."

90. D

The New Right was a label applied to Republicans elected to Congress in 1994 who attempted to implement the conservative "Contract with America"—a program of tax cuts, congressional term limits, tougher crime laws, a balanced budget amendment, and other reforms. Newt Gingrich emerged as leader of this ultra-conservative faction of the Republican Party. Bill Clinton and other centrist Democrats (A), not the "new right," formed the Democratic Leadership Conference to move the Democratic Party away from its traditional liberal agenda. The Black Caucus in Congress and other liberal members of Congress have voiced opposition to the rightward shift of the Democratic Party under Bill Clinton (B). People of different political leanings supported Clinton's welfare reform program (C). No group of Republicans opposed the impeachment of Bill Clinton (E).

HOW TO USE THE RESULTS OF YOUR DIAGNOSTIC TEST IN YOUR REVIEW

After taking the diagnostic test, you should have an idea of what subjects you are strong in and what topics you need to study more. You can use this information to tailor your approach to the following review chapters. If your time to prepare for the test is limited, skip right to the chapters covering the aspects of U.S. history that you need to review most.

KAPLAN

Section Three

U.S. HISTORY REVIEW

CHAPTER 3

The Meeting of Three Peoples

TIMELINE

1492	Columbus discovers America
1494	Treaty of Tordesillas signed
1521	Cortés conquers Mexico
1522	Magellan circumnavigates the globe
1532	Pizarro defeats Incas
1565	St. Augustine established
1680	Pope's Rebellion takes place

IMPORTANT PEOPLE, PLACES, EVENTS, AND CONCEPTS

Columbus	Crusades	caravel	Black Legend
Mayas	Renaissance	Ferdinand and Isabelle	Pope's Rebellion
Incas	Age of Exploration		St. Augustine
Aztecs	Prince Henry the Navigator	Treaty of Tordesillas conquistadors	

"The Spanish have a perfect right to rule these barbarians of the New World and the adjacent islands, who in prudence, skill, virtues, and humanity are as inferior to the Spanish as children to adults, or women to men, for there exists between the two as great a difference as between savage and cruel races and the most merciful, between the most intemperate and the moderate and temperate and, I might even say, between apes and men."

—Juan Gines Sepulveda, 1547

INTRODUCTION

The exploration and settlement of the New World is often dated from the voyage of **Christopher Columbus** in 1492. However, centuries before Columbus and his crew set foot on the soil of the New World, others had begun the long and arduous journey across the Bering Straits from Asia through Alaska and down through North and South America, settling throughout these two continents. The first contact the Europeans had with this New World occurred with the voyages of the Norsemen, most notably **Leif Ericson**, to Newfoundland around the 1000s. This settlement was fleeting and of little consequence to Europe. By the time Columbus reached the New World in 1492, some rather sophisticated civilizations had already been established there, including the empires of the Incas, Aztecs, and Mayas, along with the mainly tribal civilizations scattered throughout what is now the United States. Despite Sepulveda's comments on the barbaric nature of these peoples, quoted above, the Europeans found people who had built large cities, possessed organized governments, had made advances in science, and had established economies. Despite these advanced civilizations, the Europeans overwhelmed the native inhabitants of the Americas through their transmission of disease, their trickery, and their advanced weaponry.

NATIVE PEOPLES OF THE AMERICAS ON THE EVE OF EUROPEAN CONTACT

When the European arrived in the New World, they found advanced civilizations with great cities, religious centers, irrigation systems, road networks, and commerce. Some civilizations, like the Mayas of the Yucatan Peninsula and Central America, had developed hundreds of years before their arrival and were already in decay by the time the Europeans arrived. The Mayas used written language, higher mathematics, and a calendar more accurate than the European one.

The central plateau of Mexico had been a center of civilization for centuries before the European arrival. There the Europeans encountered the Aztecs, a people who had moved from the north to conquer the peoples of central Mexico and build a strong centralized empire. Their beautiful capital city of Tenochtitlán (the site of Mexico City) was one of their finest accomplishments.

The Andes Mountains of South America were also a cradle of civilization. There the Europeans encountered the Incas, whose pyramidal society mirrored the feudal society of Europe. The Incas' vast empire, stretching from Colombia to Bolivia and Chile was held together by an extensive road system linking the high valleys of this mountainous region.

Native American Tribes of North America

The tribes of North America were scattered across the continent and differed from one another in how they lived, governed, and survived. Most of the tribes were **nomadic** people who worked together using the environment for survival. A large tribe could number as many as 10,000 people. The tribes had established governments, in many cases democratic in their form, with the chief being elected by the tribesmen and women. In many of these tribes, women performed vital roles not only in traditional positions as homemakers and mothers, but also as political forces within the tribes. The Native Americans used items not known to the Europeans, such as tobacco and corn. They also created medicines from plants and used many animal products for survival. Many tribes had written language and crafted tools and weapons used for survival. It was a communal society, one in which people helped each other when necessary.

As in other societies, the Native Americans were protective of the land they occupied and some conflicts arose among the tribes. The greatest difficulty among these tribes, which would later lead to their defeats by European settlers, was their lack of unity. Although the **Iroquois Confederation** was a confederacy—that is, a political organization of tribes loosely bound together—the Native Americans never formed a viable, united force to combat the Europeans, and later the Americans, as the new settlers' hunger for land increased.

EUROPE AND THE BACKGROUND OF EXPLORATION

The **Crusades** of the 1100s catapulted the people of Europe out of the Dark Ages and into the **Renaissance**. Europeans tasted the knowledge and products of the people from the East, increasing their desire for silks and spices from the Eastern world. The desire for an all-water route to the Far East led to the **Age of Exploration** and the ultimate discovery of the New World.

Spain and Portugal were the leaders in the Age of Exploration. Both states had developed strong national governments, were located on the Atlantic Ocean, and had the advantage of easy access to the water. **Prince Henry the Navigator**, son of the Portuguese rulers, opened a school for navigation and geography in 1416. He financed expeditions and encouraged exploration. The invention of the **caravel**, a fast-moving sailing ship, allowed the Portuguese to explore down the African coast. The Spanish enjoyed similar political stability when **Ferdinand of Argon** and **Isabelle of Castille** ascended to the Spanish throne in the late 15th century. With the expulsion of the **Moors** from Granada in 1492, a new spirit of Spanish nationalism developed which encouraged exploration. The voyage of Columbus was financed by Ferdinand and Isabelle.

In 1494, the **Treaty of Tordesillas** was signed between Portugal and Spain, basically dividing the world between them: a line drawn north to south between the 46th and 47th meridian marked the dividing line between Spanish and Portuguese exploration. The Spanish explored to the west of the line while the Portuguese explored to the east. This explains the heavy Spanish influence in the most of Western Hemisphere, and the heavy Portuguese influence in Brazil, Africa, and the Far East.

The **conquistadors** of Spain were considered cruel conquerors, who tortured the native populations, stole their gold, and infected them with smallpox. This has been called the **Black Legend**. The Spanish adopted a system called **encomienda**, which allowed the colonists to exploit the native population for labor, provided there was an attempt to convert the native population to Christianity. In 1680, **Pope's Rebellion** occurred when the Pueblo Indians attempted to end the missionary efforts to suppress their native religion.

Along with disease, the Spanish brought with them cattle, swine, horses, and sugarcane. The mingling of the native population and the Spanish resulted in a new race known as the **mestizos**. **St. Augustine**, in what is now Florida, was settled by the Spanish in 1565 and became the oldest permanent European settlement in the land that is today the United States.

The English did not enter into the Age of Exploration until **Elizabeth I** became Queen in 1588. Much of the English exploration of the New World occurred in the areas unexplored by the Spanish and Portuguese, most notably in the Northeastern part of the North America. Jamestown, founded in 1607 at the mouth of the Chesapeake, became the first permanent English settlement in North America. As a result of English exploration, a new nation was born that was destined to become a dominant force in the world.

The French joined the British as late arrivals to the New World. They explored mainly the northern parts of North America, most notably Canada, where the first French settlement of Quebec was established in 1608. The proximity of the French and British settlements led to conflicts in North America, foreshadowing the larger conflict between the British and French in North America between 1754 and 1763.

Explorer	Explored for	Date	Accomplishment
Bartholomeu Diaz	Portugal	1488	explored southern tip of Africa
Vasco da Gama	Portugal	1498	reached India around Africa
Christopher Columbus	Spain	1492	reached the Americas
Vasco Balboa	Spain	1513	discovered the Pacific Ocean and claimed all the lands that touched it for Spain
Juan Ponce de Leon	Spain	1513	explored Florida
Ferdinand Magellan	Spain	1519	first to circumnavigate the globe
Hernan Cortés	Spain	1521	conquered Mexico
Francisco Pizarro	Spain	1532	conquered the Incas of Peru
Hernando de Soto	Spain	1539	discovered the Mississippi River
Francesco Coronado	Spain	1540	explored Arizona and New Mexico; discovered the Grand Canyon of the Colorado River
Juan Rodriquez Cabrillo	Spain	1542	explored the California coast
Don Juan de Onate	Spain	1598	explored northern Mexico and the Rio Grande Valley
Giovanni Cabot	England	1497	explored northern coast of North America
Giovanni de Verrazano	France	1524	explored the eastern part of present-day United States
Jacques Cartier	France	1534	explored the St. Lawrence River
Robert de La Salle	France	1680	traveled down the Mississippi River

AFRICA AND THE SLAVE TRADE

For many years prior to the exploration of the New World, Arab and African traders participated in the slave trade. Africans were first bought by the Portuguese to search for gold in the areas under exploration. However, as the sugar industry developed, the Portuguese began to import slaves to work on the sugar plantations of Brazil. The Spanish, Dutch, French, and British adopted the Portuguese plantation system as they established sugar plantations in the West Indies. This resulted in as many as 40,000 slaves coming to the New World by 1600.

The English settlers in North America became involved in slave trade in the mid-1600s as a result of the raising of tobacco, a labor-intensive crop. By 1612, John Rolfe had perfected tobacco production after experimenting with strains of the plant that local Indians had been growing for years. The development of rice, indigo, and, later, cotton, contributed to increased numbers of slaves in British North America.

RESULTS OF EXPLORATION

The Age of Exploration, while profoundly impacting the native peoples of the newly discovered lands, also affected the European nations. Fundamentally, exploration had taken place for gold, glory, and God. This led to economic changes in Europe that ushered in the beginnings of **capitalism** and the development of **mercantilism**, an economic system in which the colony exists for the good of the mother country by providing raw materials for the mother country and a market for its products.

New products such as corn, tobacco, beans, tomatoes, and potatoes were introduced to the European markets. At the same time, the native populations were introduced to European goods, such as horses and gunpowder. They were also introduced to European diseases, which all but annihilated the native populations.

The introduction of African slavery to the New World established the chattel slavery that would lead to racism and bloodshed as the New World developed.

Finally, with the desire for more gold, greater riches, and power in the New World, rivalries developed among the colonizing nations as they competed for control over these new lands. Eventually, the British won the battle for North America, giving birth to a new nation.

SUMMARY

The Age of Exploration grew out of a need for an all-water route to the East so that the Europeans could access the goods available from that region. What they discovered instead was a vast new land, populated by people who had established their own governments and culture. The meetings of these people altered the lives of the people in both the Old and New Worlds. The Europeans were about to embark on an experience yet to be duplicated in history.

THINGS TO REMEMBER

- **Capitalism:** An economic system in which the production and distribution of goods is determined by individual consumer preference. It is characterized by the free-enterprise system, competition, profit motive, and pricing based on the laws of supply and demand.

- **Encomienda:** A policy developed by the Spanish in the 1500s in which the Spanish settlers in the New World were permitted to use Native American labor if the settlers promised to attempt to Christianize them. It led to the exploitation of the Native Americans.

- **Mercantilism:** A economic system in which a colony exists for the good of the mother country. The colony's role is to provide raw materials for the mother country (especially products that the mother country cannot produce itself) and serve as a market for the goods produced in the mother country.

- **Mestizos:** The mixed race of people that developed as a result of the intermarriage of the Spanish and Native American populations in the 16th and 17th centuries.

REVIEW QUESTIONS

1. Which of the following events occurred LAST?

    (A) establishment of St. Augustine
    (B) establishment of Jamestown
    (C) establishment of Quebec
    (D) signing of the Treaty of Tordesillas
    (E) discovery of America by Columbus

2. The most compelling reason for European exploration in the 1400s was the

    (A) desire to Christianize new lands
    (B) increased need for labor
    (C) need for new lands to support growing populations
    (D) desire for an all water route to the East
    (E) desire for religious freedom

3. The exploration of the New World

    (A) led to the rise of capitalism
    (B) provided the raw materials needed for the New World to further its development
    (C) provided markets for goods produced in the Americas
    (D) allowed for excess African population to be sent to the New World
    (E) ended the economic system known as mercantilism

4. The first permanent European settlement in the territory that would become the United States was

    (A) Plymouth
    (B) Jamestown
    (C) St. Augustine
    (D) Santa Fe
    (E) New Amsterdam

ANSWERS AND EXPLANATIONS

1. C

Quebec, the first permanent French settlement in North America, was founded in 1608. St. Augustine, the first European settlement in the United States, was established by the Spanish in 1565. Jamestown was established by the British in 1607. Columbus set foot on the shores of the New World in 1492. The Treaty of Tordesillas was signed in 1494.

2. D

The Crusades had led to a desire for goods from the East. Because of the control of the Mediterranean by the Italian city-states and the difficulty of overland transport of goods from the Far East to Europe, the Europeans were searching for an all water route to the East. The desire to spread Christianity to the new lands developed after these new lands were discovered. There was sufficient population to meet the labor needs in Europe. The need for labor developed later as a result of the new trade and products found in these new lands. The desire to relieve overcrowding in Europe became a problem for the British in the late 1500s when economic problems developed in England. It was not a reason for the early exploration by Spain and Portugal. Finally, the desire for religious freedom led colonists to settle in the New World, but was not a major reason for the initial exploration.

3. A

The development of markets and trade led to the rise of a market economy known as capitalism. It also led to the beginnings of a modern banking system. Raw materials were provided by the New World for manufacture in the mother countries, and the Americas provided a market for goods produced by the mother countries. The need for African labor developed because of the development of sugar plantations in the West Indies. These Africans, however, did not represent excess population. Mercantilism, the economic system by which the colonies exist for the good of the mother country, developed as a result of exploration.

4. C

St. Augustine was settled by the Spanish in 1565. Plymouth was settled by the English in 1620. Jamestown, the first permanent English settlement in the New World, was established in 1607. Santa Fe was established by the Spanish in 1610. The Dutch founded New Amsterdam (now New York) in 1624.

CHAPTER 4

The Colonial Period

TIMELINE

1558	Elizabeth I becomes Queen of England
1585	Roanoke Colony founded
1607	Jamestown founded
1612	John Rolfe perfects tobacco raising
1619	First slaves brought to the colonies • Virginia House of Burgesses established
1620	Mayflower Compact signed • Plymouth Colony founded
1622	First Anglo-Powhatan War takes place
1624	Virginia becomes a royal colony • Dutch settle New Netherlands
1630	Massachusetts Bay Colony founded by Puritans
1634	Maryland founded by Lord Baltimore
1636	Rhode Island established by Roger Williams • Harvard College founded to educate young ministers
1637	Pequot Wars take place
1643	New England Confederation established
1644	Second Anglo-Powhatan War takes place
1649	Maryland Act of Toleration passed

1664	New York acquired from the Dutch
1675	King Philip's War occurs
1676	Bacon's Rebellion occurs
1681	Pennsylvania established by William Penn
1686	Dominion of New England created under the leadership of Sir Edmund Andros
1691	Massachusetts Bay Colony becomes a royal colony
1692	Salem Witch Trials take place
1693	William and Mary College founded
1696	Barbados Slave Codes of 1661 adopted by South Carolina
1702	New Jersey becomes a royal colony
1703	Delaware granted an assembly by the crown
1712	North Carolina officially separates from South Carolina
1733	Georgia founded by James Oglethorpe

IMPORTANT PEOPLE, PLACES, EVENTS, AND CONCEPTS

Lost Colony

Jamestown

John Smith

Anglo-Powhatan Wars

Plymouth

Separatists

Mayflower Compact

Wampanoag Indians

John Rolfe

Nathaniel Bacon

Bacon's Rebellion

William Berkeley

Virginia House of Burgesses

Barbados Slave Codes

Lord Baltimore

Maryland Act of Toleration

James Oglethorpe

Great Migration

John Winthrop

Salem Witch Trials

Roger Williams

Fundamental Orders of Connecticut

New England Confederation

Metacom/King Philip

Dominion of New England

Peter Stuyvesant

William Penn

"I marvel not a little … that since the first discovery of America … that we of England could never have the grace to set fast footing in such fertile and temperate places are left as yet unpossessed by them [the Spanish and Portuguese]. But … I conceive great hope that the time approacheth and now is that we of England may share and part stakes [divide] (if we will ourselves) both with the Spaniards and the Portuguese in part of America and other regions as yet undiscovered."

—Richard Hakluyt, 1582

INTRODUCTION

When the British decided to join the Spanish and Portuguese in the exploration of the New World, little did they know that they were planting the seeds for a future world power. As 16th century English scholar Richard Hakluyt indicated, there still existed in the New World vast expanses of land that had not been claimed by the colonial powers. These areas lay north of the Florida border and extended into Canada. The British heeded Hakluyt's advice and ventured into these unclaimed areas to meet the challenges of national greatness, to bring gold to the crown, and to spread Christianity.

There were many reasons why the time was right for the British to become involved in empire building:

- **The defeat of the Spanish Armada** by the British in 1588 marked the beginning of the decline of Spain as a world power and of its domination in North America. It also sparked a feeling of nationalism within England and signaled the beginning of English domination of the seas. The decline in Spanish presence and the growing control of the Atlantic Ocean by the British encouraged investors and adventurers to come to the New World.

- The British population had been steadily growing, reaching about four million by 1600. This created widespread economic hardships. The New World presented a greater opportunity for many to acquire land and wealth.

- Because of the movement of **enclosing** land for sheep grazing, many farmers became tenants, working the land for landlords. For tenant farmers living in poverty, the New World offered them economic relief and the possibility of owning their own land.

- An **economic depression** in the wool industry in England in the 1550s led to overcrowding of the cities and jails with job seekers and debtors.

- By the 1600s, the British difficulties with the **Irish** ended. The battle between the Catholic Irish and the Protestant Queen Elizabeth ended in the crushing defeat of the Irish. This allowed the crown to concentrate on overseas exploration.

- Existence of old feudal laws such as **primogeniture**, by which only the firstborn son could inherit the family wealth, encouraged many young men to seek their fortunes in the New World where land was plentiful and wealth could be accumulated.

- The British were seeking **markets** for their goods, as well as resources to furnish British industries.

- The **Protestant Reformation** and **Henry VIII**'s break with the Catholic Church gave rise to a religious conflict. This led people to the New World in search of religious freedom.

- The new type of business organization called the **joint stock company** provided the financial support for these ventures in the New World. An organization in which investors pooled their money for a share of the profits, the joint stock company was responsible for the settlements of Jamestown and Plymouth.

EARLY COLONIAL SETTLEMENTS

The British government granted charters for the purpose of establishing colonies in the New World. There were basically three types of colonies established. A **proprietary colony** was owned by a person or group who appointed the governor for the colony, while a **royal colony** was controlled by the crown, with the governor appointed by the crown. **Self-governing colonies** chose their own governors but still functioned under the auspices of the king.

Jamestown

The first attempt to establish an English colony in the New World was made in 1583 by **Sir Humphrey Gilbert** in the area of Newfoundland but it was unsuccessful. Another attempt was made in 1585 by **Sir Walter Raleigh**, off the coast of Virginia on Roanoke Island. Dubbed **"The Lost Colony,"** the settlement seemingly disappeared around 1591.

In 1607, the **Virginia Company of London**, a joint stock company, received a charter from James I to settle in the New World. The most significant aspect of the charter was that the English settlers were guaranteed to have the same rights in the New World as they would have enjoyed in England. Most of those who left England to voyage to the New World were single men who were seeking gold and the elusive passage to the East Indies.

On May 24, 1607, 100 men left for the New World from England. Only 60 arrived in Jamestown, where they faced disease, malnutrition, starvation, and attacks from Native Americans. The colony was saved when **Captain John Smith** took command, forcing the men to work for food.

Some of the hostility between the Native Americans and the settlers diminished through the efforts of **Pocohantas**, the daughter of Powhatan, who reportedly saved John Smith from death at the hands of the Native Americans. (She later married John Rolfe, who would later perfect the raising of tobacco.)

In 1610, the British crown sent Lord De La Warr to deal with the continuing Native American problem. The First **Anglo-Powhatan War** was fought in 1622, and the Powhatans were

Jamestown vs. Plymouth

- Founded by single men searching for gold
- Bad relationship w/ N. Americans

- Founded by Puritans searching for religious freedom
- At 1st, a good relationship w/ N. Americans

The Colonial Period

harshly treated by the English. In 1644, the Powhatan tribe lost their lands to the settlers in the Second Anglo-Powhatan War. The Indians were segregated from the white population of the colony. By 1685, the Powhatan tribe was virtually extinct due to disease and their inability to unite against the settlers. In the settlers' minds, the Native Americans were expendable.

Plymouth Colony

It was against the backdrop of the Protestant Reformation and Henry VIII's break with the Catholic Church in the 1530s that **Plymouth** Colony was founded. There were some in English society who wanted the Church of England to be cleansed or purified of Roman Catholic rituals.

In 1608, a group of **Separatist Puritans** left England for Holland, where they hoped to practice their religion without the threat of James I. However, they were dissatisfied with life in Holland because they feared their children were becoming "Dutchified," and they negotiated with the Virginia Company of London for a charter and passage to the New World. Leaving Plymouth, England, with 102 people aboard the *Mayflower*, the Separatists came to the New World with their families and strong religious beliefs. Before disembarking, 41 male adults aboard the ship signed a compact (agreement) in which they agreed to follow the rules set by the majority. The **Mayflower Compact** was not a constitution; rather it was an agreement for cooperation among the participants. **John Carver** was elected as the first governor of Plymouth. Upon Carver's death a year later, **William Bradford** became governor and served until 1657.

By 1621, unlike the more negative experience in Jamestown, Plymouth Colony was a thriving community with a bountiful harvest and a decent relationship with the Native Americans. The **Wampanoag Indians** had befriended the New England colonists with the help of **Squanto**, a Native American. **Massasoit**, the chieftain of the Wampanoag Indians, signed a treaty of friendship with the Plymouth Puritans in 1621. However, during the Great Migration of the 1630s, the demand for land and food by the settlers strained their relations with the Native American tribes.

SOUTHERN COLONIES

Virginia, Maryland, North Carolina, South Carolina, and Georgia formed the Southern colonies of the British Empire.

Virginia

Growing out of the Jamestown settlement founded by the Virginia Company of London, Virginia was a proprietary colony until 1624 when it became a royal colony. Characterized by a warm climate and fertile soil, Virginia became the leading producer of tobacco in the colonies. **John Rolfe** perfected tobacco growing by 1612, turning Virginia into a **one-crop**

economy. Because tobacco depleted the soil of its nutrients, the colonists searched for more land to grow their crop, increasing the tension between the Native Americans and the colonists.

The growth of tobacco also increased the need for labor. The **headright system** was developed in order to encourage people to come to Virginia. Under this system, 50 acres of land were given to any person who paid for the passage of another to Virginia. This resulted in large grants of land being given to those who could afford to pay the passage for others to the New World. This led to an extensive number of people who came to the New World as **indentured servants**. These people would negotiate a contract with a person before they left Europe. The patron paid the passage of the indentured servant to the New World and, in return, the indentured persons agreed to work for the patron for a specified number of years. Upon completion of those years, the servant received from their patron their freedom and usually a grant of land. By 1700, there were over 100,000 indentures in the New World, and approximately three-quarters of all those who immigrated to Virginia and Maryland were indentured.

In 1670, the Virginians reassessed their desire to use indentured servants. In 1676, a group of freedmen led by **Nathaniel Bacon**, many of them former indentured servants, protested the Native American policies of longtime Virginia governor **William Berkeley**. They felt that Berkeley's policy toward the Indians was too lenient and that his policies hurt the lives of freedmen and disrupted the fur trade. The rebellion eventually ended when Nathaniel Bacon died from illness. However, the colonists began to fear indentured servants and turned to African slaves for their labor needs. Although the Dutch had sold the first Africans in Virginia in 1619, **Bacon's Rebellion** helped turn the tide toward large-scale slavery in Virginia.

Concentrated mostly in the sugarcane fields of Barbados, African slavery developed slowly in the English colonies. By the 1650s, the majority of the population of Barbados consisted of African slaves, as compared to only approximately three percent of the Chesapeake populations. With the development of tobacco as the chief source of economic wealth in Virginia and the reduction in the number of indentured servants, Virginia began importing slaves, mostly from the West Indies. By 1700, the slave population of Virginia was five times higher than it was in 1670. By 1750, more than half of Virginia's population was comprised of slaves.

The **Virginia House of Burgesses**, organized in 1619 to run Virginia's government, was comprised of burgesses (representatives to the House) who were elected by male landholders to represent the interests of the colonists. This rudimentary beginning of representative democracy was controlled by the influential large landowners, among them the family of George Washington.

Maryland

The fourth colony founded in the New World was Maryland. It was settled by **Lord Baltimore** in 1634 as a proprietary colony and a haven for Catholics. Like Virginia, Maryland employed the headright system.

(handwritten margin note: indentured servants led by Nathaniel Bacon)

As the colony developed, a large number of Protestants arrived. Among fears that this growing number would thwart religious freedom for the Catholics, the **Maryland Act of Toleration** was passed in 1649. Under its provisions, Maryland offered religious toleration to all Christians but declared that the death penalty would be used as punishment for any person who denied the divinity of Jesus. In effect, this denied religious freedom to Jews and atheists. It was eventually repealed. At the time of the American Revolution Maryland had more Catholics than any other colony.

Carolina

Founded in 1670 and named for Charles I, Carolina was established as a proprietary colony for the purpose of supplying food to the sugar plantations in Barbados and silk, wine, and olive oil to England. However, the warm and humid climate of Carolina was unsuitable for the production of these goods. Charles Town (Charleston) became the leading port city of the South.

Rice became the cash crop of Carolina, in addition to indigo. Both increased the need for labor, most of which was obtained from Africa. Many of the African slaves were experienced in growing rice in their own countries and seemed to be resistant to malaria, a deadly disease carried by mosquitoes.

In 1696, Carolina officially adopted the **Barbados Slave Codes of 1661**. Originally passed by the British to control the slaves on the West Indian plantations in Barbados, these harsh rules placed the slave completely under the control of the master. These codes became the basis of the type of chattel (property) slavery that developed in the colonies. By the early 1700s, African slaves outnumbered whites in Carolina.

North Carolina

Because of the many large plantations that had developed in Carolina, smaller farmers moved northward in search of land. This northern migration led to the establishment of the colony of North Carolina, which was officially separated from South Carolina in 1712. Characterized by an independent spirit, North Carolina was considered to be irreligious and defiant. The more rugged mountain terrain led to the development of smaller farms, producing a less aristocratic society than those of neighboring Virginia and South Carolina. There was also less need for slave labor. This spirit of independence served as an impetus for resistance to British authority in the 1770s.

Georgia

Founded in 1733, Georgia was the last English colony founded in the New World. **James Oglethorpe**, an Englishman interested in prison reform, sought to create a refuge for imprisoned debtors. The king granted a proprietary charter to Oglethorpe and also funded part of the establishment of Georgia to create a defensive buffer from both the Spanish in Florida and the French in Louisiana. Georgia was the only colony to receive this type of funding.

Savannah grew as another urban center in the South and Georgia provided religious toleration to all except for Catholics. Georgia had fewer slaves than its other Southern counterparts.

NEW ENGLAND COLONIES

Founded as a refuge for religious zealots, the New England colonies developed a distinct character throughout the 1600s and 1700s. Beginning with the founding of Plymouth Colony by the Pilgrim Separatists in 1620, the development of these colonies was marked by growth in education, thriving economies, and less demand for slavery.

Massachusetts Bay Colony

Known as the **"Bible Commonwealth,"** Massachusetts Bay was founded by Puritans who desired to reform the Church of England from within and to practice their religion freely. The Puritans left England in 1630 with a royal charter that allowed them to establish a colony in the New World. This charter differed from other royal charters in that the Puritans could determine the headquarters of the Massachusetts Bay Company. As a result, the headquarters were established in the New World away from the watchful eye of the crown.

During the **Great Migration** of 1630s, over 70,000 people left England for the New World. Many of these settlers were prosperous and well-educated. They came with their families to establish new homes in a colony that many viewed as a new religious experiment.

John Winthrop served as the colony's first governor, establishing a **theocracy** (church-state) there. Membership in the Puritan's essentially Calvinist church was extremely important in that only freemen who belonged to a Puritan congregation could vote in colonial matters. Only "visible saints" (people whose behavior demonstrated God had saved them) were allowed membership in the church, as stressed by Calvinist doctrine. Religious leaders such as John Cotton believed that government existed to enforce God's law. These religious leaders wielded great power, although the congregation did have the ability to hire and fire their ministers and to set their salaries.

The Puritans believed in hard work as a way to fulfill God's will for them. This idea would develop into what has become known as the "Protestant Ethic" in America, whereby hard work is encouraged within the society. However, not all agreed with this religious structure. In 1638, Anne Hutchinson was banished from the colony when she challenged the belief that a holy life was a sign of salvation.

New Englanders, at this time, were generally superstitious and often blamed their misfortunes on people whom they believed were possessed by the devil. In Massachusetts, a person found guilty of being a witch was subject to death. In 1692, the **Salem Witch Trials** took place in Salem, Massachusetts. Several adolescent girls from Salem accused a number of older women of casting spells. Many of the accused were members of prominent Salem families, leading some historians to conclude that class differences may have been involved in some of the accusations. In all, 20 women were killed as a result of these superstitions.

Rhode Island

Salem minister **Roger Williams** was banished from Massachusetts Bay for his support of a complete break from the Church of England and his disagreement with the colony's policy of no compensation for land acquired from the Native Americans. Williams also believed that there was no place for the church in matters of the state. He contended that civil government should not interfere in religious matters. This belief in the separation of church and state became a cornerstone of the American Constitution in 1787. Rhode Island enacted simple **manhood suffrage** with no property qualifications until several years after its founding.

In 1644, Rhode Island received a charter from Parliament, becoming a colony known for its freedom of opportunity and separation of church and state. Ironically, in spite of their independent outlook, Rhode Islanders became the leading importers of African slaves to the colonies.

Connecticut

In 1662, Connecticut became a royal colony when Hartford, New Haven, and other smaller colonies along the Connecticut River merged. Hartford was founded in 1635 by **Thomas Hooker**, a Boston Puritan. New Haven was founded by discontented Massachusetts Bay Puritans in 1638. In 1639, the **Fundamental Orders of Connecticut** was drafted, becoming the first written constitution in the New World. Provisions of these Fundamental Orders were incorporated into the Connecticut State Constitution after the Revolutionary War. Connecticut was also known for its **Blue Laws** that dictated how people should behave.

New Hampshire

Absorbed by the Massachusetts Bay Colony in 1641, New Hampshire was granted a royal charter in 1679. New Hampshire, along with the rest of New England, boasted fishing, shipbuilding, and a fur trade as its economic mainstays.

NEW ENGLAND AND COLONIAL UNITY

One of the most important contributions of the New England colonies to the development of an American nation was their early attempt at colonial unity. Spurred by their problems with Native Americans, the colonies, with the help of the crown, attempted to unify for defensive purposes.

The New England Confederation

In 1637, the Pequot Indians attacked the settlers along the Connecticut River. The English responded with the virtual slaughter of the Pequot tribe. A shaky peace existed between the settlers and the Native Americans after this incident, but the concern over problems with

Native Americans led to the establishment of the **New England Confederation** in 1643. Its purpose was to establish a colonial defense, against not only the Native Americans but also the Dutch and the French. This marked the first attempt at any intercolonial cooperation.

By 1675, the Indians attempted to unify under Massosoit's son, **Metacom**, whom the settlers called **King Philip**. Metacom coordinated attacks against New England villages, but was eventually defeated by the British.

The Dominion of New England

In 1686, the British crown coerced the colonies into another form of intercolonial union called the **Dominion of New England**. Led by Sir Edmund Andros, the Dominion restricted town meetings; controlled the courts, press, and schools; and revoked land titles. It also taxed the colonies without the consent of their elected assemblies and enforced the **Navigation Acts**.

However, during 1688–1689, James II was deposed in the Glorious Revolution and replaced by **William and Mary**. Aware of the limitation of their power, William and Mary implemented the policy of **salutary neglect**, wherein the British Crown ignored the violations of British trade policies by the colonists. This resulted in a decrease of the English government's involvement with the colonies. The Dominion collapsed and Massachusetts Bay became a royal colony in 1691.

THE MIDDLE COLONIES

Set between industrious, independent-minded, and church-dominant New England and the cash crop, aristocratic Southern society, the Middle Colonies shared characteristics of both.

New York

In 1623–1624, the Dutch West India Company created the first Dutch permanent settlement in **New Netherlands**, with the purchase of Manhattan Island from the Indians. A diverse area, New Netherlands had a large aristocratic contingent. New Netherlands boasted of **patroonships**, large estates along the Hudson River, which were given to promoters who agreed to settle fifty people in these areas. The Dutch government sent in their military under the command of **Peter Stuyvesant**, who successfully secured the colony for the Dutch. However, in 1664, **Charles II** gave a land grant of this area to his brother, the **Duke of York**, and sent a British squadron to secure the grant. Stuyvesant surrendered to the British.

New York remained under the influence of large landowners and therefore had a sizeable aristocratic class. It was, however, a very cosmopolitan area through which many immigrants entered the New World.

Pennsylvania

In the mid-1660s, a group of religious dissenters known as the Quakers sprang up in England. This "religious society of friends" questioned both religious and civil authority, refused to support the Church of England, and practiced **pacificism**, the nonviolent means of achieving goals. **William Penn** embraced the Quaker faith and petitioned the king for a place for these Quakers to settle so that they could practice their beliefs freely.

In 1681, Penn received a large land grant from the king as settlement for a payment of money that the crown owed his deceased father. Pennsylvania (Penn's Woodland) attracted settlers with its liberal land policies and high tolerance for differences among people. It also enjoyed a friendly relationship with the Indians due to compensatory land policies. **Philadelphia**, a leading urban center and known as the **"City of Brotherly Love,"** became the meeting place from which the American Revolution was born.

New Jersey

In 1664, the Duke of York granted an area of land southwest of New York to two noble proprietors. Settled by a large number of New Englanders seeking suitable land, as well as Quakers seeking refuge, West New Jersey was sold by one of the proprietors to Quakers in 1674. East New Jersey also eventually was acquired by the Quakers; the crown combined the two areas in 1702 and established New Jersey as a royal colony.

Delaware

Made up of three counties and founded by Swedes, Delaware remained under the control of the governor of Pennsylvania until the American Revolution. Named in honor of Lord De La Warr, the harsh military governor of Jamestown who had dealt with the Powhatan Indian problem in 1610, Delaware eventually was given the right to establish its own assembly in 1703.

SUMMARY

Geographical conditions, motivations for settlement, and religious values contributed to the variety of political, social, and economic developments within the British colonies in America. As intercolonial trade developed and the British government implemented a policy of salutary neglect, the foundation for the future conflicts between England and the colonies began to form. Like a developing child in the absence of parental authority, the colonies looked to themselves for survival. When mother England attempted to regain control of the colonies, the child rebelled.

THINGS TO REMEMBER

- **Headright system:** A land policy developed in the 1600s in Virginia and Maryland designed to encourage settlement in the New World. It promised 50 acres to any person who paid his own passage to the New World. It also promised an additional 50 acres to any person who paid the passage of someone else to the New World. Indentured servants were brought to the New World under this system.

- **Indentured servants:** A practice used in colonial America in which a person entered into a contract for a specified period of time with another in exchange for the payment of his or her passage to the New World. The indentured servant was usually promised some land after the time of the indenture was fulfilled.

- **Joint stock company:** A company that developed in the early 1600s in England wherein a group of investors pooled their money to finance exploration of the New World. The investor would receive a portion of the profits resulting from the exploration of the New World based on the number of shares of stock (ownership) he or she had.

- **Patroonship:** Large plantation-type farm established by the Dutch along the Hudson River in the 1600s.

- **Primogeniture:** the practice of granting the firstborn son the right to all the inheritance of the parent's estate, rather than subdividing it and giving portions to all offspring

- **Proprietary colony:** A type of colony that was settled by a group of investors and in which the governor of the colony was chosen by the proprietors.

- **Royal colony:** A type of colony controlled by the king. The crown chose the governor to run the colony.

- **Salutary neglect:** The British policy of the 17th century in which the British were lax in the enforcement of laws in the colonies, thereby allowing the colonies to develop without much interference from the British government. After the French and Indian War, this policy changed to one of involvement, leading to the American Revolution.

- **Self-governing colony:** A type of colony in which the people of the colony chose the governor of the colony. Rhode Island was a self-governing colony.

- **Theocracy:** A system of government in which the religious leaders rule; a church-state, where the church is the government, is an example.

REVIEW QUESTIONS

1. The settlements of Jamestown and Plymouth differed in that

   (A) Jamestown was settled by Pilgrims, while Plymouth was settled by Puritans

   (B) the settlers of Jamestown were married with families, while the settlers of Plymouth were mostly single males

   (C) the settlers of Jamestown were largely single men seeking gold and adventure, while the settlers of Plymouth were mostly family units seeking religious freedom

   (D) Jamestown was a royal colony, while Plymouth was settled by individuals without any connection to the crown

   (E) Jamestown enjoyed a good relations with the Native Americans, while Plymouth colony was under constant attack from the Native Americans

2. Which person is correctly associated with a colony?

   (A) John Smith—Plymouth Colony

   (B) James Olgethorpe—Georgia

   (C) John Rolfe—Carolina

   (D) Lord Baltimore—North Carolina

   (E) Jonathan Winthrop—Connecticut

3. The headright system

   (A) was an example of the Barbados Slave Codes

   (B) referred to the number of people aboard a ship traveling from England to the New World

   (C) was a form of slavery

   (D) helped to populate the colonies of Virginia and Maryland

   (E) increased the number of slaves imported to the New World

4. The major crops grown in the Southern colonies

   (A) were used within the colonies

   (B) were sold as exports

   (C) depended on small farmers as the major producers

   (D) made the Southern colonies the "bread basket" of the English colonies

   (E) increased the number of indentured servants necessary to produce these crops

ANSWERS AND EXPLANATIONS

1. C

The early settlers who arrived in Jamestown in 1607 were largely single males who were interested in finding gold, while the settlers in Plymouth were religious separatists who traveled with families seeking a new place to practice their religion. Plymouth was settled by the Pilgrims but Jamestown was settled by the joint stock company known as the Virginia Company of London. Both were proprietary colonies, and both colonies experienced harsh conditions when they first settled.

2. B

James Olgethorpe founded Georgia as a refuge for imprisoned debtors. Georgia also served as a defensive buffer from the Spanish in Florida. John Smith was the leader of the Jamestown (not Plymouth) colony and was largely responsible for its survival. John Rolfe perfected the production of tobacco in Virginia, Lord Baltimore founded Maryland as a refuge for Catholics, Jonathan Winthrop was governor of the Massachusetts Bay Colony, and Thomas Hooker founded Connecticut.

3. D

The headright system was employed by Virginia and Maryland to encourage settlement in those areas. According to this system, a person would receive 50 acres of land for every person whose passage to the New World he or she paid. This led to large landholdings in these areas. This system was not designed to keep a count of the number of immigrants. Although some considered indentured servitude a form of white slavery, the headright system was based on a contract between patron and indentured servant. The Barbados Slave Codes were passed in 1661 by the British government and later adopted by South Carolina for the purpose of controlling African slaves.

4. B

The crops produced in the Southern colonies, such as tobacco, rice, and indigo, were mainly for export to England. This was different from other colonies at that time. These crops were grown by large planters. Smaller farmers produced other crops that were less labor intensive. The southern colonies' crops increased the number of African slaves needed, not indentured servants, to fill the labor demands. The Middle Colonies produced large amounts of grain and became the "bread basket" of the colonies.

CHAPTER 5

Colonial Society in the 1700s

TIMELINE

1730	The Great Awakening begins
1734	Peter Zenger arrested for libel
1754	Benjamin Franklin proposes the Albany Plan of Union • French and Indian War commences
1763	Treaty of Paris signed, ending the French and Indian War • Pontiac attacks British fort near Detroit • Proclamation of 1763 issued

IMPORTANT PEOPLE, PLACES, EVENTS, AND CONCEPTS

Great Awakening	Middle Passage	George Washington	French and Indian War
Jonathan Edwards	Triangular Trade	Benjamin Franklin	Proclamation of 1763
George Whitefield	power of the purse	Albany Plan of Union	
Old Lights	Peter Zenger	Treaty of Paris (1763)	
New Lights	Seven Years' War		

"The American is a new man, who acts upon new principles; he must therefore entertain new ideas, and form new opinion. From involuntary idleness, servile dependence, penury, and useless labor, he has passed to toils of a very different nature, rewarded by ample subsistence."

—Michel-Guillaume Jean de Crevecoeur, c. 1770

INTRODUCTION

By 1750, the English colonists who settled in the New World were remarkably different from the colonists who had arrived in the 1600s. As they became "American," life on the frontier removed the aristocratic barriers that existed in Europe, creating an environment that made men equal in their battle with the elements. The many non-British immigrants to the New World created diversity within the colonies and spawned a new population of mixed European ancestry. By 1750, the English accounted for less than half of all immigrants. Other groups included Scots-Irish, Germans, Irish, Scottish, Welsh, Dutch, and French. African slaves accounted for the highest number of immigrants, with the exception of the English.

The policy of **salutary neglect**, practiced after **William and Mary** ascended to the throne in 1688, left the colonists free to develop in their own style. When England attempted to reinstate its authority after the French and Indian War in 1763, the colonists resisted this perceived intrusion. During this century of development, the British provided the protection and governmental structure that allowed for the growth of the British Empire in North America, but the end of the war marked a turning point in the relationship between Britain and its American colonies. This change signaled the beginning of the end of British control of the American colonies.

COLONIAL SOCIETY BY 1750

The colonies had developed a very definite class structure by 1750. Free from the class structure of England and Europe, they found themselves in a more **socially mobile** society. This afforded them the ability to improve their positions. Basically a pyramid society developed with the large landholders, aristocrats, and clergy at the top of the pyramid, followed by professional men, yeoman farmers, lesser tradesmen, and hired help, in that order. Beneath these groups were the indentured servants and women, who experienced less social mobility. At the bottom of the pyramid were the slaves. The Native Americans were not assimilated into this class structure.

The Role of Clergy and Religion

As the colonies grew and pushed westward, the influence of religion appeared to diminish. In the 1730s and 1740s a religious revival known as the **Great Awakening** began in Massachusetts. **Jonathan Edwards**, the foremost American theologian of the time, stirred congregations with his preaching; his most famous work, *Sinners in the Hands of an Angry God,* characterized the fire-and-brimstone sermons he delivered. In 1734, the English preacher **George Whitefield** began to arouse crowds of people with his emotional theatrics. He traveled throughout the colonies preaching a message of religious revival.

The Great Awakening was a significant movement in colonial history because it:

- Diminished the role of the Anglican clergy, who split into two groups: the **Old Lights** were clergy who supported existing traditions, while the **New Lights** defended the Great Awakening
- Led to the development of new religions, creating greater competition among the churches for worshippers
- Led to the establishment of New Light universities such as Princeton, Brown, Rutgers, and Dartmouth
- Brought American theology to Europe through the teachings of Jonathan Edwards
- Involved all areas of the American colonies, the first such movement to do so

Slavery

In 1619, slaves were first brought to the colonies, and slavery grew as tobacco and rice production increased. Unlike indentured servants, who negotiated contracts for length of service with the promise of freedom, and in some cases land, African slaves were forced into service in the New World.

The journey of a slave began in Africa, where Africans were captured by slave hunters, sometimes with the help of African tribesmen. The captured Africans were placed in a holding pen and then boarded on **slavers**, ships bound for the Americas. This **Middle Passage,** as the journey across the Atlantic Ocean was called, was cruel and harsh. Upon their arrival in the Americas, the slaves were auctioned off, laboring in the fields, houses, or other capacities. To keep slaves under control, many colonies prohibited people from teaching them to read or write. Many slaves were branded, whipped, threatened with separation from their families, or sold to other owners. Unlike the indentured servant, the slave had little hope for freedom or land ownership. In spite of these hardships, a distinctive slave culture emerged.

The selling of slaves became part of a system called **Triangular Trade.** Molasses and sugar were imported from the West Indies to the northern colonies, where they were processed into rum. The rum was sold in West Africa to slave traders in return for slaves. The slaves were then transported to the West Indies, where they were sold in exchange for molasses and sugar for the colonies. Rhode Island became the largest trader of slaves in the colonies, although it had little need for slaves. By 1750, slaves constituted almost half the population of Virginia, while they outnumbered whites in South Carolina by two to one.

Development of Industry and Commerce

By 1750, 90 percent of American colonists were engaged in agriculture. There was also a steady growth of colonial cities such as Boston, New York, and Charlestown. Tobacco was the staple crop of Virginia and Maryland. Grain exports had grown, beaver hats and rum were popular, and iron forges had sprung up in Valley Forge, Pennsylvania. There was spinning, weaving, lumbering, and naval stores (tar, pitch, rosin, and turpentine used in shipbuilding). When Britain began having difficulty absorbing the products of the colonies, the colonists looked to trade with other countries. As the British attempted to control this commerce, it became a source of contention between Britain and the colonies after the French and Indian War.

Political Development

Using English **democracy** as background, the colonists developed their own democratic style. All the colonies had colonial assemblies, many with two-house (bicameral) legislatures. One house was usually appointed by the king or proprietors, while the other was elected by the citizens. The colonies enjoyed the **power of the purse**, that is, the governors were paid by the colonists. In New England, the **town meeting** was a living example of **direct democracy**.

In 1734, **Peter Zenge**r, the publisher of a newspaper that criticized the royal governor of New York, was arrested for seditious libel (making a false accusation). The colonial jury at his 1735 trial found him not guilty despite the royal judges opposing opinions. This was seen as a great victory for freedom of the press, which emboldened the colonists to speak out more freely against royal policy.

Education and Culture

Boys were the main recipients of the higher education available in the colonies. Harvard, William and Mary, and Yale had been founded in the 1600s to train ministers. Many well-to-do colonists traveled to England to study. New England boasted of good primary and secondary schools, while the South depended more upon private tutors.

Distinguished American painters emerged in the 1700s, most notably John Trumbull, Charles Peale, Benjamin West, and John S. Copley. In literature, Phillis Wheatley, an African American slave, wrote poetry and Benjamin Franklin published his *Poor Richard's Almanac.*

THE FRENCH AND INDIAN WAR (1754–1763)

The problems in Europe and Britain continually impacted the lives of the American colonists. In 1756, when the **Seven Years' War** erupted between France and England, and their allies, some skirmishes had already taken place in the colonies. Known as the French and Indian War in the colonies, it resulted in France's removal from Canada, further expanding British domination over North America.

Seven Years war = French & Indian war
(known in Europe)   (known in colonies)

In 1754, **George Washington** was sent by the Virginia governor to evaluate French strength in the Ohio Valley. Washington and his men shot the French leader and retreated to **Fort Necessity,** which they had hastily erected. The French returned and captured Washington and his men, who were later released. However, the English retaliated by uprooting the French Acadians and scattering them around the colonies.

In 1754, in another attempt to ward off the French threat, **Benjamin Franklin** proposed the **Albany Plan of Union,** designed as a defensive union for the colonies. The plan was to allow the colonists to raise money from taxes for their defense and to deal with the Indian problems and settlement of western lands. It was rejected by many colonies, which balked at giving up control, particularly of western lands. It was nonetheless a small step toward colonial unity.

The British government sent Major General Edward Braddock, who, along with George Washington, attempted to stop the French threat. Defeated at Fort Duquesne, the British won the war after William Pitt was appointed government minister by King George II in 1757. Pitt fully committed Britain to the war. This strategy was aimed at Canada. Victories at Louisbourg, Quebec, and Montreal removed the French from Canada.

In 1763, the **Treaty of Paris** was signed, ending the French and Indian War. According to the treaty, England received India and all of the land in North America east of the Mississippi River. The French threat to the English colonies in North America had been removed. In addition, Spain, an ally of France, was stripped of Florida (which went to Britain), but it was eventually given New Orleans and Louisiana, including the Mississippi River.

There were several significant results of this war:

- With the French threat gone, the colonists were eager to settle new lands across the Appalachian Mountains. However, this led to problems with Native Americans. In a last-ditch effort to prevent the spread of the settlers across the Appalachians, **Pontiac**, the Ottawa chief, led an attack against British posts in the Ohio Valley and along the frontier settlements. The Native Americans were eventually defeated by the British military and the settlers. To avoid further problems with the Native Americans, the British government issued the **Proclamation of 1763**. It prohibited the colonists from settling land beyond the Appalachian Mountains and required those settlers already there to leave. This infuriated the colonists, who defied the proclamation.

- The colonists found that they shared many common interests and goals. On the battlefields and in the taverns where they met, they exchanged information and ideas.

- Britain's significant struggle to defeat the French proved that it was possible to beat the British.

- The British treasury was depleted and England looked to the colonies to share some of the burden for the protection it had provided. Many colonists felt no such obligation.

- Valuable military experience was gained by the colonists.

SUMMARY

Throughout the 1600s and 1700s, the colonists adapted to life in the New World. Separated from the watchful eye of the British government by over 3,000 miles of ocean, the colonies emerged as self-reliant, independent-minded entities whose people enjoyed the freedoms that distance provided. The French and Indian War marked a change in the relationship between England and its American colonies. Although proud of their British heritage at the successful completion of the war, the colonists became discontent with British policies they perceived as stunting their growth. The increased involvement of the British in colonial affairs led to the events that culminated in the American Revolution in 1776.

THINGS TO REMEMBER

- **Democracy:** A system of government in which the power to rule comes from the people.

- **Direct democracy:** A type of democracy in which the people vote on the actions of the government, rather than electing representatives.

- **Social mobility:** A term used to describe the ability of people to move within the social framework of a society. If the social system provides opportunities for a person born into a lower social class to move to an upper one, or vice versa, a characteristic of the society is social mobility.

- **Universal suffrage:** The condition when all adults in a democracy are granted the right to vote.

- **Universal manhood suffrage:** The condition when all male adults in a democracy are granted the right to vote.

REVIEW QUESTIONS

1. The social structure that emerged in the colonies by 1750 differed from the social structure in Europe in that the colonial social structure

   (A) lacked an aristocratic class
   (B) allowed for greater social mobility than in Europe
   (C) included the Native Americans
   (D) placed the clergy in the middle class
   (E) did not include indentured servants

2. One of the significant effects of the Great Awakening was that it

   (A) was a religious revival carried to the colonies from Europe
   (B) led to less competition among churches for worshippers
   (C) led to the founding of Harvard and Princeton
   (D) lessened the influence of the clergy in the colonies
   (E) was led by the American theologian, George Whitefield

3. The Middle Passage referred to the

   (A) crossing of the Atlantic by the Pilgrims
   (B) conversion of people to the "elect" of the Puritan faith
   (C) journey of African slaves from West Africa to the New World
   (D) journey to heaven after death
   (E) transporting of rum across the Atlantic Ocean to Africa as part of Triangular Trade

4. The trade in slaves, rum, and molasses that took place during the 1700s between the colonies, Africa, and England was called

   (A) the Commercial Revolution
   (B) mercantilism
   (C) rum running
   (D) barter
   (E) Triangular Trade

ANSWERS AND EXPLANATIONS

1. B

There was greater social mobility in the colonies than in Europe and England, as the environment seemed to serve as an equalizer for people. The greater availability of land in the colonies allowed for more people to acquire property. There was a definite aristocratic class, consisting of the large landowners. The clergy occupied the top of the colonial social pyramid, along with the aristocrats and large landowners, and indentured servants were in the lower class in colonial society but were higher than slaves in the system. Native Americans remained outside the colonial social structure.

2. D

The Great Awakening was the religious revival that took place in the colonies during the 1730s and 1740s. It resulted in a split in the clergy between the Old Lights, who were more traditional, and the New Lights, who embraced the religious revivalism of this time. The congregation began to scrutinize the clergy. The Great Awakening began in the colonies and influenced European theology. More churches were formed as a result of splits in the Congregationalists and Presbyterians. Princeton was founded as a result of the Great Awakening, but Harvard had been founded in 1636, the first American college in the New World. Jonathan Edwards was the American theologian associated with leading the Great Awakening, and George Whitefield was an English clergyman who was responsible for the revivalist type of preaching that occurred during the movement.

3. C

The Middle Passage was the harsh and difficult journey made by Africans who were being shipped to the New World as slaves. Choices (A), (B), and (D) are not related to this question at all. Triangular Trade included the Middle Passage as only *part* of the process.

4. E

Triangular Trade involved the exchange of rum from the colonies for slaves in West Africa. Slaves were transported to the West Indies where they were sold for molasses and sugar, which were in turn transported to the colonies to be processed for rum, which was sold in West Africa. The Commercial Revolution took place in Europe, beginning in the 1400s. Mercantilism refers to an economic system in which the colony exists for the good of the mother country; the colony becomes the chief market for goods made by the mother country, while it supplies resources necessary to the mother country. Rum running refers to the sale of rum, usually illegally, and barter is a form of exchange or trade.

CHAPTER 6

The American War for Independence

TIMELINE

1651	First of a series of Navigation Acts passed
1733	Molasses Act passed
1754	French and Indian War begins
1760	George III becomes King of England
1763	Treaty of Paris ends French and Indian War • Proclamation of 1763 issued
1764	Sugar Act passed • Currency Act passed
1765	Quartering Act passed • Stamp Act passed • Declaration of Rights and Grievances issued • Stamp Act Congress meets • Sons and Daughters of Liberty formed
1766	Stamp Act repealed • Declaratory Act passed • Townshend Acts passed
1769	Writs of Assistance issued
1770	Boston Massacre occurs • Townshend Acts repealed, except for the tax on tea
1773	Tea Act passed • Boston Tea Party takes place
1774	Intolerable (Coercive) Acts passed • Quebec Act passed • First Continental Congress called
1775	Battle of Lexington and Concord takes place • Battle of Bunker (Breed's) Hill occurs • Second Continental Congress called

1776	Thomas Paine's *Common Sense* published • Declaration of Independence issued
1777	Second Battle of Saratoga occurs
1778	French declares war on England, joins U.S. efforts
1779	Spain declares war on England
1781	Cornwallis surrenders at Yorktown • Articles of Confederation written
1783	Treaty of Paris is signed, ending the Revolutionary War

IMPORTANT PEOPLE, PLACES, EVENTS, AND CONCEPTS

John Locke

virtual representation

actual representation

mercantile system

Navigation Acts

Molasses Act

Proclamation of 1763

King George III

Sugar Act

Currency Act

Quartering Act

Stamp Act

Declaration of Rights and Grievances

Stamp Act Congress

Sons and Daughters of Liberty

Townshend Acts

Writs of Assistance

Crispus Attucks

Boston Massacre

Tea Act

Samuel Adams

Boston Tea Party

Intolerable Acts

First Continental Congress

Lexington and Concord

Second Continental Congress

George Washington

Battle of Bunker (Breed's) Hill

Thomas Paine

Declaration of Independence

Thomas Jefferson

General William Howe

Treaty of Paris (1783)

"Resolved, That these United Colonies are, and of right ought to be, free and independent States; That they are absolved from all allegiance to the British Crown; and that all political connection between them and the State of Great Britain is, and ought to be, totally dissolved."

—Richard Henry Lee, 1776

INTRODUCTION

With the words quoted above, the English colonies in America began the process of severing their ties with England. While supported by only about one-third of the populace, the founding fathers proceeded to draft a formal declaration of independence that set forth their philosophy of government and their grievances against the king. The British practice of mercantilism and the change in British policy from salutary neglect to involvement after the French and Indian War had infuriated the colonists. Yet, the colonists appeared to regard Britain as a domineering mother who refused to allow her children to grow up.

COLONISTS PROTEST BRITISH ACTIONS

The conflict between Britain and its American colonies revolved around two main issues: political power and taxation. The philosophers of the Enlightenment, such as **John Locke**, had developed ideas of government that dealt with popular consent and limitation of power. The colonists believed that they had certain basic rights as Englishmen and that the British crown was denying them these very basic rights.

Taxation was a key issue in the conflict between England and the colonies. The colonists believed that Britain did not have the right to tax them because they were not represented in Parliament. The British government argued that the colonists, in fact, were represented by **virtual representation**; each member of Parliament represented all Englishman, no matter where they lived. The colonists, on the other hand, desired **actual representation**, wherein they were entitled to a member of Parliament from the colonies to represent colonial interests.

There were also other factors. Colonial planters and merchants were upset with the economic restraints placed on them by the British. Under the mercantile system, the colony existed for the good of the mother country; British economic restrictions were designed to make sure the colonial economy benefitted England. Among the most important restrictions on the colonists were the restrictions on trade with other nations that hurt colonial businesses.

There was also **social discontent** in the colonies. The nonpropertied class and poorer groups viewed revolution as a means to acquire more land and a greater say in government, as it would take such benefits away from the privileged classes. In addition, there were many immigrants to the colonies who had no particular loyalty to the British crown. The Scotch-Irish had disputed with the English for many years on the British Isles and the German and Dutch immigrants did not share the culture or customs of the English.

Finally, the colonies had by now developed a **national consciousness**. The lives of the American colonists greatly differed from their brethren in England. There was a lack of common interests and goals shared between the two groups.

From the end of the French and Indian War in 1763 until 1776, when independence was declared, the attempts by the king to control the American colonies resulted in increased hostility and the eventual dissolution of Britain's control of its American colonies.

British Action and Colonial Reaction

Beginning in 1651, the British passed a series of **Navigation Acts** that restricted colonial trade. The colonists were forbidden to export sugar and tobacco to any country other than England, and all goods had to be shipped on British ships. The **Molasses Act** in 1733 placed a tax on molasses. Due to the policy of **salutary neglect**, the colonists smuggled products and disregarded regulations without serious attempts on the part of the crown to enforce the laws.

After the French and Indian War in 1763, the British crown issued the **Proclamation of 1763** which forbade the colonists from crossing the Appalachians for the purpose of settlement. The colonists also ignored this order.

In 1760, **George III** was crowned King of England. He desired greater control over the colonies. After the French and Indian War, he felt that the colonies should shoulder some of the monetary burden for fighting the war—a war which he felt greatly benefited the colonies.

In 1764, under the British minister **Lord Grenville**, the **Sugar Act** was passed, placing a tax on sugar, molasses, textiles, coffee, iron, and other goods imported to the colonies. The British crown also began to enforce the laws, ending the colonial practice of smuggling. Also passed in 1764 was the **Currency Act**, which forbade the colonies from issuing their own paper money. In addition, the colonists were made to pay all taxes in gold and silver. This drained money from the colonies.

When there appeared to be some resistance to these measures, the British government passed the **Quartering Act** in 1765 by which the colonists were directed to provide barracks and supplies for British troops stationed in the colonies. This created more tension.

In 1765, Parliament passed the **Stamp Act**, placing a tax on licenses and liquor, and requiring that a stamp be placed on all newspapers and legal documents. Protesting this direct tax, the colonists issued the **Declaration of Rights and Grievances** in 1765, which stated that only colonists had the right to tax colonists. In addition, they asserted that the British should not try colonial cases in admiralty courts.

In 1765, 27 delegates from nine colonies met in the **Stamp Act Congress** to determine a response to these British actions. This first step toward a united colonial response was significant. Crying, "Taxation without representation is tyranny," the colonists enacted a **nonimportation agreement**, that is, a colonial boycott of British goods. In addition, the **Sons and Daughters of Liberty** were formed to disseminate information on actions being taken by the colonies. The British, under great pressure, repealed the Stamp Act in 1766. However, they reasserted their right to legislate for the colonies "in all cases whatsoever" by the passage of the **Declaratory Act**.

In 1766, a series of acts were passed by Parliament at the request of **Lord Townshend**, the successor to Lord Grenville. Collectively known as the **Townshend Acts**, they placed a tax on glass, lead, paint, paper, and tea. The colonists again were enraged and refused to pay the tax. They also began another boycott of British goods.

The people in Boston were especially vocal in their protests, and they smuggled tea into the city. The British government issued the **Writs of Assistance** in 1769, which allowed for a search of colonial homes. British troops were sent into Boston, leading to a series of clashes between the colonials and the British soldiers. On March 5, 1770, British troops fired on a group of colonists who had been harassing British soldiers. This clash between British troops and the citizens of Boston ended in the death of **Crispus Attucks**, a colonial black, and two others. British **Captain Thomas Preston** and his soldiers were placed on trial for this **Boston Massacre**. Ably defended by John Adams and Josiah Quincey, Preston and all but two of his soldiers were acquitted of all charges.

The Townshend Acts were repealed in 1770 on all items except tea. The colonists began to form **Committees of Correspondence** to spread propaganda and disseminate information.

The **Tea Act** of 1773 was an agreement between the British crown and the East India Company that allowed the latter to sell tea directly to the colonies. Although the price of tea was reduced, the colonial tea merchants were faced with bankruptcy. One response was to boycott tea, but **Samuel Adams** led a group of protesters who dumped a shipment of tea into Boston Harbor. The **Boston Tea Party** resulted in the passage of the **Intolerable (Coercive) Acts** in 1774. The British were attempting to punish this troublesome colony for its flagrant actions against British policy. These acts provided for the:

- Closing of Boston harbor
- Suspension of town meetings in Massachusetts
- Suspension of the charter of Massachusetts
- Quartering of soldiers in colonial homes
- Trials of British officials who broke the law to take place in England
- Placement of General Thomas Gage in Massachusetts to enforce the laws

In addition, the **Quebec Act** was passed as part of this act, although not a direct response by the British to the Boston Tea Party. This act guaranteed the French in Canada religious freedom and the ability to retain their customs and institutions. It was an issue that should have been dealt with by the British earlier, and the timing irritated the colonists further.

Although the Intolerable Acts were directed specifically at Massachusetts citizens as a punishment for their actions, other colonists became alarmed by the British actions. In September 1774, the **First Continental Congress** was called in Philadelphia to determine an appropriate response by the colonies for the actions and policies of the British crown. The colonists decided on a complete stoppage of trade with England, including the nonconsumption of British goods. They agreed to meet the following year.

On April 17, 1775, marked by the legendary ride of **Paul Revere** and **William Dawes**, the British attacked **Lexington** and **Concord**. The type of guerrilla warfare used by the colonists surprised the British in this first battle of the Revolutionary War.

In May of 1775, the **Second Continental Congress** was convened. By June, **George Washington** had been appointed Commander-in-Chief of the Continental army. Also in June, the **Battle of Bunker (Breed's) Hill** took place in which over 1,000 British soldiers were killed. The colonists also sent the **Olive Branch Petition** to King George, offering him peace. The king refused to read it. In January 1776, **Thomas Paine** wrote a pamphlet entitled *Common Sense*, in which he argued that the colonies were destined to be independent. In June of 1776, the Second Continental Congress agreed with Paine.

By the time the formal **Declaration of Independence** was issued on July 4, 1776, colonists **Ethan Allen** and **Benedict Arnold** had captured **Ticonderoga** and **Crown Point**; the British had burned **Falmouth;** and the Americans had attempted to take Canada, believing the French would join their struggle. By June of 1776, the Southerners had challenged the British fleet in Charleston harbor.

The Declaration of Independence

The task of writing a formal declaration of independence was delegated to Thomas Jefferson, Benjamin Franklin, John Adams, Robert Livingston, and Roger Sherman. However, **Thomas Jefferson** was the chief author.

Borrowing from the ideas of John Locke and the philosophers of the Enlightenment, Jefferson produced a document that was intended not only to declare the independence of the colonies from Britain, but also to convince fellow colonists and foreign nations, particularly France, of the just intentions of the colonies.

Beginning with the ideas of basic human rights, Jefferson determined that government obtained its power from the consent of the governed and that when it failed to exercise the will of the people, the people had right to overthrow the government. A list of grievances against George III followed this philosophical justification for independence. The document concluded, "That these United Colonies are, and of right ought to be, FREE and INDEPENDENT." With a country divided among the loyalists, the revolutionaries, and the indifferent, the American Revolution, in effect, was a civil war.

THE WAR OF INDEPENDENCE

Sorely lacking a government, the American colonies entered this war without a military, navy, trained soldiers, money, or the means to acquire these things. What they did have was a cause, the "home field" advantage, and a very capable leader in George Washington. Perhaps the greatest help the colonists had early on was the incompetence of the **British General William Howe**, who allowed Washington and his troops to escape at the Battle of Long Island.

Faced with enormous hardships, Washington led his troops in a surprise attack across the Delaware River on December 26, 1776, after which the British were defeated at the **Battle of Trenton**. Washington then moved on to garner another victory at the **Battle of Princeton**.

John Paul Jones proved to be effective against the British on the seas, harassing British merchant vessels. The **Marquis de Lafayette**, a French nobleman sympathetic to the American cause, and **Baron von Stueben** of Prussia gave valuable help to the colonies.

The turning point of the war came at the **Second Battle of Saratoga**, which took place in October of 1777. The American victory encouraged the French to give formal recognition to the independent colonies and to provide aid. The French fleet arrived in July of 1778 and the French declared war against Britain. By June of 1779, Spain declared war on Britain but did

[handwritten margin note: French begin to aid colonists to declare war against Britain]

not join the war in the American colonies. When the British, under the command of **General Cornwallis**, surrendered at **Yorktown** in October of 1781, they realized that a defeat was possible. Faced with the growing French threat to England itself and the fatigue of the English people with this ongoing conflict with the colonies, the British sought peace with the Americans in February of 1782.

The Treaty of Paris (1783)

In addition to British recognition of the United States as free and independent, the Treaty of Paris:

- Established the boundaries of the United States; the Mississippi River became the western boundary, and North Florida, the southern boundary
- Allowed the British to retain control of Canada; however, Florida, which had been under British control since 1763, was given to Spain
- Required that the colonists return the property of loyalists and permitted the British to collect debt owed to them by the United States
- Allowed the Americans to share the fisheries in Newfoundland

However, many of the provisions of this treaty were not fully carried out by either side. Those unresolved issues eventually led to the **War of 1812** between England and the United States.

SUMMARY

Fought for a variety of political, economic, and social reasons, the American War of Independence proved that the American colonies had simply come of age. No longer the infants of the century before, these people had reached young adulthood, eager to be out on their own. When mother England attempted to prevent this, the colonies rebelled. In the words of John Adams in 1818, "The Revolution was effected before the war commenced. The Revolution was in the minds and hearts of the people."

THINGS TO REMEMBER

- **Virtual Representation:** The idea that each member of the British Parliament represented all Englishman, regardless of location.

- **Navigation Acts:** Laws made by the British government restricting colonial trade of sugar and tobacco to any country other than England or by any means other than on British ships.

- **Boston Tea Party:** A defiant act of the colonies against the British government and their tea trade agreement with East India, which was causing colonial tea merchants to go bankrupt. Protesters dumped an entire shipment of tea into the Boston Harbor.

REVIEW QUESTIONS

1. The British government countered the colonists' argument that they were not represented in Parliament and, therefore, could not be taxed by Britain, with the idea of

    (A) actual representation
    (B) virtual representation
    (C) divine right rule
    (D) mercantilism
    (E) a classed society

2. The French and Indian War, which ended in 1763, was significant because it

    (A) removed the Native American threat from the colonies
    (B) severely drained the British treasury
    (C) opened up new lands west of the Mississippi River
    (D) gave Florida to England
    (E) signaled a shift in the British policy of salutary neglect to one of British involvement in the affairs of the colonies

3. The Intolerable Acts passed in 1774

    (A) affected all the colonies in British North America
    (B) affected only the city of Boston
    (C) resulted in the suspension of the charter of Massachusetts
    (D) led to Shays's Rebellion
    (E) were a direct result of the Townshend Acts

4. Thomas Paine's pamphlet, *Common Sense*, was significant because it

    (A) outlined the reasons for the ratification of the Constitution
    (B) outlined the reasons colonial independence from Great Britain was a logical step for the colonies to take
    (C) was rejected by the colonists as a piece of propaganda
    (D) stated a belief in democracy
    (E) was written by a high-ranking British official who supported colonial independence

ANSWERS AND EXPLANATIONS

1. B

The British argued that all Englishmen were represented in Parliament by virtual representation no matter where they lived. The colonists, on the other hand, argued that they wanted actual representation, with a colonial representative in the Parliament. Divine Right Rule refers to the belief that kings received their power to rule from God. Mercantilism was an economic system in which the colonies existed for the good of the mother country by creating a favorable balance of trade for the mother country. A classed society existed in the colonies, but the issues of class and representation were not argued by Britain and the colonies.

2. E

The French and Indian War marked the end of the British policy of salutary neglect and marked the beginning of more involvement by the British crown in the affairs of the colonies. Native Americans were not removed as a threat to the colonies. In fact, the British government issued the Proclamation of 1763 that forbade the colonists from settling beyond the Appalachian Mountains largely due to the threat of Indian attacks. Although the British treasury was, in fact, drained, the significance of the war lay more in the changed British policy. New lands were opened up east of the Mississippi River, not west of the Mississippi River. Florida was given to Spain, not England.

3. C

The Intolerable Acts, also known as The Coercive Acts, affected the colony of Massachusetts. The charter of Massachusetts was suspended and Boston Harbor was closed. The other colonies were not directly impacted by these acts. All of Massachusetts was affected by these laws, and Boston Harbor was closed. Shays's Rebellion occurred in 1787, when Daniel Shays, a farmer from Massachusetts, led an uprising against the state of Massachusetts over taxation. His actions led to the calling of the Constitutional Convention, the purpose of which was to revise the Articles of Confederation. The Townshend Acts were passed in 1766 and placed a tax on glass, lead, paint, paper, and tea. They were repealed in 1770 on all items except tea.

4. B

Thomas Paine's *Common Sense* highlighted the arguments that made colonial independence the "common sense" thing to do. Its purpose was to convince the colonists of the correctness of seeking independence from Britain. *The Federalist Papers*, written by Alexander Hamilton, James Madison, and John Jay in 1788, was designed to convince the states that had not yet ratified the Constitution to do so. Thomas Paine was an impoverished, self-educated person who had arrived in the American colonies the year before he wrote *Common Sense*.

CHAPTER 7

Experiments in Government

TIMELINE

1781	Articles of Confederation adopted
1783	Treaty of Paris signed, ending the Revolutionary War
1785	Land Ordinance enacted
1786	Shays's Rebellion occurs
1787	Northwest Ordinance enacted • Constitutional Convention held
1788	Constitution ratified • George Washington inaugurated as first president of the United States
1791	Bill of Rights adopted

IMPORTANT PEOPLE, PLACES, EVENTS, AND CONCEPTS

Articles of Confederation

Land Ordinance of 1785

Northwest Ordinance

Shays's Rebellion

Constitutional Convention

James Madison

George Washington

Benjamin Franklin

Great Compromise

Three-fifths Compromise

Commerce and Slave Trade Compromise

Electoral College

Antifederalists

Patrick Henry

Federalists

Alexander Hamilton

John Jay

The Federalist Papers

Bill of Rights

"Dr. [Benjamin] Franklin, looking toward the President's chair, at the back of which a rising sun happened to be painted, observed to a few members near him, that painters had found it difficult to distinguish in their art a rising from a setting sun. 'I have,' he said, 'often in the course of this session. . . looked at that [sun] behind the President without being able to tell whether it was rising or setting. But now, at length, I have the happiness to know that it is a rising and not a setting sun.'"

—James Madison, from his notes on the Constitutional Convention, 1787

INTRODUCTION

When New Hampshire became the ninth state to ratify the Constitution on June 21, 1788, the most enduring living blueprint for government was established for the United States. However, the accomplishment of this task strained the very fiber of the new nation, threatening dissolution, as Benjamin Franklin feared. The willingness of the Founding Fathers to compromise for the sake of the Union allowed for the successful completion of this task and for the sun to rise above the United States of America.

THE ARTICLES OF CONFEDERATION ← *unicameral legislature*

Once the colonies had determined to be independent of Great Britain, the task of establishing a government to run the United States became a necessity. Suspicious of a government in which a great deal of power would be centralized at the expense of state power, the states approved the **Articles of Confederation,** which took effect in 1781. In this **confederate** form of government, the states agreed to " . . . enter into a firm league of friendship," with the Congress permitted to exercise only those powers that had specifically been delegated to it by the Articles.

During this "critical period" in American history, the Articles had weaknesses that hampered efficient operation of the government. With no provisions for an executive branch, the Articles lacked the ability to enforce the laws that Congress passed. The failure to include a judicial branch to interpret the law made each state the ultimate interpreter. The Congress had no power to collect taxes, raise a military, coin money, or regulate interstate commerce.

In addition, the Congress was a **unicameral** legislature (one house), with each state having only one vote. Nine out of thirteen votes was necessary to pass legislation and a unanimous vote of the states was required to amend the Articles, further hampering the lawmaking process.

Despite these flaws, the Articles of Confederation established a government that successfully conducted the War of Independence and negotiated the Treaty of Paris in 1783, ending the war. The crowning glory of the Articles was the actions taken by the Congress concerning the **Western lands** acquired through the peace treaty with England. Under the **Land Ordinance of 1785**, the area of the Northwest Territory was divided into townships that were six miles square and further subdivided into 36 one-acre tracts. The 16th section was set aside for a public school.

The second, and perhaps most important, land decision was the **Northwest Ordinance of 1787**, which systematically set the guidelines for future states. It provided that:

- No less than three nor more than five states were to be formed in the Northwest Territory.

- When one of the territories had 60,000 inhabitants, it could become a state in the Union equal to the other existing states, and the inhabitants of that new state were to enjoy all the same rights and privileges of those who lived in the original states.

- Religion was to be practiced freely without interference from the government.

- The Indians were to be treated with "the utmost good faith."

- Slavery was prohibited in these new states, thus stemming the spread of slavery into this new territory.

The Articles of Confederation were a measure that allowed for the new states to remain united, and they served as a transition government until the states realized the need to create a stronger central government better able to execute the law.

THE WRITING OF THE CONSTITUTION

Shays's Rebellion

In 1786, **Daniel Shays** led 1,200 armed followers in an attack on the federal arsenal at Springfield, Massachusetts. With his farm about to be foreclosed because of owed back taxes, Shays and the other farmers demanded cheap paper money, reduced taxes, and a suspension of mortgage foreclosures. This was a local rebellion directed against the Massachusetts government, which had used the taxes to pay off debts from the Revolutionary War. The rebellion was crushed by the Massachusetts militia.

However, **Shays's Rebellion** captured the attention of the citizens of the United States. Fearful that this type of uprising might spread, George Washington, John Adams, and other Founding Fathers encouraged a meeting to discuss the weakness of the Articles of Confederation. In 1787, with 12 of the 13 states represented (Rhode Island was the exception), the **Constitutional Convention** met in Philadelphia for the purpose of *revising* the Articles of Confederation. However, instead of carrying out a revision of the Articles, the members of the convention scrapped the Articles and created a new Constitution under a cloud of secrecy. Shays's Rebellion had served as a catalyst for change.

Bundle of Compromises

Much of what is known about the Constitutional Convention is based upon the journals kept by **James Madison** during the convention. Called the **"Father of the Constitution,"** Madison provided later generations with a glimpse of what occurred in 1787. **George Washington** led the convention as its president, and **Benjamin Franklin** was the oldest member there. Noticeably absent were John Adams and Thomas Jefferson, who were serving the government abroad.

Many of the states still jealously guarded their individual powers. The sectional differences that had developed over the years of their existence created situations that nearly dissolved the Union.

The convention determined that the Articles were ineffective and elected to establish a **federal system** of government in which there would be a **division of powers** between the states and the central government. Both the states and the central government were given specific powers by the new Constitution. There was also a **separation of powers** within the central government, meaning that the central government was to be composed of an **executive** branch, to enforce the laws; a **legislative** branch, to write the laws; and a **judicial** branch, to interpret the laws. A system of **checks and balances** was built in to prevent any one branch from becoming too powerful. An **amending process** was included, as well as the addition of a "necessary and proper" clause (**elastic clause**), which allowed Congress additional powers based on the **delegated powers** specifically granted them by the Constitution.

The major compromises of the Constitutional Convention included:

- **The Great Compromise:** Based on the **New Jersey Plan** proposed by **William Patterson** and the **Virginia Plan** proposed by **James Madison**, the Great Compromise provided for a **bicameral legislature** (two houses) consisting of a **Senate** and **House of Representatives**. The number of representatives in the House was to be determined by population, and these representatives were to be elected by the people every two years. The Senate was composed of two representatives from each state, elected every six years by the state legislature. One-third of the Senate was to be elected every two years. Direct election of senators did not take place until the **17th Amendment** was added to the Constitution in 1913.

- **Three-fifths Compromise:** The question of representation raised another problem: who was to be counted for the purposes of representation and taxation? The Southern states favored the inclusion of slaves in the population count for the purposes of representation but not taxation, while the Northern states desired the exclusion of slaves from the population count for the purposes of representation but not taxation. This issue nearly caused the collapse of the Constitutional Convention and the Union. The delegates reached a compromise that provided that every five slaves were to be counted as three white men; that is, each slave counted as three-fifths of a person for purposes of representation and taxation.

- **Commerce and Slave Trade Compromise:** The issues of slavery and slave trade led the delegates to a third major compromise. The Convention determined that

Congress should have the power to regulate foreign trade. However, Congress was forbidden to interfere with slave trade for 20 years or to place taxes on exports, a provision favored by the South. Congress was permitted to place an import tax of 10 dollars on each slave brought into the country. The need for unity among the states outweighed the need for insisting upon the abolition of slavery at this time. However, the issue of slavery was far from settled.

 Other Provisions: There were other significant provisions of the Constitution. The president and vice-president were to be elected by the **Electoral College**, instead of by popular vote, for four-year terms. This provision was an attempt to prevent what some felt was **mobocracy,** or rule by the masses. The Constitution was to take effect upon **ratification**, or approval, by nine of the thirteen states.

Debate Over Ratification

The Constitution was an attempt by the Founding Fathers to preserve their positions in society. In doing so, they created a doctrine that supported **minority rights**. However, there were those who vehemently disagreed with the work of the Constitutional Convention. **Antifederalists** and old revolutionaries, like **Patrick Henry** and **Samuel Adams**, felt that the Constitution compromised the goals of the American Revolution and gave too much power to the central government. They pointed out the lack of a "bill of rights" to protect individual rights. They objected to the secrecy in which the meeting was conducted and to the fact that the delegates had created a new government rather than revise the old. On the other hand, **Federalists**, like **Alexander Hamilton**, **James Madison**, and **John Jay,** defended the Constitution as a document that was designed to prevent a tyranny of power. In a series of essays, known as *The Federalist Papers* and published in a two-volume book called *The Federalist*, they outlined their reasons for believing that the Constitution should be ratified. Considered by some to be nothing more than propaganda pieces designed to convince those states that had refused to ratify the Constitution, the essays offer insights into the thinking of the men who designed the government.

On June 21, 1788, nine states had ratified the Constitution, thus establishing it as the law of the land. The holdout states of Virginia, New York, North Carolina, and Rhode Island reluctantly ratified the Constitution because of the realization that they could not exist apart from the other states. Their approval, however, was contingent on an addition of a **Bill of Rights** to protect individual liberties and states' rights.

Bill of Rights

Adopted in 1791, the Bill of Rights constituted the first ten amendments to the Constitution. These amendments protected the basic human rights including freedom of speech, press, religion, and assembly; the right to bear arms; the right of citizens to trial by jury and just punishment. In addition, **Amendment X** provided for the protection of states' rights. According to this amendment, any power not specifically delegated to the Congress or specifically denied to the states by the Constitution was reserved to the states. This **reserved power clause** served to reassure the states that they were protected from the tyranny of a too powerful central government.

SUMMARY

No longer a "firm league of friendship," the Constitution created "a more perfect union" which now had a flexible, organized, and viable government. It had taken the states the transition period of the Article of Confederation to allow them to accept this more tightly organized set of laws. Many were disappointed with this Constitution, while others embraced it. However people felt, the government moved forward under the guidance of **George Washington**, the revered leader of the Revolution and the first president of the United States. Far from united, the states turned to the task of building a nation. Like toddlers learning how to walk, this union stumbled many times before it was able to walk on its own.

THINGS TO REMEMBER

- **Bicameral legislature:** A legislature composed of two houses. The U.S. Congress, composed of the Senate and the House of Representatives, is an example.

- **Checks and balances:** The system built into the U.S. Constitution in which the three branches of government (legislative, executive, and judicial) have separate and equal powers that are limited and dependent upon each other. It is also called **separation of powers**.

- **Confederation:** A type of government characterized by a loose alliance of states leading to a weak central government and strong state governments. This was the type of government that existed under the Articles of Confederation.

- **Delegated powers:** Powers given to the national/federal government that are specifically stated in the Constitution. They are found in Article I Section 8 of the Constitution and may also be known as expressed or enumerated powers.

- **Division of powers:** The characteristic of a federal system of government in which power is distributed between central and local governments. This distribution of power usually is established through some outside source, usually a constitution, as is the case in the United States.

- **Elastic clause:** This clause, found in the last paragraph of Article I Section 8 of the U.S. Constitution, allows Congress to make laws not specifically delegated to them by the Constitution, but which may be "necessary and proper" to carry out its **delegated powers**. (Also referred to as **"implied powers"** or the **"necessary and proper clause."**)

- **Implied powers:** See *elastic clause*.

- **Ratification:** The formal or official approval for a constitution or amendment.

- **Reserved powers clause:** Found in the 10th Amendment, it provides that any powers not specifically given to the central government nor specifically denied to the state governments by the Constitution are powers that the states are granted. For example, the power to develop an educational system is granted to the states as a result of the reserved powers clause.

- **Separation of powers:** The system built into the U.S. Constitution in which the three branches of government (legislative, executive, and judicial) have separate and equal powers that are limited and dependent upon each other. It is also called **checks and balances.**

- **Unicameral legislature:** A legislature composed of only one house or chamber.

REVIEW QUESTIONS

1. One of the challenges facing the delegates to the Constitution Convention in 1787 was

   (A) where the seat of government was to be located
   (B) the role of the cabinet in the executive branch of government
   (C) the fear of military rule to control the mobs
   (D) the need to balance governmental powers and states' rights
   (E) the need to crush Shays's Rebellion and other similar protests that had been occurring at the time

2. One of the most notable achievements of the Articles of Confederation was its

   (A) ability to enforce the laws of the land
   (B) legislation concerning the settlement of the territories acquired from Great Britain at the end of the Revolutionary War
   (C) ability to deal with foreign and domestic commerce
   (D) the establishment of a system of checks and balances
   (E) the flexibility it built into the government by the simple amending process that it established

3. To convince the states to ratify the Constitution, James Madison, Alexander Hamilton, and John Jay wrote

   (A) the Bill of Rights
   (B) the Northwest Ordinance
   (C) *The Federalist Papers*
   (D) the pamphlet *Common Sense*
   (E) the Great Compromise

4. Which statement best characterizes the attitude of the delegates to the Constitutional Convention toward the issue of slavery?

   (A) The delegates were indifferent to the issue of slavery.
   (B) The delegates recognized the need for the expansion of slavery as the nation grew.
   (C) The delegates treated slavery as a political issue because it threatened the unity of the nation.
   (D) There was a deep concern among the delegates for the plight of the African slave.
   (E) The Southern states viewed their role with the slaves as a paternalistic one.

ANSWERS AND EXPLANATIONS

1. D

One of the greatest fears of the members at the Constitutional Convention was the usurping of the power of the states by the central government. This was the reason that the states adopted the Articles of Confederation in 1781. New York was chosen as the capital, but Washington, DC, became the capital when Alexander Hamilton and Thomas Jefferson agreed to move the capital to the Potomac River if Jefferson accepted Hamilton's proposal on assumption, part of Hamilton's financial program. The cabinet was part of the unwritten Constitution as the country developed; Washington established this precedent. There was a fear of a growth of tyranny in the government because of the fear of a strong central government. However, the fear of military rule because of a need to control mobs was nonexistent. Shays's Rebellion, which occurred in Massachusetts in 1787, was crushed by the local Massachusetts militia. It acted as a catalyst for the calling of the Constitutional Convention. However, it was a local rebellion and there were few others at the time.

2. B

The Land Ordinance of 1785 and the Northwest Ordinance of 1787 provided for the orderly settlement of the Northwest Territory, which the United States had acquired at the end of the Revolutionary War. The government under the Articles of Confederation lacked the ability to enforce law. It also had little ability to control foreign and domestic commerce, and had no provisions for checks and balances since it did not have separate executive and judiciary branches. Although its amending process was simple in design, a unanimous vote was required of the states in order to change the Articles of Confederation. That was not simple to achieve.

3. C

The Federalist, or *The Federalist Papers*, were penned by Hamilton, Madison, and Jay to convince some states, particularly New York, Virginia, Rhode Island, and North Carolina, to accept the new Constitution in 1787. The Bill of Rights, the first ten amendments to the Constitution, was added to the Constitution in 1791 but was not written by these three men. The Northwest Ordinance was written under the Articles of Confederation and provided for the orderly settlement of the Northwest Territory. *Common Sense* was written by Thomas Paine to convince the people of the colonies to rebel against the British government. The Great Compromise took place during the writing of the Constitution and provided for a bicameral legislature.

4. C

The issue of slavery was dealt with as a political issue because the more emotional discussion of the treatment of slaves and the plight of the slaves almost led to the dissolution of the Union during the Convention. Therefore, these aspects of slavery were set aside for the sake of the preservation of the Union. The delegates were far from indifferent on the issue of slavery, however. The Northwest Ordinance of 1787, written under the auspices of the Articles of Confederation, had provided for no further expansion of slavery into the new territory. The delegates viewed slavery as an institution that would probably die on its own. The discussion over the plight of the slaves was shelved when it was clear that this could cause the break-up of the Union. The paternalistic view of slavery developed later on in the 1800s as the Southerners attempted to justify the continued existence of slavery.

CHAPTER 8

The Federalist Era

TIMELINE

1789	Washington inaugurated as the first president of the United States • French Revolution begins • Judiciary Act passed by Congress
1791	Bill of Rights added to the Constitution • Hamilton's financial program approved by Congress
1793	Reign of Terror begins in France • France declares war on England
1794	Whiskey Rebellion occurs • "Citizen Genêt" tries to recruit Americans to invade Florida and Louisiana • Jay Treaty signed • Battle of Fallen Timbers takes place
1795	Treaty of Greenville signed
1796	John Adams elected president
1797	XYZ Affair occurs • Navy Department established
1798	Alien and Sedition Acts passed by Congress
1798–99	Virginia and Kentucky Resolutions published
1800	Thomas Jefferson elected president

IMPORTANT PEOPLE, PLACES, EVENTS, AND CONCEPTS

George Washington

Federalists

Alexander Hamilton

Judiciary Act

Bill of Rights

10th Amendment

Thomas Jefferson

Bank of the United States

Hamilton's financial program

McCulloch v. Maryland

John Marshall

Whiskey Rebellion

Democratic-Republicans

French Revolution

Proclamation of Neutrality in 1793

Citizen Genêt

John Jay

Pinckney's Treaty

Treaty of Greenville

Washington's Farewell Address

election of 1796

John Adams

Talleyrand

XYZ Affair

Napoleon Bonaparte

election of 1800

Alien and Sedition Acts

Virginia and Kentucky Resolutions

James Madison

"I was summoned by my country, whose voice I can never hear but with veneration and love…."

—George Washington, First Inaugural Address, April 30, 1789

INTRODUCTION

With the humble words of his first inaugural address, **George Washington** became the first president of the United States of America. A hero of the Revolutionary War, Washington had been elected unanimously by the electoral college. John Adams became the vice president. Much of the presidency had been designed with Washington in mind. Honest and forthright, Washington's presence enabled a faltering republic to plant its feet more firmly in the world. By the end of his eight years in office, the republic had grown significantly, but the French Revolution and its aftermath placed the United States in a difficult position, one that threatened the very existence of the republic.

WASHINGTON'S ADMINISTRATION (1789–1797)

The new Constitution had met with a mixed reaction from the populace. The **Federalists** supported the idea of a strong central government. When George Washington took office in 1789, there were many issues that had to be addressed. One of the greatest challenges faced by the first administration was building a true union of states. With the country still very sectional and states' rights oriented, Washington and his Secretary of the Treasury, **Alexander Hamilton**, engineered the country toward greater unity. Washington was in the unique position of defining the role of the president in this new republic; he was confronted with the need to establish a judiciary and a viable economic system, organize a system of defense, and respond to the events of the French Revolution. The actions taken by Washington established precedents for future presidents.

Domestic Accomplishments of the Washington Administration

To assist him in the challenges that he faced, Washington established a **cabinet**, that is, a group of advisers. Although not included in the written Constitution, the cabinet, like political parties, became part of the **unwritten Constitution**. Presidents following Washington created new cabinet positions as the country expanded and the need for additional advisers was perceived as necessary. The members' of Washington's cabinet included:

- Thomas Jefferson—Secretary of State
- Alexander Hamilton—Secretary of the Treasury
- Henry Knox—Secretary of War
- Edmund Randolph—Attorney General

In 1789, the **Judiciary Act** was passed; this organized the federal court system. The first ten amendments were added to the Constitution in 1791 with the ratification of the **Bill of Rights**, establishing basic rights for the people of the United States. It also established the **reserved powers** of the states with the inclusion of the **10th Amendment**.

Perhaps the most pressing issue was the debt the government owed to foreign nations and individual citizens. Alexander Hamilton devised a **financial program,** the aim of which was to re-establish the credit of the United States. It was based on the idea of funding and assumption, the development of trade and commerce, and the establishment of a national bank. According to the program, the U.S. government was to pay off foreign debt and domestic debt through an exchange of old bonds for new ones, which were to be redeemed at a future date (funding). The U.S. government also was to "assume" the debt that the states owed to foreign nations. Funding and assumptions gave bondholders, both domestic and foreign, a stake in the success of the United States so that their bonds would have value. Money was to be raised for the government through **excise taxes** (added taxes on goods and services) and **tariffs** (taxes on imports). The tariff would encourage the growth of industry and commerce by discouraging the purchase of foreign goods.

The most controversial part of this financial program dealt with the establishment of the **Bank of the United States**, which was to be funded through a sale of stocks in the bank. "BUS" was to issue bank notes and serve the government as its bank. Since it was owned by private investors, it was presumed that they would want the Bank and the U.S. government to succeed in order to make a profit on their investment.

Thomas Jefferson reacted negatively to this plan. A champion of an agrarian society, Jefferson viewed BUS as an organ of the upper class in the United States. As an advocate of states' rights, Jefferson viewed the financial program as a weakening of states' power now that they were tied by this financial program to the central government. He argued that BUS favored the North and not the South since most Southern states had already paid their debt and most investors in BUS would come from the North.

Perhaps Jefferson's most compelling argument against the Bank was that it was unconstitutional. According to Jefferson, there was no provision in the Constitution for the establishment of the Bank. He was a **strict constructionist**, that is, he believed that the Constitution must be interpreted word by word. Hamilton, on the other hand, represented the **loose constructionist**, or a person who believed that there was flexibility within the Constitution. Hamilton argued that the **implied powers** clause (elastic clause) gave the government the right to establish the Bank because of the powers delegated to Congress that allowed them to regulate trade and collect taxes.

To convince Jefferson to accept the government's assumption of state debts, Hamilton worked out a deal with him for the establishment of the nation's capital on the Potomac River. Congress enacted **Hamilton's financial program** in 1791.

The Supreme Court upheld the constitutionality of the Bank of the United States in the case of *McCulloch v. Maryland* in 1819. When the state of Maryland imposed a tax on BUS in an attempt to destroy it in that state, **Chief Justice John Marshall** declared that the Bank was constitutional, and in keeping with the implied powers clause. He thus validated the Bank and strengthened the power of the federal government.

In 1794, the **Whiskey Rebellion** occurred when Pennsylvania farmers, unhappy with the excise tax placed on whiskey, refused to pay the tax. The ability of the government to levy and collect taxes was being tested. Washington, at the beckoning of Hamilton, sent out federal troops to crush the rebellion. The rebellious farmers dispersed and the government under the Constitution had demonstrated its power to enforce the law.

The differences between Hamilton's and Jefferson's views of the role of the government in the lives of people gave rise to **political parties**. Hamilton, a Federalist, distrusted the masses and viewed the government at its best when it appeared strong. Hamilton believed that the president should hold his position for life. Jefferson, on the other hand, professed trust in the educated and informed masses and believed in rotation of political office. Those who followed Jefferson, including James Madison, became known as Antifederalists, **Democratic-Republicans,** or simply Republicans.

Foreign Affairs

The **French Revolution**, which began in 1789 with the storming of the Bastille, divided the people of the United States. The split between Hamilton and Jefferson became more evident as events unfolded.

There was great sympathy in the United States for the French when the revolution for democracy began, but that sympathy diminished as the revolution changed. In 1792, France declared war on Austria and, in 1793, Louis XVI was beheaded, and the Reign of Terror began.

The Democratic-Republicans were generally sympathetic to the French. They believed that the 1778 Franco-American treaty of alliance should be honored. The Federalists, supporters of Great Britain, believed that the United States had no business in supporting the French, especially after France declared war on Great Britain in 1793.

Washington, realizing the folly of U.S. involvement in this conflict, issued the **Proclamation of Neutrality** in 1793, which declared that the United States favored neither England nor France in this conflict. He also warned American citizens not to take sides in the conflict.

In the meantime, French nationalist Edmund Genêt, known as **Citizen Genêt**, tried to recruit Americans into the army for the purpose of invading Spanish Florida and Louisiana. This proved an embarrassment to the supporters of France.

The British presented another problem for the Americans. The British ignored U.S. neutrality through seizure of American vessels and **impressment** of U.S. seamen; they removed American sailors from American vessels and forced them into the service of the British navy. They also incited the Native Americans in the northwest, where the British had kept soldiers even after the Revolution. Sentiments were rising against the British, and the divide between British and French supporters widened.

In 1794, Washington sent **John Jay**, Chief Justice of the Supreme Court, to London to negotiate a peace with England. In **Jay's Treaty**, the British promised to withdraw its forces from U.S. soil and to pay damages for the seizure of American ships. The United States promised to pay all debts still owed to British merchants from the Revolution. However, there was no agreement on the issues of impressment and freedom of the seas. The treaty was unpopular in the United States, but served to keep the United States out of war, a crucial accomplishment.

When Jay's Treaty was signed, the Spanish feared that the British and Americans were planning an alliance. They therefore negotiated **Pinckney's Treaty of 1795**, whereby Spain gave up their land east of the Mississippi River and north of Florida, with the 31st parallel as the northern boundary of Florida. The Mississippi River was also opened up to American traders.

The problem with the Native Americans in the Ohio Valley led to a conflict between the United States and the **Miami Confederacy**, northern Native American warriors in Ohio, whom the British were inciting against the Americans. In the **Battle of Fallen Timbers,** fought in 1794, General "Mad" Anthony Wayne crushed these northwestern Indian tribes. Via the **Treaty of Greenville**, signed in 1795, the Miami Confederacy gave up their claims to the Ohio country, lands rich in furs.

As the situation between France and England grew in intensity, the presidential election of 1796 took place. Washington had decided to retire after serving two terms in office, thus setting the precedent for a two-term presidency, which remained unbroken until Franklin D. Roosevelt's election to a third term in 1940. Following the victory for John Adams, Washington said farewell to the nation he had so valiantly served. In his **Farewell Address**, Washington urged the United States to remain neutral, to be friendly to all nations, and to take advantage of its geographical distance from Europe.

THE ADMINISTRATION OF JOHN ADAMS (1797–1801)

Foreign Affairs

The political differences that existed between Hamilton and Jefferson had a great impact on the **election of 1796**. Anti-Jefferson, Hamilton attempted to influence the election to assure that Jefferson was not elected. When the votes were counted, **John Adams** was elected president and Jefferson was elected vice president, a Federalist and Democratic-Republican, respectively.

The Adams administration was plagued with continuing English and French problems. In 1797, in an attempt to negotiate a peace with France, Adams sent a delegation of Americans headed by John Marshall to France, to meet with the French Minister **Talleyrand**. Upon the Americans' arrival, the French demanded a payment of $250,000 for the right to speak with Talleyrand. The **XYZ Affair**, as it was known, infuriated the people of the United States and they began to call for war with France. With that in mind, Congress established the Navy Department and expanded the tiny navy of the United States. The United States Marine Corps was established and Congress authorized the raising of an army of 10,000 men.

The Jeffersonian Republicans opposed the idea of war with France. Adams, understanding the impact a war would have on the United States, decided to try again to negotiate with the French. His efforts were met with success in the signing of the **Convention of 1800**. With **Napoleon Bonaparte** now in power in France, the Franco-American alliance was dissolved and the United States agreed to pay for the damages to U.S. shipping. Considered a sellout by the Federalists, this move cost Adams the presidency in the **election of 1800** but saved the country from a destructive war. It also paved the way for the **Louisiana Purchase**, which took place in 1803.

Domestic Affairs

To weaken the Democratic-Republicans and their vocal opposition to Adams and the Federalists, Congress passed a series of acts known as the **Alien and Sedition Acts** in 1798. These acts included the:

- **Naturalization Act**, which required that a person must be in the United States for 14 years before becoming a naturalized citizen. Since most immigrants were Democratic-Republicans, this act would considerably reduce their ranks.

- **Alien Act,** which gave the president the power to deport foreigners deemed dangerous to the peace and safety of the United States.

- **Sedition Act,** which provided for fines or imprisonment for anyone who used language that stirred discontent or rebellion in the government.

The response of the Democratic-Republicans to these acts came in the form of the **Virginia and Kentucky Resolutions**, written by **James Madison** and **Thomas Jefferson,** respectively. Published in 1798–1799, these resolutions stated that the Constitution was a compact (contract) between the states and the central government and that when the central government violates the contract, the states have the right to judge the constitutionality of the laws being passed. The Kentucky Resolution took it one step further by stating that the state was able to declare a law null and void and, therefore, unenforceable. This doctrine of **nullification** became a basic principle used by the Southern states in justifying their secession from the Union in 1860.

SUMMARY

The political lines had been drawn. The Alien and Sedition Acts and the Virginia and Kentucky Resolutions had demonstrated clearly the difference in the philosophy and thinking between the Federalists and the Democratic-Republicans. The doctrine of nullification became the cornerstone of the American Civil War, which was not the intended result of either Jefferson or Madison.

The efforts of Washington and Adams to keep the United States out of war with France and England bought valuable time for the country to grow and develop a better defensive position. The solidifying of the power of the central government through Hamilton's financial program and the demonstration of governmental force in the Whiskey Rebellion allowed the Constitution to take hold and become the law of the land.

THINGS TO REMEMBER

- **Cabinet:** A body of advisers to a head of state. The U.S. president's cabinet consists of the heads of the various departments plus other advisers.

- **Excise tax:** A tax that is added onto to the price of goods produced, sold, or distributed within a country; for example, sales tax.

- **Loose constructionist:** A person who believes in the broad interpretation of the U.S. Constitution, that is, that the Constitution does not have to be interpreted word by word. Alexander Hamilton supported this idea.

- **Protective tariff:** A tax placed on imports; its purpose is to make domestic goods cheaper to keep out foreign goods. See **tariff**.

- **Strict constructionist:** A term used to describe a person who believes that the Constitution must be interpreted word by word. Thomas Jefferson believed in strict construction of the Constitution.

- **Tariff:** A tax on imports (goods coming into a country). Tariffs were advocated by Alexander Hamilton in 1792 and favored by the supporters of the American System to pay for internal improvements and protect U.S. industry. Tariffs were often a main issue in Jacksonian and Gilded Age politics.

REVIEW QUESTIONS

1. Washington's administration was significant because it

   (A) dealt successfully with the problems between England and France
   (B) dealt effectively with political parties
   (C) was the first administration and thus set precedents for future administrations
   (D) supported the British after the French declared war on Great Britain in 1793
   (E) established a strong political base for the Democratic-Republicans

2. All of the following were part of Hamilton's Financial Program EXCEPT

   (A) the establishment of the capital of the United States in Washington, DC
   (B) the funding of the domestic and foreign debt of the United States
   (C) the assumption of state debt
   (D) the levying of excise taxes and tariffs
   (E) the establishment of the Bank of the United States

3. In his *Farewell Address*, delivered in 1796, George Washington counseled the United States to

   (A) choose sides carefully in the conflict between England and France
   (B) build a strong Navy
   (C) remain neutral when it came to the conflict in Europe
   (D) support England in the conflict with France
   (E) support John Adams and his incoming administration

4. Thomas Jefferson's objection to the Bank of the United States centered around his belief in

   (A) loose construction of the Constitution
   (B) implied powers
   (C) the idea that the Bank favored the wealthy Southern planters
   (D) nullification of federal laws by the states
   (E) strict construction of the Constitution

ANSWERS AND EXPLANATIONS

1. C

Washington defined not only the role of the president but also established other precedents to be followed by future generations, including such things as the establishment of the cabinet. The problems between England and France continued to impact the United States until the War of 1812. Washington was distressed by the rise of political factions within his administration. The Federalists and Democratic-Republicans continued to fight over governmental issues during his administration. These two political parties were well established by the Election of 1800. Washington announced the Proclamation of Neutrality in 1793, which notified the world of the decision of the United States to remain out of the conflict in Europe. Washington was not a believer in any political parties.

2. A

The placement of the United States capital on the Potomac was part of an agreement made between Hamilton and Jefferson to convince Jefferson to accept the assumption portion of Hamilton's financial plan. Choices (B), (C), (D), and (E) were all parts the Financial Program.

3. C

Washington's *Farewell Address* reiterated Washington's belief that the United States should remain neutral and isolationist, particularly concerning the problems in Europe. Therefore, choices (A) and (D) are incorrect. John Adams established the Navy Department and increased the size of the navy. Washington did support John Adams, but his *Farewell Address* concerned did not address this issue.

4. E

Thomas Jefferson believed that the Constitution must be interpreted word for word. He objected to the Bank of the United States because no part of the Constitution allowed the government to establish a bank. Hamilton, on the other hand, believed in loose construction of the Constitution and cited the implied powers clause to support the establishment of the Bank of the United States. Jefferson felt that the Bank favored the more industrial north. The doctrine of nullification was written by Jefferson in the Kentucky Resolution, part of the Virginia and Kentucky Resolutions written by Madison and Jefferson in response to the Alien and Sedition Acts passed in 1798.

CHAPTER 9

The Republicans in Power, 1800–1824

TIMELINE

1800	Thomas Jefferson elected president
1803	Louisiana Purchase made • *Marbury v. Madison* decision
1805	Treaty signed with Tripoli
1807	Embargo Act passed
1808	James Madison elected president
1810	*Fletcher v. Peck* decision
1812	United States declares war on England
1814	Francis Scott Key composes the "Star-Spangled Banner" • New England states meet at Hartford Convention • Treaty of Ghent signed
1816	James Monroe elected president • Tariff of 1816 passed • Second Bank of the United States chartered
1818	Rush-Bagot Agreement signed
1819	Adams-Onis Treaty signed • *Dartmouth College v. Woodward* decision • *McCulloch v. Maryland* decision
1820	Missouri Compromise preserves balance of power in Congress
1823	Monroe Doctrine proclaimed
1824	*Gibbons v. Ogden* decision
1825	Erie Canal completed

IMPORTANT PEOPLE, PLACES, EVENTS, AND CONCEPTS

election of 1800

Thomas Jefferson

Federalists

James Madison

Republicans

John Adams

midnight appointments

Marbury v. Madison

John Marshall

Four Pillars of Posterity

Louisiana Purchase

Napoleon Bonaparte

Embargo Act of 1807

Macon's Bill No. 2

War of 1812

William Henry Harrison

Tecumseh

Tippecanoe

Fort McHenry

Francis Scott Key

Hartford Convention

Treaty of Ghent

Rush-Bagot Agreement

Adams-Onis Treaty

James Monroe

Henry Clay

The American System

Tariff of 1816

Fletcher v. Peck

Dartmouth College v. Woodward

McCulloch v. Maryland

Gibbons v. Ogden

Monroe Doctrine

Missouri Compromise

"Let us, then, fellow-citizens, unite with one heart and one mind. . . . We have been called by different names brethren of the same principle. We are all Republicans, we are all Federalists."

–Thomas Jefferson, First Inaugural Address, 1801

INTRODUCTION

With 35 votes in the House of Representatives, Republican **Thomas Jefferson** was elected president of the United States in the **election of 1800**; Federalist **Aaron Burr** was elected vice-president. Labeled by some as **"The Revolution of 1800,"** the election of Jefferson marked a peaceful transition of government from the **Federalist** Party to the **Republican** Party. Jefferson's election was dismaying to Federalists; in the end, however, Jefferson acted more like a Federalist than a Republican in many cases.

JEFFERSON'S ADMINISTRATION (1801–1809)

Domestic Affairs

According to Jefferson's first inaugural address, the agenda for his administration involved creating a "wise and frugal government" which would establish order in society based on the Bill of Rights and equal protection under the law. He also vowed to protect states' rights. To aid him in these tasks, he selected **James Madison** as his secretary of state and **Albert Gallatin** of Pennsylvania as his secretary of the treasury.

Jefferson replaced many Federalist office holders with **Republicans**. He allowed the Alien and Sedition Acts to expire and reduced the number of years necessary for naturalization. In addition, Jefferson retired the public debt, cut executive offices, reduced the regular army and the navy, and improved the state militias.

He also ignored John Adams's **"midnight appointments"** to the federal courts, resulting in the landmark Supreme Court case of *Marbury v. Madison* in 1803. Shortly before Jefferson was inaugurated, **John Adams** had tried to fill the federal courts with Federalist judges. Adams's secretary of state, John Marshall, was to have delivered the appointments, but he failed to do so. Jefferson's secretary of state, James Madison, *refused* to do so. One of the judges that was to have been appointed, William Marbury, sued Madison. **John Marshall**, chief justice of the Supreme Court, ruled that a portion of the **Judiciary Act of 1789**—the part that allowed the Supreme Court jurisdiction in this case—was unconstitutional. Marshall, by this action, established the power of **judicial review**, which allows the Supreme Court to declare acts of Congress and the president unconstitutional. He thus expanded the power of the court, a far more important outcome than Jefferson had anticipated.

Jefferson left untouched many Federalists programs established under the first two administrations. The **Bank of the United States** remained undisturbed until 1811, when its charter expired. He supported the growth of the **"Four Pillars of Posterity,"** which had been part of Hamilton's financial program: manufacturing, commerce, navigation, and agriculture.

The crowning achievement of Jefferson's administration was the **Louisiana Purchase** in 1803. Seeking to establish his empire in Europe, **Napoleon Bonaparte** agreed to sell a large expanse of land, known as the **Louisiana Territory**, to the United States. Jefferson, a **strict constructionist**, understood that, similar to the problem faced when establishing the Bank of the United States, there was no provision in the Constitution which allowed for land purchases by the government. He bought Louisiana anyway and justified his actions using the same arguments Hamilton and the Federalists had used to establish the Bank of the United States: the power to purchase land was **implied**, based on the **elastic clause**. Jefferson received much criticism from both the Federalists and the Republicans for his actions. Once it was purchased, Jefferson sent **Lewis and Clark** to explore the land. The territory of the United States doubled in size, and the control of the Mississippi River, vital to Western development, belonged to the United States.

Foreign Affairs

It was the area of foreign affairs that was most troublesome for Jefferson, who espoused a policy of nonintervention. Four years after sending a fleet to deal with the **Barbary Pirates** in 1801, Jefferson signed a treaty with Tripoli that ended the practice of paying tribute to allow American ships to travel through the Mediterranean Sea.

Jefferson's greatest challenge was the continual harassment of American ships by both England and France. In 1807, the frigate *U.S.S. Chesapeake* was attacked by the British near Norfolk, Virginia. Jefferson responded by ordering the **Embargo Act of 1807**, by which U.S. ships were not permitted to leave U.S. harbors. This was met with opposition from the people of the United States because of its detrimental effects on trade and commerce.

THE WAR OF 1812

Despite the increased popularity of the Federalists, **James Madison**, a Republican and Jefferson's secretary of state, won the presidency in 1808. As the hostilities between England and France increased, the United States moved closer to war. In 1812, Napoleon tricked Madison into believing that France would end its harassment of America at sea when he agreed to the provisions of **Macon's Bill No. 2**. According to Macon's Bill the United States was to resume trade with the first nation, either England or France, that pledged to end its harassment of U.S. shipping.

There were many reasons the United States declared war against Great Britain in June of 1812:

- The newly elected representatives to Congress, or War Hawks, who were mainly from the West, saw war with England as a way to conquer Canada.

- Westerners were unhappy with the situation with the Native Americans, whom they believed to be working with the British against the American settlers. In 1809, General **William Henry Harrison**, governor of the Indiana Territory, duped the Indians into signing away tribal land. **Tecumseh**, a Shawnee Indian, attempted to form a confederation of tribes to fight the advances of the whites; however, in a premature attack launched by Tecumseh's brother, the Native Americans were defeated at **Tippecanoe** by Harrison. Some of their recovered weapons had come from Canada, increasing the War Hawks' desire for war against Britain and conquest of Canada.

- Anti-British feeling increased with the **impressment** of U.S. seamen, who were removed from American ships and forced to serve on British ships.

Without a real navy, a real strategy, or a national bank, the United States was unprepared for the war. As a result, the British gained control of much the Ohio Valley and burnt Washington, DC. But they failed to seize Baltimore, and the American victory at **Fort McHenry** in Baltimore harbor inspired **Francis Scott Key** to write the "*Star-Spangled Banner*," which became the national anthem.

Ironically, New England, the area most involved in shipping and commerce, opposed the war. They feared the diminishment of their power in Congress as new Western states were admitted to the Union. In 1814, the New England states met at the **Hartford Convention** where they proposed a number of amendments to the Constitution that attempted to reduce the power of other sections of the country. However, the war was over by this time. The convention resulted in a hostile reaction from the rest of the country, and the virtual death of the Federalist Party.

In 1814, the **Treaty of Ghent** was signed between the United States and Great Britain. It provided for a *status quo ante bellum*, meaning that the territory held by Britain and the United States was to return to the way it was before the war. Therefore, no land changed hands. The issues of impressment and freedom of the seas were not addressed.

The **War of 1812**, often called "Mr. Madison's War," had many significant results:

- It opened the way for a new relationship between England and the United States. In 1815, the United States signed a commercial treaty with England, and in 1818, the **Rush-Bagot Agreement** was signed, which involved the fortification of the Great Lakes. The northern boundary of Louisiana was set, and the United States and England agreed to jointly occupy the Oregon Territory for 10 years.

- The Embargo led to development of U.S. industries, and the country began to look within itself for the goods and services it required.

- The absence of Britain and Spain, from whom Florida had been purchased in 1819 via the **Adams-Onis Treaty**, left the United States free to expand.

- A new spirit of nationalism developed from what is sometimes called **"The Second War of Independence."**

THE ERA OF GOOD FEELING

The American System

In 1817, **James Monroe**, a Virginia Republican, became president of the United States. His term in office marked a period of time during which the United States grew from within. **Henry Clay**, becoming ever prominent on the political scene, proposed the idea of the **American System**. He believed that the industrial North would become the manufacturing center for the United States while the South and West would raise the raw materials and food supply of the country. In order to accomplish this, it was necessary to improve transportation, set up a national banking system, and levy **protective tariffs**—that is, taxes on imports high enough to keep out competitive foreign goods. Revenue from the protective tariffs was to be used for internal improvements, such as roads.

The **Tariff of 1816** was passed and was not significantly high, but by 1828, the tariff was raised considerably, drawing objection from the South and West. A **national road** was constructed from Maryland to Illinois, and, 1825, the **Erie Canal** was completed. In 1816, Congress chartered the **Second Bank of the United States,** which issued paper money that could be used in all places.

John Marshall and the Supreme Court

Serving as chief justice of the Supreme Court for 34 years, John Marshall shaped the Court and solidified the power of the central government. Some significant cases from his tenure as chief justice include:

- *Marbury v. Madison* (1803)—This case established the principle of judicial review.

- *Fletcher v. Peck* (1810)—This case involved a contract between a state and individuals concerning a land grant. The contract was upheld, and this case marked the first time the Court declared a state law unconstitutional, stating that a state cannot pass laws which violate the federal Constitution.

- *Dartmouth College v. Woodward* (1819)—Dartmouth College, having been granted a charter at its founding by royal authority, sued when the state of New Hampshire attempted to alter that charter. The state contended that no contract existed, as defined by the Constitution. The Supreme Court ruled in favor of Dartmouth. This established the idea that states cannot interfere with contracts between states and corporations.

- *McCulloch v. Maryland* (1819)—This case involved a branch of the Bank of the United States that was being heavily taxed by the state of Maryland. Declaring that "the power to tax is the power to destroy," Marshall declared the Bank of the United States constitutional and extended the authority of federal law over state law.

- *Gibbons v. Ogden* (1824)—This involved a contract for a ferry service on the Hudson River. The Court established the federal government's power to regulate **interstate commerce** (commerce among the states). **Intrastate commerce** (commerce within the state) remained under the control of the states.

THE MONROE DOCTRINE

With the defeat of Napoleon in 1815, the United States feared that Spain and Portugal might attempt to regain control of their colonies in the Americas that had become independent. The Russians had also been increasing their influence from Alaska to California. Responding to these fears in a speech to Congress in 1823, President Monroe presented the United States' policy concerning interference in the Americas. He stated that:

- The Americas were closed to further colonization.

- The United States would not interfere with already existing colonies in the Americas.

- The United States would not interfere in European affairs. Likewise, the Europeans were to stay out of the affairs of the Americas.

- Actions taken by the Europeans to colonize the Western Hemisphere, or any attempt to interfere with the newly independent nations, would be considered by the United States to be dangerous to the people of the United States.

The Monroe Doctrine disturbed the European nations, none of whom took action against the policy due to their belief that the British supported it. The Monroe Doctrine became the basis for American policy concerning the Western Hemisphere.

THE MISSOURI COMPROMISE

In 1819, the issue of slavery became a national debate when Missouri applied for admission into the Union as a slave state. This admission would have affected the balance of power in the Senate, which was shared equally between North and South. When Maine applied for admission as a free state, a compromise was reached under the leadership of Henry Clay. Maine entered the Union as a free state, while Missouri entered as a slave state, thus preserving the balance in Congress. In addition, slavery was forbidden north of the 36° 30' north latitude line, except for the southern boundary of Missouri. This measure preserved the Union, but the debate over slavery continued.

SUMMARY

The Republicans who led the United States from 1800 to 1824 guided the country through further growth and development from 13 individual entities into a whole nation. With the peaceful transition of government in 1800, the development of nationalism after 1812, and the establishment of the Constitution of the United States as the guiding light for the rule of law, the country began its journey as an adult in the world.

The country turned inward for a few decades as it completed its **"manifest destiny,"** to expand westward and occupy the lands from the Atlantic to the Pacific. The looming issue of slavery occupied the national mind for many years to come. Unfortunately, the euphoria of this "Era of Good Feeling" gave way to the anger and bloodshed of the 1860s.

THINGS TO REMEMBER

- **Impressment:** The policy used by the British before the War of 1812 wherein the British stopped U.S. vessels and removed sailors from them to be used on British naval vessels. It was also used to a limited extent by the French during this same time period. It was one of the causes of the War of 1812.

- **Interstate commerce:** Trade that takes place between states. Under the U.S. Constitution, the power to regulate interstate commerce is delegated to the Congress.

- **Intrastate commerce:** Trade that takes place within the boundaries of a state. Under the U.S. Constitution, the power to regulate intrastate commerce is delegated to the states.

- **Judicial review:** The principle that the Supreme Court has the power to review laws passed by Congress and actions taken by the president to determine whether or not they are consistent with the Constitution. The Supreme Court can declare a law or Presidential action unconstitutional, thereby nullifying it.

REVIEW QUESTIONS

1. The Election of 1800 has often been termed the "Revolution of 1800." This refers to the fact that it

   (A) marked the first election of a non-Virginian to the presidency since the establishment of the Constitution

   (B) was a peaceful transition of the control of the presidency from a Federalist to a Democratic-Republican

   (C) changed the process of electing the President

   (D) resulted in the election of the first non-Christian to the presidency

   (E) was the first election in which the western section of the country was very influential

2. The Supreme Court case of *Marbury v. Madison* (1803) was significant because it

   (A) gave more power to the Republicans

   (B) established the right of the federal government to control interstate commerce

   (C) supported the doctrine of states' rights

   (D) gave the states the power to control interstate commerce

   (E) established the court's power of judicial review

3. The Missouri Compromise (1820) provided for all of the following EXCEPT

   (A) the extension of slavery into the Northwest Territory

   (B) for Missouri's entrance into the Union as a slave state

   (C) for Maine's entrance into the Union as a free state

   (D) that there was to be no slavery north of the 36° 30' north latitude line

   (E) that slavery was to be permitted south of the 36° 30' north latitude line

4. The Monroe Doctrine

   (A) was enforced by England

   (B) created a sphere of influence for the United States in the Western Hemisphere

   (C) expelled all European nations from the Western Hemisphere

   (D) reiterated the United States' policy of involvement in world affairs

   (E) was part of the American System proposed by Henry Clay

ANSWERS AND EXPLANATIONS

1. B

The Election of 1800 marked a change from Federalist control of the White House to Democratic-Republican control. This transition took place peacefully. However, Jefferson kept many Federalist programs and used the Federalist argument of implied powers to justify the Louisiana Purchase. John Adams was from Massachusetts and was elected in 1796; Jefferson was elected in 1800 and he was a Virginian. The electoral process was not changed in this election. Jefferson was believed to be an agnostic or atheist. There were people who objected to him on these grounds, but this is not the reason for calling his election the "Revolution of 1800." The west had not yet become influential by 1800; when Andrew Jackson was elected in 1828, the west was more involved.

2. E

John Marshall, chief justice of the Supreme Court in 1803, used the case of *Marbury v. Madison* to establish the Court's power of judicial review whereby the Supreme Court can declare a law passed by Congress and signed by the president as unconstitutional, and therefore null and void. This case arose from John Adams's Midnight Appointments. *Gibbons v. Ogden* (1824) established the right of the federal government to control commerce between and among the states (interstate commerce), while giving the states the control of commerce within the states (intrastate commerce).

3. A

The Missouri Compromise did not extend the practice of slavery into the Northwest Territory. The Northwest Ordinance of 1787 had barred slavery from that territory. The Missouri Compromise dealt with the admission of Maine and Missouri into the Union, with Missouri as a slave state and Maine as a free state. It also banned slavery from the area of the Louisiana Purchase north of the 36° 30' north latitude line.

4. B

The Monroe Doctrine of 1823 forbade future colonization in the Western Hemisphere and warned the Europeans powers not to interfere in the affairs of the Americas. Thus, it created a sphere of influence for the United States in the Americas. Supported by England, the Monroe Doctrine required no enforcement. The colonies already held by the European nations in the Americas were not to be interfered with under the terms of the Monroe Doctrine, and it appeared to be more a policy of isolation than a policy of involvement. The American System proposed by Henry Clay was a vision for the United States in which the United States would become more self-sufficient, but this was not part of the Monroe Doctrine.

CHAPTER 10

Jacksonian Democracy, 1824–1836

TIMELINE

1824	John Quincy Adams wins in a disputed presidential election
1828	South Carolina Exposition and Protest written in protest of Tariff of Abominations
1830	Indian Removal Act passed • Webster v. Hayne debate takes place • Trail of Tears begins with Choctaws
1832	*Worcester v. Georgia* decision • South Carolina nullifies Tariff of 1832 • Jackson vetoes Bank Bill
1836	Specie circular issued • Martin van Buren elected president
1837	Panic of 1837 begins

IMPORTANT PEOPLE, PLACES, EVENTS, AND CONCEPTS

Andrew Jackson

John Quincy Adams

Daniel Webster

disputed election of 1824

Henry Clay

corrupt bargain

American Plan

Indian Removal Act

Trail of Tears

Bank War

Whigs

Panic of 1837

John C. Calhoun

South Carolina Exposition and Protest

Tariff of Abominations

Robert Y. Hayne

Tariff of 1832

Nullification Crisis

Ordinance of Nullification

Nullification Proclamation

Force Bill

Compromise of 1833

"Our white brethren have more knowledge than we and they are better skilled in traveling and commencing new settlements. Why then do they not go and possess that good land for themselves?"

—*Cherokee Phoenix*, 1830

INTRODUCTION

Andrew Jackson—hero of the Battle of New Orleans, Indian fighter, duelist, and owner of hundreds of slaves—has been proclaimed as the defender of the common man. Both **John Quincy Adams** and **Daniel Webster**, two of Jackson's biggest rivals, were antislavery, opposed to unlimited expansion to the West, and supported government aid to build industry and transportation. They were proclaimed as aristocrats who favored the rich. The three major issues of the time—the National Bank, Native American rights, and the Constitutional nature of federal power—found these major players on surprising sides.

ELECTION OF 1824

John Quincy Adams, James Monroe's Secretary of State, assumed he would be the leading candidate for the Republican nomination for the presidency in 1824. Three other candidates gained the support of their states, however: Kentuckian **Henry Clay**, former speaker of the House; a Georgian, William H. Crawford, Monroe's Secretary of the Treasury; and Andrew Jackson, "Old Hickory," from Tennessee. Jackson won a plurality of both the popular vote and the electoral vote, throwing the **disputed election of 1824** into the House of Representatives. Adams came in second to Jackson with about one third fewer popular votes, and Crawford was third. Since only the top three could compete according to the 12th Amendment, Clay supported Adams. Each state received one vote, and Adams won by one vote. There had been earlier rumors that Adams was making a deal for Clay to be Secretary of State, so when Adams appointed Clay after the election, the Jacksonians accused them of conducting a **corrupt bargain.** Adams agreed with Clay's **American Plan**, which would provide government aid for **internal improvements** like roads and canals, supported by tariffs. Adams' supporters could have disagreed with the Jacksonians—was it corrupt to get the support of someone who agrees with you?

ELECTION OF 1828

General Andrew Jackson won the election of 1828 with 56 percent of the popular vote. The bitter campaign had focused on the 1825 "corrupt bargain," along with Adams's inability to relate to the voters, Jackson's killing of six deserters in 1815 during an unsanctioned attack on the Creek Indians, and the revelation that Jackson had married before his bride was divorced. Jackson opened up the White House to Western supporters who streamed in unannounced throughout his terms of office. Unlike Adams, he gave them jobs. Thus was born what is now known as the **spoils system.**

INDIAN REMOVAL

Claiming he wanted to preserve their culture, Andrew Jackson supported the **Indian Removal Act of 1830**, which required the deportation of the Native Americans beyond the Mississippi River into present-day Oklahoma. Seventeen thousand Cherokee who knew how to argue against their "white brethren" brought a key case, ***Worcester v. Georgia***, to the Supreme Court in 1832. They had adopted white dress, created a constitution, published a newspaper (the *Phoenix*), and kept black slaves. Chief Justice Marshall ruled that the Cherokees were an independent nation over which the laws of Georgia could "have no force." The president challenged Marshall to "enforce" his ruling. Georgia removed the Cherokee in 1838 with federal troops. Beginning with the Choctaws in 1831, Native Americans were forced to trek 1,200 miles, burying their dead along this **Trail of Tears**. The Seminoles in northern Florida waged a seven-year war into the 1840s before removal, fighting alongside runaway slaves.

BANK WAR

State power versus federal power was once again a key issue when Andrew Jackson attacked the "monster" Second Bank of the United States. Chartered for 30 years in 1816, the Second Bank was funded by the national government in combination with a private corporation. The bank kept the currency stable and issued loans to entrepreneurs. In 1832, Bank president Nicholas Biddle, along with Senators Henry Clay and Daniel Webster, supported an early recharter of the Bank to undercut Jackson's support in the 1832 election. The Bank charter renewal passed the Congress with considerable Democratic (Jacksonian) support, but Jackson vetoed the Bank Bill, claiming it was an economic monopoly and an unconstitutional aggrandizement of federal power. Jackson's veto escalated the **Bank War**, sustaining his already high popular support.

"King Andrew"

Since 1828, those in opposition to Jacksonian Democrats had been calling themselves "National Republicans." Soon after the veto, however, Webster and Clay began calling themselves **Whigs**, recalling the revolutionary opposition to King George III. "King Andrew" (Jackson) defeated Clay in the 1832 election with 55 percent of the popular vote.

Panic of 1837

Upon his return to office in 1833, Jackson began to take the federal deposits out of the Bank, placing them in "pet" state banks. Without the stabilizing weight of the Second Bank of the United States, interest rates soared and worthless paper notes were everywhere. To curb the inflation, Jackson issued a *specie circular*, which required that all Western lands be paid for with precious metal, but hard currency could not cover the overheated market in the West. The lack of sound money combined with the inflation and an international crisis produced a five-year depression called the **Panic of 1837**.

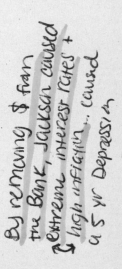

By removing $ from the Bank, Jackson caused extreme interest rates + high inflation... caused a 5 yr Depression

NULLIFICATION AND SLAVERY

South Carolina Exposition and Protest

The drama over the power of the federal government continued. **John C. Calhoun**, vice president under Jackson until 1832, wrote the **South Carolina Exposition and Protest** against the Tariff of 1828. The tariff's rates were so high that southerners called it the **Tariff of Abominations**. The government raised so much money that it had the first surplus ever (and the last one until 2000). Calhoun, the former nationalist and supporter of the American Plan who had believed that tariffs and internal improvements would bind the country together, turned sectionalist. In an argument similar to Jefferson's 1798 Kentucky Resolution, the Exposition stated that since the states made a compact, the states could dissolve it, or make "null and void" any federal law that was contrary to their interests. The Exposition argued that the Tariff of Abominations favored the North and threatened South Carolina by forcing them to pay high prices for imports. Following this **Compact Theory**, South Carolina could declare the tariff unconstitutional and not collect it.

The Webster-Hayne Debate

Massachusetts Senator Daniel Webster forced Senator **Robert Y. Hayne**, protégé of **John C. Calhoun**, to debate over slavery and nullification. Hayne argued for the Compact Theory, claiming that South Carolina could decide when to follow a federal law on the tariff. Webster proved that the controversy over the tariff and nullification was a stand-in for a debate over slavery and secession. In his **Second Reply to Hayne**, Webster denounced slavery and argued that the Union was formed by the whole people in *conventions* (see Article VII of the Constitution), and therefore the state *governments* were actually not parties to a compact. Sovereignty resided in the people, and armed defense of secession was treason. His summary was on the lips of many a Northern soldier during the Civil War: "Liberty and Union now and forever, one and inseparable." These questions were resolved only on Civil War battlefields.

Nullification Crisis

When the state of South Carolina passed an **Ordinance of Nullification** of the new **Tariff of 1832**, Jackson responded with a **Nullification Proclamation** (1833), denouncing it as secession and treason. In the **Force Bill,** Jackson threatened to send troops and arranged to collect the tariff in the sea, but Henry Clay sponsored a substitute tariff which provided for gradual reduction in the rates. South Carolina accepted this **Compromise of 1833**.

SUMMARY

The Whigs and Democrats had supporters in both the North and South. Whigs supported the U.S. Bank and internal improvements, and the Democrats favored state, not federal, economic power. Complications arose around slavery. Clay, a Whig slaveholder, arranged the Compromise of 1833, while Webster, also a Whig, fought relentlessly against nullification. For the Democrats, John C. Calhoun threatened nullification to defend the interests of the "peculiar institution." Democratic President Jackson, also a slaveholder, defended federal power against nullification, but arranged the dispossession of the Indians and destroyed the Bank—both actions against the rulings of the (federal) Supreme Court. How long could the parties hold together, North and South, if their members disagreed?

THINGS TO REMEMBER

- **Compact Theory:** The idea that the Constitution was created by the states and so the states could dissolve it. This was advocated first by Madison and Jefferson in 1798 in the Virginia and Kentucky Resolutions, and later by Robert Y. Hayne in his debate with Daniel Webster in 1830. John C. Calhoun, in the Carolina Exposition and Protest (1828) and the South Carolina Ordinance of Nullification (1832), was also a proponent of the Compact Theory. The Confederate States also supported the Compact Theory.

- **Internal improvements:** The building of canals, railroads, and turnpikes at state or federal expense. These were part of the American Plan that became an important part of the Whig program of the 1830s. Internal improvements were also supported by the National Republicans and the Republicans under Lincoln. Proposals for federal financing of internal improvements generally called for funding these with tariffs.

- **Spoils system:** The practice of victorious candidates distributing government jobs to friends and supporters rather than to the most qualified people. Andrew Jackson gave his supporters the spoils of victory whereas John Quincy Adams by and large did not.

- **Specie circular:** Coins or gold and silver money, also called "hard money."

REVIEW QUESTIONS

1. The Whigs were

    (A) a Northern party
    (B) a Southern party
    (C) a pro-Bank party
    (D) a pro-nullification party
    (E) a pro-Indian removal party

2. Who accused John Quincy Adams of making a "corrupt bargain"?

    (A) Henry Clay
    (B) Daniel Webster
    (C) William Crawford
    (D) Andrew Jackson
    (E) James Monroe

3. Who did not support the idea of nullification?

(A) John C. Calhoun
(B) Thomas Jefferson
(C) James Madison
(D) Robert Hayne
(E) Daniel Webster

4. A tariff would protect

(A) cloth made in New England
(B) cloth made in England
(C) cotton grown in the South
(D) wheat grown in the West
(E) corn grown in New England

ANSWERS AND EXPLANATIONS

1. C

The Whigs formed out of the fight over the Bank, which they supported along with internal improvements. The Whigs and the Democrats were both North *and* South parties, so nullification does not apply. Indian Removal favored those wanting land in the West, something the Whigs were opposed to, but most Congressmen favored it.

2. D

The controversy arose when the election of 1824 was thrown into the House of Representatives because neither Jackson, Adams, nor Crawford had a majority of electoral votes. Jackson thought he deserved to be president and accused Clay and Adams of making a deal: Clay would support Adams for president if Adams would appoint Clay Secretary of State. Webster and Clay favored Adams. Crawford had had a stroke, and Monroe is never mentioned in this controversy.

3. E

Nullification was the doctrine that a state could declare a federal law unconstitutional and not obey it, make it "null and void." Anti-nullification, Daniel Webster debated Hayne, who supported Calhoun's resurrection of the nullification doctrines of '98. The idea originated in 1798 when Madison and Jefferson first wrote the Virginia and Kentucky Resolutions asking other states to support them in nullifying the Alien and Sedition Acts.

4. A

A tariff is a tax on imports that protects domestic products. The key domestic industry was New England cotton manufacturing. To protect New England cloth, British cloth was taxed so that Americans would buy cheaper New England cloth. American wheat, corn, and cotton needed no protection.

CHAPTER 11

Growth, Slavery, and Reform, 1800–1850

TIMELINE

1793	Cotton gin invented
1801	Interchangeable parts exhibited
1807	Fulton perfects the steamboat
1811	National road begun
1817–25	Erie Canal built
1820s–30s	The height of the Second Great Awakening
1821	United States consists of 12 slave states and 12 free states
1829	David Walker's appeal published
1831	Nat Turner Rebellion takes place • *Liberator* published
1840	Liberty Party splits the American Anti-Slavery Society
1844	Samuel F. B. Morse invents the telegraph
1840s	American Renaissance in literature takes place
1848	Convention held at Seneca Falls • Martin van Buren runs for president on Free Soil ticket
1860	United States consists of 15 slave state and 23 free states • 4 million slaves exist

IMPORTANT PEOPLE, PLACES, AND EVENTS

Transportation Revolution

National Road

Robert Fulton

Erie Canal

Cyrus McCormick

John Deere

Elias Howe

Samuel F. B. Morse

Black Belt

Ralph Waldo Emerson

Henry David Thoreau

American Renaissance

Second Great Awakening

Temperance Movement

Convention in Seneca Falls

William Lloyd Garrison

American Anti-Slavery Society

Nat Turner

"Go down Moses, way down in Egypt land
Tell old Pharaoh: Let my people go."

—Negro Spiritual

INTRODUCTION

From 1800 to 1860 there were upheavals in the modes of transportation, industry, and agriculture. These changes resulted in clashes in religion and politics, both inside and outside the halls of Congress. A distinctive American literature also developed out of this ferment.

GROWTH

The South

The **cotton gin**, invented by **Eli Whitney** in 1793, separated the seeds from cotton fiber at 50 times the manual rate. Using the cotton gin on the difficult **short staple** inland cotton enabled the slave South to grow from six to 15 states by 1860. Cotton production rose from two million pounds in 1790 to more than a billion pounds by 1860. By 1840, the United States was already producing 60 percent of the world's cotton.

The North

By 1860, the growth of the North had far outstripped that of the South. Between 1790 and 1860, the population of New York City grew from 33,000 to 816,000, while Charleston, South Carolina's only increased from 16,000 to 42,000. There were more jobs and opportunities in the North, so immigrants flocked to the North and West to work in factories, on farms, and in their own businesses.

The Transportation Revolution and the First Industrial Revolution

The growth in the North and West accelerated because of the building of roads, steamboats, and canals, or the **Transportation Revolution**. Construction of the (federal) **National Road** began in 1811 in Cumberland, Maryland, and was completed in Vandalia, Illinois in 1838. The steamboat, perfected by **Robert Fulton** in 1807, provided more rapid transportation on rivers and lakes. The (New York State) **Erie Canal** (1817–1825) stretched from Albany to Buffalo, connecting to New York City via the Hudson River. By 1837 there were 3,000 miles of canals, creating sites for cities like Rochester, New York, which forced production of food, houses, and schools. Jobs grew exponentially. This explosion in jobs and consumer goods created what has been called a **market revolution**, requiring farmers to specialize in grain or dairy, forcing **artisans** (hand craftsmen) to compete with assembly line production, and making products cheaper and more plentiful. New England financiers founded cotton mills in Lowell, Massachusetts in the 1820s providing jobs for young New England farm women.

Inventions

Cyrus McCormick's mechanical reaper (1830s) and **John Deere's** steel plow (1837) set the stage for the late 19th century expansion of agricultural production. Similarly, the sewing machine, invented by **Elias Howe** in 1846 and perfected by I. M. Singer, provided the basis for expansion in the garment industry after the Civil War. The railroad came to America in 1828, but many hundreds of thousands of miles of track would not be laid until the 1860s. However, **Samuel Morse's** telegraph, first used in 1844, was expanded to 23,000 miles of wire by 1853. **Assembly lines**, in which workers made parts of a shoe and handed the work on to the next man sped up production, as did the manufacture of Eli Whitney's machine-made **interchangeable parts** (1801).

SLAVERY

Slaveholders

As cotton production moved west, slaves were sold from the Upper South of Virginia and Maryland to the Lower South of Alabama, Mississippi, and Louisiana, breaking up families in large numbers. The **Black Belt**, named after the dark fertile soil in the Lower South, contributed to the $194,440,000 worth of cotton production in 1859. Cotton accounted for 50 to 60 percent of total U.S. exports. Slave owners comprised only one-fourth of the population, but **planters**, those who owned 20 or more slaves, were overwhelmingly the Southern representatives in Congress and the state legislatures.

Slaves

More than half of the four million slaves in 1860 worked in cotton while the rest grew rice, tobacco, sugar, and hemp. Living in quarters among themselves, the field hands developed a culture based on both their African heritage and their American experience. They developed a **culture of the quarters** in which they told each other stories about tricking their masters and sang Bible-influenced spirituals asking to "Let my people go." Slave sabotage was widespread, and running away, even among house slaves, occurred with surprising frequency, given the severe punishment it might entail.

REFORM

The Second Great Awakening

As the society was split apart along the canals, people began to follow the revival movement of **Charles Grandison Finney**. By the late 1820s Western New York came to be called the "burned-over district." Finney led weeks-long tent meetings converting thousands to prepare for the coming of Christ. Historians have connected the growth of social reform with this **Second Great Awakening**.

Social Reforms

The movements for reform were part of a "Benevolent Empire." In 1837, **Horace Mann** began campaigning for the development of public common schools as well as normal schools for teachers. In 1843, **Dorothea Dix** succeeded in convincing the state of Massachusetts to improve treatment of the mentally ill, who had been placed in prisons with criminals. The **Temperance** Movement succeeded in preventing the manufacture of spirits in Maine in 1851. In 1848, **Elizabeth Cady Stanton** organized the **Convention in Seneca Falls** in New York to address women's rights and suffrage.

Antislavery Strategies

Arthur and Lewis Tappan and **William Lloyd Garrison**, supporters of immediate **abolitionism,** founded the **American Anti-Slavery Society** in 1833. Maintaining in his *Liberator* that slavery was a sin and that the Constitution that protected it trampled on the Declaration's phrase "all men are created equal," pacifist Garrison distributed 1.1 million pieces of literature in 1835. Black newspaper editor **David Walker** wrote an "Appeal to the Coloured Citizens of the World," warning that without equality blacks would rebel. Both Garrison and Walker opposed the **colonization** strategy of Henry Clay's American Colonization Society, which advocated sending freed blacks to Liberia in Africa. Gradual **abolitionism** was adopted by many Northern states after the Revolution, whereby any child born to a slave after 1790, for example would be freed at the age of 21. The most dramatic actions were taken by conspirators Gabriel Prosser in 1800, Denmark Vesey in 1822, and the leader of the 1831 Southampton, Virginia slave rebellion, **Nat Turner,** who led a group of slaves in killing some 60 whites. Turner believed he was called by God to destroy slavery.

LITERATURE

The questions of slavery and societal reform influenced several key literary figures of this period. **Ralph Waldo Emerson**, lecturer and poet of the transcendentalist movement, wrote an essay called *Self-Reliance* (1841) which argued that we all possess a natural ability to understand and perfect the world by relying on our higher instincts. **Henry David Thoreau**, also influenced by **transcendentalism**, published a call for a return to the simple life in *Walden* (1854). In *On Civil Disobedience* (1849), he advocated noncooperation with evil. **Walt Whitman's** *Leaves of Grass* (1855) was a free verse explosion of democratic self-expression. **Herman Melville's** *Moby-Dick* (1851) was an epic novel describing an individual's struggle with nature and fate. Finally, **Nathaniel Hawthorne's** *Scarlet Letter* (1850) was a psychological novel about Puritan mores set in 17th-century Massachusetts. This extraordinary flowering of literary genius has been called the **American Renaissance**.

SUMMARY

The extraordinary level of political activity by ordinary men and women from the 1820s through the 1840s, along with the first Western president's Andrew Jackson invitations to the men with "mud on their boots" to come to the White House and enjoy the "spoils" of victory (chapter 10), have encouraged some historians to label this period the Age of the Common Man. Reform also extended to the right to vote: white manhood suffrage became more common by the 1830s. However, the expansion and the increasing harshness of slavery in the South, in combination with the removal of the Indians and the disorienting growth of the market economy, have prompted other historians to call it simply the Jacksonian Era.

THINGS TO REMEMBER

- **Abolitionism:** The movement to end slavery. There were many points of view on the subject. Immediate abolitionism advocated ending slavery everywhere and refused to cooperate with the political process (William Lloyd Garrison). Political abolitionism advocated an end to slavery everywhere as well, but its adherents worked through the political process and ran for political office (Charles Sumner). **Gradual abolitionism** advocated freeing slaves at the age of 21 who were born after a certain date (James Tallmadge).

- **Artisan:** A skilled worker who had learned his trade from a master as an apprentice. Shoemakers, bakers, blacksmiths, and carpenters were artisans.

- **Assembly line:** A method of mass production whereby the products are moved from worker to worker, with each person performing a small, repetitive task on the product and sending it to the next for a different part until the finished item is assembled. In the 18th and 19th centuries in America, assembly lines did not move; instead, workers handed the product from one to the next.

- **Colonization:** The political position advocating sending free blacks to Liberia in Africa in order to reduce the number of them in the country—the more blacks that were freed, the fewer there would be in America. It was a way of alleviating the danger of slave insurrection. Henry Clay was an advocate of colonization, as was Lincoln, until, as president, he issued the Emancipation Proclamation.

- **Cotton Gin:** A machine that separates seeds from the cotton. The short-staple cotton that grew inland in the South's **Black Belt** could be cleaned profitably only with the cotton gin. The invention of the cotton gin allowed cotton cultivation to spread, enabling slavery to move from the coast of Georgia and South Carolina across the South to Mississippi and Louisiana.

- **Culture of the quarters:** The traditions, language, and modes of behavior of the field hands who lived in the slave quarters. They practiced many forms of resistance to the wills of their masters, told each other African-derived tales, sang spirituals, and practiced their own African- and Christian-derived religion.

- **Interchangeable parts:** Machine-made or standardized parts which could be put together to make a product. Eli Whitney demonstrated to President John Adams in 1801 how a box of guns could be disassembled and reassembled randomly. Each part must be precision-made so that it will fit with any other precision-made part. Before Whitney's invention came into widespread use, parts were handcrafted to each other to fashion a gun or other machine. Interchangeable parts were used in **mass production** in the late 19th century.

- **Planter:** A slave owner in early Virginia or Maryland; later, according to the census, a man who owned 20 or more slaves.

- **Short staple cotton:** Cotton that grew inland in the **Black Belt** of the South, an area characterized by its dark soil. Short-staple cotton could not be grown profitably until the **cotton gin** was invented.

REVIEW QUESTIONS

1. The Erie Canal connected

   (A) North to South
   (B) Midwest to South
   (C) Northeast to West
   (D) Southeast to West
   (E) Southeast to Northeast

2. Match the reform to the reformer.

   V) Mental institutions   1) William Lloyd Garrison
   W) Abolitionism   2) Charles Grandison Finney
   X) Suffrage   3) Horace Mann
   Y) Education   4) Dorothea Dix
   Z) Religion   5) Elizabeth Cady Stanton

   Answer choices:
   (A) V-4, W-1, X-3, Y-2
   (B) V-3, X-5, Y-4, Z-2
   (C) V-4, W-1, X-5, Z-2
   (D) W-1, X-5, Y-2, Z-4
   (E) W-5, X-1, Y-2, Z-4

3. In the South,

   (A) all whites held slaves
   (B) slaves told each other Bible stories
   (C) slaves rarely ran away
   (D) there were no free blacks
   (E) all slaveholders were rich

4. The cotton gin

   (A) produced cotton cloth faster
   (B) planted cotton seeds faster
   (C) was a curse to the planters
   (D) allowed cotton to be grown profitably further North
   (E) allowed cotton to be grown profitably further West

ANSWERS AND EXPLANATIONS

1. C

The Erie Canal connected Albany to Buffalo on Lake Erie, which connected to the Old Northwest via other canals and the Great Lakes. The Hudson River connected Albany to New York City. The connection led to the economic and then political isolation of the South from the West.

2. C

Dorothea Dix worked to improve treatment of the mentally ill. William Lloyd Garrison helped found the American Anti-Slavery Society in 1833. Elizabeth Cady Stanton worked for women's rights and suffrage. Charles Grandison Finney helped lead the Christian revival movement. Horace Mann campaigned for public common schools and normal schools for teachers.

3. B

Slaves learned Christianity from whites and used it to develop their own theology of liberation. The spiritual "Go Down Moses" was written by slaves. Many spirituals were songs of freedom. Slave owners made up only one fourth of the population of the South. Running away was common among slaves, despite harsh penalties. Also, some blacks in the South were not slaves.

4. E

The cotton gin separated the seeds from the cotton fiber by forcing the fiber through a series of comblike teeth. The cotton that grew near the coast (SC and GA) was characterized by long fiber or long staple cotton, from which the seeds came out more easily. The cotton that could be grown further inland was short staple and was much more difficult to de-seed. The cotton gin enabled short staple cotton to be grown profitably in the Black Belt, further West.

CHAPTER 12

Expansion, Conflict, and Compromise, 1820–1850

TIMELINE

1821	Mexico gains independence from Spain
1836	Texas—the Lone Star Republic—declares independence • House of Representatives imposes gag rule
1840	Harrison runs Log Cabin Campaign • American Anti-Slavery Society splits, forming the Liberty Party
1844	James K. Polk elected president
1845	Texas admitted to the Union • Mexican War begins
1846	Wilmot Proviso passes in the House, fails in the Senate
1848	Treaty of Guadalupe-Hidalgo signed • Gold found in California • Whig Zachary Taylor elected president
1850	Clay introduces Compromise • Taylor dies, Millard Fillmore becomes president • Compromise passed

IMPORTANT PEOPLE, PLACES, EVENTS, AND CONCEPTS

"No Irish Need Apply" (NINA)	Non-Cooperators	Treaty of Guadalupe-Hidalgo	Gold Rush
gag rule	Lone Star Republic	Wilmot Proviso	Fugitive Slave Law
Anti-Masonic Party	James K. Polk	Free Soil Party	Stephen Douglas
American Party	Nueces River	Compromise of 1850	Millard Fillmore
Liberty Party	General Zachary Taylor		

"There shall be no slavery or involuntary servitude in any territory acquired from Mexico."

—David Wilmot, 1846

INTRODUCTION

The national controversies during the Jackson administration (1828–1836) were, as we saw, disagreements over the extent of federal versus state power (see chapter 10). These were fueled by the growing economic divisions between the North and the South. After 1836 these divisions produced serious sectional conflicts in Congress, the war with Mexico, and disputes over the admission of California. Could the federal government quiet the controversies?

THE ROOTS OF CONFLICT

Both North and South were growing apart, though the North was growing much faster as business there expanded. Immigrants from Ireland poured into the cities for work, escaping anti-Catholic persecution as well as starvation in the potato famine of 1845. Discrimination was rife (**"No Irish Need Apply"**), but they found work as maids, seamstresses, or laborers. The Germans received a warmer welcome; some had skills and started farms in the West. The South, too, was forced to expand as soil in the East became depleted. Also, bigger profits could be made using more slaves on more land. Both sections grew on the basis of opposing labor systems: the North expanded its **wage (free) labor,** while the South moved its **slave labor** to the West.

Slavery and Congress

Abolitionists mounted petition campaigns to abolish slavery in Washington, DC. Southern Congressmen of course were opposed to this proposal. Afraid that the petitions would dominate the debate, the Democrats passed a motion in the House of Representatives to "table" (ignore) them at the beginning of each session. This **gag rule** lasted from 1836–1844.

Political Parties

The Democrats and Whigs spanned the North and the South (see chapter 10), which kept the questions of slavery out of the spotlight. They began using nominating conventions in the 1830s, which had been developed by the **Anti-Masonic Party**. The **American Party** was a vicious anti-immigrant, anti-Catholic group. Its members were called the **Know-Nothings** because when asked about their secret organization they would say "I know nothing."

Abolitionists

The abolitionists distributed their denunciations of slavery through the mail, but the Democrats under Jackson and Martin Van Buren instructed postmasters to block them from going to the South. Then, in 1840, a group of **political abolitionists** split the American Anti-Slavery Society, forming the **Liberty Party**, because they wanted to run James G. Birney for president. William Lloyd Garrison, leader of the Non-Cooperators, would not run candidates under the slave-supporting Constitution.

Texas

After their Revolution against Spain in 1821, Mexico invited U.S. citizens (Tejanos) into the state of Texas, but they violated Mexican antislavery laws and created further tensions by refusing to assimilate. Texas, or the **Lone Star Republic**, declared independence in 1836 and, despite a setback at the Alamo, won independence from Mexico.

The Elections of 1840 and 1844

The Whigs won a pro–common man **Log Cabin Campaign** with William Henry Harrison, the hero of Tippecanoe, but John Tyler of Virginia became president in 1841, after Harrison died. In 1844, Henry Clay ran an anti-Texas campaign against the Democrat **James K. Polk**, whose expansionist slogans were "54° 40' or fight," to annex the Oregon Territory, and "Texas is Alone but not Deserted." Polk won. The day before he took office. the Democratic Congress voted to annex Texas.

EXPANSION

Manifest Destiny

Expansion to the West was not only driven by competing labor systems and immigration, but also by the American ideology of **Manifest Destiny**. Editor John O'Sullivan believed that it was not only America's obvious fate "to o'er spread the continent," but that Americans would bring democracy to a larger number of people and a greater expanse of land.

Polk challenges mexico by sending US soldiers to California...when mexico attacks, Polk retaliates & uses it as an excuse to take CA.

The Mexican War

Polk tried to buy California from Mexico as soon as he entered office. The Mexicans refused to sell or to recognize American claims to the Rio Grande River as the border of Texas. They considered the **Nueces River**, 130 miles north, the proper border. Impatient because of British interest in California and Texas's concern over its territory, Polk sent **General Zachary Taylor** into the disputed area and waited. In April 1846 the Mexicans attacked, and Polk declared that they had attacked Americans on "American soil." The **Treaty of Guadalupe-Hidalgo** signed in 1848 gave California, Texas, New Mexico, Arizona, Nevada, Utah, and parts of Colorado to the United States. The United States paid $15 million to Mexico thereafter calling the conquered territory the "Mexican Cession."

The Free Soilers

During the War, **David Wilmot**, Democratic Representative from Pennsylvania, introduced an amendment to a war appropriations bill that stated that there should be "no slavery or involuntary servitude in any territory acquired from Mexico." Although it failed in the Senate, this **Wilmot Proviso** stated the kernel of the **Free Soil position**: there should be no extension of slavery to the West. The **Free Soil Party** (1848–1854) formed around this kernel with members ranging from men like Wilmot, who did not think blacks equaled whites, to the great abolitionist orator and runaway slave Frederick Douglass.

THE COMPROMISE OF 1850

Gold in California

Gold was discovered at Sutter's Mill in California in January 1848, and by late 1849 the settlers had written a free state constitution. The number of slave states equaled the number of free states, so that the admission of California would tip the balance in the Senate. Proslavery Southerners had called for a meeting to consider secession, if the Wilmot Proviso passed. Northern antislavery forces had elected Free Soil representatives to Congress. The voting on issues pertaining to slavery was by section, not party. In the face of these difficulties, the House of Representatives took nearly three weeks and 63 votes to elect a speaker.

Clay's Compromise

While the House was attempting to organize, Senator Henry Clay proposed a compromise package to Senator Daniel Webster, which he hoped would satisfy majorities in the House, the Senate, and the nation:

- California would be admitted as a free state.
- Slavery would remain in Washington, DC, but the slave trade (selling slaves) would be prohibited.

- The territories of New Mexico and Utah would have no restrictions on slavery, but slavery questions would be decided later.

- A new, strengthened **Fugitive Slave Law** would be enforced, wherein federally appointed commissioners were given authority to force citizens to capture runaway slaves.

Webster agreed to support the resolutions. In the debate, Senator John C. Calhoun, too sick to deliver his own speech, predicted that the Union would dissolve unless a Constitutional amendment was passed that would give the South a veto over all sectional questions. Webster answered Calhoun on March 7 in a speech that called for the Compromise as the only way to save the Union. "I speak not as a Massachusetts man but as an American . . . . There can be no such thing as peaceable secession." Debate could not produce a majority. However, **Stephen Douglas,** the Democratic senator from Illinois, arranged for separate votes on each aspect of the Compromise. A second factor aiding passage was the support of the new Whig president, **Millard Fillmore,** as Zachary Taylor, elected in 1848, had died in July 1850.

SUMMARY

Politics combined with economics and ideology to produce clashes that portended war. Acquiring territory had always created conflict with the Native Americans, but now it was causing fundamental conflicts among whites. If the slavery questions in Utah, Arizona, and New Mexico were to be decided later, had anything been solved? Was there a compromise if it was not passed as a package? Historian David Potter called it the Armistice of 1850. So far, the Union was preserved, but slavery in the territories was the chief concern of Congress throughout the 1850s. The cease-fire lasted until April 12, 1861.

THINGS TO REMEMBER

- **Free labor:** Labor in which the worker can leave whenever he or she wishes (as opposed to slave labor). Wage labor or work for pay is free labor.

- **Free Soil position:** The political idea that the West should be free of slavery. In 1846 David Wilmot wrote the proviso that there "shall be no slavery or involuntary servitude in any territory acquired from Mexico," which galvanized the antislavery forces in Congress. The question of slavery in the Old South was not addressed in the Free Soil position.

- **Manifest Destiny:** The political belief that America's obvious future was to "o'er spread the continent," in the words of John O'Sullivan in 1846. A corollary was that Americans would bring democracy to the ignorant and inferior peoples of the West. The Mexican War was the classic consequence of manifest destiny.

REVIEW QUESTIONS

1. The Irish

   (A) settled in cities
   (B) became farmers
   (C) were skilled workers
   (D) were Protestants
   (E) were highly educated

2. The gag rule was favored the most by

   (A) Northerners
   (B) Southerners
   (C) Whigs
   (D) Democrats
   (E) Anti-Masons

3. Manifest Destiny involved

   (A) slavery
   (B) anti-slavery
   (C) tariff protection for New England manufacturing
   (D) expansion to the West
   (E) Native American rights

4. David Wilmot, author of the Wilmot Proviso (1846), was a Congressman from

   (A) California
   (B) South Carolina
   (C) Pennsylvania
   (D) North Carolina
   (E) Kansas

ANSWERS AND EXPLANATIONS

1. A

The Irish had been poor tenants who grew potatoes in gardens around their cottages for their food. They were not skilled workers or farmers in the usual sense. They were mostly Catholics who settled in New York, Boston, and other Northern cities.

2. B

The gag rule (1836–1844) suppressed the discussion of petitions regarding slavery (usually abolitionist petitions to abolish slavery in Washington, DC) in the House of Representatives. Southerners were the gag rule's strongest supporters. Anti-Masons had no strong position on slavery, and Democrats and Whigs could be from the North or the South and thus did not all agree on this issue. However, some Northern Democrats voted for the gag order because they feared discussion of this issue would divide Congress and not allow other business to get done.

3. D

Manifest destiny was the belief in the inevitable expansion of the U.S. Northerners *and* Southerners were in favor of expansion, and some from each side were opposed. However, there was no official "Northern" or "Southern" position on expansion. Expansion to new land was in conflict with the interests of the Native Americans.

4. C

Pennsylvania Democrat David Wilmot wrote a proviso quoted at the beginning of this chapter which passed in the House but failed in the Senate. It was a statement of the free soil position. By and large, Northerners were against the expansion of slavery to the West, and Southerners were not. Thus southern states North and South Carolina are not good answers, and California and Kansas were not states in 1846.

CHAPTER 13

Slavery and the Road to Disunion, 1850–1861

TIMELINE

1850	Fugitive Slave Law passes, wreaking havoc in the North
1852	*Uncle Tom's Cabin* published in book form • Franklin Pierce elected president
1853	American Party dominates the Whigs in many Northern states
1854	Kansas-Nebraska Act passed • Republican Party formed
1856	John Brown leads attacks on farmers in "Bleeding Kansas" • James Buchanan elected president
1857	Supreme Court decides Dred Scott case
1858	Abraham Lincoln and Stephen Douglas debate for Illinois senate seat
1859	John Brown organizes raid on Harper's Ferry
1860	Abraham Lincoln nominated by Republicans • Democratic Party splits into Douglas and Breckinridge wings • John Bell forms Constitutional Union Party, making a four-way election • Abraham Lincoln elected • South Carolina secedes in December, followed by the rest of the Southern tier

IMPORTANT PEOPLE, PLACES, EVENTS, AND CONCEPTS

Uncle Tom's Cabin	American Party	Roger Taney	James Breckinridge
Stephen Douglas	John Fremont	Harper's Ferry	national slave code
popular sovereignty	Bleeding Kansas	Abraham Lincoln	Southern tier
Kansas-Nebraska Act	border ruffians	Lincoln-Douglas Debates	
Republican Party	John Brown	"A house divided against itself cannot stand"	
	Dred Scott case		

We protest the Kansas and Nebraska Bill which excludes "immigrants from the Old World and free laborers from our own States", converting that "vast unoccupied" area "into a dreary region of despotism, inhabited by masters and slaves."

—adapted from the *Appeal of the Independent Democrats,* January 24, 1854

INTRODUCTION

From 1850 to 1861 the national discussion was dominated by the controversy over slavery. Literature, Congress, the territories, the parties, the Supreme Court, and the presidential election of 1860 were all arenas for the debates. In the past, some historians have blamed sectional differences, abolitionists, or the fight over states' rights for the Civil War. The consensus is now that slavery was behind all the controversies.

CONFLICTS OVER SLAVERY

Uncle Tom's Cabin

The firestorm that grew as a result of the Fugitive Slave Law was fueled by **Harriet Beecher Stowe's** book, *Uncle Tom's Cabin*, which depicted the fate of runaways and the experience of slavery in heart-wrenching language. The popularity of the book and the plays based on it have been included as causes of the Civil War. **Free blacks** and runaways alike were captured on the streets of Northern cities, creating riots between the slave catchers and the abolitionists trying to protect the accused blacks.

The Kansas-Nebraska Act

In Congress, Illinois Democratic Senator **Stephen Douglas** introduced a bill to organize the territory called Kansas and Nebraska. In an attempt to please all sides, he based the admission of states in the territory on a principle called **popular sovereignty**. The bill stated that "All questions pertaining to slavery in the Territories . . . are to be left to the people residing therein . . . ." Southern senators forced Douglas to include a repeal of the Missouri Compromise line in his bill so that they could have a chance at expanding slavery. It was then that the "independent Democrats" wrote that the repeal of the Missouri Compromise was "a gross violation of a sacred pledge" because it would turn Kansas into a "dreary region of despotism inhabited by masters and slaves."

The Old Parties Split

President Pierce signed the **Kansas-Nebraska Bill**, but not before "anti-Nebraska" meetings and petitions signed by thousands of northern Democrats and Whigs splintered the two major parties in the North into the popular sovereignty and free-soil groups. The meetings, begun in Ripon, Wisconsin in 1854, formed the basis of the **Republican Party**, whose main slogan expressed the **Free Soil position**: no extension of slavery to the West.

The Whig Party virtually disappeared during the battle over the bill. In 1852, the **nativist** anti-Catholic, anti-immigrant **American Party**, or Know-Nothings, had attracted many Northern Whigs. The Kansas-Nebraska issue took precedence in 1854, however, forcing the nativists to take sides on the question of slavery. When the Northern Whigs joined the Republicans or the Douglas Democrats in the North, the only remaining political party with a presence both in the North and the South was the Democratic Party. The Republicans, of course, had no support in the South. In 1856, the Republicans ran **John Fremont**, or "the Pathfinder," an explorer of California, for president. Pennsylvania Democrat **James Buchanan**, who favored popular sovereignty, won the election with a majority only in the South.

Bleeding Kansas

In Kansas, Douglas's solution to allow the voters to decide the slavery question produced a miniature civil war. Even though the majority of settlers in Kansas were antislavery, most boycotted the election because the questions in the referendum on the Lecompton Constitution did not exclude slavery. In order to bolster their numbers, the pro-slavery **border ruffians** brought in residents of Missouri and used names from the Cincinnati, Ohio, city directory as "votes." In this atmosphere, after proslavery forces sacked the city of Lawrence in 1856, militant abolitionist **John Brown** led a small group in brutally murdering five proslavery farmers who lived along Pottawatomie Creek. Both sides engaged in acts of violence in **"Bleeding Kansas"** that resulted in about 200 deaths in the next few years. Kansas was admitted to the union as a free state in 1861.

The Dred Scott Case (1857)

In the **Dred Scott case**, Supreme Court Chief Justice **Roger Taney** tried to resolve all the conflicts over slavery. Scott had been a slave in Missouri, and had traveled with his master as a free man in the states of Illinois and Michigan. He later sued for his freedom in Missouri since he had been free during his "sojourn." Taney's decision answered three main questions: Was Scott a citizen and could he sue? Did Scott's sojourn in free territory make him free? And could Congress prohibit slavery in the territories? In an anti-Northern ruling Taney and the Supreme Court answered "no" to all three. The third "no" made the Missouri Compromise and the political positions of "popular sovereignty" and "no extension of slavery" unconstitutional. The first "no" asserted that blacks were property, rather than citizens of the states, and that they had "no rights which a white man was bound to respect."

Raid on Harper's Ferry

In 1859, John Brown led a group of five blacks and 17 whites to foment an uprising of slaves by taking over the federal arsenal at **Harper's Ferry,** Virginia. Brown was soon overpowered by troops led by J. E. B. Stuart and Robert E. Lee. It was later discovered that a group of New England abolitionists had financed Brown. As he walked to the gallows, Brown handed this note to his jailer: "I, John Brown, am now quite certain that the crimes of this guilty land will never be purged away but with blood." Southerners blamed him for initiating violence, while abolitionists celebrated the eloquence and courage of this man who believed that, like Nat Turner, he was driven by God's word.

LINCOLN AND SECESSION

The final arena for the conflict was the presidential election. **Abraham Lincoln** became the candidate of the Republican Party in 1860. He took the position that, although slavery should not go into the territories, he would not interfere where it already existed. Two years previously, in the **Lincoln-Douglas Debates** during a campaign to represent Illinois in the Senate against the leading Northern Democrat, **Stephen Douglas**, Lincoln had stated of the country that, "**A house divided against itself cannot stand** . . . It will become all one thing, or all the other." These positions—"no slavery in the West" and the "house divided" idea— taken together, would effectively cut the slave South out of the future growth of the nation if Lincoln were to win.

The Election of 1860

When the Democrats met to choose a candidate, the winner was Stephen Douglas, who advocated the popular sovereignty position. Militant Southerners walked out, forming a Southern Democratic Party, and nominated **James Breckinridge** of Kentucky. Breckinridge called for a **national slave code** to make slavery legal in all the states. The last North-South party had split. Ex-Whig **John Bell** formed a fourth party called the **Constitutional Union**

Party based on a vague position of the "union as it was." The two positions in the political middle, Douglas and Bell, were ground down to dust and the electoral vote majority went to Lincoln, while Breckinridge picked up the second highest number of electors. Since Lincoln won by calling for no extension of slavery to the West, South Carolina and the whole **Southern tier**, including Georgia, Florida, Alabama, Mississippi, Louisiana, and Texas, all voted for **secession** (to leave the Union) before Lincoln took office in March of 1861.

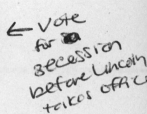

← vote for secession before Lincoln takes office

SUMMARY

It was the interests of the sections regarding slavery that drove the events leading to the political separation of the South from the North. From the fight over Kansas to the election of the Republican president, fueled by the fight over fugitive slaves and the controversy over Dred Scott, the same debate intensified in different forms until the Southern states declared independence as a revolutionary act. The secessionists wanted to preserve and spread their "peculiar institution."

THINGS TO REMEMBER

- **Free blacks:** Blacks who had been freed from slavery or were not born slaves. They lived in the cities and countryside in both the North and the South. In 1860 there were about 500,000 free blacks evenly divided between the North and the South.

- **Nativism:** The political and social conviction that only white Protestant Americans deserved civil rights and employment. Nativists tried to prevent the Irish and the new immigrants of the 1880s–1920s from becoming citizens or entering the country. The Know-Nothings and the Ku Klux Klan of the 1920s were nativists.

- **Popular sovereignty:** (1) The political theory that the people hold the fundamental power in a **democracy**. (2) The proposal by Stephen Douglas in the 1854 Kansas-Nebraska Act stating that the people of the territory of Kansas and Nebraska could decide through their representatives whether or not to include slavery in their constitutions.

- **Secession:** The political act of leaving the Union. The Southern states formed their own country during 1860–1861 after they seceded from the United States.

REVIEW QUESTIONS

1. Place these events in chronological order:

    I. Kansas-Nebraska Act
    II. Missouri Compromise
    III. secession
    IV. Bleeding Kansas
    V. *Uncle Tom's Cabin* published

    Answer choices:
    (A) II, V, IV, I, III
    (B) III, II, I, IV, V
    (C) V, IV, I, II, III
    (D) II, V, I, IV, III
    (E) V, I, II, III, IV

2. Which position had the most unpredictable outcome?
    (A) "No extension of slavery to the West"
    (B) supporting a national slave code
    (C) popular sovereignty
    (D) immediate abolition
    (E) gradual abolition

3. The Know-Nothings were
    (A) pro-immigrant
    (B) anti-immigrant
    (C) supported by slaveholders
    (D) supported by Catholics
    (E) supported by the Ku Klux Klan

4. Why did the Southern states secede after the election of 1860?
    (A) They were attacked.
    (B) The tariff was too high.
    (C) They wanted to preserve slavery.
    (D) Virginia encouraged them.
    (E) They had lost Missouri.

ANSWERS AND EXPLANATIONS

1. D

The correct order is the Missouri Compromise (1820), *Uncle Tom's Cabin* (1852), the Kansas Nebraska Act (1854), Bleeding Kansas (1856), and secession (1860 and 1861). Bleeding Kansas has to come after the people in the territory try to make a constitution, and secession is the act after Lincoln is elected. The Missouri Compromise was 30 years before, but to be repealed it had to come before the Kansas Nebraska Act. *Uncle Tom's Cabin* is a reaction to the Fugitive Slave Act, which was part of the Compromise of 1850.

2. C

Stephen Douglas used popular sovereignty in order to get the territory settled as quickly as possible. The reason there was so much fighting in Kansas was that Douglas left the question of slavery to be decided by the settlers. That is not a clear answer. Each of the other choices is more definite: for slavery (B), against all slavery (D), against slavery in the West (A), or for getting rid of slavery by having children of slaves become free at the age of 21 after a certain date (E).

3. B

The Know-Nothings were an anti-immigrant and anti-Catholic group who were also in the American Party. These nativist groups (pro-native-born American) were almost all in the Northeast and destroyed the Whig Party, not the Democrats. The Ku Klux Klan, though they might have supported them, didn't exist until 1866.

4. C

In order to maintain slavery, slave states had to expand to the West or become a minority in both houses of the U.S. congress. When Lincoln was elected it was clear they could not expand enough to maintain parity with the North. Missouri was in dispute all through the Civil War, and Virginia was supposedly reluctant to secede. The South attacked the North (not the other way around), and the tariff was an issue in the 1830s, not the 1860s.

CHAPTER 14

The Civil War, 1861–1865

TIMELINE

1861	Lincoln makes first inaugural address • Fort Sumter attacked • Upper South secedes • Southern capital moves from Montgomery, Alabama to Richmond, Virginia • First Battle of Bull Run takes place
1862	Battle of Antietam takes place • Second Battle of Bull Run takes place
1863	Emancipation Proclamation takes effect • Blacks recruited for Union army • Battles of Gettysburg and Vicksburg take place • Lincoln makes Gettysburg Address
1864	Sherman takes Atlanta and marches to the sea • Lincoln re-elected
1865	13th Amendment passed by Congress • Lee surrenders at Appomattox Courthouse • Lincoln assassinated • 13th Amendment adopted by states

IMPORTANT PEOPLE, PLACES, EVENTS, AND CONCEPTS

Abraham Lincoln

Confederate government

Jefferson Davis

Fort Sumter

Richmond

border states

peace Democrats

war Democrats

copperheads

Garrisonians

General Robert E. Lee

General Thomas "Stonewall" Jackson

General George McClellan

General Ulysses S. Grant

General William Tecumseh Sherman

Monitor

Merrimac (*Virginia*)

Battles of Bull Run

Emancipation Proclamation

Sherman's march to the sea

Appomattox Courthouse

Gettysburg Address

13th Amendment

John Wilkes Booth

"Fondly do we hope, fervently do we pray, that this mighty scourge of war may speedily pass away. Yet, if God wills that it continue until all the wealth piled by the bondsman's two hundred and fifty years of unrequited toil shall be sunk, and until every drop of blood drawn with the lash shall be paid by another drawn with the sword, as was said three thousand years ago, so still it must be said 'the judgments of the Lord are true and righteous altogether.'"

—Abraham Lincoln, Second Inaugural Address, March 4, 1865

INTRODUCTION

More than 620,000 Americans died in the Civil War—more than in any war until the Second World War. The conflicts over state power versus federal power, in existence from earliest days of the republic, came to a head in 1861 concerning the fate of slavery in the West. When Lincoln was inaugurated seven states had seceded, but there was still no war.

THE BEGINNING OF WAR

Lincoln's First Inaugural Address

In his **first inaugural address,** on March 4, 1861, President **Abraham Lincoln** attempted to convince the South that **secession** was not only illegal but impossible. His key task was to protect the Union. He believed in the **Theory of Perpetual Union**: that the Continental Congress had predated the Constitution and no state could break the Union "contract" by itself. The main dispute was whether slavery should extend to the West. There was no cause to fight, because he had promised not to attack slavery in the South. Peace, however, could last only to the point of rebellion, since his presidential oath was to "defend the Union."

[handwritten: 11 states in confederacy]

SECESSION

The **Confederate government** had formed on February 9, 1861 with former Mississippi Senator **Jefferson Davis** as president and its capital in Montgomery, Alabama. However, **Fort Sumter,** in the harbor of Charleston, South Carolina, was still loyal to the Union. Major **Robert Anderson** refused to surrender to the state militia, but he needed supplies. Trying to prevent a fight, Lincoln notified South Carolina that he would send supplies, but not troops. Nevertheless, Davis ordered the fort to be bombarded on April 12. Anderson held out for 34 hours, before surrendering. Virginia, Tennessee, North Carolina, and Arkansas all seceded after the attack, bringing the number of states in the Confederacy to 11. Davis's capital subsequently moved to **Richmond**, Virginia.

[handwritten: new southern capital]

THE BALANCE OF FORCES

Economics

In industry, merchant shipping, guns, and agriculture, the North out-produced the South by overwhelming proportions. The South recruited 80 percent of its white men to military service, while the North was able to mount even larger armies with only 50 percent of its men.

Government

The North had the advantage of a centralized government while the South had trouble with the believers in states' rights. The Confederacy lost West Virginia, which refused to secede along with Virginia. Similarly, non–cotton producing areas of northern Alabama and East Tennessee were pockets of opposition to Confederate rule. Lincoln kept the **border states** of Maryland, Delaware, Missouri, and Kentucky loyal to the Union. **Garrisonians** were constantly calling for Lincoln to free the slaves and the Northern Democrats were divided; some were for the war (**"war Democrats"**), some wanted to make peace with the Confederacy (**"peace Democrats"**), and some were actively disloyal to the union, (**"copperheads"**).

Military

The South had more talented generals than the North; **Robert E. Lee** and **Stonewall Jackson** were among them. Lincoln fired generals until he found **Ulysses S. Grant** who, along with **William Tecumseh Sherman** and **Phillip Sheridan**, won the war by following the president's strategy of putting "all their men in." Union General **George McClellan** was an excellent organizer of troops but was reluctant to put them into battle.

The South had the advantages of defending their own land, short supply lines, and a revolutionary cause. If they could preserve their army, they could win. The North tried to capture the South's capital, Richmond, and to destroy the Confederate Army.

The Union's naval blockade could not prevent all shipping, but the North did capture major ports including New Orleans. The Confederates had commerce raiders that destroyed merchant ships. The famous battle off the coast of Virginia in 1862 between the two ironclads, the *Monitor* of the North, and the former Northern ship the *Merrimac* (renamed the *Virginia)*, ended in a draw.

The Armies

Both the North and the South drafted men and allowed richer men to pay others to substitute for them. One white man on every Southern plantation with 20 or more slaves was exempt. The poor on both sides could call it "a rich man's war and a poor man's fight." The 1863 Irish laborers' anti-draft riot in New York City turned into an attack on blacks. Desertions were about 13 percent for the South and 9.6 percent for the North. The Union army totaled 2,100,000, of whom nearly 200,000 were ex-slaves and free blacks. The Confederates mobilized 800,000. At the very end of the war they unveiled a plan to draft slaves, but it was never put into effect.

THE WAR

Much of the war was fought in Virginia. The battles of **Bull Run**, Seven Days, and Chancellorsville were Confederate victories, while the battles of Wilderness and **Appomattox** were Union victories. Robert E. Lee, who commanded the Army of Northern Virginia, showed that he could outlast massive Union attacks both because his tactics were flexible and because the Union generals, especially George McClellan, commander of the Army of the Potomac, consistently overestimated the size of Lee's army and refused to follow up on their victories. When Lee tried to go North into Maryland in the battle of **Antietam** in September 1862, McClellan defeated him but did not follow up. Lincoln fired the timid Democratic general and at the same time issued the **Emancipation Proclamation**, a war measure which freed slaves in the states still in rebellion after January 1, 1862.

Grant and Sherman

The farthest Lee was able to go into the North was **Gettysburg**, Pennsylvania, where the Union won on July 3, 1863. **Vicksburg** in Mississippi fell to Grant on July 4. The Union armies cut the South in two by marching from Mississippi to Atlanta while simultaneously fighting in Virginia. When the South still refused to give up despite huge losses, Sherman, in his march from Atlanta to the sea (**Sherman's march to the sea**), turned from destroying only soldiers to burning the land and supplies. This was the first total war. After the capture of Richmond, Lee surrendered at **Appomattox Courthouse** on April 9, 1865.

LINCOLN AND THE POLITICS OF SLAVERY AND WAR

Lincoln identified the cause of the Union and the course of the war with God's will, or fate. At each point he attempted to hold the Union together and proceed to victory. He began with a "personal wish that all men everywhere could be free." When he sought to "preserve the Union" politically above all else at the beginning of the war, he backed the Democratic General McClellan. When the South refused to end the war between September 1862 and January 1, 1863, he fired McClellan and declared all the slaves in the counties and states still in rebellion "forever free." This Emancipation Proclamation was not immediate abolition, as the Garrisonians had been calling for, but it did change the character of the war. Now black troops could fight, however poorly paid, and England and France could no longer give the Confederates open support. In 1858, he had told the citizens of Illinois that blacks were not equal but deserved equal rights, but in his **Gettysburg Address** he hung the fate of the Union on the "proposition that all men are created equal," the postulate of democracy.

Lincoln as a Leader

By the time of his **second inaugural**, Lincoln discovered that the South would not be defeated "until every drop of blood drawn with the lash shall be paid by another drawn with the sword." If he suspended the civil liberties (right of *habeas corpus*) of copperheads, called up troops months before the consent of Congress, and refused to allow the emancipation of slaves in Missouri, he also engineered the passage of the **13th Amendment** abolishing slavery, won the votes of McClellan's men in the 1864 election, and kept the army and government intact. If some call him a racist because he would preserve the Union in 1862 "with" or "without" slavery, others would say along with abolitionist Wendell Phillips in 1863: "Abe grows." When **John Wilkes Booth** killed Lincoln on April 14, 1865, he ended the life of a man who was as big and as complex as the country he led.

SUMMARY

The South fought without shoes or food, and their smaller population severely limited their ability to muster reinforcements, but they fought for four years. Slaves ran away by the hundreds of thousands, depriving the South of its workforce and providing soldiers to the North. Lincoln freed them as **"contraband of war."** By the end of the war Lincoln could join his "personal wish" that every man "could be free" with his political duty to "preserve the Union." In his **Gettysburg Address** at the memorial to the fallen, he called for a "new birth of freedom" as the moral basis for "government by the people." For the first time, "Union" was capitalized. Slavery was destroyed, but the country was still comprised of freedmen, ex-slaveholders, ex-abolitionists, ex-Free Soilers, ex-peace Democrats, and ex-war Democrats. These political elements made for an explosive compound.

THINGS TO REMEMBER

- **Contraband of war:** Lincoln's Civil War policy of treating runaway slaves as enemy war property. He accepted the slaves as a way to hurt the Southern cause. They were freed and employed as aides to the Union army until Lincoln started recruiting back troops after the Emancipation Proclamation.

- **Theory of Perpetual Union:** Lincoln's contention that the Union pre-existed the Constitution because it began with the Articles of Association in 1774—since the states had signed on to that document, the Union could not be broken. He discussed this theory in his first inaugural address.

REVIEW QUESTIONS

1. Of the states below, of which one was President Lincoln most concerned about how the population felt about the Civil War?

    (A) Illinois
    (B) Kentucky
    (C) Georgia
    (D) Mississippi
    (E) South Carolina

2. Match the battle with its state.

V) Vicksburg	1) Georgia
W) Atlanta	2) Maryland
X) Richmond	3) Mississippi
Y) Gettysburg	4) Virginia
Z) Antietam	5) Pennsylvania

    Answer choices:
    (A) V-3, W-1, Y-5, Z-2, X-4
    (B) V-3, X-4, Y-5, Z-1, W-2
    (C) W-1, X-4, Y-5, Z-3, V-2
    (D) V-2, W-1, X-4, Y-5, Z-3
    (E) W-1, X-3, Y-5, Z-4, V-2

3. Place the following events in chronological order:

   1) Lincoln elected
   2) Lincoln took office
   3) secession of the Upper South
   4) secession of the Lower South
   5) attack on Fort Sumter

   Answer choices:
   (A) 1, 2, 5, 3, 4
   (B) 3, 4, 1, 2, 5
   (C) 4, 3, 1, 2, 5
   (D) 1, 4, 2, 5, 3
   (E) 1, 5, 3, 4, 2

4. Which is the BEST explanation for why the South lost?

   (A) They used slaves to fight.
   (B) They had poor generals.
   (C) They had weak support from the population.
   (D) They had too many deserters.
   (E) The war lasted too long.

ANSWERS AND EXPLANATIONS

1. B

Kentucky was a border state. It had slavery but it did not vote for secession. Keeping the border states in the union was one of Lincoln's chief concerns.

2. A

Vicksburg was fought in Mississippi, Atlanta was fought in Georgia, Gettysburg was fought in Pennsylvania, Antietam was fought in Maryland, and Richmond was fought in Virginia.

3. D

Lincoln was elected in November, 1860. The Lower South seceded before Lincoln took office in March, 1861. The attack on Fort Sumter, a pro-Union fort in Charleston, South Carolina, followed Lincoln's inauguration. Finally, the Upper South seceded after the attack.

4. E

The South called slaves to fight only at the very end. Their generals are usually considered better than the North's. Their support from the population was very strong and the number of deserters was only slightly more than in the North. The main reason the South lost was that their armies had been destroyed in the war of attrition.

CHAPTER 15

Reconstruction and Its Aftermath, 1865–1896

TIMELINE

1864	Wade-Davis Bill passed by Congress; vetoed by Lincoln
1865	Freedman's Bureau established • Andrew Johnson assumes the presidency after Lincoln's assassination • 13th Amendment ratified
1866	Ku Klux Klan founded • Johnson vetoes the Civil Rights Act • Tennessee readmitted to the Union • Radical Republicans override Johnson's veto
1867	Reconstruction Act passed, marking the beginning of Congressional (Radical) Reconstruction
1868	President Johnson impeached; he is acquitted by the Senate • Ulysses Grant elected president • 14th Amendment ratified
1870	15th Amendment ratified
1876	Hayes and Tilden vie for presidency in disputed election race
1877	Compromise awards Hayes the presidency and effectively ends Reconstruction
1896	*Plessy v. Ferguson* decision

IMPORTANT PEOPLE, PLACES, EVENTS, AND CONCEPTS

Thaddeus Stevens

Reconstruction

Abraham Lincoln's 10 Percent Plan

Radical Republicans

Wade-Davis Bill

13th Amendment

Ku Klux Klan

Freedman's Bureau

Civil Rights Act of 1866

14th Amendment

Reconstruction Act of 1867

Ulysses S. Grant

15th Amendment

Hiram Revels

"40 acres and a mule"

Compromise of 1877

Plessy v. Ferguson

"The whole fabric of Southern society must be changed and never can it be done if this opportunity is lost. Without this, this government can never be, as it has never been, a true republic...."

—From a speech by Thaddeus Stevens, 1865

INTRODUCTION

Radical Republican Senator **Thaddeus Stevens's** desire to see sweeping changes in the South, as evidenced by the above quote, was one of several approaches to a series of vexing questions that faced the United States when the Civil War ended. What accommodations should be made for freed men and women? How should the rebellious states be reintegrated into the Union? Should individuals who had participated in the Confederacy be considered criminals and be punished? The actual programs and legislation of the **Reconstruction** period grew out of political wrangling in Washington, but was also shaped by the aspirations and actions of those most immediately affected—the freed men and women of the South.

PRESIDENTIAL RECONSTRUCTION (1865–1867)

Lincoln's 10 Percent Plan

President **Abraham Lincoln** wanted to bring the Union back together quickly and easily. It was his opinion that Southern states had never actually seceded. They threatened to, but the federal government prevented secession by winning the Civil War. Lincoln promised to approach the Reconstruction process "[w]ith malice toward none, with charity toward all." Lincoln's "**10 percent plan**" was designed to let states re-enter the Union if 10 percent of the state's voters swore allegiance to the United States. Lincoln also intended to pardon all but the highest ranking Confederate officers. The **Radical Republicans**, who wanted a more far-reaching Reconstruction plan, passed the **Wade-Davis Bill**. This bill, which was **vetoed** by Lincoln, would have made Reconstruction the responsibility of Congress rather than of the president.

Johnson's Plan and the 13th Amendment (1865)

Lincoln was assassinated in 1865 by Southern sympathizer John Wilkes Booth before he could implement any form of Reconstruction. His successor, Vice President **Andrew Johnson** from Tennessee, lacked Lincoln's political skills. Johnson's plan allowed states to re-enter the Union if they ratified the **13th Amendment**, which prohibited slavery, and pledged allegiance to the Union. Though Johnson excluded the old slaveholding class from political participation, he did little to help the freed men and women.

Failures of Presidential Reconstruction

Events in the South following the Civil War led most Republicans in Congress, and indeed a large portion of Northerners in general, to have doubts about President Johnson's Reconstruction plan. As civil governments began to function in late 1865 and 1866, most Southern legislatures passed **black codes**, which represented an effort to define a new legal status for African Americans as subordinate to whites. The codes varied from state to state, but most restricted African Americans from carrying weapons, starting their own businesses, owning land, marrying whites, and traveling without a permit. Various codes provided for forced labor contracts for anyone found guilty of vagrancy. Black codes had the effect of restoring many aspects of slavery.

At the same time, some Southern whites used violence and terror to force freed men and women into an unequal status. The violence was most closely associated with the **Ku Klux Klan**, a secret organization formed in 1866, which often resorted to whippings, lynchings, and burning African American churches and schools. Klan members, wearing sheets to conceal their identity, targeted Republican organizations in the South and individual African Americans accused of not showing deference to whites.

CONGRESSIONAL (RADICAL) RECONSTRUCTION (1867–1877)

Many Northerners, after reading about black codes, Klan terror, and race riots in Memphis and New Orleans, concluded that "the South may have lost the war, but it won the peace." In response, Radical Republicans in Congress, with the support of many moderates, pushed through a series of measures that challenged the power of the White House, and eventually led to Congressional control over Reconstruction.

Congress Challenges the President on Reconstruction

The first major action that the radicals in Congress took was to refuse to seat the recently elected Southern legislators, many of whom had participated in the Confederacy. In early 1866, Congress voted to continue and enlarge the **Freedman's Bureau**, an agency created to help freed men and women adjust to their new lives, and to pass a **Civil Rights Act** guaranteeing African Americans citizenship. President Johnson saw these actions as a threat to his power, and vetoed both. Tensions between Congress and the president intensified as Congress overrode Johnson's vetoes.

Radicals drafted the **14th Amendment** (1866), which made "all persons born or naturalized in the United States" citizens of the country. Further, the amendment insisted that the states guarantee all people "equal protection under the law." It did not guarantee African American suffrage, but it stipulated that a state would lose a percentage of its Congressional seats if it denied male citizens the vote. Congress approved the amendment and sent it to the states for ratification. Johnson urged states to reject it on the grounds that it was too harsh on ex-Confederates and that Southern legislators had had no hand in drafting it. The 14th Amendment and the larger question of the nature of Reconstruction became contentious issues in the midterm congressional election of 1866. The Radicals gained the mandate they needed, capturing a two-thirds majority in Congress, enough to override presidential vetoes.

Republicans, with their moderate allies, exercised their newfound muscle in 1867 by adopting the **Reconstruction Act of 1867**, over Johnson's veto. The act presumed that the Southern states, with the exception of Tennessee, were without legal state governments. The 10 remaining former Confederate states were divided into five military districts, each headed by a federal military commander. To be eligible for readmission into the Union, Southern states had to call new Constitutional conventions, ratify the 14th Amendment, and guarantee African American men the right to vote.

The relationship between the president and Congress rapidly disintegrated in 1867. Congressional Republicans had passed the Tenure of Office Act to protect its allies in Johnson's cabinet. In August 1867, Johnson challenged the act by suspending Secretary of War and Radical sympathizer Edwin Stanton. Johnson's challenge of the Tenure of Office Act brought to a head the battle over Reconstruction. Radical Republicans in the House voted to **impeach** Johnson in 1868. The move to oust Johnson stalled in the Senate with one vote short of the necessary two-thirds. Johnson remained in office, but power over Reconstruction had shifted from the president to Congress.

Republican **Ulysses S. Grant** won the presidency in 1868, partly due to a half-million African American votes. Fearing—accurately—that white Southerners would try to disfranchise African Americans, the Radicals drafted the **15th Amendment**, which guaranteed African Americans the right to vote. The amendment, ratified in 1870, also affected some Northern states that previously had barred African Americans from voting.

Congressional (Radical) Reconstruction in Practice

Congressional Reconstruction, although short-lived, brought sweeping changes to the South. New state governments were formed as the Southern states rejoined the United States. African American families were reunited. Laws were passed that guaranteed equality, and new economic patterns emerged. An important task of the Reconstruction governments in the South was physically **rebuilding the South**. These governments expanded in size as they built roads, railroads, schools, and other institutions.

The tasks at hand were accomplished by an uneasy coalition of **carpetbaggers** (the derisive name for Northern whites), **scalawags** (Southern whites sympathetic to the new order), and African Americans. Some scalawags and carpetbaggers hoped to gain personally from participating in Reconstruction, while others were driven by a moral mandate.

For the first time, African Americans were elected to local office, state legislatures, and even Congress (notably **Hiram Revels**, a senator from Mississippi). In South Carolina, a state that had a majority African American population, they briefly comprised a majority in the legislature. Southern critics of Reconstruction have exaggerated the power of African Americans during the period and highlighted incidents of corruption. But Reconstruction governments, under the Republican banner, passed laws ending discrimination, built an infrastructure, and created an extensive educational system.

Economic change was slow in coming. The government never implemented their idea of distributing **"40 acres and a mule"** to freed men and women. Most African Americans soon settled into the **sharecropping** system, where African Americans (and poor whites) would farm a few acres of a large estate and give a share (probably half) of the crops to the owner. Few became landowners.

The End of Reconstruction

Reconstruction ended gradually. Southern Democrats regained power—a process they called redemption—between 1869 and 1876. The final blow to Reconstruction came as a result of the disputed presidential election of 1876. Neither the Republican candidate, Rutherford B. Hayes, nor the Democratic candidate, Samuel Tilden, received the required number of electoral votes (20 votes were in dispute). The Democrats, even though they had carried the popular vote, agreed to let Hayes occupy the White House, if the Republicans, in turn, agreed to withdraw federal troops from the South. The **Compromise of 1877** (also known as the Hayes-Tilden Compromise) thus ended Reconstruction.

THE POST-RECONSTRUCTION SOUTH (1877–1896)

With home rule in place, the so-called "redeemer governments" instituted a series of sweeping changes that again reduced African Americans to a subservient position in Southern society.

Denying African Americans the Vote

Despite the passage of the 15th Amendment, Southern governments created a series of obstacles that effectively denied African Americans the right to vote:

- States levied **poll taxes** as an obstacle to voting; most African Americans could not afford to pay the tax.
- Since African Americans were denied education during the period of slavery, they often could not pass the **literacy tests** required to be eligible to vote.
- The **grandfather clauses** allowed men to vote if their grandfather was a voter before Reconstruction. This enabled uneducated whites to get around literacy tests.

Legal Segregation

Jim Crow laws segregated whites and African Americans in public facilities such as train stations and schools. The laws were declared constitutional by the Supreme Court in ***Plessy v. Ferguson*** (1896); public accommodations, the high court ruled, could separate the races if the facilities for both were equal (thus the "separate but equal" doctrine). The South remained a segregated society, with unequal facilities, until Jim Crow laws were declared unconstitutional in the 1950s.

Violence

The Ku Klux Klan remained active, intimidating African Americans from challenging white supremacy.

SUMMARY

Reconstruction is generally considered a tragic failure, with the United States missing an opportunity to achieve full equality for African Americans. However, Reconstruction provided African Americans with such gains as public education and a degree of political participation. Many also see Reconstruction as inspiration for the civil rights movement almost a century later.

THINGS TO REMEMBER

- **Black codes:** Laws passed in the Southern states immediately after the Civil War to restrict the movements and limit the rights of African Americans.

- **Carpetbaggers:** Derisive term for Northerners who went to the South during Reconstruction to promote reform or to profit from it.

- **Grandfather clauses:** Provisions in the voting laws in Southern states following Reconstruction designed to allow whites who could not pass literacy tests to vote. The grandfather clauses gave the right to vote to people whose grandfathers had been eligible to vote—a provision of little value to African Americans because their grandfathers had been slaves.

- **Impeachment:** An indictment or formal charge brought by the legislative body against a government official, especially the president, in an attempt to remove them from office. If the House of Representatives determines that a president has committed acts that may be "high crimes and misdemeanors," he is impeached, as with the case of President Andrew Johnson in 1868 and President Bill Clinton in 1999. The Senate then conducts a trial to determine guilt; if the president is found guilty, he is removed from office.

- **Jim Crow:** The series of laws designed to create separation between the races. These were by and large Southern state laws made constitutional by the Supreme Court decision *Plessy v. Ferguson* in 1896.

- **Literacy tests:** Reading tests required in some Southern states before people were allowed to register to vote. They were mainly intended to prevent African Americans from voting.

- **Poll tax:** Tax paid by those wishing to vote in several Southern states after Reconstruction; it was designed to limit political participation by African Americans.

- **Scalawags:** Derisive term for white Southerners who cooperated with the Reconstruction governments.

- **Sharecropping:** Agricultural labor system in the South following the era of slavery wherein a sharecropper could farm a piece of land in return for giving the landowner a share, usually half, of the crop.

- **Tenant farming:** An agricultural system in which farm workers supply their own tools, rent land, and have more control over their work than agrarian wage workers.

- **Veto:** The power of the president to reject legislation. The U.S. Congress can override a veto by the U.S. president if it can pass the legislation by a two-thirds majority.

REVIEW QUESTIONS

1. The Freedman's Bureau was established to

   (A) help former slaves find jobs and protect them from discrimination
   (B) help Blacks win election to public office
   (C) help rebuild the transportation networks of the South
   (D) protect Blacks from scalawags and carpetbaggers
   (E) help former slave owners get back on their feet economically after Emancipation

2. Under the terms of the Compromise of 1877, Republicans maintained control of the White House and agreed to

   (A) transfer large sums of money to the Democratic Party
   (B) withdraw federal troops from the South
   (C) push for passage of the 15th Amendment
   (D) give Democrats control of Congress
   (E) raise tariff rates on imported goods

3. The Reconstruction Act of 1867 required that the former Confederate states, in order to gain readmission to the Union,

   (A) ratify the 14th Amendment and guarantee African American men the right to vote
   (B) end slavery
   (C) imprison former Confederate government officials
   (D) have 10 percent of their people sign a loyalty oath to the Constitution of the United States
   (E) nullify Jim Crow laws

4. Pick the correct order for the following events:

   W) Rutherford B. Hayes becomes president.
   X) The South surrenders to end the Civil War.
   Y) The act establishing Radical Reconstruction is passed.
   Z) The Emancipation Proclamation is issued.

   Answer choices:

   (A) X, Z, Y, W
   (B) W, Z, X, Y
   (C) Z, X Y, W
   (D) Z, Y, X, W
   (E) X, Y, W, Z

ANSWERS AND EXPLANATIONS

1. A

The Freedman's Bureau helped freed men and women adjust to their new lives, including finding them jobs. No accommodations were made for former slave holders. Choices (B) and (C) were both part of Reconstruction, but not the specific functions of the Freedman's Bureau. "Scalawags" and "carpetbaggers" were, generally speaking, the allies of freed men and women.

2. B

Withdrawing troops spelled the end of Reconstruction. The 15th Amendment had already been ratified. Power in Congress is determined by the number of seats each party won in elections, not backroom haggling, so control of Congress could not be given to the Democrats. The Republicans supported higher tariff rates anyway; raising them would be no concession to the Democrats. Choice (A) simply never occurred.

3. A

To be readmitted in to the Union, Confederate states had to ratify the 14th Amendment and guarantee African American men the right to vote. Slavery had already ended with the passage of the 13th Amendment. Radical reconstruction was not excessively harsh on ex-Confederates; there were no mass arrests or executions. The "10 Percent Plan" was Lincoln's idea in 1864. Jim Crow laws had not yet come into effect; that happened after Reconstruction ended.

4. C

There is a logic to the events, even if one does not know the exact dates of each event. The Emancipation Proclamation (1863) was issued during the war, so it would have to come before the South surrendering (1865). Reconstruction (1865–1877) happened after the war, and Hays came to power as part of the "Compromise of 1877," which ended Reconstruction.

CHAPTER 16

The Closing of the Frontier, 1876–1900

TIMELINE

1859	Gold discovered at Pikes Peak
1862	Homestead Act passed • Morrill Land-Grant Act passed
1864	Nevada becomes a state
1869	Transcontinental railroad completed
1872	Yellowstone National Park established
1876	Battle of Little Big Horn takes place
1887	Dawes Act passed.
1890	Battle at Wounded Knee takes place • U.S. census declares the frontier settled

IMPORTANT PEOPLE, PLACES, EVENTS, AND CONCEPTS

Exodusters

Comstock Lode

Great American Desert

reservation

Bozeman Trail, South Dakota

Lt. Col. George Armstrong Custer

Sitting Bull

Crazy Horse

Custer's Last Stand

Ghost Dance movement

Battle of Wounded Knee

Chief Joseph

Helen Hunt Jackson

assimilation

Dawes Act

Frederick Jackson Turner

"safety valve"

"In the United States a man builds a house in which to spend his old age, and he sells it before the roof is on; he plants a garden and lets it just as the trees are coming into bearing; … he settles in a place, which he soon afterwards leaves to carry his changeable longings elsewhere."

–From *Democracy in America* by Alexis de Tocqueville, 1835

INTRODUCTION

Between the end of the Civil War and the beginning of the 20th century, Americans accelerated the move to areas west of the Mississippi River. In the above quote, Tocqueville identifies a pervasive characteristic among many Americans of this period—a desire to pick up and move. The move to the West had a profound impact on America, especially on the Native American peoples who lived there.

MOVING WEST

Americans had settled just west of the Mississippi River and along the Pacific coast before the Civil War. After the war, they began populating the areas in between. Most were drawn by economic opportunity—the chance to strike it rich in mining, to begin again in agriculture, and to be their own boss. Some left farms east of the Mississippi when soil became depleted, while others escaped economic hardships in urban areas. Many African Americans left harsh conditions in the South. The movement was facilitated by the presence of precious metals, by government policies, and by the expansion of railroad lines.

Homestead Act of 1862

The **Homestead Act of 1862** was designed to encourage settlement in the West by offering 160 acres of land at no cost to **homesteaders** who paid a $10 filing fee and agreed to live on the land for five years. Much of the land ended up in the hands of speculators, who then sold it at a profit. Nonetheless, approximately 600,000 families attained land through the Homestead Act.

Morrill Land-Grant Act of 1862

The **Morrill Land-Grant Act** and similar acts transferred more than 140 million acres of federal land to the states. The states could set up land-grant agricultural colleges or sell the land. This act also tended to transfer land to the hands of speculators who profited from this government program.

"Exodusters"

After Reconstruction, some African Americans sought to escape violence and exploitation in the South by moving to the West. About 50,000 **"Exodusters"**—so called after the Biblical story of Exodus—made it to Kansas and beyond. Unfortunately, many of the economic and social patterns of the old South, including an active Ku Klux Klan, re-emerged in Kansas.

The Development of Railroads and the Destruction of the Buffalo

The completion of the **transcontinental railroad** in 1869 greatly facilitated Western settlement. The development of the railroads also played a major role in the destruction of the buffalo; while some were killed for food, many were shot for sport from train windows. Later, a market developed for buffalo leather. By 1886, few buffalo were left. The death of the buffalo had a detrimental effect on the Native American groups who depended on them.

THE TRANSFORMATION OF THE WEST

Three principal economic activities—mining, cattle ranching, and farming—drew people to, and eventually transformed, the West.

The Mining Frontier

The promise of quick wealth from gold and silver mining brought large numbers of migrants to the West. The first mining discovery was that of gold in California in 1848, followed by gold and silver strikes in present-day Colorado, Nevada, Idaho, Montana, Arizona, and South Dakota. The two most well-known strikes were at **Pikes Peak** in present-day Colorado in 1859, and the **Comstock Lode** in present-day Nevada. A pattern common to most precious metal strikes developed in the West. Tens of thousands of prospectors would flock to a strike, creating a boomtown. Some would strike it rich; most would not. After individuals extracted easily obtainable ore, large mining concerns took over the more intense underground work. Many of the would-be prospectors wound up as wage employees of these companies, as mining became big business.

The effects of the mining frontier were significant. While some mining centers quickly became ghost towns, others—such as San Francisco, Sacramento, and Denver—prospered into commercial centers. Many of these towns attracted immigrants from Europe, Asia, and Latin America. The migrations following strikes led to the rapid incorporation of some western states into the Union (such as Nevada in 1864). The increase in the supply of precious metals led to a political crisis over the value of currency in the 1890s.

The Cattle Frontier

Cattle ranching became widespread in the West after the great buffalo herds were decimated. This, combined with a growing market for beef in the East, the development of railway lines, and vast open grasslands, created ideal conditions for cattle ranching in the West. **Cowboys** would ride horses and graze large herds of cattle on the open prairie. Borrowing techniques from Mexican *vaqueros*, these cowboys would then lead the herds to towns such as Dodge City in present-day Kansas or Cheyenne in present-day Wyoming, so that the cattle could be shipped by rail to Chicago to be slaughtered. The era of the cowboy lasted only about 20 years, from the mid-1860s to the mid-1880s. Most cowboys were white, although about 25 percent were African American and about 12 percent were Mexican. The era of the cowboy ended for a number of reasons. Droughts (in 1883 and 1886) and a severe blizzard (in 1887) took their toll, but the invention of **barbed wire** proved most destructive. Developed in the 1870s by Joseph Glidden, barbed wire allowed ranchers and farmers to fence in their land, thus reducing the wide-open expanses that the long cattle drives depended on.

The Farming Frontier

Homesteaders faced difficult conditions on the **Great Plains**, including extreme temperatures, isolation, lack of water, fluctuating prices for grain, and infestation of pests such as grasshoppers. Farmers had to bust the sod—hard, compacted soil—before they could farm. New techniques such as deep plowing and new implements such as steam-powered threshers helped make farming on the Great Plains a success. By the early 20th century, the Great Plains had become the breadbasket of the United States, but in the process, farming, like mining, had become big business, after over two-thirds of the homesteaders' farms failed.

THE REMOVAL OF NATIVE AMERICANS

The Great Plains had been labeled the **"Great American Desert"** in 1820, but it was home to numerous and diverse Native American nations. As the frontier was gradually taken over by white settlers, Native Americans lost both their land and the means for their livelihood. This period saw organized resistance on the part of Native Americans, armed clashes, and a series of U.S. government policies designed to settle this issue.

Native American Nations

Several Native American nations lived on the Great Plains and in the desert regions of present-day Arizona and New Mexico. The Plains people included the Comanche, Sioux, Pawnee, Blackfoot, and Crow nations. Most were nomadic people who depended on horses, brought to the New World by the Spanish in the 1500s, for hunting and fighting. The desert nations of the Southwest included the nomadic Navaho and Apache nations, and the settled Hopi and Zuni peoples.

Reservation Policy

In 1834, the U.S. government designated the entire Great Plains as one enormous **reservation**, or land set aside for Native Americans. But as more settlers moved westward, the federal government, beginning with negotiations at Fort Laramie and Fort Atkinson in 1851, adopted a policy of assigning different Native American nations specific areas with definite boundaries. This policy proved difficult to enforce, as most Plains nations were nomadic and followed migrating buffalo. In addition, many Native American nations never signed treaties, and many of the Native American "chiefs" who did sign did not represent their nations. So as Native Americans continued hunting on traditional lands, clashes occurred with miners and settlers.

Warfare on the Great Plains

A series of clashes between Native Americans and U.S. troops had tragic results for the former. One by one, Native American nations succumbed to the superior firepower of the U.S. government.

- *The Sand Creek Massacre* (1864): The Colorado militia, led by Colonel John M. Chivington, massacred over 400 men, women, and children of the Cheyenne nation at the village of Sand Creek in present-day Colorado.

- *Defeat of the Sioux* (1865–1890): Conflicts first occurred between whites and members of the Sioux nation after the U.S. government built the **Bozeman Trail** (in present-day Wyoming) through prized Sioux hunting grounds. After over a year of fighting, the Great Sioux War ended in a stalemate. The Treaty of 1868 closed the Bozeman Trail and stipulated that the Sioux live on a reservation along the Missouri River in present-day South Dakota. But the clashes did not end. Gold was discovered on Sioux land, and prospectors clamored for land. After having visions of victory, Sioux chief **Sitting Bull** and troops led by **Crazy Horse** defeated **Lt. Col. George Armstrong Custer**, killing him and all of his men at Little Bighorn (in present-day Montana) in 1876. Later that year, U.S. forces, exacting revenge for **"Custer's Last Stand,"** succeeded in defeating the Sioux. A few remaining Sioux, inspired by Sitting Bull and the **Ghost Dance** religious movement, resisted being driven from their ancestral lands, but the movement was put down with the killing of 200 Sioux at **Wounded Knee** in 1890.

- *The Nez Percé*: There were peaceful relations between the whites and the Nez Percé (of present-day Washington, Oregon, and Idaho) until gold was discovered on Nez Percé land in 1860. Faced with forcible removal, **Chief Joseph** and the Nez Percé prepared to leave peacefully for the reservation. U.S. troops were misinformed about Joseph's intentions, however, and attacked the Native Americans. Pursued by the U.S. army, the Nez Percé retreated more than 1,000 miles and were finally defeated just short of the Canadian border in 1877.

The Politics of Reform

Some whites were troubled by the U.S. government's violations of treaties and its policy of forcing Native Americans onto reservations. **Helen Hunt Jackson's** exposé, *A Century of Dishonor,* drew people's attention to the plight of Native Americans. Many reform-minded Americans thought the solution to Native Americans' problems was **assimilation**—adopting the cultural practices of whites and converting to Christianity. This impulse led to the **Dawes Act** of 1887, which was designed to break up tribal units, giving individual families a small plot of land and making them U.S. citizens after 25 years of adopting "the habits of civilized life." The policy proved to be a failure and was abandoned in the 1930s.

The Closing of the Frontier?

By 1890, the U.S. Census Bureau declared that the frontier had been settled. While this was perhaps overstating the case (homesteading continued into the 20th century, and even today vast areas of the West not suited to agriculture are still unsettled), the notion troubled some Americans, including the historian **Frederick Jackson Turner**. The "Turner thesis" held that the existence of an unsettled frontier had profoundly and positively shaped the character of Americans. It encouraged Americans to be innovative and individualistic, and allowed for a high degree of social mobility. The frontier contributed to social peace in the East, by providing a **"safety valve"** for disgruntled urbanites. Many aspects of the Turner thesis have since been refuted. For instance, in the late 1800s it was more common for people to move from rural areas to industrial cities. The fear of a closed frontier also led to popular pressure for preserving wild areas in the West, which resulted in the organization of some of the early national parks (**Yellowstone** in 1872 and **Yosemite** in 1890).

SUMMARY

The settlement of West has assumed mythic proportions in American culture. But while the myth of the lone prospector or homesteader starting anew has some truth, these individuals quickly gave way to big business as mechanization and modernization required funding beyond the reach of most individuals. The impact of the settlement of the West on Native Americans was very real. A way of life was virtually destroyed.

THINGS TO REMEMBER

- **Barbed wire:** An invention of the 1870s, barbed wire enabled farmers to enclose land and prevent the long cattle drives that cowboys conducted.

- **Cowboys:** Cattle handlers who drove large herds across the southern Great Plains. The era of the cowboy lasted from 1870 to the late 1880s.

- **Homesteaders:** Settlers who were granted plots in the West, usually of 160 acres, under the Homestead Act of 1862.

- **Transcontinental railway:** The railroad route connecting the Atlantic and Pacific Oceans that was completed in 1869.

REVIEW QUESTIONS

1. Which of the following was not a major reason for the movement of large numbers of people from the east of the Mississippi River to the west of it during the second half of the 19th century?

   (A) People were interested in the free land provided by the Homestead Act.

   (B) The completion of the first transcontinental railroad made doing business out west economically feasible.

   (C) People were trying to escape the air and water pollution common in the cities of the East.

   (D) Soil was becoming depleted in the East.

   (E) Strikes of gold and silver lured prospectors out West.

2. The Dawes Act

   (A) forced Native Americans to be removed from their traditional home lands

   (B) allowed Native Americans to practice their traditional ways within the confines of their reservations

   (C) encouraged Native Americans to own individual plots of land which they and their families would cultivate

   (D) allowed Native Americans to establish gambling casinos on their land

   (E) outlawed the ceremonial Ghost Dance

3. The purpose of the Homestead Act was to

   (A) attract people to settle in the West

   (B) promote the development of railroad building in the West

   (C) raise revenue for the federal government

   (D) preserve open lands in the West for future generations to enjoy

   (E) transfer large tracts of land to giant agricultural concerns

4. "Exodusters" were

   (A) mormons who made the journey from the East to Utah

   (B) ministers who were part of the Second Great Awakening

   (C) native Americans who were forced off their land by the Indian Removal Act

   (D) African Americans who fled the South in the post Civil War period

   (E) farmers who fled the "Dust Bowl" during the 1920s and 1930s

ANSWERS AND EXPLANATIONS

1. C

Though cities were becoming crowded during the last decades of the 19th century, and some people noted the declining air quality of industrial cities, air and water pollution were not major reasons for people to move out West. The other answer choices all accurately describe motivations that people had for leaving the older communities in the East and venturing West.

2. C

The Dawes Act should be associated with the idea of assimilating Native Americans into mainstream white American culture. Choice (A) would be the answer to a question about the Indian Removal Act of 1830. Choice (B) would answer a question about the Indian Reorganization Act of 1934. State and federal courts (including the Supreme Court) ruled in the 1980s that Native Americans could operate casinos on the basis of self-determination and sovereignty. The Ghost Dance, which inspired resistance to federal incursions, was outlawed in the 1880s, but not by the Dawes Act.

3. A

The government hoped to attract people to the West by offering them free land if they made a commitment to stay there for five years. The government did promote railroad development in the West by granting land to the railroad companies, but not through the Homestead Act. The land was given away; it did not directly raise money for federal government. The act encouraged settlement, not preservation, of lands in the West. The government did later move to preserve some Western lands through the creation of national parks. Choice (E) sounds plausible, because much of the homesteaded land did eventually end up in the hands of large farming concerns, but this was not the purpose of the act.

4. D

The term "Exodusters" is derived from the biblical story of Exodus, in which the Hebrews escaped unbearable conditions in Egypt and eventually made it to the Promised Land. Conditions in the post-Reconstruction South rapidly declined for African Americans, politically, economically, and socially. Mormons made the initial journey to Utah in the 1840s, but they were not referred to as "exodusters." The Second Great Awakening preachers did travel from town to town to spread "good word" but they did not evoke the idea of an exodus to a promised land. The term "Trail of Tears" is associated with the removal of Native Americans as a result of the Indian Removal Act of 1830. And the migration of poor farmers (many of them "Okies," from Oklahoma) to California during the Depression is not usually associated with the Biblical story of Exodus.

CHAPTER 17

Industry, Big Business, and Labor Unions, 1865–1900

TIMELINE

1859	First oil well drilled in Titus, Pennsylvania
1869	Transcontinental railroad completed • Knights of Labor founded
1877	Nationwide railway strike takes place
1881	Standard Oil Trust established
1883	Standard "railroad" time goes into effect
1886	American Federation of Labor founded • Haymarket Riot occurs
1887	Interstate Commerce Commission established
1890	Sherman Anti-trust Act passed
1892	Homestead strike takes place
1894	Pullman strike occurs

IMPORTANT PEOPLE, PLACES, EVENTS, AND CONCEPTS

oil	Andrew Carnegie	Knights of Labor	Industrial Workers of the World
steel	Carnegie Steel	Terrence Powderly	
"railroad time"	John D. Rockefeller	American Railway Union	Great Railroad Strike
Credit Mobilier Scandal	Standard Oil Trust		Haymarket Riot
	Ida Tarbell	Eugene V. Debs	Homestead Strike
Jay Gould	Sherman Antitrust Act (1890)	American Federation of Labor	Pullman Strike
		Samuel Gompers	"New South"

"You have no right to be poor. It is your duty to be rich.... It is cruel to slander the rich because they have been successful. They are not scoundrels because they have gotten money. They have blessed the world."
—from the speech "Acres of Diamonds," by the Rev. Russell H. Conwell, 1900

INTRODUCTION

The United States went from being primarily a rural nation after the Civil War to the world's leading industrial power by the 1920s. This period is often known as America's **second industrial revolution** (the first began in the 1820s with the development of a mechanized textile industry in New England). Essential to this transformation was the use of new technologies to increase productivity. Several factors contributed to this change, including an abundance of natural resources, an available labor source, a host of new inventions, and rapidly expanding markets. The effects of industrialization were profound. Reverend Conwell, in the quote above, sings the praises of industrial giants. Huge corporations developed, wielding unprecedented power. Labor relations became increasingly quarrelsome, and a reform movement developed to challenge the power of the new large corporations. America became a more urban nation as farmers and immigrants were drawn to industrial work.

NEW TECHNOLOGIES

Mass Production

New techniques were introduced in the post–Civil War period that greatly increased productivity. Giant factories brought many operations under one roof. Standardized, interchangeable parts were introduced to a variety of processes. Factories became more mechanized as machines, rather than workers, began to make products. The cigarette-making machine is a good example. These **mass production** techniques brought a flood of goods to the market.

Natural Resources and Industrial Development

Anthracite coal was the most important fuel of the second industrial revolution. The burning of coal was used to generate steam. Steam engines replaced water, animal, and human power in a number of operations.

Oil and oil refining became important in the post–Civil War period as kerosene, a byproduct of oil, was used to light lamps. In 1859 **Edwin L. Drake** successfully used steam power to drill for oil in Titusville, Pennsylvania, making it practical to access large amounts of oil from beneath the earth's surface. Oil, second only to coal in importance as a fuel during the last part of the 19th century, would become even more important in the 20th century with the development of automobiles.

Steel—which is produced by removing impurities from iron and adding alloying elements— became cheaper and more available as a result of the **Bessemer process**, developed in the 1850s. Steel, more flexible and stronger than iron, became an important material in barbed wire, plows, rails, bridges, and tall buildings.

Railroads

Perhaps the most important technological development of the 19th century was the railroad. Railroads allowed for the transportation of agricultural products, raw materials, and manufactured goods over great distances, creating, in effect, a national rather than local economy. The companies that built and operated the railroad lines amassed enormous power and became embroiled in scandal and accusations of abusive practices.

Americans clamored for a route to the West before the Civil War. The first **transcontinental railroad**, using Chinese and Irish immigrant workers, was completed when the Union Pacific, building westward from Nebraska, and the Central Pacific, working eastward from California, met at Promontory Point, Utah in May 1869. In the following decades other lines were completed to the Pacific Ocean.

Railroad companies lobbied the government to create standard time zones, to end the confusion of time being slightly different from town to town. The creation of **"railroad time"** in 1883 demonstrated the enormous power of the railroad companies.

The unbridled power of the railroad companies was evident in the **Credit Mobilier Scandal** (1867). Stockholders in the Union Pacific railroad set up a construction company to lay track at inflated costs. These stockholders would gain the windfall profits for themselves. They also offered stock to congressmen to keep them quiet.

Railroad companies also abused their power by fixing prices and charging exorbitant fees. Farmers in the West had to pay the fees because they needed to get their crops to market, and often only one line would serve an area. Railroad practices were a focus of agrarian protest movements.

THE RISE OF BIG BUSINESS

Just as with the railroad industry, the economy became increasingly dominated by a few very large companies. A few of these companies exercised near-total control of certain industries; their owners exercised enormous control, both in the economy and in the political sphere. Reformers made some mostly unsuccessful attempts to check the power of these corporate giants. Contemporaries and historians have debated how these owners should be remembered.

Methods of Control

Owners of large corporations used a variety of methods to gain and maintain control of a particular industry. Companies *combined*, or merged, to form larger companies. A **horizontal monopoly** involved several companies in the same business combining, effectively controlling an industry. **Vertical integration** occurred when a company gained control of the various aspects of an industrial process; for example, from the mining of raw materials to transportation to manufacturing to distribution. A **trust** was formed when competing companies would create a single board of trustees which would oversee operations of the various companies. Thus, control was more tightly exercised and competition was reduced.

"Captains of Industry" or "Robber Barons"

Observers at the time had mixed feelings about the emerging class of corporate giants. Some marveled at the technological wonders and abundant consumer goods produced by industry. Others saw the dangers and abuses of power exercised by these **"robber barons."**

Jay Gould is generally regarded as the most ruthless business owner of this era. He gained this reputation through bribery, threats, and conspiracy against competitors. His operations included railroad speculation, stock trading, tanneries, and newspaper publishing. History has looked more favorably on **Andrew Carnegie**.

Carnegie, a Scottish immigrant, illustrated the so-called "rags-to-riches" story, as he rose from being a child employee in a cotton mill to exercising control of the steel industry. Carnegie invested money in new technologies in his steel mills, and consequently lowered production costs. He gained control of all aspects of steel production, from mining iron to controlling railroads, creating a vertically integrated company. Carnegie is known for his philanthropy; he donated his entire fortune to public libraries, museums, concert halls, and institutes of higher education.

John D. Rockefeller achieved a monopoly in the oil-refining business through horizontal integration. Rockefeller's company, **Standard Oil**, went from refining 2 to 3 percent of crude oil in the United States in 1870 to over 90 percent of it a decade later. He pushed out competitors through a variety of methods, such as arranging rebates with freight lines. His techniques were exposed by muckraker **Ida Tarbell** in her 1904 book *The History of the Standard Oil Company*, though Rockefeller defended them as legal and fair.

Attempts at Reform

The government responded to popular pressure to rein in the power of big business with the **Sherman Anti-trust Act** (1890), which stated that any attempt to interfere with free interstate trade by forming trusts was illegal. However, it proved to be difficult to enforce.

LABOR CONFLICTS (1877–1914)

Although big business became increasingly profitable in the post–Civil War period, many workers believed their lives were growing more difficult and less rewarding. They were also threatened by the growing power of industrial giants and the new methods of production, which removed any semblance of control they had over the work process. Owners of large corporations, on the other hand, believed that in an intensely competitive economy, they had to maintain, or even cut, wages, while at the same time increasingly mechanize the work process. As a result, a series of intense labor battles occurred between 1877 and the turn of the century.

Conditions in Factories

Factory workers were routinely subject to long hours (12 or more per day), repetitive and often dangerous work, and low pay. Factories lacked ventilation and light. There were no medical, unemployment, disability, or retirement benefits. Child labor was common. Women and children tended to make even less money than men.

Formation of Unions

To improve their lot, workers formed **unions**, organizations that could negotiate with owners for better pay and conditions. Unions could use a variety of techniques to press their case, but striking (stopping work) proved to be the most successful in the long run.

Industrial unionists believed that the key to success lay in organizing skilled and unskilled workers in a specific industry. An important early **industrial union** was the **Knights of Labor**. The union was open to men and women of all races and skill levels. It advocated arbitration rather than striking. It grew under **Terrence Powderly's** leadership in the 1880s, but declined by the century's end. Another example was the **American Railway Union**, which was founded by **Eugene V. Debs**. Industrial unionism would not achieve great success until the 1930s.

The **American Federation of Labor**, founded by **Samuel Gompers** in 1886, was a coalition of **craft unions**. Craft unions, such as Gompers's cigar makers' union, attempted to organize skilled workers in a particular field. The AFL encouraged strikes and was largely successful in winning improvements for its workers.

After the disastrous Pullman strike (see below), Eugene Debs came to believe that the problems that workers faced were inherent in the capitalist system itself. He and others turned to **socialism**, a political ideology that advocated the eventual end of the private enterprise system and the advent of a worker-run society. The more radical labor union, **Industrial Workers of the World**, under the banner "One big union," combined socialist and anarchist ideas but failed to attract a mass following.

Significant Strikes and Incidents

The **Great Railroad Strike** (1877) began when workers went on strike in West Virginia to protest a wage cut. The strike spread from New York to San Francisco, virtually halting rail traffic in the United States. President Hayes called in military troops to put down what is the closest the United States has ever come to a **general strike** (a cessation of work by the majority of workers in every industry).

The **Haymarket Riot** (1886) began as a peaceful demonstration for the eight-hour day. After a rally protesting police violence was ordered to disperse, someone threw a bomb. The police fired into the crowd. A total of seven police officers and four others were killed. Eight anarchists were tried, with little evidence; four were executed. The incident turned many people away from the labor movement and crippled the Knights of Labor.

The **Homestead Strike** (1892) against the Carnegie Steel Company was broken up by gun-wielding private Pinkerton guards (labor spies). A daylong gun battle left 10 dead. The Carnegie plant reopened after the National Guard was sent in. The strike was a thorough defeat for Carnegie's workers. Indeed, in its wake the entire steel industry had rid itself of union activity by 1900.

The Pullman Palace Car Company built luxurious sleeper cars for the railroads. Its workers lived in what was touted as a model community of the same name near Chicago. When Pullman announced a wage cut, the workers were incensed. The **Pullman Strike** (1894) began when Debs organized a nationwide sympathy strike of workers who handled Pullman cars. The federal government issued an injunction against the strike because, it claimed, the mail was stopped. President Cleveland sent in troops to break up the strike.

Management Resists Demands by Organized Labor

The outcome of a particular strike depended on a number of factors, including the strength of the union, the condition of the economy, and the strategy of management. **Yellow-dog contracts** mandated that employees agree not to join unions. Owners also hired replacement workers, called **"scabs"** by unions. Finally, employers circulated **blacklists** of "troublemakers," who were not to be hired.

Government Supports Management

In general, local, state, and federal governments used their power to side with the owners of companies. As with the Pullman strike, the government often issued orders, or **injunctions**, for a particular strike to end. Once an injunction against a strike was issued, strikers were considered lawbreakers and were subject to arrest or the use of force by police officers or federal troops. At times strikers armed themselves as well, but they were outmatched by the firepower of the government.

The Supreme Court asserted that strikes violated the Sherman Anti-trust Act on the grounds that they were combinations in restraint of free trade. The act was used more frequently against labor unions than against trusts.

INDUSTRY AND THE SOUTH

The South was much slower to industrialize than the North, despite the hope of some Southerners to create a **"New South"** in the 1870s. The South had fewer cities and lacked money to invest in industry. What money that did exist was invested in rebuilding after the Civil War. Also, fewer Europeans immigrated to the South. The South remained agricultural, with Northern-owned railroads exerting control over transportation and Northern corporations resisting competition from the South. Late in the century the South developed furniture and textile industries, as well as a steel industry in Birmingham, Alabama, but eventually even these came under the control of Northern capital.

SUMMARY

The "second industrial revolution" dramatically changed the American economy, as small manufacturers gave way to powerful corporations. Americans began to purchase most of the goods they used, rather than making or growing them at home. A national, and eventually international, economy was created. Some workers and farmers feared—and organized against—the growing power of the corporate giants that came to dominate America in the late 19th century. In the labor battles, the tactics of owners, along with the government's cooperation, tilted the scales in favor of management.

THINGS TO REMEMBER

- **Anthracite coal:** A type of coal, noted for being hard and clean burning coal.

- **Blacklist:** A list, circulated among potential employers, of alleged "troublemakers" not to be hired.

- **Craft unionism:** The movement to form labor organizations made up of skilled workers within a particular field.

- **Horizontal integration:** The joining together of companies engaged in similar business practices to create a virtual monopoly.

- **Industrial unionism:** The movement to form labor organizations that represent every worker in a single industry regardless of his or her level of skill.

- **Injunction:** A court order stopping a specific act, often used against unions to end a strike.

- **Mass production:** Techniques used in industry to produce large quantities of goods using interchangeable parts and moving assembly lines. Elements of mass production were developed in the 19th century; the process was perfected by Henry Ford in the 1910s.

- **Robber baron:** Critical term for the owners of the big business of the Gilded Age who accumulated great wealth and power.

- **Scab:** Derogatory term used by the labor movement to describe workers who cross picket lines.

- **Socialism:** An economic system in which the state controls the production and distribution of certain products deemed necessary for the good of the people.

- **Trusts:** Large corporations created by the consolidation of competing companies to form a monopoly or near monopoly.

- **Unions:** Worker organization formed to press for workplace demands such as better wages and safer working conditions.

- **Vertical integration:** The joining together of companies to control all aspects of the production process of an item, from the mining or growing of materials, through production and distribution of the final product.

- **Yellow-dog contract:** Agreements employers forced potential employees to sign in which the employees agreed not to join unions or go on strike.

REVIEW QUESTIONS

1. "Yellow dog" contracts

   (A) required African Americans to agree to work as sharecroppers
   (B) were the result of collective bargaining by unions and owners
   (C) were part of the strategy used by owners to prevent the establishment of unions
   (D) were welcomed by craft unions
   (E) were emblematic of Gilded Age corruption

2. The Bessemer process created an inexpensive way to

   (A) refine oil
   (B) assemble the parts of an automobile
   (C) create steel
   (D) harvest corn and wheat
   (E) generate electricity

3. The Sherman Anti-trust Act

   (A) was used successfully to break up trusts
   (B) was welcomed by Andrew Carnegie
   (C) was consistent with the philosophy of Social Darwinism
   (D) was used most effectively against striking unions
   (E) strengthened the Clayton Anti-trust Act

4. An important trend that characterized American society during the Gilded Age was

   (A) harmony and peace at industrial sites
   (B) clean, efficient government
   (C) a decline of rail transportation and an increase in truck and automobile use
   (D) the continuation of rural traditions
   (E) a growing economy

ANSWERS AND EXPLANATIONS

1. C

Some employers required potential employees to sign "yellow dog" contracts before hiring them. These contracts stated that the employee would not join a union. Unions opposed these contracts, and they were eventually declared illegal. "Yellow dog" contracts were forced upon potential employees—they were not the result of negotiations. No specific legislation required African Americans to work as sharecroppers. However, many of the black codes made owning property difficult for African Americans. No legitimate union would welcome "yellow dog" contracts. The contracts are not examples of corruption; they were not secret contracts involving kickbacks or slush funds.

2. C

The Bessemer process allowed for the inexpensive processing of iron into steel. As a result, steel became a more common building material, and was used extensively on bridges and skyscrapers. No one person is associated with developing the oil refining process, but Rockefeller is associated with bringing the industry under his control. Ford is associated with developing the process for mass producing automobiles, thus reducing the costs. Cyrus McCormick invented the mechanical reaper in the 1850s, making harvesting grains easier and cheaper. Edison built the first commercial electric generating station in New York City in 1882.

3. D

The Supreme Court ruled that strikes were illegal combinations which stood in the way of free trade, making the Sherman Anti-trust Act an effective tool to block striking unions. The Sherman Anti-trust Act of 1890 was not very successful in breaking up trusts; vague wording rendered it ineffective. In general, the owners of big business, such as Andrew Carnegie, were opposed to government attempts to rein in their power. A strict adherent of Social Darwinism would reject any attempt by the government to interfere in or regulate the economy. The stronger Clayton Anti-trust Act was passed in 1914.

4. E

Industrial expansion fueled an overall growth in the American economy. The era was fraught with battles between labor and owners. Government during the Gilded Age was known for its corruption, most notably during the Grant administration and during "Boss" Tweed's reign in New York City. Choice (C) is incorrect for the Gilded Age; it would be correct if the question were about the post–World War II period. Though rural traditions might have held on in pockets of America, the era is noted more for change than tradition.

CHAPTER 18

Society and Culture in the Gilded Age, 1865–1900

TIMELINE

1844	Samuel F. B. Morse develops the telegraph
1851	Young Men's Christian Association opens
1873	Comstock Law enacted
1876	Central Park completed • Baseball's National League founded
1879	First Woolworth "five-and-dime store" opens
1883	Brooklyn Bridge opens
1886	Statue of Liberty dedicated
1889	Hull House founded in Chicago by Jane Addams and Ellen Gates
1892	Ellis Island opens
1893	Chicago World's Fair takes place
1894	Alexander Graham Bell develops the telephone
1895	Coney Island opens
1897	First U.S. subway opens in Boston

IMPORTANT PEOPLE, PLACES, EVENTS, AND CONCEPTS

Gilded Age	Ellis Island	Jacob Riis	Comstock Law
Tammany Hall	Brooklyn Bridge	Jane Addams	Young Men's Christian Association
"Boss" William M. Tweed	skyscraper	Hull House	
	Otis's elevator	Thomas Edison	Mark Twain
Thomas Nast	Frederick Law Olmsted	Samuel F. B. Morse	dime novels
Statue of Liberty		Alexander Graham Bell	social Darwinism
Emma Lazarus	Central Park		gospel of wealth

"The vast populations of these cities are utterly divorced from the genial influences of nature…. All the sweet and joyous influences of nature are shut out from them. Her sounds are drowned by the roar of the street and the clatter of the people in the next room…. Her sights are hidden from their eyes by rows of high building…."

—from *Town and Country*, by Henry George, 1898

INTRODUCTION

There is a long tradition of anti-urban sentiment among American intellectuals, as is shown in the quote from Henry George above. As America became more industrial, such sentiments seemed increasingly anachronistic. The nation experienced a series of profound changes between the Civil War and the turn of the 20th century. First, the standard of living in the United States rose dramatically, but the rise was uneven: a fabulously wealthy elite came to dominate the economy and politics while grinding poverty persisted. In fact, this era is often referred to as the **Gilded Age**—implying a thin gold veneer covering a cheap base. Second, the United States was changing from a rural, agricultural nation to an urban one. Third, new inventions, fruits of industrial progress, changed the way Americans lived their lives. Many of the cultural products of this era reflect these changes.

URBANIZATION

Cities grew rapidly during the Gilded Age. Rural Americans and European immigrants were drawn to industrial jobs in cities. Some critics, such as **Henry Adams**, a descendent of the Presidents Adams, saw urbanization as a disease. Reformers attempted to create antidotes for urban problems.

Politics: The Age of Tammany Hall

Political corruption, common in the United States during the Gilded Age, was especially rampant in cities. Most cities were run by **political machines**, well-run party organizations that got their people elected; ideology was not important. At their best, the leaders elected via political machines provided needed services to immigrants and the poor. At their worst, the machine leaders amassed great wealth and power through theft, kickbacks, and intimidation. The most notorious machine was New York City's Democratic Party. Its most infamous "boss," **William M. Tweed**, and headquarters, **Tammany Hall**, have become bywords for corruption. Tweed was eventually brought down, in large part, as a result of a series of cartoons by the most well-known cartoonist of the 19th century, **Thomas Nast**.

Immigration

One of the most significant trends of the Gilded Age was the large number of immigrants who entered the United States. The **"new immigration"** involved mainly Southern and Eastern Europeans and Asians, while the "old immigration" (1840s–1880s) consisted mainly of Northern and Western Europeans (primarily Irish and German). Catholic Italians, Eastern European Jews, and Slavs filled urban ethnic enclaves such as New York's Little Italy and the Lower East Side. Immigrants were generally drawn to the economic opportunities of the United States; many Jews left Russia to avoid anti-Semitic massacres known as pogroms. The **Statue of Liberty**, a gift from France, was installed in New York harbor in 1886 with a poem by **Emma Lazarus** celebrating America's role as a destination for immigrants. In 1892, **Ellis Island** opened as an immigrant-admitting station.

The Growth of the Physical City

Cities grew outward and upward during the Gilded Age. The **Brooklyn Bridge** was an engineering marvel at the time it was completed in 1883. Designed and completed by John Roebling and his son Washington, it connected the then-independent cities of Brooklyn and New York. **Skyscrapers** were not a possibility until the development of steel-skeleton construction and the **elevator**, developed by **Elisha Otis** in 1857. The lack of affordable space in urban cores made tall buildings economically desirable. The "walking city" rapidly gave way to a complex network of neighborhoods and districts divided by class, race, ethnicity, and function. A series of innovations in public transportation in the 19th century made this transformation possible. Horse-drawn streetcars gave way to cable cars (1880s), which gave way to electric trolleys (1890s). The first subway opened in Boston (1897); New York was soon to follow (1906). Department stores such as Macy's in New York, Wanamaker's in Philadelphia, and Marshall Field's in Chicago (all founded in the 1870s and 1880s) developed the idea of providing, under one roof, the goods that a variety of specialty shops had previously sold. Many cities, sometimes reluctantly, built parks to provide space for leisure activities and fresh air. **Frederick Law Olmsted** is most closely linked to the parks movement. He designed New York City's **Central Park** (completed in 1876).

Urban Poverty

Overcrowding and grinding poverty were endemic to growing cities of the Gilded Age. Areas in the Lower East Side in New York had the highest densities in the world. Various reform movements sprung up in response to the dramatic rise of urban poverty. Many reformers were inspired by the **social gospel** movement: the belief that religious institutions should work to improve society as well as attend to people's spiritual needs. *How the Other Half Lives* (1890), by **Jacob Riis**, drew many people's attention to the conditions of the poor with wrenching photographs. New York passed the **Tenement Law** in *1879*, which mandated that every room in an apartment have an outside window and that buildings meet plumbing and ventilation standards. The **dumbbell tenement** grew out of this law, wherein buildings were designed to conform to the standards while cramming the largest number of people into the smallest amount of space. **Jane Addams** organized **Hull House** (1889), a **settlement house** in Chicago, which served as a community center and home for poor immigrants (mostly women and children). The **Settlement House Movement** established centers in many cities to help the poor. Settlement house workers tended to be college-educated women.

Challenges of Urban Life

Gilded Age cities were growing at a faster rate than municipal services. Consequently, a series of urban problems developed: trash in the streets, lack of water, crime, lack of sewage treatment, and fire. The political machines that ran cities often seemed overwhelmed by these problems. Slowly reformers pushed for municipal services. New York created a modern police force in the 1840s; other services followed in the post–Civil War period.

THE IMPACT OF INVENTIONS

The post–Civil War period saw an explosion of inventions. Between 1800 and 1860, the U.S. Patent Office issued over 36,000 patents; over the next 40 years it would issue 500,000 more. These technological advances had a major impact on American life. Observers commented on the ingenuity of Americans.

Electricity

The production and distribution of electrical power was made safer and less expensive after the Civil War. During the 1880s, electricity became available to people in major cities. Electricity made possible a host of changes in people's lives. Thomas Alva Edison was most responsible for bringing electrical power and its applications to the public. He created the first modern research lab, employing hundreds of employees and receiving patents for hundreds of inventions, including the incandescent light bulb, which replaced gaslights. Also important were electric printing presses and sewing machines. Many rural areas would not get electricity until the 1920s and 1930s.

Communication

A series of inventions changed the way humans communicated with one another. The first important innovation in communication was the **telegraph**, developed by **Samuel F. B. Morse** in 1844. Morse code, a series of long and short electric impulses, was used by Western Union (1870) to send millions of messages over wires. **Alexander Graham Bell** developed the "talking telegraph" or **telephone** in 1876. American Telephone and Telegraph was founded in 1884; by 1900, 1.5 million Americans had telephones. The development of the **typewriter** in the 1860s transformed office work. The **linotype machine** (invented in 1885) allowed printers to quickly create type for printing. This greatly reduced the cost of producing newspapers and magazines.

THE CHANGING AMERICAN SOCIETY

Morality

A series of crusades were launched during the Gilded Age to regulate activities that some saw as immoral or dangerous. These crusades can also be seen as an assault on immigrant and working class customs and activities. By far the most popular moral crusade was the anti-alcohol, or **temperance**, movement, which would finally achieve success in 1920. The largest temperance group was the **Women's Christian Temperance Union** (founded in 1874). **Anthony Comstock** was the most well-known crusader against gambling, prostitution, and obscenity. He was incensed at the increasing divorce rate and the availability of birth control. The **Comstock Law** (1873) made it illegal to send material deemed obscene, including information about birth control, through the mail.

Leisure

Americans tended to have more leisure time by the end of the century. Americans pursued leisure activities such as baseball and bicycling in the Gilded Age. The founding of the **Young Men's Christian Association** (1851) reflected the concern both for physical fitness and moral uplift. Americans flocked to the Chicago World's Fair of 1893 where neoclassical architecture and processed foods were on display.

Literature

Literacy rates rose during the Gilded Age as more Americans attended school for longer periods of time. With literacy rising and the cost of producing books and periodicals falling, more Americans were reading. Unlike the sentimental literature of the antebellum period, **realist** writers attempted to portray life, even its seamier side, in a direct way. William Dean Howells wrote about the plight of factory workers in *A Hazard of New Fortunes* (1885), and **Henry James** wrote about the life of the upper class in *The Bostonians* (1886). Edward Bellamy, in his novel *Looking Backward, 2000–1887* (1888), imagined someone looking back from the future and finding that the problems caused by industrialization had been solved by a socialist government.

Stephen Crane's *The Red Badge of Courage* (1895) depicted the horrors of the Civil War. **Mark Twain**, who drew on the local customs and color of the Mississippi River culture, produced two of the most important classics in American literature, *The Adventures of Tom Sawyer* (1876) and *The Adventures of Huckleberry Finn* (1884). **Edith Wharton** exposed the foibles of upper class New York in *The House of Mirth* (1905) and **Willa Cather's** *O Pioneers* (1913) and *My Antonia* (1918) portrayed life on the plains.

Art

Realism also influenced American artists. Most important among realist artists were **Thomas Eakins** and **Winslow Homer**. Also, the ashcan school of painting, with its direct representations of urban poverty, developed during the period.

The Popular Press

New printing presses were able to mass-produce books, and inexpensive **"dime novels,"** with themes of adventure, crime, or the West, became the rage. Newspaper publishing, headquartered in New York City, became big business. **Joseph Pulitzer** and **William Randolph Hearst** emerged as important publishers, printing sensational, and sometimes fictionalized, accounts of events. This **"yellow journalism"** is often cited as a cause of the Spanish-American War. *Ladies' Home Journal* offered advice to middle class women. *McClure's* and *Harper's Weekly* published feature articles about contemporary problems.

Cultural Justifications for Industrial Growth

There were many Gilded Age–era ideologies and writings that saw the amassing of wealth by industrial titans in positive terms.

The owners of large corporations justified their practices with the philosophy of **social Darwinism**. Writers such as **Charles Graham Sumner** applied to the human world observations of the natural world made by Charles Darwin. Darwin had observed that in nature, those members of a species which are best adapted to a particular environment are more likely to survive into adulthood and pass on their genes to the next generation. Social Darwinists saw this "survival of the fittest" model as applicable to human society, where a competition for success favors the cleverest and strongest. The rich and the poor, therefore, deserved their respective positions. Such a philosophy supported a *laissez-faire* philosophy where the government played little or no role in intervening in the economy.

Most of the owners of big business were churchgoing Protestants. The idea of the **gospel of wealth**, which was the title of a book by Andrew Carnegie, saw the accumulation of wealth as a positive sign from God.

Popular literature of this era, especially the stories of **Horatio Alger**, told "rags-to-riches" stories in which a poor boy, through honesty, thrift, and a bit of luck, achieves great success in life. The implication of these books, such as *Ragged Dick* (1868), was that wealth was within everyone's reach.

SUMMARY

During the Gilded Age, American society had to deal with some dramatic upheavals as a predominantly rural, homogeneous people faced the promise and peril of an urban, diverse, and industrial society. New patterns of life emerged as new inventions, consumer goods, and cultural products became available. America became a wealthy and confident nation during this period, ready to assume a more prominent role in world affairs.

THINGS TO REMEMBER

- **New immigration:** The wave of immigration from the 1880s to the 1920s of Eastern and Southern Europeans, contrasted with the "old" immigration of Northern and Western Europeans.

- **Political machines:** Political party organizations that run cities and are often associated with corruption and undemocratic practices. The most notorious example was New York's Tammany Hall Democratic club of the Gilded Age.

- **Realist movement:** Art and literature that seek to depict the commonplace in a plausible and direct manner.

- **Settlement house movement:** The movement of mostly college-educated women designed to provide shelter, cultural activities, and services to the poor. The height of the movement occurred in the late 19th and early 20th centuries.

- **Social gospel:** Also called "applied Christianity," this reform movement, driven by Christian teachings, sought to relieve the suffering of the poor.

- **Telegraph:** Developed by Samuel F. B. Morse in 1837, the telegraph allowed for communications over long distances by tapping out coded messages to be carried over wires.

- **Temperance movement:** The 19th and early 20th century movement to limit or outlaw the drinking of alcoholic beverages. The movement achieved its ultimate success with the passage of the 18th Amendment—or Prohibition—which went into effect in 1920.

- **Yellow journalism:** Sensationalistic, lurid, and often falsified accounts of events printed by newspapers and magazines to attract readers.

REVIEW QUESTIONS

1. Pick the choice which matches the author with the book he or she wrote.

   X) Stephen Crane   1) *My Antonia*
   Y) Willa Cather   2) *The House of Mirth*
   Z) Henry James   3) *The Bostonians*
                         4) *The Red Badge of Courage*

   Answer choices:
   (A) X-4; Y-2; Z-1
   (B) X-2; Y-1; Z-3
   (C) X-4; Y-1; Z-3
   (D) X-3; Y-2; Z-4
   (E) X-2; Y-1; Z-4

2. The "new immigrants" of the late 19th and early 20th century were primarily

   (A) Anglo-Saxons
   (B) Irish refugees from the potato blight
   (C) from within the Western hemisphere
   (D) Eastern and Southern Europeans
   (E) exiles leaving the United States

3. Pick the answer that matches the person with the idea or movement he or she is associated with.

   X) Charles Graham Sumner   1) the gospel of wealth
   Y) Jane Addams   2) social Darwinism
   Z) Andrew Carnegie   3) pragmatism
                               4) the settlement house movement

   Answer choices:
   (A) X-1; Y-2; Z-3
   (B) X-2; Y-3; Z-4
   (C) X-2; Y-4; Z-1
   (D) X-3; Y-4; Z-1
   (E) X-3; Y-1; Z-2

4. Urban political machines during the Gilded Age

   (A) were scorned by immigrant groups who were cheated by graft and corruption
   (B) were usually associated with the Republican Party
   (C) often formed alliances with the Women's Christian Temperance Union
   (D) often provided a social safety net in an age when welfare did not yet exist
   (E) were eliminated by the Pendleton Act

ANSWERS AND EXPLANATIONS

1. C

Stephen Crane wrote *The Red Badge of Courage*, a novel that takes place during the Civil War; Willa Cather wrote *My Antonia*, a novel of frontier life; and Henry James chronicled the life of upper class Boston in *The Bostonians*. *The House of Mirth*, which chronicled high society and the clashes between tradition and modernity, was written by Edith Wharton.

2. D

Between 1880 and the Emergency Quota Act in 1921, the largest number of immigrants came from Eastern European countries such as Russia and Poland, as well as Italy. Anglo-Saxons comprised the first European immigrant group to come over, primarily during the colonial period. Irish refugees from the potato blight came over during the 1840s and 1850s. Immigration from within the Western hemisphere is a phenomenon of the later part of the 20th century, especially after 1965. There was never a significant movement of people out of the United States, even among freed slaves returning to Africa.

3. C

Charles Graham Sumner is the most prominent proponent of social Darwinism. Jane Addams is the person most closely identified with the settlement house movement. Andrew Carnegie wrote a book entitled *The Gospel of Wealth*. William James is associated with the pragmatist philosophical movement.

4. D

Immigrants received benefits, from jobs to money, which cemented their loyalty to the political machines. The urban political machines of the Gilded Age, especially New York's Tammany Hall, were associated with corruption, but immigrant groups stayed loyal to these machines. Urban politics from the Civil War until today have generally been dominated by the Democratic Party, not the Republicans. The political machines, with their strong working class and immigrant support, would not support the temperance movement. The Pendleton Act applied to the federal government—specifically to the way in which civil service employees were selected.

CHAPTER 19

Politics of the Gilded Age, 1877–1900

TIMELINE

1877	*Munn v. Illinois* decision
1883	Pendleton Act passed
1886	*Wabash v. Illinois* decision
1887	Interstate Commerce Commission established
1892	Populist Party formed
1893	Panic of 1893 begins
1894	Coxey's Army marches to Washington, DC
1896	William Jennings Bryan runs for president on Democratic ticket with Populist support

IMPORTANT PEOPLE, PLACES, EVENTS, AND CONCEPTS

Populist movement

William Jennings Bryan

"waving the bloody shirt"

spoils system

Mugwumps

Pendleton Act

Panic of 1893

Coxey's Army

Granger movement

Granger laws

Munn v. Illinois

Wabash decision

"Cross of Gold" speech

"You come and tell us that the great cities are in favor of the gold standard; we reply that the great cities rest upon the broad and fertile prairies. Burn down your cities and leave our farms, and your cities will spring up again as if by magic; but destroy our farms and the grass will grow in every city street in the country . . . ."

—from the "Cross of Gold" speech by William Jennings Bryan, 1896

INTRODUCTION

Gilded Age politicians have not fared well in history books. The era was rampant with corruption, as politicians were tempted by the great wealth amassed by industrialists. Further, little real leadership came from the White House. The most potent political movement of the Gilded Age was the **Populist movement**—the agrarian uprising that **William Jennings Bryan** appealed to in the speech quoted above.

NATIONAL POLITICS

Political Parties

A **two-party system**, essentially still in effect today, developed during the Civil War period. Although the Democrats and the Republicans attracted roughly similar numbers of voters, the Republicans held onto the White House from Lincoln's administration through Woodrow Wilson's election in 1912, with the exception of Grover Cleveland's two nonconsecutive terms. Republicans dominated most Northern states, while Democratic had strength in the Southern states and in industrial cities. While no major issue polarized the parties as slavery had in the past, there were still differences. Republicans tended to push for laws limiting what they saw as immoral behavior—notably, drinking. They also were in favor of restrictions on immigration. Democrats, with more support from immigrants and workers, tended to oppose laws limiting "immoral" behavior, or **blue laws.** Strong in the rural South, Democrats tended to hold traditional rural positions, such as favoring a low tariff and limiting the role of government. The cautious Republican candidates for the White House were more likely to "wave the bloody shirt"—to emphasize the Democrats' role in supporting secession and plunging the nation into war—than to engage in heated ideological debate.

The Forgotten Presidents

The presidents of the Gilded Age—Rutherford B. Hayes (1877–1881), James A. Garfield (1881), Chester A. Arthur (1881–1885), Grover Cleveland (1885–1889 and 1893–1897), and Benjamin Harrison (1889–1893)—are sometimes referred to as the "forgotten presidents." Their individual accomplishments might not stand out, but a familiarity with the issues of the age and their context is important.

Gilded Age = Political Corruption

Politics, Big Business, and Corruption

Politics in the Gilded Age was largely dominated by big business. The government essentially professed a **laissez-faire**, or hands off, approach to business. While it is true that government did not regulate business, it did aid it in several ways, such as with high **protective tariffs** and subsidies to railroads. Several scandals involving government corruption epitomized the era.

The Spoils System

The **spoils system**—the practice of assigning civil service jobs to party loyalists—had been a contentious issue as far back as the Jackson administration. However, its prevalence during the Gilded Age aroused indignation. Many "good government" Republicans, who became known as **"Mugwumps,"** broke with their party in 1880 out of disgust with the spoils system and supported the Democratic candidate. Republican candidate Garfield won, but was assassinated four months after taking office by a party loyalist who felt he had been passed over for a position. Garfield's assassination brought the issue of the spoils system to the fore; the **Pendleton Act** (1883) was passed to create a civil service based on merit rather than patronage.

Tariffs

As industry grew, **protective tariffs** became a contentious issue. Republicans generally supported higher tariffs to benefit American industry; Democrats generally supported consumer-friendly lower tariffs. Republican President Harrison, for instance, dramatically raised the tariff.

The Panic of 1893

During the **Panic of 1893**, thousands of businesses collapsed, banks closed their doors, and unemployment soared. The *laissez-faire* approach of Gilded Age government was evident in the lack of a response to the terrible depression following the Panic. Jacob Coxey organized a group, **Coxey's Army**, to march to Washington, DC (1894) to protest President Cleveland's seeming insensitivity.

UNREST AMONG FARMERS (1867–1896)

The **Populist Party** of the late 19th century posed one of the most formidable challenges to the two-party system. The origins of the movement, and of the **Granger movement** and the alliance movement which preceded it, can be traced to a series of difficulties farmers faced in the second half of the 19th century. These problems included the pricing practices of the railroads, debt, and deflation. The decline of the movement can be attributed to its inability to forge links with discontented workers in urban centers.

"Mugwumps": good gov't Republicans who split w/ their party b/c of spoils system & supported Democratic candidate

The Grange

The Grange, a farmer organization founded in 1867, organized opposition to railroad practices, banks, and grain wholesalers. Many western states passed **Granger laws** to regulate railroad rates. The Supreme Court upheld a state's right to regulate railroad rates, and indeed to regulate private industry, in the case of ***Munn v. Illinois*** (1877). In the 1886 ***Wabash decision***, however, the Supreme Court ruled that states could not set rates on commerce *between* states—a damaging decision to the Granger movement. The federal government set up the nation's first independent regulatory agency, the **Interstate Commerce Commission**, in 1887 with mixed results. It wasn't until Theodore Roosevelt's administration that the ICC had real teeth.

The Populist Party

In 1892, a more significant agrarian formation—the Populist Party—developed as the Grange declined in influence. Western farmers found themselves in an economic bind. Mechanization may have increased production, but this led to a decrease in the prices farmers received for their crops. At the same time, farmers went into debt buying expensive new farming equipment. In addition, a tight money supply in the United States caused **deflation**. While deflation benefited consumers, it was deadly for farmers. First, lowered prices meant farmers got less money for their crops. As a result, it was more difficult for farmers to pay off their debts to creditors. The strong dollar made it seem like farmers were paying back more than they had borrowed (leaving interest aside).

The platform of the Populist Party, therefore, included a call to increase the money supply. The **gold standard**, in which the amount of money in circulation is tied to the amount of gold in the treasury, was seen as the enemy. The Greenback Party had advocated simply printing paper money backed by nothing. The Populist platform called for backing money with silver as well as gold, hence the party nicknames **"Bimetallists"** and **"Free Silverites."** In addition, the platform called for a graduated income tax, direct election of senators, an eight-hour day, restrictions on immigration, and secret ballots (all of which were eventually adopted). It also called for nationalizing banks, railroads, and telegraph lines (none of which were adopted). Frustration among workers and farmers mounted during the depression that resulted from the Panic of 1893, but the Populist program did not gain the support of most workers. In 1896, the Populists and the Democratic Party jointly nominated William Jennings Bryan for president. He attacked the gold standard in his **"Cross of Gold" speech.** Bryan's loss in the election signaled the end of the Populist challenge.

SUMMARY

The intense labor battles and the agrarian unrest of the Gilded Age shed light on tensions that existed within American society. Organized labor failed to make substantial gains. In fact, unions would not enjoy a larger degree of success until the Wagner Act is passed, ensuring laborers' right to organize. The farmer alliances of the 19th century were short-lived. The Populists were not able to become a viable third party or forge significant links with urban workers. Though its influence waned as power shifted from the farm to the city, many Populist initiatives were taken up by the Progressive movement and eventually were adopted.

THINGS TO REMEMBER

- **Bimetallists:** Grangers, Populists, and agrarian activists of the late 19th century who advocated basing money on silver as well as gold. Also called Free Silverites.

- **Blue laws:** Laws enacted in many states based on religious bans of personal behavior deemed immoral; for example, laws prohibiting the sale of alcohol on Sundays.

- **Free Silverites:** Populists and "Silver Democrats" who in the 1890s argued in favor of an immense increase in silver coinage as a way of stimulating a faltering economy. Also called Bimetallists.

- **laissez-faire:** Government policy of noninterference in business practices and in individuals' economic affairs; literally translated as "to let do."

- **Protective tariff:** A high tax placed on imports; its purpose is to make domestic goods cheaper than foreign goods, thus "protecting" domestic industry.

- **Two-party system:** A political system dominated by two parties. Voters' reluctance to support third parties reinforces the two-party system. The first two-party system, dating back to the 1790s, included the Federalist and Republican Parties. The current two-party system of Democrats and Republicans dates from the Civil War.

REVIEW QUESTIONS

1. The term "spoilsmen" is most appropriately applied to

   (A) politicians who supported civil service reform
   (B) miners who destroyed important natural areas
   (C) generals who profited off of America's victory in the Spanish-American War
   (D) urban "bosses" who received kickbacks from contracts between the government and private firms
   (E) party loyalists who expected jobs in exchange for their political work

2. "Coxey's Army" was

   (A) a disgruntled band of poor farmers and indentured servants in colonial Virginia
   (B) a group of farmers who protested the excise tax on whiskey during Washington's administration
   (C) an African American regiment that fought in the Civil War
   (D) an agrarian protest movement against the government's inaction in the wake of the Panic of 1893
   (E) World War I veterans who marched to Washington, DC, during the depression to demand their bonus payments

3. A major source of farmers' problems in the late 19th century was

   (A) the inability to attain new, mechanized farm equipment
   (B) a declining urban market for their goods
   (C) inflation due to an increase in the money supply
   (D) the unwillingness of the next generation to stay in farming
   (E) overproduction and lowered prices on their crops

4. "Granger laws," passed in several states in the 1870s and 1880s,

   (A) outlawed the sale and consumption of alcohol on a county-by-county basis
   (B) increased the supply of money
   (C) established homesteading on the Great Plains
   (D) regulated rates railroads could charge farmers
   (E) reformed electoral practices

ANSWERS AND EXPLANATIONS

1. E

The term is derived from the war adage, "to the victor goes the spoils." The implication is that the winner of an election is entitled to appoint his men to government positions. The "spoilsmen" were the benefactors of this system. "Spoilsmen" did not want to see the spoils system ended through civil service reform. There is not a common term used to describe miners who cause ecological damage, nor is there evidence of substantial war profiteering following the Spanish-American War. Urban "bosses" and their kickbacks refers to some of the corrupt political machines that ran cities during the Gilded Age, such as Tammany Hall in New York, run by "Boss" Tweed.

2. D

Coxey's army, led by Jacob Coxey, marched on Washington to protest Cleveland's laissez-faire approach to the depression following the Panic of 1893. Most of the other choices refer to other protests in American history. Choice (A) describes Bacon's Rebellion, choice (B) describes the Whiskey Rebellion and choice (E) describes the Bonus March. The most famous African American regiment in the Civil War was the 54th Massachusetts Infantry.

3. E

Ironically, mechanization and the increased yields of American farms in the late 19th century proved to be problematic, as prices fell and farmers were unable to repay the loans they had taken out to buy the new equipment. Farmers often want inflation so that they can more easily pay off loans for farm equipment and land. Farmers were generally able to obtain loans for new farm equipment. The urban market was not on the decline; cities were growing rapidly in the late 19th century. The problem of the next generation's unwillingness to stay in farming has been more pronounced during the 20th century, as many former farming towns have become virtual ghost towns.

4. D

The Grange was a farmers' organization that was very concerned with railroad abuses. Granger Laws were early attempts to move away from a laissez-faire approach to the economy. "Dry laws" or "blue laws" pertained to the outlawing of the consumption of alcohol. The Grangers *did* want an increase in the money supply, but that is not what Granger laws refer to. Great Plains Homesteading is a reference to the Homestead Act of 1862. Reformed electoral practices could refer to a whole host of measures pushed by the Populists and later by the Progressives.

CHAPTER 20

Imperialism, 1880–1914

TIMELINE

1893	Queen Lilioukalani of Hawaii overthrown
1896	William McKinley elected president
1898	Hawaii annexed • United States declares war on Spain • Battle of San Juan Hill forces Spain to surrender
1899	Open Door policy on China adopted
1900	Boxer Rebellion occurs
1901	Theodore Roosevelt assumes presidency
1902	Rebellion in the Philippines is put down by the United States
1903	Panama "revolts" against Columbia • Hay-Bunau-Varilla Treaty negotiated
1904	Roosevelt Corollary to the Monroe Doctrine issued
1914	Panama Canal completed

IMPORTANT PEOPLE, PLACES, EVENTS, AND CONCEPTS

Albert Beveridge	Jose Marti	Rough Riders	Insular Cases
Admiral Alfred T. Mahan	Governor Valeriano "Butcher" Weyler	rebellion in Philippines	spheres of influence
Josiah Strong	yellow journalism	Platt Amendment	Open Door policy
Queen Lilioukalani	de Lome letter	Guantanamo Bay, Cuba	Boxer Rebellion
Sanford Dole	*Maine*		Panama Canal Zone
Spanish-American War	Emilio Aguinaldo	Foraker Act	Roosevelt Corollary
			Anti-Imperialist League

"It seems to me that God, with infinite wisdom and skill, is training the Anglo-Saxon race for an hour sure to come in the world's future . . . There are no more new lands. The unoccupied arable lands are limited and soon will be taken . . . Then will the world enter upon a new stage of its history—the final competition of races, for which the Anglo-Saxon race is being schooled."

–Josiah Strong, *Our Country: Its Possible Future and Its Present Crisis*, 1885

INTRODUCTION

In the years after the Civil War, Americans settled the lands between the Mississippi River and the Pacific Ocean. But toward the end of the century, the United States, as Josiah Strong predicted in the quote above, looked overseas and became an **imperialist** nation. A series of factors led the United States to become imperialist, and a series of issues emerged once the United States gained an empire.

CAUSES OF AMERICAN IMPERIALISM

There are several reasons the United States entered the imperialist race:

- *Industrial development:* As an industrial power, the United States needed raw materials, some of which could not readily be obtained within the country. Also, American industrialists were looking for new markets to which they could export their manufactured goods. **Albert Beveridge**, an Indiana senator, argued for an imperialist policy on economic grounds.

- *Military considerations:* The United States saw itself in competition with European powers. Admiral **Alfred T. Mahan** argued that America needed to expand its military, especially its navy, in order to protect shipping lanes. Mahan specifically urged the government to establish coaling stations throughout the world (such as Hawaii), to establish military bases in the Caribbean, to build a canal through Panama, and to build a modern navy.

- *Social reasons:* Some people, such as **Josiah Strong**, believed in the superiority of the Anglo-Saxons. Implicit in this racist notion was the idea that non-white peoples were incapable of governing themselves. Others felt that the next logical step in fulfilling the nation's manifest destiny was overseas expansion. Some Protestants felt a responsibility to bring their God to those whom they considered heathens. It was also argued that the superiority of the country's democratic institutions required the United States to play a more active role in the world.

- *Pro-imperialist presidents:* The election of 1896 brought the pro-business and expansionist **William McKinley** (Republican) to office. McKinley was assassinated after re-election in 1901. The equally expansionist **Theodore Roosevelt** took office and occupied the White House until 1909; he was followed by fellow Republican and expansionist **William H. Taft**.

THE UNITED STATES AS AN IMPERIALIST POWER

The United States had acquired contiguous territory from the time of the Louisiana Purchase, but it did not look abroad until the 1880s.

Hawaii

One of the first overseas acquisitions of the United States was **Hawaii**. American business interests looked to Hawaii and its sugar crop in the middle of the 19th century. American businessmen played an increasingly important economic, and even political, role on the islands, and in 1887 they pressured the king to give the planters special privileges, including sole voting rights. The next Hawaiian ruler, **Queen Lilioukalani**, challenged the growing power of the planters. The planters rebelled, and the U.S. military intervened on their behalf (1893). In 1898, Hawaii was **annexed** by the United States.

The Spanish-American War

Cuba had been a colony of Spain for centuries. By the 1860s an independence movement had developed, but it failed to achieve its goal. In the meantime, U.S. businesses became interested in Cuban sugar. In 1895, **Jose Marti** again raised the cry of independence. Spain responded with severe measures. Spanish governor Valeriano Weyler placed many people in concentration camps, and many died from harsh conditions.

A number of events led to U.S. participation in the war:

- *Yellow journalism:* **"Butcher" Weyler's** actions were recounted in the daily newspapers in the United States. Sensationalistic **"yellow journalism"** aroused the sympathy of the American public for the Cubans fighting for independence from a

European power. Many Americans recalled the nation's own struggle for independence from Great Britain.

- *The de Lome letter:* A letter written by **Enrique Dubuy de Lôme**, the Spanish minister to the United States, criticized President McKinley for being weak and ineffectual. The letter was intercepted by Cuban rebels and leaked to the press. It angered many Americans.

- *The* Maine *sinks:* An explosion occurred in the Havana harbor, sinking the U.S. battleship *Maine* and killing 260 people. The press and the U.S. government immediately blamed Spain, and vowed revenge. A later investigation showed that the explosion happened from within the ship and was probably an accident.

Despite Spanish concessions, the United States declared war on Spain in 1898. Much of the fighting took place in the Spanish colony of **the Philippines**. Commander **George Dewey** and rebel leader **Emilio Aguinaldo** defeated Spanish troops there. In Cuba, **Theodore Roosevelt** and his **Rough Riders** won the **battle of San Juan Hill** and forced the Spanish to surrender.

The **Treaty of Paris** (1898) stipulated that Cuba would become independent, that **Guam** and **Puerto Rico** would become U.S. possessions, and that the United States would pay Spain $20 million for the Philippines.

Aftermath of the Spanish-American War

The war created a small, yet far-flung, empire for the United States. The country ran into a series of difficulties in governing its possessions, but it emerged as a powerful nation.

- Although the United States fought side-by-side with Filipino rebels during the Spanish-American War, it did not grant the Philippines independence. Many Americans favored granting independence, but McKinley argued that the Philippines was not ready for that responsibility. Emilio Aguinaldo led a fierce **rebellion in the Philippines** against the United States that lasted three years (1899–1901), far longer than the Spanish-American War. After 300,000 Filipino casualties, the rebels capitulated. The Philippines was not granted independence until 1946.

- Cuba received its independence after the Spanish-American war, but the United States insisted that the Cuban constitution contain a provision, the **Platt Amendment**, which gave the United States the right to intervene in Cuban affairs and to maintain a naval base on the island. The amendment compromised Cuba's independence. U.S. troops intervened on three separate occasions when it perceived that its investments were threatened, making Cuba a **protectorate** of the United States. Some historians see these incursions as sources of anti-American feelings that came to the fore when Fidel Castro led a successful revolution in 1959. The United States still maintains a naval base at **Guantanamo Bay**.

- Many Puerto Ricans hoped for independence, and some argued for U.S. statehood, but the American government rejected both. The **Foraker Act** (1900) denied U.S. citizenship to Puerto Ricans, while allowing the president of the United States to appoint Puerto Rico's governor and members of the upper house of the legislature. In the **Insular Cases**, the U.S. Supreme Court ruled that "the Constitution does not follow the flag"—that is, constitutional rights don't necessarily apply to people living in U.S. territories. Over the years, Puerto Rico evolved into its present commonwealth status, wherein Puerto Ricans select their own leaders and have U.S. citizenship rights.

The Open Door Policy in China

With the United States in possession of Hawaii and the Philippines, interest in trading with Asia was strong. **China**, with its vast population and nearly nonexistent industrial capacity, seemed like a logical market for U.S. goods. The major European powers, with similar interests in China, had carved out **spheres of influence** there, wherein a particular country had exclusive trading rights. The United States thought the most productive strategy was to push for all nations to have equal access to China. This became known as the **Open Door policy**. The United States gained some clout in China by helping to suppress the anti-Western **Boxer Rebellion** (1900). The European powers acquiesced to U.S. demands.

The Panama Canal

Under President Theodore Roosevelt, the United States embarked on building a canal across **Panama** to connect the Pacific and Atlantic Oceans. Such a canal would facilitate trade between Asia and the east coast of the United States and would also allow for more rapid deployment of U.S. forces. When Colombia, which controlled Panama at the time, was slow in negotiating with the United States, the United States encouraged a rebellion of Panamanians against Columbia. U.S. warships aided the rebels, and Panama became independent. The new nation quickly negotiated the **Hay-Bunau-Varilla Treaty** with the United States that granted the latter the 10-mile-wide **Canal Zone**. The huge construction project lasted 10 years and cost over 5,000 lives. The **Panama Canal** has greatly increased U.S. power, and was returned to Panama's possession in 1999 as part of a treaty worked out by President Carter in 1977.

The Roosevelt Corollary

Theodore Roosevelt advocated a more active role for the United States in Latin America. Determined to protect U.S. interests and investments, he argued that the United States should "speak softly and carry a big stick." The **Roosevelt Corollary** to the Monroe Doctrine set forth that the United States would not only see European intervention in Latin America as a threat, but it would intervene if U.S. investments were threatened. The nation would, in effect, act as an "international police force" in Latin America.

William H. Taft, Dollar Diplomacy, and Anti-Imperialists

Taft, the Republican who succeeded Roosevelt, continued Roosevelt's interventionist policies (for example, Nicaragua in 1911). Critics of U.S. imperialism used the term **"dollar diplomacy"** to imply that business interests drove U.S. foreign policy. Some Americans, notably novelist **Mark Twain** and politician **Carl Schurz,** questioned America's imperialist policies. The **Anti-Imperialist League** pointed out the racist assumptions in the belief that native peoples could not govern themselves. The league argued that U.S. policy should not function to protect the investments of the wealthy.

SUMMARY

The actions of the United States from the 1890s to the outbreak of World War I established the country as a presence on the international stage. The United States successfully opened new markets to its substantial industrial output. While the country often relied on armed force, like its fellow imperialist powers in Europe, it made an effort to avoid direct control over foreign lands; rather, it attempted to establish a series of relationships that safeguarded U.S. interests. While such actions enhanced the country's power and wealth, they were often met with hostility abroad. Clearly, the policies implemented during this period marked the end of U.S. isolationism.

THINGS TO REMEMBER

- **Annexation:** The process of acquiring new territories.

- **Dollar diplomacy:** Derisive term for U.S. foreign policy in the early 20th century designed to protect the investments of U.S. corporations in Latin America.

- **Imperialism:** A policy of empire building in which a nation conquers other nations with an aim toward increasing its power and controlling those nations. This was a cause of World War I.

- **Protectorate:** A country whose affairs are partly controlled by a stronger country. The United States established several protectorates, such as Cuba, in the 20th century.

REVIEW QUESTIONS

1. The Platt Amendment and the Roosevelt Corollary are similar in that they both

    (A) pushed the Progressive agenda into new areas.

    (B) were welcomed by American anti-imperialists who believed in self-determination for all people.

    (C) led to war with European powers.

    (D) expanded the role of the United States in foreign nations.

    (E) were attacked by critics who argued that the president was assuming too much power.

2. The Spanish-American War is often considered a turning point in U.S. history because it

    (A) helped spark an industrial revolution.

    (B) ushered in a period of isolation from world affairs for the United States.

    (C) made the United States a significant imperialist power.

    (D) led to the formation of the League of Nations.

    (E) ended the period of laissez-faire and led to greater government involvement in economic matters.

3. The Open Door policy

    (A) divided China into spheres of influence.

    (B) allowed for U.S. intervention in Cuban affairs.

    (C) stated that the United States reserves the right to intervene in the affairs of Latin American nations.

    (D) called for free trade with Africa.

    (E) called for equal access to trade with China for all nations.

4. Alfred Mahan is best known in American history for his argument that

    (A) the Philippines should have been granted independence after the Spanish-American War.

    (B) non–Anglo-Saxon peoples are genetically inferior and therefore incapable of self rule.

    (C) the United States should develop its naval power and establish overseas colonies if it hopes to be a world power.

    (D) Jim Crow laws served the interests of both African Americans and whites in that they maintained social order and harmony.

    (E) the power of the industrial giants needed to be reigned in if America were to maintain its democratic government.

ANSWERS AND EXPLANATIONS

1. D

The years just before and just after 1900 marked an increase in U.S. involvement in world affairs. The Platt Amendment was put into the Cuban constitution at the behest of the United States. It stated that the United States reserves the right to intervene in Cuban affairs. The Roosevelt Corollary to the Monroe Doctrine states that this right extends to all the nations of Latin America. The United States has exercised this right both in Cuba and throughout Latin America when it perceives its interests are threatened. Although some Progressives supported U.S. expansion overseas, this was not central to the "Progressive agenda." Further, the undemocratic implications of both the Platt Amendment and the Roosevelt Corollary rankled many Progressives. For similar reasons choice (B) is wrong. These two documents compromised self-determination for Cuba and indeed for all of Latin America. Anti-imperialists would certainly oppose them. The one instance in which Latin American affairs led to war with a European power—the Spanish American War—preceded both the Platt Amendment and the Roosevelt Corollary. Neither raised questions of presidential power; both had congressional approval.

2. C

The United States gained an empire as a result of the Spanish-American War. The United States played a more aggressive role in world affairs after this war. If anything, industrialization was a cause of the war, not a result. The war ushered in a period of increased U.S. intervention in the world, not isolation. World War I, not the Spanish-American War led to the formation of the League of Nations. The U.S. government was never fully separate from the economy, as a true laissez-faire policy would require. Alexander Hamilton was an early advocate of government intervention in the economy. It is true that over time, the level of government intervention has increased. Perhaps the most pronounced expansion of government policies into the economy occurred during the New Deal.

3. E

In the 1800s, the major European powers had divided China into spheres of influence, within which a particular European power would have exclusive trading rights. The United States did not have a sphere of influence, so it proposed that all of China be open to all nations for trade. This is the essence of the Open Door policy. U.S. intervention in Cuban Affairs refers the Platt Amendment and the United States' reserving the right to intervene in the affairs of Latin American countries refers to the Roosevelt Corollary. Free trade with Africa was not a major U.S. government pronouncement.

4. C

Mahan urged the United States to build up its naval strength and to become an imperialist power. He and Josiah Strong are often cited as promoters of U.S. imperialism. An anti-imperialist, such as Carl Schurz or Mark Twain, would have taken the position in choice (A). Choice (B) was an argument made by many Americans, such as Josiah Strong and proponents of social Darwinism. The Democratic Party, more than the Republicans, held the position expressed in choice (D) during the period between Reconstruction and the New Deal. Choice (E) is a position taken by Socialist Eugene V. Debs and muckraker journalists of the Progressive Era.

CHAPTER 21

The Progressive Era, 1900–1920

TIMELINE

1900	Hurricane in Galveston leads to calls for better municipal government
1901	Theodore Roosevelt assumes presidency
1906	Pure Food and Drug Act passed
1908	*Muller v. Oregon* decision
1910	NAACP founded
1911	Triangle Factory fire spurs workplace reforms
1912	Progressive (Bull Moose) Party formed • Woodrow Wilson elected president
1913	16th Amendment ratified • 17th Amendment ratified • Underwood Tariff passed • Federal Reserve Act passed
1914	Federal Trade Commission created • Clayton Antitrust Act passed
1920	19th Amendment ratified, giving women the right to vote

IMPORTANT PEOPLE, PLACES, EVENTS, AND CONCEPTS

John Dewey	recall	"trustbuster"	Federal Trade Commission
Upton Sinclair	17th Amendment	conservation	
Pure Food and Drug Act	19th Amendment	16th Amendment	Clayton Antitrust Act
	Triangle Factory fire	Bull Moose Party	W. E. B. DuBois
Frank Norris	*Muller v. Oregon*	Underwood Tariff	
Florence Kelly	Roosevelt's "Square Deal"	Federal Reserve Act	Booker T. Washington
Robert LaFollette			

"There are—in the body politic, economic, and social—many and grave evils, and there is an urgent necessity for the sternest war upon them. There should be relentless exposure of and attack upon every evil man, whether politician or businessman; every evil practice, whether in politics, in business, or in social life . . . ."

—From a speech by President Theodore Roosevelt, 1906

INTRODUCTION

The United States experienced intense industrialization, rapid urbanization, and the growth of big business during the late 19th century. The labor movement and the populist movement each attempted, with mixed results, to address some of the dislocations and problems caused by these changes. In addition, an assortment of middle class men and women put forth a series of proposals for incremental reforms to improve various aspects of American society. Many reformers approached social ills with the zeal of crusaders, as is exhibited in the above quote from Roosevelt. Though not affiliated with a single group, nor even united by ideology, these reformers and their campaigns together embodied the **Progressive movement**.

BACKGROUND AND INFLUENCES

The Progressive movement can trace its origins to a number of sources. Many Progressive activists were influenced by the philosophical movement associated with **John Dewey** and William James known as **pragmatism**. Dewey, the most important 20th-century American philosopher and education theorist, argued that government actions should be judged by the good they do for society. The Progressive movement also was influenced by the more general trend, especially in the business world, toward greater efficiency. Just as efficiency experts streamlined business operations, they could also propose solutions to some of society's problems. Many Progressives were religious leaders who believed in a **"social gospel"**—that religious institutions should be improving society as well as attending to spiritual matters. Finally, the movement drew inspiration from the **Populist movement** (see chapter 19) and the **Socialist Party** (see chapter 17), heeding the call to address social ills, but rejecting the sweeping changes proposed by these movements.

PROGRESSIVE REFORMERS

Progressive reformers tended to be middle class city dwellers. Many were professional people: doctors, social workers, scientists, and managers.

Muckrakers

Muckrakers were journalists who exposed a variety of problems to the public. Their exposés appeared in magazines such as *Collier's* and *McClure's* as well as in books and novels. Their work often led to reforms. Writers Jacob Riis, Lincoln Steffens, and Ida Tarbell fall into this category. **Upton Sinclair's** fact-based novel, *The Jungle* (1906), graphically described the unsanitary conditions in the meatpacking industry. The novel led to the passage of the **Pure Food and Drug Act** and the **Meat Inspection Act** (both in 1906). **Frank Norris's** *The Octopus* (1901) described the power of the railroads over the farmers of the West.

Women

Women were active in the Progressive movement for two main reasons. First, many women were discontented with laws and practices that discriminated against them. Second, women were rising in status as educational opportunities opened for them, yet they were denied the right to participate in the electoral system. The Progressive movement was an avenue for women to participate in public issues. **Florence Kelly**, who had lived in Hull House, was instrumental in pushing for improved factory conditions in Illinois.

PROGRESSIVE ISSUES

Better Government

Progressives worked on making government on all levels more efficient and more democratic.

City government: The origins of the push for municipal government reform can be traced to the aftermath of a hurricane in Galveston, Texas, in 1900. After the local **political machine** proved incapable of dealing with the disaster, there were calls for a more efficient and professional form of city government. First in Galveston and then elsewhere, political machines were replaced with nonpartisan **commissioners** who were selected to run the various city departments (such as sanitation, fire, water, or parks). Also, many cities replaced their mayor with a **city manager** hired by the city council.

State government: The campaign to reform state government started in Wisconsin and was initiated by **Robert LaFollette**, a Progressive who was elected governor on the Republican ticket in 1900. The reforms he initiated were imitated in many states, and were intended to take power away from entrenched political machines and put it into the hands of the citizenry. The **direct primary** allowed people, instead of parties, to decide who the candidates would be for general elections. The **initiative** allowed citizens to introduce legislation by gaining a certain number of signatures. The **referendum** allowed citizens to directly enact pieces of legislation through voting on ballot questions. Finally, the **recall** allowed citizens to cut short a politician's term by calling for a special election.

National government: The Progressives helped to push through the **17th Amendment** (ratified in 1913), which took the election of senators out of the hands of state legislatures and put it into the hands of the people.

Women's suffrage: Progressives joined the women's suffrage movement, which had been agitating for extending voting privileges to women since at least the Seneca Falls Conference (1848). The first successes were in Western states. By 1914, 11 states had given women the right to vote. The **19th Amendment**, which gave all women the right to vote, was ratified in 1920.

Consumer Protection

The Pure Food and Drug Act and the Meat Inspection Act were just two of the numerous measures designed to protect consumers from unscrupulous or dangerous business practices. America moved away from the adage, *caveat emptor* ("let the buyer beware"). New laws, some state and some federal, called for truthful labeling of food and drugs, regulation of the insurance industry and stricter building codes.

Protecting Workers

The publication of Upton Sinclair's *The Jungle* highlighted the unsafe conditions in many factories. Progressives pressed many states to pass workers' compensation laws, which provided money to workers injured in industrial accidents. States also passed laws limiting work hours, calling for factory inspections, and creating more sanitary conditions.

The worst industrial accident in American history occurred in 1911 when 146 garment workers died in a fire at the Triangle Shirtwaist Company in New York City. The owners had locked most of the doors to keep the workers in and union organizers out. The event galvanized the labor movement, leading to public protests and an investigation by New York State that led to stricter fire codes, a shorter work week for women and minors, and the abolition of labor for those under the age of 14.

Progressive reformers paid special attention to addressing workplace issues relating to women and children, two groups seen as especially vulnerable to exploitation. An Oregon law limiting women to a 10-hour workday was challenged in the courts by employers. The Supreme Court upheld the law in *Muller v. Oregon*, thus setting a precedent of the Supreme Court using its power for social reform. John Spago's book, *The Bitter Cry of Children*, drew attention to the issue of child labor. By 1914, most states had enacted minimum age laws for the workplace.

PROGRESSIVE PRESIDENTS

Presidents **Theodore Roosevelt** (Republican, 1901–1909) and **Woodrow Wilson** (Democrat, 1913–1921) both enacted reforms that many Progressives had been pushing for. To a lesser degree, William H. Taft (Republican, 1909–1913) also was influenced by the Progressive movement.

The Roosevelt Administration

Theodore Roosevelt called his agenda the "**Square Deal**"—a belief in equal opportunity and adherence to the spirit of the law.

Roosevelt is known as the "**trustbuster**" for the enthusiasm with which he went after conglomerates using the Sherman Antitrust Act. He targeted "bad" (corrupt or unethical) trusts, such as Northern Securities Company, a railroad company. He also successfully pushed for passage of the **Hepburn Act** (1906), which strengthened the Interstate Commerce Commission of 1887.

Roosevelt's other main area of activity was **conservation**: protecting the environment. An outdoorsman, Roosevelt tripled the amount of land set aside for national forests, created the **National Conservation Committee**, and publicized the conservationist cause.

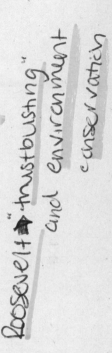

Roosevelt "trustbusting" and environment conservation

The Taft Administration

Though Taft was selected by Roosevelt to be his successor (Taft had been his secretary of war), he was more conservative than his predecessor. Taft's conservatism was evident in the controversy over tariffs. Progressives had been pushing for lower tariffs to benefit consumers, while conservatives generally supported higher tariffs to protect American industry from competition. The **Payne-Aldrich Tariff** was a compromise measure, barely lowering tariffs, yet Taft signed it. The **16th Amendment**, ratified during Taft's administration, allowed for the federal income tax.

The Election of 1912

Tensions within the Republican Party became evident during the election of 1912. Roosevelt and fellow Progressive Republicans were dissatisfied with Taft's conservatism. When Roosevelt was defeated by Taft for the Republican nomination, he and his allies formed the Progressive Party, also known as the **Bull Moose Party.** The Bull Moose Party embraced much of the Progressive agenda, but was unable to run a successful campaign. As a result of the division in the Republican Party, the Democratic candidate Woodrow Wilson won the election.

The Wilson Administration

Only the second Democrat to be elected president since the Civil War, Woodrow Wilson, while perhaps best known for his role in the peace following World War I, was also instrumental in several important Progressive-era reforms. Wilson's drive to lower the tariff succeeded with the **Underwood Tariff** (1913). He argued that lower tariffs would increase trade and force businesses to be more efficient and competitive. Probably Wilson's most significant domestic initiative, the **Federal Reserve Act** (1913) was meant to address four weaknesses in the American banking system: the lack of a flexible currency, the lack of stability in times of crisis (periodic "panics"), the lack of central control over banking practices, and the concentration of financial power in New York City. The **Federal Reserve Bank**, created by the act, was able to regulate the money supply through a series of financial mechanisms. As a result of this act, 12 districts were created, each with a branch of the "Fed," throughout the country. The **Federal Trade Commission** (1914) was created to investigate dishonest and unscrupulous business practices. It has the power to order companies to halt such practices. The **Clayton Antitrust Act** (1914) attempted to provide the government with a tool to challenge monopolistic practices, and was stronger than the Sherman Antitrust Act. The act was welcomed by organized labor because it specifically stated that it shall not be used "to forbid the existence and operation of labor . . . organizations," as the Sherman Act did.

AFRICAN AMERICANS IN THE PROGRESSIVE ERA

Progressives largely did not address one of the most serious areas of injustice in America at the time—discrimination against African Americans. With the support of the *Plessy v. Ferguson* decision (1896), most Southern states had Jim Crow segregation laws. An early significant feature film, D. W. Griffith's ***Birth of a Nation*** (1915), was a racist depiction of Reconstruction that glorified the Ku Klux Klan. President Wilson especially disappointed African American leaders when he segregated government offices. Two leading African American activists proposed divergent solutions to these problems. **W. E. B. DuBois** helped found the **NAACP** (National Association for the Advancement of Colored People) in 1910. He argued that African Americans should press for an immediate end to segregation and for economic and political justice. He urged that African American intellectuals, the "talented tenth," to take the lead in the struggle. **Booker T. Washington** was seen as more of an accommodationist. He argued that rather than challenge the status quo, African Americans should seek to improve their individual lot through hard work and job training.

SUMMARY

The Progressive era established a more activist government, ending the more hands-off approach that typified 19th-century policies. The agenda of the Progressive movement was not hostile to business; in fact, many felt that eliminating the abusive practices of business would restore people's faith in the free market system. The movement helped make the political process more open and democratic. Some aspects of the Progressive agenda became part of the New Deal in the 1930s.

THINGS TO REMEMBER

- **Direct primary:** Early 20th-century election reform that allowed citizens rather than political machines to choose candidates for public office.

- **Initiative:** Progressive political reform in the early 1900s that enabled voters to introduce legislation.

- **Muckrakers:** Journalists of the Progressive era who exposed urban poverty, unsafe working conditions, political corruption, and other social ills.

- **Pragmatism:** Philosophical movement, with deep roots in the United States, which holds that truth emerges from experimentation and experience rather than from abstract theory; it is associated with William James and John Dewey.

- **Progressive movement:** Middle class reform movement of the first decades of the 20th century that sought to widen political participation, eradicate corruption, and apply scientific and technological expertise to social ills.

- **Referendum:** Progressive-era reform that created a mechanism for voters to approve or reject legislation placed on the ballot. It was designed to weaken the power of entrenched political machines.

REVIEW QUESTIONS

1. The devastation caused by a hurricane and flood in Galveston, Texas, in 1900 led to calls for

   (A) the replacement of political machines with more efficient and professional forms of municipal government
   (B) federal projects to divert rivers and build levees
   (C) people to abandon seaside cities and move to higher elevations
   (D) a federal income tax
   (E) a religious reawakening to allay fears of divine punishment

2. The Progressive movement could most accurately be described as a

   (A) working class response to low wages and long hours
   (B) conservative reaction to immigration
   (C) middle class response to urbanization and industrialization
   (D) rural response to falling farm prices and powerful banks
   (E) Southern response to the power of Northern politicians

3. Theodore Roosevelt used his position as president to

   (A) push for measures to protect the environment
   (B) advance a socialist agenda
   (C) reform the banking system
   (D) convince Americans to join World War I
   (E) argue for a strict interpretation of the Constitution

4. The passage of the Federal Reserve Act was important because it

   (A) made up for revenue lost by the Underwood Tariff
   (B) centralized financial power in one city—New York
   (C) allowed the president to set interest rates
   (D) created a mechanism to regulate the money supply
   (E) nationalized banks in the United States

ANSWERS AND EXPLANATIONS

1. A

The political machine in Galveston was unable to deal with the crisis at hand, and many reformers saw this as evidence that these machines had outlived their usefulness. Calls for federal projects (B) are associated with the New Deal. Abandoning seaside communities (C) never occurred in any significant way. A federal income tax (D) was instituted in 1913 with the passage of the 16th Amendment after protectionist tariffs were reduced. A religious awakening (E) did not occur as a result of the hurricane.

2. C

The movement was inspired and guided by middle class teachers, doctors, social workers, and other professionals. Choice A could describe the labor movement or the Communist or Socialist parties. The most extreme reactions to immigration were seen in the Know-Nothing Party of the 1850s and the Ku Klux Klan of the 1920s. Choice (D) describes the Populist movement.

3. A

Theodore Roosevelt is known for championing environmental conservation. He helped bring thousands of acres under federal jurisdiction. No president advanced a socialist agenda (B), although President Franklin Roosevelt was accused by conservatives of doing so. President Wilson, not Theodore Roosevelt, reformed the banking system (C) with the Federal Reserve Act and argued for U.S. intervention in World War I (D). A strict interpretation of the Constitution (E) is most closely associated with President Jefferson.

4. D

The main purpose of the Federal Reserve Bank (the Fed) is to regulate the money supply, primarily by raising or lowering its interest rate for loaning money. The federal income tax made up for revenue lost by tariffs. The Federal Reserve Act was also designed to decentralize financial power, making (B) incorrect. The president appoints the head of the Fed, but cannot set interest rates or manipulate the bank himself, making (C) wrong. And banks have never been nationalized in the United States (E).

CHAPTER 22

The United States and World War I, 1914–1920

TIMELINE

1914	Archduke Ferdinand of Austria assassinated • War in Europe begins
1915	*Lusitania* sinks • *Arabic* sinks
1916	Germans attack the *Sussex* • *Sussex* Pledge accepted
1917	Germany announces the resumption of unrestricted submarine warfare • Zimmermann Note intercepted • United States enters World War I • Wilson writes Fourteen Points
1918	Germany and the Allies sign armistice
1919	Treaty of Versailles signed, ending World War I
1920	United States rejects Treaty of Versailles • League of Nations formed
1921	United States signs separate peace with Germany

IMPORTANT PEOPLE, PLACES, EVENTS, AND CONCEPTS

Triple Entente

Triple Alliance

Archduke Franz
Ferdinand

U-boat

Kaiser Wilhelm II

Lusitania

Arabic

Sussex Pledge

Woodrow Wilson

Zimmermann Note

Bolsheviks

Vladimir Lenin

liberty bonds

Committee of
Public Information

Civilian Council of
National Defense

War Industries
Board

National War Labor
Board

Food
Administration

propaganda

Espionage and
Sedition Acts

*Schenck v. United
States*

Oliver Wendell
Holmes

Admiral Sims

General John
Pershing

Fourteen Points

League of Nations

Article X

Treaty of Versailles

reparations

Henry Cabot Lodge

"It is a war against all nations. . . . The challenge is to all mankind . . . Our
motives will not be revenge of the victorious assertion of the physical might of
the nation, but only the vindication of right, of human right of which we are only
a single champion."

–President Woodrow Wilson, April 2, 1917

INTRODUCTION

The war message of Woodrow Wilson was idealistic in its themes and set the tone for the U.S.
involvement in World War I. At the peace table, the allied nations viewed President Wilson
with suspicion. His attempt to establish an international organization to prevent future wars
was met with resistance by the American people, indicating the people's fear of war and their
desire to remain isolated in the aftermath of World War I. In the end, the failure of the
country, and the world, to heed Wilson's advice contributed to the rise of Hitler and a much
greater conflagration.

THE WORLD AT WAR

Years of suspicion and competition among the European nations for colonies and markets
ultimately led to the outbreak of World War I. The rise of **nationalism**—and **imperialism**—
in Europe stirred anger and hostility among the countries. In addition, a system of **alliances**
had formed. The **Triple Entente (Allies)** consisted of England, France, and Russia; Germany,
Austria-Hungary, and Italy made up the **Triple Alliance (Central Powers)**. Finally, an
increasing **militarism**, caused by the desire to dominate trade and protect trading routes,
spurred a great arms race and provided the equipment necessary to conduct a war.

The spark that ignited the powder keg that had been growing through the years came in the form of a political assassination. In June 1914, **Archduke Franz Ferdinand** (the heir to the Austrian Empire) and his wife were killed in Sarajevo, a province of Bosnia, by Gavrilo Princip, a member of a Serbian nationalist society known as the Black Hand. Austria-Hungary responded by declaring war on Serbia. Since Serbia was an ally of Russia, the Russians sent troops to help Serbia. Germany then declared war on France, Russia's ally. Great Britain, an ally of France, declared war on Germany. World War I had begun.

THE UNITED STATES REMAINS NEUTRAL

World War I differed from previous wars in that new technology was implemented. The Germans had perfected the **U-boat**. When Great Britain established a blockade along the German coast, **Kaiser Wilhelm II** of Germany announced that any ships carrying goods to Great Britain would be sunk. In 1915, a German submarine sank the British liner the *Lusitania,* which the Germans believed was carrying contraband goods. More than 100 Americans died in this attack. Three months later, the Germans sank another British ship, the *Arabic.* The United States protested, and Germany agreed not to sink any more liners without warning. However, in March of 1916, the Germans attacked the *Sussex*, a French passenger ship with Americans on board. Germany agreed to the **Sussex Pledge**, which provided that no more attacks would take place on unarmed vessels—but only if the United States could persuade Britain to lift the blockade.

The British intercepted a telegram from German Foreign Minister Arthur Zimmermann to the government of Mexico that encouraged an alliance between the two countries. Germany pledged to support Mexico in regaining control of Texas, New Mexico, and Arizona. This **Zimmermann Note**, published in newspapers in March of 1917, further pushed the United States toward war with Germany.

In an attempt to gain world support against the Germans, Wilson encouraged a negotiated peace settlement that included provisions for establishing a world organization to maintain and support peace, disarmament, and democracy. However, in March of 1917, the kaiser announced the resumption of unrestricted submarine warfare. Wilson knew that U.S. participation in this war was inevitable. Wilson wished to defeat the Germans and make "the world safe for democracy." On April 2, 1917, the United States entered World War I.

In November of 1917, the Russian Bolsheviks, under the leadership of Vladimir Lenin, overthrew the czar. The Russians eventually withdrew from the war and signed a separate peace with Germany.

"OVER THERE": THE UNITED STATES AT WAR

Preparation for the war was fast and furious. To finance the war, liberty bonds were issued. A **Committee of Public Information** was organized and a **Civilian Council of National Defense** was established. In 1917, the **War Industries Board** was established under the leadership of **Bernard Baruch** to convert industry to wartime production. Women left their traditional roles at home to work in industry. In 1918, the **National War Labor Board**, headed by former President William Taft, was established to deal with labor disputes. The **Food Administration**, headed by Herbert Hoover, helped to regulate food supply for the troops by encouraging people to give up certain items. A **Fuel Administration** was also organized to deal with energy demands by allocating scarce supplies of coal. The **propaganda** machine kicked into gear, encouraging men to enlist in the military.

In 1917 and 1918, the **Espionage and Sedition Acts** were passed, which fined or jailed people who interfered with the draft, or with the sale of government bonds. It also provided for the punishment of people who were disloyal or spoke out against the war effort. This act led to a Supreme Court case that would establish the doctrine of "clear and present danger"—*Schenck v. United States* (1919). Charles Schenck, the general secretary of the Socialist Party, distributed leaflets in front of an army recruiting station in an attempt to discourage men from entering the military. Schenck claimed that he had the right to do this because he was protected by the 1st Amendment right to free speech. Supreme Court Justice **Oliver Wendell Holmes** disagreed. The Court upheld the conviction of Schenck under the Espionage Act of 1917, stating that "When a nation is at war many things that might be said in time of peace . . . will not be endured."

Songs such as George M. Cohan's "Over There" inspired Americans as they ventured to make "the world safe for democracy." However, they were sorely disappointed when the hardships of war affected their lives. The number of American lives lost may have been small compared to the losses of the other participating countries, but it nevertheless greatly impacted the view of the American people toward participation in future wars.

America's help in the war effort turned the tide of victory in favor of the Allies. Under the leadership of **Admiral Sims** at sea and **General John Pershing** on land, the Allies were victorious, most notably at battles in Chateau-Thierry, Belleau Wood, and Reims. The United States also participated in air battles, a new phenomenon in warfare.

On November 11, 1918, an **armistice** (truce) was signed between the Germans and the Allies. World War I had ended.

WILSON, PEACE, AND THE LEAGUE OF NATIONS

In addition to suffering a tremendous loss of life, the European nations had been destroyed physically. They sought revenge against Germany for its aggression. In contrast, the United States had been little touched by the war, except for the U.S. casualties. This difference affected the peace negotiations that took place in Versailles, France in 1918.

In January of 1918, before World War I ended, Wilson announced his vision for peace. His **Fourteen Points** centered on preventing future wars by examining the actions that had caused World War I. Wilson proposed:

- The end of secret alliances
- Freedom of the seas
- Establishment of equality in trade
- Arms reduction
- Self-determination for nations
- The return of Alsace-Lorraine to France
- The establishment of a **League of Nations** as a general association to deal with world problems before these problems led to war

Wilson himself attended the peace conference, attempting to convince Italy, France, and Great Britain to accept his Fourteen Points. Instead, the Allies wanted revenge against the Germans and accepted only a few of the Fourteen Points, including **Article X**, which called for the League of Nations to be established. Wilson was disappointed. As a result of the **Treaty of Versailles**, signed on June 28, 1919, nine new nations were created, and the boundaries of other nations changed. The British and French were given temporary **mandates** (colonies) over Turkish areas until they were ready for self-rule. Germany was stripped of its army and required to pay **reparations**, or war damages, to the Allied nations. Germany was held completely responsible for the war.

When Wilson returned to the United States, the Senate, led by **Henry Cabot Lodge**, a Republican from Massachusetts, rejected the treaty. They objected to Article X, fearful that membership in the League of Nations would lead the country into another war. Wilson refused to compromise and took his case (unsuccessfully) to the American people. Although Congress, at the urging of Wilson, defeated a number of amendments or **reservations** that Lodge had added to the treaty, the Senate failed to ratify it with the necessary two-thirds votes. Wilson's unwillingness to compromise had defeated the Treaty of Versailles. The United States signed a separate peace with Germany in 1921 and never participated in the League of Nations.

SUMMARY

Wilson's failure to gain approval for the Treaty of Versailles undermined any positive effects the League of Nations might have had. The harshness of the treaty placed Germany in an economic depression that led to a depression in Europe and the Great Depression in the United States in 1929. It also created a fertile breeding ground for Adolf Hitler and his supporters. Wilson's desire to participate in a "war to end all wars" was not accomplished.

THINGS TO REMEMBER

- **Alliances:** A grouping of nations where each one pledges mutual support to the others. This support is usually defensive in nature. The formation of alliances was an underlying cause of World War I.

- **Imperialism:** A policy of empire building in which a nation conquers other nations or territories with the goal of increasing its power and expanding the area it controls. This was a cause of World War I.

- **Militarism:** The development of large military forces, not only for defense of the nation, but for possible aggression into other nations. It was one of the causes of World War I.

- **Nationalism:** A strong feeling of pride in and devotion to one's nation. For people under the control of a foreign power, nationalism is expressed as a desire that one's nation should become a free and independent country. For people who already live in an independent country, it is expressed as a belief that one's nation should be made greater and more powerful. Nationalism contributed to the problems that led to World War I.

REVIEW QUESTIONS

1. All of the following led to World War I EXCEPT:

    (A) the rise of capitalism
    (B) the formation of alliances
    (C) imperialism
    (D) the desire for self-determination among nations
    (E) extreme nationalism

2. The immediate cause of the United States' entrance into World War I was the

    (A) assassination of Archduke Franz Ferdinand of Austria
    (B) announcement by Germany of the use of unrestricted submarine warfare
    (C) sinking of the *Lusitania*
    (D) Zimmermann Note
    (E) attack on Pearl Harbor, Hawaii

3. Woodrow Wilson's Fourteen Points, written in 1918, aimed to

    (A) guarantee that all people live under a democracy
    (B) spread the United States' influence in the world
    (C) shift United States policy from isolation to involvement
    (D) establish a peacekeeping force in Europe
    (E) prevent future wars by rectifying the causes of World War I

4. Henry Cabot Lodge objected to the League of Nations on the grounds that it

    (A) violated the Constitution
    (B) might lead the United States into future wars
    (C) was too idealistic to be workable
    (D) was to be located outside of the United States
    (E) violated the principals of self-determination

ANSWERS AND EXPLANATIONS

1. A

The rise of capitalism, an economic system based on free enterprise and competition, was not a cause of World War I. Answer choices (B), (C), (D), and (E) were all causes of World War I. The rise of militarism was the other main cause of World War I.

2. B

Germany announced that it would resume unrestricted submarine warfare and violate the Sussex Pledge, which was the immediate reason for the United States' entry into World War I. The assassination of Archduke Franz Ferdinand of Austria by a Serbian nationalist was the immediate cause of World War I in Europe, but not the reason the United States entered the war. The sinking of the *Lusitania* occurred in 1915 and some Americans were killed. However, the United States didn't declare war until 1917. The Zimmermann Note was intercepted in 1917 but was not the immediate cause of the United States' entry into the war; the issue of freedom of the seas and submarine warfare was. The attack on Pearl Harbor, Hawaii was the immediate cause of the United States' entry into World War II.

3. E

Wilson's Fourteen Points examined the causes of World War I with the hope of preventing future wars. Wilson desired to maintain peace with the principals of his Fourteen Points. Although Wilson would have loved to see democracy everywhere in the world, the principal of self determination was set forth, allowing nations to choose their own government. The United States was not interested in using its influence around the world to bring great changes. The people of the United States were still basically isolationists. It desired to remain isolationist, as evidenced by the rejection of the League of Nations and the Treaty of Versailles. There was no talk of maintaining peacekeeping forces in Europe.

4. B

Lodge objected to Article X in the Treaty of Versailles, which established the League of Nations. He felt that the United States' participation in the League of Nations would lead the United States into war again. There was no Constitutional argument against the League. Although some considered Wilson idealistic (C), this was not Lodge's criticism of the League of Nations. Location of the League was not an issue, and the League was not imposing government on any nations, and therefore was not a violation of self determination.

CHAPTER 23

Tradition and Change in the 1920s

TIMELINE

1913	Henry Ford introduces the assembly line at his automobile plant
1915	Modern Ku Klux Klan founded
1919	18th Amendment ratified • Strike wave breaks out
1920	Warren G. Harding elected president
1921	Washington Naval Conference called • Emergency Quota Act passed
1922	Fordney-McCumber Tariff passed
1923	Calvin Coolidge assumes presidency
1924	Teapot Dome scandal occurs • Dawns Plan enacted
1925	Scopes trial takes place
1927	*The Jazz Singer*, first "talkie" movie, opens • McNary-Haugen bill vetoed by Coolidge • Sacco and Vanzetti executed • Lindbergh makes trans-Atlantic flight
1928	Herbert Hoover elected president • Kellogg-Briand Pact signed
1933	21st Amendment ratified; 18th Amendment repealed

IMPORTANT PEOPLE, PLACES, EVENTS, AND CONCEPTS

Margaret Sanger

F. Scott Fitzgerald

"return to normalcy"

Washington Naval Conference

Teapot Dome scandal

Dawes Plan

Eugene V. Debs

Kellogg-Briand Pact

Sinclair Lewis

welfare capitalism

Henry Ford

Model T

buying on credit

flappers

Great Migration

Red Scare

Palmer raids

nativism

Emergency Quota Act

National Origins Act

Sacco and Vanzetti trial

"100 percent Americanism"

Herbert Hoover

Calvin Coolidge

Robert LaFollette

Warren Harding

Prohibition

Scopes trial

Ku Klux Klan

Babe Ruth

Charles Lindbergh

"Lost Generation" writers

Harlem Renaissance

"It was the best of the nationally advertised and quantitatively produced alarm clocks, with all modern attachments, including cathedral chime, intermittent alarm, and a phosphorescent dial. Babbitt was proud of being awakened by such a rich device . . . ."

"He sulkily admitted that there was no more escape, but he lay and detested the grind of the real-estate business, and disliked his family, and disliked himself for disliking them."

—from *Babbitt* by Sinclair Lewis, 1922

INTRODUCTION

The United States moved in different directions in the 1920s. Great changes were afoot: technological innovations, the immigration of Eastern and Southern Europeans, the growing importance of cities, the migration of African Americans from the rural South to the urban North, changing gender roles, changing standards of moral behavior—all these created an America very different from its 19th century counterpart. At the same time, traditional ways of seeing the world and conservative politics were reasserted in the 1920s with new enthusiasm. These tensions are evident in the excerpt above from **Sinclair Lewis's** *Babbitt* as well as in a number of social and political issues which have come to define the era.

POLITICS: THE RETURN TO NORMALCY

In his campaign for the presidency in 1920, Republican nominee **Warren Harding** promised a **"return to normalcy."** This was both a rejection of the activist government of the Progressive era and a call to isolate America from war- and revolution-torn Europe. The Republicans controlled the White House from Harding's victory in 1920 until Herbert Hoover's defeat in 1932.

The Harding Administration

The Harding Administration is best known for its policy of **isolationism**, its ties with big business, and its scandals. Harding handily defeated the Democratic candidate in the election of 1920. Socialist candidate Eugene V. Debs, running from prison (where he was sent for an Espionage Act conviction), received a little over 900,000 votes. Harding argued against President Wilson's Progressive domestic agenda. In 1921, the United States called the **Washington Naval Conference** of major powers with interests in Asia (excluding communist Russia). The United States, Great Britain, Japan, France, and Italy agreed to scrap a percentage of their existing battleships, cruisers, and aircraft carriers. Fearing a flood of goods from a revived postwar Europe, Congress passed the **Fordney-McCumber Tariff** (1922), which raised tariff rates. This tariff act, which was especially high on agricultural goods, is seen as an expression of America's desire to isolate itself from Europe.

The Harding administration was embroiled in a number of scandals. The most notorious was the **Teapot Dome scandal** (1921–1923). It involved bribery and the transfer of rights to precious oil reserves at Teapot Dome, Wyoming. The whole affair, when made public, demonstrated the administration's shaky ethical foundation, as well as its pro-business slant, although Harding himself was not personally involved.

The Coolidge Administration

President Harding died, apparently from a heart attack, in 1923; Vice President **Calvin Coolidge** finished the term. In the election of 1924, the Democratic Party was divided at its 1924 convention between its Eastern wing, which was in favor of repealing Prohibition and condemning the Ku Klux Klan, and its more fundamentalist conservative Western/Southern wing. The party settled for an unknown conservative as its standard bearer. Meanwhile, a new Progressive Party saw an opening, with the major parties putting forth relatively conservative platforms, and ran **Robert LaFollette** from Wisconsin again. Though LaFollette received an impressive five million votes, Coolidge won the election handily.

Coolidge's conservative *laissez-faire*, pro-business approach to governing was evident in a number of actions. The president, who proclaimed that "the chief business of the American people is business," twice vetoed (in 1927 and 1928) the **McNary-Haugen Bill**, which would have provided price supports to struggling farmers, an idea that would gain currency during the New Deal.

Perhaps the most contentious foreign relations problem the country faced in the 1920s was international debt. The United States had loaned England and France about $10 billion during World War I. The Europeans, in a precarious economic situation, resented U.S. insistence on payments. Americans, on the other hand, expected repayment as a matter of course. Complicating the situation was Germany's inability to pay reparations to England and France. The **Dawes Plan** (1924) was the U.S. plan to provide loans to Germany so it could stabilize its currency and continue its reparations payments, which, in turn, would enable England and France to pay off loans to America. This cycle of money transfers benefited U.S. banking interests.

The Kellogg-Briand Pact (1928) outlawed war, but it was little more than a statement of intent with no powers of enforcement. The pact, along with the Washington Naval Conference, reflected the naïve hope that America could avoid international entanglements through dramatic gestures and good intentions.

The Election of Herbert Hoover (1928)

The campaign in 1928 again reflected many of the tensions evident in 1920s American society. The Democrats ran New York Governor Alfred Smith, but his thick New York accent and Catholicism may have alienated some Americans, who could hear the presidential candidates on the radio for the first time. Republican **Herbert Hoover's** call for "a chicken in every pot" tapped into the seeming prosperity of the decade and contributed to his victory.

ECONOMIC CONDITIONS

The **"Roaring Twenties"** were characterized by a seemingly strong economy. After a brief recession following World War I (1919–1922), the economy recovered and grew, remaining strong until the stock market crash of 1929. The growth of the economy was based on increases in efficiency, manufacturing output, and consumption. The government made a point of keeping taxes down, foreign goods out, and profits up. The stock market soared, but few seemed to notice signs of danger, such as increased consumer debt and a struggling agricultural sector.

Increasing Production

America became the world's leading manufacturer in the 1920s. Big business succeeded thanks to a weak union movement, an increase in efficiency, and a vital consumer sector.

In 1919, immediately following World War I, American workers, who had been forbidden to strike during the war, launched one of the largest strike waves in U.S. history, with over 4 million workers participating in over 3000 strikes. The most significant incidents were the **Seattle general strike** and the **Boston police strike**. After 1919, union membership declined as employers pushed for **open shops** (nonunion workplaces). To head off efforts at unionization, employers used paternalistic techniques that became known as "welfare capitalism." Such efforts included safety programs and medical insurance. Organized labor would not rebound until the New Deal.

An industry buzzword in the 1920s was "efficiency." **Efficiency** experts saw traditional methods of production, especially those based on craft knowledge, as hopelessly outdated, and attempted to remake the shop floor. These experts were inspired by the work of **Frederick Winslow Taylor**, who developed the field of scientific management (Taylorism). Time and motion studies using stopwatches were employed to increase efficiency.

The Automobile

The advent of the automobile had a huge impact on American society and the man most responsible for bringing the automobile to the masses was **Henry Ford**. Ford had revolutionized the production process by introducing an **assembly line** at his Highland Park, Michigan plant in 1913. While the pace of work, now determined by the speed of the conveyor belt rather than of the workers, could be exhausting, and the work itself could be repetitive and mind-numbing, production rates soared. Ford implemented a $5 a day wage— then a considerable sum—for loyal workers to cut down on attrition. The end product was the Model T Ford, and each year the Model T was exactly the same, down to the color (black). General Motors improved on Ford's ideas and began introducing different colors in 1925. Ford belatedly followed suit, introducing his Model A in a variety of colors in 1927.

The impact of the automobile on American society was staggering. Development patterns changed, as people no longer had to live near an urban core or a suburban train station. The car brought greater independence to women and young people, and reduced the sense of isolation for rural families. Automobiles became a status symbol and a symbol of the success of American industry. In the 1920s over 80 percent of the world's automobiles were in the United States. It was the auto industry that led the overall growth of the American economy in the 1920s.

Consumerism

The economic growth of the 1920s was largely driven by consumer spending. Electricity became widely available: About two-thirds of homes had electricity by the close of the '20s. Many electric appliances were introduced or popularized during the decade, including the vacuum cleaner, toaster, refrigerator, washing machine, and radio.

Developed in tandem with new consumer products was a more sophisticated and widespread **advertising** industry. Tapping into Freudian psychology and a general sense of unease in a changing world, ads went beyond a simple description of a product. New products, advertising assured, could help one find a mate or keep friends. Doctors and other experts in ads assured the public that a particular product was essential. Not having the right product could entail being ridiculed or being seen as behind the times.

To facilitate spending, **consumer credit** was greatly expanded. **Installment plans** allowed people to put some money down and pay the rest, with interest, later. Some saw the increased use of credit as symptomatic of careless spending and indicative of a superficial prosperity.

Expansion of Big Business

The trend toward greater consolidation in business that was evident in the late 1800s continued into the 1920s. Oligopolies of a few large corporations controlled most major industries, such as the automobile industry. Corporations raised most of their money through the sale of stocks and bonds. Consequently, the demand for corporate loans decreased. Banks, therefore, invested their funds in the stock market. The dangers of this strategy became evident when the market crashed in 1929.

Agriculture

Farmers suffered a series of setbacks in the 1920s that prevented them from sharing in the prosperity of the decade. As Europe recovered from World War I, the overseas market for U.S. agricultural products dried up. Further, farmers had difficulty repaying loans they had taken out to mechanize their farms. President Coolidge twice vetoed legislation intended to help farmers.

SOCIETY IN THE 1920s

The automobile, the increased availability of electricity, and other technological advances dramatically changed America. Also important were several social trends that are often associated with the move toward modernity.

Changing Expectations for Women

The **19th Amendment** (ratified in 1920), which gave women the right to vote, did not create profound changes in the political climate, as women did not vote as a block. But the right to vote was one of a host of changes in the 1920s which had the overall effect of opening doors and expanding acceptable modes of behavior for women. Women had more opportunities for asserting their independence in the 1920s. More women entered the workforce than previously had, gravitating toward "women's professions" such as office work, teaching, and social work. Marriage was increasingly based on the choice of the two people involved rather than of their families, and more liberal divorce laws permitted women to end marriages more easily. Also, women could achieve a greater degree of sexual liberation as birth control became more readily available. Fashions were less constricting as well. Gone was the Victorian matronly style of petticoats and corsets, to be replaced by the more youthful and rebellious ideal of the **"flapper."** This ideal valued shorter, even boyish, hair, waistless dresses cut above the knee, and a degree of self-assuredness. Flappers, more likely to be found in urban settings, even began smoking and drinking in public.

The Great Migration

Production in war-related industries expanded during World War I, but new workers were hard to find. Immigration from Europe dried up during the war, and when the United States entered the war, many young men entered the army. As a result, half a million African Americans made the move from the rural South to the urban North in the 1910s. This **Great Migration** continued in the 1920s; by the end of the decade about 40 percent of America's 12 million African Americans lived in cities. This migration was also fueled by such "push" factors as Jim Crow discrimination and low-paying jobs in the South, combined with bad cotton crops in 1915 and 1916. While African Americans did find work in war-related industries in the North, they still suffered discrimination and violence. Over 25 race riots erupted in Northern cities in 1919. America also became a more urban nation in the 1920s. Led by New York and Philadelphia, America's cities drew rural migrants as well as European immigrants.

TRADITION AND REACTION

Conservative tendencies are evident in several developments as many Americans seemed uncomfortable with the march of modernity.

The Red Scare

Following World War I, American politics tended to move in a more conservative direction, a trend exemplified by the so-called "**Red Scare**." The Red Scare was both a government attempt to expose and punish communists, anarchists, and radicals, and a grassroots fear of the spread of a worldwide communist revolution. Two sets of circumstances set the stage for the Red Scare. First, in 1917, communists staged a successful revolution in Russia. They publicly expressed their hopes for a general uprising of workers in industrialized countries, and in 1919 they organized the Communist International to help achieve that goal. Second, the strike wave of 1919 convinced some that a communist uprising was imminent, though only a small minority of the strikers had any connection with the Communist Party or with anarchist groups.

The Red Scare was characterized by "**Palmer raids**," investigations of labor leaders and radicals, named after U.S. Attorney General A. Mitchell Palmer. Government agents raided homes, union halls, offices, and meetings, often without warrants, in their search for communist subversion.

Nativism

Anti-immigrant sentiment, or **nativism**, had been present in the United States at least as far back as the first large waves of Irish immigration in the 1840s and '50s. It gained strength during the latter part of the 19th century as Eastern and Southern Europeans began immigrating to the United States. Protestants feared an influx of Jews, Catholics (Poles and Italians), and members of the Eastern Orthodox Church (Russians and Slavs). Organized labor feared that an influx of unskilled workers would drive wages down and make organizing unions more difficult. And some Americans simply resented so many people with different ways and languages entering the United States.

As European immigration increased after World War I, Congress established a quota system with the **Emergency Quota Act** (1921). The act set quotas for different nationalities based on the number of people from that nationality that had lived in the United States in 1890, thus discriminating against new immigrant groups. The **National Origins Act** of 1924 tinkered with this formula, but the net result was a dramatic decrease in European immigration from 1921 until 1965, when the Immigration Act ended the national origins quota system.

The Sacco and Vanzetti Case

In the atmosphere of the Red Scare and intense nativism, two Italian workers with anarchist sympathies, **Nicola Sacco** and **Bartolomeo Vanzetti**, were arrested in 1920 for the murder of a factory paymaster and a guard, and for stealing the payroll. Even though the case against the two was weak and the judge made prejudicial comments, the two were found guilty. The case provoked demonstrations both at home and abroad against the verdict and the sentence—the death penalty—which was carried out in 1927.

The Ku Klux Klan

As African Americans began leaving the South in large numbers as part of the Great Migration, the modern **Ku Klux Klan** was born (1915). By 1923, the new Klan boasted five million members (probably an exaggeration). The organization was strongest in the South, but its strength also was felt in the Midwest and Pacific Northwest. The Klan was devoted to **"100 percent Americanism."** This entailed opposition to African Americans and Catholics, as well as to Jews and immigrants in general. It also stood for fundamentalist Protestantism, Prohibition, and what it saw as traditional moral values. The organization resorted to repressive tactics, including cross burnings and lynchings, largely directed at African Americans.

Prohibition

The **18th Amendment**, which banned the manufacture, sale, or transportation of alcoholic beverages, took effect in 1920. The specifics of **Prohibition** and its enforcement were delineated in the **Volstead Act**, which was passed in 1919, just before Prohibition became the law of the land. The temperance movement had gained strength in the 20th century as conservatives from the rural South and West associated alcohol with urban depravity and immigrant vices. Prohibition proved very difficult to enforce. **Bootleggers** (illegal distributors of alcohol) and **speakeasies** (secret clubs that served alcohol) became common features of life in the 1920s and symbolized the futility of Prohibition. The 1932 victory of the Democrats led to the passage of the **21st Amendment** (1933), which repealed the 18th Amendment and ended America's "noble experiment."

The Scopes Trial

Perhaps the best illustration of the tensions in American society in the 1920s was the **Scopes trial**. Conservative fundamentalist Protestants, led by **William Jennings Bryan**, had been pushing for the elimination of evolution from high school biology curricula. Fundamentalists believed in a literal interpretation of the Bible and saw Darwinian evolution as a threat to their belief system. They were successful in Tennessee, which passed legislation prohibiting the teaching of evolution in 1925. The American Civil Liberties Union was eager to challenge the law, and found a biology teacher, John Scopes, who was willing to break the law to create a test case. Scopes was found guilty in a case that attracted national attention, as Bryan argued against evolution and the well-known lawyer Clarence Darrow defended Scopes's right to teach it.

CULTURE OF THE 1920s

Americans, with more leisure time and more money in the 1920s, were much more apt to participate in mass culture than were previous generations. Movie attendance soared. Sound was first used in a feature movie in 1927's *The Jazz Singer*, followed a year later by **Walt Disney's** *Steamboat Willie*, the first movie with Mickey Mouse. Baseball was very popular—the public was captivated by the achievements of Yankee great **Babe Ruth**. Radio, an infant medium in 1920, was enormously popular by the close of the decade. Americans read tabloid newspapers, such as the *New York Daily News*, which featured sensationalized accounts of the day's events, including **Charles Lindbergh's** solo flight across the Atlantic (1927). *Time* magazine, started by Henry Luce in 1923, attempted to interpret current events. The public seemed especially captivated by fads, such as flagpole sitting and dance marathons.

Some American writers became disillusioned with rampant materialism and were disgusted by small-town provinciality. Many members of this **"Lost Generation"** also wrote about the cruelty and seeming meaninglessness of World War I. **F. Scott Fitzgerald's** *The Great Gatsby*, which portrayed the emptiness of the lives of the wealthy and privileged, came to define the era. **Sinclair Lewis's** novels, notably *Main Street* and *Babbitt*, ridiculed the narrowness and materialism of the middle class. **Ernest Hemingway's** *A Farewell to Arms* critiqued the glorification of war.

The **Harlem Renaissance**, arriving on the heels of the Great Migration, was a creative outpouring among African American writers, artists, and musicians. Foremost among poets was **Langston Hughes**; significant jazz musicians were **Louis Armstrong** and **Duke Ellington**; **Bessie Smith** was a well-known blues singer. During this time period, Marcus Garvey's "back to Africa" movement gained a following among African Americans.

SUMMARY

Americans grappled with the significance of the changes that shook the country in the 1920s. Some found solace in tradition, religion, and rural values, while others welcomed the changes. While society moved in new directions, the political trend was toward conservatism. Economic growth seemed limitless, but the shaky foundations of the economy would become evident in the coming decade.

THINGS TO REMEMBER

- **Advertising:** The promotion of products in various media. Modern advertising, employing psychology, expert testimony, and other innovations, developed in the 1920s.

- **Assembly line:** A method of mass production whereby the products are moved from worker to worker, with each person performing a small, repetitive task on the product and sending it to the next for a different part until the item is assembled. In the 18th and 19th centuries in America, assembly lines did not move; instead, workers handed the product from one to the next. Car manufacturer Henry Ford invented the moving assembly line in the early 20th century.

- **Bootleggers:** People who illegally manufactured, sold, or transported alcoholic beverages during the Prohibition period.

- **Installment plans:** The practice of paying for goods at regular intervals, usually with interest added to the balance, associated with consumption in the 1920s.

- **Isolationism:** The belief that the United States should not be involved in world affairs.

- **Speakeasies:** Illegal bars and saloons that operated during Prohibition.

REVIEW QUESTIONS

1. The National Origins Act of 1924

   (A) favored immigration from all parts of Europe because America needed European workers

   (B) greatly reduced the number of immigrants from Eastern and Southern Europe

   (C) favored immigration from Asia and Africa because the immigrants were likely to work for low wages

   (D) had little impact on the flow of immigrants into the United States

   (E) led to an immigration movement of United States residents back to Europe

2. This African American leader thought the way for African Americans to improve their position in American society was to gain vocational training to obtain jobs in agriculture, craft work, and manufacturing.

   (A) Booker T. Washington

   (B) W. E. B. DuBois

   (C) Marcus Garvey

   (D) Malcolm X

   (E) Martin Luther King Jr.

3. Margaret Sanger is best known for

   (A) being the first female cabinet member in a presidential administration

   (B) devoting her adult life to pushing for women to have the right to vote

   (C) advocating prohibition

   (D) singing jazz songs

   (E) opening the first birth control clinic in the United States

4. Which of the following was not a cause of the Great Migration?

   (A) the need for workers in munitions plants during World War I

   (B) lynchings in Southern towns

   (C) Jim Crow laws

   (D) the Great Depression

   (E) the failure of the cotton crops in the 1910s

ANSWERS AND EXPLANATIONS

1. B

The National Origins Act was an expression of nativism and isolationism. It was designed to reduce immigration in general, but had the largest impact on immigrants from Southern and Eastern Europe. The immigration acts of the 1920s reduced the number of immigrants allowed into the United States. The National Origins Act favored the "older" immigrant groups—that is, those who had a sizable presence in the United States before 1890. It had a major impact on immigration into the United States. There was never a sizable movement of people out of the United States.

2. A

Washington is often contrasted with W. E. B. DuBois, who argued for a more political, direct challenge to racism in the United States. Garvey is associated with the "back to Africa" movement. Malcolm X is associated with Black nationalism and would chafe at Washington's accommodationist platform. King believed in pushing for equality and justice, not in accepting the prevailing racial hierarchy.

3. E

Sanger is the person most closely identified with promoting birth control. Francis Perkins was the first female cabinet member (A) and Elizabeth Cady Stanton and Susan B. Anthony were leaders of the Women's Suffrage Movement (B). Women, more than men, supported prohibition (C), but there is not one nationally recognized leader associated with the movement. Bessie Smith and Ella Fitzgerald were well known jazz singers of the decade.

4. D

The Great Depression occurred a short time after the Great Migration. Choice (A) would be considered a "pull" factor, drawing African Americans to the North. Answer choices (B), (C), and (E) are all "push" factors, convincing many African Americans that life in the South was intolerable.

CHAPTER 24

The Crash, the Depression, and the New Deal

TIMELINE

1928	Herbert Hoover elected president
1929	The Great Depression begins
1932	Reconstruction Finance Corporation established • Norris–La Guardia Anti-Injunction Act passed • Franklin D. Roosevelt elected president
1933	Bank holiday declared • New Deal programs begin • Agricultural Adjustment Act passed • Banking Act (Glass-Steagall) enacted • Federal Deposit Insurance Corporation established • Federal Emergency Relief Administration established • National Industrial Recovery Act passed • Civilian Conservation Corps forms
1935	Social Security Act passed • National Labor Relations Act passed • National Industrial Recovery Act declared unconstitutional • Emergency Relief Appropriations Act passed • Works Progress Administration formed
1936	FDR elected to second term as president • AAA declared unconstitutional • FDR attempts his Court Packing Scheme
1937	Farm Security Administration established
1938	Fair Labor Standards Act passed
1940	FDR elected to an unprecedented third term as president

IMPORTANT PEOPLE, PLACES, EVENTS, AND CONCEPTS

Herbert Hoover

Black Tuesday

"trickle down" theory

Reconstruction Finance Corporation

National Industrial Recovery Act (NIRA)

Norris–La Guardia Anti-Injunction Act

Franklin D. Roosevelt

bank holiday

New Deal

Social Security Act

alphabet agencies

yellow dog contracts

Bonus Army

" . . . Let me assert my firm belief that the only thing we have to fear is fear itself–nameless, unreasoning, unjustified terror which paralyzes needed efforts to convert retreat into advance."

—Franklin D. Roosevelt, First Inaugural Address, March 4, 1933

INTRODUCTION

With the nation in the throws of the worst depression in history, Franklin D. Roosevelt assumed the presidency of the United States, bringing hope and reassurance to a frightened populace. Taking immediate action by declaring a bank holiday, Roosevelt went on to change the very fabric of how government relates to those being governed. To some, FDR was a savior, while others preferred to have the government remain at a distance from the lives of the people. FDR's New Deal brought relief to some but remained limited in its effectiveness.

CAUSES OF THE DEPRESSION

In November of 1928, **Herbert Hoover** stated that the nation was " . . . nearer to the final triumph over poverty than ever before in the history of any land." Ironically, less than a year later, the United States was plunged into a depression in which the unemployment rate almost reached 25 percent.

Throughout the 1920s, the country enjoyed a period of prosperity. Businesses were expanding, unemployment was low, the work week was reduced from 60 hours to 44 hours per week, real income had increased by 10 percent, and there was a great deal of investing in the stock market. Even life expectancy had increased.

On October 29, 1929, known as **Black Tuesday**, the stock market crashed. In effect, the value of the companies in which people had invested by purchasing a share of **stock** (ownership in the company) had declined. This caused a great many people to lose their fortunes. Banks failed, the amount of money in circulation declined, and millions were unemployed.

The causes of the Great Depression were many. They included:

- **Overproduction and underconsumption:** There were too many goods being produced and not enough people buying the goods. Farmers, in particular, had not enjoyed the prosperity of the 1920s. After World War I, the demand for farm products decreased, while the supply remained the same. Prices for farm products fell, forcing many off their land and into tenant farming.

- **Speculation** was rampant. People and banks had invested in companies whose earning power was questionable. Many of these were bogus companies. This resulted in the overpricing of stocks, leading to the collapse of the stock market.

- **Margin buying** had substantially increased, particularly in the area of stock purchases. People were permitted to buy stocks on **margin**; they paid for only part of the stock, planning to pay the remainder when the price of the stock increased. However, when the stock prices dropped, people were called upon to pay for the balance of the stock cost which they owed, and they simply didn't have the money.

- Unsound bank practices led to the closure of many banks, with a tremendous loss of money to the depositors.

- New methods of production caused **technological unemployment**: people lost their jobs when machines did the work they used to do.

- High tariffs made U.S. products unwelcome abroad.

- The severe depression in Europe decreased the demand for American goods abroad.

Although depressions had occurred before in America's history, the magnitude of the Depression of 1929 startled the American people. Hoover's reaction to it cost him the election of 1932.

HOOVER'S RESPONSE TO THE CRISIS

By 1932, Herbert Hoover was leading a nation crippled by the Depression. "Hoovervilles," communities of people living together in vacant lots, sprung up throughout the country. A staunch advocate of free enterprise, Hoover believed that when business was successful, wealth would **"trickle down"** to the individual workers. In addition, Hoover was a believer in **rugged individualism**, the idea that individuals have the ability to improve their lives with little interference from the government. Hoover, therefore, was reluctant at first to interfere with the problems created by the Depression and many felt he was not making any attempt to meet the challenges presented by the depression. But he did take action; however, it was too little, too late.

Hoover's first step was to give aid to the railroads, banks, and rural credit corporations with the hope that these industries would recover and relieve unemployment. This kind of government involvement was a new step for the United States. Congress also voted huge sums of money to be used for public works. **Hoover Dam** on the Colorado River was built as a result.

In 1932, at Hoover's request, Congress established the **Reconstruction Finance Corporation (RFC)**, which gave loans to businesses, states, and local governments. Also that same year, the **Norris–La Guardia Anti-Injunction Act** was passed, ending **yellow dog contracts** (those contracts which employees were made to sign stating they would not join a union). It also prevented the courts from issuing an **injunction** forbidding workers from striking, boycotting a company's goods, or picketing.

These measures, it was hoped, would help the economy to recover and end the depression. Although not successful, the steps taken by the Hoover administration paved the way for the more aggressive measures of the New Deal.

ROOSEVELT'S NEW DEAL

In the summer of 1932, a group of World War I veterans—the **Bonus Army**—marched on Washington seeking past pay owed to them by the government. Disgusted with this episode and Hoover's perceived indifference to the plight of the people, the American people overwhelmingly elected **Franklin D. Roosevelt** to the presidency in November 1932.

His first action as president was to declare a **bank holiday** to examine bank practices before reopening them. He then called Congress into special session and enacted his program, called the **New Deal**. Based on the idea of **"priming the pump,"** that is, using government money to generate money, a number of government programs were established. These programs were designed to bring immediate **relief** to the hungry and unemployed, to assist in the **recovery** of help businesses and individuals, and to **reform** the areas that had contributed to the depression. Many government agencies and pieces of legislation emerged from the New Deal. Because each was referred to by acronym, these agencies became known as **"alphabet agencies."** Many of these programs provided not only relief but also recovery and reform. They are generally divided as follows:

Relief

Federal Emergency Relief Administration (1933)—FERA gave federal money to the states and cities to feed the needy and pay for public works projects.

National Industrial Recovery Act (1933)—NIRA was designed to reduce unemployment by asking employers to spread out the work as much as possible. The National Recovery Administration asked industry to reduce competition and to regulate wages and hours. Labor was granted the right to organize and bargain collectively. The Supreme Court declared this act unconstitutional in 1935.

Public Work Administration (1933)—The PWA was established under the NIRA. Secretary of the Interior Harold Ickes distributed over three billion dollars in work relief programs for roads and public buildings.

Civilian Conservation Corps (1933)—CCC provided employment for young men in the areas of forestry, flood control, and soil conservation.

Fair Labor Standards Act (1938)—This act set a minimum wage at 25 cents per hour and a work week of 44 hours. It also outlawed labor for children under 16 years of age.

Recovery

Agricultural Adjustment Act (1933)—AAA paid farmers to reduce production and offered aid to them. It was declared unconstitutional by the Supreme Court in 1936.

The Tennessee Valley Authority (1933)—TVA examined and developed the resources in the Tennessee Valley.

Emergency Relief Appropriations Act (1935)—ERAA established work programs financed by the federal government. This included the **Works Progress Administration** (WPA), which employed manual laborers to build roads, bridges, and public buildings. In addition, the WPA supported the arts and literature with such projects as the Federal Writes Project, Federal Music Project, Federal Arts Project, and Federal Theater Project.

Farm Security Administration (1937)—FSA provided low-interest, long-term loans to tenant farmers to help them buy their own homes.

Reform

Banking Act of 1933 (Glass–Steagall Act)—This act provided for banking reform and set up the **FDIC**.

Federal Deposit Insurance Corporation (1933)—FDIC insured bank deposits up to $5,000 to encourage people to use the banks.

Security and Exchange Act (1934)—This act created the Security Exchange Commission (SEC) to police the activities of the stock market.

Social Security Act (1935)—This act provided for payment by the government to individuals who were unemployed, crippled, blind, or old. It also provided aid for dependent mothers and children.

National Labor Relations Act (1935)—NLRA was passed after the NIRA was declared unconstitutional. It recognized the right of labor to organize and bargain collectively, and had the power to force unions and employers to engage in collective bargaining.

REACTION TO THE NEW DEAL

When FDR was re-elected in 1936, he believed that he had received a mandate from the people to continue the New Deal. Because some of the legislation that had been passed under the New Deal was later declared unconstitutional by the **Supreme Court**, FDR proposed a change to that institution. Since there were nine justices sitting on the Court and six of them were over 70 years of age, FDR asked Congress to approve legislation that would allow for the appointment of one new justice for every justice over 70. The proposal also provided that the number of justices sitting on the Court was to be limited to 15. Congress was aghast at this proposal. If this **court packing scheme** had been approved, FDR would have been able to appoint six new justices, presumably ones who favored the New Deal. Despite the rejection of this scheme by Congress, no other New Deal legislation was declared unconstitutional by the Supreme Court.

By 1937, the United States suffered yet another downturn in the economy. With unemployment still very high, it was clear that the New Deal had had a limited effect. In an effort to prime the pump even more, Roosevelt suggested deficit spending to jumpstart the economy. Although Congress approved limited measures, the real end to the depression came when the United States became involved in World War II.

SUMMARY

The Depression and the New Deal represent a huge change in how the government functioned. The idea of rugged individualism was abandoned in favor of a fuller participation of the government in the lives of its citizens. This idea that government could give money directly to the people to improve their lives was radical and innovative.

Many were frightened by the idea of a move toward **socialism**, which they perceived the New Deal to be indicative of. The expansion of the role of the president—especially when FDR ran for a third term—was another cause for concern. Yet FDR gave people hope that a better day was dawning. He made people believe that the government cared about their plight, thereby diffusing any attempt to topple the government. When World War II became a reality, the country moved out of depression. Roosevelt again inspired faith and hope in the existing democracy of the United States.

THINGS TO REMEMBER

- **Court packing scheme:** President Roosevelt's attempt in 1936 to push a judicial reform bill through Congress that would allow him to appoint six new Supreme Court justices sympathetic to his New Deal.

- **Margin buying:** The practice of buying stock on credit. People pay a small percentage of the price of the stock hoping that it will go up in value and that they can use that money to pay the balance they owe. This practice contributed to the Stock Market Crash of 1929.

- **Rugged individualism:** A belief in the ability of people to achieve success in difficult times by calling on their own abilities and resources without the interference of the government. Herbert Hoover subscribed to this notion; it affected the development of governmental policies during the early part of the Depression of 1929.

- **Socialism:** A type of economic system in which the state controls the production and distribution of certain products that they deem as necessary for the good of the people.

- **Speculation:** A term used to describe an investment made in something whose future is uncertain. It usually refers to high-risk investment with a reward that can be great—if the investment is successful. It contributed to the Stock Market Crash of 1929.

- **Technological unemployment:** The idea that the machine eliminates the need for human employment—that the development of new machine-based methods of work can lead to workers' losing their jobs.

REVIEW QUESTIONS

1. A major cause of the Depression of 1929 was

    (A) too few dollars in circulation

    (B) overproduction and overconsumption of goods, creating a shortage of goods

    (C) overproduction and underconsumption of goods, causing the prices of goods to decrease

    (D) an increase in the number of exports

    (E) low tariffs

2. When Herbert Hoover was elected President in 1928, the United States economy appeared to be in a

    (A) depression

    (B) recession

    (C) period of prosperity

    (D) recovery

    (E) bank crisis

3. FDR and Herbert Hoover differed in that

    (A) FDR believed in rugged individualism while Herbert Hoover believed that the individual was capable of raising himself/herself above the depression

    (B) Herbert Hoover believed that the government and the people had a duty to help those suffering from the depression, while FDR believed in laissez-faire

    (C) FDR supported the idea of "priming the pump" with government money to end the depression, while Herbert Hoover believed in direct relief to the people suffering from the depression

    (D) Herbert Hoover believed in rugged individualism, while FDR believed in "priming the pump" with government funds to end the depression

    (E) FDR was willing to take control of legislation to end the depression even without the support of Congress, while Herbert Hoover believed in expanding the powers of the presidency to deal with the depression

4. Franklin D. Roosevelt's Administration began with

    (A) a court packing scheme

    (B) an end to speculation in stocks and the Stock Market

    (C) a decrease in unemployment

    (D) the establishment of the Social Security System

    (E) a bank holiday

ANSWERS AND EXPLANATIONS

1. C

The Depression of 1929 was caused by too many goods (overproduction) being available without enough people willing to buy them (underconsumption). This led to falling prices. Too many dollars in circulation lead to inflation, but there are too few dollars in circulation during a depression. Overproduction and overconsumption are mutually exclusive, that is, overconsumption would mean that people would buy all the goods being produced. If goods are being exported, then goods are being sold. This is healthy for an economy. The tariffs (taxes on imports) were high at this time, which led to other nations keeping out U.S. goods from their countries, contributing to the Depression.

2. C

Herbert Hoover's election occurred during a period of prosperity. That makes answers (A), (B) and (D) incorrect. There appeared to be no bank crisis (E) at the time of Hoover's election in 1928.

3. D

Hoover believed that the individual was capable of great achievement and had the ability to rise above the depression. FDR, on the other hand, believed that people needed assistance to get out of the depression, and believed that the government should prime the pump, or place dollars into the economy that would stimulate industry and create more dollars. Choice (A) states that both believed in rugged individualism, which is incorrect. FDR did not believe in laissez-faire, that is, little or no government interference in business, as demonstrated by his New Deal programs. FDR believed in pump priming, while Hoover believed that the government should not give direct relief to the people. FDR, in his first Inaugural Address, made it clear that he was going to take action whether the Congress agreed or not. Hoover was reluctant to take on greater power as President.

4. E

The first act of the FDR administration was to declare a bank holiday. The court packing scheme did not occur until 1936. Controls were placed on the securities market by the New Deal. Employment increased gradually due to the New Deal programs and ultimately, World War II. The Social Security System *was* established, but not until 1935.

CHAPTER 25

Politics and Society in the 1930s

TIMELINE

1933	Hitler comes to power in Germany • Unionized workforce at 3 million
1935	Concert by Marian Anderson on the steps of the Lincoln Memorial • Huey Long is assassinated
1936	Beginning of sit-down strike at General Motors • Franklin Roosevelt elected to a second term
1937	CIO expelled from AFL
1941	Roosevelt issues executive order banning discrimination in government jobs • Unionized workers at 10.5 million

IMPORTANT PEOPLE, PLACES, EVENTS, AND CONCEPTS

National Industrial Recovery Act (NIRA)

Wagner Act

Congress of Industrial Organizations

United Auto Workers

Communist Party

Popular Front strategy

American Liberty League

Father Charles Coughlin

Upton Sinclair

Francis Townsend

Huey Long

Eleanor Roosevelt

Marian Anderson

"Black Cabinet"

Scottsboro Boys

Frances Perkins

Indian Reorganization Act

"Once in khaki suits, gee we looked swell
Full of that Yankee-Doodly dum
Half a million boots were slogging through Hell
And I was the kid with the drum
Say, don't you remember, you called me 'Al'—
It was 'Al' all the time
Say don't you remember, I was your pal—
Brother, can you spare a dime."

—Excerpt from the song "Brother, Can You Spare a Dime" by Yip Harburg, 1932

INTRODUCTION

Franklin D. Roosevelt's New Deal was not without important context. A variety of participants—political groupings, unionized workers, even the first lady—responded to the economic crisis of the 1930s in different ways, and helped to shape the direction and content of New Deal legislation. Further, the culture of the 1930s also reflects responses to the Great Depression. Yip Harburg's song, quoted above, expresses the frustration of a generation that came of age during World War I.

GROWTH IN THE 1930s

Organized Labor

The **Wagner Act**, implemented after NIRA (see chapter 24) was shot down by the Supreme Court, legalized union membership in the United States. As a result, union membership, which had been falling in the 1920s, rose from 3 million in 1933 to 10.5 million by 1941. By the end of World War II, 36 percent of nonagricultural American workers belonged to a union.

Industrial Unionism

The drive to organize workers led to tensions within the labor movement. The 50-year-old **American Federation of Labor** (AFL), a coalition of craft unions, had never shown much interest in organizing unskilled assembly line workers. Labor leaders such as **John L. Lewis** of the United Mine Workers wanted the AFL to do more in this growing sector of the labor force. In 1935, Lewis and other leaders from primarily unskilled unions formed the Committee for Industrial Organization within the AFL. The Committee's task of organizing basic industries met the ire of AFL leadership, which ordered it to disband in 1936. When it refused, the AFL expelled the Committee unions in 1937. In 1938, the Committee reconstituted itself as the independent **Congress of Industrial Organizations** (CIO).

The CIO and the Sit-down Strike

The growth of the CIO was phenomenal. It had already boasted of 1.8 million members when it was expelled from the AFL in 1937; by 1941 it had 5 million, more than the AFL. While unions were legal in America, employers were still under no compulsion to accept union demands. A wave of strikes ensued in the late 1930s. A new, militant tactic that CIO unions engaged in was the **sit-down strike**, where workers stopped work and refused to leave the shop floor, thus preventing the employer from reopening with replacement workers (or "scabs" in the parlance of the labor movement). The most famous sit-down strike took place at the General Motors plant in Flint, Michigan in the winter of 1936–1937. The strike resulted in General Motors recognizing the **United Auto Workers** as the bargaining unit for its 400,000 workers.

POLITICAL DEVELOPMENTS OF THE 1930s

The Growth of the Communist Party

The **Communist Party** had never found a large following in the United States, but in the 1930s it attracted new members and exerted influence beyond its numbers. Some Americans were impressed with the achievements of the Soviet Union; others simply felt that the capitalist system was not working. The Communist Party also attracted potential members by dropping talk of impending revolution, and adopting Stalin's **"Popular Front"** strategy of cooperating with a spectrum of antifascist groups and governments, including Roosevelt's New Deal.

Opposition to the New Deal

Some conservative critics saw the New Deal as socialism in disguise. They thought that the New Deal had pushed the government too far into new realms. Roosevelt's **court packing scheme** seemed especially heavy-handed. The most prominent group on the right was the **American Liberty League**, which consisted primarily of conservative businessmen. **Father Charles Coughlin**, using his popular national radio show, accused Roosevelt of being a Communist and a dictator.

Although Roosevelt could count on the support of the Communist Party, other voices from the left criticized the New Deal as being overly cautious. **Upton Sinclair** (author of *The Jungle*) ran for governor of California in 1934 under the banner **"End Poverty in California,"** proposing more sweeping, somewhat socialistic solutions. **Francis Townsend**, also from California, proposed a tax to generate enough money to give everyone over 60 years old a monthly stipend. The most serious threat to Roosevelt from the left came from **Huey Long**, the flamboyant populist governor, and then senator, from Louisiana. His **"Share Our Wealth" Society** proposed breaking up the fortunes of the rich and distributing them to everyone else. He talked of running against Roosevelt in 1936, but was assassinated in 1935.

CULTURE OF THE 1930s

Cultural developments of the 1930s must be seen in the context of the economic hardships of that decade. Some cultural products offered escape from the drudgery of everyday life, while others looked squarely at the plight of the downtrodden.

Movies

The movie industry, which had entered the **"talkie"** era in the late 1920s, thrived during the Great Depression (approximately 65 percent of the American public went to the movies every week). Escapist musicals with lavish sets and spectacular numbers, such as *Golddiggers of 1939* and *42nd Street*, proved popular. The Marx Brothers produced and starred in comedies such as *Monkey Business* and *Duck Soup*, while Charlie Chaplin's *Modern Times* satirized the capitalist system. Some movies attempted to grapple with the wrenching public issues of the time. *The Grapes of Wrath*, the film version of John Steinbeck's novel, chronicled the conditions of dust bowl farmers fleeing to California, while Frank Capra's *Mr. Smith Goes to Washington* depicted the triumph of a decent, "everyman" politician.

Radio

Radio, which had become fashionable in the 1920s, continued its popularity in the 1930s. Americans listened to weekly serials such as *The Shadow* and *The Lone Ranger*, comedians such as Jack Benny and George Burns, soap operas, and big band and classical music. Radio and movies tended to create a more homogenous culture in the United States.

Literature

Pearl Buck's *The Good Earth*, a story of peasants in China, John Steinbeck's tale of the dust bowl, *The Grapes of Wrath*, and Margaret Mitchell's account of the Old South, *Gone With the Wind*, have endured as classics of 1930s literature. Several novels of the decade reflected the influence of the Communist Party on American culture. There were antifascist novels, like *It Can't Happen Here* by Sinclair Lewis, and Proletarian literature such as Jack Conroy's novel *The Disinherited* and Clifford Odets's play *Waiting for Lefty*.

THE DEPRESSION AND SOCIAL GROUPS

African Americans

African Americans, in a vulnerable position in American society before the Depression, were especially hard hit by the economic difficulties of the 1930s. Many New Deal programs ignored African Americans, such as the Agricultural Adjustment Act, which did not help tenant farmers. Roosevelt was leery of losing the support of the Southern wing of the Democratic Party, so he did not put African Americans on the New Deal agenda. Neither did he endorse federal anti-lynching legislation (which was never passed).

First Lady **Eleanor Roosevelt** and Interior Secretary **Harold Ickes** championed the civil rights cause. The most dramatic gesture made by Eleanor Roosevelt was her organizing of a concert by African American singer **Marian Anderson** in 1935 on the steps of the Lincoln Memorial after Anderson was blocked by the Daughters of the American Revolution from performing at their concert hall.

President Roosevelt formed a "**black cabinet**" of advisers and in 1941 issued an executive order banning discrimination in government jobs. African Americans switched their allegiance from the Republican party (the party of Lincoln) to the Democratic party.

The limits of the justice system in terms of treating African Americans fairly was demonstrated in the highly publicized "**Scottsboro Boys**" case (1931–1935). Eight African American youths were convicted of rape in Alabama on flimsy evidence. The Communist Party supplied lawyers during the appeal stage, but several of the defendants served lengthy prison sentences.

Women

Women suffered a double burden during the Depression—they were responsible for putting food on the table during difficult times, but they were scorned if they took a job outside the home (the argument was that they were taking jobs away from men). Further, New Deal programs tended to slight women: The CCC was only for men, and NIRA set lower wage levels for women than for men. Nonetheless, individual women such as **Frances Perkins**, the first female cabinet member (Secretary of Labor) and Eleanor Roosevelt, an extremely active and public first lady, opened doors for women in general. Despite criticism, more women were working outside the home in 1940 than in 1930.

Native Americans

New Deal legislation profoundly affected Native Americans. The **Indian Reorganization Act** largely undid the assimilationist Dawes Act by recognizing tribal ownership of reservation lands.

Mexican Americans

Many Mexicans had moved to the southwest United States in the 1920s to work in agriculture. These Mexican Americans saw their wages plummet in the 1930s, and New Deal programs did little to help. For instance, the CCC and the WPA excluded migrant farm workers by requiring a permanent address.

SUMMARY

While the realities of daily life for millions of Americans during the 1930s was grim, the decade also saw an outpouring of political and creative energy. The New Deal itself and Roosevelt's "can-do" attitude inspired hope in people. New Deal legislation encouraged union organizing on an unprecedented scale. While Roosevelt's program did not initially address the particular problems of African Americans in this country, African Americans themselves pushed civil rights onto the national agenda, and laid some of the groundwork for the civil rights movement. Women, as a group, did not make significant gains in breaking down gender stereotypes, although they would during World War II. Americans participated in mass entertainment, keeping the movie industry healthy. Much of the literature of the decade, including that written from a left wing perspective, showed a renewed appreciation for America and its people—especially as storm clouds gathered over Europe.

THINGS TO REMEMBER

- **Lynching:** The killing of African Americans, usually by hanging, carried out by white mobs primarily in the southern states.

- **Sit-down strike:** Technique of the labor movement in the 1930s that entailed stopping work but not leaving the factory floor, as owners were not able to hire replacement workers so long as the workers occupied the shop floor.

- **Talkies:** Motion pictures with sound; *The Jazz Singer* (1927) was the first movie to use sound in a significant way.

REVIEW QUESTIONS

1. Which of the following organizations, born in the 1930s, focused on organizing unskilled workers?

   (A) The Congress of Industrial Organizations

   (B) The Industrial Workers of the World

   (C) The Knights of Labor

   (D) The American Federation of Labor

   (E) The Communist Party

2. Pick the answer that correctly matches the artist and the cultural product they created:

X) John Steinbeck	1) *Mr. Smith Goes to Washington*
Y) Frank Capra	2) *The Good Earth*
Z) Margaret Mitchell	3) *The Grapes of Wrath*
	4) *Gone With the Wind*
	5) *Waiting for Lefty*

   Answer choices:

   (A) X-2; Y-4; Z-5

   (B) X-3; Y-2; Z-4

   (C) X-5; Y-2; Z-2

   (D) X-3; Y-4; Z-1

   (E) X-3; Y-1; Z-4

3. Sit-down strikes proved to be a successful strategy for some unions in the 1930s primarily because they

   (A) were enthusiastically supported by the Roosevelt administration

   (B) prevented damage to company property

   (C) prevented the factory owners from carrying on production with strikebreakers

   (D) tended to gain public sympathy

   (E) were protected by federal legislation

4. The National Industrial Recovery Act and the Wagner Act both dealt with the issue of

   (A) the government's right to set price controls

   (B) employers' rights to exclude women from their workforce

   (C) workers' rights to organize unions

   (D) states' rights to regulate interstate trade

   (E) corporations' rights to cooperate in setting industry-wide standards

ANSWERS AND EXPLANATIONS

1. A

The Congress of Industrial Organizations. While the Industrial Workers of the World and the Knights of Labor did attempt to organize unskilled workers, both of those choices, as well as the AFL, date back to the 19th century. The Communist Party was a political group in the 1930s, not a union, although it supported organized labor.

2. E

Mr. Smith Goes to Washington is a film about a decent politician. *The Grapes of Wrath* is the most important novel about the suffering caused by the depression. *Gone With the Wind* is an important, and somewhat racist, account of life in the "old South." *The Good Earth* is a novel by Pearl Buck about peasants in China, and *Waiting for Lefty* is a working class play by Clifford Odets.

3. C

The strikes closed down factories, such as the General Motors facility in Flint, Michigan. Roosevelt supported organized labor, but not specifically sit-down strikes, which were not protected by law, making (A) and (E) incorrect. Choice (D) is incorrect because the public's reaction was mixed—some saw the sit-down strikers as lawbreakers. Even if some sectors of the public supported the sit-down strikes, that is not what made them successful. Strikers had no vested interest in protecting company property, making (B) incorrect.

4. C

The Wagner Act was passed after NIRA was declared unconstitutional. Both make it clear that workers have the right to organize into unions. Roosevelt thought that if workers were in unions they would win higher wages and have greater purchasing power. Some sections of NIRA established prices on products (A), but the Wagner Act did not. While there was pressure during the depression on women to give up their jobs so that men could work, there was no specific legislation excluding women from the workforce (B). The Supreme Court dealt with the question of interstate trade in two decisions, *Munn v. Illinois* (1877) and *Wabash v. Illinois* (1886). The first upheld the states' right to regulate railroads; the second held that only Congress could regulate interstate trade.

CHAPTER 26

World War II: From Neutrality to Hiroshima, 1936–1945

TIMELINE

1921	Washington Conference held
1922	Mussolini and Fascist Party gain control of the Italian government
1931	Japan invades Manchuria
1932	United States issues Stimson Doctrine
1933	Hitler appointed chancellor of Germany
1934	Johnson Debt-Default Act passed
1935	Neutrality Act passed
1937	Second Neutrality Act passed • Japan sinks *Panay*
1938	Munich Pact signed • Stalin establishes Communist dictatorship in USSR • Franco comes to power in Spain
1939	More Neutrality Acts passed
1940	USSR attacks Finland • Hitler attacks Denmark, Norway, Belgium, and the Netherlands • Hitler invades France • FDR elected to third term as president
1941	Lend-Lease Act passed • Atlantic Charter written • First peacetime draft established • Pearl Harbor attacked by the Japanese

1942	Rommel's Afrika Korps defeated in Operation Torch
1944	Invasion of Normandy • FDR elected to unprecedented fourth term as president
1945	FDR dies • V-E day in Europe (May 8) • Atomic bomb dropped on Hiroshima (August 6) • Nagasaki bombed (August 9) • Japan surrenders (August 14)

IMPORTANT PEOPLE, PLACES, EVENTS, AND CONCEPTS

Franklin D. Roosevelt

Washington Conference

Benito Mussolini

Adolf Hitler

Munich Pact

Joseph Stalin

General Francisco Franco

Neutrality Acts

Lend-Lease Act

Atlantic Charter

draft

Stimson Doctrine

Panay

Pearl Harbor

War Production Board

Revenue Act

Smith-Connolly Act

Rosie the Riveter

A. Philip Randolph

Fair Employment Practices Commission

Japanese internment

Korematsu v. the United States

George Marshall

Dwight D. Eisenhower

Operation Torch

General Rommel

D-Day

Harry Truman

V-E Day

Douglas A. MacArthur

Admiral Nimitz

Manhattan Project

Hiroshima

Nagasaki

"To the Congress of the United States: Yesterday, December 7, 1941—a day which will live in infamy—the United States of America was suddenly and deliberately attacked by naval and air forces of the Empire of Japan."
—Franklin D. Roosevelt, War Message, December 8, 1941

INTRODUCTION

Franklin D. Roosevelt delivered the above war message to arouse the American people's desire to fight for freedom and liberty. "Surprised" by the Japanese attack on Pearl Harbor, the United States was thrust into the world quarrel. The country found itself fighting a two-front war, but the vast oceans to the east and west protected the country from physical damage. The cost in American lives, however, was great.

As a result of World War II, the social fabric of the United States changed. Women and blacks demanded their rightful place in society. The horrors of the Holocaust raised awareness of how prejudice impacts a society. The bombings of Hiroshima and Nagasaki ushered in the nuclear age and the United States emerged as a world power. Never again would the United States be removed from world events.

THE WINDS OF WAR IN EUROPE

In 1921, the **Washington Conference** was held to deal with the problems in the Far East. There were several important treaties signed at this conference, including one to protect the territorial integrity of China and to respect each nation's possessions in the Far East. In addition, the **Five Power Pact**, signed by the United States, Great Britain, Japan, France, and Italy, attempted to limit the size of fleets and new shipbuilding for military purposes.

However, this spirit of cooperation was short-lived. In 1922, the **Fascist Party,** under the leadership of **Benito Mussolini,** gained control of the Italian government. He dissolved labor unions, abolished any opposing parties, and suspended freedom of the press. He wished to create a Roman Empire. In 1934, Italy invaded Ethiopia, which was annexed in 1936.

In 1933, **Adolf Hitler** was appointed chancellor of Germany by President Paul von Hindenburg. When Hindenburg died, Hitler solidified his power, desiring to make Germany a world power. Representing the ideas of the **Nazi Party** (Nationalist Socialist German Workers' Party), Hitler arrested his opponents and enlarged the German army.

In 1934, the United States passed the **Johnson Debt-Default Act**, which forbade the sale of U.S. securities to any nation that failed to pay its war debts to the United States. This created economic hardship in Germany, opening the way for Hitler to gain power.

In an effort to avert war with Germany, European countries adopted a policy of **appeasement.** In 1938, the **Munich Pact**, signed by Great Britain, France, Italy, and Germany, gave the **Sudetenland** to Germany in exchange for a promise of no further acts of aggression. In March of 1939, Germany invaded Czechoslovakia.

In August of 1939, the USSR, under **Joseph Stalin**, signed a **nonaggression treaty** with Germany, clearing the way for Germany to pursue its aggressive policy in Europe. That September, Germany invaded Poland and the war in Europe began, as France and Britain were allied with Poland.

The **Spanish Civil War** ended in 1939 with **General Francisco Franco** becoming the dictator of Spain. He sold arms and supplied men to the Germans and Italians. To avert war, the United States and the other European countries took no action against Franco as he destroyed democracy in Spain and supported Hitler and Mussolini.

By 1940, the USSR had attacked Finland in an effort to use it as a buffer from Hitler. Hitler took Denmark and Norway, followed by the Netherlands and Belgium. In June of 1940, Hitler invaded France, a move that stunned the United States.

THE U.S. RESPONSE TO PEARL HARBOR

The United States, during this period of growing aggression, attempted to remain neutral in its quest to stay out of the European war. With no desire to repeat World War I and a severe economic depression consuming its time, the United States looked from afar at the events in

Europe. With these winds of war blowing in Europe, the American people elected FDR to an unprecedented third term as president, believing that, given the circumstances, changing leaders midstream was not wise.

There was a slow movement toward U.S. involvement in World War II from 1933–1941, as evidenced by the following:

The **Neutrality Acts** (1935 and 1937) forbade U.S. citizens from selling or transporting arms or munitions to, making loans to, or traveling on ships of nations at war. In addition, it established a **"cash and carry"** system: Any belligerent nations that wished to purchase any goods, other than munitions, from the United States had to carry these goods on their own ships. This provision clearly favored the Allied nations, since Britain's navy was still a force to be reckoned with in the Atlantic.

The **Neutrality Acts of 1939** permitted the purchase of war materials from the United States on a cash and carry basis, again clearly favoring the Allied nations. In addition, it banned American merchant ships from traveling into war zones that were determined by the president.

The **Lend-Lease Act** (March 1941) made the United States the "arsenal of democracy," as the president was given the power to "lend, lease, or exchange" war materials with nations whose struggle against aggression was seen as vital to the security of the United States. By July 1941, FDR permitted convoys to escort lend-lease ships; by November, merchant ships were permitted to be armed.

In the **Atlantic Charter** (August 1941), the United States and Great Britain agreed on the following:

1. Neither the United States nor Great Britain was seeking to gain new territory as a result of the war.

2. There should be no territorial changes without the agreement of the people being governed.

3. People have the right to choose their own form of government.

4. Nazi tyranny must be destroyed.

5. Freedom of the seas must be preserved.

6. There was a need for greater disarmament.

Congress, after much debate, adopted the first peacetime **draft** (September 1941). Men between the ages of 21 and 35 were required to serve in the military for one year.

Clearly, the United States was moving toward involvement in this struggle. Its citizens, however, were still reluctant to abandon **isolationism.**

The Japanese, in the meantime, had seized the Chinese province of Manchuria in 1931, changing its name to **Manchukuo.** The League of Nations condemned this action. The United States, in the **Stimson Doctrine** of 1932, condemned Japan's actions and noted that these actions violated existing treaties, and imposed sanctions against the Japanese, which were ignored by other countries. In 1937, the *Panay*, a U.S. gunboat, was sunk by Japan on a river in China. The Japanese apologized and paid an indemnity to the Untied States. However, on December 7, 1941, the Japanese attacked **Pearl Harbor** in Hawaii, and the United States finally entered the war.

THE HOME FRONT

Several steps were taken to mobilize the United States for war:

The **War Production Board** was established to convert the country's production from peacetime to wartime.

The **War Food Administration** was established to handle the food supply for troops and civilians.

The **War Manpower Commission** was established along with the **Office of Scientific Research and Development**.

The **Office of Price Administration** was an important agency established to control prices.

The **Revenue Act of 1942** increased the income tax. By 1944, a standard payroll deduction had been established.

In 1943, the **Smith-Connolly Act** was passed, authorizing the government to seize any plant or mine that was idled by a strike and affect the war effort. It expired in 1947.

The **Office of War Mobilization** was established to monitor the industrial production of the nation.

Over 6 million women were brought into the workforce. **"Rosie the Riveter"** was a common sight. Many women also served in the armed forces, although they were not subject to the draft.

There was a great African American migration as blacks sought jobs in the war plants. In 1941, **A. Philip Randolph**, head of the Brotherhood of Sleeping Car Porters, threatened to march on Washington to demand equal opportunity for blacks in war jobs and in the armed forces. FDR issued an executive order prohibiting discrimination based on race. The **Fair Employment Practices Commission** was established, and organizations such as the **NAACP** (National Association for the Advancement of Colored People) and **CORE** (Congress of Racial Equality) increased their membership.

Mexican workers crossed the borders to work in American plants, and many Native Americans left the reservations to aid in the war effort. Over 25,000 of them served in the armed forces.

Japanese Americans, on the other hand, suffered great discrimination, as evidenced in California with the establishment of **Japanese internment** camps. Fearful that the Japanese in America would spy for Japan, U.S. officials seized their property and forced them into holding areas. In the case of *Korematsu v. the United States* (1944), the Supreme Court upheld the government's right to do such things to the Japanese Americans because of the extraordinary times. Those who were interned would not receive any compensation until 1988.

THE UNITED STATES AT WAR IN EUROPE

U.S. battles were led by **George Marshall**, chief of staff of the U.S. army, and **General Dwight D. Eisenhower**, commander of the European front. **General Bernard Montgomery** led the British efforts in Europe.

In 1942, the Soviets defeated the German army at Stalingrad. In North Africa, **Operation Torch** saw the defeat of German **General Rommel's Afrika Korps,** leading the Axis powers to lose control of Africa and the Mediterranean. In Italy, Mussolini was arrested by the king of Italy, only to be rescued by the Germans. Mussolini was eventually killed by the Italian underground in 1945.

Perhaps the biggest Allied effort was the **invasion of Normandy** on June 6, 1944—**D-Day**. It was the largest amphibious operation in history. By September 1944, France, Belgium, and other areas of Europe had been freed from German control. The Germans were defeated at the bitter **Battle of the Bulge** on the Belgian border and were soon in full retreat.

In 1944, Franklin Roosevelt, in failing health, won a fourth term as president of the United States. On April 12, 1945, Roosevelt died suddenly of a cerebral hemorrhage, and Vice President **Harry S. Truman** assumed the presidency.

The end of the war in Europe came when the Allied troops moved east across Europe, while the Soviets moved westward toward Berlin. In April 1945, these troops met on the Elbe River. Crushed on both sides, Hitler committed suicide, and on May 7, 1945, Nazi Germany surrendered to General Eisenhower. On May 8, 1945, **V-E Day** ("Victory in Europe") was celebrated as the European war ended.

THE UNITED STATES AT WAR IN THE PACIFIC

The Pacific was a cause of great concern, as Japan had expanded its control over Hong Kong, French Indochina, Malaysia, Burma, Thailand, the Dutch East Indies, Guam, and Wake Island. In addition, **General Douglas MacArthur**, commander of the American forces in the Pacific, had been forced from the Philippine Islands.

In 1942, the United States bombed Tokyo and halted an attempt by the Japanese to seize Australia. The Japanese, in addition, suffered a heavy defeat at Midway Island.

Under an island-by-island plan to defeat the Japanese, U.S. forces won at **Guadalcanal**, providing them with a valuable air base. **Admiral Nimitz**, leading the American fleet, along with MacArthur on land, defeated the Japanese on the Solomon, Gilbert, and Marshall Islands. The Japanese suffered a crushing defeat in the **Battle of the Philippine Sea** and used kamikaze (suicide) pilots in the **Battle of Leyte Gulf**.

Despite Japan's heavy losses, the leadership in Japan was reluctant to surrender. When Truman became president, he was informed of the U.S. government's secret **Manhattan Project**, which had designed an atomic bomb. On August 6, 1945, the United States dropped an atomic bomb on **Hiroshima**, resulting in nearly 130,000 casualties and the leveling of 90 percent of the city. On August 8, 1945, the Soviets entered the war against Japan. The following day, with no response from Japan, a second bomb was dropped on **Nagasaki**, killing or wounding over 75,000 people. Japan surrendered on August 14, 1945, after the Allies agreed to allow the Japanese **Emperor Hirohito** to remain on the throne as a nominal emperor. The war in the Pacific was over.

SUMMARY

Justified or not, the atomic bombings of Hiroshima and Nagasaki dramatically ended the Second World War. Much of territorial Europe had been destroyed, the horrors of the Holocaust were revealed, and Japan was in shambles. The Soviet Union and the United States emerged as the two world powers, and the clash of these two giants lay ahead as peace negotiations took place. A war of political philosophy and territorial control was about to take place under the threat of atomic annihilation. The **Cold War** had already begun.

THINGS TO REMEMBER

- **Appeasement:** The policy practiced by the European nations prior to World War I wherein they made concessions to aggressive nations—particularly, Hitler's Germany—in hopes of satisfying the demands of that nation and ending further aggression.

- **Isolationism:** The belief that the United States should not be involved in world affairs.

- **Nonaggression treaty:** A treaty in which the parties agree not to attack the other unless they are attacked first.

REVIEW QUESTIONS

1. The Washington Conference, held in 1921, resulted in

   (A) an undermining of the authority of the United Nations
   (B) Treaties of disarmament among Great Britain, Japan, and the United States
   (C) an end to Japanese aggression in China
   (D) the development of the Stimson Doctrine
   (E) the rise of Mussolini in Italy

2. The United States demonstrated its support for the Allies before it entered World War II by

   (A) the announcement of the Stimson Doctrine
   (B) its reaction to the sinking of the *Panay* by Japan
   (C) the adoption of the policy of Lend-Lease
   (D) its participation in the League of Nations
   (E) its participation in the Washington Conference in 1921

3. All of the following were principles outlined in the Atlantic Charter by FDR and Winston Churchill EXCEPT:

   (A) freedom of the seas

   (B) self-determination

   (C) disarmament

   (D) the destruction of Nazi tyranny

   (E) territorial aggrandizement by Great Britain and the United States

4. Which of the following was a result of the Munich Pact of 1938?

   (A) The rise of Franco in Spain

   (B) The nonaggression treaty signed between the USSR and Germany in 1939

   (C) The German invasion of Czechoslovakia in 1939

   (D) V-E Day

   (E) The Atlantic Charter

ANSWERS AND EXPLANATIONS

1. B

The Washington Conference resulted in treaties reaffirming the Open Door Policy in China and disarmament among the participating nations. The United States, Japan, Great Britain, Franc,e and Italy agreed to limit their fleets and shipbuilding for military use. The United Nations was not established until after World War II. The Japanese violated the treaties of the Washington Conference when it invaded Manchuria in 1931. The Stimson Doctrine was a response by the United States government to the attack by Japan on Manchuria in 1931. Mussolini came to power in 1922 but not as a result of the Washington Conference.

2. C

The United States had clearly chosen sides with the passage of the Lend-Lease Act in 1941. The Stimson Doctrine was the response of the United States to the Japanese invasion of Manchuria. The attack on the *Panay* resulted in the Japanese paying an indemnity to the United States. The United States Senate rejected the Treaty of Versailles that ended World War I. It also rejected any participation by the United States in the League of Nations. The United States *did* participate in the Washington Conference in 1921, but this was long before the problems with Hitler arose.

3. E

Great Britain and the United States clearly stated that they wished no territorial aggrandizement as a result of the war, that is, they were not seeking new territory. Choices (A), (B), (C), and (D) were all stated principles of the Atlantic Charter.

4. C

The Munich Pact gave Hitler the Sudetenland, an area on the western part of Czechoslovakia. In less than six months, Hitler had taken all of Czechoslovakia. Franco came to power in Spain in 1939 at the end of the Spanish Civil War. There was a nonaggression treaty signed by the USSR and Germany after Stalin came to power. The war in Europe did not end (V-E Day) until 1945. The Atlantic Charter resulted from a meeting between Winston Churchill and FDR in 1941.

CHAPTER 27

The Cold War, 1945–1963

TIMELINE

1943	Teheran Conference takes place
1945	Yalta and Potsdam Conferences take place
1947	Truman Doctrine implemented • Marshall Plan implemented • National Security Act passed, creating the Department of Defense
1949	Berlin Airlift established • NATO created
1950	Korean War begins
1953	Ethel and Julius Rosenberg executed
1954	SEATO created
1955	Warsaw Pact created • Geneva Summit takes place
1956	War erupts over Suez Canal
1957	*Sputnik* launched
1960	Russia captures U.S. U-2 spy plane
1961	Berlin Wall erected • Unites States invades Cuba's Bay of Pigs
1962	Cuban Missile Crisis occurs

IMPORTANT PEOPLE, PLACES, EVENTS, AND CONCEPTS

Tehran Conference

Yalta Conference

Potsdam Conference

Harry Truman

Soviet satellite nations

iron curtain

Soviet bloc

Truman Doctrine

Marshall Plan

Berlin Airlift

North Atlantic Treaty Organization (NATO)

Warsaw Pact

Korean War

Douglas MacArthur

Dwight Eisenhower

Southeast Asia Treaty Organization (SEATO)

Nikita Khrushchev

Geneva Summit

Berlin Wall

Suez Crisis

Eisenhower Doctrine

Fidel Castro

Bay of Pigs

John F. Kennedy

Cuban Missile Crisis

National Security Act

Central Intelligence Agency (CIA)

Smith Act

Dennis v. United States

Alger Hiss

Ethel and Julius Rosenberg

Sputnik

Joseph McCarthy

"From Stettin in the Baltic to Trieste in the Adriatic, an iron curtain has descended across the Continent . . . . I am convinced that nothing they [the Communists] so much admire as strength, and there is nothing for which they have less respect than weakness, especially military weakness."

—Winston Churchill, 1946

INTRODUCTION

In 1945, the Allied victors sought to create a lasting peace, but mistrust between the Soviet Union and the Western nations made this goal difficult to achieve. Although this mistrust grew into hostility, it never resulted in a tragedy such as World War II. Yet this "cold" struggle between East and West was no friendly rivalry. The **Cold War** was a battle of words and propaganda, involving competition in weaponry, science, and culture, and in obtaining influence among nations—both old and new—in Africa, Asia, and Latin America. Indeed, it was a war in many ways. The two new superpowers, the United States and the Soviet Union, had very different philosophies about human rights, economics, and politics. Each superpower had friends in Europe. Much of the rest of the world became a "battleground" in which each of them would compete for prestige, favors, and control.

AGREEMENTS DURING WORLD WAR II (1943–1945)

Although the United States, Great Britain, and the Soviet Union were allies during the war, much mistrust arose among them that made them uneasy partners. The reasons were primarily philosophical, political, and historical:

- Communist theory held that capitalist nations were enemies, and asserted that communism would one day spread over the earth.

- Ever since the Communists came to power in Russia in 1917, leaders of the Western capitalist democracies, such as the United States and Britain, viewed them as threats, and said as much.

- There had been Allied support of the anti-Communist White Army during the Russian Civil War (1918–1921). The United States and Great Britain landed troops on Russian soil during this conflict, prompting fears of an invasion.

- The United States did not officially recognize the USSR until 1933.

- The dictatorial, police-state policies of the USSR were in sharp contrast with the democratic ideals of Western nations.

The only real bond that held these three nations together was their opposition to Nazi Germany. Once that bond dissolved, the old suspicions and fears resurfaced. Decisions made in three conferences during the closing years of the war, as well as those made shortly thereafter, laid the groundwork for the Cold War by dividing Europe into two specific spheres of political influence: communist and democratic.

The Teheran Conference (1943)

The first conference took place in **Teheran**, Iran in 1943. Participants were Soviet Premier **Joseph Stalin**, U.S. President **Franklin D. Roosevelt**, and British Prime Minister **Winston Churchill**. At that meeting, Stalin agreed to bring the USSR into the war against Japan once Germany was defeated. In return, the United States and Britain agreed to open a second front in France, thus forcing the Nazis to divide their army. Stalin, however, rejected the proposal to open another front in Eastern Europe, as he feared that this would have given America and Britain greater influence in the region.

The Yalta Conference (February, 1945)

The second conference took place at **Yalta** (Crimea) in February of 1945. While they agreed on the establishment of the United Nations, the complete **"de-Nazification"** of Germany, and the creation of four occupation zones (United States, Great Britain, France, and the USSR) within that nation, the Allies soon disagreed on the post-war fate of Eastern Europe. Stalin claimed that Eastern Europe, which was already occupied by Soviet troops, was vital to the USSR's security, as Russia had been invaded through this region for centuries. He insisted that the Soviet Union be given some measure of control over the area. Both Roosevelt and Churchill objected. Finally it was agreed that free general elections would be held in the region's nations as soon as possible.

The Potsdam Conference (July, 1945)

The last meeting of the three Allies took place in **Potsdam,** Germany in July of 1945. At this meeting, the only original member present was Stalin; Roosevelt had died and Churchill had lost that year's election in Britain. The United States was represented by the new president, **Harry Truman,** and Great Britain by its new Prime Minister, **Clement Atlee.** Even though there was once again general agreement on matters concerning Germany, Eastern Europe was still a sensitive issue. Vague assurances about free elections there were all that Stalin would offer the Western Allies.

SOVIET SATELLITES IN EASTERN EUROPE

The Emergence of the Iron Curtain

With the spirit of cooperation slowly disappearing after the Potsdam Conference, Stalin ignored the previous agreements. He forced Communist dictatorships on the Eastern European nations of Poland, Romania, Bulgaria, and Hungary, beginning in 1945. Independent local Communist regimes had established themselves in Yugoslavia, Czechoslovakia, and Albania. They were friendly with the USSR. The Western Allies were infuriated with the creation of these **Soviet satellite nations** (smaller nations controlled by a larger one). Truman denounced the new governments, while Churchill added a new phrase to the world's political vocabulary. He warned of an **"iron curtain"** dividing a free and democratic West from an East under totalitarian rule. Stalin thereupon labeled the Western democracies as the enemies of Communism. While not all the Eastern European Communist leaders were obedient to Stalin, their nations nevertheless became known as the **Soviet Bloc,** or Eastern Bloc. This grouping, also called the Communist Bloc, stood in contrast to the Western Bloc, or the "Free World" Bloc. At the United Nations, for example, the Western Bloc would usually support the United States on certain issues, while the Eastern Bloc would support issues promoted by the USSR.

The Division of Berlin

The breakdown of cooperation between the former World War II allies was felt most strongly in Germany, which was still divided into **zones of occupation.** Berlin, the former German capital city, which was within the Soviet zone, was itself divided into four occupation sectors. Access to the individual sectors was possible only through the Soviet zone. In 1947, the British, French, and U.S. zones joined together for economic reasons. With this union, the Western powers took the first steps toward creating the nation that was to become known as West Germany.

The Policy of Containment

Shortly after World War II ended, Communist rebels, with Soviet backing, captured northern Greece. This led to the Greek Civil War (1945–1948). Similar rebellions took place in Turkey and Iran. In response to these acts of Soviet-supported aggression and expansion of influence, President Truman announced a policy to be known as the **Truman Doctrine**. This policy aimed to support any free nation trying to resist being forcibly taken over by another power. As a result of this policy, the United States sent military and economic aid to assist those countries fighting Communist forces. This Truman Doctrine was part of a new American policy known as **containment**. As stated in 1947 by an American diplomat, **George Kennan**, the Containment Theory claimed that only through determined and continued resistance could the advance of Soviet power and influence be stopped. Communism, Kennan believed, had to be "contained" where it already existed and not be allowed to spread. Communism and Soviet power were viewed, in a sense, as contagious diseases. These diseases had to be contained before they "infected" other parts of the globe.

This Containment policy was further pursued with the **Marshall Plan**. As proposed by Secretary of State **George Marshall** in 1947, this plan was a broad program of economic assistance that aimed to help Europe recover from the devastation of World War II. Marshall feared that if economic conditions became bad, particularly in Western Europe, successful Communist revolutions might occur there. Only Western European nations accepted Marshall Plan aid; Stalin did not permit any Soviet satellite nations to request such assistance. Both the Truman Doctrine and the Marshall Plan were highly successful. By 1948, the Communist rebellions in Greece, Turkey, and Iran had been defeated, and the Western European nations underwent a remarkable economic recovery.

The Division of Germany

As tensions in Germany grew more severe, the Soviets cut off all access routes between Berlin and the Western occupation zones in June, 1948. This trapped the Westerners living in the city. In response, the United States established the **Berlin Airlift**, wherein food, fuel, and supplies were flown into the Western sector of the city. With the Berlin Airlift making the Soviet blockade ineffectual, Russia decided not to escalate the crisis and reopened the access routes in May 1949. A month later, the Western Allies established the Federal Republic of Germany, or **West Germany**, as it came to be known. The Soviets responded by creating an **East Germany**, or German Democratic Republic, in their zone.

The Creation of NATO

The mounting antagonism in Europe between the East and West gradually led to military alliances. In April of 1949, representatives of 12 Western nations signed the North Atlantic Pact. This was a mutual defense agreement—if one nation is attacked, the others will come to its aid—between the United States, Great Britain, France, Belgium, the Netherlands, Luxembourg, Denmark, Norway, Iceland, Canada, Italy, and Portugal. In 1952, Greece and Turkey joined, followed by West Germany in 1955. The **North Atlantic Treaty Organization (NATO)** was established to coordinate the activities of the alliance and to counter any acts of Soviet expansionism in Europe.

The Creation of the Warsaw Pact

The Soviets responded to West Germany's joining NATO with the creation of the **Warsaw Pact** in 1955. This was a military alliance of the Soviet Union with Albania, Bulgaria, Czechoslovakia, East Germany, Hungary, Poland, and Romania. Yugoslavia, under independent Communist leader Tito, refused to join.

THE ARMS RACE

Both alliances now began to stockpile huge quantities of arms. They enlarged their armed forces, increased military spending, and sent spies into each other's member nations. Thus, as the 1950s came to a close, it appeared that a frightening repetition of history was happening. The two military alliances were reminders of the "two armed camps" that existed before World War I. Both the Triple Alliance and the Triple Entente claimed to be merely defensive in nature—that is, each would fight only if attacked by the other. A similar policy was stated by NATO and the Warsaw Pact nations. Yet, the existence of these two groupings made the world more alarmed than was the case with the earlier alliances, for these reasons:

- NATO and the Warsaw Pact had many more member nations.
- Their armed forces were larger.
- Their weapons were newer and more deadly. Air forces, intercontinental missiles, and atomic power came to be possessed by both sides.
- Fear and distrust on both sides were enormous. The West was upset with the USSR's post–World War II expansion into Eastern Europe, Stalin's treachery, and the messianic belief of the Communists that spoke of inevitable world domination. The Soviets claimed that the Western powers were "ganging up" on them. NATO was seen as a threat to the Soviets, reminiscent of two previous invasions of Russia from the West (Napoleon in 1812, and Hitler in 1941).

The Korean War and the Creation of SEATO

The Cold War was not confined only to Europe. The East versus West, Communism versus Free World division was also evident in Asia. The rise of Communist regimes under **Mao Zedong** in China (1949) and **Kim Il-Sung** in North Korea (1949) created panic in the West. These nations were friendly with the USSR, taking similar anti-Western and anti-American stances. When North Korea attacked South Korea in 1950, United Nations forces led by the United States went to war. The conflict became known as the **Korean War** (1950–1953). Initially, the North Korean army overran much of South Korea. Chinese troops crossed the Yalu River and inflicted heavy casualties upon the anti-Communist forces. However, **General Douglas MacArthur**, who was in command of the U.S. troops, engineered a brilliant amphibious attack at **Inchon**. The success of this attack forced a retreat by the Communist armies and resulted in a stalemate in the fighting. Nevertheless, major disagreements broke out between MacArthur and President Truman. One of these concerned MacArthur's wish to take the war into China. Ultimately, Truman, in his constitutional capacity as

Commander-in-Chief of U.S. armed forces, dismissed MacArthur. In 1953, near the village of **Panmunjoun**, an **armistice agreement** was signed that brought a temporary halt to the fighting. No formal peace treaty has ever been signed.

North Korea had received weapons from the USSR as well as from Communist China. Even with such help, North Korea failed to conquer the South. Therefore, the United States and its allies considered this failure a result of the successful application of the Containment policy. They had stopped Communist expansion and re-established the status quo (existing state of affairs) that existed before the war.

The United States, having successfully protected a nation from Communist domination, became more convinced of the importance of practicing Containment. In 1954, President **Dwight Eisenhower** expanded the Western anti-Communist alliance system with the creation of the **Southeast Asia Treaty Organization** (**SEATO**). This included the United States, Great Britain, France, Australia, New Zealand, the Philippines, Thailand, and Pakistan. Modeled after NATO, it was justified by what Eisenhower termed the **"domino theory."** Akin to a row of dominoes, Asian nations could collapse. This could happen if, one by one, each fell to Communist expansion.

It was in Southeast Asia itself, where fear of **"falling dominoes"** amidst Cold War tensions erupted into another "hot war." This was in Vietnam. (See chapter 31 for details.)

The Policy of Peaceful Coexistence

In 1953, Stalin died and control of the USSR went to a more moderate leadership. The new Soviet leader, **Nikita Khrushchev**, adopted a policy labeled **"Peaceful Coexistence."** This was a policy of peaceful competition between the East and the West that would be based on greater achievement as a means of influencing nonallied nations (**"Third World"** nations). In 1955, President Eisenhower and the leaders of Great Britain and France held a summit with Khrushchev in Geneva, Switzerland. Known as the **Geneva Summit**, it was a breakthrough in trying to resolve the East-West tensions that existed at the start of the Cold War in 1945.

Continued Tension over Berlin

In November of 1958, Berlin once again became a source of tension. Khrushchev started a campaign to change the status of Western involvement in the city by demanding that the Western powers remove all military equipment and personnel in six months; otherwise, he would turn over the city to East Germany. He was aware that the East German government was not recognized by the Western nations. When these nations refused to comply, Khrushchev did nothing to carry out his threat. A scheduled 1960 summit meeting in Paris between Eisenhower and Khrushchev was cancelled, due to Russia's capture of an American U-2 spy surveillance plane while it flew over Soviet territory. Khrushchev was furious and demanded an apology. Eisenhower refused, but promised to suspend such spy missions.

Soviet pressure concerning West Berlin resumed in 1961. This was seen dramatically in the construction of a wall between West and East Berlin. The **Berlin Wall** closed off the border between the free area and the Communist area, and aimed to prevent East Germans from fleeing to the West. Although the Wall was viewed as a stark symbol of Communist oppression, the Western powers did nothing to affect its construction. Until its destruction in 1989, the Wall was often the scene of both successful and unsuccessful escapes into West Berlin.

OTHER GLOBAL SIGNS OF THE COLD WAR

Europe

Events elsewhere in Europe, and in 1956 in particular, cooled U.S. and Soviet relations. In Hungary, the nation's Communist rulers sought to reduce their connection with the Soviet Union. Angered by such action, the USSR sent in troops to quell any activity that was deemed anti-Soviet. Many Hungarians were killed in what became known as the **Hungarian Revolution** of 1956. Although the Western powers condemned this Russian invasion, they sent no aid to Hungary. In Poland, workers' resentments resulted in rioting. Stability was restored when the Communist rulers gave in to some of the demands.

The Middle East

The Middle East was also an area of concern in The Cold War. Egyptian President Gamal **Abdel Nasser** sought assistance from both the United States and the Soviet Union to construct a large dam on the Nile River at Aswan. As a "Third World" nation, Egypt supposedly claimed to be in neither the Free World bloc nor the Communist bloc, but it also shrewdly recognized the competition by both blocs to win favor in third world countries. It ultimately accepted Soviet aid for the dam in 1956. In that same year, Nasser's attempt to nationalize the **Suez Canal** led to war. Britain and France, owners of the canal, attacked Egypt. Israel, which had suffered repeated terrorist raids by Egypt along its borders, joined them. President Eisenhower was angered by this action, since the United States was not consulted beforehand by Britain and France, America's two main allies. In addition, Eisenhower feared that the Soviets would send military help to Egypt, especially since Egypt was crushed during the fighting. Pressure from the United States and from the United Nations brought about a cease fire and the removal of foreign forces from Egypt.

Worried about expanding Russian influence in the Middle East, President Eisenhower announced in 1957 that the United States would send armed forces to any nation there that asked for help against Communist threats. Labeled as the **Eisenhower Doctrine**, it was applied successfully in Lebanon in 1958.

Latin America

Cold War tensions in Latin America led to the most potentially dangerous U.S.-Soviet military confrontation outside of Europe. In 1959, **Fidel Castro** led a successful revolution against the government headed by **General Fulgencio Batista**. Initially, the United States welcomed Castro's victory and recognized his government. Soon, however, this friendly attitude began to change. Castro's undemocratic policies (i.e., restricting civil liberties), economic actions (i.e., nationalizing industries), and foreign relations conduct (i.e., aligning with the USSR and Communist China) greatly disturbed the Eisenhower administration. Many Cubans fled the island, settling mainly in Florida and vowing to depose Castro one day. The United States began to see Cuba as a base for Communist operations and as a security threat to the Western Hemisphere, and thus formed a force of Cuban exiles to overthrow Castro. They landed in Cuba at the **Bay of Pigs** in April of 1961, during the presidency of **John F. Kennedy**, and were soundly defeated by Cuba.

Consequently, Castro's anti-American stance grew stronger, as did his ties with the Soviet Union. Russia gave him vast quantities of conventional arms and sent many military and technical advisers. They also began to build missile launching pads for intermediate-range missiles. President Kennedy called on Khrushchev to dismantle the missile bases and warned that any nuclear attack from Cuban soil would result in a full-scale U.S. retaliation on the Soviet Union itself. Furthermore, Kennedy ordered a naval blockade to prevent Russian ships from bringing any more weapons to Cuba. The U.S. policy was successful, as Khrushchev had the missile bases torn down. In turn, Kennedy promised not to invade Cuba and to remove American missile bases in Turkey. The world was spared a nuclear catastrophe.

SUMMARY

The Cold War split the post–World War II globe into two antagonistic and contentious groupings. The struggle between these two camps created an arms race marked by hatred and fear. The world stood on the brink of a third world war.

THINGS TO REMEMBER

- **Cold War:** The conflict between the Soviet Union and the United States from the end of World War II until the collapse of the Soviet Union (1991). It was characterized by harsh rhetoric, technological rivalry, an arms buildup, and proxy wars in developing countries.

- **Containment:** The post–World War II U.S. policy that sought to prevent the spread of Communism.

- **Domino Theory:** The Eisenhower-era theory that one Communist country would infiltrate or influence its neighbors, supporting insurrection there and causing them to become Communist too. They would fall like a series of dominoes standing close together. Kennedy, Johnson, and Nixon also subscribed to this theory, a version of containment.

- **Summit meeting:** A conference attended by leaders of two or more nations.

REVIEW QUESTIONS

1. NATO was formed primarily to stop the spread of Communism in

   (A) Asia

   (B) Europe

   (C) South America

   (D) Africa

   (E) the Middle East

2. In the years after World War II, President Truman's foreign policy was focused chiefly on

   (A) nuclear testing

   (B) economic growth in underdeveloped countries

   (C) containment of international Communism

   (D) diplomatic relations with Eastern European nations

   (E) creation of cultural links with Red China

3. The reaction by Western Europe to the Berlin Blockade was the

   (A) invasion of East Germany

   (B) threat to increase nuclear arms

   (C) use of spy satellites

   (D) boycott of Soviet goods

   (E) Berlin Airlift

4. For Western Europe, The Marshall Plan provided

   (A) military assistance

   (B) cultural links

   (C) technology

   (D) economic aid

   (E) medical goods and equipment

ANSWERS AND EXPLANATIONS

1. B

NATO stood for North Atlantic Treaty Organization, and was signed by the United States and eleven Western European nations. It was a defensive alliance that aimed to counter an "armed attack ... in Europe or North America."

2. C

As the greatest external fear of the United States after World War II was the spread of Communism, Truman took appropriate measures. These included signing the NATO treaty, pledging economic and military aid to nations facing the threat of Communism (Truman Doctrine), and sending troops to fight in Korea. Issues regarding nuclear testing (A) and underdeveloped countries (B), although important, did not receive as much attention as did the threat of Communism. Given the tensions of the Cold war and the anti-American attitudes in Eastern Europe (D) and Red China (E), we did little to promote ties with them.

3. E

The purpose of the Berlin Airlift was to fly food and supplies into West Berlin. This was the sector (part) of Berlin to which the Soviets had cut off all land access. The allies did not attempt to pursue any of the actions described in the other choices.

4. D

The Marshall Plan was designed to prevent the spread of Communism. It realized that Communism often grew in areas experiencing poverty, hunger, and wartime devastation. Accordingly, the Plan provided over $12 billion in U.S. economic aid to Europe. It was not designed to do anything else, although other programs provided U.S. military assistance for western European nations and established cultural links between the United States and Europe.

CHAPTER 28

Affluence and Conservatism, 1946–1960

TIMELINE

1946	4.6 million workers go on strike • Republicans gain control of Congress
1947	Truman Doctrine announced • Taft-Hartley Act passed
1948	Alger Hiss case goes to trial
1950	Korean War begins • McCarren Internal Security Act passed over Truman's veto
1952	Eisenhower elected president
1953	Julius and Ethel Rosenberg executed • Truce ends the Korean War
1954	Army-McCarthy hearings take place • First McDonald's opens
1955	AFL and CIO merge
1956	Elvis Presley appears on *The Ed Sullivan Show*
1957	*Sputnik* launched by USSR

IMPORTANT PEOPLE, PLACES, EVENTS, AND CONCEPTS

Truman's Fair Deal

Dixiecrats

Strom Thurmond

Henry Wallace

Richard Nixon

"Checkers speech"

Sputnik

Communist Party

Federal Employee
Loyalty Program

McCarren Internal
Security Act

House Un-
American Activities
Committee (HUAC)

Alger Hiss case

Rosenberg case

Senator Joseph
McCarthy

Taft-Hartley Act

John Kenneth
Galbraith

Levittown

G.I. Bill

Interstate Highway
Act

redlining

Dr. Benjamin Spock

Betty Friedan

Elvis Presley

Paul Goodman

C. Wright Mills

Beat movement

Allen Ginsberg

Jack Kerouac

"In the councils of government, we must guard against the acquisition of unwarranted influence, whether sought or unsought, by the military-industrial complex. The potential for the disastrous rise of misplaced power exists and will persist."

—from President Dwight D. Eisenhower's Farewell Address, 1961

INTRODUCTION

The repercussions of the **Cold War** with the Soviet Union were felt in America in the 1950s. As the United States rose to the status of superpower, the importance of the military and of military production grew, as the above quote by President **Dwight Eisenhower** indicates. Suspicions developed about domestic Communists and radicals. The 1950s are known as a time of social conformity and political conservatism. Consumer items fueled steady economic growth from the late 1940s until the early 1970s. Also, the first glimmering of dissenting voices, which would come to define the 1960s, were heard.

POLITICAL DEVELOPMENTS

The Truman Years (1945–1953)

President **Harry S. Truman** continued many of Franklin Roosevelt's New Deal initiatives under the name **Fair Deal**. But Truman, not nearly as skilled politically as Roosevelt had been, had difficulty implementing his program. In 1946, his popularity plummeted and the Democrats lost control of Congress.

Truman survived a difficult election in 1948. Conservative Southern Democrats, angered by the party's support for civil rights, broke away, formed the **Dixiecrat Party**, and ran **Strom Thurmond** for president. Meanwhile the left wing of the party abandoned Truman and joined Roosevelt's third vice president, **Henry Wallace**, who ran for president with a new Progressive Party.

The Eisenhower Years (1953–1961)

A Republican was in the White House for the first time in 20 years when Dwight Eisenhower (nicknamed "Ike") was elected in 1952. Ike's running mate was **Richard Nixon**, who had previously gained exposure in the Alger Hiss case (see below). A pattern of ethical lapses by Nixon first emerged in accusations that he had a secret slush fund. He successfully defended his reputation in the **"Checkers speech."**

Ike, like the Republicans of the 1920s, was pro-business. Eisenhower had reservations about Senator Joseph McCarthy's anti-Communism crusade (see below), but generally kept quiet as he saw the political usefulness of McCarthyism. In his oft-cited farewell address, he warned against the power of the military-industrial complex.

The announcement that *Sputnik*, a Soviet satellite, had successfully orbited the earth challenged American confidence. In response, the United States passed the **National Defense Education Act** (1958) to adequately prepare a future generation of scientists and technicians.

Anti-Communism

Anti-Communism was a backdrop for much of the 1950s. Whereas antiradical feelings have been present in America as far back as the "Red Scare" of the 1920s, the stock of the Communist Party actually rose during the Depression and World War II. However, anti-Communism grew to a fevered pitch with Soviet-American relations deteriorating, China becoming a Communist nation (1949), and North Korea attacking South Korea (1950). The suspicions intensified into a crusade that not only targeted Communists, but also threatened the public's civil liberties. Three areas came under special scrutiny: the entertainment industry, the teaching profession, and government employees.

Truman initiated the **Federal Employee Loyalty Program** (1947) to investigate federal employees for Communist ties, and also to quiet Republican critics who accused him of being "soft on Communism."

Congressional Republicans did not think Truman's loyalty program went far enough. Over Truman's veto, they passed **McCarren Internal Security Act** (1950), which made it a crime to plan for the replacement of the U.S. government with a dictatorship.

The **House Un-American Activities Committee (HUAC)** investigated many facets of American society, notably the entertainment industry. A group of movie directors, actors, and writers, known as the **Hollywood Ten**, refused to cooperate and were jailed for contempt (1947). The investigations had a chilling effect, as Hollywood shied away from any subject that might be deemed controversial. Hollywood executives maintained a **blacklist** of supposed "subversives" who were not to be hired.

Many feared that the Soviet Union would obtain information about producing the atomic bomb from U.S. spies. **Alger Hiss**, a State Department employee, was accused of spying for the Soviet Union (1948) and was then convicted of perjury. The most famous spy case involved **Julius and Ethel Rosenberg**, who were accused of passing atomic secrets to the Soviets. Despite public protests, both were executed in 1953.

Anti-Communism came to be synonymous with Republican Senator **Joseph McCarthy** after he claimed to have a list of State Department employees who were Communists (1950). His wild accusations against virtually anyone who disagreed with him, his smear campaigns, and his recklessness eventually led to his undoing. When he opened investigations against the Army (1954), the Senate and the public had had enough of his crusade and **"McCarthyism"**; the Senate passed a censure motion against him in 1954.

ECONOMIC GROWTH

After a brief recession following World War II, the United States began the longest period of economic growth in its history as more Americans achieved middle class status. Many pockets of the country, however—notably, large segments of the African American community—did not share in this prosperity.

Workers in the Postwar World

Truman lifted wartime price controls and prices soared. Wages, however, did not. In response, in 1946, workers participated in a huge strike wave, with over 4.6 million workers on strike. These strikes were largely successful in bringing higher wages to industrial workers. The government responded with the anti-union **Taft-Hartley Act**, which sent workers in essential industries back to work and required union leaders to sign a non-Communist oath. The union movement was strengthened by the merger of the AFL and the CIO in 1955.

Consumerism

From 1946 into the 1950s, American families purchased consumer items at unprecedented rates. Shopping malls made shopping easier; status consciousness seemed to make it necessary. The production and sale of dishwashers, power tools, automobiles, and televisions (to name a few items) prevented the usual economic downturn associated with the conversion from a wartime to a peacetime economy and kept the American economy humming until the early 1970s. Americans also purchased more goods from branches of national chains. The most successful chain of franchises was **McDonald's**. **John Kenneth Galbraith**, in his 1958 book, *The Affluent Society*, saw a danger in affluence in the private realm at the expense of the public realm. He encouraged the wealthiest society in the world to do more to eradicate poverty within its borders.

SOCIAL TRENDS IN THE 1950s

The Baby Boom

Marriage and birth rates, which had been declining because of the difficulties and uncertainties of the Depression and World War II, rose dramatically in the 1950s and into the 1960s. The children of these new families are known as the **"baby boom"** generation.

The Move to Suburbia

Though **suburbs** date back to the 19th century, the 1950s saw a mass exodus from city to suburb. Suburban developments helped ease the housing shortage following World War II. **William Levitt** applied mass production techniques to housing, building communities of nearly identical houses on former agricultural land near big cities. The first **Levittown** was built on Long Island, New York. The Servicemen's Readjustment Act, or **G.I. Bill** (1944), provided low interest loans to would-be homeowners. The **Interstate Highway Act** of 1956 built thousands of miles of interstate highways and facilitated the commute from suburb to city. The act was accompanied by a dramatic increase in car ownership. During World War II, the movement of African Americans from the rural South to the urban North continued. After the war, many white families, alarmed to find African Americans as neighbors, moved to the suburbs—a trend known as **"white flight**." While the suburbs helped many Americans fulfill the "American Dream," others were not so sanguine. Some critics took issue with **"redlining**," covenants in some communities that prohibited selling homes to African Americans. **Malvina Reynolds's** song *Little Boxes* criticized the monotony of suburban homes and the conformity of the suburban lifestyle. Others bemoaned the neglect of the urban centers left behind.

Gender Roles

The ideal of the 1950s woman was a suburban housewife. Women were expected to happily hand over their wartime jobs to returning soldiers, and to devote themselves to childrearing. **Dr. Benjamin Spock's** best-selling *Common Sense Book of Baby and Child Care* encouraged women to devote themselves full time to mothering. He also discouraged spanking, and advised parents to let children's curiosity guide their development. **Betty Friedan** was an early feminist who challenged prevailing notions of gender. She identified a malaise that many 1950s women felt in her book *The Feminine Mystique* (1963) and critiqued the straightjacket that society had created for women.

The ideal 1950s man was the breadwinner who did not make waves at work. This pressure to **conform** was critiqued in several books including **Sloan Wilson's** novel *The Man in the Grey Flannel Suit* (1955).

1950s CULTURE

Several developments in the 1950s have come to define mass culture in the second half of the 20th century.

Television

First demonstrated to the public at the 1939 New York World's Fair, **television** became a dominant medium in the 1950s, deeply cutting into the movie-going audience. Television settled into a few predictable genres by the late 1950s: suburban comedies, such as *Father Knows Best*, westerns, and crime dramas. Television also brought advertising into the home, fueling consumerism.

The Youth Market

Society and young people themselves began to see the **teenage** years as a distinct stage in life in the 1950s. These young people were sometimes seen as problematic, as evident in the hand wringing over **juvenile delinquency**. The movie *Rebel Without a Cause*, starring **James Dean**, dealt with troubled teens. But marketers tried to capitalize on this age group by aiming products and advertising at the teenager.

Rock and Roll

Teenagers gravitated to a new music, dubbed **rock and roll**. Using electric instruments and drawing on a variety of genres—such as rhythm and blues—African American, and then white, artists produced a new and popular sound. **Chuck Berry** is perhaps the most important rock and roll innovator, but the most popular performer, by far, was **Elvis Presley**. Presley, who appeared on *The Ed Sullivan Show* in 1956, brought rock and roll to a mass audience and almost singlehandedly redefined postwar American popular culture.

Dissent

Not everyone subscribed to the suburban ideal of conformity and consumerism. Many people felt anxious about the threat that nuclear weapons posed or were distressed over the disregard for free expression implicit in McCarthyism.

Paul Goodman's *Growing Up Absurd* (1960) critiqued the expected roles for young people, and **C. Wright Mills's** *The Power Elite* (1956) examined the methods used by the "ruling class" to dominate society. Both became important texts for the New Left of the 1960s.

The **Beat literary movement** flaunted convention and embraced spontaneity, jazz, alcohol and drug use, and open sexuality, thus setting it apart from 1950s ideals. Prominent beats included poet **Allen Ginsberg**, whose *Howl*, a long poem attacking contemporary American society, was confiscated by the police for obscenity, and **Jack Kerouac**, whose *On the Road* is often considered the most important Beat text.

SUMMARY

In many ways the 1950s was America's moment in the sun. Its economic growth was unchallenged, and its military might far surpassed the rival Soviet Union. Even culturally, the influence of the United States was beginning to be felt abroad. New Deal liberalism was in retreat in the 1950s, as increased consumer spending and a tenacious anti-Communist movement created a conservative atmosphere.

THINGS TO REMEMBER

- **Anti-communism:** Opposition to communism. Extreme anti-communism was manifested in the "Red Scare" of the 1920s and McCarthyism of the 1950s.

- **Blacklist:** A list of persons, often secretly circulated, who are disapproved of and are to be denied employment or other benefits.

- **Baby boom:** The generation of children born between the end of World War II and 1964.

- **Consumer society:** The result of a general shift in society in the 1920s characterized by a greater emphasis on purchasing goods.

- **Juvenile delinquency:** A term coined in the 1950s to describe illegal or undesirable behavior by **teenagers**.

- **Loyalty oaths:** An element of President Truman's 1947 Federal Employees Loyalty and Security Program which was designed to weed out communists and other "subversives" from government employment.

- **McCarthyism:** Anti-Communism crusade of the 1950s led by Republican Senator Joseph McCarthy characterized by irresponsible accusations and smear campaigns.

- **Rock and roll:** Popular music genre, with roots in African American rhythm and blues and "doo-wop," that developed in the 1950s and was popularized by Elvis Presley.

- **Suburbia:** Residential communities near large urban centers. Although suburbs existed in the 19th century, they became a widespread social phenomenon in the 1950s.

- **Teenagers:** Teenagers, as an identifiable social group, emerged in the 1950s. Teenagers were seen both as a problematic, rebellious grouping, as well as a target for new products and cultural offerings.

- **White flight:** The exodus of white middle class families from cities to suburbia following World War II and the migration of African Americans to urban centers.

REVIEW QUESTIONS

1. Julius and Ethel Rosenberg were tried for and found guilty of

    (A) spying for Nazi Germany
    (B) inciting opposition to World War II
    (C) being Communists
    (D) providing information about the atomic bomb to the Soviet Union
    (E) violating tax laws

2. Which of the following was *not* considered an important factor in the rise of suburbia after World War II?

    (A) the building of new highways
    (B) the G.I. Bill
    (C) the construction of new train lines
    (D) white flight
    (E) a housing shortage in cities following World War II

3. All of the following are associated with the anticommunist movement of the late 1940s and 1950s except the

    (A) hearings of the "Hollywood Ten"
    (B) trial of Julius and Ethel Rosenberg
    (C) McCarren Act
    (D) G.I. Bill
    (E) Army-McCarthy hearings

4. William Levitt is often compared to Henry Ford because they both

    (A) invented new products that changed American society
    (B) standardized production of particular products
    (C) used extensive government funding to advance particular projects
    (D) created products that only the wealthy could afford
    (E) publicly supported the rise of Fascism in Europe

ANSWERS AND EXPLANATIONS

1. D

Julius and Ethel Rosenberg were accused of passing atomic secrets to the Soviets. There are no high profile cases involving Americans spying on Nazi Germany (A). The Rosenbergs—loyal Communists—would not protest U.S. involvement in World War II (B). There were only a few isolated cases of people being arrested under the Smith Act for opposition to U.S. involvement in the war. Though many people were arrested and tried for simply being members of the Communist Party in the 1950s (C), the Rosenbergs were convicted of spying, and were sent to the electric chair as punishment. Choice (E) might refer to Al Capone, a major gang leader during the Prohibition era, who was convicted of tax evasion despite reports of far more serious crimes.

2. C

Very few new train lines were built in the 20th century. While some suburbs were on train lines, this was not a major factor for the development of suburbia after World War II. All the other answers were major factors in the development of suburbia. The federal government built new interstate highways, and local governments also funded expressways. The G. I. Bill provided loans to returning soldiers to purchase new homes, allowing many to leave the city. "White flight" was the term to describe the abandonment of cities by middle class white families when African American families moved into the neighborhood. Because little new housing had been built since before the Depression, there was a severe housing shortage following the war—thus creating a demand for suburban housing.

3. D

The anticommunist impulse cast its shadow over many facets of American life in the late 1940s and 1950s, but the G. I. Bill occurred before the movement gained strength, and was concerned with the nonpolitical task of helping G. I.s adjust to civilian life. Hollywood was a prime target of anticommunism because of its ability to reach the public (A). The Rosenbergs (B) were accused of spying for the Soviet Union and were executed. The McCarren Act (C) was a broad act aimed at eliminating threats to the nation's security; it was passed over Truman's veto. And the Army-McCarthy hearings (E) involved McCarthy's accusations of Communist infiltration of the Army.

4. B

Ford standardized car production with the assembly line and Levitt standardized home production, allowing workers to go from home to home and do the same task repeatedly. (A) is wrong because Levitt and Ford did not invent, respectively, the home and the car; rather they changed the way these products are produced. While the government provided some funds for suburban development in the 1950s, Levitt's houses did not depend on extensive funding, and Ford received no funding whatsoever, making (C) incorrect. Both Levitt's houses and Ford's cars were affordable to people of moderate means, making (D) incorrect. Though Ford was a known and published anti-Semite, he was largely quiet in the 1930s as the Nazis solidified power in Germany, and Levitt said little publicly about the state of the world, making (E) incorrect.

CHAPTER 29

The Kennedy and Johnson Years

TIMELINE

1960	Kennedy elected president
1961	23rd Amendment ratified • Peace Corps established
1962	*Baker v. Carr* decision
1963	Nuclear Test Ban Treaty signed • Kennedy assassinated • Johnson assumes presidency
1964	Johnson elected president • 24th Amendment ratified • "War on Poverty" declared
1965	Immigration Act ends quotas • Medicaid and Medicare programs established • Elementary and Secondary Education Act enacted
1966	*Miranda v. Arizona* decision
1967	25th Amendment ratified • Six-Day War in the Middle East
1968	Johnson declines to run for re-election

IMPORTANT PEOPLE, PLACES, EVENTS, AND CONCEPTS

John F. Kennedy

Baker v. Carr

Alliance for Progress

Peace Corps

Berlin Wall

Nuclear Test Ban Treaty

Lyndon B. Johnson

Lee Harvey Oswald

Earl Warren

Barry Goldwater

Elementary and Secondary Education Act

Office of Economic Opportunity

Miranda v. Arizona

Immigration Act of 1965

Six-Day War

hotline

23rd, 24th and 25th Amendments

> "We stand today at the edge of a New Frontier—the frontier of the 1960s—a frontier of unknown opportunities and perils—a frontier of unfulfilled hopes and threats."
>
> —John F. Kennedy, 1960

> "And so, my fellow Americans: Ask not what your country can do for you—ask what you can do for your country."
>
> —John F. Kennedy, 1961

> "This nation, this generation, in this hour has man's first chance to build a Great Society, a place where the meaning of man's life matches the marvels of man's labors."
>
> —Lyndon B. Johnson, 1964

INTRODUCTION

John F. Kennedy and Lyndon B. Johnson came from different parts of America, had different temperaments, lifestyles, and upbringings. Each sought to impart his own imprint on the nation; both faced unexpected events that greatly impacted their respective presidencies.

THE KENNEDY ADMINISTRATION (1961–1963)

The Election of 1960

At its convention 1960, the Democratic Party chose **John F. Kennedy** from Massachusetts and Lyndon B. Johnson from Texas for its ticket. Both had been in the Senate; Kennedy also had served in the House of Representatives. Their campaign, run against the Republican ticket of Richard Nixon and Henry Cabot Lodge, was marked by the first televised presidential candidate debates in history. The Democrats prevailed with a victory margin of less than one percent of the popular vote, although the electoral vote was 303–219. At 43 years old, Kennedy became the youngest president elected in U.S. history, and the first Roman Catholic in that office.

Domestic Issues

The **Civil Rights Movement**—focusing on the removal of barriers to equality and respect for black Americans—was the main domestic concern of the Kennedy administration. (Further discussion of the Civil Rights Movement can be found in the next chapter.)

Kennedy's attempts to introduce social reforms affecting health care, housing, and education were turned down by Congress. His main problem, even though there were Democratic majorities in both houses of Congress, rested with opposition from Republicans and Southern Democrats. However, many of these proposals did receive passage later in the Johnson administration.

Other noteworthy domestic developments in the Kennedy years:

The **23rd Amendment**, ratified in 1961, permitted voters in Washington, DC, to participate in presidential elections. Washington, DC, was granted three electoral votes.

In *Baker v. Carr* (1962), a historic split decision affecting reapportionment of legislative districts, the Supreme Court held that federal courts would now have jurisdiction over (power to decide on) cases in which state apportionment formulas were being challenged. Such challenges sought to ensure that legislative district representation would be based fairly—on population, rather than on political concerns.

Foreign Affairs

The Cold War's continuance was the backdrop for major challenges. The most significant were those that involved Russia and the **Cuban Missile Crisis**. Other Cold War–related items include the following:

Through the **Alliance for Progress** program (1961), Kennedy hoped to stem Communist expansion in Latin America by providing funds for economic development. The funds would come from public and private sources in the United States, Japan, Western Europe, and some Latin American nations, for improvements in schools, transportation, housing, and public health. The program had mixed results. Some money went for useful purposes, while other funds went to authoritarian governments and their armed forces.

The Peace Corps (1961), as approved by Congress, was designed to send American civilian volunteers to developing nations. The volunteers would aid local citizens in Africa, Asia, and Latin America in such fields as education, health, technology, and agriculture. The Peace Corps still exists and has been judged successful.

On a symbolic trip to the **Berlin Wall** (1963), Kennedy made an inspiring speech. He spoke of the American willingness to defend the city, asserting that he too was "a Berliner."

With the **Nuclear Test Ban Treaty** (1963), the United States and the USSR agreed to stop nuclear testing in the atmosphere, in space, and underwater. Over 100 other nations also signed the treaty; the only nuclear powers at the time who did not were France and Communist China.

President Kennedy involved the nation in a **space program** that was aimed at placing a person on the moon. This commitment was spurred by the launch of a man into space by the Soviets in 1961. By 1969, American astronauts had landed on the moon.

In the case of **Vietnam**, Kennedy believed, as did Eisenhower, in the **domino theory**. He sent military advisers to South Vietnam to help keep the nation free from Communism. His role in affecting Vietnam policy was minimal, as he was assassinated in 1963.

Assassination of Kennedy

While in a motorcade in Dallas, Texas on November 22, 1963, President Kennedy was hit by two rifle bullets. He died within an hour, whereupon Vice President **Lyndon B. Johnson** was sworn in as President. **Lee Harvey Oswald**, who had allegedly fired at the president from a book depository, was arrested for his murder. While being led to a jail, Oswald himself was shot and killed by Jack Ruby.

President Johnson appointed a commission, headed by Supreme Court Chief Justice **Earl Warren**, to investigate the assassination. Its conclusions, presented in September 1964, were that Lee Harvey Oswald acted alone, and there was no conspiracy. Although the findings have generally been accepted, they remain controversial, with various alternative theories purported about the events surrounding the assassination. No hard evidence exists, however, to conclusively prove any of them.

THE JOHNSON ADMINISTRATION (1963–1969)

The Election of 1964

Upon a smooth transition to the presidency, Johnson saw fit to press Kennedy's goals for social welfare legislation and civil rights. Riding a tide of sentiment and popular support, he ran for chief executive in his own right in 1964 against Arizona Senator **Barry Goldwater**. He crushed Goldwater, winning 61 percent of the popular vote and gaining the electoral vote by 486–52.

Domestic Issues

As an effective politician who promised to make America a **"Great Society,"** Johnson was able to achieve many legislative successes. Some of these were in areas in which his predecessor had initiated proposals but been unable to get them passed. The **Elementary and Secondary Education Act** (1965) provided federal aid of over one billion dollars to school districts so that "every child can find knowledge to enrich his mind and enlarge his talents." The bill also required that schools accepting the money make good faith attempts at integration. The Health Insurance Act for the Aged (1965), an amendment to the Social Security Act, established **Medicare** and **Medicaid**. Medicare made provision for certain types of health care to people over 65; Medicaid would give funds to states in order to help the needy and poverty-stricken of any age who were not covered by Medicare. **VISTA** (1965), Volunteers in Service to America, would serve as a domestic Peace Corps. The volunteers would be trained to assist groups such as the mentally ill, the elderly, and migrant workers.

"The War on Poverty" was the slogan for grouping together the major social welfare goals of the Johnson administration. The key measure was the **Economic Opportunity Act** of 1964. It created the **OEO (Office of Economic Opportunity)**, which did such things as establish job and work training classes, and provide loans to small businesses that hired the unemployed. One OEO agency was VISTA. Other OEO programs included Operation Head Start (aid to preschoolers from poor families) and the Job Corps (vocational training for school dropouts). A new cabinet post, the **Department of Housing and Urban Development**, was created in 1966. HUD was designed to coordinate federal involvement with housing improvements and urban development projects.

On the heels of the *Baker v. Carr* decision (1962), the Supreme Court went further in trying to make for equality in legislative representation. In *Wesberry v. Sanders* (1964), the Court held that congressional districts in a state must contain "as nearly as practicable" the same number of voters. The case established the principle of "one person, one vote."

During the 1960s the Supreme Court, under Chief Justice Earl Warren, took a broad (liberal) approach in deciding cases concerning the **Bill of Rights** (the first 10 amendments). Labeled as "activist," the Supreme Court made major pronouncements in the following cases:

- The *Mapp v. Ohio* (1961) decision held that any evidence unreasonably acquired by the police cannot be admitted as evidence in a trial. This became known as "the exclusionary rule."

- In *Engel v. Vitale* (1962), the Court ruled that the reading of a nonsectarian prayer in a public school violates the 1st Amendment.

- In *Gideon v. Wainright* (1963), it was decided that a person who cannot afford a lawyer has the right to have the state furnish him with one in a criminal case.

- *Escobedo v. Illinois* (1964) resulted in the ruling that a person charged with a crime has the right to be told he can have a lawyer prior to being questioned.

- The *Miranda v. Arizona* (1966) decision set the precedent that the police must inform a person accused of a crime of his right to remain silent, as well as any other rights, prior to any questioning.

Foreign Affairs

The single most crucial foreign policy challenge to the Johnson administration rested with the escalating violence in **Vietnam**. The failed attempts to meet this challenge are what finally influenced Johnson not to seek re-election in 1968. (For in-depth details, see the chapter devoted to the Vietnam War.)

The Immigration Act of 1965 ended quotas based on national origin. The applicant's occupation and skills would now be the main criteria for admission to the United States. Preference was now given to those applicants who already have relatives in the United States.

In the **June (Six-Day) War** in 1967, Israel achieved an astounding victory over several Arab nations bent on its destruction. It was during the fighting that President Johnson spoke with Soviet Premier Alexei Kosygin in the first use of the **"hotline."** This link was created between Washington, DC, and Moscow for use in emergency situations. Both leaders agreed not to send military aid into the region, and to work for a cease fire.

SUMMARY

Both Presidents Kennedy and Johnson had visions for America that involved fighting Communism abroad and, at home, making Americans healthier, safer, better educated, and more secure economically.

THINGS TO REMEMBER

- **Great Society:** The name used by the administration of President Lyndon B. Johnson to describe its domestic programs.

- **Medicaid:** A program providing health care for the needy (people who lived below the poverty level) who were not covered by **Medicare**.

- **Medicare:** A program providing health insurance and health care for people over the age of 65.

- **New Frontier:** The name used by the administration of John F. Kennedy to describe its proposed programs for the nation.

- **War on Poverty:** A slogan used by President Lyndon B. Johnson to describe his goal of ending poverty in the United States.

REVIEW QUESTIONS

1. Which of the following is associated with the Kennedy administration?

   (A) Medicare
   (B) Medicaid
   (C) Alliance for Progress
   (D) the 24th Amendment
   (E) The ESEA

2. *Baker v. Carr* was concerned with

   (A) the Bill of Rights
   (B) presidential succession
   (C) criminal rights
   (D) the poll tax
   (E) legislative reapportionment

3. Which of the following proposed that the nation declare a "war on poverty"?

   (A) John F. Kennedy
   (B) Richard Nixon
   (C) Barry Goldwater
   (D) Lyndon B. Johnson
   (E) Earl Warren

4. According to the Immigration Act of 1965, the main criteria for admission to the United States would be based on an applicant's

   (A) gender
   (B) race
   (C) country of origin
   (D) occupation
   (E) education

ANSWERS AND EXPLANATIONS

1. C

The Alliance For Progress was an idea of John Kennedy's. All of the other choices refer to programs initiated during Johnson's administration.

2. E

This Supreme Court case was initiated as a challenge to malapportioned legislative districts. Presidential succession (B) and the poll tax (D) were never issues in a Supreme Court case. The Bill of Rights (A) and criminal rights (C) deal with protection of basic rights and were not issues in this case.

3. D

This phrase was used by the Johnson administration to emphasize its attempt to end poverty in the United States. Presidents Kennedy (A) and Nixon (B) and presidential candidate Goldwater (C) used other slogans in their political careers. As a judge, Earl Warren (E) never made any proposals for the nation.

4. D

Occupation became the chief criteria under this act, discontinuing discriminatory criteria that had been used in other immigration legislation, such as race (B) and country of origin (C). To use gender (A) would have also been discriminatory, and would not have been acceptable given the mood of the nation in the 1960s. Education (E) was not as important as were particular occupations that were in short supply in the nation

CHAPTER 30

The Civil Rights Movement, 1954–1968

TIMELINE

1944	Black troops drive tanks in the Battle of the Bulge
1948	President Truman desegregates the Army
1954	Supreme Court decides *Brown v. Board of Education of Topeka*
1955	Montgomery Bus Boycott occurs
1957	Southern Christian Leadership Conference (SCLC) founded • Little Rock Central High School integrated for one year
1960	Sit-ins take place in Greensboro, North Carolina • Student Nonviolent Coordinating Committee (SNCC) founded
1961	Freedom Rides take place
1962	James Meredith enters University of Mississippi protected by 5,000 federal troop
1963	Birmingham desegregation campaign launched • Martin Luther King Jr. writes "Letter from Birmingham Jail" • March on Washington occurs • 16th Street Baptist Church (Birmingham) bombed by Ku Klux Klan • Medgar Evers, field secretary of the NAACP, assassinated • John F. Kennedy assassinated
1964	Civil Rights Act passed • "Freedom Summer" • Mississippi Freedom Democratic Party (MFDP) denied seats at Democratic Party Convention

1965	Voting rights activists march from Selma to Montgomery • Voting Rights Act passed • Watts Riot takes place • SNCC split by Black Power advocates • Malcolm X assassinated
1967	Urban riots take place
1968	Martin Luther King assassinated • Robert F. Kennedy assassinated • Civil Rights Act of 1968 passed

IMPORTANT PEOPLE, PLACES, EVENTS, AND CONCEPTS

NAACP

Brown v. Board of Education of Topeka

Thurgood Marshall

Earl Warren

Martin Luther King Jr.

Montgomery Bus Boycott

Rosa Parks

Southern Christian Leadership Conference (SCLC)

Birmingham desegregation demonstrations

Eugene "Bull" Connor

Letter from Birmingham Jail

"I Have a Dream" speech

March on Washington

march from Selma to Montgomery

Voting Rights Act

"We Shall Overcome"

de facto segregation

de jure segregation

Student Nonviolent Coordinating Committee (SNCC)

Freedom Rides

Congress of Racial Equality (CORE)

Freedom Summer

Bob Moses

Stokely Carmichael

Ku Klux Klan (KKK)

Medgar Evers

13th Street Baptist Church

Fannie Lou Hamer

Andrew Goodman, Michael Schwerner, James Chaney

National Advisory Commission on Civil Disorders (Kerner Commission)

Malcolm X

Little Rock Central High School

James Meredith

Civil Rights Acts

Mississippi Freedom Democratic Party (MFDP)

"But the one thing we did right
Was the day we started to fight,
Keep your eyes on the prize,
Hold on, hold on"

—From traditional freedom song, "Keep Your Eyes on the Prize"

INTRODUCTION

The **Civil Rights Movement** set the stage for the progress and turmoil of the 1960s. Despite the American creed of "equality for all" **segregation** or other forms of discrimination reigned in the South and in many places in the North from the 1870s to the late 1960s. The Civil Rights Movement—the collective action of masses of ordinary people—was the key force in eliminating **Jim Crow**. The federal government enacted reforms, but it was the blacks and their white allies who kept their **"eyes on the prize"** of equality, who forced the changes in government and society, and who changed themselves in the process. This was the **Second Reconstruction** after the defeat in 1877.

ROOTS OF THE CIVIL RIGHTS MOVEMENT

The modern Civil Rights Movement had its roots largely in the ideas of Frederick Douglass, W. E. B. DuBois, A. Phillip Randolph, and the experiences of soldiers and workers in industrial plants during World War II. Douglass was the leader of forthright post–Civil War protest, DuBois was a founder of the **NAACP,** and A. Phillip Randolph was the activist who called for mass marches to end discrimination.

World War II

After participating as fighter pilots and fighting against the Nazis in key tank units in the Battle of the Bulge, African American soldiers found it demeaning and infuriating to return to the state laws that segregated everything from schools to water fountains in the South. Activist Randolph had forced President Franklin D. Roosevelt to employ blacks in the defense industries during the war, and President Harry Truman desegregated the armed forces by 1948.

Brown v. Board of Education

The NAACP began bringing school discrimination cases to the Supreme Court in the 1930s and 1940s, the most important of which was *Brown v. Board of Education of Topeka, Kansas* (1954). Linda Brown had been denied admission to her local elementary school in Topeka because she was black. NAACP lawyers led by **Thurgood Marshall** (who would later become the first black Supreme Court Justice) successfully argued the case using the results of psychological and sociological studies showing that segregation affects the ability of African American children to learn. Chief Justice **Earl Warren** led the Court to overrule *Plessy v. Ferguson* (1896), concluding "that the doctrine of separate but equal has no place" in public schools. What seemed like a clear federal stand encouraged civil rights workers to press for equality.

School Desegregation

In the course of school desegregation, African Americans faced the same resistance from whites and the federal government as they had in their attempts to integrate public facilities. The *Brown* decision had called for change, but the Court was unwilling to rush, and the ex-Confederate states stalled as much as they could. In Little Rock, Arkansas, nine black students entered **Central High School** only after President Eisenhower sent in the Army to protect them. They spent that school year in class with whites, but the next year Governor Orville Faubus closed down the school to prevent further integration. In 1962, President Kennedy sent 5,000 federal troops to protect **James Meredith** when he entered the University of Mississippi. A majority of the public schools in the South were not desegregated until the 1970s. *Brown* only set the stage for demonstrations; it did not ensure change.

MARTIN LUTHER KING JR.

Montgomery Bus Boycott

The groundbreaking work of Reverend **Martin Luther King Jr.** as a leader began in Montgomery, Alabama, in the winter of 1955. As the new pastor in Montgomery with a Ph.D. in theology from Boston University, King inspired confidence and determination in the 40,000 African Americans who refused to ride city buses on a segregated basis. On December 1, 1955, **Rosa Parks**, a committed activist for many years, was arrested for refusing to give her seat to a white man. By the next day, no African American person rode the public buses, as the Women's Political Council had distributed 30,000 leaflets calling for a boycott. For eleven months, the African American community either walked or arranged carpools to get to work. After suffering bombings, arrests, and direct threats by the Ku Klux Klan, the Montgomery Improvement Association succeeded when the Supreme Court ordered desegregation of the buses in Montgomery. In 1957, King helped to found the **Southern Christian Leadership Conference** (SCLC) to coordinate action against segregation after the success in the Montgomery Bus Boycott. As the name implies, the SCLC, like much of the movement, used the church as an organizational base.

Birmingham Desegregation Demonstrations

In 1963, King led a campaign to force the city government of Birmingham, Alabama, to take down the "whites only" signs. When **Eugene "Bull" Connor,** the city's Commissioner of Public Safety, used fire hoses and attack dogs to disperse demonstrating students, it was shown on national television, shocking the nation. During these demonstrations Martin Luther King was arrested. King wrote the **"Letter from Birmingham Jail"** in which he explained that waiting for segregation to end would only prolong the suffering of his people. The nonviolent demonstrations were justified, he said, because they hurried the achievement of equal rights. Activists were breaking unjust laws for morally right reasons and prepared to serve time in jail for their beliefs.

Marches in Washington and Selma

On August 28, 1963, King gave the **"I Have a Dream" speech** to the **March on Washington**, where 250,000 people had gathered to demonstrate for jobs and freedom. Echoing his abolitionist ancestors who stood on the premise of the Declaration of Independence, King called for America to fulfill its promise of equality for all.

In 1964, King won the Nobel Prize for Peace, but in the next years he met some of the bloodiest opposition of all. The pictures on television of the **march for voting rights from Selma to Montgomery**, Alabama, in 1965 made it look like a war zone, with the police using tear gas, billy clubs, and guns. This publicity produced a response from President Johnson: He called for a **Voting Rights Act** (1965) to assure that all citizens could register and have their votes counted. When he introduced the bill to Congress, Johnson quoted the Civil Rights anthem, **"We Shall Overcome."**

King's Assassination

King was assassinated in 1968 while leading demonstrations in Memphis, Tennessee, for higher pay for sanitation workers. He had come to the realization that job discrimination and *de facto* neighborhood housing discrimination were at least as important as the Jim Crow (*de jure*) segregation he had been battling since 1955. Similarly, he had turned publicly against the war in Vietnam (1967), partially because the expenses for the war were draining money needed for social programs.

STUDENT NONVIOLENT COORDINATING COMMITTEE

In 1960, following student-led **sit-ins** desegregated lunch counters in Greensboro, North Carolina, SCLC member **Ella Baker** helped establish the **Student Nonviolent Coordinating Committee** (SNCC). By October of that year, more than 112 sit-ins took place in Southern cities.

Freedom Rides

SNCC had black and white student members who participated in the **Freedom Rides** of 1961. The **Congress of Racial Equality** (CORE) led by **James Farmer** organized a campaign to desegregate bus stations and rest stops from Washington, DC to New Orleans that had "whites only" waiting rooms, bathrooms, and lunch counters. The activists were beaten so severely that CORE was ready to give up. SNCC completed the ride despite more beatings and fire bombings. **John Lewis**, currently a congressman from Atlanta, was a leader in the Freedom Rides and at the Selma march where SNCC provided the shock troops to bear the brunt of the attacks during the demonstrations.

Freedom Summer

In the **Freedom Summer** of 1964, SNCC organized a group of 300 students from the North and South to come to Mississippi to help African Americans register to vote. SNCC brought many people to the polls who had never to registered before, due to poll closings, literacy tests, and fear of retribution.

Black Power

In 1966 SNCC split along racial lines when **Stokely Carmichael** began to advocate **black power** in economic and political terms. He said there was no room for whites in SNCC because blacks had to make decisions for themselves. Not all blacks followed the separation, but it created a significant rift in the Civil Rights Movement.

VIOLENCE

The violence during this period was one of the most divisive factors. It was perpetrated by the **Ku Klux Klan**, the police and the FBI (who were sometimes allied with the Klan), and by African Americans in reaction to police attacks and the lack of socioeconomic equality. The violence created **white flight** from the cities, leaving the inner cities even more impoverished.

Violence by the Klan and its Allies

Medgar Evers, a leader of the NAACP in Mississippi, was shot in 1963. Two weeks after the peaceful March on Washington, the Klan threw a bomb into the **16th Street Baptist Church** in Birmingham, Alabama, killing four teenage girls. Three students who were working to register black votes, **Andrew Goodman**, **Michael Schwerner**, and **James Chaney**, disappeared at the beginning of Freedom Summer; their bodies turned up in a river, where Klansmen had thrown them after lynching them. Numerous other bodies were discovered in the weeks followed. **Fannie Lou Hamer**, a sharecropper participant in the Freedom Summer, was beaten severely for registering to vote. Finally, during the same summer, **Viola Liuzzo**, a white woman from Detroit, was shot while riding in her car with an African American man in Mississippi.

Urban Riots

There were civil disturbances, variously called **urban riots** or rebellions, in Harlem, Watts (Los Angeles), and Detroit. In 1966, 43 cities experienced riots; in 1967, the number rose to 167 cities. The attacks centered on the businesses in the black areas and the police and firefighters who tried to protect them. Social inequality and the expectations that the civil rights victories had raised fueled the anger of the disadvantaged. The 1968 **National Advisory (Kerner) Commission on Civil Disorders** convened to discover why there was so much violence, stating that America was "two societies separate and unequal," and that the plight of African Americans was largely unknown to whites. It concluded that the richest nation on earth could correct these inequalities. In the next month Martin Luther King Jr. was shot, spawning more riots.

Malcolm X

Malcolm X, born Malcolm Little, was a complex figure who evolved through many political positions. He is most famous for his statement "By any means necessary," which referred to African American self-defense. In his career he became successively a thief, a Black Muslim (Nation of Islam), an orthodox Muslim, and finally, a fighter for human rights who wanted to bring the United States before the United Nations on charges of racism. Malcolm did not believe in turning the other cheek; but, despite his reputation, he also did not want to initiate violence. After he left the Black Muslims, Malcolm called for the ballot, and said that if denied this right, African Americans would use the bullet. He was assassinated by followers of the Black Muslims in 1965.

ROLE OF GOVERNMENT

In general, the federal government reacted to the pressure from the grass roots: SNCC, SCLC, NAACP, and CORE. The two Civil Rights Acts (in 1957 and in 1960) were unenforceable calls for voting rights and desegregation, but the **1964 Civil Rights Act,** passed after a 57-day filibuster by Southern senators, did include strong provisions for integration of public accommodations as well as an unnoticed clause for women's rights. Kennedy had been unable to pass the bill, but Johnson forced it through, using his considerable political skills and trading on sympathy for the assassinated president.

During the 1960 campaign Kennedy had claimed that he would end discrimination in housing with "the stroke of a pen." Only after thousands of pens had been sent to the White House did he issue the order. The **24th Amendment,** outlawing **poll taxes,** was passed in 1964, and the **Voting Rights Act** (1965) was passed in response to the demonstrations in Selma, which had provoked so much violence.

Johnson's "Great Society" was in large part a civil rights program. The Office of Economic Opportunity (1964) was part of the War on Poverty. A series of executive orders banned discrimination and called for affirmative action. The Equal Employment Opportunity Commission (1965) was designed to enforce civil rights laws. Congress passed the last major piece of civil rights legislation, the **Civil Rights Act of 1968,** against housing discrimination, but it could not obtain a majority without an anti-riot amendment attached, signalling the end of liberal dominance on civil rights.

SUMMARY

The gains of the Civil Rights Movement are evident in every aspect of American life—from an increasing acceptance of black leaders in politics, sports, the arts, and intellectual pursuits to a change in the language from "negro" to "black" to "African American," and an acceptance of the rights of minorities to be represented on television. Regardless of what business leaders have thought about discrimination, they have had to pay attention to diversity. The Black Power Movement laid the basis for a widespread acceptance of black pride that changed hairstyles and self-images. Jesse Jackson, leader of the Rainbow Coalition, ran a serious primary campaign for president in 1984, gaining the respect of the more established leaders of the Civil Rights Movement. Most white southerners reacted against the Second Reconstruction by switching to the Republican Party, helping to elect Republican presidents from Nixon and Reagan to G. H. W. Bush and G. W. Bush. The backlash against the gains of blacks and other minorities began a **culture war** that is still being fought today.

THINGS TO REMEMBER

- **Black power:** The political advocacy of black-owned businesses and independent black political action. Stokely Carmichael first used the term in a position paper for the Student Nonviolent Coordinating Committee in 1965.

- **Civil Rights Movement:** The organizations and events in the 20th century that collectively pressured the federal, state, and local governments and businesses to grant equal rights to blacks and other minorities.

- **Culture wars:** The political events of the 1960s divided the country in many ways. There were pro-Vietnam hawks and anti-Vietnam doves; those who supported the counterculture of liberated sex and drugs and those who did not; those who favored American involvement in anticommunist foreign interventions and those who did not; and those who favored the civil rights revolution and those who did not. The conflicts within American culture between groups promoting competing views of American social and political values have been called cultural wars.

- **Jim Crow:** The series of laws designed to create separation between the races. These were by and large Southern state laws made constitutional by the Supreme Court decision *Plessy v. Ferguson* in 1896.

- **Second Reconstruction:** The Civil Rights Movement of the 1950s and 1960s was called the "Second Reconstruction" because the first Reconstruction in the 1860s and 1870s had not brought equality for blacks.

- **Sit-ins:** A form of nonviolent protest used by antiwar and antisegregation activists. Protesters would take over buildings, camp out in front of administration offices, or sit at lunch counters and demand to be served on an integrated basis. The first sit-ins were civil rights demonstrations at lunch counters in Greensboro, North Carolina in 1960.

- **Urban riots:** The series of violent reactions to police brutality, poor living conditions, assassinations, and high unemployment from 1964–1968. The National Advisory Commission on Civil Disorders (Kerner Commission) called them a reaction to rising expectations of the Civil Rights Movement. They were a cause of white flight from the cities to suburbia.

REVIEW QUESTIONS

1. Which organization was not involved in the Civil Rights Movement?

    (A) SNCC
    (B) UFW
    (C) CORE
    (D) SCLC
    (E) NAACP

2. Place these Civil Rights milestones in chronological order.

    1) Montgomery bus boycott
    2) Birmingham desegregation demonstrations
    3) voting rights march from Selma to Montgomery
    4) *Brown v. Board of Education*
    5) Greensboro lunch counter sit-ins

    Answer choices:
    (A) 1, 4, 2, 5, 3
    (B) 4, 1, 5, 2, 3
    (C) 4, 5, 1, 2, 3
    (D) 5, 2, 4, 1, 3
    (E) 1, 5, 4, 3, 2

3. The goal of the Freedom Rides was to desegregate

    (A) lunch counters
    (B) school buses
    (C) bus stations
    (D) interstate buses
    (E) trains

4. The landmark *Brown v. the Board of Education* Supreme Court decision on school desegregation was based on

    (A) the 14th Amendment equal protection clause
    (B) the 13th Amendment, which ended slavery
    (C) the 5th Amendment due process clause
    (D) the Bill of Rights
    (E) the doctrine of strict scrutiny

ANSWERS AND EXPLANATIONS

1. C

The United Farm Workers were a mainly Chicano union of lettuce and grape workers and not a Civil Rights organization for black equality, as the other choices were.

2. B

Brown vs. the Board of Education, 1954; Montgomery bus boycott, 1955; sit-ins at lunch counters in Greensboro, 1960; Birmingham desegregation demonstrations, 1963; Selma march, 1965.

3. C

Blacks and whites rode interstate buses together in 1961 and integrated bus stations and highway rest stops from Washington, DC to New Orleans. CORE and SNCC both participated.

4. D

The Warren Court's unanimous decision in 1954 was based on psychological studies on the equal protection clause of the 14th Amendment. The Court relied on sociological psychological studies that showed that African American children had feelings of inferiority and that separation was harmful and prevented blacks from equal opportunity in society. Strict scrutiny (a highly rigorous level of evaluation of a rule) was not mentioned. The 13th Amendment and the Bill of Rights (the first ten amendments to the Constitution) had no relevance to this case.

CHAPTER 31

The Vietnam War, 1954–1975

TIMELINE

1954	France defeated at Battle of Dien Bien Phu • Geneva Accords • Ngo Dinh Diem installed as prime minister of South Vietnam
1956	Elections for the reunification of Vietnam canceled
1957	Vietcong begin actions in South
1960	Eisenhower sends 3,000 military advisers to South Vietnam
1963	Kennedy sends an additional 13,000 advisers to South Vietnam • Buddhist monks begin self-immolation • CIA allows anti-Diem *coup d'état* results in Diem's murder
1964	Gulf of Tonkin Incident and Resolution • First bombings of North Vietnam
1965	First anti-war demonstration by Students for a Democratic Society in Washington, DC • First teach-in at University of Michigan, Ann Arbor • First draft board sit-in at University of Michigan SDS in Ann Arbor, Michigan • Vietnam Day Committee (VDC) demonstrations in Berkeley, California • President Johnson begins escalation of war
1967	More than 500,000 troops in Vietnam • Simultaneous demonstrations of 500,000 in New York and San Francisco
1968	Tet Offensive takes place • Johnson declines to run for second full term • Demonstrations at Chicago Democratic Convention • Nixon elected on "peace with honor" platform

1970	Nixon bombs and invades Cambodia and Laos • Demonstrations at Kent State University; four students killed by National Guard
1971	Daniel Ellsberg gives Pentagon Papers to the *New York Times* • *New York Times Co. v. United States* decision
1973	Cease fire in Vietnam; the United States agrees to withdraw in 60 days
1975	North Vietnamese troops enter Saigon, rename it Ho Chi Minh City

IMPORTANT PEOPLE, PLACES, EVENTS, AND CONCEPTS

self-immolation of Buddhist Monks

Ho Chi Minh

Dien Bien Phu

Geneva Accords

Ngo Dinh Diem

National Liberation Front (NLF)

Vietcong

military advisers

Lyndon B. Johnson

Gulf of Tonkin Incident

Gulf of Tonkin Resolution

booby traps

tunnels

Ho Chi Minh Trail

General William Westmoreland

Robert McNamara

William J. Fulbright

Tet

Clark Clifford

Eugene McCarthy

Richard Nixon

"Peace with Honor"

Vietnamization

Cambodia and Laos

Kent State University

Pentagon Papers

New York Times Co. v. United States

War Powers Act

26th Amendment

prisoners of war (POWs)

missing in action (MIA)

> "You can kill ten of my men for every one I kill of yours, but even at those odds you will lose and I will win."
>
> —Ho Chi Minh

INTRODUCTION

Americans were first introduced to Vietnam in 1963 when the newspapers showed a picture of a seated Buddhist monk who had **immolated** (sacrificed) himself by igniting his gasoline-soaked robes. This protest against the U.S.-supported government of South Vietnam was a dramatic introduction to a series of world-changing events. Nearly 30 years after the end of the war, there are still liberals who steadfastly maintain that President Kennedy would not have pursued the war. There are also conservatives who still argue that the United States pulled out without really fighting hard enough. Nearly sixty thousand Americans and more than 2,000,000 Vietnamese (both North and South) died in the conflict.

THE GROWING AMERICAN INVOLVEMENT IN VIETNAM

France ruled Vietnam from the 1890s to 1954, when the Communist and nationalist leader, **Ho Chi Minh**, led a successful war of liberation. After fighting a guerrilla war that began in 1948, the Vietnamese General Vo Nguyen Giap forced the French to surrender at **Dien Bien Phu**.

The Geneva Accords

France and its ally Great Britain along with the victorious Vietnamese and their allies, the Soviet Union and China, agreed to divide the country into North (Communist) and South (pro-West). There were to be elections in 1956 to decide whether it should be reunited. The United States attended the conference in Geneva, Switzerland, but did not sign the **Geneva Accords** of 1954.

The Eisenhower and Kennedy Administrations

Presidents Dwight D. Eisenhower and John F. Kennedy held to the standard Cold War theory of **containment**, and their **domino theory** followed from it: If one country fell to communism, its neighbors would follow. Eisenhower installed a **"puppet" regime** in South Vietnam headed by **Ngo Dinh Diem,** who had supporters in the old, pro-French bureaucracy. Ho Chi Minh ruled in the North. Since the United States assumed that Ho Chi Minh would win in the 1956 referendum, it prevented the elections from taking place. Opposed to the U.S.-supported South Vietnamese government and supported by the North were the National Liberation Front and the Vietcong. Both were organizations of communists and nationalists who wanted to rid the country of foreign control.

As the internal conflict in South Vietnam increased, Eisenhower sent 3,000 **military advisers** to the Diem government. Kennedy sent an additional 13,000. They were called "advisers," but they also fought in combat. In his inaugural address, Kennedy had stated his version of the **Truman Doctrine**: "Let every nation know, whether it wishes us well or ill, that we shall pay any price . . . support any friend, oppose any foe . . . in order to assure the survival . . . of liberty."

Diem was unable to control the South because of the work of the Vietcong and the anger of the Buddhist majority. The burning monks had protested because only Catholic interests, former French supporters, were represented in the government. In 1963, South Vietnamese military officers led a *coup d'état* against the Diem government; President Kennedy had instructed the Central Intelligence Agency (CIA) not to oppose or interfere with such a move. Diem was killed in the *coup*.

The Lyndon Johnson Administration

The new president, **Lyndon B. Johnson**, a Texan, wanted to be greater than Franklin Roosevelt. He was a political maneuverer *par excellence* who was accused of being an ignorant cowboy. According to the anti-war Kennedy liberals he "dragged the country into Vietnam." But Johnson took the advice of the whole Harvard-educated Kennedy cabinet, comprised of intellectuals and corporate executives. It wasn't until 1968 that any of these "wise men" changed their minds about the war.

In the 1964 election, Johnson and the liberal Senator Hubert Humphrey ran against Barry Goldwater, the standard bearer of the ideological conservatives. Goldwater believed in a strong-arm foreign policy and extreme free enterprise economics. Johnson ran as a peace candidate, saying he would never send "boys" to Asia but during the campaign he began to bomb North Vietnam.

The Gulf of Tonkin Resolution

American destroyers in the Gulf of Tonkin (near the Northern capital of Hanoi) had been attacking targets in North Vietnam. In a midnight speech President Johnson announced that the Vietnamese had shot at the U.S. boat, the *Maddox*, and called the attack "unprovoked" and "unequivocal." Such an attack probably never took place; no damage had been done to the *Maddox* and at Senate hearings chaired by Senator J. William Fulbright in 1966, no attack could be proven. As a result of the "attack," Johnson asked Congress for an authorization to "repel any armed attack against the forces of the United States." This **Tonkin Gulf Resolution** (1964) passed in Congress with only two dissenting votes. Although not a declaration of war, it provided Johnson with permission to bomb the North, which he did immediately. Johnson used the **Gulf of Tonkin Incident** to justify a major escalation to the war. Today both the incident and the resolution remain sources of controversy.

THE WAR

The Enemy

Movies such as *Full Metal Jacket*, which shows the frightening experience of guerrilla war fought in a jungle in which the enemy could be anywhere, and *Good Morning Vietnam*, in which the main character discovers that his best friend in Saigon is a member of the Vietcong, portray a reality only the soldiers could describe.

The Vietcong and their numerous supporters fought with **booby traps** and homemade weapons that could overturn tanks or kill soldiers with sharp poisoned sticks. Women and children would plant bombs in cities while riding bicycles. Under their villages the Vietcong built **tunnels** many hundreds of miles long for hiding, storing supplies, and living for months at a time. The North Vietnamese sent supplies to the South by truck and by mule, and on the backs of soldiers, men, and women. The routes were collectively called the **Ho Chi Minh Trail**. The NLF and the North Vietnamese received aid from Russia and China, but it was the support of the people of Vietnam for the cause of independence that allowed Ho Chi Minh to say, "You can kill ten of my men for every one I kill of yours, but even at those odds you will lose and I will win."

War Strategies

The Vietnamese wanted independence, but the Americans wanted a pro-West South Vietnam. After Diem was killed, the United States installed a series of generals and colonels to run the government. America tried to force Ho Chi Minh to give up the South. After the Tonkin Gulf Incident, Johnson sent 185,000 troops in 1965, and kept **escalating** the number until it reached 543,000 in 1969. Many of these young men were drafted, prompting more demonstrations. General **William Westmoreland** kept calling for more and more troops, claiming they were winning because they killed more Vietnamese everyday. Johnson tried to bomb the North into submission in prolonged bombing raids such as Rolling Thunder. U.S. troops tried to **defoliate** (eliminate) the jungle with **Agent Orange**, and to terrorize the population with **napalm**, a jellylike substance that would burst into flames after it stuck to its victim. The expression, "We had to destroy the village in order to save it," characterizes the American war effort.

The War on Television

Night after night there were scenes on the TV news of soldiers fighting in the jungle or being interviewed about how they felt. Also broadcast were pictures of body bags of dead U.S. soldiers—more than 100 for weeks in a row—but, as General Westmoreland said, the Vietcong body count was always many times more. This was the first television war; many people blamed the anti-war protests on the TV coverage.

THE GROWING ANTI-WAR PROTEST

As the war escalated, the protests grew apace. There were **teach-ins** to learn about Vietnam history and the role of America in the world. Students held **sit-ins** to protest the war—to obstruct the work of draft boards (University of Michigan); to stop the CIA from recruiting on campus (Columbia University); to stop buses from taking recruits to military bases (University of California at Berkeley); to stop weapons research (University of Michigan and Princeton); to protest against the manufacturer of napalm, Dow Chemical Company, (University of Wisconsin); and to try to eliminate the Reserve Officers Training Corps (ROTC) from many campuses. There were demonstrations twice a year in Washington, DC, from 1965 to 1970, which grew to many hundreds of thousands of people. In 1967 there were simultaneous marches of 500,000 people each in New York and San Francisco. In these demonstrations, the chants were "Hey, Hey LBJ, How many kids did you kill today," "Out Now," and, after 1968, "Ho, Ho, Ho Chi Minh, the NLF is gonna win!" Some men burned draft cards, or refused to be drafted and went to jail, and more than 30,000 of them went to Canada. No matter where Johnson, or later Nixon, went, there would be demonstrators. One of Johnson's aides called this the "imprisonment in the White House."

Tet

In 1968, Secretary of Defense **Robert McNamara** had said that the **"light is at the end of the tunnel,"** or victory was near in Vietnam. Events proved him disastrously wrong. A cease-fire was planned for the Vietnamese New Year, **Tet**. The respite was broken by simultaneous attacks on more than 100 cities and towns, including Saigon, the capital of South Vietnam, where the radio station and the CIA headquarters were taken over. There was news footage of General Westmoreland defending his headquarters in Saigon with a pistol. Americans had thought that the United States controlled the cities, if not the jungle. Now it was clear that the Vietnamese could coordinate a devastating attack in the cities, just when McNamara had said the end was near.

The consequences of the Tet Offensive were momentous. The government and the Army were immediately discredited, and Johnson's "wise men" began to see that the war was unwinnable. It caused **Clark Clifford**, a presidential adviser since the late '40s, to turn to a policy of withdrawal instead of continuous escalation. He convinced most of Johnson's senior advisers of this, and they brought Johnson himself to this point of view. Johnson decided it was time for peace and arranged for a peace conference with the Vietnamese, both North and South.

The 1968 Election

The 1968 election was one of the most turbulent in American history. During the primaries there were two peace candidates in the Democratic Party in addition to Johnson. **Robert Kennedy** began a run late in the season, and **Eugene McCarthy**, an anti-war senator from Minnesota, had started a youth campaign to end the war, gathering support by having his workers go door to door all over the country. In the first primary, McCarthy received a much larger percentage of the vote than Johnson anticipated, showing LBJ that the president no longer had control of his party. Johnson decided not to run for re-election. In his dramatic speech to the nation on April 1, 1968, Johnson called for peace negotiations and in one short paragraph at the end of a 4,000-word speech he announced that he "would not seek another term" as president. This opened the door for Robert Kennedy, Eugene McCarthy, and Governor George Wallace of Alabama (who ran on the American Independent Party platform).

Martin Luther King Jr. and Robert Kennedy were killed in April and June, respectively. The riots that occurred after King's assassination were a violent prelude to demonstrations that rocked the August Democratic Convention in Chicago. Television viewers saw unprovoked police attacks on demonstrators as thousands tried to get into the convention to nominate Eugene McCarthy. They chanted the "whole world is watching" as they were being beaten. The Democrats nominated Hubert Humphrey, who felt it necessary to defend his role as vice-president. He promised negotiations when many of his liberal colleagues were calling for immediate withdrawal.

Richard Nixon and Spiro Agnew were nominated by the Republicans. Nixon promised **"Peace with Honor."** He said he spoke for the **silent majority** and that he would "bring us together." The election was extremely close in popular votes: Nixon won with 43 percent to Humphrey's 42 percent, and Wallace got 13 percent.

NIXON AND THE WAR

War Strategy

Nixon had ran as a peace candidate; once in office, however, he began to implement the plan outlined by Clark Clifford. There would be a gradual withdrawal of American troops, but the strategy was to **"Vietnamize"** the war: U.S. troops would train the South Vietnamese to fight on their own while the United States would support them with bombing raids. In the meantime, America would try to win the "hearts and minds" of the Vietnamese people. Nixon also had Secretary of State **Henry Kissinger** arrange invasions and bombings of **Cambodia and Laos**, designed to destroy the Ho Chi Minh Trail. These prompted huge demonstrations, including the **Kent State** University demonstration (1970) at which the National Guard killed four students.

Domestic Strategy

To reduce protests and wind down the war, Nixon ended the draft. First he introduced a lottery, but then he phased it out until America had an all-volunteer army. Nixon's attempt to unite the country was an utter failure. It is not clear that anyone could have brought together the prowar **hawks** and the anti-war **doves**, but calling the demonstrators "bums," making an enemies list of reporters and dissenters, and giving the names to the FBI for investigation and harassment did not endear him to his opponents.

The Pentagon Papers

Much of the true story of Vietnam and America was revealed in the **Pentagon Papers**, which were leaked to the *New York Times* in June of 1971 by a Pentagon employee named **Daniel Ellsberg**. In 7,000 pages of documentation secretly ordered by Robert McNamara, the Papers revealed that the Johnson administration had been lying about the success of the war. They revealed that the CIA analysis had concluded that the war was unwinnable, but president after president ignored their advice and went ahead with it. Nixon decided that this information was too damaging to publish, so he tried to stop its publication. The Supreme Court ruled against him in the landmark decision of *New York Times Co. v. United States*. A free press was more important than keeping secrets of the government that did not pose a threat at the moment.

THE END OF THE WAR

Nixon was re-elected in 1972 in a landslide win against the anti-war candidate, **George McGovern**, but his relations with Congress were becoming more and more troubled. Having been lied to too many times, the Senate refused to allow more funds for new actions in the war, but Nixon continued to bomb in Cambodia and to mine Haiphong Harbor in the North. Despite this, the North would not give in. Finally, Henry Kissinger arranged a cease-fire in January of 1973; troops were to be withdrawn within 60 days. There were still some forces left behind, but South Vietnam had to fend for itself from that point forward. On April 27, 1975, North Vietnamese forces marched into Saigon and changed its name to Ho Chi Minh City. The war was over.

RESULTS

Politically, the Vietnam War resulted in The **War Powers Act** (1973), which prevented the president from sending troops to a foreign country for more than 60 days without a vote by Congress. The war also resulted in the voluntary army and the **26th Amendment** of the Constitution (1971), which reduced the voting age to 18. Most of the student protesters of the '60s—and many of the draftees—could not vote.

The issue of the **prisoners of war** (POWs) and those **missing in action** (MIAs) lasted well into the 1980s as a campaign issue. Conservatives, and some relatives of MIAs, lobbied Congress and the presidents to investigate the whereabouts of those soldiers who had never come home.

The controversy about how the war was fought and whether the United States could have won continues to this day. General Westmoreland maintained that the war was lost because he was not given the support he needed from Congress and from the American people. This **Vietnam Revisionism** still had many adherents in 2000, at the 25th anniversary of the defeat of South Vietnam.

SUMMARY

Political thinkers believe the **culture wars** of the 1960s were still working themselves out during the Clinton administration. One source of these cultural conflicts was how to understand the Vietnam War. Were the protests justified? Should we distrust the government? Is America a good country, an imperialist monster, or something in between? One way to understand Vietnam is to compare it to the American Revolution. Britain was the most powerful country of the 1770s, and America fought an eight-year guerrilla war against them. The British could have sent more troops to America after Yorktown, but there was a powerful opposition in George III's government that favored withdrawal. America won that war, but the British still teach it much differently than we do.

THINGS TO REMEMBER

- **Domino theory:** The Eisenhower-era theory that one Communist country would infiltrate or influence its neighbors, supporting insurrection there and causing them to become Communist too. They would fall like a series of dominoes standing close together. Kennedy, Johnson, and Nixon also subscribed to this theory, a version of containment.

- **Doves:** Those who were against the Vietnam War in the 1960s. The opposite of hawks.

- **Escalation:** An increase in number, volume, scope. In reference to the Vietnam War, it refers to the increase in the number of troops and the intensity of involvement by the United States.

- **Guerrilla war:** Hit-and-run tactics combined with hiding and ambushing the enemy. The soldier would live off the land and the population in an area so that he need not carry many supplies. The Americans learned this from the Indians in colonial times and used it during the Revolution. The Vietnamese used it against the Americans in the Vietnam War.

- **Hawks:** Those who were pro–Vietnam War in the 1960s. The opposite of doves.

- **Puppet regimes:** A government controlled behind-the-scenes by another power. During the Vietnam War, South Vietnam's governments were installed and controlled by the United States; Ngo Dinh Diem and General Thieu, leaders of South Vietnam, were American puppets.

- **Teach-ins:** A form of educational protest at universities. The practice began in 1965 at the University of Michigan in Ann Arbor, when professors and students analyzed U.S. foreign policy and debated with each other and—only in the earlier days of the war—with government representatives.

- **Vietnam revisionism:** The political position that claimed that we could have won the Vietnam War if we had declared war, put in more troops, had had a more unified country, or had given our generals free reign to fight. These positions are called revisionist because the consensus among historians and politicians was that we had lost the war and that the war was unwinnable.

REVIEW QUESTIONS

1. Put the following events in order from oldest to most recent.

   1) Geneva Accords
   2) Tonkin Gulf
   3) Dien Bien Phu
   4) The Tet offensive
   5) Assassination of Ngo Dinh Diem

   Answer choices:
   (A) 2, 3, 4, 1, 5
   (B) 4, 3, 2, 5, 1
   (C) 3, 1, 5, 2, 4
   (D) 3, 1, 4, 2, 5
   (E) 2, 3, 5, 1, 4

2. Nixon's policy in Vietnam was called

   (A) Rolling Thunder
   (B) Vietnamization
   (C) containment
   (A) immediate withdrawal
   (E) pacification

3. Vietnam revisionism was a belief that

   (A) immediate peace was necessary
   (B) America lost the war because of a lack of Congressional support
   (C) the demonstrators lost the war
   (D) the Army did not fight hard enough
   (E) the Vietnamese were tougher than we had expected

4. In 1968 President Johnson did not run for reelection because

   (A) he had already served two full terms
   (B) he had lost the New Hampshire primary
   (C) he wanted to negotiate a peace
   (D) his health was failing
   (E) Eugene McCarthy came in a close second in the New Hampshire primary

ANSWERS AND EXPLANATIONS

1. C

The French were defeated at Dien Bien Phu in 1954. The Geneva Accords were signed soon after. Diem was killed in 1963. The Tonkin Gulf Resolution was passed in 1964, during the campaign of Johnson against Goldwater. The Tet offensive occurred in 1968, before Johnson decided not to seek another term.

2. B

Vietnamization was the slow withdrawal of troops and the increased bombing to try to win more before leaving Vietnam. Rolling Thunder and Pacification were Johnson policies, Containment was Truman, and immediate withdrawal was a radical demand.

3. B

The general opinion among political thinkers is that Vietnam was an unwinnable war. The Revisionists contend that Congress did not give the military enough support. Such people believe that the demonstrations had no affect and they also believe the army fought hard, but was not permitted to fight long enough.

4. E

Johnson did not try to run for reelection because he was losing decisive control of his party. The anti-war forces (McCarthy and Kennedy) were gaining strength. He had not served two terms and he was not sick. He wanted to negotiate a peace, but that was not a reason to drop out of the election; he could have negotiated a peace while campaigning.

CHAPTER 32

Cultural and Social Change in the 1960s

TIMELINE

1960	Joan Baez's first record becomes a hit, Folk Revival takes off
1962	Port Huron Statement of Students for a Democratic Society written • "Blowin' in the Wind" written by Bob Dylan • Pete Seeger's "If I Had a Hammer" becomes a hit for Peter, Paul, and Mary
1964	Free Speech Movement (FSM) at the University of California, Berkeley • Beatles appear on *The Ed Sullivan Show*
1965	"Like a Rolling Stone" becomes a big hit for Bob Dylan • "I Can't Get No Satisfaction" becomes a big hit for the Rolling Stones • "Tracks of My Tears" becomes a big hit for Smokey Robinson
1966	Black Panther Party founded • United Farm Workers sign first contract
1967	Summer of Love
1968	SDS sponsors a protest at Columbia University, more than 700 arrested • Demonstrations held at Chicago Democratic Convention
1969	Woodstock Festival takes place
1973	Stand-off at Wounded Knee—American Indian Movement (AIM)

IMPORTANT PEOPLE, PLACES, EVENTS, AND CONCEPTS

"Freedom Now!"

Paul Goodman

Erich Fromm

Students for a
Democratic Society
(SDS)

Port Huron
Statement

"Let the People
Decide"

Weathermen

Free Speech
Movement (FSM)

Mario Savio

Abbie Hoffman

Yippies

Black Panthers

Huey Newton

Cesar Chavez

United Farm
Workers of America

American Indian
Movement

Motown

Joan Baez

Bob Dylan

Beatles

Rolling Stones

Ravi Shankar

John Coltrane

psychedelic rock

Woodstock

Timothy Leary

"Turn on, Tune in,
Drop out"

hippies

Haight-Ashbury

"There is a time when the operation of the machine becomes so odious, makes you so sick at heart, that you can't take part . . . You've got to put your bodies upon the gears and upon the wheels, upon the levers . . . and you've got to make it stop. And you've got to indicate to the people who run it . . . that unless you're free, the machine will be prevented from working at all!"

—Mario Savio, Berkeley, California 1964

INTRODUCTION

The protesters of the 1960s were ordinary people who were agents of change. In order to understand the decade, we must understand their origins and the nature of their mission. Underlying the optimism of the youth was the postwar boom and its contrast with the depression culture of their parents. The key was a new sense that society was in flux, and the baby boomers, the largest generation ever, could direct its development. Some were moved by John Kennedy's words, " . . . ask what you can do for your country," but many others regarded **Freedom Now!** of the SNCC, "Let the People Decide" of the SDS, or "Turn on, Tune in, Drop out" of Timothy Leary as the paths to follow.

THE POLITICAL ACTIVISTS

Moral and Intellectual Roots

The roots of the protests were moral, intellectual, and cultural. The moral roots came from the actions and purposes of the Civil Rights Movement. The intellectual sources came from the analyses of four main thinkers. In *The Power Elite* (1956), C. Wright Mills contended that the United States was a class society controlled by a small group of moneyed men. In *Contours of American History* (1961), William Appleman Williams argued that not only had America always been undemocratic, it had also been imperialist. **Paul Goodman**, in *Growing Up Absurd* (1960), and **Erich Fromm,** in *The Sane Society* (1955) and *The Art of Loving* (1956), gave psychological permission to the baby boomers to express their authentic (natural) feelings against what they saw as a puritanic and shallow capitalist society in which everything was for sale. The four writers encouraged free expression both intellectually and sexually, advocating useful (productive) work that would build community cohesion and provide opportunities for all to grow.

Cultural Roots

The cultural roots of the 1960s were in the hipster world of jazz and blues. The many uses of "man"—for "you" or as a substitute for "lord"—are familiar examples. The casual acceptance of marijuana as a recreational drug went as far back as the 1920s, when Louis Armstrong's smoking habits became public. The world of the Beats, which was derived from the cool jazz lifestyle, came into the '60s through **Allen Ginsberg's** poem "Howl" (1955), and **Jack Kerouac's** novel *On the Road* (1951). Finally, **Aldous Huxley's** *Doors of Perception* (1954) introduced hallucinogenic drugs to the baby boomers.

POLITICAL ORGANIZATIONS

Students for a Democratic Society

The founding document of **Students for a Democratic Society (SDS)** was the **Port Huron Statement** (1962) which, like Paul Goodman, called for "educative . . . creative work" that would help realize man's potential for "self-direction and self-understanding." SDS wanted to **"let the people decide"** in both the economic and political spheres. Tom Hayden and Paul Potter, early leaders of SDS, watched in amazement as their group of less than 100 students from the University of Michigan seemed to grow by itself into an organization of 142,000 by 1967. They called SDS a **New Left** organization to differentiate themselves from the Communist and Socialist organizations of the 1930s–1950s that had a heritage of Stalinism and old disputes that never seemed to be resolved. They mobilized on campuses and organized for community development in Cleveland, Ohio, and Newark, New Jersey. When the Vietnam War did not end in response to their demonstrations, some members of the leadership called for violence against what they called the "monster United States war machine," splitting SDS up into factions in June 1969. One splinter group was the **Weathermen,** who decided to become terrorists in America in order to save the world from more Vietnams. They derived their name from a line by Bob Dylan: "You don't need a weatherman to know which way the wind blows." Four Weathermen died in an explosion in a townhouse in Greenwich Village, New York City. SDS terrorism died with them.

The Free Speech Movement

The Free Speech Movement of the University of California at Berkeley grew directly out of civil rights demonstrations at hotels in San Francisco. The university administration suspended some students for distributing pro-demonstration literature on campus. In protest, hundreds of students took over the main classroom building. This signaled a new era: They were not only fighting for the right to express themselves politically, but they were also demanding to be treated with respect. The chancellor, Clark Kerr, had called the university a "huge machine." However, **Mario Savio**, a philosophy graduate student, in his famous speech, said he was so "sick at heart" at the repression of his ideas and actions that he was willing to put his "body upon the gears and upon the wheels, upon the levers . . . to make it stop" until he was free. This inspired students all over the country to take power into their own hands and to shape their schools and the society to their ideals. The Free Speech Movement of 1964 grew into an anti-war organization called the **Vietnam Day Committee** (**VDC**) (see the chapter on the Vietnam War).

Yippies

The gifted activist and comedian **Abbie Hoffman** and his partner Jerry Rubin organized a group of anarchists to oppose the war in Vietnam and the stodgy-minded conformity of consumer culture. These **Yippies** (Youth International Party) poured garbage bags full of dollar bills from the balcony onto the floor of the New York Stock Exchange. They also protested against the war by marching with pictures of Lyndon Johnson upside down. Hoffman wrote *Steal this Book* in 1971.

Black Panthers

The **Black Panthers** of Oakland, California were the most contradictory of all the organizations of the 1960s. They were an inspiration to many white and African American radicals because they seemed ready to put their lives on the line. **Huey Newton**, Bobby Seale, and Eldridge Cleaver were all strong personalities who carried unconcealed weapons. They demanded a socialist America that would protect all its citizens from violence and poverty. In the meantime, they would protect their community and provide free breakfasts for poor African American children, so they could go the school and learn. Their speeches were long harangues, serious and hilarious by turns. Some of the Black Panthers were also selling heroin or were involved with other serious crime.

United Farm Workers and the American Indian Movement

Cesar Chavez organized Chicano (Mexican) migrant farm workers in California. They formed a union, the **United Farm Workers of America** (1966), and called for boycotts of grapes and lettuce. Dennis Banks, a Chippewa, and Russell Means, a Sioux, led the **American Indian Movement** to obtain equal rights for Native Americans. They led a protest at the historic site of the **Wounded Knee** Massacre (1889) in 1973.

CURRENTS IN HISTORY WRITING

The ideas of the 1960s influenced historians: they now discussed history in terms of change caused by conflict and the actions of ordinary people. This is called **conflict historiography**. Everything no longer "turned out for the best" in their view, and not everyone agreed with the presidents. Slavery and the lives of African Americans, women, and minorities were treated much more extensively.

MUSIC

Motown

The **Motown** record company was owned and operated by Barry Gordy, a black entrepreneur. Its distinct Motown sound of Smokey Robinson's "Tracks of My Tears" and the Supremes' "Stop in the Name of Love," combined with the Memphis sound of Otis Redding's "Try a Little Tenderness" and Wilson Pickett's "Mustang Sally" produced a constant stream of hits.

Joan Baez and Bob Dylan

Joan Baez was the 19-year-old symbol of the folk revival. Her crystalline voice made converts by the thousands from 1958–1961. Her albums were best sellers; other popular and more mainstream successes included Peter, Paul, and Mary, the Kingston Trio, and, later, **Bob Dylan**. Dylan had studied folk, blues, rock, and Ginsberg and Kerouac. He absorbed all these influences and churned out songs and poems concerning current events, as well as his personal relationships. Dylan's two most famous songs were "Blowin' in the Wind," about the ills of racism and war (which became a big hit when Peter, Paul, and Mary sang it in 1963), and "Like a Rolling Stone" (which was his first folk-influenced rock hit). "Like a Rolling Stone" was a description of how hard it is to make choices for yourself when you have no one to take care of you.

The Beatles and the Rolling Stones

In 1964, the British group **the Beatles** played on *The Ed Sullivan Show*, a television variety program. Their appearance was a teen sensation, but the Beatles became a phenomenon unlike any other group of teen idols. They developed a musical and intellectual depth far beyond their initial impression. From "I Want to Hold Your Hand," a simple love song, to "Eleanor Rigby," an ominous tune about a lonely old lady played with quirky rhythms on the cellos and violins, the Beatles opened up a wide new space for popular music, taking their gravity from Dylan and their music from folk and the blues.

The blues singer Muddy Waters received widespread recognition only after British rock star **Mick Jagger** explained that he had named his band the **Rolling Stones** after one of Waters's songs. The Stones played a raw kind of rock that was extremely intense, like the blues, and was often tinged with a violence and hostility that most of the Beatles' songs lacked. The sexual references in "I Can't Get No Satisfaction" (1965) and the dark references in "Street Fighting Man" or "Sympathy for the Devil" (1968) were anthems for the Weathermen. Their music helped set the tone for a knifing by a member of the Hell's Angels motorcycle gang at an outdoor concert in Altamont, California in 1969.

Ravi Shankar, John Coltrane, and Psychedelic Music

Interest in Eastern philosophy extended to a fascination when the classical music of India was brought to America by the master musician **Ravi Shankar**. The jazz virtuoso and innovator **John Coltrane** was also heavily influenced by Indian music. His successive recordings of the showtune "My Favorite Things," from 1960 to his death in 1967, show a reach for meaning through his music similar to those who seek justice or personal truth. Lastly, rock and roll reflected the drug experience in **psychedelic rock** through such songs as the Beatles' "Lucy in the Sky with Diamonds," Jimmy Hendrix's "Purple Haze," or the lengthy improvisations of the Grateful Dead.

Monterey and Woodstock

In 1967 and 1969, two immense gatherings of music lovers occurred in Monterey, California and **Woodstock**, New York. The first was an outdoor concert at which British and American white rock stars played along with Jimmy Hendrix, Otis Redding, and Ravi Shankar. Woodstock, in 1969, was a concert in which drugs and nudity were prevalent. So many hundreds of thousands of people showed up that it was constantly on the verge of chaos. The fact that no one died has been attributed either to the magic of the '60s or to sheer luck.

HIPPIES

The hippies, who followed the LSD guru (leader) **Timothy Leary**, were readers of the Eastern philosophies of Hinduism, Buddhism, Zen Buddhism, and Taoism. In *The Way of Zen* (1958) Alan Watts explained the thinking of the East that emphasized reaching inner peace (contentment) through meditation and spontaneous expression. In an analysis that criticized the Judeo-Christian tradition, Watts argued that instead of being separate from nature and each other, we are all one. Timothy Leary believed that LSD could create the experiences of self-knowledge and contentment that Eastern holy men sought. The **hippies** who followed him and his **"Turn on, Tune in, Drop out"** philosophy did just that: They dropped out of the competitive culture, dressed up in bright colors, tuned into their own feelings, and believed they could change the world by not participating. Some joined **communes** in which they tried to live simple lives on farms or as scavengers in cities. They held **be-ins** in San Francisco and New York City in which they experienced their togetherness in parks. The hippies flocked to a small San Francisco district called **Haight-Ashbury** in the summer of 1967, the **Summer of Love**. "Love is all you need," chanted the Beatles.

SUMMARY

At the height of the protests, a "movement culture" developed; thousands of people would turn out for demonstrations in any city in the country. Those who participated in demonstrations had experienced a sense of empowerment; they knew they were makers of history and agents of change. Hundreds of thousands of young people and their allies were listening to the same music, from Dylan to the Beatles, from Hendrix to the Stones. Everyone seemed to be dancing to Smokey Robinson. The movement lost its steam by the early '70s: The war was not ending but the draft was, so only those most committed to radical change were participating in anti-war activities. The music became less urgent and less spontaneous, and disco took over. But the culture of the country had been changed fundamentally. Now there were those who favored the changes in the 1960s and those who did not. New conflicts were on the way, while the war in Vietnam continued and equal opportunity was still not a reality.

THINGS TO REMEMBER

- **Conflict historiography:** Historiography is the study of how history is written. Historians of the 1950s—consensus historians—in general argued that America was the world's great democracy that only did good in the world and had no conflicts at home. Largely due to the efforts of the Civil Rights and Anti-war Movements, the issues and facts about slavery, racial and gender discrimination, riots, radicals, etc., have been important parts of U.S. history curriculum in schools since the late 1960s and early 1970s. Similarly, while consensus historians of the 1950s emphasized compromise as the key characteristic of change in American history, conflict historians believe that change occurs through conflict between opposing forces.

- **New Left:** Organizations such as the underground press, Students for a Democratic Society and its offshoots, and women's groups (like the Red Stockings) that were interested in social change but uninterested in the debates over whether to support Russia as a socialist country. These organizations did not require their followers to support the Stalinist practices of the Communists: They were not explicitly socialist, even though many in the organizations were socialists. They tried to differentiate themselves from the debates over totalitarianism by claiming that America did not need a police state to enforce economic and political equality. They rejected the "old left" of Stalinism.

REVIEW QUESTIONS

1. Which was the most important reason for the early growth of
   Students For a Democratic Society (SDS) and the Free Speech
   Movement (FSM)?

   (A) drugs
   (B) government lies
   (C) the high divorce rate
   (D) optimism caused by the postwar boom
   (E) the nuclear threat

2. Which did the Beatles influence the LEAST?

   (A) Students For a Democratic Society (SDS)
   (B) American rock and roll
   (C) hippies
   (D) Timothy Leary
   (E) yippies

3. Match the book and the author:

   A) *Growing Up Absurd*   1) Alan Watts
   B) *The Power Elite*   2) Abbie Hoffman
   C) *The Art of Loving*   3) Paul Goodman
   D) *The Way of Zen*   4) C. Wright Mills
   E) *Steal This Book*   5) Eric Fromm

   Answer choices:
   (A) A-3, B-4, C-5, E-2
   (B) B-4, C-1, D-4, E-2
   (C) B-5, C-1, D-3, E-2
   (D) A-5, B-4, D-1, E-2
   (E) B-4, C-3, D-1, E-2

4. The key reason for the slowing of the protests after 1971 was that

   (A) America was winning in Vietnam
   (B) the government became more responsive
   (C) the draft ended
   (D) all the major battles had been won
   (E) the government cracked down on protesters

ANSWERS AND EXPLANATIONS

1. D

The postwar boom created a sense of optimism that characterized the student movement. The nuclear threat was not as important. Lies and drugs did not come until later.

2. A

SDS was a political organization; the Beatles did not encourage political action. The drugs and music of the other choices were closer to the Beatles' ideas. The Yippies combined fantasy and politics and drugs.

3. A

Paul Goodman wrote *Growing up Absurd*; C. Wright Mills wrote *The Power Elite*; Eric Fromm wrote *The Art of Loving*; Abbie Hoffman wrote *Steal This Book*; Alan Watts wrote *The Way of Zen*.

4. C

When the draft wound down, so did the majority of protesters. America was never winning in Vietnam, Nixon increased the bombing so the moves toward peace were never apparent, the war had not ended by 1971, and government harassment never stopped the protests.

CHAPTER 33

Politics and Society, 1968–1980

TIMELINE

1968	Richard Nixon elected president
1969	Apollo Mission lands on moon
1970	Environmental Protection Agency established
1971	Ping Pong Diplomacy opens relations with the People's Republic of China
1972	*Roe v. Wade* decision • Equal Rights Amendment (ERA) passed by Congress • Watergate Hotel broken into • Nixon re-elected
1974	*United States v. Nixon* decision • Articles of Impeachment passed by House Judiciary Committee • Nixon resigns, Gerald Ford takes office • Ford pardons Nixon
1976	Jimmy Carter elected president
1978	Beginning of steep rise in gasoline prices • *University of California v. Bakke* decision • Camp David Accords negotiated • ERA fails to win 38 votes

IMPORTANT PEOPLE, PLACES, EVENTS, AND CONCEPTS

Warren Burger

Roe v. Wade

University of California v. Bakke

Betty Friedan

National Organization of Women (NOW)

Equal Rights Amendment (ERA)

Earth Day

Rachel Carson

Environmental Protection Agency (EPA)

New Federalism

OPEC

Henry Kissinger

Ping Pong Diplomacy

détente

ABM Treaty

SALT

shuttle diplomacy

Salvador Allende

The Committee to Re-Elect the President

Watergate

John Mitchell

Bob Woodward and Carl Bernstein

cover-up

smoking gun

Saturday Night Massacre

United States v. Nixon

Gerald Ford

Jimmy Carter

Camp David Accords

Iran Hostage Crisis

"The President has only 12 votes in the Senate. He has lied to me …. [and] to my colleagues for the last time."

—Senator Barry Goldwater, 1974

INTRODUCTION

The heady times of the 1960s profoundly influenced the next decades. If the Anti-war Movement could be credited with bringing down Lyndon Johnson, it could also take credit for the atmosphere that made the reporters and Congress pursue Nixon in Watergate. Similarly, Nixon's anger at the student "bums" and his adult "enemies" were key motivations for the actions of the Watergate conspirators. The second wave of feminism and the environmental movement were continuations of the methods and thinking of the Civil Rights, Anti-war, and Student Movements. There was a turn to the right, but each step was fought in the streets and in the halls of Congress.

SOCIAL ISSUES

Desegregation of Schools

In 1968, segregation was still a reality by law (*de jure*) in the South and by neighborhood (*de facto*) in the North. When Nixon took office, 67 percent of African Americans in the South attended school without white classmates, but by 1974 that had changed to 10 percent. In the North, however, about half of all children attended segregated schools. Mass marches and boycotts had forced change in the South, but in Boston a **backlash** in 1974 produced an opposition to busing for racial balance. **White flight** from urban areas in the North produced black majorities in the cities, leaving a deteriorating tax base, poor schools, and inadequate services.

Supreme Court Decisions

Although Chief Justice **Earl Warren** resigned in 1969, the Supreme Court continued to expand on his decisions under **Warren Burger**. *Furman v. Georgia* (1972) declared the death penalty unconstitutional. *Roe v. Wade* (1973) legalized abortion in early pregnancy. *Regents of the University of California v. Bakke* (1978) granted the use of affirmative action as long as there were no quotas involved.

Nixon's appointees, William H. Rehnquist and Lewis Powell, were key figures in turning the court against its Warren precedents in the 1980s. Justice Harry Blackmun, a third Nixon appointee, became more liberal, defending *Roe* and *Furman*.

FEMINISM

The **Second Wave of Feminism** began in the late 1960s among radicals in the Anti-war and Civil Rights Movement and spread through an informal network of small group meetings. At these **consciousness raising groups**, women discovered that their personal difficulties in breaking out of the traditional roles of housewife were society-wide political obstacles. The analyses in **Kate Millet's** *Sexual Politics* (1970), which described the oppression of housewives and how women were portrayed in literature and psychology, and **Betty Friedan's** *The Feminine Mystique* (1963) lent ammunition to the burgeoning movement. With the founding of the **National Organization of Women** (**NOW**) in 1966, and the publication of *Ms.* magazine in 1972, the movement gained organizational bases that could sponsor demonstrations and exchange ideas. Between 1975 and 1988, women employed as physicians went from 13 percent to 20 percent; as bus drivers, from 37.7 percent to 48.5 percent; and as telephone operators, from 93.3 percent to 89.8 percent. The issues of rape, abortion, and spousal abuse became common topics of conversation, and the government passed laws to protect the economic, civil, and educational rights of women. Women were also entering the mainstream of sports on the strength of these laws.

Equal Rights Amendment

Passed by Congress in 1972, the **Equal Rights Amendment** (**ERA**) stated simply that "equality of rights under law shall not be abridged by the United States or any state on account of sex." Only 35 of the necessary 38 states passed it by 1978. The successful opposition included a group of women led by **Phyllis Schlafly**, a conservative intellectual and political activist.

The Fight over Abortion

Pro-choice activist lawyers had won *Roe v. Wade* in the Supreme Court on the basis of the 4th Amendment right of privacy. **Pro-life** opposition claims that abortion was murder often reflected the religion-based viewpoint, which argued that the fetus was a sacred human life.

THE ENVIRONMENT

Activism regarding the environment and nuclear power were also continuations of the movements of the 1960s. On April 25, 1970, the first **Earth Day** was celebrated on college campuses all over the country. There were sit-ins, teach-ins, and celebrations of clean air and fresh water as a way to build a safe legacy for themselves and future generations. The threats to health and well being described in the *Population Bomb* by Paul Ehrlich (1968) and the threat of pesticides pointed out in *Silent Spring* by **Rachel Carson** (1962) represented a new approach to environmentalism. These warnings were quite different from the call for the preservation of natural beauty and space for recreation advocated by Theodore Roosevelt, John Muir, and John Burroughs in the early 20th century. Congress responded in 1970 with passing a Clean Air Act and establishing the **Environmental Protection Agency** (**EPA**) and Occupational Health and Safety Administration, the latter of which dealt with automobile and factory emissions, solid wastes, and the health of workers in factories and offices.

THE ECONOMY

Richard Nixon began the Republican campaign to reduce the size of the federal government with his revenue-sharing **New Federalism** programs. These provided block grants to states, allowing them to decide how money was to be spent. The inflation that started as a result of the Vietnam War produced an unusual combination of high prices and high unemployment called **stagflation**. Finally, the oil embargo organized by the **Organization of Petroleum Exporting Countries** (**OPEC**) created an ongoing energy crisis during the 1970s.

FOREIGN AFFAIRS

Nixon has been credited with uncommon expertise in foreign affairs, excluding Vietnam. He and his secretary of state, **Henry Kissinger**, arranged the opening of diplomatic relations with the People's Republic of China. Discussion began when the ping pong teams of the United States and China played against each other in 1971. **"Ping Pong Diplomacy"** successfully exploited the rift between the Soviet Union and China, which had been in existence since 1959. Full diplomatic relations waited until 1979. The policy of **détente**, or a lessening of tensions in the Cold War, was intended to reduce the balance of terror with the USSR and other nuclear powers. The main agreements were the **Anti-Ballistic Missile** (**ABM**) **Treaty**, to limit defensive missiles, and the **Strategic Arms Limitation Treaty (SALT)**, to limit offensive missiles.

Israel engaged in two major wars in which it fought Egypt and other Arab nations—the Six-Day War in 1967, and the Yom Kippur War in 1973. Kissinger helped dampen the tensions through **shuttle diplomacy** (traveling back and forth among the combatants), but not before U.S. support of Israel prompted an Arab oil embargo. The energy crises of the early and late '70s had their roots here.

THE WATERGATE SCANDAL

The scandal began as a scheme to create the biggest win possible in the 1972 election. The **Committee to Re-Elect the President** (**CREP**), called CREEP by opponents, had bugged the offices of the Democratic Party campaign headquarters in the Watergate Hotel and office building in Washington, DC in June of 1972. One of the "burglars," who had worked for the CIA, was an employee of CREP and had in his pocket the telephone number of **John Mitchell**, the former U.S. attorney general and head of Nixon's 1972 campaign. The revelations that followed, brought out by *Washington Post* reporters **Bob Woodward** and **Carl Bernstein**, as well as by Senate investigations and confessions of participants trying to bargain for shorter sentences, amounted to a collection of wrongdoing going back many years. The scandal involved hundreds of thousands of dollars in payoffs for silence, stolen information from a psychiatrist's office, the planting of false information in newspapers about opponents, and a convoluted cover-up of illegal activities.

Nixon and Watergate

The key question, according to Republican Senator Howard Baker of the Senate Watergate Committee, was: "What did the president know and when did he know it?" Tapes of White House conversations, arranged by Nixon, revealed that despite his repeated denials, he did have full knowledge of the activities of the burglars. In the **smoking gun tape** it was revealed that he had also ordered the CIA to stop an independent FBI investigation into Watergate matters. The president could now be charged with obstruction of justice. Obtaining the tapes was a major constitutional battle. Nixon claimed that executive privilege permitted him to withhold them from Congress and the courts. After forcing out two attorneys general in the **"Saturday Night Massacre"** because they would not fire the special prosecutor, Nixon had to appoint a second prosecutor and take his case to the Supreme Court. In *United States v. Nixon* (1974), the court ruled against the president. He was now facing the possibility of impeachment, and he lacked support in the Senate. Conservative **Barry Goldwater** explained that "the President has only 12 votes in the Senate. He has lied to me . . . [and] to my colleagues for the last time."

Nixon and Ford

After Nixon resigned in August of 1974, **Gerald Ford** of Michigan became president. Nixon's longtime vice president, Spiro Agnew, had resigned in disgrace in 1973 after it was revealed that he had accepted bribes as governor of Maryland. Ford entered office with the soothing words that the "long national nightmare is over," but then he shocked the country when he pardoned Nixon after only a few months in office.

THE CARTER ADMINISTRATION

In the 1976 election, former Democratic Governor of Georgia **Jimmy Carter**, who ran as an anti-DC "outsider," beat Gerald Ford in the wake of Watergate and the pardon, but only with 50.1 percent of the vote. Carter promised "never to lie" to the American people and to cut government spending and waste. One of his first tasks in office was to begin the process of deregulating the airline industry. Inflation had reached 13 percent, and oil prices soared as OPEC limited production and American gas-guzzling cars ate up fuel. He tried to discuss the inability of the country to deal with its problems as a loss of faith and a "malaise," but it did nothing to lift his poor ratings.

Foreign Affairs

Carter negotiated the return of the Panama Canal to Panama by the end of the century, but his biggest triumph was the negotiation of the 1978 **Camp David Accords**: Egypt recognized Israel and won the return of the Sinai. Carter recognized the democratically elected pro-Cuba **Sandinista** government of Nicaragua (1979), and maintained a position on human rights that condemned the USSR for its treatment of dissidents and Jews and for its invasion of Afghanistan.

The **Iran Hostage Crisis** proved to be Carter's undoing, however. The new fundamentalist Shiite Muslim Khomeni government in Iran (1979) blamed the United States for selling arms to the deposed shah. Fifty-two American embassy workers were taken hostage by angry students with the support of the Khomeni government. They spent 444 days in captivity and were only released on the day **Ronald Reagan** was inaugurated in 1980.

SUMMARY

There was more to the 1960s than Vietnam. The conservatives learned at least as much as the liberals from the mass movements. New laws were enacted, accompanied by public discussions of race, gender, government lying, environmental damage, and the dangers of nuclear power. *All the President's Men* (1974), by Carl Bernstein and Bob Woodward, told the story of Watergate. Conservatives and Northern white workers, who were hurt by stagflation, fought back with an intensity that shocked liberals who assumed that American history always went their way. Phyllis Schlafly helped defeat the ERA, while integration, affirmative action, and the right to have an abortion were under attack. The government was still the protector of the unions, but Nixon's New Federalism and Carter's deregulations were portents of the future.

THINGS TO REMEMBER

- **Backlash:** The reaction of some whites to the Civil Rights Movement and the urban riots of the 1960s. The formerly solid–Democratic South started voting Republican following the gains of the Civil Rights Movement in the 1960s and many whites sent their kids to private school instead of letting them sit next to blacks in public schools in both the North and South. Many whites left the cities for the more homogeneous suburbs, and attitudes about African Americans taking advantage of affirmative action and welfare became widespread among whites.

- **Consciousness raising groups:** An organization and discussion method employed by feminists in the late 1960s and early '70s in which women would exchange experiences of discrimination, read radical analyses of oppression, and develop an understanding that it was the patriarchal or sometimes capitalist society that was causing their insecurity and lack of advancement in the business and academic world, not their own actions or lack of them. They developed the slogan "the personal is political."

- **Pro-choice:** The political position that favors abortion on demand.

- **Pro-life:** The political position that opposes abortion.

- **Second Wave of Feminism:** The first wave was in the 1830s through the early 20th century when the radicals Elizabeth Cady Stanton, Susan B. Anthony, and Lucretia Mott advocated equality, employment, education, and suffrage. The second wave, which advocated these same ideas (except suffrage, which had been won in 1920), came about in the late 1960s and early 1970s. Betty Friedan, Gloria Steinem, Susan Brownmiller, and Kate Millet were all Second Wave feminists.

- **Stagflation:** The economic state in which prices are rising (inflation) and unemployment is high, producing stagnation of growth.

- **White flight:** The exodus of white middle class families from cities to suburbia following World War II partially caused by the migration of African Americans to urban centers.

REVIEW QUESTIONS

1. Which of the following statements from the Seneca Falls Declaration of 1848 was NOT a concern of the feminist movement of the 1970s?

   I. He has usurped the prerogative of Jehovah himself, claiming it as his right to assign for her a sphere of action, when that belongs to her conscience and to her God.

   II. He has endeavored, in every way that he could, to destroy her confidence in her own powers, to lessen her self-respect and to make her willing to lead a dependent and abject life.

   III. Now, in view of this entire disfranchisement of one-half the people in this country, we insist that [women] have immediate admission to all the rights and privileges which belong to them as women.

   (A) I
   (B) II and III
   (C) III
   (D) I and III

2. The Carter Administration faced

   (A) the Iran-Contra scandal
   (B) the energy crisis
   (C) record deficits
   (D) Iraq's invasion of Kuwait
   (E) revolution in Jamaica

3. Nixon resigned because

   (A) he was impeached
   (B) the Senate voted to impeach him
   (C) there were too many demonstrations
   (D) he was threatened with impeachment and did not have support in the Senate
   (E) he had lied to Congress

4. Match the author with the book:

A) Rachel Carson	1) *Sexual Politics*
B) Betty Friedan	2) *All the President's Men*
C) Kate Millet	3) *The Population Bomb*
D) Paul Ehrlich	4) *Silent Spring*
E) Carl Bernstein and Bob Woodward	5) *The Feminine Mystique*

Answer choices:

(A) A-4, B-1, D-2, E-3

(B) B-1, C-5, D-2, E-3

(C) B-5, C-3, D-4, E-2

(D) A-1, C-5, D-3, E-2

(E) A-4, B-5, C-1, D-3

ANSWERS AND EXPLANATIONS

1. C

The Seneca Falls Declaration of 1848, written by Elizabeth Cady Stanton, called for much more than suffrage, though suffrage was the most notable feature of the document at the time. By the 1970s, suffrage, discussed in choice (III), was not an issue because women obtained the right to vote in 1920 with the 19th Amendment. (I) refers to God—not a primary preoccupation of the modern feminist movement—but it also addresses the existence of separate sphere of activity which confined women. (II) parallels a central argument of Betty Friedan's Feminine Mystique, an important book for the feminist movement of the 1970s.

2. B

Oil prices got very high in the middle and late '70s. The Iran-Contra occurred in 1985 in the Reagan administration. The invasion of Iraq was in 1990 in George H. W. Bush's presidency. There was a Revolution in Haiti (1990), not Jamaica.

3. D

Nixon was not impeached; he was threatened with impeachment because the House Judiciary Committee passed articles of impeachment and the House was expected to vote to impeach him. He resigned because, if impeached, he would have been convicted in the Senate and would have had to leave office. Impeachment is a two-part process that starts in the House of Representatives. He would have been tried in the Senate. There were no significant anti-Nixon demonstrations and he was not found guilty of lying to Congress.

4. E

Rachel Carson wrote *Silent Spring*; Betty Friedan wrote *The Feminine Mystique*; Kate Millet wrote *Sexual Politics*; and Paul Ehrlich wrote *The Population Bomb*. Carl Bernstein and Bob Woodward wrote *All the President's Men*.

CHAPTER 34

The Triumph of Conservatism, 1980–1992

TIMELINE

1980	Ronald Reagan elected
1981	AIDS epidemic discovered • PATCO strike broken
1982	Boland Amendment passed • Sandra Day O'Connor appointed to Supreme Court
1985	Iran-Contra diversions begin
1987	Stock market crashes
1988	George H. W. Bush elected
1989	Berlin Wall destroyed
1991	Desert Storm invasion takes place • Clarence Thomas appointed to Supreme Court • Soviet Union breaks up

IMPORTANT PEOPLE, PLACES, EVENTS, AND CONCEPTS

Ronald Reagan

The Great Communicator

yuppies

PATCO

C. Everett Koop

"Just Say No" campaign

Sandra Day O'Connor

William Rehnquist

Iran-Contra scandal

Oliver North

Contras

Sandinista

Boland Amendment

back channel operations

Mikhail Gorbachev

peristroika

glasnost

evil empire

Strategic Defense Initiative (SDI), or "Star Wars"

voodoo economics

Geraldine Ferraro

Persian Gulf War

Saddam Hussein

Desert Storm

Clarence Thomas

"Mr. Gorbachev, tear down this wall."

—Ronald Reagan, Berlin, 1987

INTRODUCTION

Ronald Reagan was called **"The Great Communicator"** because he connected with voters. He was called the Teflon president because no matter what went wrong during "his watch," it never seemed to affect his approval ratings. Reagan was a free-market thinker who had the support of the religious Right. Fundamentalist Christians led by **Pat Robertson** and **Jerry Falwell** organized mail order fund-raising campaigns on behalf of their extremely active supporters. Their rallying cry was **"family values"**: they favored prayer in the schools and repression of homosexuality; they were antifeminist and anti-abortion. The stage was set for an all-out assault on liberalism.

ELECTION OF 1980

The campaign for presidency, which took place during the **Iran Hostage Crisis** of 1979–1980, pitted Ronald Reagan, former conservative governor of California, against President Jimmy Carter. Blaming Carter for inaction, and convincing voters that he would do better—by reducing government and by restoring America's respect around the world—Reagan, the new outsider, and George H. W. Bush won by 489 to 49 electoral votes. However, only 52.3 percent of eligible voters came to the polls. Reagan seemed decisive, in strong contrast to Jimmy Carter.

DOMESTIC AFFAIRS

Reaganomics

In his first inaugural Reagan contended that "In this present [inflationary] crisis, government is not the solution to our problem." To get government out of the way he proposed cutting income and capital gains taxes. This **supply-side** theory of economics—**Reaganomics**—would encourage the rich to invest their money in new production, create jobs and increase revenue, and balance the budget. Reagan and his economists maintained that the increased prosperity of people at the Top of society would "trickle down" to the workers and the poor at the bottom. Reagan's program caused the national debt to soar from under one trillion dollars to nearly three trillion dollars between 1981 and 1989. The double digit inflation of the Carter years had been reduced to 4 percent, but unemployment stood at 11 percent. Deep cuts in federal spending left states and cities desperate for money.

Income Disparities

Everyone did not suffer. Income distribution became increasingly skewed: The income of the poorest fifth of the population declined nearly 10 percent while that of the richest fifth increased more than 15 percent. A new group of young urban professionals, or **yuppies**, graduated from law and business schools and created a flamboyant lifestyle not seen since the Gilded Age. Lawyers arranged leveraged **buy-outs** (mergers) of businesses, making money for some stockholders while creating extensive job losses. The savings and loan banks were deregulated, spawning new millionaires, but the real estate market went sour in the late '80s, causing large numbers of these banks to fail. Congress agreed to have the taxpayers **bail out** the banks in order to protect the reckless investments of a few. There was a severe stock market crash possibly caused by electronic (computer) trading in 1987.

An Attack on Unions

Just as his administration began, Reagan refused to negotiate with the **Professional Air Traffic Controllers' Organization (PATCO)**, which had gone on strike for better wages and reduced work hours. He broke the union: strikebreakers could now legally be hired as replacement workers. Competition with Japan, Germany, and Korea had resulted in the loss of many American jobs and a record trade deficit. Reaganomics had created mainly low wage positions in the service industry. The new jobs paid 5 or 6 dollars per hour, as opposed to industrial jobs which had paid 10 to 15 dollars per hour.

Health and the Environment

Ronald Reagan appointed **C. Everett Koop** surgeon general in 1981. AIDS had been discovered in 1981, but because it was initially found in gay men, it was ignored. An educator, Koop fought for the protection of children and adults from AIDS and the effects of smoking. James Watt, head of the **Environmental Protection Agency**, created political firestorms by attempting to undo clean air regulations and the sanctity of national parks, opening them up to mining and timber development. First Lady Nancy Reagan led a campaign to reduce drug use among young people; she asked them to **"Just say no."**

The Supreme Court

Reagan appointed Antonin Scalia, a professor at Yale Law School, to the Supreme Court. Scalia believed in **original intention**, a concept claiming that a justice could know the ideas of the framers of the Constitution and had no authority to change these. Also appointed were **Sandra Day O'Connor**, the first woman justice, and Chief Justice **William H. Rehnquist**, a conservative who led the Court in limiting access to abortion and remedying civil rights violations.

FOREIGN POLICY

It was in foreign policy that Reagan experienced his greatest triumphs. The new prime minister of the Soviet Union, **Mikhail Gorbachev**, had introduced *perestroika*, a move toward private ownership, and *glasnost*, a move toward openness of speech and the press. These changes created a democratic ferment in the totalitarian state. Reagan welcomed this new openness and even backtracked from his former characterization of the USSR as an **"evil empire."** However, his most dramatic statement was his demand in Berlin in 1987: "Mr. Gorbachev, tear down this wall." Many political analysts claimed that Reagan accelerated the process that ended the Cold War by calling for the **Strategic Defense Initiative** (**"Star Wars"**) missile shield in space, which forced the failing Soviets to keep pace with American arms buildup.

THE IRAN-CONTRA AFFAIR

With the Iran-Contra affair, the Reagan administration was involved in a scandal comparable to Watergate. Reagan's National Security Council, run by Robert MacFarlane and John Poindexter, with Colonel **Oliver North** as their subordinate, developed a scheme in 1985 to arrange the release of hostages in Lebanon and at the same time give aid to the anti-Communist **Contras** in Nicaragua.

In conjunction with the CIA, North arranged for arms to be sold to Iranians, who would intervene with the Lebanese to release hostages. North then used the money to fund the anti-**Sandinista** Contras in Nicaragua. This scheme broke Reagan's pledge that he would never negotiate with terrorists, and violated the **Boland Amendment** forbidding military aid without congressional approval. In order to conceal these "back channel" operations, North organized shredding of documents, and Poindexter misled Congress. All the principals pled guilty or were convicted of perjury. North's conviction was overturned on a technicality. Reagan denied that there was an exchange of arms for hostages. The final report by **Independent Counsel** Lawrence Walsh, released in 1994, concluded that "although it seems obvious that President Reagan made hopelessly conflicting statements . . . it would be impossible to prove beyond a reasonable doubt that any misstatement was intentional or willful."

ELECTION OF 1988

Though George H. W. Bush was a loyal vice-president, before Reagan's nomination in 1980 he called the supply-side policies **"voodoo economics."** In 1984, Reagan and Bush beat Walter Mondale and **Geraldine Ferraro**, the first woman vice-presidential candidate, 59 percent to 41 percent. Bush had been a national political figure as a member of the House of Representatives, director of the CIA, and ambassador to the United Nations. Coming from a wealthy and liberal Republican family, he initially supported abortion rights and Keynesian economics, but his success with Reaganomics reoriented his politics.

In 1988 George H. W. Bush promised no new taxes and a "kinder, gentler" nation. Charity with a "thousand points of light" would substitute for the "tax and spend" habits of the Democrats. For his running mate, Bush chose Senator Dan Quayle of Indiana, a conservative supporter of "family values." Bush accused his opponent, Massachusetts Governor Michael Dukakis, of being a "card-carrying" member of the American Civil Liberties Union, and Bush's supporters ran vicious attack ads that Dukakis never adequately responded to. Liberals were now objects of derision. Bush-Quayle won 56 percent of the vote, but only 50 percent of the eligible voters came to the polls.

THE FIRST BUSH PRESIDENCY

Desert Storm

The **Persian Gulf War** (1991) was the major event of the Bush administration. **Saddam Hussein** of Iraq had threatened to invade oil-rich Kuwait. Bush saw a threat to America's ally, Saudi Arabia. Discarding sanctions, he announced, "This will not stand," and submitted a resolution to Congress under the **War Powers Act**. In the **Desert Storm** invasion, Bush forced Hussein out of Kuwait. He claimed "we" had "put Vietnam behind us." He had not only cooperated with Congress, but the United States had won, and the protests were nearly nonexistent. Bush proclaimed a new World Order, since Communism had fallen in Eastern Europe (1988) and in the Soviet Union (1990).

The Bush Legacy

When Thurgood Marshall resigned as Supreme Court justice, Bush appointed the African American conservative judge **Clarence Thomas**. During the stormy confirmation hearings, he was accused of sexual harassment by Anita Hill, an African American law professor who had been his employee at the Equal Employment Opportunity Commission. Americans were forced to confront racism, disagreements among African Americans, and women's issues. Federal debt grew to new heights during Bush's single term, prompting him to go back on his promise not to raise taxes. The supply-side ideologues denounced him. Despite his defeat of Saddam Hussein and the successful invasion of Panama to capture the drug-dealing dictator **Manuel Noriega**, Bush could not regain the support of the American people.

SUMMARY

During the age of Reagan, the economy endured wide fluctuations. In 1984 and 1988, the rich were gaining confidence and voted overwhelmingly for the Republicans. Simultaneously, unemployment was high, and the trade deficit and federal and state debt had all skyrocketed. The gap between rich and poor was growing at an enormous rate. Supporters of family values seemed to be the most prominent group in the political arena, and Reagan remained the Great Communicator. The Republicans seemed to have the support of the majority, but women voted for the Democrats in higher percentages (this is referred to as a **gender gap**). If only half of eligible voters went to the polls, could elections indicate what the majority thought? How would the Democrats cope with the voters' shift to the right? In the next period Americans had to deal with the huge national debt, the legacy of Watergate, and the consequences of the '60s culture wars.

THINGS TO REMEMBER

- **Bailouts:** The policy of supplying government support for corporations when they are in severe financial trouble. The Chrysler Corporation, for example, got a $1.5 billion bailout in 1980, and the savings and loan banks received at least $159 billion during the bailout of the late 1980s.

- **Family values:** The political position advocated by Jerry Falwell, Pat Robertson, and other conservative Republicans emphasizing a life of religious observance along with no drugs, no divorce, no abortions, no homosexuality, no working mothers, and no sex before marriage.

- **Gender gap:** The difference in the votes of men and women. Often men vote Republican in larger numbers than women, who are more likely to vote Democratic, producing a gender gap.

- **Independent counsel:** A prosecutor chosen by a panel of three judges (appointed by the attorney general) to investigate wrongdoing in the executive branch. Established after the Watergate scandal, it was designed to prevent conflict of interest within the executive branch. This law was used extensively to investigate the Iran-Contra scandal during the Reagan administration, and the Whitewater and Lewinsky affairs during the Clinton administration.

- **Supply-side economics:** The theory that the path to economic growth is through tax cuts for the rich who will then invest in new businesses and expand old ones, employing new workers as a result.

REVIEW QUESTIONS

1. Ronald Reagan was called the Great Communicator because

   (A) he always told the truth
   (B) he memorized his speeches
   (C) he connected with people
   (D) he had been an actor
   (E) it was his nickname as a radio announcer

2. Supply-side economics was designed to

   (A) increase demand by cutting taxes
   (B) provide more goods and services
   (C) provide money for new business investment by cutting taxes
   (D) make government grow
   (E) cut the size of the government

3. Who did not vote for Bush in large numbers in 1988?

   (A) Southerners
   (B) women
   (C) those with high income
   (D) residents of Maine
   (E) Reagan Democrats

4. Which issue is least emphasized by "family values" advocates?

   (A) abortion
   (B) stay-at-home mothers
   (C) religion
   (D) homosexuality
   (E) education

ANSWERS AND EXPLANATIONS

1. C

All the answers are true except (A) and (E), but (C) is the reason he was called the Great Communicator. It was never clear just how much he remembered from Iran Contra (A). He instilled a confidence in people that they responded to. Reagan had been a baseball radio announcer.

2. C

Supply-side programs cut the taxes of the rich so that they would start new businesses. This was supposed to increase employment, and then the supply of goods. Demand-side would be employing people directly, as the Keynesians and Franklin Roosevelt had done.

3. B

Bush's lack of support among women was called the gender gap. Bush had home-state support in Maine and Texas where he had residences. Southerners had been voting for Republicans since Nixon; the rich voted for the Republicans; and many Democrats who had crossed over for Reagan ("Reagan Democrats") voted for Bush in 1988.

4. E

The family values advocates wanted to put prayer in schools, but they did not have a particular view of education, as they did of abortion, sexuality, and their wish to keep women as housewives.

CHAPTER 35

America at the
Turn of the Century

TIMELINE

1992	Bill Clinton elected president
1993	Paula Jones accuses Clinton of sexual harassment • Ruth Bader Ginsberg appointed justice of the Supreme Court • Stephen Bayer appointed justice of the Supreme Court
1994	Rise of the New Right • Kenneth Starr appointed as independent counsel to investigate Whitewater • Brady Bill signed • Contract with America developed • Wye Memorandum signed
1995	Dayton Accords signed
1996	Clinton elected to second term as president
1997	Clinton testifies before a federal grand jury investigating the Lewinsky affair
1998	House of Representatives impeaches Bill Clinton
1999	Clinton tried and acquitted by the Senate
2000	George W. Bush wins contested election • Clinton issues pardons
2001	Terrorists attack the World Trade Center and the Pentagon

IMPORTANT PEOPLE, PLACES, EVENTS, AND CONCEPTS

Bill Clinton

Al Gore

Madeleine Albright

Hillary Rodham Clinton

New Democrats

Brady bill

Newt Gingrich

conservative Right

Contract with America

Whitewater

Kenneth Starr

Paula Jones

Monica Lewinsky

William Rehnquist

Oklahoma City bombing

NAFTA

World Trade Organization

Somalia

Jean-Bertrand Aristide

Bosnia

Kosovo

Slobodan Milosevic

Wye Memorandum

The Dayton Accords

U.S.S. Cole

Election 2000

George W. Bush

Jeb Bush

Katherine Harris

computer revolution

Immigration Reform and Control Act

global warning

Osama bin Laden

"Thomas Jefferson believed that to preserve the very foundations of our nation, we would need dramatic change from time to time. Well, my fellow citizens, this is our time. Let us embrace it."

—William Jefferson Clinton, First Inaugural Address, January 21, 1993

INTRODUCTION

When Bill Clinton was elected president in 1992, the people of the United States hoped that this new president would invigorate the nation and lead it into the 21st century. The first president to be born after World War II, Clinton faced a world without a Cold War and computer revolution that was changing society. Blessed with a booming economy, Clinton retained his popularity despite becoming the first president to be impeached since Andrew Johnson in 1868. Issues such as health care reform, welfare reform, gays in the military, and AIDS presented great challenges for his administration. After 12 years of Republican presidents, the American people desired a fresh approach to these difficult problems. They wanted to "embrace" change and, to them, Bill Clinton personified that change.

CLINTON AS PRESIDENT

Bill Clinton painted himself as a moderate Democrat in the election of 1992. The governor of Arkansas, Clinton portrayed himself as a Washington outsider, more conservative than the liberals in the Democratic Party. For his running mate, he chose **Albert Gore**, a senator from Tennessee with long-standing ties to Washington. **Ross Perot** ran as an independent and received more votes than any third-party candidate since Theodore Roosevelt and the Progressives. **George H. Bush**, the Republican candidate and incumbent president, lost the election to Clinton.

The Early Years

The Clinton presidency was marked by tremendous highs and incredible lows. The early perceptions of Clinton's first administration was that of a leader unfamiliar with the workings of Washington who seemed to surround himself with an inexperienced and somewhat incompetent staff. However, Clinton's cabinet reflected a desire to create more diversity and included African Americans, Latinos, and women. **Janet Reno** became the first woman attorney general; later, **Madeleine Albright** became the first woman secretary of state. Clinton chose his wife **Hillary Rodham Clinton** to lead the task force to reform health care.

These early months were marked with challenges. He ran into difficulty not only with the Republicans in power, but also with the Democrats. There were many staunch Democrats, many of whom believed that Clinton had sold them out, as his legislative decisions as a **"New Democrat"** appeared to be more moderate than they desired. When there was resistance to Clinton's early support for gays in the military, Clinton modified his policy to call for a "don't ask, don't tell" philosophy. He also used his executive power to ease some of the restrictions on abortion counseling and the importation and use of RU-486, a French "abortion pill." In February of 1993, Clinton signed the **Brady Bill** into law, providing for aid to municipalities for police, the building of prisons, and the establishment of crime prevention programs.

The Rise of the Conservative Right

The midterm elections held in November 1994 sent a clear message to Clinton: the country was displeased with the his administration and its poor leadership on important issues. The Republicans gained control of Congress for the first time in 40 years. This new Congress had a voice in **Newt Gingrich**, the Speaker of the House of Representatives. Exemplary of the thinking of the **conservative Right**, the Republicans issued a **"Contract with America,"** which proposed such things as congressional term limits, an amendment to the Constitution requiring a balanced budget, and various tax cuts. The debates over this contract highlighted the differences between the Democrats and the Republicans. Clinton's refusal to support the contract resulted in a battle over the budget in 1995, leading to the virtual shutdown of the government.

Clinton the Man

The problems of Clinton's personal life plagued him through much of his two terms. In 1994, a special counsel was chosen to head the investigation of **Whitewater**, a real estate deal that involved a possible funneling of money to Clinton's campaign in Arkansas. **Kenneth Starr** headed this investigation as an independent counsel. The investigation was closed in 2000, with Clinton and his wife not charged with any wrongdoing. However, Bill Clinton was disbarred in Arkansas.

Perhaps the darkest hours for Clinton involved his sexual life. Accused by Paula Jones of sexual harassment in May of 1991, before he became president, Bill Clinton then found himself being investigated concerning his sexual relations with a White House intern, Monica

Lewinsky. Appearing on national television, Clinton denied ever having "...sexual relations with that woman." In August 1997, Clinton testified before a federal grand jury about this relationship with Lewinsky. He was accused of lying under oath, and Independent Counsel Kenneth Starr turned his attention to this affair. The Starr Report accused Clinton of obstructing justice and tampering with witnesses. On December 19, 1998, the House of Representatives voted to impeach Clinton on charges of perjury and obstruction of justice. In January, 1999, the impeachment trial of Bill Clinton was held, with Chief Justice William Rehnquist presiding. After much testimony and debate, Bill Clinton was acquitted of the charges and remained president of the United States.

Domestic Affairs

During the early Clinton years, a growing anti-government movement developed, which led to a 1993 confrontation in **Waco, Texas,** where government agents stormed the compound of an armed religious cult. Two years to the date after that incident, a federal building in **Oklahoma City** was bombed by **Timothy McVeigh,** killing 169 people. Clinton's handling of this tragedy boosted his popularity as the election of 1996 approached.

Clinton battled the Congress on welfare reform as the Republicans supported an end to the **Aid to Dependent Children** program. Clinton and Congress finally agreed on the **Personal Responsibility and Work Opportunity Act,** which shifted more of the responsibility for welfare programs to the individual states. It also provided minimum aid to all children in need.

The booming **economic expansion,** fueled by the growing "dot-com" companies, was a highlight of the Clinton campaign as the election of 1996 approached. They could boast the lowest unemployment rates in recent history and a growing middle class. The polls showed that more people felt that they were better off since Clinton had taken office. With Americans feeling confident about the economy, along with the president's personal charm and charisma (despite the personal problems that plagued him), Clinton won a decisive victory over **Robert Dole,** the Republican senator and majority leader of the Senate. Dole won only 11 states, and Clinton won 379 electoral votes to Dole's 159.

The election of 1996 resulted not only in the Republicans' failure to gain the presidency, but also in their loss of seats in Congress, sending a clear signal that the country was not happy with the ultraconservative Republicans. Newt Gingrich resigned as speaker of the house and a more moderate approach to solving the country's problems was adopted.

Foreign Affairs

In the area of foreign affairs, Clinton's success was mixed. Bill Clinton was a staunch supporter of **NAFTA, the North American Free Trade Agreement,** which was signed into law in 1994. It provided for the lifting of trade restrictions, including the lowering or eliminating of the tariffs between the United States and its neighbors, Mexico and Canada, over the next 15 years. He also supported the establishment of a **World Trade Organization**.

Clinton sent more U.S. troops abroad in peacetime than any other president. In 1993, as part of a peacekeeping mission, he sent American troops to **Somalia** in East Africa. The U.S. military restored **Jean-Bertrand Aristide** to power in Haiti in 1994. American troops were also part of NATO peacekeeping forces sent to **Bosnia** because of ethnic conflicts in that area of the world. As part of a NATO operation in 1999, Clinton also committed American troops to end the **ethnic cleansing**, or slaughtering, of **Albanians** in **Kosovo**, which appeared to have been ordered by the Serbian President **Slobodan Milosevic**. At press time, Milosevic was on trial at the Hague for war crimes stemming from this incident.

In the Middle East, in 1994, Clinton helped to engineer an accord dealing with Palestinian self-rule between Israeli leader **Yitzhak Rabin** and Palestinian leader **Yasser Arafat**. Israeli Prime Minister **Benjamin Netanyahu** and Yasser Arafat signed the **Wye Memorandum**, in which Israel agreed to withdraw troops from parts of the West Bank. In 1995, the **Dayton Accords** were signed, bringing an end to years of civil war among the Muslims, Croats, and Serbs in Bosnia. Finally, Clinton normalized relations with **Vietnam**, more than 25 years after the last American troops left that country.

The Clinton administration was marred by a terrorist bombing of the **World Trade Center** in 1993 by Muslim extremists, as well as the bombings of U.S. embassies in Africa, and the bombing of the ***U.S.S. Cole*** in Yemen harbor in 2000. These terrorists actions were connected to the work of Islamic fundamentalists led by **Osama bin Laden** and his **al Qaeda** group. The United States' response to these incidents was limited.

The Clinton administration's accomplishments, although often overshadowed by his personal problems, included a comprehensive welfare reform bill, a balanced budget, a booming economy, and a relatively peaceful world. Despite Clinton's personal failings, he enjoyed tremendous popularity during his presidency.

THE CONTESTED ELECTION OF 2000

Bill Clinton was unable to run for a third term as president in 2000 because of the 22nd Amendment to the Constitution. His vice president, **Al Gore,** ran against the Republican governor of Texas, **George W. Bush**, son of former President **George H. W. Bush**. When the television news channels predicted that Gore had won the state of Florida, it appeared that he had won the election. However, within a short time, these TV stations retracted their predictions and stated that the race in Florida was too close to call. What resulted was five weeks of uncertainty as the Florida ballots were in dispute. What complicated this situation was that George W. Bush's brother, **Jeb**, was governor of Florida.

Florida's secretary of state, **Katherine Harris**, a Republican, was in charge of the Florida election process. Gore asked for a recount of certain counties, but the Bush team challenged the recount as well as the decision the Supreme Court of Florida made in ordering a recount. When the court challenges continued and the Florida votes remained in dispute, the decision was finally made by the U.S. Supreme Court. In the ***Bush v. Gore*** case, the Supreme Court, in a 5–4 vote, ruled that the different methods used in the various counties of Florida for recounting the vote violated the Equal Protection Clause under the 14th Amendment. The court determined that since there was no clear-cut state standard for determining the intent of the Florida voters, a hand count of the disputed votes would be unconstitutional. Bush, who had maintained a 537-vote lead in the popular vote in Florida, therefore, won the **plurality** (most) of votes in that state and all 25 electoral votes. With this victory, George W. Bush followed in the footsteps of his father George H. W. Bush, as he was sworn in as president, only the second son of a former president to do so. **John Quincy Adams**, son of John Adams, the president from 1797–1801, had followed his father into that office in 1824, also as a result of a disputed election.

THE GLOBAL ECONOMY

The development of **multinational corporations** has led to a more global economy. Due to the growth of computers and rapid communication systems, companies can develop business sites throughout the world. **Mergers** took place between companies that have traditionally done business in one area of the world. For example, U.S. car manufacturer **Chrysler** merged with the German-based **Daimler** Corporation. Each brought their markets to this marriage of companies. By creating multinational corporations, many companies can avoid tariffs and some regulations which affect profitability.

The Internet and the Computer Revolution

The success of the U.S. economy during the Clinton years can be attributed, in part, to the **computer revolution**. The information superhighway, known as the **Internet,** has changed the way people and businesses communicate and store information. The **Microsoft Corporation** has revolutionized how communication is carried on. From schools to businesses to government, Americans have become involved with computers. Although initially causing **technological unemployment**, or loss of jobs due to increased use of new technology, the computer has opened up many new jobs in computer-related fields. Chat rooms, email, and instant messages have become part of everyday language. The development of interactive classrooms has changed how people learn; college courses can be conducted via the Internet. Even the military has been impacted by this new technology. Weapons such as smart bombs are computer guided, and information about events is almost instantaneous.

The stock market boom of the 1990s reflected the growth of this new technology. **"Old economy" stocks** were replaced by **"new economy" stocks** in personal stock portfolios. The rise in the value of these new economy stocks led to investment by ordinary people who developed a "get rich quick" attitude. The market boom of the 1990s has slowed and many "dot-com" companies have gone out of business. The future remains uncertain, but the changes that technology has brought to the lives of people will continue to be a significant factor in the years to come.

MULTICULTURALISM

In the 1980s and 1990s, the United States experienced a tremendous growth in the number of people immigrating to the country. Many immigrants were from Asia and Latin America, in contrast to the mostly European immigrants that arrived in the early 1900s. The reasons for coming to the United States still center around the many opportunities that the country affords people.

However, there are many who wish to close the door on immigration. In 1986, Congress passed the **Immigration Reform and Control Act**, which punishes employers who hire undocumented workers. California attempted to stem the tide of immigration from Mexico by voting to deprive illegal immigrants of benefits, such as education and medical care.

ECOLOGICAL CHALLENGES AT THE DAWN OF A NEW CENTURY

The issues of energy and **ecology** have become increasing difficult to balance. The Republican administration of George W. Bush has repeatedly called for exploration in preserved lands in Alaska to find new sources of oil. The environmentalists fear that this exploration will destroy the pristine environment of this area. The issue of **global warming** is another point of contention. Although scientists seem uncertain as to the degree or existence of global warming, the nations of the world are involved in dialogues to deal with this situation.

One thing is certain: the increased demand for energy will require new supplies to be tapped. Nuclear energy is efficient and clean, but people fear the possible problems of nuclear meltdown. Coal is plentiful, but it pollutes the air, and while companies have the capabilities to clean it up, this would be at a great cost. The balance of nature and oil drilling is under debate, and the country must address this issue as it moves through the 21st century.

TERRORISM IN THE 21st CENTURY

On the morning of September 11, 2001, the lives of thousands were changed in a flash as the world began its most crucial battle of the new century. The World Trade Center in New York City and the Pentagon in Washington, DC, were attacked by terrorists presumably under the direction of the notorious Muslim extremist **Osama bin Laden** and his **al Qaeda** network.

The young presidency of George W. Bush faced its greatest challenge: Declaring a "war on terrorism" against terrorists and nations that support them while emphasizing a respect for the religion of Islam and the people who embrace it, President Bush has prepared the United States for a long, protracted battle against terrorism throughout the world. The United States first invaded Afghanistan, where al Qaeda had its operations base. Afghanistan's Taliban government was toppled and a new leadership was put into place. Then President Bush requested military action against Saddam Hussein's leadership in Iraq. However, there was no evidence that Iraq was involved in the terrorist attacks on the United States, and thus, the United Nations Security Council would not support this initiative. But U.S. and British forces attacked Iraq in March of 2003 despite that fact. The subsequent war against Iraq has resulted in the deposition of the Hussein regime and the occupation of Iraq while they try to devise new leadership. However, the anti-U.S. sentiment and opposition from militant Iraqi groups has increased dramatically, and the success of the United States depends on worldwide support. But much of the world and the American public are against the war, and it was under this heightened anti-war/pro-war dichotomy in the U.S. that the Presidential elections of 2004 were held. John Kerry, the Jr. Senator from Massachusetts, was the democratic candidate running against George W. Bush. Although Senator Kerry garnered a lot of support and stood for a new and hopeful approach against the increasingly violent war in Iraq, the country was split 50/50 for each candidate. And on November 2, 2004, the American public voted to re-elect George W. Bush 51 percent to 49 percent.

SUMMARY

The administration of Bill Clinton was an active one. Charismatic and human, Clinton grew into the presidency, developing into a self-assured, world leader. However, many of his accomplishments were overshadowed by questionable judgments in his personal life.

The new administration of George W. Bush has been challenged to protect the United States from the attempts of extremists who wish to destroy the American way of life through terrorism. Bush faces the problems of protecting the United States, exercising leadership in a world torn by political and ethnic strife, and restoring the economy to prosperity. The 21st century will pose many important challenges for the people of the United States and the world.

THINGS TO REMEMBER

- **Ecology:** The study of the environment.

- **Ethnic cleansing:** A policy in which one people or a group within a nation attempts to destroy people whose ethnic background differs from theirs.

- **Impeachment:** An indictment or formal charge brought by the legislative body against a government official, especially the president, in an attempt to remove the person from office. If the House of Representatives determines that a president has committed acts which may be "high crimes and misdemeanors," he is impeached, as with the case of President Andrew Johnson in 1868 and President Bill Clinton in 1999. The Senate then conducts a trial to determine guilt; if the president is found guilty, he is removed from office.

- **Multiculturalism:** The presence of many different ethnic groups within a society.

- **Multinational corporations:** Corporations, usually large ones, who have established businesses in many different countries around the world.

REVIEW QUESTIONS

1. Bill Clinton's presidency was marked by

   (A) a period of prosperity for the nation

   (B) an absence of political dissension between the Republicans and the Democrats

   (C) peace between the Israelis and the Palestinians

   (D) an isolationist foreign policy

   (E) the passage of the Contract with America

2. The people of the United States demonstrated their disapproval of Clinton's first two years in office by

   (A) holding demonstrations in Washington to express their displeasure

   (B) appointing a special counsel to investigate Bill Clinton

   (C) electing Republicans to Congress in 1994

   (D) electing New Democrats to Congress in 1994

   (E) impeaching Bill Clinton

3. Bill Clinton supported free trade policies by signing the

   (A) free trade agreement with France

   (B) North American Free Trade Agreement

   (C) Dayton Accord

   (D) order imposing sanctions on Japanese trade with the United States

   (E) agreement to establish multinational companies

4. The Election of 2000 was significant because

   (A) the Supreme Court of Florida decided the election

   (B) Katherine Harris, a Democrat, validated the election

   (C) Al Gore won more popular votes than George W. Bush, but lost the election

   (D) Jeb Bush, the brother of George W. Bush, was governor of Florida

   (E) George W. Bush was the first son to follow his father into the presidency

ANSWERS AND EXPLANATIONS

1. A

The eight years of Bill Clinton's terms were marked by a high period of prosperity. Employment was high, businesses were growing, and the dollar was strong. There was much political disagreement between the Democrats and Republicans as demonstrated by the battles over the budget, welfare reform, and the impeachment. The Wye Memorandum was an agreement signed between Israeli Prime Minister Benjamin Netanyahu and Palestinian leader Yasser Arafat. It authorized Israel to withdraw troops from parts of the West Bank. However, the conflict between the Palestinians and the Israelis was not resolved. Bill Clinton's Administration took a very active role in foreign affairs, and therefore, can not be considered isolationist. The Contract with America was composed by the Republicans in 1994 but was never passed. Clinton battled the Republicans over this Contract, which resulted in the Republicans withholding their approval of the federal budget in 1995. This battle virtually shut down the government.

2. C

The midterm Congressional elections of 1994 elected enough Republicans to make them the majority in Congress, a clear message to Clinton about the American peoples' displeasure with his administration. There were no demonstrations in Washington, DC to show the displeasure of the people. The special counsel, Kenneth Starr, was appointed by a panel of judges. Bill Clinton was impeached by the House of Representatives, but that didn't happen until his second term as president.

3. B

Bill Clinton was a strong proponent of the North American Free Trade Agreement (NAFTA). There were no new free trade agreements with France. The Dayton Accords were signed in 1995, ending years of civil war among the Muslims, Croats, and Serbs in Bosnia. Bill Clinton threatened to place economic sanctions on Japanese products if the Japanese did not open its doors to American goods. However, had these sanctions been ordered they would have been a step away from free trade. Multinational corporations have developed as a result of economic conditions, not as a result of any specific agreement to establish them.

4. C

Al Gore won more popular votes than George W. Bush but failed to win the presidency because he did not win a sufficient number of electoral votes. The United States Supreme Court ruled on the constitutionality of recounting votes in Florida, impacting the outcome of the election. Although the Florida Supreme Court had ruled prior to the U.S. Supreme Court's decision, it was not the deciding decision for the election. Katherine Harris, the secretary of state of Florida and a Republican, was responsible for certifying the election in Florida. Jeb Bush, George W. Bush's brother, was the governor of Florida, but that fact does not make the election most significant. George W. Bush is the second son to follow his father into the presidency. John Quincy Adams, in 1824, followed his father, John Adams, who was president from 1797–1801.

Section Four

PRACTICE TESTS

HOW TO TAKE THE PRACTICE TESTS

Before taking a practice test, find a quiet room where you can work uninterrupted for one hour. Make sure you have several No. 2 pencils with erasers.

Use the answer grid provided to record your answers. Guidelines for scoring your test appear on the reverse side of the answer grid. Time yourself. Spend no more than one hour on the 90 questions. Once you start the practice test, don't stop until you've reached the one-hour time limit. You'll find an answer key and complete answer explanations following the test. Be sure to read the explanations for all questions, even those you answered correctly.

Good luck!

HOW TO CALCULATE YOUR SCORE

Step 1: Figure out your raw score. Refer to your answer sheet to determine the number right and the number wrong on the practice test you're scoring. You can use the chart below to figure out your raw score. Multiply the number wrong by 0.25 and subtract the result from the number right. Round the result to the nearest whole number. This is your raw score.

SAT Subject Test: U.S. History Practice Test 1

Number right	Number wrong	Raw score
☐	$- \left(0.25 \times \square \right) =$	☐

Step 2: Find your practice test score. Find your raw score in the left column of the table below. The score in the right column is an approximation of what your score would be on the SAT Subject Test: U.S. History.

A note on your practice test scores: Don't take these scores too literally. Practice test conditions cannot precisely mirror real test conditions. Your actual SAT Subject Test: U.S. History score will almost certainly vary from your practice test scores. However, your scores on the practice tests will give you a rough idea of your range on the actual exam.

Conversion Table

Raw	Scaled	Raw	Scaled	Raw	Scaled	Raw	Scaled	Raw	Scaled	Raw	Scaled
90	800	72	770	54	680	36	580	18	470	0	350
89	800	71	760	43	670	35	570	17	460	−1	350
88	800	70	760	52	670	34	570	16	460	−2	340
87	800	69	750	51	660	33	560	15	450	−3	340
86	800	68	750	50	660	32	550	14	450	−4	330
85	800	67	740	49	650	31	550	13	440	−5	330
84	800	66	740	48	650	30	540	12	430	−6	320
83	800	65	730	47	640	29	540	11	430	−7	320
82	800	64	730	46	640	28	530	10	420	−8	310
81	800	63	720	45	630	27	520	9	410	−9	310
80	790	62	720	44	630	26	520	8	410	−10	300
79	790	61	710	43	620	25	510	7	400	−11	300
78	790	60	710	42	610	24	510	6	390	−12	290
77	790	59	700	41	610	23	500	5	390	−13	280
76	780	58	700	40	600	22	490	4	380	−14	280
75	780	57	690	39	600	21	490	3	370	−15	270
74	780	56	690	38	590	20	480	2	370	−16	270
73	770	55	680	37	580	19	480	1	360	−17	260

Answer Grid
Practice Test 1

1. (A) (B) (C) (D) (E)	31. (A) (B) (C) (D) (E)	61. (A) (B) (C) (D) (E)
2. (A) (B) (C) (D) (E)	32. (A) (B) (C) (D) (E)	62. (A) (B) (C) (D) (E)
3. (A) (B) (C) (D) (E)	33. (A) (B) (C) (D) (E)	63. (A) (B) (C) (D) (E)
4. (A) (B) (C) (D) (E)	34. (A) (B) (C) (D) (E)	64. (A) (B) (C) (D) (E)
5. (A) (B) (C) (D) (E)	35. (A) (B) (C) (D) (E)	65. (A) (B) (C) (D) (E)
6. (A) (B) (C) (D) (E)	36. (A) (B) (C) (D) (E)	66. (A) (B) (C) (D) (E)
7. (A) (B) (C) (D) (E)	37. (A) (B) (C) (D) (E)	67. (A) (B) (C) (D) (E)
8. (A) (B) (C) (D) (E)	38. (A) (B) (C) (D) (E)	68. (A) (B) (C) (D) (E)
9. (A) (B) (C) (D) (E)	39. (A) (B) (C) (D) (E)	69. (A) (B) (C) (D) (E)
10. (A) (B) (C) (D) (E)	40. (A) (B) (C) (D) (E)	70. (A) (B) (C) (D) (E)
11. (A) (B) (C) (D) (E)	41. (A) (B) (C) (D) (E)	71. (A) (B) (C) (D) (E)
12. (A) (B) (C) (D) (E)	42. (A) (B) (C) (D) (E)	72. (A) (B) (C) (D) (E)
13. (A) (B) (C) (D) (E)	43. (A) (B) (C) (D) (E)	73. (A) (B) (C) (D) (E)
14. (A) (B) (C) (D) (E)	44. (A) (B) (C) (D) (E)	74. (A) (B) (C) (D) (E)
15. (A) (B) (C) (D) (E)	45. (A) (B) (C) (D) (E)	75. (A) (B) (C) (D) (E)
16. (A) (B) (C) (D) (E)	46. (A) (B) (C) (D) (E)	76. (A) (B) (C) (D) (E)
17. (A) (B) (C) (D) (E)	47. (A) (B) (C) (D) (E)	77. (A) (B) (C) (D) (E)
18. (A) (B) (C) (D) (E)	48. (A) (B) (C) (D) (E)	78. (A) (B) (C) (D) (E)
19. (A) (B) (C) (D) (E)	49. (A) (B) (C) (D) (E)	79. (A) (B) (C) (D) (E)
20. (A) (B) (C) (D) (E)	50. (A) (B) (C) (D) (E)	80. (A) (B) (C) (D) (E)
21. (A) (B) (C) (D) (E)	51. (A) (B) (C) (D) (E)	81. (A) (B) (C) (D) (E)
22. (A) (B) (C) (D) (E)	52. (A) (B) (C) (D) (E)	82. (A) (B) (C) (D) (E)
23. (A) (B) (C) (D) (E)	53. (A) (B) (C) (D) (E)	83. (A) (B) (C) (D) (E)
24. (A) (B) (C) (D) (E)	54. (A) (B) (C) (D) (E)	84. (A) (B) (C) (D) (E)
25. (A) (B) (C) (D) (E)	55. (A) (B) (C) (D) (E)	85. (A) (B) (C) (D) (E)
26. (A) (B) (C) (D) (E)	56. (A) (B) (C) (D) (E)	86. (A) (B) (C) (D) (E)
27. (A) (B) (C) (D) (E)	57. (A) (B) (C) (D) (E)	87. (A) (B) (C) (D) (E)
28. (A) (B) (C) (D) (E)	58. (A) (B) (C) (D) (E)	88. (A) (B) (C) (D) (E)
29. (A) (B) (C) (D) (E)	59. (A) (B) (C) (D) (E)	89. (A) (B) (C) (D) (E)
30. (A) (B) (C) (D) (E)	60. (A) (B) (C) (D) (E)	90. (A) (B) (C) (D) (E)

Practice Test 1

1. The British settled in North America in the 17th century for all of the following reasons EXCEPT:

   (A) Primogeniture laws prevented some young men from acquiring wealth in England.
   (B) There was an increase in the population of England, which caused severe economic hardship.
   (C) The defeat of the Spanish Armada in 1588 created a spirit of nationalism in England and weakened Spanish influence in North America.
   (D) Educated Englishmen wanted to create a democracy that would serve as an example for other nations.
   (E) A depression in the woolen industry left England with high unemployment.

2. The period from 1781 to 1787 is often called the Critical Period because

   (A) the United States lacked strong leaders
   (B) the Articles of Confederation had created a weak government that threatened the continued existence of the United States
   (C) the British presence in the United States remained a powerful force that threatened the country
   (D) French Huguenots had moved into the Ohio Valley, threatening American settlements there
   (E) of continuous attacks by Native Americans on Western settlements, slowing Westward expansion

GO ON TO THE NEXT PAGE

3. One of the events which led Kansas to be called "Bleeding Kansas" in 1856 was

(A) the fight by the free African American, Shadrach, against men enforcing the Fugitive Slave Law

(B) the sack of Lawrence by pro-slavery men

(C) John Brown's storming of a federal arsenal at Harper's Ferry

(D) the Fugitive Slave Law's effect on the carrying out of popular sovereignty

(E) the growth of the Second Great Awakening revival movement in the Burned-Over District

GO ON TO THE NEXT PAGE

THE BOSSES OF THE SENATE.

4. The cartoon above could most accurately be interpreted as

(A) criticism of senators from agricultural states who opposed the growth of industry

(B) praise for the Senate for working in harmony with big business

(C) an expression of frustration at the inability of the Democrats and the Republicans to work together to pass meaningful legislation

(D) criticism of the state of politics in which powerful trusts dominate democratic institutions such as the Senate

(E) a call to abolish the Senate in favor of a more democratic House of Representatives

GO ON TO THE NEXT PAGE

5. The development of barbed wire in the second half of the 19th century was most significant in the history of the West because it

(A) was used along railroad tracks to prevent animals from going onto the tracks

(B) enclosed Native American reservations, preventing mingling between Native Americans and whites

(C) enabled farmers to enclose their land thus preventing cowboys from taking cattle on long runs

(D) allowed prospectors to protect their strikes from competitors

(E) was used to build a fence between Mexico and the United States to prevent illegal immigration into the United States

6. John Dewey and other progressive educators of the early 20th century argued that the main function of education should be to

(A) create a future generation of mathematicians and scientists

(B) prevent children from getting into mischief on the streets

(C) teach children the importance of rote memory

(D) instill in children a respect for God, country, and family

(E) impart to the young the skills needed to participate in democracy

7. The novel *It Can't Happen Here* by Sinclair Lewis

(A) warned Americans in the 1920s that excessive buying on credit could lead to an economic crisis

(B) described what the United States would look like if communists led a successful revolution in the 1950s

(C) imagined a fascist takeover in the United States in the 1930s

(D) addressed the danger of nuclear war in the 1960s

(E) woke Californians up in the 1970s to the dangers of a devastating earthquake

8. In public, Truman justified his decision to drop the atomic bomb on Hiroshima and Nagasaki in 1945 by arguing that

(A) these cities were industrial centers that helped the Japanese war effort

(B) these cities were relatively sparsely populated

(C) it would prevent the Soviet Union from attempting to seize land in Asia

(D) American strength would increase in Asia

(E) the American people were war weary

9. Which of the following was least likely to provoke a direct military confrontation between the U.S. and the USSR?

(A) the Berlin Airlift of 1948

(B) the Cuban missile crisis of 1962

(C) the Soviet suppression of the Hungarian revolt in 1956

(D) the construction of the Berlin Wall in 1961

(E) the Korean War of 1950 to 1953

GO ON TO THE NEXT PAGE

10. The Kerner Commission published a report concerning violence in America which stated that

    (A) immigrants were the source of conflict and should barred from entry into the United States

    (B) unions should be made illegal because they had been infiltrated by the Communist Party

    (C) violence is caused by young people and when the population gets older after the baby-boom, the level of violence would go down

    (D) the death penalty would deter the high levels of violence against police officers

    (E) the main cause of the urban riots of the 1960s was the economic and social gulf between races

11. Slavery and indentured servitude in colonial America differed in that most indentured servants

    (A) were promised great financial compensation for their service

    (B) were coerced into service

    (C) received land after completion of their terms of indenture

    (D) came voluntarily

    (E) were considered members of their master's family

12. In addition to improving the credit of the United States, Alexander Hamilton's financial program, approved by Congress in 1791,

    (A) increased the power of the states

    (B) strengthened the political power of the common people

    (C) increased the power of the presidency

    (D) created support for the success and growth of the United States

    (E) decreased the political differences between the Federalist Party and the Democratic-Republican Party

13. Jefferson acted more like a Federalist than a Democratic-Republican when he

    (A) voted to establish the Bank of the United States

    (B) purchased the Louisiana Territory

    (C) commissioned Lewis and Clark to explore the Louisiana Territory

    (D) wrote the Virginia and Kentucky Resolutions along with James Madison

    (E) supported the idea of nullification

14. At the beginning of the Mexican War in 1846 when "American blood was spilled on American soil," General Zachary Taylor and his troops were

    (A) in California waiting for the Mexicans to sell the Texas Territory

    (B) north of the Rio Grande River in territory claimed by both Mexico and the United States

    (C) in New Mexico marching toward Texas attempting to resolve the border dispute between Texas and New Mexico

    (D) on a ship sailing toward Texas

    (E) in the Utah Territory at President Polk's request

GO ON TO THE NEXT PAGE

15. In the Platt Amendment, incorporated into Cuba's 1901 constitution, Cuba promised to do all of the following EXCEPT

    (A) allow the United States to intervene militarily in Cuba
    (B) set aside revenue to pay off debts to the United States
    (C) refrain from signing treaties detrimental to U.S. interests
    (D) provide land for American bases
    (E) grant the United States exclusive trading privileges in Cuba

16. The Japanese attack on Pearl Harbor resulted in all of the following EXCEPT

    (A) U.S. entry in World War II
    (B) hostility toward Japanese people in the United States
    (C) women entering the work force in large numbers in the United States
    (D) an end to segregation in the armed forces
    (E) an end to the Great Depression

17. Although congress had not declared war, President Truman sent U.S. armed forces to aid South Korea—an action he believed the he was empowered to take based on

    (A) powers granted presidents in the United Nations Charter
    (B) a joint resolution of Congress
    (C) a constitutional power of the presidency
    (D) a special U.S. treaty with South Korea
    (E) the U.S. commitment under the NATO agreement

18. What major consequence occurred as a result of the break-in at the Watergate Hotel?

    (A) The *New York Times* began publishing the Pentagon Papers.
    (B) President Reagan had to discuss the diversion of money to the Contras.
    (C) President Nixon resigned.
    (D) The truth about the Gulf of Tonkin Incident was revealed.
    (E) The October Surprise was revealed and Carter's efforts to free the hostages in Iran were given new respect.

19. The Equal Rights Amendment (ERA) was defeated because

    (A) Congress would not pass it
    (B) it was held to be unconstitutional
    (C) not enough state legislatures passed it
    (D) Betty Friedan opposed it
    (E) Richard Nixon vetoed it

GO ON TO THE NEXT PAGE

KAPLAN

20. President Clinton's position on gun control and law enforcement were reflected in his

    (A) support for the Contract With America
    (B) appointment of Sandra Day O'Connor to the Supreme Court
    (C) approval of the Dayton Accords
    (D) signing of the Brady Bill
    (E) support from the National Rifle Association

21. All of the following statements represent ideas expressed in the Declaration of Independence EXCEPT:

    (A) Governments derive their power to rule from the consent of the governed.
    (B) People have the right to overthrow a government which does not fulfill the will of the people.
    (C) People have the unalienable right to own property.
    (D) All men are created equal.
    (E) George III has committed egregious acts against the colonies.

22. In order to gain Thomas Jefferson's support for the assumption of state debts by the national government, Alexander Hamilton agreed to

    (A) modify his financial program
    (B) the placement of the capital of the United States on the Potomac River
    (C) support Jefferson's election in 1800
    (D) help negotiate a peace treaty with England
    (E) withdraw his support for excise taxes on goods made in the United States

23. The concept of "redemption" in the politics of the post–Civil War period refers to

    (A) a religious awakening among Northerners in regard to the evils of racism
    (B) washing away the sins of the South's illegal rebellion
    (C) the physical rebuilding of the infrastructure of the South following the Civil War
    (D) atoning for the fraternal violence of the Civil War
    (E) white Southerners retaking power in the South following Reconstruction

24. President McKinley publicly justified U.S. annexation of the Philippines on the grounds that

    (A) the United States had a responsibility to uplift the Filipinos
    (B) a plebiscite indicated Filipino preference for U.S. rule
    (C) a failure to do so would open the way for a Marxist regime
    (D) the Philippines were spoils of the Spanish-American War
    (E) America needed raw materials from the Philippines

25. The Hepburn Act, pushed through Congress by President Theodore Roosevelt, was significant in that it

    (A) strengthened the Interstate Commerce Commission
    (B) created the United States Forest Service
    (C) empowered the Department of Agriculture to inspect meat
    (D) strengthened the Sherman Anti-trust Act
    (E) made child labor illegal

GO ON TO THE NEXT PAGE

26. An important effect of the increase of open shops and "company unions" in the 1920s was

    (A) a weakening of the agricultural sector of the economy
    (B) an increase in the purchasing power of workers
    (C) a strengthening of the Democratic Party
    (D) a weakening of the labor movement
    (E) improved working conditions

27. To make America "the Great Society" was a pronouncement concerning

    (A) Richard Nixon's ideas on federalism
    (B) John F. Kennedy's initiatives on Civil Rights
    (C) Gerald Ford's fight against inflation
    (D) Lyndon B. Johnson's plan to fight poverty
    (E) Jimmy Carter's goals concerning education

28. The presidency of Lyndon Johnson was dominated by issues involving Vietnam after he

    (A) coined the phrase *domino theory* and sent advisors to South Vietnam
    (B) pledged to support French forces in Vietnam
    (C) signed the Geneva Accords
    (D) "Vietnamized" the war
    (E) proposed the Tonkin Gulf Resolution

29. The economic condition of "stagflation" of the early 1970s can best be described as

    (A) deflation and low productivity
    (B) high productivity and high prices
    (C) high inflation and high unemployment
    (D) high prices and low productivity
    (E) low prices and high productivity

30. The Iran Hostage Crisis of 1979–1981

    (A) reflected resentment of the U.S. support of the Shah of Iran
    (B) aided Jimmy Carter's bid for re-election in 1980
    (C) increased American prestige
    (D) heightened Cold War tensions
    (E) caused a global oil crisis

31. A provision of the charter issued by the British government for the establishment of the colony of Virginia was that

    (A) full rights of English citizenship would be extended to English settlers
    (B) Virginia would enjoy complete autonomy under the policy of salutary neglect
    (C) Virginia would choose the location of its seat of government separate from England
    (D) Virginia would be under the strict control of the royal governor
    (E) Virginia would establish its own form of government, independent of the British crown

32. In response to colonial actions to protest British policies after the French and Indian War, the British government did all of the following EXCEPT

    (A) repeal the Stamp Act
    (B) reaffirm its right to legislate for the colonies
    (C) sign a nonimportation agreement
    (D) order the quartering of troops in the colonies
    (E) pass the Intolerable Acts

GO ON TO THE NEXT PAGE

33. Who most strongly opposed colonization of free blacks in Liberia in the 19th century?

    (A) Henry Clay
    (B) Daniel Webster
    (C) James Monroe
    (D) Marcus Garvey
    (E) David Walker

34. In the years between the Civil War and 1900, the South

    (A) developed an extensive railroad network
    (B) remained primarily agricultural with a few pockets of industry
    (C) became economically independent from the rest of the United States
    (D) encouraged higher tariffs to prevent foreign cotton from coming into the country
    (E) experienced the same economic progress as did the North

35. In the early 20th century, the Progressive movement advocated reform in all of the following areas EXCEPT:

    (A) the power of trusts
    (B) conditions for factory workers
    (C) political corruption
    (D) segregation of the races in public facilities
    (E) problems of democratic participation

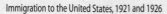

Immigration to the United States, 1921 and 1926

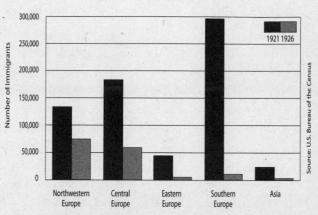

36. The trend illustrated by the graph above could best be explained by

    (A) a sharp downturn in the U.S. economy, which discouraged potential immigrants
    (B) the rise of totalitarian regimes in Europe, which restricted the number of people allowed to leave
    (C) legislation in the United States, which restricted the number of immigrants allowed into the United States
    (D) German submarine warfare, which targeted ships leaving Europe bound for the United States
    (E) industrial growth in Europe, which absorbed rural workers

37. To protect citizens from bank failures, Franklin D. Roosevelt and Congress established the

    (A) National Industrial Recovery Act (NIRA)
    (B) Securities and Exchange Commission (SEC)
    (C) Federal Deposit Insurance Corporation (FDIC)
    (D) Social Security Administration
    (E) Federal Reserve System

GO ON TO THE NEXT PAGE

38. Which of the following statements is true of the Gulf of Tonkin Resolution of 1964?

(A) It passed both the Senate and the House without any dissenting votes.

(B) It contributed to President Johnson's slim margin of victory in the 1964 election.

(C) It was a declaration of war that Congress passed after much debate.

(D) In retrospect it is clear that the resolution was justified by clear evidence of North Vietnamese aggression.

(E) It gave President Johnson a "blank check" to retaliate against the North Vietnamese.

GO ON TO THE NEXT PAGE

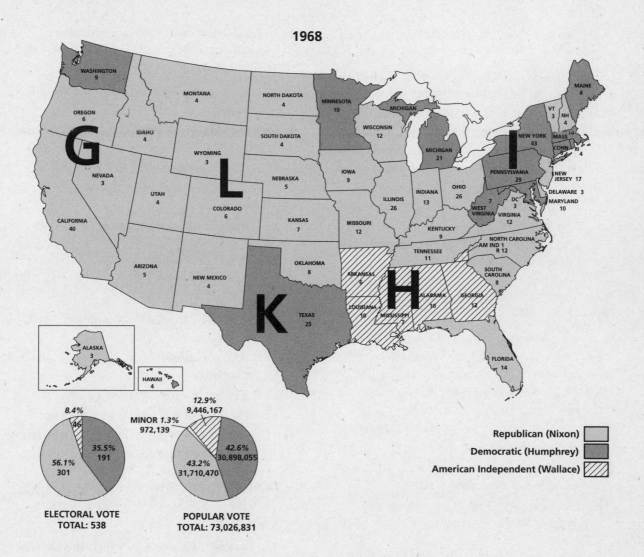

1968

Republican (Nixon)
Democratic (Humphrey)
American Independent (Wallace)

ELECTORAL VOTE
TOTAL: 538

POPULAR VOTE
TOTAL: 73,026,831

39. In the map of the 1968 election above which
area shows the effects of the backlash against
Civil Rights?

(A) K

(B) L

(C) G

(D) H

(E) I

40. The Weathermen, who were in the news in the 1960s and early 1970s, were

    (A) radical black nationalists who believed in power to the black people
    (B) radical terrorists who opposed the Vietnam War
    (C) environmental activists who opposed the pollution caused by automobiles
    (D) a rock and roll group who were precursors to punk rock and heavy metal groups
    (E) a commune that called for love and peace and living in the outdoors

41. Key components of Henry Clay's American System included

    (A) a strict interpretation of the Constitution and rapid Western expansion
    (B) a high protective tariff and internal improvements
    (C) the development of Southern industry and Northern agriculture
    (D) the elimination of export taxes and of the international slave trade
    (E) exclusive government ownership of canals and the national bank

42. Which of the following is NOT true of John Quincy Adams?

    (A) He was the only President to serve in the House of Representatives after he left the presidency.
    (B) He was an ardent opponent of the Gag Rule.
    (C) He supported scientific research.
    (D) He was the only son of a president to attain the presidency himself.
    (E) He argued for the freedom of the slaves on the ship Amistad.

43. In his debates against Senator Stephen Douglas in 1858, Abraham Lincoln held the position that slavery

    (A) should be abolished in the whole United States
    (B) should be abolished immediately in the South
    (C) should be abolished in California
    (D) should not spread to the Western territories
    (E) was not an important question

44. President Lincoln's ideas about Reconstruction were based on the theory that the Confederate states

    (A) should be treated as conquered territories
    (B) could be admitted to the Union only by Congress
    (C) had never actually left the Union
    (D) must grant full equality to all people
    (E) should be barred indefinitely from being part of the United States

45. In his futuristic novel, *Looking Backward 2000–1887*, published in 1888, Edward Bellamy

    (A) described a world in which the United States exercised unrivaled naval power
    (B) scolded the South for enacting Jim Crow laws and tolerating the lynching of African Americans
    (C) imagined a world in which socialism and harmony replaced the antagonisms of the Gilded Age
    (D) discussed the potential benefits of having a single tax on unimproved lands
    (E) warned readers about the dangers of totalitarian regimes

GO ON TO THE NEXT PAGE

46. The "Turner Thesis," put forward by historian Frederick Jackson Turner in the 1890's held that

    (A) Darwin's ideas about the natural world could be applied to human communities
    (B) America, if it hoped to compete with European powers, must build up its navy and acquire overseas colonies
    (C) it was the "manifest destiny" of the United States to expand from the Atlantic to the Pacific Ocean
    (D) the frontier experience had produced a practical, self-reliant people who valued individualism and freedom
    (E) slavery had developed an excessively negative reputation, and that African Americans had been better off under slavery than living in the Jim Crow South

47. What was the main goal of the Truman Doctrine?

    (A) Elimination of communism
    (B) Implementation of the "Domino Theory"
    (C) Containment of communism
    (D) Reconstruction of Western Europe after World War II
    (E) Assistance to British colonies in Africa

48. Dr. Benjamin Spock was significant in the 1950s because he

    (A) found a cure for childhood polio
    (B) popularized a more lenient approach to child rearing
    (C) was accused of passing atomic secrets to the Soviet Union
    (D) performed the first human heart transplant
    (E) encouraged the use of tranquilizers among suburban housewives

49. All of the following influenced the hippies of the 1960s EXCEPT

    (A) Gregory Corso's poetry
    (B) Rachel Carson's warning about the environment
    (C) Timothy Leary's ideas on drugs
    (D) Allen Ginsberg's poetry and ideas
    (E) Phyllis Schlafly's ideas on women

50. Which of the following was a result of George H. W. Bush's reversal of his pledge not to raise taxes?

    (A) The country went into severe recession.
    (B) He said the country had finally "kicked the Vietnam syndrome."
    (C) Inflation became the main problem of the 1990s.
    (D) He lost the support of the core of Republican loyalists.
    (E) He was able to finance the invasion of Panama without endangering the economy.

GO ON TO THE NEXT PAGE

JOIN, or DIE.

51. The drawing above was suggesting that the American colonists

(A) support the Dominion of New England
(B) join the New England Confederation
(C) send representatives to the First Continental Congress
(D) approve the Albany Plan of Union
(E) revise the Articles of Confederation

52. Which of the following statements about the Louisiana Purchase is correct?

(A) It expelled the British from North America.
(B) It contributed to peace with the Native Americans of the Ohio Valley.
(C) It demonstrated President Jefferson's willingness to negotiate with the King of Spain.
(D) It doubled the size of the United States.
(E) It was an unconstitutional act committed by President Jefferson and Congress.

53. The term "Manifest Destiny," used in 1846 by newspaper editor John L. O'Sullivan, could best be described as a policy that would

(A) bring democracy to the West and expand the territory of the United States
(B) remove the French from Oregon
(C) increase immigration from Europe
(D) push the Spanish out of Texas
(E) protect Indian culture

54. All of the following statement about African American troops in the Civil War are true EXCEPT:

(A) They fought on the front lines in battles.
(B) They received equal pay to the white troops throughout the war.
(C) They were always under the command of white officers.
(D) Many of them were runaway slaves who were called "contraband" by Lincoln.
(E) They often served as workers in the rear of battles.

55. The event that brought the issue of civil service reform to the fore during the Gilded Age was

(A) the Credit Mobilier scandal
(B) a report in McClure's magazine chronicling the extent of the patronage system
(C) a series of pointed cartoons by Thomas Nast
(D) the assassination of President Garfield
(E) the large number of civil servants fired by Democratic President Cleveland when he assumed office

GO ON TO THE NEXT PAGE

56. Willa Cather's *My Antonia* and Mark Twain's *The Adventures of Tom Sawyer* are similar in that both

    (A) showed the effects of slavery and racism on American society
    (B) focused on the difficulties of immigrants in adjusting to American life
    (C) presented the culture and customs of particular regions of the United States
    (D) failed to gain popular acclaim in their authors' lifetimes
    (E) alerted Americans to the wretched conditions in the factories

57. The event that immediately precipitated the Spanish-American War was

    (A) the nationalization of U.S. sugar plantations by Spain
    (B) the murder of Cuban nationalist leader Jose Marti
    (C) the sinking of the U.S. battleship *Maine* in the Havana harbor
    (D) a dispute involving the border between Mexico and the United State
    (E) Spain's refusal to allow the United States to build a canal through Panama

58. The Agricultural Adjustment Act of 1933 was an attempt to increase farm prices by

    (A) restricting farm production through voluntary cooperation by farmers
    (B) increasing farm production to meet growing demand
    (C) reducing farm production by paying farmers to plant fewer crops
    (D) lowering the tariffs to increase the sale of agricultural products abroad
    (E) teaching farmers industrial skills so that they could leave the land

59. Which of the following is true about both the American Revolution and the Vietnam War?

    (A) The United States was victorious in both wars.
    (B) Both were essentially wars against domination by an overseas power.
    (C) Both were civil wars between North and South.
    (D) Both the United States in 1779 and South Vietnam in 1972 received military support from France.
    (E) Both were traditional wars fought by traditional armies.

60. Which statement explains why gay rights organizations opposed the policy adopted during the Clinton administration regarding gays in the military?

    (A) It prohibited gays from serving in the military.
    (B) It prohibited gays from serving in combat.
    (C) It provided for segregation of gay troops.
    (D) Its frank acceptance of gay soldiers endangered public support.
    (E) It did not protect openly gay soldiers from discrimination.

61. Bacon's Rebellion of 1676 was significant in that it

    (A) led the colonies to recruit a greater number of indentured servants
    (B) caused the death of Governor Berkeley of Virginia
    (C) contributed to an increase in Indian uprisings in Virginia
    (D) created fear of additional rebellions by former indentured servants
    (E) was the largest slave rebellion in U.S. history

GO ON TO THE NEXT PAGE

62. Peter Zenger's trial in 1734 was significant in that it

(A) laid the groundwork for freedom of the press in the future United States

(B) exposed corruption in the British government

(C) led to reforms within the British government concerning rule of the colonies

(D) involved a jury composed of British officials

(E) resulted in the execution of Peter Zenger

63. In which of the following pairs of events did the first cause the second?

(A) John Quincy Adams signed the *Specie Circular*—the United States entered a depression.

(B) John C. Calhoun wrote the Nullification Proclamation—Virginia joined with Kentucky against the Sedition Act.

(C) Daniel Webster opposed the Bank of the United States—Andrew Jackson issued the *Specie Circular*.

(D) Tariff of 1828 passed—Martin Van Buren elected president.

(E) Andrew Jackson vetoed the Bank Re-charter Bill—the Whig Party formed.

64. Sherman's March to the Sea during the Civil War is significant because

(A) it was the first major victory by Union forces

(B) it was a major victory for African American troops

(C) It was the turning point of the war

(D) it was the final battle of the war

(E) it was the first example of total war

65. During Presidential Reconstruction, Congressional Republicans opposed Andrew Johnson's policy of

(A) letting former members of the Confederacy run the new postwar state governments

(B) guaranteeing suffrage to African Americans

(C) requiring each former Confederate state to ratify the 14th Amendment

(D) banning former members of the Confederacy from voting and holding office

(E) granting each freedman 40 acres and a mule

66. The Dawes Severalty Act of 1887 was passed by Congress in response to pressure from

(A) large mining interests that wanted to exploit Native American reservation lands

(B) Native Americans who thought the plan for gradual assimilation offered their best hope for survival

(C) the U.S. military, which was seeking revenge for "Custer's Last Stand"

(D) reform-minded whites trying to solve the "Indian problem" by promoting Native Americans' assimilation

(E) buffalo hunters who wanted unlimited access to buffalo herds

GO ON TO THE NEXT PAGE

67. The 1919 Treaty of Versailles ending World War I

    (A) did not create a lasting peace as envisioned by Woodrow Wilson in his Fourteen Points
    (B) gave the United States temporary control of a portion of Germany
    (C) was endorsed by the United States because it attempted to contain communism
    (D) led to the immediate emergence of the United States as a world power
    (E) did not include any ideas put forward by Woodrow Wilson in his Fourteen Points

68. The Red Scare of 1919–1920 was, in part, a response to the

    (A) labor unrest that produced a nationwide strike wave
    (B) rise of fascism in Europe
    (C) teaching of Charles Darwin's theory of evolution
    (D) rebirth of the Ku Klux Klan
    (E) temperance movement and its success in establishing Prohibition

69. Because of his belief that the New Deal had not accomplished its goals, Francis Townsend proposed a plan to

    (A) use nonviolent civil disobedience to oppose racial segregation
    (B) send aid to anti-fascist groups in Europe
    (C) force all "subversive" groups to register with the government
    (D) ban women from working outside the home until all able-bodied men had work
    (E) provide a monthly stipend to everyone in the United States over 60 years old

70. Which of the following was the most important factor in John F. Kennedy's victory over Richard Nixon in 1960?

    (A) Americans' disappointment with the results of the Korean War
    (B) Kennedy's superior showing in a televised debate
    (C) Nixon's World War II record
    (D) The Watergate investigation
    (E) Kennedy's record as governor of Massachusetts

71. Portugal led the way in exploration in the 1400s because of

    (A) its inland location requiring it to find an overland route to the Indies
    (B) government stability and the invention of the caravel
    (C) the signing of the Treaty of Tordesillas with Spain
    (D) the marriage of Ferdinand and Isabella
    (E) the success of Columbus's voyage to the New World

72. An important achievement of George Washington's first term of office, 1789–1793, was the

    (A) establishment of a cabinet to act as advisors
    (B) purchase of Florida from Spain
    (C) suppression of a rebellion of Massachusetts farmers
    (D) passage of the Alien and Sedition Act
    (E) formation of a political party to oppose Alexander Hamilton

73. Which statement most closely reflects William Lloyd Garrison's view of slavery?

   (A) The only solution to the slavery question is a federal slave code.
   (B) Slavery must immediately be abolished in all areas of the United States.
   (C) There should be no extension of slavery to the territories in the West.
   (D) The question of slavery should be settled by popular sovereignty.
   (E) The question of slavery in the territories of the West should be decided in the future.

74. In the Dred Scott case of 1857 the Supreme Court included which idea as part of its decision?

   (A) Separate but equal facilities are constitutional.
   (B) An African American had no rights a white man was bound to respect.
   (C) The state of Georgia has no jurisdiction over the Cherokee which is a separate nation.
   (D) Interstate commerce is not within the jurisdiction of the states, but of the federal government.
   (E) Separate but equal facilities are inherently unconstitutional.

75. Black Codes, passed in many Southern states in 1865 and 1866,

   (A) helped freed men and women find employment and land after emancipation
   (B) were intended to recreate the plantation economy without slavery
   (C) were supported by Harriet Tubman and Frederick Douglass
   (D) were opposed by President Andrew Johnson
   (E) were declared unconstitutional by the Supreme Court

76. "Having behind us the producing masses of this nation and the world, supported by the commercial interests, the laboring interests, and the toilers everywhere, we will answer their [the wealthy classes'] demand for a gold standard by saying to them: You shall not press down upon the brow of labor this crown of thorns, you shall not crucify mankind upon a cross of gold."

   In this 1896 speech, William Jennings Bryan is advocating

   (A) government subsidies to farmers
   (B) free and unlimited coinage of silver
   (C) passage higher protective tariffs
   (D) reduction of the work day to eight hours
   (E) the enactment of laws restricting immigration

77. The Hay-Bunau-Varilla Treaty of 1903 is significant because it

   (A) ended the Spanish-American War
   (B) paved the way for the Panama Canal project
   (C) established commonwealth status for Puerto Rico
   (D) added the Mexican Cession to U.S. territory
   (E) gave United States companies exclusive rights to the Guatemalan banana trade

GO ON TO THE NEXT PAGE

78. President Wilson's unwillingness to compromise over the issue of the League of Nations resulted in

    (A) a surge in popular support for his resolve

    (B) his loss of the presidency in the election of 1920

    (C) the rejection of the Treaty of Versailles by the European nations

    (D) the failure of the Senate to approve the Treaty of Versailles

    (E) an increase in power of the Democratic party

79. At the Yalta Conference of 1945, President Franklin D. Roosevelt was most worried about the views expressed by

    (A) Joseph Stalin on Eastern Europe

    (B) Charles de Gaulle on Western Europe

    (C) Winston Churchill on the Irish question

    (D) Mao Zedong on Chinese relations with Japan

    (E) Kim Il Sung on the unification of Korea

80. The United States became politically involved in Vietnam immediately after

    (A) France was defeated by the Vietminh

    (B) China threatened Taiwan

    (C) Great Britain partitioned India

    (D) North Korea attacked South Korea

    (E) Japan relinquished its control over Vietnam following World War II

81. When Europeans arrived in the Americas in the 15th and 16th centuries, they found

    (A) established societies that contained various forms of government

    (B) scattered tribes of lawless, nomadic people

    (C) extensive trade being carried on in African slavery

    (D) hostile, unwelcoming tribes

    (E) wild horses in abundance

82. Henry Clay, "The Great Compromiser," was instrumental in engineering compromises which resulted in all of the following EXCEPT

    (A) Missouri being admitted to the Union

    (B) Rutherford B. Hayes becoming president

    (C) resolution of the nullification crisis

    (D) California being admitted to the Union

    (E) Maine being admitted to the Union

GO ON TO THE NEXT PAGE

83. "I consider the tariff as the occasion rather than as the cause of the unhappy state of things. The truth can no longer be disguised that the peculiar domestic institution of the southern states and the consequent direction which her soil and climate have given to her industry has placed them in regard to taxation and appropriation in opposite relation to the majority of the nation."

Which of the following statements are supported in the above quote from John C. Calhoun?

    I. The existence of slavery is the result of nature and geography.

    II. Sectionalism was based on slavery, not states' rights.

    III. The tariff was the most important cause of sectional tensions.

    IV. The majority of the nation agreed with the southern viewpoint on slavery.

(A) I and III

(B) II and IV

(C) I and II

(D) II and III

(E) III and IV

84. The Industrial Workers of the World was known for being

(A) a company union, set up and funded by large corporations, to calm worker discontent

(B) a craft union, which avoided unskilled workers in organizing drives

(C) a Gilded Age union more ready to compromise than strike

(D) the most militant and anti-capitalist union of the late 1800s and early 1900s

(E) a secret brotherhood responsible for the Haymarket Affair

85. All of the following are reasons for the United States entry into World War I EXCEPT

(A) the sinking of the Lusitania

(B) the interception of the Zimmerman Note

(C) German violation of freedom of the seas

(D) the desire to make "the world safe for democracy"

(E) the American commitment to the Triple Alliance

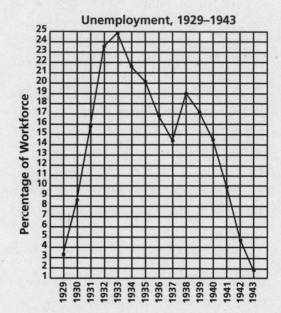

86. Based on the graph above, which statement best explains the changes in the unemployment figures between 1941 and 1943?

(A) The programs of the New Deal were effective in ending the Depression of 1929.

(B) The United States had become involved in World War II.

(C) More women had found employment outside of the home.

(D) New technology had developed which led to greater employment.

(E) The Depression was more severe most economists realized.

GO ON TO THE NEXT PAGE

87. The Stimson Doctrine of 1932 called for

    (A) an economic boycott of all German goods by the allied nations
    (B) a pledge by the allied nations to respect the territorial integrity of China
    (C) a cease-fire in China
    (D) a condemnation by the United States of Japan's actions in Manchuria
    (E) a call for an end to Italy's aggressive policies in Africa

88. The Soviet Union responded to the formation of the North Atlantic Treaty Organization (NATO) by

    (A) providing military assistance to the Southeast Asian Treaty Organization (SEATO)
    (B) forming the Warsaw Pact
    (C) giving financial aid to Central Treaty Organization (CENTO)
    (D) joining the Alliance for Progress
    (E) sending advisors to the Organization of American States (OAS)

89. In the "Checkers speech," Richard Nixon

    (A) denied allegations that he had improperly received gifts during his 1952 bid for the vice-presidency
    (B) accused John F. Kennedy of being "soft on communism" during the 1960 campaign for president
    (C) announced his policy of "Vietnamization" of the Vietnam War in 1969
    (D) called for normalizing relations with China in1972
    (E) declared, in 1974, that he "was not a crook," in response to allegations of wrongdoing in connection with the Watergate scandal

90. Of the following ideas, which was NOT part of the *Brown v. Board of Education of Topeka* decision?

    (A) Education is the most important function of local government.
    (B) The original intent of the 14th Amendment was to end school segregation.
    (C) The doctrine of "separate but equal" fosters feelings of inferiority in African American children.
    (D) Schools should be integrated "with all deliberate speed."
    (E) Education is the basis of success in our society.

STOP!

If you finish before time is up, you may check your work.

Answer Key
Practice Test 1

1. D	31. A	61. D
2. B	32. C	62. A
3. B	33. E	63. E
4. D	34. B	64. E
5. C	35. D	65. A
6. E	36. C	66. D
7. C	37. C	67. A
8. A	38. E	68. A
9. E	39. D	69. E
10. E	40. B	70. B
11. D	41. B	71. B
12. D	42. D	72. A
13. B	43. D	73. B
14. B	44. C	74. B
15. E	45. C	75. B
16. D	46. D	76. B
17. C	47. C	77. B
18. C	48. B	78. D
19. C	49. E	79. A
20. D	50. D	80. A
21. C	51. D	81. A
22. B	52. D	82. B
23. E	53. A	83. C
24. A	54. B	84. D
25. A	55. D	85. E
26. D	56. C	86. B
27. D	57. C	87. D
28. E	58. C	88. B
29. C	59. B	89. A
30. A	60. E	90. B

ANSWERS AND EXPLANATIONS

1. D

The British settlers who came to the New World did not intend to build a model democratic society. They came for the reasons stated in (A), (B), (C), and (E). Primogeniture (A) refers to the medieval law by which only firstborn sons are permitted to inherit the family estate. Therefore, many second sons came to the new world in search of wealth. The growth of the English population (B) and the failure of the woolen industry (E) led people, particularly debtors, to seek a new life in the New World. The defeat of the Spanish Armada by England (C), during the reign of Queen Elizabeth I, developed a spirit of nationalism that contributed to England's decision to explore the New World.

2. B

The Critical Period is particularly associated with the problems involved in the establishment of a new government for the newly freed colonies. The Articles of Confederation established a loose league of friendship that created a weak central government. The absence of an executive and a judiciary jeopardized the existence of the United States because of the inability of Congress to enforce and interpret laws. There were many strong leaders at the time (A). Although British troops retained a presence in the United States after the French-American victory at Yorktown in 1781, these troops were not influential in the establishment of a government for the new colonies. The French (D) were not a threat to American settlements at the time. Although some hostility between settlers and Native Americans did exist (E), this was not particularly pronounced or critical during this period.

3. B

Bleeding Kansas refers to the Kansas Territory during a mini-civil war over the fate of slavery. Popular sovereignty, allowing voters to approve or reject slavery, could not resolve the slavery question if people fought instead of voting. About 200 were killed before Kansas became a state in 1862. The first major act was the destruction of the anti-slavery town of Lawrence (called the sack of Lawrence). John Brown's raid on Harper's Ferry (C) was in Virginia in 1859. The Fugitive Slave Law (D) was part of the Compromise of 1850, and had nothing directly to do with Bleeding Kansas. Shadrach (A) was a victim of the Fugitive Slave Law who was kidnapped in Boston in 1851 by his African American friends and spirited away before the magistrate knew what happened. The Burned-Over District (E) was in western New York, not Kansas.

4. D

Many people were concerned over the growing power of trusts, which were a form of monopoly control in business. Trusts seemed to wield nearly limitless power. Early in the 19th century, Southern agricultural states often opposed pro-industry legislation (A), such as the protective tariff, but the cartoon is clearly not sympathetic to business. The juxtaposition of massive trusts and puny senators does not imply equal status or harmony (B). The senators are not identified by party (C). Few people were calling for the abolition of the U.S. Senate (E), although some were calling for the direct election of senators by the voters to make them more responsive to the people.

5. C

The cowboy era ended for a number of reasons, but barbed wire played a significant part. It allowed ranchers and farmers to enclose their lands, making long cattle runs unfeasible. Barbed wire was not significant in any of the ways indicated in the other choices. Railroad companies (A) would not have gone out of their way to protect wild animals. Reservations (B) were not enclosed by barbed wire. Miners (D) used means other than barbed wire to protect their claims. Parts of the border between the United States and Mexico (E) has been fortified with fences that no doubt include barbed wire, but that is a 20th century phenomenon.

6. E

Dewey wanted education to move away from rote memorization and to prepare young people to be active participants in democracy. In fact, the Students for a Democratic Society cite him as an inspiration to the call for participatory democracy in the 1960s. The emphasis on science and mathematics (A) characterized Cold War initiatives of the 1950s. Progressive educators wanted education to be meaningful, not simply a means of keeping children off the street (B), and not to focus on memorization (C). Conservatives, not progressives, would want education to focus of God, country, and family (D).

7. C

Lewis's novel served as a warning as fascism was gaining ground in Europe and demagogues were gaining adherents in the United States. The other answer choices were not highlighted in major American novels.

8. A

Truman justified the dropping of the atomic bomb by stating that Hiroshima and Nagasaki were industrial cities fueling the Japanese war effort. He also argued that dropping the bomb would shorten the war and save American lives. These cities both had large populations (B). Many critics felt that the bomb was intended to send a message (C) to the Soviet Union, but Truman did not use this as a justification in public for his decision. Likewise, if Truman was interested in expanding American influence in Asia (D), he would not have publicly stated this as a justification for the atomic bombing of Japan, nor would he have cited American war weariness as a justification (E).

9. E

The Korean War involved direct engagement between U.S. forces and those of North Korea and China, but not the Soviet Union. The Berlin Airlift (A), the Cuban missile crisis (B), the Soviet suppression of the Hungarian revolution (C), and the construction of the Berlin Wall (D) all resulted in eyeball-to-eyeball standoffs that almost led to armed conflict between the United States and the Soviet Union, as each had specific interests that were threatened.

10. E

The 1968 National Advisory (Kerner) Commission on Civil Disorders, convened to discover why there was so much urban violence in the 1960s. Its report stated that America was "two societies separate and unequal," and that the plight of African Americans was largely unknown to whites. However, it concluded that the richest nation on earth could correct these inequalities. The commission reached liberal social and economic conclusions, thus it did not blame immigrants (A), or unions (B), or call for the death penalty (D). The young people (C) certainly were participants in the riots, but the social and economic factors were the primary causes according to the report.

11. D

Indentured servants came to the new world voluntarily, agreeing, through a contract, to work a certain length of time in exchange for passage to the New World. Indentured servants (other than prisoners) were not forced to sign a contract of indenture (B). Indentured servants were not promised any financial compensation, nor did they receive any (A). In fact, some called it "white slavery." Although indentured servants were often promised land after the completion of their contract (C), many never received any. Many indentured servants were treated harshly by their sponsors; they were seldom considered members of their master's family (E).

12. D

Hamilton's efforts at funding the U.S. government and assumption of state debts from the war of independence cemented the loyalty of wealthy individuals, states, and foreign powers to the success of the United States. Hamilton was not an advocate of strong state governments (A) and his program had the effect of binding these new states to the success of the Union. He feared rule by the common people, or "mobocracy" (B) and his program did nothing to strengthen popular control. Hamilton increased the power of the central government and established the Bank of the United States, but his economic plan did not lead to an increase in the power of the presidency itself (C). Hamilton's financial program heightened, rather than diminished, differences between the two political parties (E).

13. B

Jefferson, a Democratic-Republican and a strict constructionist in regard to constitutional issues, used the same justification for the Louisiana Purchase that Hamilton, a Federalist and loose constructionist, had used to justify the establishment of the Bank of the United States. Both relied on the "elastic clause" of the Constitution to justify their actions. The Bank of the United States (A) had been part of Hamilton's economic program; Jefferson was opposed. Lewis and Clark's journey (C) was not a partisan issue. The Virginia and Kentucky Resolutions (D) were written in response to the Federalist-supported Alien and Sedition Acts, passed during the administration of John Adams, a Federalist. Nullification (E) was part of the Kentucky resolution and was a strong statement of states' rights, consistent with the political philosophy of the Democratic-Republicans.

14. B

Zachary Taylor was the general who James K. Polk sent to provoke war with Mexico in 1846. The territory between the Nueces River in Texas and the Rio Grande to the South was disputed. It was claimed by both Mexico and the United States. The Mexicans shot at Taylor—who was on the land they claimed. The provocation worked and the war did not end until 1848. The quote in the question was by Polk who claimed that the border of Texas was the Rio Grande so that it was "American soil." In 1846, California (A), New Mexico (C) and Utah (E) were not "American soil"; they were territories gained after the Mexican War in the Treaty of Guadalupe-Hidalgo in 1848. There was a border dispute between New Mexico and Texas, but Taylor did not negotiate that. Taylor was a general, not an admiral in the Navy, so (D) is not correct.

15. E

The United States would not have insisted on exclusive trading rights (E) because it supported free trade. This is evident in the Open Door Notes, written the same year in regard to China. The 1901 Platt Amendment seriously compromised Cuba's independence following the Spanish-American War. All the other choices contributed to this compromise of independence.

16. D

The attack on Pearl Harbor did not result in the end of segregation in the armed forces. Segregation ended after World War II. The attack did result in the U.S. declaration of war against Japan thrusting the United States into World War II (A). The Pearl Harbor attack brought distrust and hostility towards Japanese-Americans, who were interned during World War II (B). As factories stepped up production of war equipment, women entered the work force (C) and the unemployment rate declined bringing the Depression came to an end (E).

17. C

Under his Constitutional power as Commander-in-Chief of the armed forces, the President has the authority to order troops into combat. The U.S. president has no power under the UN Charter (A), although the UN Charter was used as the legal basis for the American military involvement in the Korean War. No Congressional Resolution was passed at the onset of the Korean War (B). The United States had no mutual security treaty with Korea (D). Korea was not a member of NATO, the North Atlantic Treaty Organization (E).

18. C

The break-in at the Watergate Hotel in 1972 was the beginning of the Watergate Scandal, which forced Richard Nixon to resign. The Pentagon Papers (A) were leaked to the *New York Times* by the Pentagon researcher Daniel Ellsberg, an action not directly related to the Watergate break-in, although Nixon's "plumbers" also broke into Daniel Ellsberg's psychiatrist's office in an attempt to discredit Ellsberg. The Reagan administration's (B) Iran-Contra scandal came to light in 1984, a decade after Watergate. The truth about the Gulf of Tonkin Incident (D) was revealed in Senate hearings led by William Fulbright. The October Surprise (E) was an accusation that Ronald Reagan's aides foiled negotiations between President Carter and the Iranians to free the hostages in Teheran, so that Carter would lose the election of 1980. It did not involve a break-in and was not revealed in time to save Carter's reputation.

19. C

Only 35 state legislatures passed the ERA. To achieve passage, the amendment needed the approval of 38 state legislatures, since 38 represents the required three-fourths of the 50 states. Congress (A) passed the amendment by the required two-thirds majority of each house. If it had passed, it would have become part of the Constitution and could not be declared unconstitutional (B). Betty Friedan (D), a women's rights advocate, was in favor of the amendment. Presidents don't sign or veto constitutional amendments (E).

20. D

In 1994, Clinton signed the Brady Bill which provided for stricter gun control and other crime prevention measures. The Contract with America (A) was a Republican program, while Clinton was a Democrat. Sandra Day O'Connor (B) was the first woman appointed to the Supreme Court in 1981. She was appointed by Ronald Reagan, not Clinton. The Dayton Accords (C) were signed in 1995 to end the civil war in Bosnia. The National Rifle Association (E) is a pro-gun organization, which did not support Clinton's position.

21. C

Although John Locke discussed individual rights as "life, liberty, and property," the Declaration of Independence discussed the right of individual rights as "life, liberty, and the pursuit of happiness." "Property" was omitted. The other choices were clearly stated by Jefferson in the Declaration of Independence.

22. B

Hamilton knew that he needed Jefferson's support to carry out his financial program, so he compromised on the location of the permanent capital, agreeing to locate it in the South on the Potomac River. Hamilton did not modify his economic program (A), including his support for excise taxes. (E). He did support the candidacy of his archenemy Jefferson in the election of 1800 when that election was thrown into the House of Representatives for resolution (C), but this occurred almost a decade after he had implemented his financial program. Hamilton was pro-British, while Jefferson was more supportive of the French Revolution. Hamilton would not be conceding anything to Jefferson by working out a treaty with England (D).

23. E

"Redemption" is the term Southern Democrats used to describe their return to power, with the implication that the terrible wrong of

Reconstruction has finally been eradicated. The change to Democratic control signaled the end of the social programs and laws that had offered freedmen and women a degree of social equality during the Reconstruction period. The rebuilding of the South (C) is an aspect of reconstruction itself—although the term "reconstruction" is not restricted to the physical rebuilding of the South. "Redemption," though it has religious overtones, is a political movement; it is not a religious movement (A), (B), (D).

24. A

McKinley argued that the Philippines were not ready for self-government and American control was needed to improve their situation. No vote occurred in the Philippines (B). Marxist regimes (C) became a concern for the United States later in the 20th century—especially after World War II, but not in 1898. War spoils (D) and raw materials (E) would not be justifications that McKinley would publicly give for annexation.

25. A

This 1904 act, along with the 1903 Elkins Act, dealt with railroad regulation. Neither act went as far as some Progressives, such as Robert LaFollette, wanted, but they did strengthen the Interstate Commerce Commission. Theodore Roosevelt was closely linked with the environmental conservation movement. He expanded the acreage of the national forests, but the Forest Service had been created earlier (B). Meat inspection (C) was addressed in the Meat Inspection Act of 1906. Clayton Anti-trust Act (1914), passed during the Wilson administration, strengthened the Sherman Anti-trust Act (D). Child labor (E) was addressed in the Keating-Owen Child Labor Act (1916), which was later struck down by the Supreme Court.

26. D

An open shop is a non-union shop. Company controlled unions and benefit plans initiated by management, which came to be known as welfare capitalism, undermined calls for a union by the workers. Both open shops and company unions weakened the labor movement, which lost ground from 1920 until the New Deal. A weakened labor movement meant that working conditions (E) did not improve and wages (and thus purchasing power) did not increase (B). The agricultural sector did become weaker as the decade wore on, but that was largely due to overproduction (A). The Democrats failed to capture the White House and remained the minority party during the conservative 1920s (D).

27. D

The goal and slogan of "the Great Society" reflected Johnson's hope to improve the standard of living for all Americans. Nixon's ideas on federalism (A) were known as "New Federalism." There is no name for Kennedy's Civil Rights agenda (B) nor Carter's education agenda (E). Ford's fight against inflation (C) was called "Whip Inflation Now."

28. E

The Tonkin Gulf Resolution was gave the president the unrestricted right to defend American interests in Vietnam. Johnson escalated the war rapidly after his election in 1964. The war dominated his administration, influencing his decision not to run for a second full term in 1968. The term "domino theory" was coined by President Eisenhower, the first president to send troops—which he called "advisors" (A). Harry Truman sent money to aid the French (B) but no troops. The United States never signed the Geneva Accords of 1954 (C), which split Vietnam into North and South Vietnam and called for elections. It was President Nixon's policy to "Vietnamize" the war (D), which was a strategy to increase the bombing and turn over the fighting on the ground to the South Vietnamese.

29. C

"Stagflation" was an economic condition characterized by low productivity caused by unemployment along with inflation. This unusual combination of economic conditions was called stagflation. Economic theory failed to explain how, in the early 1970s, the unemployment level could be high while, at the same time, prices increased at a rapid rate. Standard economic theory held that inflation (a rise in prices) was pushed by high wages: when workers have more money they spend more, raising prices. If unemployment is high, according to this theory, the total amount of wages should be low, bringing prices down. The other answer choices do not describe the economic conditions of the early 1970s.

30. A

The students who occupied the United States Embassy in Iran were angered at the United States support of the deposed Shah of Iran. One major reason Jimmy Carter was not re-elected in 1980 (B) was his inability to resolve the hostage crisis. American prestige was severely damaged (C) since the superpower was unable to rescue the hostages. Cold War tensions (D) did not increase, nor did a global oil crisis (E) develop during the hostage crisis (an oil crisis occurred earlier—in 1971–1973).

31. A

The charter issued by the British Crown for the settlement of the Virginia colony guaranteed to the colonists the rights of Englishmen. The colonies were not autonomous (B). The policy of salutary neglect developed after the Glorious Revolution of 1688. Only the Massachusetts Bay Colony charter provided for a specific place for the seat of the government to be located (C). The royal governors (D) often had limited control since the colonists possessed the power of the purse, that is, they paid the salaries of the royal governors. The government in Virginia was established under the authority of the British Crown (E).

32. C

The nonimportation agreements were the colonists' reactions to the Stamp Act not a British reaction to American protests. These agreements were signed by merchants in major ports, such as Boston and New York, who agreed that they would not buy goods from the British. The British did repeal the Stamp Act (A) in response to colonial

protest. However, the British also passed the Declaratory Act of 1765 (B) which reaffirmed the right of the British to legislate for the colonies. The British quartered troops (D) in the colonies in 1765 when the Quartering Act was passed in response to colonial unrest. The Intolerable Acts (1774) (E) were passed by the British government in response to the Boston Tea Party.

33. E

David Walker was opposed to colonization. In the famous sentence, often quoted in textbooks, he opposes colonization saying he was born here and was as American as anyone, and that he would fight for his freedom if denied it. Colonization was a 19th century scheme to get rid of slavery by freeing slaves and sending them to Africa. (Not back to Africa—the people concerned were born in America for the most part.) This would reduce the black population in America and reduce the possibility of rebellion by getting rid of the "dangerous" element: free blacks. Henry Clay (A), Daniel Webster (B), and James Monroe (C) supported colonization. Marcus Garvey (D), a leader of the Back to Africa movement in the 1920s, probably would have supported colonization of Liberia too.

34. B

Despite the hopes of southern moderates that a "New South" would emerge in the post-Reconstruction years, the South failed, for the most part, to industrialize and develop economically until the post–World War II period. Pockets of industry did develop in the 1800s, most notably in Birmingham, Alabama. For this reason, the development of an extensive railroad network (A) and parallel economic growth (E) did not take place. Since the South had little industry it was dependent on the rest of the country (C). Foreign cotton was not coming into the United States because domestic cotton was plentiful and cheap. There was no need for tariffs (D). The industrial North, not the South, was in favor of high tariffs on manufactured goods.

35. D

In general, the Progressive movement accepted the prevailing racist notions about segregation. The most vivid example of this was Wilson's resegregation of government offices. The Progressive movement made strides on all of the other issues. The Clayton Anti-trust Act addressed the issues of the monopolistic business practices (A). State minimum wage laws addressed the conditions (B) of factory workers. Lincoln Steffens's Shame of the Cities exposed municipal corruption (C). The 17th amendment provided for the direct election of senators (E).

36. C

The graph clearly shows that European immigration, especially immigration from southern and eastern Europe, dropped between 1921 and 1926. The cause of the drop is the anti-immigration legislation of the 1920s. The United States did not experience a drop in the economy in the 1920s (A)—industrial production expanded. Totalitarianism (B) did emerge in Russia and Italy in the 1920s, but these regimes did not implement excessively restrictive migration policies. The Soviet Union did severely limit migration later— from Stalin's rule until Gorbachev's glasnost policies. German submarine warfare (D) occurred during World War I, not in the 1920s. Europe was rebuilding during the 1920s (E) and did not experience the level of industrial expansion as did the United States

37. C

The FDIC was established under the Banking Act (Glass-Steagall) Act of 1933 to protect depositors' money. NIRA (A) dealt with standards of production and business practice. The SEC (B) regulated the sale of stocks and bonds. Social Security (D) was established to provide direct relief to individuals, in particular the elderly and disabled. Established in 1913 under President Woodrow Wilson, the powers of The Federal Reserve System (E) were broadened in the 1930s. The "Fed" monitors the money supply and banking practices.

38. E

The Gulf of Tonkin Resolution gave Lyndon Johnson the permission to strike at will to protect American interests in Vietnam. However, it was not a declaration of war (C). Only two senators (A) voted against it. Contrary to what Congress and the American public had been lead to believe, there was no clear evidence of North Vietnamese aggression to justify the resolution (D). This lack of clear evidence emerged during Senate hearings in 1966. Johnson won a landslide (B) against Barry Goldwater in 1964, but Vietnam was not a big issue in the United States until 1965.

39. D

The 1968 election was a three-way race with Governor George Wallace of Alabama running against Richard Nixon and Hubert Humphrey. After Reconstruction, the ex-Confederate states became the Solid (Democratic) South. Setting up barriers to block blacks from voting kept them all in the Democratic column. During the Second Reconstruction there was the "backlash" against Democratic-sponsored civil rights legislation. George Wallace's ("Segregation Now, Segregation Forever") victories in section H above were the result of this backlash against the Democratic Party. In subsequent elections many white Democrats in the South began to switch to the Republican Party.

40. B

The Weathermen were a small faction of Students for a Democratic Society that resorted to terrorism in 1969 to oppose the Vietnam War. Four of their members were killed by a bomb that exploded in a townhouse in Greenwich Village, New York City. Black nationalists (A) were the Black Panthers. The environmentalists who upset the auto industry (C) were known as Nader's Raiders, after consumer advocate Ralph Nader. They were not a rock and roll group (D) and rejected the commune movement (E).

41. B

Henry Clay believed that the United States could become self-sufficient through the "American System." The North would produce industrial goods; the South would supply the raw materials, while the West would supply food for the country. Revenue could be raised through a high protective tariff that would keep out competition and help domestic industry to develop. Excise or sales taxes would be placed on certain goods and the revenues from these taxes and tariffs would be used for internal improvement, such as roads and canals. The bank would keep currency stable and would invest in internal improvements. The plan for the American System required a loose interpretation of the Constitution (A), because canals and roads were not mentioned in the document. Clay did not promote southern industry (C). Export taxes (D) are forbidden by the Constitution and not part of Clay's plan and the international slave trade was ended in 1808 (before Clay's plan). The canals and the Bank of the United States would be jointly controlled by the government and private owners (E).

42. D

Until the election of George W. Bush, John Quincy Adams was the only son of a president to become president. He was an intellectual out of his natural environment as president, but he really came into his own as a member of the House of Representatives (A). He was an anti-slavery man, so he opposed the Gag Rule (B) but was not an abolitionist. He supported scientific research (C) including an astronomical observatory, and he defended the Amistad captives (E) before the Supreme Court.

43. D

Lincoln and the Republican Party held that there should be no extension of slavery to the territories in the West. This position did not endorse abolition (A), nor did it consider the South (B). There was no slavery in California (C) since it came in as a free state in 1850. Lincoln claimed Douglas did not hold that slavery was a serious issue (E) because he advocated popular sovereignty and did not seem to care whether slavery existed in any state.

44. C

Lincoln argued that the southern states had never left the Union. Individuals in those states rebelled, but the states had never legally left. Therefore, using his power as commander-in-chief during wartime, Lincoln issued his Proclamation of Amnesty and Reconstruction in Dec. 1863 in which he set the terms for the rebellious states to form new state governments. If the states had left the Union, as the Radical Republicans claimed, then it was Congress' job to readmit them and determine the conditions under which they would be readmitted. So the argument was political as much as it was legal. The Radical Republicans held that the South should be treated as a conquered territory (A), that only Congress can admit states (B), and that the South must grant equality to freed men and women (D). No one maintained that the Southern states should be barred from readmission to the United States (E). The debate concerned how readmission would take place.

45. C

Bellamy's utopian novel, which described the benefits of socialism, inspired over 100 Bellamy Clubs devoted to implementing Bellamy's ideas. Questions of naval power (A) or race (B) were not included in the novel. Others addressed these issues in the late 19th century. Imperialists, such as Alfred T. Mahan, supported an expansionistic foreign policy, while several African American writers and activists, notably Ida B. Wells, Booker T. Washington, and W. E. B. DuBois, addressed issues of race in America around the turn of the 20th century. It was Henry George in *Progress and Poverty* in 1879 who proposed a single tax on unimproved land (D) to ensure that land be used for the common good instead of for speculation.

Totalitarian regimes (E) are a 20th century phenomenon, the dangers of which are the subject of anti-utopian novels such as George Orwell's *1984* written in 1948.

46. D

The Turner thesis held that the pioneering experience gave Americans a sense of optimism and individualism. Social Darwinism (A) was most closely associated with the writer William Graham Sumner. It was Alfred T. Mahan who pushed forcibly for an expansionist foreign policy and a strong navy (B). "Manifest Destiny" (C) was an idea held by a large cross section of the American population in the 19th century. Turner was not known for being an outspoken on issues of race (E).

47. C

President Harry S. Truman sought to contain the spread of communism. In 1947, his request for funds to preserve the independence of Greece and Turkey from communist subjugation was approved by Congress. Although the elimination of communism (A) was an ultimate U.S. goal, the Truman Doctrine only sought to contain it. The Domino Theory (B) was a belief expressed by President Dwight D. Eisenhower in 1953 and is most closely associated with the effects of the spread of Communism in Southeast Asia. Although the United States helped in the rebuilding efforts in Europe (D) during Truman's administration, the Truman Doctrine was aimed specifically at containing communism. The Truman Doctrine was specifically targeted at Greece and Turkey and not at the British colonies in Africa (E).

48. B

Dr. Spock encouraged 1950s parents to treat their children with warmth and understanding, to refrain from spanking and scolding, and to breastfeed. Some conservatives blame him for creating a generation of undisciplined ne'er-do-wells who rebelled against their elders in the 1960s. Dr. Jonas Salk (A) developed a vaccine for childhood polio and Julius and Ethel Rosenberg (C) were accused of spying. The first human heart transplant (D) was done in 1967 in South Africa. The use of tranquilizers by women (E) reflects a trend among psychologists in the 1950s, rather than a breakthrough by a specific doctor.

49. E

Phyllis Schlafly was a conservative Republican and anti-feminist whose ideas were diametrically opposed to the views of hippies. Corso (A) and Ginsberg (D) were members of the Beat Generation, which was a precursor to the hippie movement. Rachel Carson (B), author of *The Silent Spring*, was a founder of the environmental movement. Timothy Leary (C) advocated use of the hallucinogenic drug LSD. Hippies followed these leaders and their ideas.

50. D

Bush promised not to raise taxes during his successful campaign for president in 1988. Many attribute Bush's loss to Clinton in 1992 to his reneging on this pledge because he had lost his conservative core of support. The economy began to rebound (A). The statement about the Vietnam syndrome (B) had to do with the lack of significant domestic or Congressional opposition to the Gulf War. Inflation (C) was an economic problem of the 1970s, not the 1990s. The invasion of Panama (E) did not cost enough to endanger the economy.

51. D

The drawing represented Benjamin Franklin's proposal for the Albany Plan of Union in 1754 to provide for colonial defense. The date and name under the drawing help to identify the purpose of the cartoon. The Dominion of New England (A) was established in 1686 by the British crown to control the New England colonies. It was headed by Sir Edmund Andros, who restricted town meetings and controlled the courts. The New England Confederation (B) was formed in 1643, to establish colonial defenses, not only against the Indians but also against the Dutch and French. It marked the first attempt at intercolonial cooperation. The First Continental Congress (C) was called in 1774 to discuss colonial response to the Intolerable Acts. The Articles of Confederation (E) was the frame of government passed in 1781.

52. D

The Louisiana Purchase doubled the size of the United States. The British were not expelled from North America (A); they retained colonies in Canada. The Louisiana Purchase had nothing to do with the problems with Native Americans in the Ohio Valley (B), which continued after 1803. The agreement was made with Napoleon, not the King of Spain (C). Jefferson, as a strict constructionist, was faced with the dilemma of whether it was constitutional for Congress to purchase land (E). He cited the elastic clause, the basis of a loose interpretation of the Constitution, to justify the purchase. This was a legitimate constitutional position, though contrary to the one he had held regarding the creation of the Bank of the United States.

53. A

Manifest Destiny was the idea that it was the obvious (manifest) fate of the United States to "O'er spread the Continent," a statement by John O'Sullivan in 1846. He said that United States would be doing a good deed by bringing democracy to the peoples of the West. At the time, the French (B) were not in Oregon (the English claimed it). Immigration from abroad (C) was not a tenet of Manifest Destiny—movement to the West by Americans was. The Spanish (D) had not been in Texas since 1821. Native American culture (E) was not a concern of the people who wanted their land.

54. B

There was considerable pay and supply discrimination against the African American troops, who did not receive equal pay until late in the war. They fought on the front lines in battle (A), although not until after the Emancipation Proclamation. They were always under the direction of (C) white officers. Before they fought, slaves who ran away from the South were considered "contraband of war" (D) by Lincoln. He accepted them behind Northern lines as a way to steal Southern "supplies." These men and women worked behind the lines (E) for the army from the beginning of the war.

55. D

President Garfield was assassinated by a party loyalist who felt he had been passed over for a job. The attention generated by the event led to the passage of the Pendleton Act (1883), which attempted to create a civil service based on merit rather than patronage. The Credit Mobilier scandal (A), which was exposed in 1872, concerned corruption in railroad construction as well as in the Grant Administration. *McClure's* magazine (B) was known for printing muckraking articles in the early 20th century, notably Ida Tarbell's expose of the Standard Oil Company (1902–1905). Thomas Nast (C) was probably the most influential political cartoonist in U.S. history. He was most prolific in the 1860s and 1870s and was best known for bringing down "Boss" William Tweed of New York City. Whenever a new party wins the White House, there is a change in personnel. This was the case with Cleveland (E), but it was not seen as a catalyst to civil service reform.

56. C

Regional literature was a staple of the 19th century. Many of Cather's stories chronicled the difficulties of frontier life on the plains of Nebraska, while Twain described life in the Mississippi River Valley. Twain's work examined issues of race in the United States (A), but issues of race are not central to Cather's work. Also, both writers wrote after slavery had ended. While much of Cather's work, notably *O! Pioneers* (1913) and *My Antonia* (1918), dealt with Slavic immigrants (B) who settle on the Great Plains, Twain's characters are virtually all native born Americans. Both writers achieved critical and popular success in their lifetimes (D). Neither writer made industrial conditions a central concern of his or her work (E).

57. C

The explosion on the *Maine* was later found to have occurred from within the vessel, probably originating in the coal room, but at the time the "yellow press" left little doubt that the culprit was Spain. (A) and (B) did occur in the years before the Spanish American War and contributed to the sentiment that the United States get involved in Cuba, but the final spark was the sinking of the *Maine*. A border dispute (D) was a factor contributing to the Mexican War of 1846–1848, but not the Spanish-American War (1898). Spain had lost control of Panama long before the United States considered building a canal there (E). In 1902 it was Colombia that was reluctant to allow the United States to build a canal through what was at that time the Colombian province of Panama; as a result, the United States supported the independence of Panama, but this was unrelated to the Spanish-American War.

58. C

The Agricultural Adjustment Act of (AAA) of 1933 subsidized farmers who planted fewer crops. It was hoped that a smaller supply would increase farm prices. This was not a voluntary program (A). An increase in crops (B) would depress prices further. The AAA did not propose a lowering of tariffs (D); nor did it encourage farmers to leave the land (E).

59. B

Both the British in America and the Americans in Vietnam were trying to maintain control of overseas lands against the armed rebellion of inhabitants of those lands who wanted to expel the overseas power. The United States did not win in Vietnam (A); it was forced to withdraw in 1973. Although the United States had a North and a South in the 18th century (C), the American colonists' war for independence was not a civil war between the North and South. During the American Revolution, America was supported by France (D) informally from the beginning and officially after Saratoga; but France did

not support its former colony, South Vietnam. Although there were important traditional battles (E) both in Vietnam and in the American Revolution, most of the fighting in Vietnam was guerrilla warfare, as was much of the fighting in colonial America.

60. E

Although Clinton first proposed allowing gays to serve openly in the military, this proposal met stiff opposition in Congress and in the military. Under the compromise policy labeled "Don't Ask, Don't Tell," gay soldiers were not obligated to divulge their sexual practices, and commanding officers were not permitted to initiate investigations of soldiers' sexual lives. However, openly gay troops would still be discharged from the armed forces. This policy was criticized because it fell short of protecting the rights of gays. Gays were permitted to serve in the military (A) and engage in combat (B), and Clinton's policy did not mandate segregation (C) for homosexual soldiers. This policy was not a frank acceptance of gay soldiers (D).

61. D

Bacon's Rebellion of 1676 was led by Nathaniel Bacon, a planter who was unhappy with the Indian policies of Governor Berkeley of Virginia. He was joined in his rebellion by many present and former indentured servants. The fear of future rebellion led the colonists to turn to African slavery, over which they felt they would have greater control. Thus they did not increase recruitment of indentured servants (A). Berkeley was not killed in the rebellion (B), although Bacon did die. This had no effect on Indian uprisings in Virginia (C), and it was not a slave rebellion (E).

62. A

The colonial jury supported Zenger's freedom to print the truth. The jurors acquitted him of seditious libel (writing, printing or speaking an untruths against a public official) in 1734 because they decided that Zenger's claims about the royal governor of New York were true and therefore could not be libelous. Zenger exposed the corruption of the British government in North America, not the Church of England (B). The British crown did not implement any reforms (C) as a result of this trial. It was a colonial jury (D) that tried Zenger. Zenger was acquitted, not executed (E).

63. E

The Whig Party formed as a result of Jackson's veto of the Bank Re-charter Bill. The former National Republicans called Jackson "King" and themselves Whigs to recall the Whig Patriots who fought against the Tories of 1776. John Quincy Adams did not sign the *Specie Circular* (A), Jackson did, and the depression that occurred partially as a result took place from 1837 to 1939, years after Adams left office. Calhoun did not write the Nullification Proclamation (B), Jackson did, and the Proclamation was written, after, not before, Virginia and Kentucky joined in opposition to the Sedition Act (1798). Daniel Webster was in favor of the Bank (C). The tariff of 1828 had little to do with Martin Van Buren's election in 1836 (D).

64. E

Sherman's 285-mile March to the Sea from Atlanta to Savannah destroyed the homes and farms of slaveholders who would not give up even when they were running out of food. It was total war against the property of the enemy. The first major victory by Union forces (A) was Antietam. The first major victory in which African American troops fought (B) was Fort Wagner. The turning point of the war (C) was at Gettysburg. The final battle of the war (D) was at Appomattox Courthouse.

65. A

For Congressional Republicans, letting the former rebels run state governments meant that the North had "lost the peace" after winning the war. Andrew Johnson did not go far enough, in the eyes of the Radical Republicans, in punishing the rebellious plantation-owning class and helping freedmen and women. Letting former Confederates run new state governments demonstrates Johnson's business-as-usual approach to Reconstruction, while all the other answers represent dramatic actions in creating a new type of South—actions favored by many Congressional Republicans. The suffrage was extended to African American men (B) by the 15th ment (1870). The 14th amendment (1868) (C) extended citizenship rights to African Americans and banned many Confederates from public office (D). The idea of giving freed people 40 acres and a mule (E) was a Radical Republican idea, but it was never implemented.

66. D

The Dawes Act encouraged Native American assimilation into white culture. Ironically, it was liberal sympathizers, including Helen Hunt Jackson, author of *A Century of Dishonor*, who pushed for the measure, thinking that by accepting white ways Native Americans would break the cycle of poverty and dependence. It is seen today as a condescending, insensitive measure that ignored Native American traditions and rights. Miners (A), the military (C), and the buffalo hunters (E), did not push a measure that, at the time, was seen as a forward step for Native Americans. Native Americans themselves (B), did not, in general, support a measure that showed so little respect for traditional ways.

67. A

Wilson's Fourteen Points encouraged a just peace. He feared that a harsh treaty would lead to another war. The Treaty of Versailles led to resentment and depression in Europe, which ultimately led to the rise of Hitler and World War II. The United States occupied Germany (B) after World War II, not World War I. The policy of containment of communism (C) developed after World War II, not World War I. The United States emerged as a super power (D) at the end of World War II. Some of the ideas in the Fourteen Points (E), including the League of Nations, found expression in the Treaty of Versailles.

68. A

The Red Scare was a government crackdown on communists, anarchists, and radicals in the late 1910s and early 1920s. Some also saw it as a way to silence labor agitators. Fascists (B) came to power in Europe after the Red Scare—Mussolini in Italy in 1922 and Hitler in Germany in 1933. The Red Scare was not a response to the teaching of evolution (C), the Ku Klux Klan (D), or Prohibition (E).

69. E

Francis Townsend's $200 a month proposal influenced the passage of the Social Security Act. He was one of several leaders who proposed sweeping plans and attracted a large following. Others included Huey Long and his Share Our Wealth Society and Upton Sinclair and his End Poverty in California campaign. Nonviolent civil disobedience (A) is associated with Martin Luther King Jr., and the civil rights movement of the 1950s and 1960s. Philip Randolph threatened a mass march in Washington, DC in 1941 if President Roosevelt did not integrate defense industries. It was the Communist Party that sent aid to anti-fascist groups in Europe (B). J. Edgar Hoover, head of the F.B.I., favored registering subversive groups (C) in the 1950s. Many public figures argued that women working during the Depression were taking jobs away from men (D).

70. B

In the first televised presidential debate, Kennedy's appearance and charisma out shown Nixon's. This was judged a key factor in the presidential race. A truce had ended the fighting in the Korean War (A) in 1953. Nixon had no significant war record (C). Kennedy was a Massachusetts Senator, not a governor (D). The Watergate investigation (E) occurred more than a decade after the 1960 election.

71. B

The stable government of Portugal supported Prince Henry the Navigator, an innovator in sailing technology and the caravel, a fast sailing ship, was perfected by the Portuguese. Portugal is not inland (A) but rather on the Atlantic Ocean. The signing of the Treaty of Tordesillas (C), which split the world between Spain and Portugal did not take place until the end of the this century (1494). Ferdinand and Isabelle (D) were rulers of Spain who had no influence on the early success of the Portuguese. Columbus sailed to the New World in 1492 for Spain, not Portugal (E).

72. A

When Washington established a cabinet; he set a precedent that has been followed by all subsequent administrations. Florida (B) did not become part of the United States until 1817 as a result of the Adams-Onis Treaty. In his second administration Washington put down the Whiskey Rebellion (C) in Pennsylvania. Shays's Rebellion occurred in Massachusetts in 1787 before Washington's first term as President. The Alien and Sedition Acts (D) were passed under John Adams in 1798. Thomas Jefferson and James Madison formed a political party to oppose Hamilton (E). Washington usually supported Hamilton, but joined no political party.

73. B

William Lloyd Garrison wanted the immediate abolition of slavery throughout the United States. The creation of a national slave code (A) was advocated by John C. Breckinridge in the election of 1860. The idea of no extension of slavery to the territories in the West (C) was supported by Abraham Lincoln. Popular sovereignty (D) was the solution to the slavery question offered by Stephen Douglas, and leaving questions of slavery to be decided in the future was John Bell's position.

74. B

In the Dred Scott case (1857) Chief Justice Taney ruled that Scott had no standing to bring to bring the case because "A Negro had no rights a white man was bound to respect" and it had been that way since before the Revolution. It was the *Plessy v. Ferguson* decision (1896) that stated that separate but equal facilities were constitutional (A). It was overturned by *Brown v. Board of Education of Topeka* (E) in 1954. *Worcester v. Georgia* (1832) was the Cherokee case (C) that John Marshall decided in their favor. The decision stated that the Cherokee treaties were legal documents that the state of Georgia could not countermand. Jackson denounced the decision and ignored it, aiding Georgia in forcing Indians onto the Trail of Tears. The *Wabash v. Illinois* (1886) decision struck down state laws regulating the railroads, paving the way for the federal Interstate Commerce Act (1887).

75. B

The Black Codes restricted African Americans' freedom of movement and prevented them from starting businesses or owning land, thus making work on their old plantations the only viable option. Freed men and women (A) were aided by the Freedman's Bureau. Tubman and Douglass (C), two anti-slavery activists, did not support laws designed to restrict the freedom of African Americans. Johnson did not oppose Black Codes (D). In fact, he vetoed the Civil Rights Bill, which was Congress' attempt to eliminate the Black Codes. The Supreme Court never ruled on the constitutionality of Black Codes (E).

76. B

The excerpt is from the "Cross of Gold" speech by William Jennings Bryan, who ran for president on the Democratic ticket with the support of the Populist Party in 1896. It is one of the most cited speeches in U.S. history. The gold standard was harmful to farmers, he argued. Let money be backed by silver as well, thus allowing the government to issue more money, which would cause inflation and help debtors including most farmers. Agrarian organizations would not support higher tariffs (C); farmers generally want free trade so their products are more desirable on the international market. Though the Populist Party supported subsidies for farmers (A), an eight-hour day for industrial workers (D), and restrictions on immigration (E), this excerpt is only a critique of the gold standard.

77. B

In 1902, Colombia rejected the U.S. bid to build a canal through Panama (which was then part of Colombia). The United States, with the collaboration of Phillipe Bunau-Varilla, an official in the French company that had previously attempted to build a canal, then organized a "revolution" in Panama against Colombia. The United States immediately recognized the newly independent nation of Panama. Secretary of State John Hay quickly signed a treaty with Bunau-Varilla (who had become the Panamanian ambassador to the United States), allowing the United States to build the canal. The Treaty of Paris of 1898 ended the Spanish-American War (A). The 1900 Foraker Act established commonwealth status for Puerto Rico (C). The 1848 Treaty of Guadalupe-Hidalgo secured the Mexican Cession for the United States (D). There was no treaty with Guatemala involving banana growing (E).

78. D

Wilson's unwillingness to compromise over Article X of the peace treaty which had to do with the establishment of the League of Nations led to the rejection of the Treaty of Versailles by the United Sates Senate. The United States negotiated a separate peace with Germany in 1921. Wilson did not enjoy a surge in popularity as a result of his battle with the Senate (A), and he was a two-term president who did not run in 1920 (B). The European nations did accept the Treaty of Versailles (C). The Democrats lost the election in 1920 (E) and did not win the White House again until 1932 with the election of Franklin D. Roosevelt.

79. A

Roosevelt was concerned about the views of Stalin regarding expansion of Soviet influence in Eastern Europe. Churchill (C) generally concurred with Roosevelt on most matters. Roosevelt, Churchill and Stalin were the major figures at the Yalta Conference. Charles de Gaulle (B), Mao Zedong (D) and Kim Il Sung (E) were not at Yalta.

80. A

The United States became involved in Vietnam with the installation of Ngo Dinh Diem as a puppet leader of South Vietnam after the French military defeat at Dien Bien Phu by the Vietminh in 1954. The relationship between China and Taiwan (B), the partitioning of India in 1947 (C), and the invasion of South Korea by North Korea in 1950 (D) did not cause the United States to become politically involved in Vietnam. Japan controlled Vietnam during World War II. After World War II, France reasserted its power in Vietnam (E).

81. A

When the Europeans arrived they found advanced civilizations such as the Aztecs and Incas. Most Native Americans were not nomadic (B). The Eastern Tribes, for example, had systems of government and lived in settled communities. African slavery (C) did not exist in the Americas. Some European explorers were initially welcomed by the Indians; for example, Cortes, who destroyed the Aztec empire, received a friendly, not a hostile welcome until the Aztecs figured out his intentions (D). The Europeans introduced horses to the New World (E).

82. B

Henry Clay died in 1852, 25 years before the Compromise of 1877 placed Rutherford B. Hayes in the White House. Clay did play an important role in the Missouri Compromise of 1820 which enabled Maine (E) to become a free state in 1820 and Missouri (A) to become a slave state in 1821. Clay proposed a reduction in tariff of 1833 which convinced South Carolina to rescind its nullification ordinance (C). Clay wrote the Compromise of 1850 which admitted California as a free state (D).

83. C

Calhoun tried to shift the blame for slavery by saying it was the climate and the soil that required it. This was special pleading for protection of the "peculiar institution" of slavery. Slavery was the key issue behind sectionalism. Therefore, I and II are correct (C). Calhoun was clearer than most textbooks on this question: The tariff was not the main issue behind sectional tensions. It was only the "occasion" for sectional controversy making III a wrong choice. He knew that defending his right to own slaves did not reflect the majority view, making IV an incorrect statement.

84. D

The IWW was not a big, or even very successful, union, but it made a name for itself by being fiery and militant, with slogans such as "An injury to one is an injury to all," and "One big union." It was the most militant, not the most compromising, union of its day (C). "Company unions" (A) were not unions in the usual sense of the word, but organizations set up by management head off any union organizing drives. The American Federation of Labor, not the IWW, was a craft union (B). The IWW was not a secret brotherhood nor was it involved in the Haymarket Affair (E). Those are associated with the Knights of Labor.

85. E

The United States was not a member of the Triple Alliance which consisted of Germany, Austria-Hungary, and Italy. The British ship, *Lusitania*, was sunk (A) by German submarines, killing American passengers. In the Zimmerman Note (B) the Germans promise to aid Mexico reconquer the Southwest. This horrified Americans. The use of submarines by the Germans (C) endangered American shipping in the Atlantic. The idealist, Woodrow Wilson, viewed the war as a means of creating a more democratic world (D).

86. B

The graph indicates that there was a large drop in unemployment from 1941 to 1943. This is when the United States became more involved in World War II. The Lend-Lease Law, passed in March, 1941, established the United States as the "arsenal of democracy." The United States entered the war in December, 1941, following the Japanese bombing of Pearl Harbor. Both Lend-Lease and the U.S. entrance into the war resulted in a greater demand for labor. The chart shows that the New Deal had had a limited effect (A). Women did enter the workforce after World War II, but that is not demonstrated in the chart (C). The chart does not allude to technological innovation (D). The rising employment figures represent an end to the depression, not its persistence (E).

87. D

The Stimson Doctrine condemned the Japanese invasion of Manchuria in 1932. The United States did not boycott German goods (A) as a result of the Stimson Doctrine. The United States stressed the importance of preserving the territorial integrity of China (B), but there was no pledge by the Allied nations to protect China. The Doctrine does not include a provision for a cease-fire in China (C). Italy did, in fact, invade Ethiopia, but this did not occur until 1935 and was not the subject of the Stimson Doctrine (E)

88. B

The Soviets, regarding NATO as an offensive threat, wanted to counterbalance it with their own defensive alliance. The Warsaw Pact was formed in 1955 as a military alliance. Its members were the Soviet Union and its Eastern European satellites: Poland, East Germany, Czechoslovakia, Hungary, Romania, and Bulgaria. Two of the other groupings, SEATO (A) and CENTO (C) were created with the United States to contain the spread of Communism. The Alliance for Progress (D) promoted United States economic assistance to Latin America. The OAS (E) was established to promote economic cooperation among the nations of Latin America.

89. A

Nixon's history of questionable ethical decisions predates the Watergate scandal. During the 1952 campaign, Nixon was accused of accepting money from supporters in California and creating a "slush fund." In the "Checkers speech," Nixon sought to reassure the public that he had done no wrong. He contended that the only gift he accepted from supporters was the family dog, Checkers, and that it would break his daughter's heart to give it up. Eisenhower and Nixon won the election. Cold war posturing (B), the "Vietnamization" (C) of the Vietnam War (withdrawing U.S. troops to leave the fighting to Vietnamese forces allied with the United States), pursuing détente with China (D), and defending himself after the Watergate revelations (E) were all actions that Nixon took later during his career in politics.

90. B

Brown v. Board of Education of Topeka was NOT decided on the basis of the original intent of the 14th Amendment. There was segregation in 1868 when it was passed and the 14th Amendment was not intended to end the practice. Psychological studies by Dr. Kenneth Clark, among others, showed that black children had feelings of inferiority (C) caused by segregation. The general social questions of the importance of education, the opportunities it provided for success in society (E), and the importance of local government in controlling education (A)—were key points in the decision. The final ruling stated that segregation should be eliminated "with all deliberate speed" (D)—a contradiction that gave permission for both the movement toward desegregation and its slow speed.

HOW TO CALCULATE
YOUR SCORE

Step 1: Figure out your raw score. Refer to your answer sheet to determine the number right and the number wrong on the practice test you're scoring. You can use the chart below to figure out your raw score. Multiply the number wrong by 0.25 and subtract the result from the number right. Round the result to the nearest whole number. This is your raw score.

SAT Subject Test: U.S. History Practice Test 2

Number right	Number wrong	Raw score

$$\boxed{} - \left(0.25 \times \boxed{}\right) = \boxed{}$$

Step 2: Find your practice test score. Find your raw score in the left column of the table below. The score in the right column is an approximation of what your score would be on the SAT Subject Test: U.S. History.

A note on your practice test scores: Don't take these scores too literally. Practice test conditions cannot precisely mirror real test conditions. Your actual SAT Subject Test: U.S. History score will almost certainly vary from your practice test scores. However, your scores on the practice tests will give you a rough idea of your range on the actual exam.

Conversion Table

Raw	Scaled	Raw	Scaled	Raw	Scaled	Raw	Scaled	Raw	Scaled	Raw	Scaled
90	800	72	770	54	680	36	580	18	470	0	350
89	800	71	760	43	670	35	570	17	460	−1	350
88	800	70	760	52	670	34	570	16	460	−2	340
87	800	69	750	51	660	33	560	15	450	−3	340
86	800	68	750	50	660	32	550	14	450	−4	330
85	800	67	740	49	650	31	550	13	440	−5	330
84	800	66	740	48	650	30	540	12	430	−6	320
83	800	65	730	47	640	29	540	11	430	−7	320
82	800	64	730	46	640	28	530	10	420	−8	310
81	800	63	720	45	630	27	520	9	410	−9	310
80	790	62	720	44	630	26	520	8	410	−10	300
79	790	61	710	43	620	25	510	7	400	−11	300
78	790	60	710	42	610	24	510	6	390	−12	290
77	790	59	700	41	610	23	500	5	390	−13	280
76	780	58	700	40	600	22	490	4	380	−14	280
75	780	57	690	39	600	21	490	3	370	−15	270
74	780	56	690	38	590	20	480	2	370	−16	270
73	770	55	680	37	580	19	480	1	360	−17	260

Answer Grid
Practice Test 2

1. Ⓐ Ⓑ Ⓒ Ⓓ Ⓔ
2. Ⓐ Ⓑ Ⓒ Ⓓ Ⓔ
3. Ⓐ Ⓑ Ⓒ Ⓓ Ⓔ
4. Ⓐ Ⓑ Ⓒ Ⓓ Ⓔ
5. Ⓐ Ⓑ Ⓒ Ⓓ Ⓔ
6. Ⓐ Ⓑ Ⓒ Ⓓ Ⓔ
7. Ⓐ Ⓑ Ⓒ Ⓓ Ⓔ
8. Ⓐ Ⓑ Ⓒ Ⓓ Ⓔ
9. Ⓐ Ⓑ Ⓒ Ⓓ Ⓔ
10. Ⓐ Ⓑ Ⓒ Ⓓ Ⓔ
11. Ⓐ Ⓑ Ⓒ Ⓓ Ⓔ
12. Ⓐ Ⓑ Ⓒ Ⓓ Ⓔ
13. Ⓐ Ⓑ Ⓒ Ⓓ Ⓔ
14. Ⓐ Ⓑ Ⓒ Ⓓ Ⓔ
15. Ⓐ Ⓑ Ⓒ Ⓓ Ⓔ
16. Ⓐ Ⓑ Ⓒ Ⓓ Ⓔ
17. Ⓐ Ⓑ Ⓒ Ⓓ Ⓔ
18. Ⓐ Ⓑ Ⓒ Ⓓ Ⓔ
19. Ⓐ Ⓑ Ⓒ Ⓓ Ⓔ
20. Ⓐ Ⓑ Ⓒ Ⓓ Ⓔ
21. Ⓐ Ⓑ Ⓒ Ⓓ Ⓔ
22. Ⓐ Ⓑ Ⓒ Ⓓ Ⓔ
23. Ⓐ Ⓑ Ⓒ Ⓓ Ⓔ
24. Ⓐ Ⓑ Ⓒ Ⓓ Ⓔ
25. Ⓐ Ⓑ Ⓒ Ⓓ Ⓔ
26. Ⓐ Ⓑ Ⓒ Ⓓ Ⓔ
27. Ⓐ Ⓑ Ⓒ Ⓓ Ⓔ
28. Ⓐ Ⓑ Ⓒ Ⓓ Ⓔ
29. Ⓐ Ⓑ Ⓒ Ⓓ Ⓔ
30. Ⓐ Ⓑ Ⓒ Ⓓ Ⓔ

31. Ⓐ Ⓑ Ⓒ Ⓓ Ⓔ
32. Ⓐ Ⓑ Ⓒ Ⓓ Ⓔ
33. Ⓐ Ⓑ Ⓒ Ⓓ Ⓔ
34. Ⓐ Ⓑ Ⓒ Ⓓ Ⓔ
35. Ⓐ Ⓑ Ⓒ Ⓓ Ⓔ
36. Ⓐ Ⓑ Ⓒ Ⓓ Ⓔ
37. Ⓐ Ⓑ Ⓒ Ⓓ Ⓔ
38. Ⓐ Ⓑ Ⓒ Ⓓ Ⓔ
39. Ⓐ Ⓑ Ⓒ Ⓓ Ⓔ
40. Ⓐ Ⓑ Ⓒ Ⓓ Ⓔ
41. Ⓐ Ⓑ Ⓒ Ⓓ Ⓔ
42. Ⓐ Ⓑ Ⓒ Ⓓ Ⓔ
43. Ⓐ Ⓑ Ⓒ Ⓓ Ⓔ
44. Ⓐ Ⓑ Ⓒ Ⓓ Ⓔ
45. Ⓐ Ⓑ Ⓒ Ⓓ Ⓔ
46. Ⓐ Ⓑ Ⓒ Ⓓ Ⓔ
47. Ⓐ Ⓑ Ⓒ Ⓓ Ⓔ
48. Ⓐ Ⓑ Ⓒ Ⓓ Ⓔ
49. Ⓐ Ⓑ Ⓒ Ⓓ Ⓔ
50. Ⓐ Ⓑ Ⓒ Ⓓ Ⓔ
51. Ⓐ Ⓑ Ⓒ Ⓓ Ⓔ
52. Ⓐ Ⓑ Ⓒ Ⓓ Ⓔ
53. Ⓐ Ⓑ Ⓒ Ⓓ Ⓔ
54. Ⓐ Ⓑ Ⓒ Ⓓ Ⓔ
55. Ⓐ Ⓑ Ⓒ Ⓓ Ⓔ
56. Ⓐ Ⓑ Ⓒ Ⓓ Ⓔ
57. Ⓐ Ⓑ Ⓒ Ⓓ Ⓔ
58. Ⓐ Ⓑ Ⓒ Ⓓ Ⓔ
59. Ⓐ Ⓑ Ⓒ Ⓓ Ⓔ
60. Ⓐ Ⓑ Ⓒ Ⓓ Ⓔ

61. Ⓐ Ⓑ Ⓒ Ⓓ Ⓔ
62. Ⓐ Ⓑ Ⓒ Ⓓ Ⓔ
63. Ⓐ Ⓑ Ⓒ Ⓓ Ⓔ
64. Ⓐ Ⓑ Ⓒ Ⓓ Ⓔ
65. Ⓐ Ⓑ Ⓒ Ⓓ Ⓔ
66. Ⓐ Ⓑ Ⓒ Ⓓ Ⓔ
67. Ⓐ Ⓑ Ⓒ Ⓓ Ⓔ
68. Ⓐ Ⓑ Ⓒ Ⓓ Ⓔ
69. Ⓐ Ⓑ Ⓒ Ⓓ Ⓔ
70. Ⓐ Ⓑ Ⓒ Ⓓ Ⓔ
71. Ⓐ Ⓑ Ⓒ Ⓓ Ⓔ
72. Ⓐ Ⓑ Ⓒ Ⓓ Ⓔ
73. Ⓐ Ⓑ Ⓒ Ⓓ Ⓔ
74. Ⓐ Ⓑ Ⓒ Ⓓ Ⓔ
75. Ⓐ Ⓑ Ⓒ Ⓓ Ⓔ
76. Ⓐ Ⓑ Ⓒ Ⓓ Ⓔ
77. Ⓐ Ⓑ Ⓒ Ⓓ Ⓔ
78. Ⓐ Ⓑ Ⓒ Ⓓ Ⓔ
79. Ⓐ Ⓑ Ⓒ Ⓓ Ⓔ
80. Ⓐ Ⓑ Ⓒ Ⓓ Ⓔ
81. Ⓐ Ⓑ Ⓒ Ⓓ Ⓔ
82. Ⓐ Ⓑ Ⓒ Ⓓ Ⓔ
83. Ⓐ Ⓑ Ⓒ Ⓓ Ⓔ
84. Ⓐ Ⓑ Ⓒ Ⓓ Ⓔ
85. Ⓐ Ⓑ Ⓒ Ⓓ Ⓔ
86. Ⓐ Ⓑ Ⓒ Ⓓ Ⓔ
87. Ⓐ Ⓑ Ⓒ Ⓓ Ⓔ
88. Ⓐ Ⓑ Ⓒ Ⓓ Ⓔ
89. Ⓐ Ⓑ Ⓒ Ⓓ Ⓔ
90. Ⓐ Ⓑ Ⓒ Ⓓ Ⓔ

Practice Test 2

1. In 1500 the civilizations of Mexico and Central America differed from the civilizations of the North American Plains Indians in that the Plains Indians

   (A) were nomadic, while the civilizations of Mexico and Central America were more stable

   (B) lived in adobe houses while the natives of Mexico and Central America lived in tents

   (C) were united, while the natives of Mexico and Central America were scattered

   (D) were ravaged by European diseases, while the inhabitants of Mexico and Central America were not

   (E) assimilated into European culture while the inhabitants of Mexico and Central America did not

2. Which of the following statements concerning the New England colonies in the 17th century is true?

   (A) The New England colonies grew faster than the southern colonies through natural reproduction.

   (B) The New England colonies were more dependent on Great Britain than the southern and middle colonies.

   (C) The New England colonies were open societies with a high tolerance for those who were different.

   (D) The New England colonies had larger farms than the middle and southern colonies.

   (E) The New England colonies lacked strong leadership.

GO ON TO THE NEXT PAGE

3. Which of the following was not a PRESIDENTIAL action of Andrew Jackson?

(A) He opposed the Nullification Ordinance of South Carolina.

(B) He advocated the removal of the Cherokees to territory west of the Mississippi River.

(C) He defeated the English in the Battle of New Orleans after the War of 1812 was over.

(D) He vetoed the re-charter of the Second Bank of the United States.

(E) He appointed government workers based on party loyalty.

4. The mechanical reaper, invented by Cyrus McCormick in the 1830s, was most significant because it

(A) turned over the hard prairie soil

(B) planted seeds four times as fast as a man could do by hand

(C) aided irrigation of the arid Midwest

(D) increased cotton production

(E) cut wheat at a greater rate than the scythe

5. The phrase "With malice toward none, with charity toward all" refers to Lincoln's attitude toward

(A) Southern state legislatures, which had passed Black Codes

(B) radical Republicans in the House of Representatives after Reconstruction

(C) congressmen after they impeached Andrew Johnson

(D) the rebellious South near the end of the Civil War

(E) Senators Stephen Douglas, John C. Breckenridge, and John Bell, who had run against him in 1860

6. The "social gospel" is a term usually associated with the

(A) Second Great Awakening of the 1820s and 1830s

(B) abolitionist movement of the 1840s and 1850s

(C) urban reform movement of the 1890s and 1900s

(D) fundamentalist Christian movement of the 1920s

(E) political movement of the religious right during the1980s

GO ON TO THE NEXT PAGE

7. Which of the following is the best description of the cartoon above?

   (A) the Senate's objection to U.S. membership in the League of Nations
   (B) the debate involving the membership of the United States in the United Nations
   (C) the marriage of Woodrow Wilson
   (D) the problems of establishing economic alliances
   (E) Wilson's violation of the Constitution by his support of the League of Nations

GO ON TO THE NEXT PAGE

8. One reason President Franklin D. Roosevelt was *not* a strong advocate of civil rights for African Americans was that he

   (A) believed that the separation of the races was in the best interests of all concerned

   (B) resented the fact that African Americans voted for the Republican Party in 1936

   (C) believed the role of the federal government in society should be minimal

   (D) believed that Progressive-era reformers had successfully addressed the problem of segregation

   (E) feared losing the support of the southern Democrats in Congress

9. Which of the following cases declared that prayer in the public school was unconstitutional?

   (A) *Brown v. Board of Education of Topeka*

   (B) *Engel v. Vitale*

   (C) *Baker v. Carr*

   (D) *Miranda v. Arizona*

   (E) *Roe v. Wade*

10. When Stokely Carmichael became the leader of the Student Non-Violent Coordinating Committee in 1966, its key slogan changed from

    (A) "Freedom Now" to "Black Power"

    (B) "Self-Defense" to "Pick up the Gun"

    (C) "We Shall Overcome" to "Dare to Struggle Dare to Win"

    (D) "Tune In" to "Drop Out"

    (E) "Back to Africa" to "By Any Means Necessary"

11. Which of the following statements about 18th century America is true?

    (A) By 1750, half of all American colonists lived in cities.

    (B) By 1750, the New England colonists were exporting more than they were importing.

    (C) After 1763, the colonists were prohibited from settling beyond the Appalachian Mountains.

    (D) By 1750, slaves outnumbered whites in the colonies by 2 to 1.

    (E) By 1740, the colonists recognized Jonathan Edwards as a leader of the Old Lights.

12. The war hawks demanded war against Britain in 1812 in order to

    (A) eliminate the Native American threat in the Northwest

    (B) appease the New England states

    (C) assimilate the Native Americans into U.S. society

    (D) gain control of New Orleans

    (E) make the United States less dependent on imports

13. In explaining why the nullification of the 1828 Tariff of Abominations was justified, John C. Calhoun contended that

    (A) the people had ratified the Constitution and therefore, could decide on the constitutionality of a federal law

    (B) the states were sovereign because they had formed a compact called the Constitution

    (C) the Supreme Court had declared the Tariff of Abominations unconstitutional

    (D) Congress was sovereign and could decide on all major questions including slavery

    (E) President Andrew Jackson had been elected by the whole people and agreed with his position

GO ON TO THE NEXT PAGE

14. *Moby-Dick*, by Herman Melville, representative of the American Renaissance of the 1840s, is significant in that it

    (A) changed the attitude of the people of the United States toward the Native Americans

    (B) portrayed life in a utopian community

    (C) was an anti-slavery novel that galvanized northern opinion against the Fugitive Slave Law

    (D) opposed the narrow Puritan point of view of 17th century New England

    (E) used a predominately American occupation to explore man's struggles with the natural world and good and evil

15. In the *Plessy v. Ferguson* decision of 1896, the Supreme Court

    (A) declared that poll taxes and literacy tests were unconstitutional

    (B) declared that segregation of the races was acceptable

    (C) struck down many aspects of Congressional Reconstruction

    (D) ended segregation in public schools on the grounds that it was inherently unfair

    (E) ruled that slaves were still considered property even if they resided in a free state or territory

16. Jacob Riis's book, *How the Other Half Lives*, was significant in that it

    (A) drew the public's attention to the harsh conditions slaves lived under in the 1850s

    (B) demonstrated the double standards applied to women in American society at the turn of the 20th century

    (C) criticized the lifestyles of the upper class in the 1920s

    (D) exposed the living conditions of the urban poor at the turn of the 20th century

    (E) chronicled the lives of the poor immigrants from Asia and Africa in the 1960s

17. The American reaction to Germany's announced intention of resuming unrestricted submarine warfare, violating the *Sussex Pledge*, was to

    (A) implement the policy of appeasement

    (B) declare war on Germany

    (C) negotiate another treaty with Germany

    (D) send the Zimmermann Note to Germany

    (E) intern German immigrants in the United States

GO ON TO THE NEXT PAGE

18. Which of the following statements about American cities in the post–World War II period (1945–1970) is NOT true?

    (A) "White flight" led to a decline in property taxes and income taxes collected by municipal governments.

    (B) Large numbers of African Americans moved from the rural South to the urban North.

    (C) The Urban Renewal program was a huge success in eliminating slums and poverty in American cities.

    (D) Black neighborhoods in many Northern cities experienced a series of riots in which the frustration of Black America was expressed.

    (E) The development of shopping malls and highways had a detrimental effect on shopping districts in the centers of United States cities.

19. The primary goal of Martin Luther King Jr.'s Southern Christian Leadership Conference was to

    (A) defend black neighborhoods against police brutality

    (B) challenge segregation in the Supreme Court

    (C) use nonviolent resistance to achieve desegregation

    (D) create equal racial representation in the Democratic Party

    (E) reinvigorate the back to Africa movement

20. President Clinton was impeached by the House of Representatives because there was evidence that he had

    (A) mishandled funds in the Whitewater land development scheme

    (B) used his influence to arrange for a job for Paula Jones

    (C) misused the White House for raising funds for his presidential campaign in 1996

    (D) conducted himself in a manner that demeaned the office of the presidency

    (E) committed perjury when testifying about the Monica Lewinsky affair

21. Taverns of the 1700s were important because they

    (A) provided a place for an exchange of information among the colonists

    (B) served as one-room schoolhouses

    (C) served as targets for the temperance movement during the Second Great Awakening

    (D) were halfway houses for the poor

    (E) were places where the New England town meetings were held

22. The Great Awakening of the 1730s and 1740s was important because

    (A) it caused people to question established authority

    (B) it provided the spiritual rationale for the abolition movement

    (C) religious unification caused a reduction in the number of religious sects

    (D) religious revivalism lessened in the colonies

    (E) it led to the Salem witch trials

GO ON TO THE NEXT PAGE

23. To correct the weaknesses of the Articles of Confederation, the writers of the Constitution in 1787 included

(A) a method of amending the Constitution that required the approval of all states

(B) the addition of a Bill of Rights to protect individual citizens

(C) the establishment of a cabinet to advise the president

(D) provisions for an executive and a judicial branch of government

(E) a reserved powers clause to protect states' rights

24. The Second Bank of the United States was important in that it

(A) became a part of the Federal Reserve System of 1913

(B) was the central component of the American System supported by the Whigs

(C) was the forerunner of the pet banks of the 1830s

(D) was the substitute bank supported by Alexander Hamilton after the first Bank of the United States was rejected by Congress

(E) was struck down by the Supreme Court in the *Gibbons v. Ogden* decision

25. The acquisition of territory from Mexico as a result of the Mexican War was most significant in that it

(A) settled conflicts between the Native Americans and the U.S. government

(B) led to the acquisition of Oregon

(C) led to Bleeding Kansas

(D) provided the United States with territory to build the Panama Canal

(E) heightened sectional tensions over the issue of slavery

Resources of the North and South in the Civil War
(Represented as a ratio)

	North	South
Total Population	2.4	1
Male Population ages 18–60	4.4	1
Free Men in Military Service	1.8	1
Railroad Miles	2.4	1
Naval Shipping	25	1
Factory Production	10	1
Textile Goods	14	1
Firearms	32	1
Farm Acres	3	1
Draft Animals	1.8	1
Wheat Production	4.2	1
Corn Production	2	1
Cotton Production	1	24

26. Which statistic best explains why the North won the Civil War?

(A) Cotton Production

(B) Naval Shipping

(C) Corn Production

(D) Draft Animals

(E) Male Population ages 18–60

27. Passage of the Reconstruction Act of 1867 signaled the

(A) end of Jim Crow laws

(B) beginning of Presidential Reconstruction

(C) abolition of slavery

(D) fulfillment of Abraham Lincoln's vision for the post–Civil War South

(E) beginning of Congressional Reconstruction

GO ON TO THE NEXT PAGE

28. Which of the following statements is true of the Populist movement?

   (A) Although it began in agricultural states, it soon became a national movement of farmers and urban workers.

   (B) It endorsed the concept of the gold standard.

   (C) It rejected both the Republican and Democratic candidates for president in 1896.

   (D) Its platform in 1892 called for government ownership of banks and railroads.

   (E) It fought against inflationary policies so that consumers would not suffer economically.

29. One of the first actions taken by President Franklin D. Roosevelt after his inauguration in 1933 was to

   (A) declare a bank holiday

   (B) establish the Reconstruction Finance Corporation

   (C) establish Social Security

   (D) establish the National Recovery Administration

   (E) pack the Supreme Court

30. One of President Nixon's most important diplomatic initiatives was to

   (A) reunite Vietnam

   (B) open diplomatic relations between China and the United States

   (C) establish a forum for discussions of human rights

   (D) pressure China to recognize Taiwan

   (E) end the Cold War

31. European exploration of the Americas resulted in all of the following EXCEPT the

   (A) introduction of new products to the Americas

   (B) spread of European diseases, such as smallpox, to the Native Americans

   (C) introduction of new products to Europe

   (D) development of unified resistance by the Native Americans to European settlement

   (E) mixed-race peoples in Mexico and Central America

32. The Maryland Act of Toleration, passed in 1649, was significant in that it:

   (A) provided religious freedom to Christians

   (B) provided religious freedom to Catholics only

   (C) provided for the just treatment of Native Americas

   (D) provided religious freedom for Catholics, Jews, and Quakers

   (E) allowed atheists to deny the existence of God

33. The Battle of Saratoga was considered the turning point of the American Revolution because it

   (A) demonstrated America's naval superiority

   (B) signaled the end of loyalist support for Great Britain

   (C) led to an alliance between Spain and the colonies

   (D) prompted France to enter the war in support of the colonies

   (E) resulted in the defeat of General Howe

GO ON TO THE NEXT PAGE

34. "We demand that all immigrants to the United States reside here at least 14 years before they may apply for citizenship."

    Which party advocated the above idea as its main political position?

    (A) The Know-Nothing Party
    (B) The Whig Party
    (C) The Free Soil Party
    (D) The Democratic Party
    (E) The National Republican Party

35. Lincoln fired General George McClellan because he

    (A) marched through Georgia destroying crops and homes
    (B) would not cross the Mississippi into Vicksburg
    (C) was too timid to engage the enemy
    (D) did not train the troops properly
    (E) refused to charge up Little Roundtop at Gettysburg

36. "Sod busters" was a nickname given to

    (A) New England settlers in the 1600s
    (B) cotton growers in Texas in the 1840s and 1850s
    (C) frontier farmers on the Great Plains in the 1860s and 1870s
    (D) Dust Bowl farmers in the 1930s
    (E) Eastern farmers who were displaced by suburban development in the 1950s

37. The phrase "Speak softly and carry a big stick" originally referred to

    (A) President Theodore Roosevelt's policy in regard to Latin America
    (B) President John F. Kennedy's policy in regard to Vietnam
    (C) President Andrew Jackson's policy in regard to Native American nations
    (D) President George H. W. Bush's policy in regard to Saudi Arabia
    (E) President Dwight D. Eisenhower's policy in regard to the Soviet Union

38. Rosie the Riveter was a symbol of the

    (A) participation of women in the war effort during World War II
    (B) Women's Liberation Movement of the 1960s
    (C) new fashions for women that became popular in the 1950s
    (D) participation of women in the Industrial Revolution of the late 1800s
    (E) change that had occurred as a result of women's suffrage

39. The "War on Poverty" was an attempt by

    (A) President Richard Nixon to aid Latin American nations
    (B) President Lyndon Johnson to end hunger and economic hardship in the United States
    (C) President John F. Kennedy to aid the developing world by organizing the Peace Corps
    (D) George Marshall to feed the people of Europe after World War II
    (E) President Dwight Eisenhower to reduce the number of people on welfare

40. The Watergate scandal of 1972–1974 began with

    (A) arms shipments to rebels in Nicaragua

    (B) a break-in at a hotel in Washington, DC

    (C) the publication of secret Pentagon papers related to the war in Vietnam

    (D) a deal between Republican Party officials and railroad owners

    (E) payoffs to the government in exchange for oil drilling rights

41. Which events are correctly paired to reflect cause and effect?

    (A) The influx of Quakers to Maryland—the passage of the Maryland Act of Toleration

    (B) The expulsion of Roger Williams from Massachusetts Bay Colony—the founding of Connecticut

    (C) The development of the head-right system for acquiring land and workers—the development of slavery in South Carolina

    (D) William and Mary's ascension to the throne in England—the overthrow of the Dominion of New England

    (E) Massachusetts Governor John Winthrop's Indian Policies—the break-out of Bacon's Rebellion

42. The War of 1812 has often been called the "Second War of Independence" because it

    (A) ended the British presence in North America

    (B) resulted in the adoption of a national anthem

    (C) marked the development of the United States Navy

    (D) marked the last major conflict between England and the United States

    (E) resulted in the acquisition of new lands to further United States expansion

43. The Whig Party, which existed from 1833–1854, supported all of the following EXCEPT

    (A) re-chartering the Second Bank of the United States

    (B) raising tariffs to protect U.S. industry

    (C) admitting Texas to the United States in 1844

    (D) funding internal improvements such as canals and roads

    (E) Henry Clay for president in 1844

$100 REWARD

Ranaway from Richard's Ferry.

Culpepper Country, Va. 23rd instant.

ABRAM,

who is about 30 years old, 5 feet from 8 to 10

inches high and weighs from 175 to 180.

His complexion is dark though not black and hair long for a Negro.

He is a very shrewd fellow, and there is reason to believe he is

attempting to get to a free state.

I will give the above reward if taken out of Virginia—

$50

if taken 20 miles from home or

$20

if taken in the neighborhood.

Wm. R.J. Richards, Adm'r of Jas. Richards,

Dec'd Sept 24.

---

44. What word or words would a social historian find most useful in analyzing the above runaway advertisement?

    (A) "instant"

    (B) "Abram"

    (C) "long hair"

    (D) "shrewd"

    (E) "free state"

GO ON TO THE NEXT PAGE

45. Mechanization of agriculture in the late 1800s

    (A) brought unparalleled prosperity to U.S. farmers
    (B) drove down prices of agricultural goods
    (C) was ineffective at raising the output of farms
    (D) was confined largely to New England
    (E) was funded primarily by the federal government

46. The Progressive movement's most significant impact on American society was

    (A) eliminating corruption in the political system
    (B) convincing large segments of the working class to support socialist ideas
    (C) establishing that federal legislation can be used to regulate business
    (D) putting the issue of civil rights for African Americans on the national agenda
    (E) setting the United States on an isolationist course

47. Frank Capra was a Depression-era film director whose artistic response to the Great Depression could best be described as

    (A) elaborate musicals, such as *Gold Diggers of 1933*, with lavish dance numbers and opulent sets which suggested that better times were just around the corner
    (B) earnest films, such as *Mr. Smith Goes to Washington*, which suggested that the problems of the era could be solved by old-fashioned values rather than sweeping political or economic change
    (C) bright animated films, such as *Snow White and the Seven Dwarfs*, which offered Americans an escape from the drudgery of daily life
    (D) zany comedies, such as *Duck Soup*, which created an anarchic world that mocked authority at a time when traditional authorities seemed to be unable to provide answers to the day's problems
    (E) gritty gangster movies, such as *The Public Enemy*, which presented a lonely, often-cruel world of urban decay and violence

48. Herbert Hoover reacted to the Depression of 1929 by

    (A) doing nothing
    (B) encouraging unions to organize
    (C) establishing extensive federal relief programs to meet the emergency
    (D) building Hoovervilles to shelter the homeless in all the large cities
    (E) providing loans to industry to restart production

GO ON TO THE NEXT PAGE

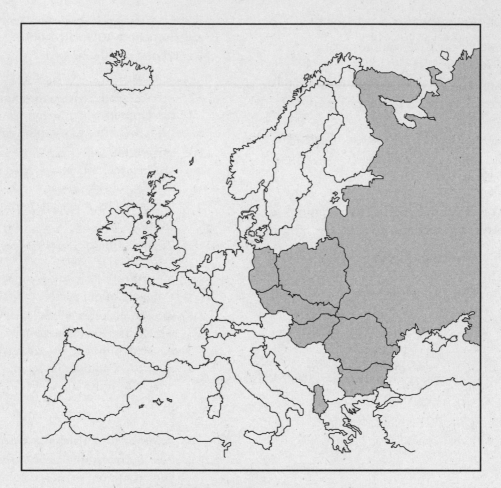

49. The shaded area in the map above shows

   (A) the Axis Powers
   (B) the Warsaw Pact
   (C) the League of Nations
   (D) the Allied Powers in World War II
   (E) NATO

GO ON TO THE NEXT PAGE

50. The mid-term congressional elections of 1994 were significant because

    (A) the Democratic Party gained control of Congress
    (B) the Republican Party gained control of Congress
    (C) the same political party gained control of the executive and legislative branch
    (D) it led to bipartisan support for the Contract With America
    (E) 18 year olds were given the right to vote in federal elections

51. Which of the following statements is true of the *encomienda* system, established by the Spanish in the New World?

    (A) Settlers were given 50 acres of land, as well as 50 acres for every person whose passage they paid to the New World.
    (B) Colonies existed for the good of the mother country.
    (C) African slaves were brought to the New World to labor on plantations.
    (D) The system resulted in the exploitation of the Native American population by the Spanish.
    (E) The mother country exported more than it imported creating a favorable balance of trade.

52. The Great Compromise, agreed upon during the Constitutional Convention,

    (A) established the executive branch of government
    (B) established the legislative branch of government
    (C) established the judicial branch of government
    (D) provided for the direct election of Senators by the voters
    (E) stipulated that slaves would be counted as three-fifths of a person for the purpose of taxation and representation

53. "Both parties deprecated war, but one of them would make war rather than let the nation survive, and the other would accept war rather than let it perish, and the war came."

    —*Abraham Lincoln,*
    Second Inaugural Address, 1865

    Which of the following statements is an accurate interpretation of the above quote?

    (A) The North was to blame for the war.
    (B) The South wanted to fight a war more than it wanted to preserve slavery.
    (C) The North wanted the South to perish.
    (D) The war started despite the efforts of both sides to avoid it.
    (E) Both sides wanted to preserve the union.

GO ON TO THE NEXT PAGE

54. In the second half of the 19th century, mining went from being an endeavor dominated by individual prospectors to one dominated by a few large corporations because

    (A) the children of prospectors lost interest in mining and sold their operations to corporations

    (B) insurance and licensing fees were beyond the reach of most individuals

    (C) the machinery required for extracting ore cost more than most prospectors could afford

    (D) the transportation costs of shipping ore became too great for individual prospectors

    (E) most of the prospectors were drafted into the Union army during the Civil War

55. The temperance movement of the 19th century

    (A) attracted little popular support

    (B) found a strong ally in the Democratic Party

    (C) rejected appeals to people's sense of morality

    (D) achieved its ultimate goal by the turn of the 20th century

    (E) had a strong appeal among women

56. The Harlem Renaissance can best be described as

    (A) a movement to gain equal access to public accommodations

    (B) an urban renewal project in northern Manhattan

    (C) a project to preserve 19th century buildings and artifacts made by free African Americans

    (D) a self-conscious effort by African Americans to promote their literature, music and art

    (E) a movement for racial integration in northern Manhattan

57. *Sarge, I'm only eighteen,*
    I got a ruptured spleen
    and I always carry a purse.
    I got eyes like a bat,
    my feet are flat,
    and my asthma's getting worse.

    Which of the following is an accurate statement about this 1964 song by Phil Ochs, "Draft Dodger Rag"?

    (A) It encouraged young men to burn their draft cards.

    (B) It encouraged young men to evade the draft by fleeing to Canada.

    (C) It was a humorous song lacking serious content.

    (D) It encouraged an anti-military attitude.

    (E) It encouraged organized protest.

GO ON TO THE NEXT PAGE

58. C. Everett Koop, President Reagan's Surgeon General, made headlines when he

    (A) called for an end to the war on drugs
    (B) resigned in protest of Ronald Reagan's environmental policies
    (C) changed the labeling on foods to show daily requirements
    (D) launched a major campaign to prevent smoking
    (E) called for new meat-inspection laws to prevent outbreaks of *E. coli*

59. When President George H. W. Bush spoke of a New World Order he was referring to

    (A) the results of the "war to end all wars"
    (B) agreements between China, the Soviet Union, and the United States
    (C) the defeat of Iraq in the Gulf War
    (D) the signing of the NAFTA (North American Free Trade Agreements) and the improved relations between Canada, Mexico, and the United States
    (E) importance of the United Nations as a force to settle international disputes after the fall of the Soviet Union

60. Which of the following statements is an accurate description of differences between immigration patterns in the late 19th century and late 20th century?

    (A) A backlash developed against the more recent immigrants, while the older immigrants were universally welcomed.
    (B) The more recent immigrants were primarily from Asia and Latin America while the older immigrants were primarily from Europe.
    (C) The older immigrants were less educated than the more recent immigrants.
    (D) The more recent immigrants are taking jobs away from people in the United States, while the older immigrants did not.
    (E) The more recent immigrants have flocked to cities, while the older immigrants flocked to rural areas.

61. The Virginia House of Burgesses and the Fundamental Orders of Connecticut were similar in that both

    (A) provide for direct democracy
    (B) provide for representative democracy
    (C) symbolized the independent spirit that existed in the American colonies
    (D) provided for universal male suffrage
    (E) were independent of the British government

GO ON TO THE NEXT PAGE

62. Thomas Jefferson and Alexander Hamilton were similar in that they both

    (A) advocated a balance between states' rights and a strong central government
    (B) supported the Bank of the United States
    (C) believed in rotation of public offices
    (D) used the elastic clause to justify actions they had taken
    (E) believed that the people were capable of making a decision if they were educated and informed

63. "We are opposed to the extension of slavery because it diminishes the productive powers of its population… It is an obstacle to compact settlements and to every general system of public institution. [If slavery goes into the territories] the free labor of all the states will not… [I]f the free labor of all the states goes there, the slave labor of the southern states will not, and in a few years the country will teem with an active and energetic population."

    —*Editorial*, New York Evening Post, *1847*

    Why will free labor not go where there is slavery, according to the above excerpt?

    (A) Because African Americans are inferior.
    (B) Free laborers are morally opposed to slavery.
    (C) Slaves work too hard and would force out free laborers.
    (D) Slaves prevent the growth of productive communities.
    (E) Free laborers do not want to work next to slaves.

64. Helen Hunt Jackson's 1881 book, *A Century of Dishonor*, chronicled the

    (A) mistreatment of Chinese laborers working on the transcontinental railroad
    (B) government's record of broken treaties and promises in regard to Native Americans
    (C) destruction of the ecology of the West by settlers and big business
    (D) conditions on cotton plantations before the Civil War
    (E) history of Spanish misdeeds in Cuba before the Spanish-American War

65. The 17th Amendment (direct election of U.S. Senators), the initiative, and the recall were all intended to

    (A) break up the power of municipal political machines, such as Tammany Hall
    (B) empower the government to challenge big business
    (C) extend civil rights to African Americans
    (D) give the people more power in the democratic process
    (E) relieve the suffering of the poor

66. Eugene V. Debs and Robert M. La Follette were similar in that both

    (A) opposed U.S. involvement in World War II
    (B) ran for president on third-party tickets
    (C) rejected sweeping challenges to the status quo
    (D) were arrested under the Espionage Act during World War I
    (E) served in Franklin D. Roosevelt's cabinet

GO ON TO THE NEXT PAGE

67. As part of President Franklin Roosevelt's plan to fight the Great Depression, the Agricultural Adjustment Act (AAA) was passed to

    (A) replace the New Deal farm price supports that had been declared unconstitutional

    (B) raise the prices of farm goods so that the farmers could survive the Depression

    (C) provide new equipment so farmers could grow more crops

    (D) give loans to farmers who planted crops that were needed in cities

    (E) ensure that all farmers who wanted to relocate to more fertile land could move without difficulty

68. The Smith Act of 1940 and the McCarran Act of 1950 are similar in that they both

    (A) were used to hamper the activities of the Communist Party

    (B) aided the development of suburbs

    (C) checked the power of large corporations

    (D) were milestones in the struggle for civil rights for African Americans

    (E) expanded the rights of people accused of crimes

69. When Gerald Ford said "the long national nightmare is over," he was referring to the end of the

    (A) Vietnam War

    (B) Cold War

    (C) Iran Hostage Crisis

    (D) Watergate Scandal

    (E) Savings and Loan Crisis

70. In his first year in office President Ronald Reagan

    (A) initiated the famous 100 days of intense legislative activity

    (B) began his program of trading arms for hostages

    (C) fired air traffic controllers who refused to end their strike for shorter hours and higher pay

    (D) invaded Iran to force the return of American hostages

    (E) launched an invasion of Cuba

71. The Mayflower Compact can best be characterized as

    (A) the first written constitution in the New World

    (B) a peace accord that settled competing territorial claims between the Puritans and Native Americans

    (C) the colonial government in Massachusetts Bay Colony

    (D) a statement of religious principles

    (E) a formal agreement signed by the Puritans that created a democratic process

72. Many historians believe that Stephen A. Douglas wrote the Kansas-Nebraska Act because he

    (A) wanted a railroad to the West that would start in Chicago

    (B) wanted votes from Easterners for a future presidential run

    (C) wanted to expand farming because he was for the Homestead Act

    (D) wanted to please the South by opening up more land for cotton farming

    (E) opposed slavery

GO ON TO THE NEXT PAGE

73. "Our government's foundations are laid; its cornerstone rests upon the great truth that the Negro is not equal to the white man, that slavery and subordination to the superior race is his natural and moral condition. This, our new government, is the first in the history of the world based upon this great physical, philosophical, and moral truth.... Our Confederacy is founded upon principles in strict conformity with these laws. This stone, which was rejected by the first builders, has become the chief stone of the new corner in our edifice."

    —*Alexander Stephens,*
    Vice President of the Confederacy,
    March 21, 1861

    Which of the following is an accurate interpretation of Alexander Stephens's statement?

    (A) Slavery would gradually end without interference from the North.
    (B) Ancient Greece and Rome were wrong to have supported slavery.
    (C) The Founding Fathers were correct on all substantive issues.
    (D) Slavery was the proper philosophical basis for the Confederacy.
    (E) Southerners seceded for primarily economic reasons.

74. A major factor leading to U.S. imperialism in the 1890s was

    (A) a political shift as the Democratic Party gained power at the expense of the Republican Party
    (B) the opportunity created for the United States as European powers began to move away from imperialist expansion and focus on internal development
    (C) the desire for new markets as industrial production outpaced domestic consumption
    (D) the need to find new lands to absorb the expanding population of the United States
    (E) a desire for fertile land, as farmland on the American mainland was becoming depleted

75. Which of the following did not reinforce white supremacist notions of race relations in the United States?

    (A) The *Plessy v. Ferguson* decision
    (B) The D. W. Griffith film, *Birth of a Nation*
    (C) The *Dred Scott v. Sanford* decision
    (D) The Niagara Movement
    (E) The Dixiecrat Party

76. A major function of the Federal Reserve System, established in 1913, was to

    (A) regulate the money supply
    (B) balance the budget
    (C) encourage industrial development
    (D) regulate the stock market
    (E) regulate foreign trade

GO ON TO THE NEXT PAGE

77. Franklin D. Roosevelt attempted to pack the Supreme Court in 1937 because

   (A) the justices were too inexperienced to deal with the Great Depression
   (B) the court had declared some New Deal legislation unconstitutional
   (C) Roosevelt felt that Congress had become more powerful than the President
   (D) the court refused to allow the President to implement the Lend-Lease Act
   (E) the court had demonstrated liberal tendencies in interpreting the New Deal legislation

78. The Senate passed a censure motion against Senator Joseph McCarthy in the wake of

   (A) accusations of financial impropriety
   (B) hearings, which implicated high-ranking members of the military
   (C) the execution of Julius and Ethel Rosenberg
   (D) the Supreme Court's opinion on the constitutionality of the House Un-American Activities Committee (HUAC)
   (E) the U.S. entry into the Korean War

79. The Immigration Act of 1965 was significant in that it

   (A) opened the door to many non-European immigrants
   (B) used racial criteria for the first time as a basis for admission to the United States
   (C) favored northern and Western Europeans
   (D) excluded unskilled workers
   (E) used IQ tests as a criterion for admission to the United States

80. United States forces in Vietnam used Agent Orange primarily to

   (A) counteract the effects of poisons used by the Vietcong
   (B) camouflage movement in the jungle
   (C) interrogate Vietcong prisoners
   (D) destroy the natural cover used by the Vietcong guerrillas
   (E) prevent the diseases carried by the insects of Vietnam

81. One of the major reasons for the development of political parties in the 1790s was that

   (A) Jefferson and Madison had developed a personal dislike for one another
   (B) support for the French Revolution eroded Washington's power
   (C) the Alien and Sedition Acts had reduced the number of immigrants entering the United States
   (D) differences had developed concerning the interpretation of the Constitution
   (E) The Articles of Confederation had created a weak central government

82. Key components of Henry Clay's American system included

   (A) a strict interpretation of the Constitution and rapid Western expansion
   (B) high protective tariffs and internal improvements
   (C) the development of Southern industry and northern agriculture
   (D) the elimination of export taxes and of the slave trade
   (E) government ownership of railroads and canals

GO ON TO THE NEXT PAGE

83. "Scalawag" was a derogatory term used by

    (A) abolitionists to describe slave catchers in the 1850s

    (B) whites in the South to describe other Southerners who cooperated with Reconstruction

    (C) Republicans to describe Federalists who cooperated with the British during the War of 1812

    (D) Westerners to describe white settlers who argued for fair treatment of Native Americans in the 1870s

    (E) union members to describe workers who crossed a picket line during the labor conflicts of the Gilded Age

84. Jose Marti and Emilio Aguinaldo are similar in that both

    (A) fought against U.S. forces in their respective countries

    (B) served as governors of U.S. protectorates

    (C) led nationalist movements in their respective countries

    (D) signed treaties allowing the United States to have a military presence in their respective countries

    (E) were leaders of the Organization of American States

85. In the 1908 *Muller v. Oregon* decision, the Supreme Court

    (A) upheld the use of the Sherman Anti-trust Act to break up trusts

    (B) forbade states from regulating railroad rates for routes between states

    (C) held that worker-protection laws do not violate the constitutional rights of employers

    (D) upheld segregation laws, if both sets of facilities are equal to one another

    (E) ruled that the government has the right to limit speech if a clear and present danger exists

86. The passage of the Emergency Quota Act in 1921 and the movement to prevent the teaching of evolution in public schools in the 1920s could best be seen as

    (A) conservative responses to social change

    (B) Marxist responses to economic dislocation

    (C) liberal responses to the rise of the Ku Klux Klan

    (D) Democratic responses to the success of the Republican Party

    (E) feminist responses to Victorian morality

87. As the civil rights movement shifted its focus to the North and issues of de facto segregation which of the following became a central issue?

    (A) separate lunch counters for African Americans and whites

    (B) segregation in department store fitting rooms

    (C) blacks and whites living in separate neighborhoods

    (D) discrimination in waiting rooms in interstate bus stations

    (E) requiring blacks and whites to use separate water fountains

GO ON TO THE NEXT PAGE

88. The Supreme Court decisions *Gideon v. Wainwright* and *Miranda v. Arizona* are significant in that they

    (A) expanded the rights of people accused of crimes

    (B) made participation in the political system easier for African Americans

    (C) strengthened the separation of church and state

    (D) established the principle of equal pay for equal work

    (E) ensured free speech during wartime

89. President Jimmy Carter broke from previous U.S. administrations in foreign policy by

    (A) promising to "walk softly and carry a big stick" in his dealings with Latin American nations

    (B) vowing to halt communist expansion in Asia

    (C) pursuing a policy of détente with the Soviet Union

    (D) linking U.S. aid to foreign nations to improvements in human rights

    (E) signing a new treaty with Panama extending U.S. control of the Canal Zone

90. All of the following were initiatives of Clinton Administration except the

    (A) Brady Gun Control Bill, which regulated handgun ownership

    (B) Personal Responsibility and Work Opportunity Act, which reformed the welfare system

    (C) Camp David Accords for peace between Israel and Egypt

    (D) commitment of 20,000 troops to Haiti to support President Bertrande Aristide

    (E) Dayton Accords for a peace settlement in Serbia

STOP!

If you finish before time is up, you may check your work.

Answer Key
Practice Test 2

1. A	31. D	61. B
2. A	32. A	62. D
3. C	33. D	63. D
4. E	34. A	64. B
5. D	35. C	65. D
6. C	36. C	66. B
7. A	37. A	67. B
8. E	38. A	68. A
9. B	39. B	69. D
10. A	40. B	70. C
11. C	41. D	71. E
12. A	42. D	72. A
13. B	43. C	73. D
14. E	44. D	74. C
15. B	45. B	75. D
16. D	46. C	76. A
17. B	47. B	77. B
18. C	48. E	78. B
19. C	49. B	79. A
20. E	50. B	80. D
21. A	51. D	81. D
22. A	52. B	82. B
23. D	53. D	83. B
24. B	54. C	84. C
25. E	55. E	85. C
26. E	56. D	86. A
27. E	57. D	87. C
28. D	58. D	88. A
29. A	59. E	89. D
30. B	60. B	90. C

KAPLAN

ANSWERS AND EXPLANATIONS

1. A

The Plains Indians moved with the buffalo. The civilizations of Mexico and Central America were centered in some of the largest cities on the continent at that time. The Plains Indians lived in tents, not adobe houses (B) and were never able to unite (C). All of the native populations of America were devastated by European diseases (D). The Aztecs did intermarry with the Spanish leading to the development of the *mestizos* (a mixed race) and a blending of cultures (E), while the Plains Indians, who did not intermarry, attempted to preserve their way of life.

2. A

The New Englanders experienced rapid population growth through natural reproduction. Unlike their southern brethren, the settlers to New England came with their families. In the 17th century, there was a shortage of women in the South. All the colonies were highly dependent on Great Britain (B) for trade and defense against their enemies. The New England colonies, with the exception of Rhode Island, were not tolerant (C) of religious differences. The New England farms (D) were smaller than those in Pennsylvania and the plantations of the South. From John Winthrop to John Adams there were many strong leaders in New England (E).

3. C

Andrew Jackson was president from 1829–1837. He was called the "Hero of New Orleans" because be defeated the British in 1814, just after the Treaty of Ghent was signed ending the War of 1812 during the presidency of James Madison. All of the rest of the choices were presidential actions of Andrew Jackson. He opposed South Carolina's Ordinance of Nullification (A) with both the Nullification Proclamation and the Force Bill. He advocated removing the Cherokees west of the Mississippi River (B) and signed the Indian Removal Act of 1830. He vetoed the re-charter of the Second Bank of the United States (D) in 1832 because he thought the bank was a monopoly favoring the wealthy. He appointed people to governmental positions based on party loyalty (E) because he wanted to reward his supporters and keep tight control of the government. His predecessor, John Quincy Adams, had been opposed to such overtly political actions.

4. E

The mechanical reaper cut wheat by using horse power and rotating blades resulting in a twelve-fold increase in production. The steel plow, invented by John Deere, turned over soil (A). The reaper did not plant seeds (B) and did not aid in the irrigation of the Midwest (C). The cotton gin, invented by Eli Whitney in 1793, led to increased cotton production (D). Mechanical harvesting of cotton developed in the middle of the 20th century.

5. D

In his Second Inaugural Address Lincoln called for a post-war reconciliation with the rebellious South. He wanted "to bind up the nation's wounds" "with malice toward none and charity for all." as a way to begin to rebuild the Union. The Second Inaugural Address was delivered in March 1865 before the Southern legislatures (A) passed Black Codes. Lincoln died on April 14, 1865. Reconstruction (B) ended in 1877 well after Lincoln's assassination. Johnson was impeached (C) in 1868 after he became president upon Lincoln's death. The candidates who ran against him (E) in 1860 were not actors on the political stage in 1865.

6. C

The "social gospel" was a movement that attempted to apply Christian values to solving the problems of labor and immigrants resulting from the industrialization and urbanization of the 1890s and 1900s. The Second Great Awakening (B) was a religious revival movement that did not specifically address social problems. The abolitionist movement (C) was not specifically a religious movement; it dealt with the slavery issue and not other social problems. The fundamentalist Christian movement (D) centered on literal interpretations of the Bible and opposed the idea of evolution; it did not address social problems in particular. The religious right political movement (E) centered on family values and not the problems of industrialization and urbanization.

7. A

This cartoonist was depicting the dispute over U.S. participation in the League of Nations (1918) and the belief that the United States would be pulled into world conflicts because of it. U.S. membership in the League is depicted as a "marriage" to the foreign nations. The League of Nations is acting as the minister who would make this marriage official, thus involving the United States in foreign entanglements. The United Nations (B) was formed after World War II, clearly out of the time frame of this cartoon. This cartoon has nothing to do with Wilson's relationship to his wife (C). While the source of controversy was the possibility of international alliances, this was not mainly an economic (D) issue. There was nothing in the Constitution (E) that would have prevented the United States from participating in the League of Nations. The United States Senate rejected the Treaty of Versailles and U.S. participation in the League of Nations.

8. E

FDR reasoned that if he pushed for civil rights and anti-lynching legislation, he would lose the support of the Southern wing of the Democratic Party and would not be able to implement New Deal programs. Roosevelt was not a white supremacist (A); Eleanor Roosevelt addressed the issues of civil rights, while FDR did not. Starting in 1936, the majority of African Americans were no longer voting Republican (B) as they had since the days of Lincoln. The New Deal was a program involving massive intervention into American society (C). Progressive reformers did not eliminate segregation from American society. In fact, they did not even address the issue (D).

9. B

Engel v. Vitale (1962) struck down voluntary prayer in public schools as a violation of the "establishment clause" of the 1st Amendment, which forbids the establishment of an official religion in the United States. The "establishment clause" put the concept of separation of church and state in the Constitution. *Brown v. Board of Education of Topeka* (A) (1954) involved the doctrine of "separate but equal" and overturned the *Plessy v. Ferguson* decision of 1896. *Baker v. Carr* (C) (1962) involved the problem of reapportionment in state legislatures. Decided by the Supreme Court in 1966, *Miranda v. Arizona* (D) held that verdicts rendered against accused criminals could not stand if the police did not inform them of their right to remain silent and to have a lawyer present during questioning. *Roe v. Wade* (E) (1973) was the decision that legalized abortion.

10. A

Stokely Carmichael was the leader of the Student Non-Violent Coordinating Committee (SNCC) who led the Black Power split in 1966. SNCC had been an organization concentrating on civil rights. The Black Power advocates changed the goals from legal rights for blacks to black economic power and black separatism. This shift in philosophy forced whites and integrationist blacks out of the organization. "Self-Defense" (B) and "Pick up the Gun" were both slogans of the Black Panther Party. "We Shall Overcome" (C) was the most famous non-violent Civil Rights Movement anthem and "Dare to Struggle Dare to Win" was a Students for a Democratic Society (SDS) slogan from 1968. "Turn on, Tune in, Drop out" (D) was Timothy Leary's slogan. "Back to Africa" was Marcus Garvey's slogan from the 1920s. Malcolm X was the advocate of making change "By any means necessary" (E) which was not a call for violence, but for self-defense.

11. C

The Proclamation of 1763 forbade the colonists from settling beyond the Appalachian Mountains. All of the other statements are untrue. In 1750, 90 percent of the colonists lived on farms (A). The colonists imported more than they exported under the mercantile system, and New England (B) was no exception. Only in South Carolina did slaves outnumber whites by the mid-1700s (D). Jonathan Edwards (E) inspired the Great Awakening and the New Lights in the 1740s.

12. A

The War Hawks, led by Henry Clay in Congress, were mainly Westerners interested in eliminating the threat of the Native Americans in the Northwest. The westerners believed that the British had incited and supplied the Native Americans against them. The War Hawks also were interested in expanding the United States into Canada. The New England states (B) opposed the War of 1812 even meeting in Hartford to protest the war in 1814. The War if 1812 was not an attempt to assimilate the Native Americans into American society (C). New Orleans, a key city at the mouth of the Mississippi River, was already under American control when the war broke out (D); it remained under American control thanks to Andrew Jackson's defeat of a British force that attacked the city. As a result of the Embargo of 1807 and the War of 1812, the United States began to develop its own industries (E). However, this was a *result* of the war not a goal of the war.

13. B

John C. Calhoun contended in the South Carolina Exposition and Protest of 1828 that the states were sovereign and had the right to rule. Since the Constitution was a compact formed by the states, the states could decide on the legality and constitutionality of federal laws. The position that the people were sovereign was a pro-national government position that Calhoun had abandoned by 1828, knowing that the majority of the country would not support his sectional interest in regard to slavery and nullification. Advocates of the national government like Daniel Webster and Henry Clay called for the Supreme Court (C) to decide on the constitutionality of the tariff, not the state legislatures, as Calhoun had advocated. Congress (D) did not support Calhoun's ideas since there was a northern majority by 1820 in the House of Representatives. He called for nullification in order to sidestep federal control. Perhaps he thought that Andrew Jackson would allow nullification since he was a slaveholder and opposed many national programs. However, since the president is chosen as a representative of the whole people (E), he represents federal not state power. Andrew Jackson strongly opposed nullification.

14. E

The American Renaissance in literature signified the worldwide acceptance of the American writers. Moby Dick was the name of the whale that obsessed the captain, Ahab, of the ship *Pequod*. It is an epic tale of the struggle between man and nature, and good and evil. While the novel included sympathetic portrayals of Native Americans (A), it did not significantly alter American attitudes toward the Native Americans. Nathaniel Hawthorne's book, *Blithedale Romance*, explores life in a utopian community (B). *Uncle Tom's Cabin*, written in 1852 by Harriet Beecher Stowe, galvanized Northern opinion against the Fugitive Slave Law of 1850 (C). *The Scarlet Letter* by Nathaniel Hawthorne portrayed the rigidity of 17th century Puritan New England.

15. B

The expression "separate but equal" originated from this decision by the Supreme Court, which gave the court's seal of approval to segregation. This decision was overturned by the court in the *Brown v. Board of Education of Topeka* (1954) (D). Poll taxes (A) were abolished as a result of the passage of the 24th Amendment (1964) to the Constitution.

Congressional Reconstruction (C) had ended by 1877, well before the *Plessy* decision of 1896. The issue of slaves as property was addressed in 1857 in the *Dred Scott v. Sanford* decision.

16. D

In his 1890 book, Jacob Riis combined narrative and photographs to vividly portray life of the urban poor. Harriet Beecher Stowe addressed the issue of harsh condition for slaves (A) in *Uncle Tom's Cabin* in 1852. The specific problems of women (B) at the turn of the 20th century was addressed by Theodore Dreiser's novel, *Sister Carrie* (1900). The lifestyles of the upper class in the 1920s (C) was the subject of the 1925 novel *The Great Gatsby* by F. Scott Fitzgerald. The chronicle of the lives of the immigrant poor from Asia and Africa in the 1960s (E) is well past the time period when Riis wrote.

17. B

The *Sussex Pledge* was a promise made by Germany to restrict the use of submarine warfare to attacks on military transports. The pledge was made before the United States became involved in World War I. When Germany announced the resumption of unrestricted submarine warfare, Wilson asked for a declaration of war against Germany. The policy of appeasement (A) was used in the 1930s to satisfy the aggressive moves of Hitler and the Axis powers. The United States did not negotiate any treaty with Germany (C) and the Germans sent the Zimmermann Note (D) to Mexico shortly after the Germans announced the resumption of unrestricted submarine warfare. The United States did not intern German immigrants (E), during World War I but did intern people of Japanese ancestry during World War II.

18. C

The Urban Renewal program was designed to tear down inner-city slums and replace them with modern housing and stores. It displaced large numbers of people and destroyed vibrant neighborhoods. It did not eliminate slums and

poverty in American cities. All of the other statements are accurate characterizations of developments in post–World War II American cities.

19. C

After the Montgomery Bus Boycott, Martin Luther King Jr. founded the Southern Christian Leadership Conference to use the methods of nonviolent resistance to integrate public facilities in the South. The Black Panther party called for defense of black neighborhoods against police brutality (A). The National Association for the Advancement of Colored People challenged segregation in the Supreme Court (B) and won the major case of *Brown v. Board of Education of Topeka* in 1954. It was the Mississippi Freedom Democratic Party (MFDP) that led the struggle for racially equal representation (D) at the 1964 Democratic Convention. There was no significant back-to-Africa movement (E) after the 1920s.

20. E

Clinton was accused of lying before a federal grand jury about the Lewinsky Affair. He was accused of perjury. The House of Representatives viewed this action as a "high crime" or "misdemeanor," an impeachable offense under the Constitution. Choices (A) and (C) were scandals of the Clinton years but were not the basis of the charges of impeachment. The Articles of Impeachment concentrated on the alleged perjury, not on securing a job for Paula Jones (B). Clinton was criticized for his poor conduct as president (D), but again, this was not an impeachable offense.

21. A

Taverns served as a meeting place where colonists from different areas could exchange information. The people discovered certain common traits in their lives. This was important during the years prior to the American Revolution. Children did not attend school in taverns (B). The temperance movement (C) did not begin until 1810. Taverns were neither halfway houses for the poor (D) nor work houses. Town meetings (E) took place in a variety of locations, most notably town halls.

22. A

Many new religions developed as a result of the Great Awakening, leading to greater competition for worshippers. This led to a loss of power for the clergy and a questioning of existing religious authority. The abolitionist movement (B) was largely a 19th century phenomenon that grew out of the Second Great Awakening. The number of religious sects increased (C). Revival meetings (D) were key experiences of the both Great Awakenings. The Salem witch trials (E) occurred in the 1690s before the Great Awakening.

23. D

Two great failings of the Articles of Confederation were its lack of an executive branch to enforce the law and a judiciary to interpret the law. The Constitution provided for both of these. The amending process described in (A) was part of the Articles of Confederation. While the Constitution provides for an amending process, it does not require a unanimous approval of the states as the Articles did. The Bill of Rights (B) was not added to the Constitution until 1791, after the Constitution was in effect. No specific cabinet positions (D) were written into the Constitution. It was developed by George Washington. The reserved power clause (E) is the 10th Amendment of the Constitution and part of the Bill of Rights.

24. B

The American System, a Whig program that originated after the War of 1812, was designed to promote industry by using the National Bank, tariffs, and internal improvements like roads and canals. The Federal Reserve System (A) was established in 1913 long after the bank was destroyed by Andrew Jackson between 1832 and 1836. Jackson placed the money from the Second Bank into "pet" or state banks (C) as a way to eliminate the federal bank. Therefore it was not a

forerunner; it was fundamentally different. The First Bank of the United States was supported by Congress (D) in 1791. The Supreme Court declared the first bank constitutional in 1819 in the *McCulloch v. Maryland* decision of 1819.

25. E

The acquisition of territory from Mexico after the Mexican War provided a place which became the center of conflict concerning the extension of slavery. The acquisition of the Mexican Territory aggravated conflicts with the Native Americans (A). The Oregon question (B) had been settled in 1846. Bleeding Kansas (C) occurred in 1856 and Kansas was acquired as part of the Louisiana Territory. Panama (D) is located in Central America.

26. E

In the end, the North won the Civil War because it could expend more men than the South. It is astonishing how the statistics overwhelmingly favor the North. The North had an advantage in naval shipping (B), corn production (C), and even draft animals in service (D), but none of these advantages were as important as the number of men the North threw into service in the war effort. The South had an advantage in cotton production (A), but this wasn't very helpful since the North produced most of the textiles and the South was running out of clothing by the end of the war. The Civil War lasted so long because the South fought so tenaciously.

27. E

The Reconstruction Act of 1867 divided the South into five military districts. While it did not go as far as some radicals had hoped, it ended Andrew Johnson's cautious reconstruction program and ushered in Congressional Reconstruction. Jim Crow laws ended (A) with protests and federal legislation in the 1950s and 1960s. Presidential Reconstruction began (B) with Lincoln's Proclamation of Amnesty and Reconstruction in

1863. The abolition of slavery (C) occurred with the passage of the 13th Amendment in 1865. We are not sure how Lincoln would have responded to post–Civil War problems because he died the month the war ended (E). However, during the war Lincoln emphasized a quick reunification rather than a prolonged period of military occupation of the South.

28. D

The 1892 Omaha platform of the Populists included some radical demands, including nationalizing banks and railroads. It rejected the gold standard (B) and it advocated inflationary policies (E) so that farmers could pay off their debts more easily and sell their crops at higher prices. It never became a national movement (A), although some of the Omaha platform was later adopted by the Progressives. Many populists supported Democratic candidate William Jennings Bryan (C) in 1896.

29. A

Franklin Roosevelt's bank holiday was one of his very first actions as President in dealing with the Depression. During the bank holiday, all banks were closed until they could be reopened on a sound financial footing. President Hoover established the Reconstruction Finance Corporation (B) in 1932. Social Security (C) was established in 1935 to protect the elderly and unemployed. The National Recovery Administration (D) was established under the National Industrial Recovery Act in 1933 after the Bank Holiday. The Court Packing scheme (E) of President Franklin Roosevelt was attempted in 1937.

30. B

Henry Kissinger, who was President Nixon's Secretary of State, arranged to meet with the Chinese during a ping-pong (table tennis) tournament in Japan in 1971. This was the beginning of the "opening to China." Nixon did not reunite Vietnam (A). North Vietnam conquered South Vietnam in 1975, and reunited the country, after American troops had withdrawn in 1974.

Jimmy Carter was associated with human rights (C), not Nixon. China tolerates Taiwan (D), but still does not recognize it as an independent political entity. The Cold War (E) did not end until 1991 with the fall of the Soviet Union.

31. D

Unity was never achieved among the Native American populations. There were new products introduced to the Americas (A), such as the gunpowder. European diseases killed off 90 percent of the native population (B). Europe did get new products from the Americas, such as corn (C). Mixed race people (*mestizo*) (E) emerged from the intermarriage of the native population and the Europeans.

32. A

The Maryland Act of Toleration provided for religious freedom to Catholics and most Christian sects. One of its clauses called for the execution of any person who denied the divinity of Christ. This eliminated Jews and atheists, making choices (D) and (E) incorrect. The Act had nothing to do with Native Americans (C).

33. D

When the Americans won the Battle of Saratoga, the French decided that the colonists might succeed in their fight against England. They joined the Americans against the British, turning the tide of the Revolution. The American forces still had limited naval power (A) compared to Great Britain and there was still a great deal of loyalist opposition (B) to the war. Spain joined the conflict against Britain but did not play a crucial role in the war in the American colonies or form an alliance with the American colonies (C). General Howe was not involved in the Battle of Saratoga (E).

34. A

The American Party, also known as the Know-Nothings, was an anti-Catholic and anti-immigrant party. It called for the extension of the residence requirement for citizenship in order to discourage the Irish and the German Catholics from becoming citizens. Such a group, including the Ku Klux Klan of the 1920s, is called "nativist" because it favored the nonimmigrant "native" Americans. The American Party's members were called "Know-Nothings" because they refused to divulge what occurred in any of their meetings, which were originally held in secret. Instead of answering questions they would say, "I know nothing." The Whig Party's (B) key proposals were a national bank and internal improvements. The Free Soil Party's (C) main positions were cheap land and opposition to the extension of slavery to the western territories. The Democratic Party (D) had an immigrant base so it did not advocate extending the residence requirement for citizenship. The National Republican Party (E) was John Quincy Adams's party and it advocated internal improvements and the national bank.

35. C

General George McClellan was unwilling to pursue the Confederates when he had the opportunity, spent too much time planning battles and did not execute them well. The famous march through Georgia (A) was led by General William Sherman. Vicksburg (B) was General Ulysses Grant's first big victory. McClellan's expertise extended to training and organizing his troops (D). General George Meade commanded the Union forces at Gettysburg (E).

36. C

Sod is the thick layer of matted grass and roots that had to be cut through (or "busted") before farming could begin. It is characteristic of the Great Plains. Soil in New England (A) and the East in general (E) does not consist of sod. (The sod used in the suburbs is especially grown for lawns.) Cotton grew in Texas (B) but normally not on soil covered with sod. The farmers of the Dust Bowl (D) were called "Okies," not "sod busters."

37. A

Although the description could apply to other presidents' actions, the phrase was coined by Theodore Roosevelt, who pursued an aggressive foreign policy in regard to Latin America. His "Roosevelt Corollary" to the Monroe Doctrine asserted America's right to intervene in Latin American nations' affairs. He was famous for this phrase. The other presidents pursued aggressive policies but did not use Roosevelt's language.

38. A

Rosie the Riveter, the woman in a World War II poster, symbolized the great numbers of women who took traditionally male industrial jobs to support the war effort during World War II. The poster is specific to World War II not the 1950s (C) or 1960s Women's Liberation Movement (B). Although women did work in factories as part of the Industrial Revolution (D), Rosie the Riveter did not appear until World War II. Women's workforce participation was not directly related to the suffrage movement (E).

39. B

The "War on Poverty" was a phrase used by the Johnson Administration to dramatize its attempt to end poverty in the United States. Aid to Latin American nations was not a Nixon initiative (A); the best known U.S. initiative to aid Latin American nations was Kennedy's Alliance for Progress. The Peace Corps (C), Kennedy's program to improve relations between the United States and the world's peoples, was never called a "war on poverty." General Marshall's work in Europe was called the Marshall Plan (D). President Eisenhower (E) did not initiate any specific anti-poverty programs.

40. B

The Watergate Hotel in Washington, DC, was the Democratic Party campaign headquarters in the 1972 campaign. The break-in was an attempt to bug the offices of the Democrats. Richard Nixon's campaign turned out to be responsible. This event and its subsequent cover-up led to Nixon's downfall. It was the Iran-Contra scandal that began with the release of documents showing that Ronald Reagan had authorized the payment of money to the Nicaraguan Contras (A) in defiance of Congressional policy. The Pentagon Papers scandal began with a leak to the *New York Times* of a secret analysis of the Vietnam War (C). The Credit Mobilier scandal, during the Ulysses Grant administration in the 1870s, dealt with kickbacks in railroad construction (D). The Teapot Dome scandal, which occurred during the Warren Harding administration in 1922, involved payoffs and fraud (E) but no break-ins.

41. D

When William and Mary ascended the throne in the Glorious Revolution of 1688–1689, the colonists overthrew the Dominion of New England. The Dominion of New England, which included New England and the other colonies north of Maryland, had been instituted in 1684 to discipline them. The Glorious Revolution gave the colonists the impetus to topple the Dominion. The Maryland Toleration Act (A) was written to protect Catholics, not Quakers. Pennsylvania, not Maryland, was founded as a haven for Quakers. The head-right system (C), which had first been developed in Virginia and Maryland, was designed to bring indentured servants to the colonies, not slaves. Governor Berkeley of Virginia was the object of Bacon's Rebellion (E), not Governor Winthrop of Massachusetts.

42. D

After the War of 1812 the British accepted the United States as a fully independent nation. It did not end British presence in North America (A); the British were still in Canada, but they did leave the forts in the Ohio Country. The "Star Spangled Banner" (B), which was later adopted as the national anthem, was written during the war; however, this did not make the United States any more independent of Britain. The United States had had a navy (C) since its founding. The war did not result in a gain of new lands (E) for the United States.

43. C

In the campaign of 1844 the Democrat, James K. Polk, favored the admission of Texas while Henry Clay, the Whig (E), opposed it because the possibility of the expansion of the country to the West opened up a chance that the Democrats would become a permanent majority. When Clay back-tracked on Texas late in the campaign, he ended up losing to Polk. The Bank of the United States (A) was one of the most important Whig issues. The Whigs supported tariffs (B) provide funds for internal improvements (D). In the Whig American Plan, both the bank and the tariff were designed to aid the development of industry.

44. D

The key word in the advertisement is "shrewd." Social historians are interested in the ideas and actions of ordinary people including masters and slaves. This master revealed an interesting contradiction when he called his slave "shrewd." If the slave is shrewd, how could the master argue that slavery was justified by the inferiority of blacks and their inability to run their own lives? Runaway advertisements are a wonderful source of information about slavery. The other choices are not as relevant in analyzing this document because they are normal expectations of the master for the runaway. "Instant" (A) means this month. "Abram" (B) was the slave's name. That he had long hair (C) would not be as important as shrewd. If he were going to a free state (E), why would that be unusual?

45. B

Mechanization increased output—a development that pushed down agricultural prices. It became increasingly difficult for farmers to repay the loans that they had taken out to buy agricultural implements and land. Because prices fell, farmers did not prosper (A). Mechanization was very effective at raising output (C). New England (D) was not the center of agricultural production in the late 1800s, the Midwest was. The government (E) did not support the farmers on a large scale until the New Deal of the 1930s.

46. C

The Progressive movement pushed through significant legislation to regulate industry, from the Meat Inspection Act of 1904 to the Clayton Anti-trust Act of 1914. Though Progressives were opposed to political corruption, they were certainly not successful in eliminating it (A). The Teapot Dome scandal of the 1920s and the Watergate scandal of the 1970s are evidence that corruption is still a part of the political system. Progressives generally opposed socialist solutions (B) and ignored the issue of race (D). Progressives tended to be internationalists rather than isolationists (E).

47. B

Frank Capra's movies are seen as optimistic and perhaps somewhat sentimental. His depictions of decent, hardworking people triumphing over special interests and greed seem to parallel the goals and worldview of the New Deal. *Gold Diggers* (1933) (A) was choreographed by Busby Berkeley. *Snow White and the Seven Dwarfs* (C) was produced by Walt Disney. *Duck Soup* (D) was a Marx Brothers movie. *Public Enemy* (E) was directed by William Wellman.

48. E

Herbert Hoover and Congress established the Reconstruction Finance Corporation in 1932 which gave government loans to businesses and railroads, hoping that this would "prime the pump" of the economy. He did not do nothing (A), but he opposed extensive relief programs (C). Roosevelt, not Hoover, encouraged unions to organize (B) in order to raise wages and increase purchasing power. Hoovervilles (D) were collections of makeshift houses built by homeless families during the Depression. They mockingly named their "communities" after Hoover.

49. B

The Warsaw Pact, signed in Warsaw, Poland, in 1955 by the Soviet Union and its satellite states in eastern Europe, formed a military alliance to balance NATO. The Warsaw Pact was signed by Albania, Bulgaria, Czechoslovakia, East Germany (German Democratic Republic), Hungary, Poland, Romania, and the USSR—all of which are shaded on this map. The Axis Powers (A) refers to Germany and its allies in World War II. The League of Nations (C), which included most of the European nations, was formed after World War I to promote peace. The Allied Powers in World War II (D) were those fighting against Germany, including Britain, France, the Soviet Union (and the United States). Formed to stop the spread of Soviet power and influence after World War II, NATO, or the North Atlantic Treaty Organization (E), was a military alliance that included most western European nations along with the United States and Canada.

50. B

The mid-term elections resulted in the Republican Party gaining control from the Democrats of the Senate and House of Representatives. This makes choice (A) incorrect. This was significant because President Bill Clinton, a Democrat, had to deal with a Republican Congress. Therefore, the executive and legislative branches of government were not of the same party. This Republicans in Congress, but not the Democrats, pursued the Contract With America (D). Eighteen year olds were given the right to vote by the 26th Amendment, ratified in 1971.

51. D

Under the encomienda system, the Spanish conquistadores exploited the labor of Native Americans in the New World; this was considered justified if an attempt was made to Christianize the laborers. It provided a way for the Spanish to enslave the Native American population. The importation of African slaves (C) was not part of the encomienda system, although in the Caribbean islands, the encomienda system was replaced by African slavery as the native population died out from disease, overwork, and warfare. The practice of granting a settler acres of land for each person whose passage they paid (A) is called the headright system. The system in which colonies exist for the good of the mother country (B) and in which the mother country attempts to maintain a favorable of trade (E) is called mercantilism.

52. B

The Great Compromise established a bicameral legislature made up of the House of Representatives and the Senate. The House satisfied large states that wanted representation to be based on population, and the Senate satisfied small states that wanted equal representation. The executive branch (A) and the judicial branch (C) were both established by the Constitution, but not by the Great Compromise. The 17th Amendment (1917) provided for the direct election of senators (D). The three-fifths compromise, also agreed upon at the Constitutional Convention, established a method for counting slaves (E).

53. D

Lincoln believed that the actions of both sides started the war and the positions of both sides produced the war. He really did not blame either side; they both deprecated war, but nevertheless "the war came." It might be true that the South wanted independence more than slavery (B), but it lost both at Appomattox and the quote does not refer to slavery. The North accepted war (A) so it did not start it. The North did not want the South to perish (C). Rather, the North wanted to preserve the Union, but the South did not (E).

54. C

During the various precious metal "rushes" and "strikes" of the 19th century, the first pieces of gold

and silver could be found along the surface or just beneath it. But soon heavy equipment was needed to dig underground mines and extract large amounts of precious metals. This was beyond the financial means of the average prospector. This progression from individual entrepreneur to large corporation is repeated in many different economic fields during U.S. history. The story of children losing interest in the family business (A) is more common to agriculture than to mining. Exorbitant insurance and licensing fees (B) are more common to the litigious 20th century than the 19th century. Transportation costs (D) were not such a concern with precious metals, which were brought to market in smaller quantities than, say, corn or lumber. The Civil War draft (E) did not significantly impact the mining industry.

55. E

Women were drawn to the temperance movement because they often bore the brunt of their husband's drunken rage. Also, it was the woman who had to put food on the table—a difficult task if her husband's paycheck had disappeared at the local pub. The movement was the largest social movement in the 19th century (A). The Democratic Party (B), with its strong working class, immigrant support, generally opposed temperance. The movement relied heavily on a particular moral code of behavior (C). The ultimate goal (D) was not achieved until 1920.

56. D

The key characters of the Harlem Renaissance were jazz trumpet player Louis Armstrong, poet Langston Hughes, and painter Jacob Lawrence. These men made a concerted effort to gain worldwide respect for African American culture. The civil rights movement of the 1950s and 1960s worked to gain equal access to public accommodations for African Americans (A). The Urban Renewal Program (B) was a federal project designed to improve city neighborhoods; it began in the 1950s. The 19th century free African

American community of Weeksville, Brooklyn, not Harlem, was discovered in 1960s. There has been a movement since the 1970s to preserve it (C). Before the 1920s Harlem was predominately white; thereafter, it became predominantly African American. Currently there is a growing white population in Harlem; however, there was no movement called the Harlem Renaissance to integrate Manhattan (E).

57. D

This song, by the folksinger Phil Ochs, proposed an individualistic way to avoid being drafted: lie. Ochs supported draft card burning (A) and probably supported fleeing to Canada (B), but neither of these are mentioned in the song. Though the song is humorous, he is serious about the message (C). He encouraged organized protest (E), and performed at many rallies, but, again, this was not the message of the song.

58. D

C. Everett Koop was the surgeon general who pushed for a ban on cigarette advertising and dealt with the early stages of the AIDS crisis. He served during the Reagan administration. The war on drugs (A), which had been going on since the Nixon administration, gained momentum under the Reagan years. Koop did not resign (B) from Reagan's administration. The labeling of foods (C) changed under Clinton and serious outbreaks of *E. coli* (E) occurred in the 1990s.

59. E

George H. W. Bush declared that the fall of the Soviet Union gave the democratic nations a chance to settle international disputes through the United Nations. The coalition led by the United States to defeat Iraq had the support of the United Nations. There was no major power to oppose United States actions after 1991, in the United Nations or anywhere else. The "war to end all wars" (A) was a slogan used to describe World War I. There have never been major agreements among China, the Soviet Union, and the United States (B). The New

World Order refers to efforts for worldwide peace not the defeat of Iraq (C), or the signing of the NAFTA agreement in 1993 (D).

60. B

Recent immigrants are less likely to be from Europe than immigrants arriving before 1921. There have been backlashes against immigrants (A) as far back as the Irish immigration of the 1840s and 1850s; they are not something new. Education varies within groups of immigrants (C), both in the early and in the late 20th century. Immigrants during both periods have been accused of taking jobs away from native-born Americans (D). The accusation is largely groundless. Most economists contend that immigration strengthens the economy. Most immigrants during both periods moved into urban areas (E).

61. B

The Virginia House and Burgesses and the Fundamental Orders of Connecticut involved the elections of representatives to carry on government. Thus, they were examples of representative democracy, not direct democracy (A). These assemblies followed the English traditions that the colonists were accustomed to, not uniquely American impulses (C). These documents did not provide for universal manhood suffrage (D). They were established with the approval of the British government (E).

62. D

Both Hamilton and Jefferson, despite their differing views on interpreting the Constitution, cited the elastic clause (the implied powers clause) of the Constitution to justify their actions. Hamilton cited it in establishing the Bank of the United States and Jefferson cited it in purchasing the Louisiana Territory. Jefferson supported states' rights; Hamilton supported a strong central government (A). Jefferson opposed the Bank of the United States (B) on the grounds that it would favor urban elites at the expense of farmers and that the Constitution did not grant Congress the power to create a national bank; Hamilton believed that a bank would aid in the economic development of the United States and would create a stable currency. Jefferson favored the rotation of public offices as a democratic measure, while Hamilton believed in retaining qualified people (C). Jefferson had a great deal of confidence in the common man (E), while Hamilton doubted the ability of the masses to decide wisely.

63. D

This editorial is an example of the free soil position which was a form of anti-slavery. The free (not slave) laboring men favored economic growth which created good jobs. Slaves prevented the rapid growth of free-enterprise. The free soil position was a compromise between abolitionists who wanted to eliminate all slavery and the people who wanted only a slavery-free West. The quote does not say that blacks are inferior (A) or make a moral criticism (B) of slavery. The quote does not say that slaves work too hard (C). In fact, it implies they do not work hard enough. The quote does not explicitly say that free laborers did not want to work next to slaves (E), although that was the case.

64. B

This important, and somewhat condescending, book brought to light many of the abuses Native Americans suffered at the hands of the U.S. government. Chinese laborers working on the transcontinental railroad were mistreated (A) and the settlement of the West did bring with it ecological costs (C), but these issues were not the subject of 19th century books. Many books, most notably the novel *Uncle Tom's Cabin*, described the conditions of slavery (D). Spanish misdeeds in Cuba were widely publicized in lurid newspaper accounts in the years leading up to the Spanish-American War (1898) (E), but no contemporary book was written.

65. D

The 17th Amendment (1917) called for the direct election of senators, the initiative allowed voters to instruct the legislature to address a specific issue, and the recall allowed voters to sign a petition to have a special election to try to unseat an unpopular politician. All were designed to put more power in the hands of the people. All were pushed by the Progressive movement. Municipal reforms, such as the commission form of government, helped break up the power of municipal machines (A). The Sherman Anti-trust Act (1890) and the Clayton Anti-trust Act (1914) were designed to check big business (B). The Reconstruction era amendments, the 13th, 14th, and 15th, were intended to expand civil rights for African Americans (C). Much of the New Deal legislation was designed to relieve the suffering of the poor (E).

66. B

Debs ran for president in 1900, 1904, 1908, 1912, and 1920 with the Socialist Party, La Follette ran for president in 1924 with the Progressive Party. Both had died by 1926, precluding opposition to World War II (A) or participation in Franklin D. Roosevelt's cabinet (E). Both favored sweeping changes to the status quo (C) and only Debs was arrested during World War I (D).

67. B

The AAA was passed in the first 100 days in order to counter the overproduction of crops that had been one of the major causes of the Depression. Farmers were given subsidies not to grow crops and to reduce their output in order to raise prices and provide them with a living. The AAA was declared unconstitutional (A) in 1936. It did not replace itself. More crops would have lowered prices (C), and since there was a surplus the idea of special loans (D) for new crops would not have been useful. The AAA was designed to help farmers hold onto the farms they had, not move to new farms (E), although some farmers who lost their farms due to foreclosure moved to California to work as farm laborers (the "Okies"). The Roosevelt administration encouraged people to move to rural areas in the beginning of the New Deal; this relocation was not a success.

68. A

The 1940 Smith Act was written to punish spies for the Nazis during World War II, but stayed on the books and was used to prosecute members of the Communist Party starting in 1949. The McCarran Internal Security Act, passed over Truman's veto in 1950, was used to prevent "subversives" from coming into the United States, and to deport immigrants if they belonged to "Communist or Communist Front" organizations. The government encouraged the development of suburbia (B) through programs such as the Federal Housing Administration (1934) and the Veterans Administration (1944). The power of large corporations (C) has largely gone unchecked in U.S. history. The Clayton Anti-trust Act of 1914 was an attempt to check their power. The Smith Act and the McCarran Act had nothing to do with civil rights for African Americans (D). These acts did not expand civil liberties for those accused of crimes (E). In fact, the McCarran Act was criticized for limiting civil liberties.

69. D

Gerald Ford became president in August 1974, after Richard Nixon resigned because he was about to be impeached for his part in the Watergate cover-up. It was a two year nightmare and Ford was hoping to heal the wounds of the scandal. The Vietnam War (A) ended in early 1974 when the United States pulled its troops out; Nixon was president at the time. The Cold War (B) did not end until 1991 during the administration of George H. W. Bush. The Iran Hostage Crisis (C) ended as Ronald Reagan took office in 1981. The Savings and Loan Crisis (E) took place during the last years of Reagan's second term.

70. C

In a test of wills in August 1981, Reagan threatened, then fired air traffic controllers and broke their union, the Professional Air Traffic Controllers Association (PATCO). It signaled an anti-union offensive that produced a sharp reduction in union membership and the legalization of replacement workers during strikes. The 100 days (A) was the famous beginning of the New Deal in 1933 under Franklin Roosevelt. The trading of arms for hostages (B) did not occur in the first year of Reagan's term, and it has never been proved that he initiated it. He did not invade Iran (D). Carter tried that, but failed. The hostages were released soon after Reagan took office. It was John Kennedy who launched an invasion of Cuba upon entering office (E); the Bay of Pigs invasion had been planned under the Eisenhower Administration.

71. E

Attempting to improve their chances of survival in the New World, the Puritans signed the Mayflower Compact. It did not create specific laws to be followed by the community, but was merely an agreement to abide by the will of the majority in establishing the colony. The first written constitution in the New World (A) is considered to be the Fundamental Orders of Connecticut, which was a comprehensive plan of government. Fighting between English colonists and Native Americans (B) only ended when Native Americans were pushed beyond European settlements; there was no successful comprehensive accord. The Mayflower Compact was signed by 41 out of the 102 people who sailed to the New World on the *Mayflower*, but it was not the basis of the government established in the Massachusetts Bay Colony (C). In fact, Plymouth Colony, founded by the Puritans on the *Mayflower*, was not originally part of Massachusetts Bay Colony, which was founded a few years after the arrival of the *Mayflower*. The Puritans wrote many documents outlining their religious beliefs and practices (D), but the Mayflower Compact was not one of them.

72. A

Stephen Douglas tried to provide the opening for a railroad route to the West that would start in his home state of Illinois. At least this is the supposition of many historians—no one knows for sure. The real problem, of course was that in order to get the swing votes of Southerners in Congress, he agreed to the repeal of the Missouri Compromise line, opening up the question of slavery in Kansas and Nebraska. Allowing the opportunity for slavery to spread north of the Missouri Compromise line is hardly an act of someone seriously opposed to slavery (E). Later in the Lincoln-Douglas debates of 1858, Lincoln tried to show that Douglas simply didn't care about slavery. There is no evidence Douglas was thinking of a Presidential bid (B) in 1854. Although a future presidential run might have been in his mind, it's unlikely the Kansas-Nebraska Act was part of any plan to get Eastern support for a presidential bid, since the Northeast overwhelmingly opposed the Kansas-Nebraska Act. There is no direct relationship between the Homestead Act (1862) and the Kansas-Nebraska Act (1854). The Act would not open up more land for cotton farming (D) since Kansas and Nebraska did not have a suitable climate for cotton production.

73. D

The Cornerstone Speech is a stark statement of racism. Not all Confederates thought that way or expressed themselves so forcefully, but this is important because it expresses the point of view of many at the top of the Confederate government. The new stone in this edifice is "the great truth that the Negro is not equal to the white man." This is not the morality of Martin Luther King, Frederick Douglas, or Abraham Lincoln. It is *his* morality. He believed in a *different* morality and philosophy. It is important to understand that people don't fight wars if they agree. They fight wars because they disagree. Stephens wanted slavery. He was not predicting it would end (A). He does not mention Greece and Rome (B) in this quote, but he does say

that that the key point is to enslave Negroes, not whites as others had done in the past. The Founding Fathers (C) were not correct if they rejected Stephens's cornerstone. He does not mention economic (E) reasons in his statement.

74. C

Most historians look at economic factors as most important in understanding why the United States became an imperialist power. Industrialization produced a desire for new markets and a need for raw materials. Throughout the 1890s, the Republicans held onto the White House (A), implementing an aggressive imperialist policy. European powers were heavily engaged in imperialism (B) as well. There was plenty of land in the continental United States to both absorb its growing population (D) and to farm (E).

75. D

The Niagara Movement grew out of a conference held by W. E. B. DuBois at Niagara Falls in 1905. The conference was made up of African Americans who favored active resistance to racism, in opposition to the accomodationist approach of Booker T. Washington. In the *Plessy v. Ferguson* decision (1896) (A), the Supreme Court gave its seal of approval to racial segregation. It is one of the most well known decisions in U.S. history. It was undone by another important decision—*Brown v. the Board of Education* (1954). *Birth of a Nation* (B) was a racist depiction of the Civil War and Reconstruction, portraying the Ku Klux Klan in a heroic light. In the Dred Scott decision (1857) (C), the Supreme Court stated that African Americans were inferior to whites. The Dixiecrat Party (E), was led by the then South Carolina Governor Thurmond who ran unsuccessfully for President that year. It broke away from the Democratic Party in 1948, perceiving that President Harry Truman was not sufficiently segregationist.

76. A

The Federal Reserve System, a Woodrow Wilson initiative, established a nation-wide banking system with a central board and 12 district banks. It regulates interest rates and the amount of money in circulation. It was the first central bank since the Civil War. The Gramm-Rudman Balanced Budget Act (B) passed in 1985 is unrelated to the Federal Reserve System. The First and Second Banks of the United States (1791–1811 and 1816–1836) were designed to encourage the growth of industry (C), but that was not the major task of the Federal Reserve. The United States was already an industrial giant by 1913. The Securities and Exchange Commission of 1934 was established to regulate the stock market (D). Foreign trade is regulated by Congress as stipulated in the Constitution (E).

77. B

The court-packing scheme of FDR in 1937 was a political maneuver by Roosevelt to ensure that no more New Deal legislation would be declared unconstitutional by the Supreme Court, which, according to Roosevelt, consisted of "nine old men." FDR asked Congress to expand the size of the Court to 15 members, allowing him to appoint one new justice for every one of the justices over 70 years of age (there were six). In this way, he hoped to gain a majority on the Court that would favor his New Deal legislation. Many members of Congress viewed FDR's attempt with dismay. The justices were not too inexperienced (A); in Roosevelt's opinion, however, they were too old. Roosevelt contended that the Court, not the Congress (C) had become too powerful. The Lend-Lease Act (D) was not opposed by the Court and since it was implemented in 1941, could not be a reason for the Court packing scheme, which occurred in 1937. In Roosevelt's opinion, the Court had not acted too liberally (E) but rather too conservatively on the New Deal legislation. The Court packing scheme was never approved by Congress but the Court began supporting New Deal legislation, nevertheless.

78. B

It was the Army-McCarthy hearings in 1954 that brought down McCarthy. He accused the Army of being soft on communism. He had gone so far with his charges of communist conspiracy that President Eisenhower found it necessary to defend the Army against McCarthy's allegations. Accusations of financial impropriety (A) were most famously made against vice presidential candidate Richard Nixon in the 1952 campaign. The Rosenberg Case (C) was not directly associated with Senator McCarthy. The Supreme Court never struck down HUAC (D). McCarthy was at the height of his power during the Korean War (E); he was censured in 1954 after the war was over.

79. A

The Immigration Act of 1965 represented a change in policy from the 1920's because it allowed large numbers of non-European immigrants to come into the country. While the National Origins Act of 1929 was narrowly based on country of origin, the 1965 act, which replaced it, was based on an overall quota system by hemisphere. The Chinese Exclusion Act of 1882 was the first racially based immigration act (B). The quota system of the 1920s favored northern and Western Europeans (C), but the 1965 act put all Europeans in the same category. Unskilled workers were not excluded (D), but skilled workers and professionals were admitted beyond their quotas. The rationale for the exclusion of Southern and Eastern Europeans in the 1920s was that they supposedly scored lower on IQ tests (E), but IQ tests have never been a criterion for permitting immigration to the United States.

80. D

Agent Orange was the toxic chemical substance used to defoliate (remove leaves from) the trees in the jungle so the Americans could see their enemy. It is now linked to cancers and other diseases among American (and presumably Vietnamese) veterans of the Vietnam War. Agent Orange was not a medicine to cure poisoning (A), nor was it used to camouflage troop movement (B). Sodium pentothal was one drug used for interrogation (C). Insects (E) must have died in the spray, but that was not the purpose for using Agent Orange.

81. D

The differing interpretation of the Constitution developed between the Federalists and Republicans during the administration of George Washington. The Federalist, led by Alexander Hamilton, believed in loose interpretation of the Constitution. The Democratic-Republicans, led by Thomas Jefferson, believed that the Constitution must be interpreted strictly. By the end of the 1790s, the party lines had been drawn culminating in the passage of the Alien and Sedition Acts by the Federalists and the Democratic-Republican response in the Virginia and Kentucky Resolutions. Further differences had developed as a result of the French Revolution. Jefferson and Madison were both Democratic-Republicans (A) and known to be friends. Washington (B) remained popular throughout his public career; the French Revolution did not diminish his popularity or power. (C) The Alien and Sedition Acts did not discourage or restrict immigration. It merely made it a longer time period before a person could become a citizen of the United States. Political parties were nonexistent at the time of the Articles of Confederation (E), which were no longer in effect during the 1790s, having been replaced by the U.S. Constitution.

82. B

Henry Clay believed that the United States could become more self-sufficient through his proposed program, called the American System. The North would produce industrial goods; the South would supply the raw materials, while the West would supply food for the country. Revenue could be raised through high protective tariffs that would keep out competition and help domestic industry to develop. Excise or sales taxes would be placed on certain goods and the revenues from these taxes and tariffs would be used for internal improvement, such as roads and canals. A national bank would keep currency stable and would invest in internal improvements. The American System required a loose interpretation of the Constitution (A), because canals, roads, and a national bank were not mentioned in the document. Clay's proposed program would not promote southern industry (C). Export taxes (D) are forbidden by the Constitution and were not part of Clay's plan. The international slave trade was ended in 1808 (E), before Clay's plan.

83. B

"Scalawag" is a derogatory term applied to southern whites who favored Reconstruction. It is derived from Scottish. White Southerners regarded the Reconstruction governments as a foreign occupying force that restricted their economic and political rights. Slave catchers (A) in the 1850s were called "man-stealers." Federalists (C) did not cooperate with Great Britain although they opposed the War of 1812. Native Americans (D) received very little sympathy from white settlers. Workers who crossed picket lines (E) were dubbed "scabs."

84. C

Both Marti and Aguinaldo were important nationalist leaders. Aguinaldo led forces in the Philippines against United States occupation in 1899 to 1901, while Marti fought against Spanish rule in Cuba in the latter half of the 19th century. Marti did not fight against the United States (A). Both Marti and Aguinaldo were nationalists fighting for independence; they did not support American occupation, nor would they serve as colonial officials for the United States (B). Marti died in 1895, before the Spanish American War, and Aguinaldo was captured by the United States in 1901. Neither signed a treaty with the United States (D). The OAS was not formed until 1948 (E).

85. C

This important decision paved the way for other legislation that set workplace regulations. Owners could no longer claim that what went on in their factories was only their business. The *Northern Securities* decision in 1904 upheld the Sherman Anti-trust Act (A). The Court stuck down state regulation of interstate railway routes (B) in the 1886 *Wabash* decision. Segregation (D) was upheld in the 1896 *Plessy v. Ferguson* decision. Wartime restrictions on speech (E) were upheld in the 1919 *Schenck v. the United States* decision.

86. A

The Emergency Quota Act was an expression of anti-immigrant sentiment and the movement to prevent the teaching of evolution was a fundamentalist Christian attack on science. Other conservative responses included the rise of the KKK and the Red Scare. Many Marxists or Socialists (B) were immigrants themselves who opposed fundamentalism and favored evolution. Liberals (C) opposed immigration restrictions and favored evolution. The Democrats (D) had a base among urban immigrants so all Democrats would not have favored the Emergency Quota Act. The Quota Act and the teaching of evolution were not examples of restrictive Victorian morality (E).

87. C

Neighborhood segregation was an example of *de facto* segregation—segregation caused by custom and economics rather than explicit law. When the civil rights movement moved to the North, it concentrated on *de facto* segregation since it was the primary form of segregation in the North. *De jure* segregation refers to segregation by law. It was common in the South while *de facto* segregation was common throughout the United States. Neighborhoods in the North and South were segregated by race because of the price of homes and the refusal of banks and mortgage brokers to give loans to blacks who wanted to move into "white" neighborhoods. Only the Southern states maintained segregation with "Whites Only" and "Colored Only" signs at lunch counters (A), fitting rooms (B), bus waiting rooms (D), and public water fountains (E).

88. A

In *Gideon*, the Court ruled that free legal counsel be supplied to those who could not afford it. In *Miranda* the Court ruled that suspects must be read their rights at the time of arrest and before questioning. The 24th Amendment struck down poll taxes, which had been an obstacle to African Americans (B) voting in the South. *Engel v. Vitale* in 1963 ruled that school prayer was unconstitutional, thus strengthening the wall between church and state (C). The principle of equal pay for equal work (D) is part of civil rights law but was not established in a Supreme Court case. While the Supreme Court limited speech during World War I (*Schenk v. United States*), it expanded wartime speech (E) during the Vietnam War in the case *Tinker v. Des Moines School District* (1969). This case dealt with wearing armbands in school in protest of the War in Vietnam.

89. D

Jimmy Carter was noted for his emphasis on pressuring despotic regimes to improve their human rights policies. Among many other actions, he criticized the Soviet Union for its treatment of Jews. Teddy Roosevelt promised to "walk softly and carry a big stick" (A) in Latin America. All the presidents from Truman to Reagan vowed to halt communist expansion (B). Détente (C) was Nixon's policy. Carter signed a treaty ending United States control of the Canal Zone (E).

90. C

The Camp David Accords were signed under the administration of Jimmy Carter in 1979. The rest of the choices were achieved during the Clinton Administration. The Brady Bill (A) was signed in 1993. The welfare reform act (B) was signed in 1996. Clinton supported democracy in Haiti (D) in 1994. Clinton arranged the Dayton Peace Accords to end the civil war in Bosnia in 1995 (E).

HOW TO CALCULATE
YOUR SCORE

Step 1: Figure out your raw score. Refer to your answer sheet to determine the number right and the number wrong on the practice test you're scoring. You can use the chart below to figure out your raw score. Multiply the number wrong by 0.25 and subtract the result from the number right. Round the result to the nearest whole number. This is your raw score.

SAT Subject Test: U.S. History Practice Test 3

Number right	Number wrong	Raw score
☐	− (0.25 × ☐)	= ☐

Step 2: Find your practice test score. Find your raw score in the left column of the table below. The score in the right column is an approximation of what your score would be on the SAT Subject Test: U.S. History.

A note on your practice test scores: Don't take these scores too literally. Practice test conditions cannot precisely mirror real test conditions. Your actual SAT Subject Test: U.S. History score will almost certainly vary from your practice test scores. However, your scores on the practice tests will give you a rough idea of your range on the actual exam.

Conversion Table

Raw	Scaled	Raw	Scaled	Raw	Scaled	Raw	Scaled	Raw	Scaled	Raw	Scaled
90	800	72	770	54	680	36	580	18	470	0	350
89	800	71	760	43	670	35	570	17	460	−1	350
88	800	70	760	52	670	34	570	16	460	−2	340
87	800	69	750	51	660	33	560	15	450	−3	340
86	800	68	750	50	660	32	550	14	450	−4	330
85	800	67	740	49	650	31	550	13	440	−5	330
84	800	66	740	48	650	30	540	12	430	−6	320
83	800	65	730	47	640	29	540	11	430	−7	320
82	800	64	730	46	640	28	530	10	420	−8	310
81	800	63	720	45	630	27	520	9	410	−9	310
80	790	62	720	44	630	26	520	8	410	−10	300
79	790	61	710	43	620	25	510	7	400	−11	300
78	790	60	710	42	610	24	510	6	390	−12	290
77	790	59	700	41	610	23	500	5	390	−13	280
76	780	58	700	40	600	22	490	4	380	−14	280
75	780	57	690	39	600	21	490	3	370	−15	270
74	780	56	690	38	590	20	480	2	370	−16	270
73	770	55	680	37	580	19	480	1	360	−17	260

Answer Grid
Practice Test 3

1. Ⓐ Ⓑ Ⓒ Ⓓ Ⓔ
2. Ⓐ Ⓑ Ⓒ Ⓓ Ⓔ
3. Ⓐ Ⓑ Ⓒ Ⓓ Ⓔ
4. Ⓐ Ⓑ Ⓒ Ⓓ Ⓔ
5. Ⓐ Ⓑ Ⓒ Ⓓ Ⓔ
6. Ⓐ Ⓑ Ⓒ Ⓓ Ⓔ
7. Ⓐ Ⓑ Ⓒ Ⓓ Ⓔ
8. Ⓐ Ⓑ Ⓒ Ⓓ Ⓔ
9. Ⓐ Ⓑ Ⓒ Ⓓ Ⓔ
10. Ⓐ Ⓑ Ⓒ Ⓓ Ⓔ
11. Ⓐ Ⓑ Ⓒ Ⓓ Ⓔ
12. Ⓐ Ⓑ Ⓒ Ⓓ Ⓔ
13. Ⓐ Ⓑ Ⓒ Ⓓ Ⓔ
14. Ⓐ Ⓑ Ⓒ Ⓓ Ⓔ
15. Ⓐ Ⓑ Ⓒ Ⓓ Ⓔ
16. Ⓐ Ⓑ Ⓒ Ⓓ Ⓔ
17. Ⓐ Ⓑ Ⓒ Ⓓ Ⓔ
18. Ⓐ Ⓑ Ⓒ Ⓓ Ⓔ
19. Ⓐ Ⓑ Ⓒ Ⓓ Ⓔ
20. Ⓐ Ⓑ Ⓒ Ⓓ Ⓔ
21. Ⓐ Ⓑ Ⓒ Ⓓ Ⓔ
22. Ⓐ Ⓑ Ⓒ Ⓓ Ⓔ
23. Ⓐ Ⓑ Ⓒ Ⓓ Ⓔ
24. Ⓐ Ⓑ Ⓒ Ⓓ Ⓔ
25. Ⓐ Ⓑ Ⓒ Ⓓ Ⓔ
26. Ⓐ Ⓑ Ⓒ Ⓓ Ⓔ
27. Ⓐ Ⓑ Ⓒ Ⓓ Ⓔ
28. Ⓐ Ⓑ Ⓒ Ⓓ Ⓔ
29. Ⓐ Ⓑ Ⓒ Ⓓ Ⓔ
30. Ⓐ Ⓑ Ⓒ Ⓓ Ⓔ

31. Ⓐ Ⓑ Ⓒ Ⓓ Ⓔ
32. Ⓐ Ⓑ Ⓒ Ⓓ Ⓔ
33. Ⓐ Ⓑ Ⓒ Ⓓ Ⓔ
34. Ⓐ Ⓑ Ⓒ Ⓓ Ⓔ
35. Ⓐ Ⓑ Ⓒ Ⓓ Ⓔ
36. Ⓐ Ⓑ Ⓒ Ⓓ Ⓔ
37. Ⓐ Ⓑ Ⓒ Ⓓ Ⓔ
38. Ⓐ Ⓑ Ⓒ Ⓓ Ⓔ
39. Ⓐ Ⓑ Ⓒ Ⓓ Ⓔ
40. Ⓐ Ⓑ Ⓒ Ⓓ Ⓔ
41. Ⓐ Ⓑ Ⓒ Ⓓ Ⓔ
42. Ⓐ Ⓑ Ⓒ Ⓓ Ⓔ
43. Ⓐ Ⓑ Ⓒ Ⓓ Ⓔ
44. Ⓐ Ⓑ Ⓒ Ⓓ Ⓔ
45. Ⓐ Ⓑ Ⓒ Ⓓ Ⓔ
46. Ⓐ Ⓑ Ⓒ Ⓓ Ⓔ
47. Ⓐ Ⓑ Ⓒ Ⓓ Ⓔ
48. Ⓐ Ⓑ Ⓒ Ⓓ Ⓔ
49. Ⓐ Ⓑ Ⓒ Ⓓ Ⓔ
50. Ⓐ Ⓑ Ⓒ Ⓓ Ⓔ
51. Ⓐ Ⓑ Ⓒ Ⓓ Ⓔ
52. Ⓐ Ⓑ Ⓒ Ⓓ Ⓔ
53. Ⓐ Ⓑ Ⓒ Ⓓ Ⓔ
54. Ⓐ Ⓑ Ⓒ Ⓓ Ⓔ
55. Ⓐ Ⓑ Ⓒ Ⓓ Ⓔ
56. Ⓐ Ⓑ Ⓒ Ⓓ Ⓔ
57. Ⓐ Ⓑ Ⓒ Ⓓ Ⓔ
58. Ⓐ Ⓑ Ⓒ Ⓓ Ⓔ
59. Ⓐ Ⓑ Ⓒ Ⓓ Ⓔ
60. Ⓐ Ⓑ Ⓒ Ⓓ Ⓔ

61. Ⓐ Ⓑ Ⓒ Ⓓ Ⓔ
62. Ⓐ Ⓑ Ⓒ Ⓓ Ⓔ
63. Ⓐ Ⓑ Ⓒ Ⓓ Ⓔ
64. Ⓐ Ⓑ Ⓒ Ⓓ Ⓔ
65. Ⓐ Ⓑ Ⓒ Ⓓ Ⓔ
66. Ⓐ Ⓑ Ⓒ Ⓓ Ⓔ
67. Ⓐ Ⓑ Ⓒ Ⓓ Ⓔ
68. Ⓐ Ⓑ Ⓒ Ⓓ Ⓔ
69. Ⓐ Ⓑ Ⓒ Ⓓ Ⓔ
70. Ⓐ Ⓑ Ⓒ Ⓓ Ⓔ
71. Ⓐ Ⓑ Ⓒ Ⓓ Ⓔ
72. Ⓐ Ⓑ Ⓒ Ⓓ Ⓔ
73. Ⓐ Ⓑ Ⓒ Ⓓ Ⓔ
74. Ⓐ Ⓑ Ⓒ Ⓓ Ⓔ
75. Ⓐ Ⓑ Ⓒ Ⓓ Ⓔ
76. Ⓐ Ⓑ Ⓒ Ⓓ Ⓔ
77. Ⓐ Ⓑ Ⓒ Ⓓ Ⓔ
78. Ⓐ Ⓑ Ⓒ Ⓓ Ⓔ
79. Ⓐ Ⓑ Ⓒ Ⓓ Ⓔ
80. Ⓐ Ⓑ Ⓒ Ⓓ Ⓔ
81. Ⓐ Ⓑ Ⓒ Ⓓ Ⓔ
82. Ⓐ Ⓑ Ⓒ Ⓓ Ⓔ
83. Ⓐ Ⓑ Ⓒ Ⓓ Ⓔ
84. Ⓐ Ⓑ Ⓒ Ⓓ Ⓔ
85. Ⓐ Ⓑ Ⓒ Ⓓ Ⓔ
86. Ⓐ Ⓑ Ⓒ Ⓓ Ⓔ
87. Ⓐ Ⓑ Ⓒ Ⓓ Ⓔ
88. Ⓐ Ⓑ Ⓒ Ⓓ Ⓔ
89. Ⓐ Ⓑ Ⓒ Ⓓ Ⓔ
90. Ⓐ Ⓑ Ⓒ Ⓓ Ⓔ

Practice Test 3

1. Roger Williams, the founder of the colony of Rhode Island, supported the idea that

   (A) civil authority should be separated from church authority
   (B) church leaders should be the leaders of the colonies
   (C) the Native American population should be resettled to the West
   (D) the theocracy that existed in Massachusetts Bay should be extended to other colonies
   (E) women should enjoy equal rights with men

2. President Andrew Jackson vetoed the Bank Re-Charter Bill because he

   (A) was a Democrat and it was a Whig measure
   (B) disagreed with the Supreme Court decision in *Marbury v. Madison*
   (C) believed that paper money was the most important element for economic success
   (D) called it a "monster" because it was a monopoly
   (E) believed it was too late to bring up the question

GO ON TO THE NEXT PAGE

3. "The government, Sir is the independent offspring of the popular will. It is not the creature of the state legislatures; nay more, if the whole truth must be told, the people brought it into existence, established it, and have hitherto supported it for the very purpose, amongst others of imposing certain salutary restraints on state sovereignties. . . The people, then, Sir, erected this government. They gave it a constitution, and in the constitution they have enumerated powers which they bestow on it."

From Daniel Webster's "Second Reply to Hayne."

What argument was Daniel Webster responding to in the above passage?

(A) The theory that the people were the source of power in the Constitution.

(B) The theory that the tariff was unconstitutional.

(C) The Compact Theory that the states were sovereign.

(D) The Theory of Perpetual Union that the union existed before the Constitution.

(E) The theory that sovereignty rests in the general government.

4. The Chinese Exclusion Act, passed in 1882, had the effect of

(A) exempting China from participation in the League of Nations

(B) dividing China into "spheres of influence"

(C) banning most Chinese people from immigrating to the United States

(D) establishing the "open door policy" in regard to trade with China

(E) raising tariffs on goods from China

5. The establishment of standard time zones occurred

(A) at the time of the American Revolution to standardize measurements in the new nation

(B) in the 1880s to facilitate scheduling of railroad lines

(C) during World War I to better coordinate the war effort

(D) in the 1920s to allow for the coordination of nationally broadcast radio shows

(E) as part of the New Deal efforts at modernization

6. Among the key components of President Theodore Roosevelt's "Square Deal" program were

(A) a national bank and internal improvements

(B) unemployment insurance and relief for poor families

(C) opposition to U.S. imperialism and autonomy for Latin American nations

(D) regulation of trusts and consumer protection

(E) racial integration in public facilities and voting rights for African Americans

7. Black Tuesday is a significant day in U.S. history because it marks the beginning of

(A) U.S. involvement in World War II in 1941

(B) the Depression of 1929

(C) the atomic age with the bombing of Hiroshima in 1945

(D) World War I in 1914

(E) the great blackout in New York City in 1976

GO ON TO THE NEXT PAGE

8. The increased membership in the NAACP and CORE during World War II resulted from the

   (A) discriminatory job practices against African Americans during World War II

   (B) Black Power movement which had developed after World War I

   (C) establishment of the Fair Employment Practices Commission

   (D) addition of Mexicans and women to the workforce during World War II

   (E) preference for Native American recruits over African American recruits during World War II

9. The main goal of the Marshall Plan was to

   (A) rebuild European economies with a recovery program

   (B) assist the agricultural economies of Latin America

   (C) give aid to those communist nations that agreed to adopt democracy

   (D) provide military aid to South Vietnam

   (E) place Japan under a "nuclear umbrella"

10. Two significant events which occurred during the administration of Ronald Reagan were

   (A) the removal of the Berlin Wall and the break-up of the Soviet Union

   (B) the Camp David Accords and Declaration of Human Rights

   (C) Watergate scandal and the opening to China

   (D) the end of the Iran hostage crisis and the invasion of Grenada

   (E) War on Poverty and the first major escalation of the Vietnam War

11. Which of the following contributed to the economic development of the colonies during the 1600s?

   I. The addition of slavery as a source of labor.

   II. The growth of trade and commerce due to good harbors and an extensive river system.

   III. The British policy of salutary neglect.

   IV. The development of universal manhood suffrage.

   VI. The Great Awakening.

   (A) I, II, III, IV, V

   (B) I, II, and III only

   (C) I, II, and V only

   (D) III, IV, and V only

   (E) I, III, and V only

GO ON TO THE NEXT PAGE

MAP
OF THE FORMER
TERRITORIAL LIMITS
OF THE
CHEROKEE "NATION OF" INDIANS
EXHIBITING THE BOUNDARIES OF THE VARIOUS
CESSIONS
OF LAND MADE BY THEM TO THE
COLONIES AND TO THE UNITED STATES
BY TREATY STIPULATIONS, FROM THE BEGINNING OF THEIR RELATIONS
WITH THE WHITES TO THE DATE OF THEIR REMOVAL
WEST OF THE MISSISSIPPI RIVER.
BY
C. C. ROYCE.

12. What incident is referred to in the map title above?

(A) King Phillip's War
(B) The Pequot War
(C) The disappearance of the buffalo
(D) The protests of Tecumseh
(E) The Trail of Tears

GO ON TO THE NEXT PAGE

13. In the post–Reconstruction South, the economic arrangement known as sharecropping involved

    (A) groups of freed African American laborers working for wages on large plantations

    (B) agricultural workers signing contracts which bound them to a particular plantation for a period of time

    (C) former slaves being granted ownership rights to tracts of land that had previously been owned by slaveholders

    (D) landowners dividing up their land and allowing growers to use plots of land in exchange for a portion of the yearly yield

    (E) the gradual transition from a purely cash-crop agricultural economy to a mixed economy of farming and manufacturing

14. The "Mugwumps" were Republican leaders who left the Republican Party in 1884 and supported the Democratic Party because they were

    (A) angry with the Republican Party for not taking a stand against the spread of Jim Crow policies in the Southern states

    (B) offered cabinet positions if the Democrat Grover Cleveland won the Presidential election

    (C) disappointed with the Republican presidential candidate's history of corruption

    (D) weary of the Republican Party's opposition to immigration

    (E) disgusted with the violence that had been done to the Native Americans of the Great Plains

15. The Social Security Act of 1935 was important in that it

    (A) offered direct relief to eligible unemployed and disabled individuals

    (B) reformed the existing federal unemployment insurance system

    (C) created a new agency to monitor investment in the securities industry

    (D) provided relief for businesses in financial trouble as a result of the Depression

    (E) succeeded in relieving the problems of the banking system

16. All of the following are reasons for the anti-immigrant sentiment that resulted in the quota system of the 1920s EXCEPT

    (A) the demand for unskilled labor in American factories decreased as World War I ended

    (B) many Americans perceived that anarchists and socialists were immigrating from Europe and contributing to social unrest in the United States

    (C) racist ideas that held Jews, Slavs, and Italians as inferior gained credence in the United States

    (D) some Protestants feared that the United States would change for the worse because of the influx of Catholics and Jews

    (E) immigrants often took positions as indentured servant which undermined the earning potential of American wage workers

GO ON TO THE NEXT PAGE

17. As a result of the Proclamation of Neutrality issued by the United States in 1939, the United States

    (A) favored the Axis powers
    (B) established a "cash and carry" system of trade with belligerent nations
    (C) withdrew from the League of Nations
    (D) was criticized by the Allies and Axis powers alike
    (E) joined the European powers in appeasing Germany

18. The immediate cause of U.S. military involvement in the Korean peninsula in 1950 was the

    (A) crossing of the Yalu River by the Chinese "volunteers"
    (B) Japanese invasion of Manchuria
    (C) creation of the DMZ (demilitarized zone) along the 38th parallel
    (D) acquisition of a nuclear weapons by North Korea
    (E) attack by North Korea on South Korea

19. As a result of President Truman's insistence that the Democratic Party include a civil rights plank in its 1948 platform

    (A) substantial numbers of white voters abandoned the Democratic Party, allowing the Republican Party to win the general election that November
    (B) Congress passed the Civil Rights Act and the Voting Rights Act within the next four years
    (C) African American activists, encouraged that civil rights was becoming part of the national debate, founded the National Association for the Advancement of Colored People
    (D) Martin Luther King Jr. was encouraged to organize the March on Washington
    (E) many Southern Democrats, or Dixiecrats, left the Democratic convention and formed the States' Rights Democratic Party

20. The Pentagon Papers contained information on all of the following presidents EXCEPT

    (A) Dwight D. Eisenhower
    (B) Richard Nixon
    (C) Lyndon Johnson
    (D) Jimmy Carter
    (E) John Kennedy

21. Columbus, Magellan, and Balboa were similar in that

    (A) their voyages were all sponsored by the Spanish government
    (B) they sailed across the Pacific Ocean
    (C) they were killed by native inhabitants of North America
    (D) they accumulated great personal wealth as a result of their explorations
    (E) they found an all-water route to the East

GO ON TO THE NEXT PAGE

22. The delegates at the Constitutional Convention agreed that

    (A) Congress would not interfere with the importation of slaves for 20 years

    (B) an import duty could not be placed on slaves brought into the United States

    (C) the government was not permitted to tax imports

    (D) slaves were to be counted as three-fifths of a person for the purposes of representation but not for the purposes of taxation

    (E) slavery was not to be prohibited in any territory acquired by the United States in the future

23. "The manhood of the slave is conceded. It is admitted in the fact that Southern statute books are covered with enactments forbidding, under severe fines and penalties, the teaching of the slave to read or to write."

    —*Frederick Douglass, 1852*

    Why did Douglass point out that there were laws against teaching slaves to read?

    (A) To show that the Southern statute books were unfair

    (B) To show that since only humans can read, slaves were men

    (C) To warn slaves that they were in danger of fines and penalties if they learned to read

    (D) To concede that the Southerners had control of the slaves

    (E) To show that the laws would not be obeyed

24. All of the following are considered factors in the collapse of Reconstruction in the 1870s EXCEPT

    (A) many Northerners simply lost interest in the issues and problems of the South

    (B) a compromise following the disputed election of 1876 committed the Republican Party to withdrawing the last troops from the South

    (C) the South had largely complied with the goals of Reconstruction and the Radical Republicans felt satisfied that fairness and equality would exist in the South

    (D) the Democrats in the South grew increasingly aggressive in asserting their right to run the governments of the Southern states

    (E) many of the leading Radical Republicans, who had guided Congressional Reconstruction, died by the 1870s

25. The Bessemer process, which was important in the industrial growth of the United States in the second half of the 19th century, involved

    (A) using time and motion studies to streamline production and eliminate inefficiencies

    (B) moving a product from worker to worker by a conveyor belt as it is being manufactured

    (C) injecting air into molten iron to remove carbon and produce steel inexpensively

    (D) connecting the various sites of an operation by telegraph wires to facilitate communication

    (E) mass producing interchangeable parts to decrease dependence on skilled craftsmen

GO ON TO THE NEXT PAGE

26. Railroads challenged several of the "Granger laws" in court, claiming that they were unconstitutional. The Supreme Court rejected this claim in *Munn v. Illinois* on the grounds that

    (A) regulating business activities for the public good is a legitimate power of the states

    (B) criticizing corporate activities is protected by the 1st Amendment

    (C) the principle of eminent domain should only be applied if an overriding public need is involved

    (D) railroad companies were not considered "citizens," and only citizens can initiate lawsuits

    (E) contracts between the states and individuals or corporations are binding

GO ON TO THE NEXT PAGE

Percent of Banks that Failed
Annually 1932–1942

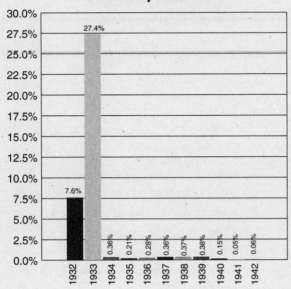

Percent of Farms Foreclosured
Annually 1932–1942

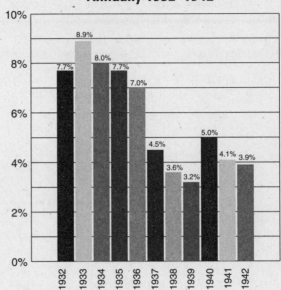

27. The conclusion that can be drawn from these charts concerning the New Deal is that it

   (A) had little effect on the amount of farmers who lost their land as a result of the Great Depression

   (B) helped protect depositors and farmers from the effects of the Great Depression

   (C) failed to prevent bank failures

   (D) had no significant effect on farm foreclosures or bank failures until the outbreak of World War II

   (E) was directly responsible for the establishment of the Federal Reserve System

GO ON TO THE NEXT PAGE

28. All of the following events contributed to Cold War tensions EXCEPT the

    (A) rejection of the Treaty of Versailles by the isolationist Senate
    (B) U.S. airlift of food to the citizens of Berlin
    (C) massive economic support for Western Europe through the Marshall Plan
    (D) united support of the Greek monarchy in 1947
    (E) the establishment of the defensive North Atlantic Treaty Organization

29. Napalm, a focus of anti-war protests during the Vietnam War, was

    (A) an explosive weapon that divided into parts killing many people
    (B) a nerve gas that paralyzed the enemy
    (C) a drug used to interrogate prisoners
    (D) a weapon that burst into flames after adhering to its victim
    (E) a class of biological weapons that caused rare diseases

30. John Coltrane and Miles Davis were innovators in the

    (A) swing music of the 1930s
    (B) folk music of the 1960s
    (C) Chicago blues of the 1950s
    (D) rock 'n' roll of 1950s
    (E) jazz music of the 1950s and 1960s

31. The Neutrality Act of 1793, Jay's Treaty of 1795 and the Convention of 1800 were all similar in that they

    (A) were negotiated during the administration of George Washington
    (B) ended the practice of impressment
    (C) allowed the United States to freely navigate the Mississippi River
    (D) were supported by the people of the United States
    (E) delayed the United States' involvement in a war

GO ON TO THE NEXT PAGE

KAPLAN

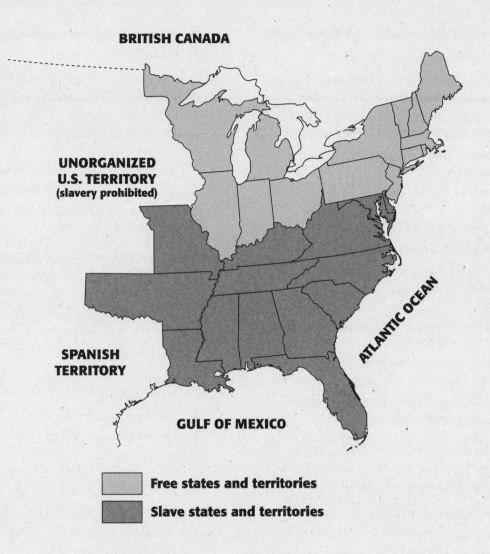

BRITISH CANADA

UNORGANIZED
U.S. TERRITORY
(slavery prohibited)

SPANISH
TERRITORY

ATLANTIC OCEAN

GULF OF MEXICO

Free states and territories

Slave states and territories

32. The map represents the United States
immediately after the

(A) Louisiana Purchase
(B) Civil War
(C) Proclamation of 1763
(D) Northwest Ordinance
(E) Missouri Compromise

GO ON TO THE NEXT PAGE

33. To become an artisan in the 1830s, one had to

    (A) study at a vocational school
    (B) attend two years of university
    (C) attend grammar school for five years
    (D) join a union affiliated with the American Federation of Labor
    (E) become an apprentice to a master craftsman

34. As part of the Compromise of 1850, the Fugitive Slave Law stated that

    (A) all African Americans were slaves
    (B) all African Americans suspected of being slaves should be brought to a trial by jury
    (C) every accused African American had the right to a defense lawyer
    (D) all citizens were responsible for catching fugitive slaves
    (E) each state had to determine whether it would comply with the law

35. The Credit Mobilier scandal of the 1870s and the Teapot Dome of the 1920s are similar in that they both demonstrate the

    (A) lack of government oversight over the savings and loan industry
    (B) cutthroat political competition between the Democrat and Republican Parties which has often resulted in underhanded campaign practices
    (C) prevalence of corrupt municipal political machines in the United States
    (D) tendency of an overzealous press to invent stories in order to sell newspapers
    (E) willingness of politicians to accept bribes from large corporations in exchange for granting these corporations political favors

36. Horizontal integration occurs in business when a company

    (A) acquires ownership or control over other companies in the same business
    (B) controls all aspects of the production and distribution of its product
    (C) creates locally owned franchises
    (D) changes its ownership from a single proprietor to a board of directors
    (E) uses scientific management techniques to increase efficiency

37. The deployment of nuclear missiles to Cuba by the Soviet Union in 1962

    (A) displayed Soviet nuclear superiority over the United States
    (B) prompted a blockade of Cuba by President Kennedy
    (C) enabled Fidel Castro to establish a dictatorship
    (D) helped Kennedy's re-election bid
    (E) caused the Bay of Pigs attack

38. Buddhist monks set themselves on fire in 1963 as a protest against

    (A) French imperialism in Vietnam
    (B) American support for Indonesian President Sukharno
    (C) the puppet Diem regime in South Vietnam
    (D) anti-Buddhist policies of the Communist leader Ho Chi Minh
    (E) the Tet Offensive, because it broke a ceasefire

GO ON TO THE NEXT PAGE

39. Andrew Goodman, Michael Schwerner, and James Chaney were lynched in Mississippi during Freedom Summer when they were attempting to

   (A) secure the admission of African Americans to the state university
   (B) desegregate city buses
   (C) desegregate lunch counters
   (D) integrate highway rest stops
   (E) help African Americans register to vote

40. When President Bill Clinton was tried by the Senate in 1999, it was necessary that

   (A) Hillary Rodham Clinton testify before the Judiciary Committee
   (B) Bill Clinton appear before the Senate
   (C) Chief Justice William Rehnquist preside over the impeachment trial
   (D) Vice President Al Gore temporarily assume the presidency
   (E) Kenneth Starr resign as Independent Counsel

41. A major reason for the founding of the Massachusetts Bay Colony in 1620 was to

   (A) provide freedom of worship for Quakers
   (B) establish profitable businesses
   (C) create a fully democratic government
   (D) provide freedom of worship for Puritans
   (E) establish a colony with complete separation of church and state

42. According to Washington's Farewell Address, United States interests would best served by a foreign policy of

   (A) involvement in world affairs
   (B) support for democratic revolutions
   (C) expansion into South America
   (D) isolation from European affairs
   (E) alliances with nations that support U.S. growth

43. Dred Scott believed that he was entitled to freedom because he lived for a period of time in

   (A) unsettled territory in the West
   (B) Illinois which had been organized under the Northwest Ordinance
   (C) Massachusetts, which had abolished slavery
   (D) Kansas, which was being organized under the policy of popular sovereignty
   (E) Missouri, where he had been born

44. Which of the following statements regarding the Confederate army's firing on Fort Sumter in 1861 is true?

   (A) Abraham Lincoln had previously sent troops to defend the fort
   (B) Jefferson Davis had offered to protect the ship that came to rescue the Union soldiers
   (C) Abraham Lincoln had previously decided to abandon the fort
   (D) Abraham Lincoln had previously sent supplies without extensive military protection
   (E) Jefferson Davis had left the decision to fire upon the fort up to the troops in Charleston, South Carolina

GO ON TO THE NEXT PAGE

45. The films, *Birth of a Nation*, directed by D. W. Griffith, and *Gone with the Wind*, based on a novel by Margaret Mitchell, are similar in that they both

   (A) revolutionized the way silent films were made

   (B) presented the old South in ways sympathetic to the former slaveholding class

   (C) were rejected by the public, but were appreciated by critics for their artistry

   (D) dealt with the tensions and conflicts of the Revolutionary War era

   (E) offered escapism to the poor during the Great Depression

46. The U.S. experiment in Prohibition, which lasted from 1920 to 1933, demonstrated that

   (A) it is difficult for the government to enforce laws that are unpopular with large segments of the public

   (B) granting women the right to vote opened the door to a variety of reforms that were previously unthinkable

   (C) the Republican Party was more in tune with popular sentiments than the Democratic Party

   (D) the power of the federal government can be successfully used to change the public's behavior

   (E) the issue of states' rights versus federal power had not yet been solved

47. Which of the following pairs of laws were enacted as part of President Lyndon Johnson's "Great Society" program?

   (A) The Interstate Highway Act and the National Defense Education Act

   (B) The Smoot-Hawley Tariff Act and the National Origins Act

   (C) The Social Security Act and the Wagner Act

   (D) The Medicare Act and the Equal Opportunity Employment Act

   (E) The Servicemen's Readjustment Act and the Taft-Hartley Act

48. All of the following are part of the Watergate Scandal EXCEPT:

   (A) The publication of the Pentagon Papers by the *New York Times* and the *Washington Post*

   (B) Saturday night massacre in which one Attorney General resigned and another was fired

   (C) Giving money to rebels in Nicaragua

   (D) The revelations of smoking gun tape which provided proof of obstruction of justice

   (E) The payment of hush money to keep conspirators quiet

49. Muhammad Ali was a significant figure in the 1960s, 70s, and 80s for all of the following reasons except

   (A) he refused to serve in the Vietnam War

   (B) he converted to Islam and adopted a Muslim name

   (C) he campaigned for Ronald Reagan in 1980

   (D) he became a symbol for civil rights

   (E) he won a gold medal at the 1960 Olympics

GO ON TO THE NEXT PAGE

50. Which of the following is a true statement in regard to foreign policy during the Clinton Administration?

    (A) The United States continued a policy of isolationism.

    (B) Clinton labeled the Soviet Union the "evil empire" to gain the support of Congressional Republicans.

    (C) Clinton sent more troops in peacetime around the world than any other President.

    (D) Clinton's policies were, by and large, opposed by the American people.

    (E) Clinton distanced the United States from NATO actions.

OGRABME, or, The American Snapping-turtle

51. The cartoonist was most likely portraying discontent over the issue of

(A) Federalist control of the judiciary

(B) state control of interstate commerce

(C) impressment of U.S. seamen by captains of British ships

(D) the Citizen Genet affair

(E) the embargo imposed by Presidents Jefferson and Madison

GO ON TO THE NEXT PAGE

52. Representative David Wilmot of Pennsylvania wrote an amendment to an appropriation bill for the Mexican War in 1846 which stated that, "there shall be no slavery or involuntary servitude in any territory acquired from Mexico." These words represented a key element of the

    (A) gradual abolitionist position of James Tallmadge
    (B) free soil idea of the moderate anti-slavery politicians
    (C) immediate abolitionism of William Lloyd Garrison
    (D) nativist platform of the Know Nothing Party
    (E) popular sovereignty position

53. Stephen Douglas's Freeport Doctrine stated that

    (A) slavery should be excluded from all territories west of the Mississippi River
    (B) the Union cannot survive half slave and half free
    (C) the Union must be preserved at all costs
    (D) liberty is more important than the Union
    (E) slavery can only exist where it has been supported by local law

54. Which of the following statements is true in regard to President Theodore Roosevelt's environmental polices?

    (A) Roosevelt rejected the notion of conservation because he allowed the "good trusts" to develop some areas in national parks for business purposes.
    (B) Roosevelt rejected any attempts at government protection of wilderness areas, arguing instead that market forces should determine land use.
    (C) Roosevelt appointed the pro-business James Watt as Secretary of the Interior, angering many environmentalists such as John Muir.
    (D) Roosevelt worked closely with the head of the U.S. Forest Service, Gifford Pinchot, to set aside land for national parks, national monuments and wildlife refuges.
    (E) While Roosevelt was an avid outdoorsman, he believed that any action on behalf of the environment should be taken at the state level.

55. *The Grapes of Wrath*, John Steinbeck's depression-era novel, chronicles the lives of

    (A) Mexican migrant farm workers
    (B) displaced Dust Bowl farmers
    (C) Southern sharecroppers
    (D) coal miners from West Virginia
    (E) unemployed autoworkers from Michigan

56. President Franklin D. Roosevelt's actions were noteworthy because he

    (A) simplified the operations of the federal government

    (B) implemented a sweeping civil rights program

    (C) extended the direct influence of the government into the lives of the people

    (D) succeeded in being elected five times to the presidency

    (E) successfully concluded World War II

57. Which of the following statements about the 1947 Taft-Hartley Act, passed by Congress over President Truman's veto, is true?

    (A) It was welcomed by the suburban developers because it earmarked large sums of money for highway construction.

    (B) It was labeled the "Magna Carta for organized labor" by AFL-CIO head George Meany because it made it legal for workers to organize unions.

    (C) It was condemned by unions because it barred closed shops and allowed the president to call an 80-day "cooling off" period before a strike could proceed.

    (D) It was supported by veterans groups because it provided aid to soldiers returning from World War II for college education and home ownership.

    (E) It was supported by the National Association for the Advancement of Colored People because it required the federal government to end racial discrimination in defense industries.

58. The Mississippi Freedom Democratic Party was formed in

    (A) 1912, to support the Progressive candidacy of Theodore Roosevelt

    (B) 1948, to support President Truman's civil rights initiatives

    (C) 1962, to support prayer in public schools

    (D) 1964, to support African American representation at the Democratic convention

    (E) 1968, to support the presidential bid of Governor George Wallace

59. Why did the Vietnamese build hundreds of miles of tunnels?

    (A) to hide from the French soldiers

    (B) to hide from the American soldiers

    (C) to prepare for military operations

    (D) to live in for months at a time

    (E) all of the above

60. The "Contract with America," put forward by Congressional Republicans in 1994, included proposals to

    (A) decrease income taxes and force welfare recipients to find work

    (B) decrease military spending and increase the education budget

    (C) protect the rights of homosexuals in the military and create a "single payer" healthcare system

    (D) reinforce the separation of church and state and reform the campaign finance system

    (E) make English the national language and eliminate bilingual education

GO ON TO THE NEXT PAGE

61. Mercantilist policies contributed to the desire of the American colonies to become independent from Britain for all of the following reasons EXCEPT

    (A) they restricted the colonies' trade with French, Dutch, and Spanish colonies in America

    (B) they restricted colonial production

    (C) they involved the exercise of British authority over the colonies

    (D) they restricted trade between the different British colonies in America

    (E) they required that colonial goods go through British ports on their way to other countries

62. The Hartford Convention of 1814 was important because it

    (A) was held by disgruntled Republicans unhappy with the War of 1812

    (B) led to the death of the Federalist Party

    (C) was supported by the South and West

    (D) led to the prominence of Henry Clay

    (E) changed the Constitution by engineering the passage of several amendments to increase the power of the state governments

63. In 1860, the Democratic Party split into two parts over

    (A) the admission of California as a free state

    (B) the Missouri question which decided fate of the Louisiana Territory

    (C) national slave codes which called for all states to have slavery

    (D) internal improvements which called for the building of the transcontinental railroad

    (E) the Second Bank of the United States leading many Democrats to join the Whig Party

64. The Civil War has been called the "Second American Revolution" because

    (A) it made the United States totally independent of Great Britain which, for the first time, accepted its former colony's political and economic independence

    (B) it eliminated the old economic system of slavery and set the country on the road to rapid and unhindered economic growth

    (C) the methods of fighting were directly inherited from the war for independence

    (D) Abraham Lincoln has been called the second George Washington because of his statesmanship and his military leadership

    (E) the problems of race, the fundamental contradiction in American society, were solved

65. The Interstate Commerce Act of 1887 and the National Industrial Recovery Act of 1933 are similar in that they both

    (A) were struck down by the Supreme Court

    (B) put into practice the theory of laissez-faire

    (C) were aimed at limiting the power of the railroad companies

    (D) extended the power of the government into the regulation of business

    (E) recognized the right of workers to form unions

66. Which of the following statements is true in regard to the role of the progressive movement in electoral politics?

    (A) It refused to work with either of the major political parties, labeling them the "parties of big business."

    (B) Reform-minded politicians in both the Democratic and the Republican Parties worked on progressive issues.

    (C) Progressives worked exclusively within the Republican Party, perceiving that the Democratic Party was controlled by special interests.

    (D) Progressive activists worked for the defeat of the Bull Moose Party in the 1912 election and worked to support the reelection of President Taft.

    (E) Progressives generally ignored the electoral arena, arguing that no meaningful change could come through the electoral politics.

67. The most significant change in voting patterns in the 1930s was the

    (A) decrease in the percentage of women who voted

    (B) shift among African American voters from the Republican to the Democratic Party

    (C) large percentage of voters attended by the Communist Party in presidential elections

    (D) overall decrease in the number of people who voted at all

    (E) large number of recent immigrants who registered with the Republican Party

68. The End Poverty in California campaign and the Share the Wealth Society, could best be described as

    (A) campaigns that argued the New Deal did not go far enough

    (B) local programs under the auspices of the New Deal

    (C) labor organizations formed by the Communist Party

    (D) conservative attacks on the "dictatorial" New Deal

    (E) women's organization that thought male dominated organizations did not understand the realities of poverty

69. William H. Whyte's 1956 book *The Organization Man* and Sloan Wilson's 1955 book *The Man in the Grey Flannel Suit* are similar in that they both

    (A) analyzed the growing sense of conformity and the loss of individualism in American society

    (B) were held up as examples of "subversive" literature by the House Un-American Activities Committee

    (C) called attention to the fact that the Soviet Union was outpacing the United States in economic output

    (D) were influential in reshaping standard curricula at American business administration programs

    (E) criticized the "beatnik" ethic of laziness, indulgence and promiscuity

GO ON TO THE NEXT PAGE

70. The Saturday Night Massacre was important in that it

    (A) exposed the role of the Ku Klux Klan as mortal enemies of the Civil Rights Movement

    (B) showed that the CIA had cooperated with the South Vietnamese to assassinate a head of state

    (C) led to the indictment of Lieutenant William Calley in connection to the killing of unarmed civilians in Vietnam

    (D) created a backlash against the insanity defense when John Hinckley was declared innocent of the attempted assassination of President Reagan

    (E) set the stage for the downfall of President Nixon

71. One of the main reasons for the writing of the Declaration of Independence was

    (A) to establish a new political philosophy

    (B) to state an existing political philosophy

    (C) to allow the colonies to obtain new lands

    (D) to gain support for the Revolution among the colonists

    (E) establish human rights

72. The Northwest Ordinance of 1787 was significant for all of the following reasons EXCEPT that it

    (A) provided for freedom of religion in the Northwest Territory

    (B) established militias for protection against the French

    (C) prohibited slavery in the Northwest Territory

    (D) encouraged the fair treatment of Native Americans

    (E) provided for the orderly settlement of the Northwest Territory

73. Which idea is most consistent with the political philosophy of Alexander Hamilton?

    (A) There should be rotation of people who hold public office.

    (B) The Constitution should be loosely interpreted.

    (C) The people can be trusted to make the right decisions if given the proper information.

    (D) All people have a right to be educated.

    (E) The states should have more power than the central government.

74. When Lincoln said "Four score and seven years ago. . .," he was reminding his audience of the

    (A) inauguration of George Washington

    (B) convening of the Constitutional Convention

    (C) writing of the Mayflower Compact

    (D) signing of the Declaration of Independence

    (E) landing at Jamestown

75. The platform of the People's (Populist) Party, ratified at its founding convention in Omaha, Nebraska in 1892, consisted of all the following demands EXCEPT

    (A) a graduated income tax

    (B) an increase in the supply of money

    (C) the eight-hour day for workers

    (D) government ownership of railroads

    (E) an end to immigration restrictions

GO ON TO THE NEXT PAGE

76. Montgomery Ward and Richard Sears both played a significant role in the history of American commerce in the 19th century by

    (A) starting chains of "five and dime" stores carrying a large variety of items

    (B) creating "lay away" plans where customers would pay a only portion of the list price upfront

    (C) creating mail order catalogs, allowing rural people to purchase a wide assortment of goods

    (D) selling mass produced items made in the Untied States instead of hand crafted items made in England

    (E) adding refrigeration to their grocery stores, allowing them to feature a variety of fresh food

77. President Theodore Roosevelt's foreign policy initiatives included all of the following EXCEPT

    (A) securing the Hay-Bunau-Varilla Treaty with Panama to build a canal through Panama

    (B) brokering a peace treaty between Russia and Japan

    (C) establishing a corollary to the Monroe Doctrine asserting the United States' right to intervene in Latin American affairs

    (D) popularizing the expression "speak softly but carry a big stick" is regard to dealing with foreign nations

    (E) negotiating a treaty with Spain following the Spanish-American War

78. President Woodrow Wilson's actions during the debate in the U.S. Senate over the ratification of the Treaty of Versailles demonstrated his

    (A) desire to compromise with Congress

    (B) all or nothing attitude in regard to acceptance of the League of Nations

    (C) dislike for the actions of the Allied nations

    (D) desire to implement an isolationist policy

    (E) unwillingness to accept loss of control over the military actions

79. U.S. foreign policy with regard to the conflicts in the Middle East since the 1960s has been an influenced by the desire to balance the

    (A) independence of Israel with the need for oil from the Arab states

    (B) rights of the Palestinians with the support for Libya

    (C) interests of Muslims and Hindus

    (D) expansionist policies of the Soviet Union and to preserve the territorial integrity of the Palestinian state

    (E) preservation of human rights with maintaining free trade

80. When many savings and loan banks in the 1980s failed, the federal government

    (A) forced the bank owners to pay the depositors their proper shares

    (B) allowed the market to take its natural course

    (C) allowed Federal Deposit Insurance Corporation to reimburse the depositors

    (D) used tax money to bail out the banks

    (E) reorganized the banking industry by passing the Glass-Steagall Act

GO ON TO THE NEXT PAGE

81. Which of the following statements regarding the American Revolution is true?

    (A) Benjamin Franklin led protests against the British in New York.

    (B) Thomas Paine established the Committees of Correspondence to disseminate information during the Revolutionary War.

    (C) John Adams defended the British Soldiers involved in the Boston Massacre.

    (D) Crispus Attucks was killed at Bunker (Breed's) Hill.

    (E) Patrick Henry was hung by the British for protesting the Tea Tax.

82. Shays's Rebellion was important in that it

    (A) highlighted the slave problems that existed in the United States in 1787

    (B) was crushed by a militia sent by the Congress under the Articles of Confederation

    (C) was a catalyst which led to the scrapping of the Articles of Confederation

    (D) led to the adoption of the Bill of Rights

    (E) was the "shot heard round the world"

83. During the John Adams administration, the Virginia and Kentucky Resolutions

    (A) introduced the idea of nullification

    (B) resolved the conflict over the Alien and Sedition Acts

    (C) were supported by the Federalists

    (D) were written by James Madison and Alexander Hamilton

    (E) were declared unconstitutional by the Supreme Court

84. In the Emancipation Proclamation, Abraham Lincoln stated that all

    (A) slaves in the states in rebellion would be freed

    (B) slaves in the border states would be freed

    (C) slaves in the United States would be free at the end of the Civil War

    (D) children born to slaves would be born free

    (E) slaves in the North would be freed

85. All of the following books could be used to justify the prevailing economic conditions in Gilded Age America except

    (A) *Risen From the Ranks* (1874) by Horatio Alger

    (B) *What Social Classes Owe to Each Other* (1883) by William Graham Sumner

    (C) *Looking Backward: 2000–1887* (1888) by Edward Bellamy

    (D) *The Wealth of Nations* (1776) by Adam Smith

    (E) *The Gospel of Wealth* (1889) by Andrew Carnegie

86. Josiah Strong and Alfred T. Mahan were American writers in the late 19th century who were noted for

    (A) opposing Jim Crow laws and lynching

    (B) exposing urban corruption

    (C) depicting regional customs and dialects

    (D) supporting an imperialist foreign policy

    (E) describing the horrors of war

87. Although the Progressive movement consisted of a diversity of interests, a common belief held by most progressives was that

    (A) the federal government should nationalize banks and major industries

    (B) state governments should take steps to overturn Jim Crow laws and to stop lynching incidents

    (C) higher tariffs should be implemented to protect U.S. businesses and preserve jobs for Americans

    (D) the role of the government should be expanded to address social and economic problems

    (E) women should honor the middle class ideals of the "cult of domesticity"

88. Which of the following is true of the 1935 Works Progress Administration?

    (A) It was struck down by the Supreme Court on the grounds that it gave legislative power to the executive branch.

    (B) It oversaw the building of massive hydroelectric plants along the Tennessee River that brought electricity to many parts of the rural South.

    (C) It established legal protections for workers organizing unions and listed unfair labor practices that employers could not use.

    (D) It rapidly created jobs in fields as varied as airport construction and mural painting.

    (E) It provided emergency assistance to banks, railroad companies, life insurance companies and other large businesses.

89. A fundamental cause of urban riots that broke out in many cities during the Lyndon Johnson administration was

    (A) the rising expectations of African Americans for an improved quality of life

    (B) despair of the poor and minorities over the draft for Vietnam

    (C) frustration of African Americans over the slow pace of change in the South regarding segregation

    (D) anger over the inability of the African Americans in the North to vote

    (E) growing feeling among African Americans that affirmative action would never be implemented

90. All of the following are challenges being faced by the United States in the 21st century EXCEPT

    (A) the danger to the Social Security system because of the graying of America

    (B) the search for a cure for AIDS

    (C) the existence of *de jure* segregation in the South

    (D) the high costs of healthcare

    (E) the lack of sufficient energy resources

STOP!

If you finish before time is up, you may check your work.

**Turn the page
for answers and explanations
to Practice Test 3.**

Answer Key
Practice Test 3

1. A	31. E	61. D
2. D	32. E	62. B
3. C	33. E	63. C
4. C	34. D	64. B
5. B	35. E	65. D
6. D	36. A	66. B
7. B	37. B	67. B
8. A	38. C	68. A
9. A	39. E	69. A
10. D	40. C	70. E
11. B	41. D	71. D
12. E	42. D	72. B
13. D	43. B	73. B
14. C	44. D	74. D
15. A	45. B	75. E
16. E	46. A	76. C
17. B	47. D	77. E
18. E	48. C	78. B
19. E	49. C	79. A
20. D	50. C	80. D
21. A	51. E	81. C
22. A	52. B	82. C
23. B	53. E	83. A
24. C	54. D	84. A
25. C	55. B	85. C
26. A	56. C	86. D
27. B	57. C	87. D
28. A	58. D	88. D
29. D	59. E	89. A
30. E	60. A	90. C

ANSWERS AND EXPLANATIONS

1.   A

Roger Williams founded the colony of Rhode Island in 1636 after he was banished from the Massachusetts Bay colony for criticizing the theocracy (church-state) that existed there. He believed in the separation of church and state. Williams did not believe that only church leaders (B) should govern the colonies; he did believe that the Native American population (C) should be treated fairly. Resettlement of the Native Americans to the west was an action taken by Andrew Jackson in the 1830s. Roger Williams did not support the theocracy in Massachusetts Bay (D) and did not wish to see that form of government extended to the other colonies. Equality for women (E) is more closely associated with Anne Hutchinson.

2.   D

Jackson, in his veto message, claimed to represent the poor and powerless and he portrayed the bank as a monster that deprived the working men and farmers of opportunities. It was not a Whig measure (A) because the Whigs came into existence as a result of the veto. The Supreme Court decision (B) that declared the Bank constitutional was *McCulloch v. Maryland*, not *Marbury v. Madison*, which established judicial review. Paper money (C) was an important element of the bank's transactions and Jackson distrusted it. The future Whigs, Daniel Webster and Henry Clay, purposely brought the re-charter up early (E) as a way to defeat Jackson in the 1832 presidential election.

3.   C

The passage is a response to the compact theory, which contended that the states had made the Constitution. Webster explained that the people were sovereign, not the states. "It is not the creature (creation) of the state legislatures." The theory that the people (A) were the source of power in the Constitution was Webster's theory, not Hayne's. Hayne maintained that the tariff was unfair to South Carolina and was unconstitutional (B), but that was not Webster's target in the quote. The

tariff is not mentioned in the quote. The theory of Perpetual Union (D) was Lincoln's theory from his First Inaugural in 1861; it was not Webster's theory. The theory that sovereignty rests in the general (federal) government (E)—that the government is more important than the people—is not a democratic idea.

4.   C

The Chinese Exclusion Act banned immigration of Chinese people to the United States, with the exception of students, teachers, merchants, and government officials. The League of Nations (A) was not founded until 1919, following World War I. In the last decades of the 19th century, European nations established "spheres of influence" in China with exclusive trading privileges (B). These spheres of influence were successfully challenged by the U.S. initiative to create an "open door" policy (D) of free trade in China at the turn of the 20th century. However, the Chinese Exclusion Act had nothing to do with either trade or tariffs (E).

5.   B

Standard time zones were created in 1883. Railroads were frustrated in trying to maintain schedules of train services when each city had a slightly different time. So the railroad companies pressured the government to create standard time zones. At the time, many were alarmed that the railroads were so powerful that they could actually have the "time" changed. Standard time could not have been an issue in 1776 (A), an era before rapid transportation or communication. The other choices, (C), (D), and (E), occurred in the 20th century, well after the creation of "railroad time."

6.   D

Theodore Roosevelt's domestic agenda was known as the "Square Deal." His domestic accomplishments include challenging "bad" trusts using the Sherman Anti-trust Act, strengthening the Interstate Commerce Commission with the Elkins Act (1903) and the Hepburn Act (1906), and setting aside millions of acres for conservation.

A national bank and internal improvement (A) were part of Henry Clay's American System. Poverty relief and unemployment insurance (B) were part of Franklin D. Roosevelt's "New Deal." Theodore Roosevelt was an enthusiastic expansionist (C). Progressives, such as Roosevelt, generally ignored issues of racial discrimination (E). African American voting rights were not addressed until after World War II.

7. B

Black Tuesday refers to October 29, 1929, when the stock market crashed signaling the beginning of the Great Depression. Japan bombed Pearl Harbor on December 7, 1941, "the day that will live in infamy," which forced the United States into World War II (A). The other days have no catch phrases associated with them.

8. A

There was a great deal of discrimination against African Americans for jobs during World War II. The National Association of the Advancement of Colored People (NAACP) and the Congress of Racial Equality (CORE) gained membership in an attempt to stem these discriminatory practices. NAACP and CORE were civil rights organizations not part of the Black Power movement (B), which began in 1965. The Fair Employment Practices Commission (C) was set up by Franklin D. Roosevelt to monitor discriminatory practices in employment it was not the cause of increased protest. The addition of Mexicans and women (D) to the workforce in World War II did not account for the rise in membership in CORE or the NAACP, which were African American organizations. The army showed no preference for Native American recruits over African American recruits (E) during World War II.

9. A

The Marshall Plan of 1947 focused on rebuilding the war torn economies of Western Europe; it was not restricted to democratic countries (C). The Marshall Plan did not include aid to Latin America (B), although the it gradually evolved into a global

U.S. foreign aid program. Aid to Latin America was emphasized in the Kennedy administration, which initiated the Alliance for Progress (1961), a foreign aid program focused on Latin America. The Eastern bloc countries were offered Marshall Plan aid, but refused it. The Marshall Plan was introduced seven years before the creation of South Vietnam (D). The United States offered protection to Japan (E) as a result of the Mutual Defense Treaty of 1952.

10. D

Ronald Reagan served as president from 1981 to 1989. The hostages were released from the American embassy in Iran on the day Reagan took office. The invasion of Grenada occurred in 1983. The fall of the Berlin Wall and the break-up of the Soviet Union (A) occurred during the George H. W. Bush administration. The Camp David Accords and Declaration of Human Rights (B) were signed during the Jimmy Carter administration. Watergate scandal and the opening to China (C) occurred during the administration of Richard Nixon. The War on Poverty and the escalation of the Vietnam War (E) occurred during the administration of Lyndon Johnson.

11. B

Slavery, the irregular coastline of eastern North America, and the British policy of salutary neglect (noninvolvement in colonial affairs prior to the French and Indian War) all led to the economic growth of the colonies. Universal manhood suffrage did not exist in the colonies (IV) and the Great Awakening (V) took place in the 1740s.

12. E

The Trail of Tears was the forced trek of the southeastern Indians, most famously the Cherokee, to the Indian Territory (Oklahoma) west of the Mississippi River. King Phillip's War (A) was the attack of the Wampanoags and Narragansett Indians on Massachusetts and Rhode Island settlement in 1675 and 1676. The Pequot War (B) was the massacre of the Pequot Indians after they attacked the Massachusetts colonists in 1637. The buffalo (C) were slaughtered by the whites as the railroads were built in the Great Plains in the 1870s, and Tecumseh (D) was the visionary Indian leader who united the Old Northwest tribes behind the Shawnee to eliminate whites once and for all. He was defeated by William Henry Harrison at Tippecanoe in 1811 and then at the Battle of the Thames in 1813 during the War of 1812.

13. D

Sharecropping was an economic arrangement that developed in the South during and after Reconstruction. Sharecroppers worked a small plot of the plantation owner's land in return for a share of the crop. Generally, sharecroppers were in perpetual debt to the landowner. African Americans tried to avoid working in "gangs" for wages on large plantations (A). The practice, in many ways, recreated the power relations of the slavery era. The signing of labor contracts (B) is associated with indentured servitude, a practice that had ended by 1800. Many freedmen and women urged the federal government to redistribute land (C) and grant ex-slaves "40 acres and a mule," but this never became a reality. Manufacturing (E) did not gain a substantial foothold in the South in the 19th century.

14. C

The "Mugwumps" were reformers in the Republican Party, who believed in good government. They were disappointed that the party had nominated James Blaine, who had accepted stocks from railroad executives in exchange for political favors when he was Speaker of the House. The "Mugwumps" decided to support the Democratic candidate in 1884, Grover Cleveland. Some Americans were disappointed that the Republicans had abandoned African Americans in the South (A), but this was not a "Mugwump" issue. "Mugwumps" did not receive, nor apparently had they been offered, cabinet positions (C) in the Cleveland administration. The Republicans tended to be more anti-immigrant in the late 19th century,

but the "Mugwumps" didn't seem to mind. Few people or groups opposed U.S. policies in regard to Native Americans in the late 1800s (E); the "Mugwumps" did not address this issue.

15. A

The Social Security Act of 1935 gave direct relief to those unable to work for a variety of reasons. Federal unemployment insurance (B) was part of the Social Security Act and did not exist before this time. The Securities and Exchange Commission (SEC) was established in 1934 to monitor investments in various securities (C). Social Security was not designed to give aid to businesses in trouble as a result of the Depression (D). The issue of banking was addressed by the Glass-Steagall Act of 1933.

16. E

Indentured servitude had ended by the middle of the 19th century. Immigrants competed for jobs with American born workers. Unskilled workers (A) did have a higher rate of unemployment than skilled workers after World War I. Many immigrants were, in fact, socialists and anarchists (B). Nativists, who generally were white Protestants of northern European heritage, believed that Italians, Slavs, Catholics in general, and Jews, (C and D) were inferior peoples who would dilute the northern European character of American culture.

17. B

The Proclamation of Neutrality established a cash-and-carry system that deemed that any nation who wished goods from the United States would have to pay cash and carry the goods on their own ships. Because of the geographical location of the Allied nations, this Proclamations of Neutrality favored England and France and not Germany and the Axis powers (A). The United States had never been a member of the League of Nations (C). The Allies supported this U.S. action (D). The United States was not trying to satisfy the Axis powers by a policy of appeasement (E).

18. E

The Korean War erupted in June, 1950 when South Korea was attacked by North Korea while Harry Truman was President. The Chinese "volunteers" (A) crossed the Yalu River in October, 1951. Japan invaded Manchuria in 1931 (B). The DMZ (C) was created as part of the truce in July, 1953. The North Korean acquisition of nuclear weapons (D) did not occur in the 1950s.

19. E

Southern Democrats, or Dixiecrats, became unhappy with the party's steps toward challenging the Jim Crow system of segregation in the South, though these steps were minor. They left the party's convention in 1948 and formed the pro-segregation States' Rights Democratic Party, which nominated Strom Thurmond for president. The Republican Dewey lost the general election to the incumbent Truman (A). The Civil Rights Act and the Voting Rights Act (B) were passed during the Johnson administration in 1964 and 1965 respectively. The NAACP (C) had formed earlier—in 1909. The March on Washington (E) did not occur until 1963, 15 years after the 1948 convention.

20. D

The Pentagon Papers were a history of Vietnam and the American involvement in Vietnam. Jimmy Carter was president after the pull out of troops from Vietnam and after the Pentagon Papers were published. Eisenhower (A) and Kennedy (E) sent 3,000 and 13,000 "advisors" to Vietnam respectively. The greatest U.S. involvement in the war was during the Nixon (B) and Johnson (C) administrations.

21. A

Columbus was credited with finding the New World. Magellan circumnavigated the globe and Balboa discovered the Pacific Ocean—all for the Spanish crown. None found an all water route to the East (E). Columbus died poor (D) and Magellan was killed in a rebellion in natives in the Philippines, not by Native American (C). Balboa and Magellan both sailed to the Pacific Ocean; Columbus did not (B).

22. A

The Slave Trade Compromise allowed the possibility for Congress to end the international slave trade after 1808. Slavery was the most volatile issue at the Constitutional Convention in 1787. An import tax (B) of $10 for every slave brought into the country could be established. At the Constitutional Convention it was also agreed that the government could tax imports (C). The Three-Fifths Compromise provided that five slaves would be counted as three white men for the purposes of taxation *and* representation (D). The prohibition of slavery in newly acquired territories (E) was the language used in the Northwest Ordinance and the Wilmot Proviso which were not part of the Constitution.

23. B

The topic of the quote is whether the slave is a man. Douglass says that the existence of the laws prohibiting slaves from reading proves his point. Since laws were passed to make sure slaves could not learn to read or write, it was clear that slaves were intelligent beings, not inherently inferior to whites. He was not showing that the statute books were unfair (A), he was using the unfair laws to prove his point. He was not warning slaves (C) since the laws were directed at whites and slaves could not, by and large, pay fines. These literacy laws were not the major form of control (D) that white Southerners had over slaves. Obeying the laws (E) was not the sense of the quote. He wasn't calling for opposition to *those* laws. He was calling for an end to the laws supporting slavery itself.

24. C

By 1877, the year the U.S. government officially ended Reconstruction, the South was not in any way complying with the goals of the Republican Party. The so-called "redeemers," the coalition of southern white elites which took power after Reconstruction, immediately set out to deny African Americans the vote—first by intimidation and fraud and then by legal maneuvers. This marked the beginning of a system of white supremacy that lasted well into the 20th century. The disputed election of 1876 (B) marked the end of Reconstruction. In a compromise arrived at just before the inauguration in 1877, the Democrats agreed to drop their challenge of the election and accept the Republican Rutherford B. Hays as president if the Republicans agreed to withdraw the last federal troops from the South. But signs of Reconstruction's eventual demise had been evident for several years. Republican politicians perceived that northern voters were tired of the "southern question" (A). Aggressive Democrats (D) had already asserted their power in several Southern states well before the compromise of 1877. By 1875, Thaddeus Stevens, Salmon Chase, and Charles Sumner had all died (E).

25. C

The Bessemer process greatly reduced the cost of producing steel. Steel, which is lighter and stronger than iron, became an important material as America industrialized. It was used extensively in rails, bridges and skyscrapers. Time and motion studies (A) are associated with Frederick Winslow Taylor and his push for scientific management. The conveyor belt (B) is associated with Henry Ford and the mass production of the automobile. After Samuel F. B. Morse developed the telegraph, its usefulness in the production process (D) became evident to a variety of large producers, but this was not related to the Bessemer process. Interchangeable parts (E) were first used by Eli Whitney in the production of muskets at the end of the 18th century.

26. A

The *Munn* decision of 1877 held that the state of Illinois was within its constitutional rights to regulate rates for storing grain in warehouses. More broadly, it upheld the power of the states to regulate private property when it is used in the public interest. The 1st Amendment was not relevant to the decision, and its protection (B) has always extended to criticism of corporate activities. Railroads used eminent domain to obtain property to build railroads (C), but this was

not the subject of the *Munn* case. Because corporations were considered citizens in legal terms (D), they did have the right to sue. The *Munn* decision did not deal with contracts (E).

27. B

The charts show the decrease in the number of bank failures and foreclosures during the course of the New Deal. The New Deal protected both depositors and farmers from the ill effects of the Depression. The chart shows the decrease in foreclosures on farms (A) from 1932 to 1939 with only a slight increase in 1941 and subsequent declines in 1941 and 1942. Bank failures dropped (C) from 7.6% in 1932 to 0.06% in 1942. The United States entered World War II in 1941 but bank failures and foreclosures had decreased (D) prior to the outbreak of the war. The Federal Reserve System (E) was established in 1913 under the Wilson Administration well before this time period, although its powers were expanded during the Great Depression. The Federal Deposit Insurance Corporation was established in 1933 under the Glass-Steagall Banking Reform Act to protect depositors' money.

28. A

The debate over the Treaty of Versailles occurred after World War I, nearly 30 years before the beginning of the Cold War. All of the other choices were significant events contributing to Cold War tensions. The Berlin Airlift (B) in 1948 was a response by the United States to the Soviet blockade of West Berlin. The Soviet Union considered the Marshall Plan (C) a plot against their economic system. The Truman Doctrine (D) and NATO (E) were policies of the United States designed to stem the spread of communism.

29. D

Napalm was a jellylike substance that stuck to its targets and then burst into flame. It was an especially horrifying aspect of the American attempt to terrorize the Vietnamese. It was not a fragmenting bullet (A), nerve gas (B) or a biological weapon (E). Napalm was not used to interrogate prisoners (D).

30. E

John Coltrane and Miles Davis were key figures in the movement toward free jazz improvisation in the 1950s and 1960s. The Swing Era (A) was during the 1930s and 40s. Folk music (B) of the 1960s tried to remain separate from jazz. The Chicago blues (C) of the 1950s influenced jazz, but not so much the other way around. The rock 'n' roll of the 1950s (D) was highly influenced by blues not jazz.

31. E

Both Washington and Adams realized the folly of United States involvement in the European conflicts of the 1790s. These agreements bought time for the United States to unify and grow. The Convention of 1800 (A) was negotiated in the Adams administration. The issue of impressment (B) was not addressed in any of these agreements. The Convention of 1800 (C) ended the undeclared war with France and eliminated the treaty of friendship of 1778. Neither Jay's Treaty nor the Convention of 1800 (D) was popular.

32. E

This map depicts the agreement reached in the Missouri Compromise of 1820. The demarcation line of 36°30' is clear on the map. The Northwest Territory (D) had already been incorporated into states, as this map shows. The Oregon Territory is not represented (B) and neither is the area of the Mexican Cession (D) or the Rocky Mountains (E).

33. E

To become an artisan one had to go through an apprenticeship with a master craftsman. Artisans included shoemakers, blacksmiths and tailors. The apprentice system was inherited from medieval times; vocational schools (A) or academic universities (B) were not part of the training. The American Federation of Labor (D), born in 1886, consisted of unions of craft workers employed in industrial settings.

34. D

The Fugitive Slave Law required that every citizen become a slave-catcher. It provoked street fights in the North between those willing to protect the accused and those who cooperated with the slaveholders. All African Americans (A) were not slaves in 1850, although many free people of color were accused of being fugitives. The law provided for neither trial by jury (B) nor defense counsel (C). As a federal law, it required compliance (E) by all the states.

35. E

The Credit Mobilier scandal involved illegal profiteering in the construction of western railroads and the Teapot Dome scandal involved the misuse of oil rich government land. In both cases, politicians accepted large amounts of money to remain silent. The Credit Mobilier occurred during the Grant administration, while the Teapot Dome scandal occurred during the Harding administration. Both administrations are associated with corruption. Troubles in the savings and loan industry (A) began after deregulation in the early 1980s. Many savings and loan companies made questionable investments, leading to over 600 savings and loans going out of business. As of 2002, the government was still bailing out the industry, the cost of which has topped $400 billion. Both scandals were more about money than politics (B). The Watergate scandal of the 1970s involved political competition. Municipal corruption (C) is usually linked with "Boss" William Marcy Tweed and Tammany Hall, the headquarters of the New York City Democratic Party. In the 1870s, Tammany Hall's pattern of corruption, kickbacks and fraud became front page news. Tweed himself died in jail in 1878. As scandals first unfold, the perpetrators of wrongdoing often try to shift the blame to an overzealous press (D), out to increase circulation.

36. A

Horizontal integration involves a company gaining control over a particular industry by acquiring competing companies or entering into a trust agreement. Successful horizontal integration can be a monopoly. The control of all aspects of production and distribution of a product (B) is called vertical integration. Franchises (C) are associated with post–World War II businesses, such as McDonald's. Many corporations in the Gilded Age changed from single proprietorships to corporations which had boards of directors (D) but this is not a horizontal integration. Scientific management (E) is associated with Frederick Winslow Taylor.

37. B

During the Cuban missile crisis, President Kennedy ordered the U.S. Navy to intercept any military equipment shipped to Cuba. There was no evidence of Soviet nuclear superiority (A). Castro's dictatorship (C) was established in 1959. Kennedy was assassinated in 1963 before he made a re-election bid (D). The Bay of Pigs attack (E) occurred in 1961, prior to the missile crisis.

38. C

In 1963 Buddhist monks in Vietnam protested the American puppet regime of Ngo Dinh Diem. The Buddhists were not fairly represented in the government and the Diem regime had been murdering them for protesting. The French (A) had been forced out of Vietnam in 1954. The Buddhists in Indonesia (B) did not protest against Sukharno; the Indonesian Communists did. Ho Chi Minh (D) was in control of North Vietnam in 1963, not the South where the monks burned themselves. The Tet Offensive (E) took place in 1968.

39. E

The Freedom Summer of 1964, organized by the Student Nonviolent Coordinating Committee (SNCC), began with the tragic murder of the three young men, Goodman and Schwerner from the North and Chaney from Mississippi. They were part of a voter registration drive to help African Americans gain more political power in the South. But it was not until further violent attacks during demonstrations at Selma, Alabama that the 1965 Voting Rights Act was passed. African American admission to the University of Mississippi (A) was opened up by James Meredith in 1962. The Montgomery Boycott in 1955–1956 won bus desegregation (B) in the capital of Alabama. Lunch counters (C) were SNCC's target in North Carolina and elsewhere, but Freedom Summer was a voting drive. SNCC also participated in Freedom Rides to desegregate interstate highway rest stops (D).

40. C

According to the Constitution, the Chief Justice of the Supreme Court must preside over a presidential impeachment trial. Hillary Rodham Clinton (A) was not called to testify, and neither was Bill Clinton (B). The Constitution does not require any particular witnesses to testify in an impeachment trial. Clinton remained president through the impeachment process, and Vice President Gore (D) did not assume presidential power. Kenneth Starr (E) did not resign but remained Independent Counsel.

41. D

The Puritans came to the New World seeking freedom of religion for *themselves*. They neither practiced nor advocated total religious freedom. Pennsylvania was founded in 1681 by William Penn as refuge for Quakers (A). When Massachusetts Bay Colony was founded, the Puritans were interested in religion, not business (B). Democracy was limited in Massachusetts Bay (C). There was no separation of church and state (E) in Massachusetts Bay, as it was a theocracy (church-state).

42. D

Washington counseled the young nation to steer clear of permanent alliances and to use the ocean as a buffer to remain uninvolved in the affairs of Europe or the world (A). He advocated neither support for democratic revolutions (B), expansion to South America (C), nor alliances with other nations for any reason (E).

43. B

Dred Scott lived in Illinois and Wisconsin with his master as a free man from 1834–1838. Illinois is part of the Old Northwest, which had been settled under the Northwest Ordinance of 1787, prohibiting slavery, and Wisconsin was a free state under the Missouri Compromise. Scott sued for his freedom upon returning to Missouri. He was trying to establish his right to be legally free because he had lived in free territory. Chief Justice Roger Taney's decision to consider him property and re-enslave him, and then to deny the right of Congress to legislate about the question of slavery, shook the nation in 1857. Scott did not go to unsettled territory in the West (A), Massachusetts (C), or Kansas (D). Missouri (E) was a slave state, and he had lived there as a slave.

44. D

Lincoln attempted to re-supply the loyal Fort Sumter in Charleston Harbor in the least provocative way. He sent supplies by sea on a lightly armed ship. He wanted the Confederates to be blamed for starting the shooting. Lincoln had not sent troops (A) to defend the fort. Jefferson Davis ordered the firing (E) and did not offer (B) to protect the fort. Abraham Lincoln did not decide to abandon the fort (C).

45. B

Birth of a Nation (1915) presented the story of the Civil War and Reconstruction from the point of view of the Confederacy and was criticized by the NAACP for its racist depiction of African Americans and its glorification of the Ku Klux Klan. *Gone With the Wind* (1939) looked back fondly on plantation life. Although *Birth of a Nation* was a silent movie, *Gone With the Wind* was not (A). Both movies were popular with the public (C). *Gone With the Wind* is one of the most watched movies ever. Although both movies are historical, neither deals with the Revolutionary War (D). *Birth of a Nation* was produced 15 years before the Great Depression.

46. A

The 18th Amendment, which outlawed the production, sale, or consumption of alcohol, was a failure. "Bootlegging" (illegally selling alcohol) and "speakeasies" (illegal clubs which served alcohol) become part of the national vocabulary as Prohibition laws were routinely flouted. The 18th Amendment, was adopted in 1919, a year before the adoption of the 19th Amendment, which granted women the right to vote (B). Also, most historians have acknowledged that women have not voted as a bloc. Both parties avoided taking a strong stand on the Prohibition issue (C). Prohibition attempted to change the public's behavior (D), but it was not successful. Prohibition was a federal initiative (E). It did not revolve around the issue of states' rights.

47. D

The "Great Society" was the major domestic program of the Johnson administration which sought to improve the standard of living of Americans through such legislation as Medicare and the Economic Opportunity Act. The Interstate Highway Act (1956) and the National Defense Education Act (1957) (A) were Eisenhower era initiatives. The Smoot-Hawley Tariff Act (1930) and the National Origins Act (1929) (B) reflected isolationist impulses of the 1920s and 1930s. The Social Security Act (1935) and the Wagner Act (1935) (C) were part of Franklin D. Roosevelt's New Deal program. The Servicemen's Readjustment Act (1944) and the Taft-Hartley Act (1947) contributed to the shaping of the post–World War II world.

48. C

Money given to the rebels or Contras in Nicaragua was part of the Iran-Contra affair during the Reagan Administration. Richard Nixon's "plumbers" broke into Daniel Ellsberg's psychiatrist's office to get "dirt" on the man who leaked the Pentagon Papers (A) to the *New York Times*. The Saturday Night Massacre (B) was the night two Attorneys General left office (one resigned and one was fired), because they refused to fire the Watergate Special Prosecutor. The Special Prosecutor had demanded Nixon turn over tapes of White House conversations. The smoking gun tape (D) was the proof that Nixon had called for the obstruction of FBI investigations into Watergate matters. Hush money (E) were payoffs to the burglars amounting to many thousands of dollars at a time.

49. C

Muhammad Ali did not campaign for the conservative Ronald Reagan. He was politically to the left. He became Muslim (B) and changed his name from Cassius Clay upon his conversion. Ali was an independent minded man who always spoke his mind about discrimination. His unflinching militancy symbolized (D) the turbulent times in which he lived. His entry into the public eye came in the 1960 Olympics (E) when he won a gold medal.

50. C

Clinton sent peacekeeping troops to Haiti, Somalia and Bosnia. His foreign policy was one of active involvement in world affairs. The policy was neither isolationist (A), nor at odds with NATO (E). The Soviet Union (B) had ceased to exist by 1991, before Clinton took office. Reagan had labeled the Soviet Union the "evil empire." Although sometimes receiving criticism for his actions, Clinton enjoyed the majority support of the American people (D).

51. E

A 90-day embargo was passed by James Madison in 1813. Both acts were passed to protect American shipping from harassment by the English and French. It is clear that the issue in the cartoon is the Embargo because "OGRABME" is embargo spelled backward. The cartoonist was portraying the discontent, particularly among New Englanders for the Embargo, which was first passed in 1807 under the administration of Thomas Jefferson. The Federalists (A) controlled the judiciary, but that is not the subject of the cartoon. The issue of the Embargo dealt with foreign commerce not interstate commerce (B). Impressment (C) of United States seamen was one of the key causes of the War of 1812, but not the subject of this cartoon. The Citizen Genet affair (D) occurred during the administration of George Washington in 1793.

52. B

The free soilers wanted to exclude slavery from the western territories, including the Mexican Cession, which the United States acquired in 1848 after the war with Mexico. They formed the Free Soil party in 1848 and many of them became Republicans after 1854. Gradual abolition (A) was an idea which was the law in many northern states in the latter part of the 18th century. It stated that all persons born to slaves after a certain date would be free at age 21 or 25. The immediate abolitionists (C), like William Lloyd Garrison and Wendell Phillips, called for an immediate end to slavery in all of the United States. The supporters of popular sovereignty (E) left the question of slavery open to the settlers.

53. E

The Freeport Doctrine was Douglas's attempt to support both the *Dred Scott* decision and popular sovereignty. It put forward the idea that the people should decide on slavery in a given territory, but he claimed that slavery could not exist without laws supporting it. This was already disproved by the presence of slaves in the territories of Kansas and Missouri before they were states. The Mississippi (A) was not a dividing line for Douglas who wanted to permit slavery in Kansas and Nebraska through popular sovereignty. Lincoln expressed the sentiments paraphrased in choice (B) in his house divided speech. (C) and (D) are paraphrases of the statements by Andrew Jackson and John C. Calhoun during the nullification crisis of the 1830s.

54. D

President Theodore Roosevelt was aggressive in setting aside tracts of land for recreation as well as for "responsible" use by industry—a strategy he called "conservation." He took a middle path between the wholesale despoliation of the environment by industrialists and loggers and those who argued for "preservation," that is preserving nature in its pristine state. He and Gifford Pinchot sought to manage the country's natural resources in a scientific, rational way. Roosevelt embraced the idea of conservation (A); he rejected the idea of preservation. He moved away from a laissez-faire approach to the environment (B). The appointment of James Watt (C) as Secretary of the Interior angered environmentalists during the Reagan administration, not during the Roosevelt administration. Roosevelt was eager to use the power of the federal government (E) in a number of fields, including conservation.

55. B

Steinbeck's classic novel shows great compassion for the Joad family, who were displaced Dust Bowl farmers. All the other groups, (A), (C), (D), and (E), suffered in the Great Depression, but *The Grapes of Wrath* concerned the migration of "Okies" to the "Garden of Eden" of California.

56. C

Franklin Roosevelt brought government more directly into the lives of the people. Roosevelt expanded the role of the federal government with the Social Security program, the Works Progress Administration, and other government construction projects. The federal government become more complex, not simpler (A), during the Roosevelt administration. Roosevelt was cautious on the civil rights front (B), as he did not want to lose the support of southern Democrats. Roosevelt was elected to the presidency four times (D), and he died before the end of World War II (E)

57. C

The Taft-Hartley Act (1947) was a Republican initiative to halt the progress of the labor movement. It outlawed many measures that had

been approved by the Wagner Act (1935), such as the use of union dues for political activities and closed shops (union only shops). It allowed the president to issue an 80-day injunction—a "cooling off" period—if he believed that a strike could harm the economy. It also can be seen as an expression of the anti-communist sentiment of the late 1940s and 1950s; union leaders has to sign anti-communist pledges. Interstate highways (A) were funded by the Federal Highway Act (1956). The Clayton Anti-trust Act (1914) was labeled the "Magna Carta for organized labor" (B) because it excluded unions from anti-trust litigation. Veterans (D) got aid from the 1946 Servicemen's Readjustment Act, or G.I. Bill. Racial integration in defense industries (E) was the result of Executive Order 8802 (1941).

58. D

Fannie Lou Hamer and the integrated Mississippi Freedom Democratic Party (MFDP) attempted to replace the segregationist regular Democrats at the Democratic Convention in 1964. The Freedom Democratic Party was an organization of activists that grew out of the voting drives in Mississippi. They failed to get the seats despite the vocal support of the national Democrats for civil rights. The 1912 candidacy of Teddy Roosevelt (A) was supported by the Bull Moose Party. There was a 1948 party (B) called the Dixiecrats which *opposed* Truman's civil rights programs. No political party was formed in 1962 (C) specifically to advance the cause of prayer in the schools. George Wallace was the leader of the Independent Party in 1968. (E).

59. E

There were tunnels all over South Vietnam, which showed the willingness of the South Vietnamese to sacrifice time, effort, and comfort for independence. These were elaborate systems in which some people lived for months. American soldiers were never sure where the Vietcong would appear because they could come out of the tunnels at them.

60. A

The "Contract with America" was a series of conservative proposals including reduced taxes, a stronger military, a reduced federal government, and welfare reform. Decreasing the military budget, increasing the education budget (B), protecting the rights of gays, creating a "single payer" or national healthcare system (C), keeping church and state separated, and reforming the campaign finance system (D) are all liberal measures, more likely to gain the support of the Democratic Party. While making English the national language and eliminating bilingual education (E) are conservative measures, they were not part of the "Contract with America."

61. D

The colonies, under the mercantilist policies of Britain *could* freely trade with each other, although not with the colonies of other European powers (A). Under the mercantilist economic system colonies exist for the good of the mother country. To prevent competition with the British, colonial production (B) was restricted by the Iron Act and the Hat Act, and colonial shipping and commerce were restricted by requiring colonial goods to go through British ports (E). These restrictions led to resentment of British authority (C) and contributed to the American colonists' desire for independence.

62. B

The Hartford Convention, held by New England Federalists in 1814 to protest the War of 1812, marked the beginning of the end of the Federalist Party. The Democratic-Republican Party (A) of Jefferson was founded in 1794 in the wake of the Jay Treaty, while the Republican Party of Lincoln was founded in 1854 in Wisconsin in the wake of the Kansas-Nebraska Act and neither of these parties was involved in the Hartford Convention. The Hartford Convention was not supported by the South or the West (C) and the New England Federalists were isolated and discredited, bringing a loss in political power for the Northeast. Henry

Clay (D) maintained his prominence as a War Hawk in Congress at this time, a situation that was not changed by the Hartford Convention. Although the Hartford Convention did come up with proposals for amendments increasing state powers (E), these were not adopted into the Constitution.

63. C

In 1860, the Southern (Breckinridge) Democrats introduced a plank into the Democratic Party platform calling for a national slave code: Slavery would be legal everywhere. The northern (Douglas) Democrats refused to pass it. One Ohio delegate said, "Gentlemen of the South, you mistake us. We will not do it!" Forty-seven southerners walked out. The Democrats tried to reunite but failed. That was the origin of the two Democratic Parties in the 1860 election. Each one of the other answer choices refers to earlier controversies. California was admitted as a free state (A) in 1850 and Missouri (B) in 1820. The issue of internal improvements (D) was a major controversy in the 1830s and it was the Republicans who called for a transcontinental railroad in the 1860 election. The bank (E) was a key issue in the 1830s.

64. B

The elimination of slavery brought the United States onto the road to world economic leadership because the existence of slavery had been holding it back according to the historians Charles and Mary Beard. They analyzed the development of the United States from an economic point of view. Full, unhindered capitalism, won in the Civil War—this was the basis of the "Second American Revolution." The War of 1812 has been called the "Second War for American Independence" (A) because Britain finally recognized that the United States was no longer her possession. Guerrilla warfare (C), which was characteristic of the patriots in the Revolution, was not a major factor in the Civil War. Historians disagree over Lincoln's ability as a military leader (D) and regardless, similarities between

Washington and Lincoln alone, would probably not be a reason to call the war the "Second American Revolution." The problems of race (E) were certainly not solved by the abolition of slavery—we are still arguing over issues from affirmative action to the flying of Confederate battle flags over state capitols today.

65. D

Both acts created regulatory bodies that oversaw business activities. The Interstate Commerce Commission regulated railroad rates while the National Recovery Administration set codes for wages, hours, and production for major businesses during the Great Depression. The Supreme Court struck down the National Industrial Recover Act (NIRA) in 1935 (A), but never heard a case challenging the Interstate Commerce Act (ICA). These acts reflected a move away from traditional laissez-faire policies (B). The NIRA was not designed to limit the power of the railroad companies (C). Section 7A of NIRA encouraged workers to join unions (E) so that they would be better able to protect their interests, while the ICA did not mention union membership.

66. B

The progressive movement was a broad movement which included both Democrats and Republicans. It was not exclusively affiliated with the Republican Party (C). In fact, of the two presidents most closely linked to the progressive movement, Theodore Roosevelt and Woodrow Wilson, one was a Republican and one was a Democrat. The progressives were not purists; they believed that working through the two major political parties (A) was an effective way of implementing reforms. They certainly did not shy away from electoral politics (E). The Bull Moose Party (D) was formed by Theodore Roosevelt and other progressive minded Republicans because they felt that President Taft was not sufficiently progressive.

67. B

This was a very important shift within the electorate. From the days of Lincoln, the "Great Emancipator," until 1932, a majority of African Americans voted for the Republican Party. But from Roosevelt's reelection in 1936 until the present day, African Americans have overwhelmingly voted for the Democratic Party, which has appeared more responsive to the needs and interests of African Americans. The percentage of women who voted (A) increased in the 1930s. The Communist Party (C) vote was always small. Even though the party gained in strength in the 1930s, as part of its Popular Front strategy, it supported Roosevelt. The percentage of actual voters in the electorate (D) increased in the 1930s. Immigrants (E), union members, African Americans and urban political machines comprised Roosevelt's New Deal coalition.

68. A

Roosevelt felt some pressure from the left, as leaders pushed agendas more radical than the New Deal. The End Poverty in California was Upton Sinclair's campaign, and the Share Our Wealth movement was Huey Long's project. The two programs were opposed to the New Deal, not part of it (B). The Communist Party had influence in some of the CIO unions in the 1930's (C), but the two programs were not labor unions. The New Deal was attacked from the right (D) by people such as Father Charles Coughlin, who had a popular weekly radio show. These programs did not have a specifically rural emphasis (E)

69. A

Whyte and Wilson criticized the sameness of American society as large corporations and suburbia came to dominate society. The two books mentioned were critical of trends within American society but they were not Marxist, nor were they labeled as such (B). The Soviet Union was not outpacing the United States in economic output during the 1950s (C). While Whyte and Wilson criticized the conformity of American society, their criticisms did not make their way into business school curricula (D). The "beatniks" (E) were criticized by the mainstream press, but not by Whyte and Wilson.

70. E

One of the major events in the Watergate scandal was the successive resignation and dismissal or Saturday Night Massacre in 1974, of two Attorney's General, Elliot Richardson and Nicholas Katzenbach. They had both refused to fire the Special Prosecutor, Archibald Cox. Nixon insisted that they fire Cox because he had ordered the president to hand over tapes of conversations between Nixon and his aides concerning the Watergate break-in and cover-up. When the story came out that Nixon was attempting to fire the head of the Watergate investigation, the call for impeachment and resignation became a firestorm. The Ku Klux Klan (A) had killed the civil rights workers, Goodman, Schwerner, and Chaney in 1963 and the young girls in the basement of a Birmingham Church the same year, but they were known as lynchings not massacres. The CIA (B) cooperated in the assassination of Ngo Dinh Diem in 1963 when John Kennedy was president. William Calley (C) was indicted for his role in the My Lai massacre in 1968. John Hinckley (D) pleaded not guilty by reason of insanity in the 1981 assassination attempt on President Reagan not on Nixon.

71. D

Since the American Revolution initially only had the support of about a third of the population in the colonies, the Declaration of Independence was written to justify independence and gain support for the American cause. The founding fathers also knew they had to appeal to the international community, notably France, to be successful against the British. This was not a new political philosophy (A) since it was borrowed by Jefferson from John Locke. The French Revolution (B) began 13 years after the signing of the Declaration of Independence. There was no mention of gaining land (C) The time for requesting concessions had

passed (E). The purpose was to break the "political bands" that joined Britain and the colonies.

72. B

The Northwest Ordinance did not have any provisions involving the establishment of militias and, after the French defeat in the French and Indian War in 1763, the French were no longer a threat in the area. The ordinance did provide for freedom for religion (A), prohibit slavery in the territory under discussion (C), encourage decent treatment of Native Americans (D), and provide for the orderly settlement of the Northwest Territory (E).

73. B

Alexander Hamilton was a loose constructionist who justified the establishment of the Bank of the United States by citing the elastic clause (implied powers clause) in the Constitution. He did not support the idea of rotation in office (A), as he believed that the president should serve for life. He generally mistrusted the masses (C) and did not support the idea of an educated populace (D). Hamilton was a strong believer in the supremacy of the central government (E).

74. D

The Gettysburg Address was delivered by President Lincoln in November, 1863, five months after the Battle of Gettysburg. A score is 20 years, so 87 years before 1863 was 1776. He was rededicating the nation to a more modern meaning of the Declaration of Independence: that African Americans and whites were created equal. Many abolitionists had been using the Declaration that way since the days of the American Revolution. It was significant that the president adopted this meaning of the Declaration and called for a "new birth of freedom." The inauguration of Washington (A) occurred in 1789, 74 years before the Gettysburg Address. The Constitutional Convention (B) was in 1787, and the Constitution does not make allusions to men being "created equal." The writing of the Mayflower Compact occurred in 1620, over 200 years before the Civil War. Although it had been interpreted as having a democratic content, it was not a statement of equality. The landing at Jamestown in 1607, also occurring over 200 years before the Civil War, was an important event in American history, but the resulting society in Virginia was not based on ideas of equality.

75. E

The Populist platform called for immigration restrictions in order to forge an alliance with urban workers. They argued that the large number of immigrants weakened the bargaining position of American workers. The wide-ranging set of demands included as graduated income tax (A), inflationary policies (B), the eight-hour day (C), and government control of railroads (D) and banks.

76. C

Ward and Sears brought the bounty of industrial America to the rural hinterland with their mail order catalogs. F. W. Woolworth opened his first of many "five and dimes" (A) in 1879. The installment plan (B), in which the consumer puts down a percentage of the cost of a product and agrees to pay the rest in installments, is associated with the 1920s. Several entrepreneurs sold mass produced American goods (D), starting in the early 19th century, and several added refrigeration to grocery stores (E) in the early 20th century.

77. E

Although Roosevelt fought in the Spanish-American War, it occurred before his presidency. Roosevelt did secure the Panama Canal Zone for the United States (A). He won a Nobel Peace Prize for his efforts at brokering a peace treaty between Japan and Russia (B). He established the Roosevelt Corollary to the Monroe Doctrine (C). At times he dispatched U.S. battleships to various parts of the world as a show of strength, exemplifying the adage "speak softly but carry a big stick" (D).

78. B

Woodrow Wilson was inflexible when it came to the debate over the Treaty of Versailles and the League of Nations. Wilson himself proposed a League of Nations in his Fourteen Points. He was unwilling to compromise (A). Although Wilson had encountered difficulty with the Allies when negotiating the peace at Versailles (C), the debate over ratification was with Congress, not the Allies. Wilson wanted the United States to participate in the League of Nations, an international body, not to isolate itself from the world (D). The League of Nations covenant, which Wilson supported, pledged each member nation to preserve the independence and territorial integrity of all the other member nations. Many isolationist Senators opposed this pledge, outlined in Article X of the covenant, on the grounds that it would limit the freedom of the United States in world affairs and affect U.S. military actions (E).

79. A

The United States has supported Israel since its beginning in 1948. However, the growing need for Arab oil has created a conflict in American foreign policy because no Arab oil state had given diplomatic recognition to Israel until 1978. The United States has never supported Libya (B). There is not a large population of Hindus (C) in the Middle East. A Palestinian state does not exist (D) and free trade (E) in the Middle East has not been a major question for the United States.

80. D

President George Bush H. W. Bush signed the biggest bailout in United States history, $159 billion, for the savings and loan banks which had been underfunded and had taken risks not seen since the 1920s. The owners of the banks (A) had not invested much of their money in their own banks and could not have paid off the debts themselves since they were so over-extended. The Federal Deposit Insurance Corporation (FDIC) (C) could not reimburse the depositors since it only insured commercial banks, not savings banks. The Glass-Steagall Act (E) which had set up the FDIC in 1933 had strictly separated the two kinds of banks as a way to prevent such disasters. It was the deregulation of the Carter and Reagan years which opened up the possibility for the crisis.

81. C

John Adams defended the British soldiers involved in the Boston Massacre. Benjamin Franklin (A) was in London for much of the 1760s, and his home was in Philadelphia, not New York. Thomas Paine (B) wrote *Common Sense* and did not establish the Committees of Correspondence. They were established by Samuel Adams. Crispus Attucks (D) was an African American killed during the Boston Massacre. Patrick Henry (E) was not executed by the British.

82. C

Shays's Rebellion led to the scrapping of the Articles of Confederation. It occurred in 1787 when farmers in western Massachusetts led by Daniel Shays protested the tax policies in Massachusetts. It raised fears of general disorder and prompted the call for a convention to revise the Articles of Confederation. Instead of revising the Articles, the convention scrapped the document and drafted the Constitution. It was not a slave rebellion (A). It was suppressed by the Massachusetts and New York militia, not a militia sent by the Congress of the Articles of Confederation (B). The Bill of Rights (D) was added to the Constitution in 1791 and did not address the issues raised in Shays's Rebellion. The "shot heard round the world" (E) occurred in Concord, Massachusetts, in 1775 and signaled the beginning of the American Revolution.

83. A

The idea of nullification was introduced in the Virginia and Kentucky Resolutions of 1798. They were written by James Madison and Thomas Jefferson, respectively, to oppose to the Alien and Sedition Acts. Jefferson contended that the states had entered into a compact forming the government and that when a federal law failed to satisfy the people of a state, that state had the right to declare the law "null and void." The theory of nullification became the basis of the South Carolina Exposition and Protest, written by John C. Calhoun in 1828, and of secession in 1860, although Jefferson did not intend that people would take the idea that far. The resolutions inflamed the conflict (B) over the Alien and Sedition Acts, because the Federalists (C) supported the Alien and Sedition Acts and the Democratic Republicans supported the Virginia and Kentucky Resolutions. Hamilton did not participate in the writing of the resolutions (D). He supported stronger federal power, not state power. The Supreme Court (E) did not rule on the resolutions.

84. A

The Emancipation Proclamation was issued in September, 1862 and went into effect January 1, 1863. It stated that slaves in states or parts of states still in rebellion as of January 1, 1863 would be freed. Though this did not immediately free any slaves because the Union government was unable to exercise power in the rebellious areas of the South, it did dedicate the war to the anti-slavery cause and freed slaves as the Union army conquered the South. Lincoln was not yet ready to free all the slaves (C). This came with the ratification of the 13th Amendment in 1865. Lincoln was still worried about the border states (B), such as Missouri and Kentucky, leaving the Union. To retain their support he did not attempt to free the slaves in loyal states. Freeing the children of slaves (D), gradual emancipation, had been the policy in many Northern states since the end of the 18th century. The Emancipation Proclamation embodied a different policy. By the time of the Civil War slavery had ceased to exist in the North (E) except for the border states.

85. C

Bellamy presented a scathing indictment of industrial capitalism, and imagined a socialist utopia in its place. All other authors could be invoked to justify the economic conditions of the Gilded Age. Alger (A) wrote "rags to riches" stories in which poor boys achieve great success with hard work and a little luck. Sumner (B) championed the ideas of social Darwinism, which saw laissez-faire capitalism as a testing ground in which the fittest survive. Smith (D) wrote in the previous century, but his description of the economy guided by market forces—the invisible hand—sat well with Gilded Age advocates of laissez-faire capitalism. Carnegie (E) supported the idea of free market capitalism, but argued that the captains of industry should give something back to the community.

86. D

Strong and Mahan were fervent expansionists. Strong argued that it was the mission of the United States to Christianize and civilize the "weaker races." Mahan argued that the United States needed to expand its naval power and take over territories in the Pacific if it hoped to achieve international prominence. Several activists opposed racism in the United States (A), such as Ida B. Wells who wrote and lectured against lynching in the South. Urban corruption (B) was the subject of Lincoln Steffens's *The Shame of the Cities* (1904). Regional novelists (C) include Mark Twain and Willa Cather. Anti-war novels (E) include *Three Soldiers*, by John Dos Passos and *A Farewell to Arms*, by Ernest Hemingway.

87. D

The progressives had a great deal of faith in the power of the government to implement reforms. These reforms included federal actions such as the Meat Inspection Act (1906) and the Federal Reserve Act (1913), which reformed the banking system, as well as state actions such as placing restrictions on lobbying in Wisconsin, the "laboratory of democracy." The nationalization of banks and industries (A) was advocated by socialists, not progressives. The progressive movement was largely silent on issues of race (B). Progressives generally wanted lower tariffs (C) to keep consumer prices from rising. Progressive era reformers such as Florence Kelley and Jane Addams challenged traditional ideas about "feminine" behavior (E).

88. D

The WPA, an important New Deal program, employed over 8 million people between 1935 and 1943. The WPA built schools, libraries, and hospitals; employed writers, photographers, and artists; and created a vast array of public works projects. The Supreme Court (A) struck down the National Industrial Recovery Act, not the WPA, in 1933 because it gave the president law making powers. Hydroelectric dams (B) were built along the Tennessee River by the Tennessee Valley Authority (1933). The Wagner Act (1935) established legal protections for workers (D). Assistance to big business (E) was provided by Hoover's 1932 Reconstruction Finance Corporation.

89. A

The Kerner Commission on urban violence concluded that it was the rising expectations among African Americans in the North for a wider range of opportunities that caused the riots in the Watts neighborhood of Los Angeles in 1965 and Detroit in 1967. The draft (B) for Vietnam was not a major issue before 1967 and the riots in African American urban neighborhoods began before that date. The riots were in the North and West not in the South (C) in the early 1960s. African Americans were not barred from voting in the North (D). Affirmative Action (E) was not an issue in America until the Nixon Administration (after 1969).

90. C

De jure segregation refers to segregation grounded in law. Segregation laws were declared unconstitutional in 1954 and were eliminated during the 1950s and 1960s by civil rights demonstrations and court decisions. *De facto* segregation still exists in many cities. The issues of an aging America (A), the challenges of the AIDS crisis (B), problems in the health care industry (D) and energy requirements (E) continue to be pressing issues in the United States.

Glossary

abolitionist

one who favors the end of slavery

abomination

a vicious or vile action that is met with great distaste

affirmative action

policies of the government aimed at increasing access to jobs, schooling, and opportunities to people previously discriminated against

agrarian

pertaining to farming or agriculture

anarchist

an individual who advocates the overthrow of all government

annex

the act of taking a smaller territory into a larger one

antebellum

before the war; usually used with regard to the time before the Civil War

anti-Semitic

one who is prejudiced against Jews

apologists

those in the South who justified slavery by claiming African Americans were better off under the current system than left on their own

appeasement

a policy of giving into modest demands of an enemy to hold off potential conflict

apportionment

The proportional distribution of the number of members of the U.S. House of Representatives on the basis of the population of each state

arbitration

the settlement of a dispute by a third, unbiased party

armistice

a suspension of fighting; a cease-fire

arsenal

a stockpile of weapons or a place for making and storing weapons

artisans

those considered skilled in certain industries such as metal work, carpentry, or printing

autocrat

a ruler having unlimited power; a despot

bandwagon

a political cause that draws increasing numbers of proponents due to its success

bicameral

composed of or based on two legislative chambers or branches

blasphemy

a contemptuous or profane act, utterance, or writing concerning God or a sacred entity

blitzkrieg

Hitler's tactic of "lightning war," which involved swift action against the enemy

bond

an interest-bearing note issued by the government which guarantees repayment at a set date

boycott

to refrain from engaging, purchasing, or trading with another in an expression of protest

bracero

a Mexican farm worker brought to the United States to work during World War II

buying on margin

the act of purchasing stock on credit

capitalism

an economic system in which the means of production and exchange are controlled by individuals

caravel

any of several types of small, light sailing ships, especially one with two or three masts and lateen sails used by the Spanish and Portuguese in the 15th and 16th centuries.

carpetbagger

a Northern Republican who moved South for financial and political gain

ceded

given or surrendered to another, possibly by treaty

charter

a written grant from the sovereign power of a country conferring certain rights and privileges on a person, a corporation, or the people

closed shop

a workplace in which workers must join the labor union as a condition of employment

collective bargaining

employees and management negotiating wages, working conditions, and work hours

confederation

an alliance or body of states loosely united for common purposes

conscription

compulsory enrollment of men in the armed forces

constituents

the voters or citizens of a particular region who are represented by an elected official

conquistador

a Spanish conqueror of the Americas

conversion experience

a rite of passage for Calvinists who publicly confessed all sins to become one of the "elect"

corollary

an inference that follows proof from a previous instance

coup

the overthrow of a ruling party/person by a small group illegally and/or by force

de facto

"in fact"; usually with regard to segregation

de jure

"in law"; usually with regard to laws passed for segregation

demography

the study of the characteristics of human populations, such as size, growth, density, distribution, and vital statistics

depression

a prolonged period of declining economic activity characterized by rising unemployment and falling prices

détente

a period of relaxed tensions between countries

direct primary

an election in which registered members of the party elect their party nominees for office

dissent

to object or disagree

domestic

of or relating to a country's internal affairs

duty

money collected by government from a tariff

egalitarian

upholding the equality of all people

elect

according to Calvinists, those who have been chosen by God for salvation

elite

a group or class of persons or a member of such a group or class, enjoying superior intellectual, social, or economic status

emancipation

to free from slavery or bondage

embargo

a prohibition or ban; usually used with regard to trade or shipping

encomienda

the Spanish labor system whereby individuals were bound to unpaid labor but were not legally owned by a master

enfranchisement

giving the right to vote

entrepreneur

a person who engages in a risky business adventure

established church

a church that is officially recognized and protected by the government

excise tax

a fee collected on goods and services bought and sold within a country

executive privilege

the claim by a president that certain information should be kept from Congress

expatriates

individuals who have chosen to leave their native country in favor of living abroad

fascism

a dictatorial form of government that glorifies military service and nationalism

filibuster

the act of Congressmen of delaying a vote or action by refusing to release the floor during debate

Fire Eaters

term used by Northerners to name Southern slavery advocates

foreclosure

the repossession of a property by a lender after a borrower fails to pay on the loan

fugitive

an individual who flees danger or capture

Fundamentalism

a religious movement or point-of-view characterized by a return to rigid adherence to fundamental principles

genocide

the systematic extermination of a race or ethnicity by another group

gentry

people of gentle birth, good breeding, or high social position; usually owned land

ghetto

an area where ethnic minorities are forced to live in either by law or discrimination

graft

the use of one's position to gain money or property illegally

greenback

paper currency in the United States that replaced specie before the founding of the Federal Reserve

Gross National Product (GNP)

the sum of all goods and services produced both within and abroad by citizens of a country in a given year

guerrilla warfare

irregular, paramilitary units operating in small bands in occupied territory using subversive tactics to surprise the enemy

hard money

limited currency with high value

headright system

a system of obtaining land in colonial times in which one received 50 acres of land for every emigrant to America one sponsored

heresy

an opinion or a doctrine at variance with established religious beliefs

hierarchy

a system that places things in graduated order, from lowest to highest

homestead

a single-family home or farm

horizontal integration

a single company controls one aspect of the manufacture of a product

ideology

the body of ideas and beliefs that represent a culture or large group

impeach

to charge a government official with a criminal offense

imperialism

a policy of extending a country's authority over a foreign country by acquisition or colonization

impress

to force into military service

incumbent

an individual running for an office they currently hold

indentured servant

a person who is bonded or contracted to work for another for a specified time, in exchange for learning a trade or travel expenses

indigenous

native to a particular region

inflation

an increase in the value of currency relative to the cost of consumer goods

infrastructure

the basic structure needed for the functions of a society; usually refers to transportation, sanitation, and communication

initiative

process by which voters can propose legislation and place that law on a ballot in a popular election

insurrection

the act or an instance of open revolt against civil authority or a constituted government

isolationist

an individual who would rather remain uninvolved in world affairs

Jim Crow

the practice of legal racial segregation

jingoism

extreme nationalism coupled with an aggressive foreign policy stance

joint-stock companies

a company that has some features of a corporation and some features of a partnership

laissez faire

the belief that government should refrain from interfering in business and the economy

landslide

the winning of an election by a large margin

literacy test

an exam given to individuals to prove they were literate before they could register to vote

lynching

the illegal act of putting to death a person accused of committing a crime; usually conducted by mobs

mandate

a command or instruction given by the electorate to their representative

martial law

military occupation imposed upon an area when civilian resources have failed or collapsed

martyr

an individual who makes a great sacrifice to further a cause; one who chooses death rather than renouncing beliefs

materialism

a belief that the accumulation of possessions is more important that spiritual pursuits

matrilineal

relating to, based on, or tracing ancestral descent through the maternal line.

mercantilism

the belief that all economic activity should be for the good of the whole (country) rather than for the individual

mercenaries

foreign soldiers hired to serve in the military

Mestizo

a person of mixed racial ancestry, especially of mixed European and Native American ancestry

mobilization

government organization of the nation for war

mudslinging

unsubstantiated accusations and attacks on a political opponent

mulatto

an individual of African and European ancestry

nation-state

a political society that combines a central government with cultural unification

nationalism

devotion to the interests or culture of one's nation

nativism

the policy of upholding the rights of native citizens over those of immigrants

naturalization

the process of immigrants gaining legal citizenship

nullify

to declare a law void

oligarchy

rule by a few

omnibus bill

a potential law that includes a variety of topics under one name

pacifist

an individual who is opposed to all war

pardon

the act of releasing an individual from responsibility for a crime

partisan

supporting a particular political party

patronage

the support of a cause through financial gifts

peculiar institution

a name given to slavery by Southern apologists

political machine

an organization controlled through spoils and patronage

poll tax

a tax levied on individuals before they could vote

pool

an alliance of competing companies to set prices and split profits by sharing customers

pork barrel

Congressional appropriations for political gain in a particular constituency

precedent

a decision or action that establishes a standard for future instances

predestination

the doctrine that God has foreordained all things, especially that God has elected certain souls to eternal salvation

primogeniture

the right of the eldest child, especially the eldest son, to inherit the entire estate of one or both parents

proclamation

an official announcement

propaganda

information or materials provided by the proponents or opponents of an idea to influence public thought

proprietary colony

a settlement in a region granted by a king or queen to a legal owner

proviso

a clause within a document that stipulates an exception or restriction

pump-priming

the increase in government spending to stimulate the economy

puppet government

a government that is controlled by outsiders

quota

a proportional share of something to a group or members of a group; an allotment

ratification

the act of approving and giving formal sanction of

recall

the act of removing a public official from office by a vote of a specified number of citizens

referendum

the submission of a law directly to the voters for approval or denial

reparations

money, goods, or services paid by a government for destruction and damage caused during a war

republic

a government whose power rests in a citizenry who is entitled to vote, is represented by those they vote for, and usually has a president rather than a monarch as head

Rustbelt

states in the Northeast and Midwest which were once prosperous steel producers

scabs

replacement workers during a strike

scalawag

a white Southerner who supported Radical Reconstruction

secession

the withdrawal from an alliance or association

sect

a group of people forming a distinct unit within a larger group by virtue of certain refinements or distinctions of belief or practice

secular

of the world rather than of the church or spirit

sedition

the act of incitement of rebellion against the government

segregation

the act of separating; usually regarding race and ethnicity

siege

the surrounding and blockading of a city, town, or fortress by an army attempting to capture it

self-determination

the belief that people should have the opportunity to decide their own form of government

sharecropper

an individual who receives land on credit and pays back debt with a share of the crop yield

socialist

an individual who believes that business and the economy should be controlled by the community not individuals

soft money

plentiful currency with low value

sovereignty

power vested in an independent government

speakeasies

illegal bars and clubs where liquor was sold during Prohibition

specie

coined (gold, silver, or other metal) currency

speculation

risky business transactions on the bet of quick or considerable profit

sphere of influence

a region controlled by the influence of other powerful nations

spoils system

the practice of the winning political party rewarding supporters with jobs regardless of qualifications

stagflation

a combination of high unemployment and high inflation

stalwart

an individual who has unwavering support for a party or cause

strike

an action by organized labor to stop work in order to force management to negotiate

subversion

a systematic attempt to overthrow or undermine a government or political system by persons working from within

suffrage

the right to vote

Sunbelt

states along the South and Southwestern United States

tariffs

taxes placed on imported goods

temperance

the belief in moderation, particularly with regard to alcohol

tenant farmer

a person who leases land from a landowner

tenement

an urban multifamily housing unit

theocracy

a government by the church leaders

trust

an organization of corporations where stock holders have traded their stocks for trust certificates

tycoon

a wealthy and powerful business person

urbanization

the growth of cities

utopian

seeking perfection in society

vertical integration

a single company controls all aspects of manufacturing

Vietnamization

President Nixon's policy of turning over the Vietnam War to the South Vietnamese

virtual representation

the political practice of a small group of people being elected to speak for a larger group

wildcat bank

uncontrolled and unregulated Western banks of the 1800s whose speculation and unsafe practices helped spur the Panic of 1819

writ of habeas corpus

from the Latin "of the body," a formal order requiring the presentation of the accused before a judge to be charged with a crime or released from custody

yellow-dog contracts

agreements that forced employees to promise never to join a union in order to gain or maintain employment

yeomen

non-slave owning farmers

Index